LIFESPAN HUMAN DEVELOPMENT

Suzanne Simar

LIFESPAN HUMAN DEVELOPMENT

Fourth Edition

Anne V. Gormly

Trenton State College

David M. Brodzinsky

Rutgers University

Holt, Rinehart and Winston, Inc.
New York   Chicago   San Francisco   Philadelphia
Montreal   Toronto   London   Sydney   Tokyo

Publisher   **Susan Driscoll**
Acquisitions Editor   **Susan Arellano**
Developmental Editor   **Jane Knetzer**
Photo Research   **Cheryl Mannes**
Special Projects Editor   **Jeanette Ninas Johnson**
Manager of Production   **Angelo Puleo**
Text and Cover Design   **Caliber Design Planning**
Design Supervisor   **Louis Scardino**

Printed in the United States of America

Gormly, Anne V.
    Lifespan human development. -- 4th ed. / Anne V. Gormly, David M.
Brodzinsky.
      p.   cm.
    Rev. ed. of: Lifespan human development / David Brodzinsky, Anne
V. Gormly, Sueann Robinson Ambron. 3rd ed. c1986.
    Bibliography: p.
    Includes indexes.

    1. Developmental psychology.   I. Brodzinsky, David.   II. Ambron,
Sueann Robinson. Lifespan human development.   III. Title.
BF713.A46 1989
155--dc19   88-7586
                                                                     CIP

ISBN 0-03-023427-1

9 8 0 1 069 9 8 7 6 5 4 3 2 1

Holt, Rinehart and Winston, Inc.
The Dryden Press
Saunders College Publishing

PREFACE

Ten years have passed since the first edition of *Lifespan Human Development* was published. During that time, our text has undergone a series of changes with each edition that have built on its strengths and contributed to its overall quality. Our aim is to introduce and weave together the basic concepts, principles, and theories that describe the physical, cognitive, social, and personality changes that occur during significant periods of growth across the lifespan. We discuss topics and issues related to the changes in life from conception to death, yet *Lifespan Human Development* can be covered in a semester course.

This book may be used for courses without prerequisites, and in which many students are encountering the basic concepts of psychology for the first time. Each technical term is introduced with a clear, concise definition followed by concrete applications and illustrations. This book provides a solid foundation in modern psychological and developmental theory and research, and provides practical implications of research—it tells the reader about the children and adults they meet in everyday life. Presented in this way, the study of human development provides an essential background for students in psychology, nursing, education, social welfare, and home economics; for workers in community service; and for parents and prospective parents.

Changes in This Edition

Every chapter has been rewritten to include a stronger emphasis on the lifespan approach. An attempt has been made to relate developmental changes in one period in the lifespan to other periods and to take into account the influence on human development of several changing systems. In Chapter 1, we begin with a discussion of the themes and challenges in the study of lifespan development. Such issues include: What is the best way to study and measure changes across the lifespan? What is the impact of physical, social, and cultural changes on human development? Can people of all ages change their behavior, or is remediation only possible in the early part of the lifespan?

We have updated the research and included new topics, making the strong research base of the third edition even stronger. Over 350 new citations have been made, 85 percent of these from journal articles or books published since 1980. New topics include, for example, the use of surrogate mothers and alternate means of conception, foster care, children's perception of reality, bilingualism, single and stepparent families, the impact of AIDS, physical fitness, leisure activities, stress, sex education, early retirement, Alzheimer's disease, and caring for dying children and their families.

The learning aids have been enhanced with the addition of *Human Development in Practice* boxes that present material of particular interest to students majoring in nursing and education. New "Pauses for Thought," questions inserted throughout each chapter, stimulate critical thought and discussion.

We have improved the running glossary by adding more terms, and we have included an end-of-text glossary as well. The photographs in this edition have been carefully selected to illustrate the text and to serve as a memory aid for important concepts. Color photographs and new graphics make the fourth edition an exciting and appealing book to look at as well as to read.

Pedagogical Features

Readability   The readability of the book is promoted, first, by careful organization: Topics follow logically, and each is given an accurately descriptive heading. Second, the text is written to present even the most abstract concepts in lively prose that is easy to retain. Numerous colorful examples emphasize and clarify ideas. Finally, important technical terms are introduced in bold type, defined immediately in the text and again in the running glossary and the end-of-text glossary.

Part Openers   Each section is introduced by a short explanation of the developmental issues that will be addressed in subsequent chapters. These openers serve as a guide from one developmental period to the next.

Chapter Outlines and Opening Vignettes   At the beginning of each chapter, the reader is given a preview in outline form of the major topics and issues included in the chapter. The outline is followed with a warm, real-life example of typical behavior appropriate to the age and aspect of development presented in the chapter.

Human Development in Practice   Distributed throughout the text are boxed features presenting material of particular interest to students studying nursing and education. However, the real-life applications are relevant and of interest to all readers. A list of topics included in the boxed features follows the Table of Contents.

Pause for Thought   Strategically placed in several spots within each chapter, these "Pauses" are designed to stimulate critical thought and application of textual material. Instructors may want to use selected "Pauses" as lecture openers, as catalysts for class discussion or debate, or as essay questions on an exam.

Summaries and Further Readings   Every chapter concludes with a summary, organized into short, coherent paragraphs, that provides a handy review for the student. Also following each chapter is a list of annotated readings that will lead interested students to more information.

Observational Activities   At the end of each chapter, activities relate chapter contents to real-life experiences with children and adults. The observational activities also help stimulate classroom discussion.

Running Glossary   The chapter-by-chapter glossary, a lifespan dictionary in miniature, defines all important terms in the margin of the page on which the term is first introduced. The glossary item is also listed alphabetically in the end-of-text glossary.

Supplements   Instructors will find the accompanying *Instructor's Manual* helpful in arranging their curricula. The Manual, written by Anne Gormly, contains suggestions for lecture topics, films, classroom discussions and activities, as well as multiple-choice test items and essay questions. The test questions are available in computerized form. The accompanying self-scoring *Study Guide* for students contains for each chapter an outline of topics, summary of key concepts, key terms and phrases, review questions, exercises, and a quiz including true-false, sentence completion, multiple choice, and matching questions. Answer keys provide immediate feedback to the student. In addition, 50 color transparencies and 100 color slides are available from the publisher.

Organization of the Book

The fourth edition features eight major parts, introduced by a discussion of issues, theories, and methods in Chapter 1. With the exception of Part Eight, which covers death, dying, and bereavement, each part covers the physical, cognitive, personality, and social development of the individual in one of the broad stages of growth.

Chapter 1, "Lifespan Development: Issues, Theories, and Methods," deals with the concerns of lifespan developmental psychology, summarizes major theories of development, and provides an overview of how research on human development is conducted.

Part One, "The Beginning: Conception through Infancy," follows the development of the individual from conception through the second year of life. Chapter 2 describes the mechanisms of genetics, the many dimensions of prenatal development, and the birth process. Chapter 3 describes the characteristics of the newborn and the infant's rapid physical and cognitive development during the first two years of life. The infant's social and personality development are described in Chapter 4, which also includes a discussion of early language behavior.

Part Two, "Preschool Years," takes the child to age five or six. Physical, cognitive, and language development are detailed in Chapter 5, and personality and social development are presented in Chapter 6.

Part Three, "Middle Childhood," follows the developing person through the grade-school years to pubescence. Chapter 7 describes physical growth, cognition, and learning, and Chapter 8 examines personality and social development.

Part Four, "Adolescence," treats the physical changes that occur at puberty and their effects on the individual's personality and social life. Chapter 9 describes the adolescent's attainment of physical maturity, as well as changes in cognitive and moral–ethical development. In Chapter 10, the issues of identity and personality are explored.

Part Five, "Early Adulthood," presents the major developmental tasks confronting people as they make the transition to adulthood. Chapter 11 focuses on physical, cognitive, and personality changes experienced by young adults, and Chapter 12 examines parenting and family relations and occupational development.

Part Six, "Middle Adulthood," takes the individual through the middle years of adult life, from approximately 40 to 65 years of age. Physical, cognitive, and personality development are described in Chapter 13. Chapter 14 examines midlife marital and family relations as well as experiences and adjustments at work.

Part Seven, "Late Adulthood," completes the lifespan with chapters on aging. Chapter 15 explores various factors that influence physical and cognitive adaptation in the later years as well as issues of identity and personality adjustment among the elderly. Chapter 16 focuses on family life, social relations, and adjustment to retirement.

Part Eight, "The Final Stage of Life," includes Chapter 17 that discusses the changes that occur as people die and experience bereavement. The impact of death on individuals of different ages across the developmental lifespan is described and completes the text.

Special Note to Students

This is a book about life, some of which you have already experienced, some of which is ahead of you. Some of you may be interested in the material on human development because you want to figure out or explain your own development (or perhaps that of your roommate, friend, or relative). Many of you may be just as eager to learn about the years ahead. Some of the material that you will read about in these 17 chapters will not stay in your immediate memory after this course is finished (it is hoped that you will remember most of the material until you have taken your final exams). Some time in the future, however, you will no doubt find yourself in real-life situations with infants, children, and other adults of varying ages and will remember *something* about what you have read. It is then that you will be glad that you have kept your textbook as a reference. If and when you have children of your own to bring up, you may find yourself devouring the pages in Parts One, Two, Three, and Four. If you are working with the elderly or perhaps living with your aging parents, then Parts Seven and Eight may become your favorite chapters. We hope that you will find this text enjoyable and informative.

We would welcome any suggestions or comments you have about our text. Please send them to the Psychology Editor, Holt, Rinehart and Winston, 111 Fifth Avenue, New York, New York 10003.

About the Authors

We thought you would like to know a little bit about your authors. Anne V. Gormly, full professor at Trenton State College in Trenton, New Jersey, holds a Ph.D. in Personality from the University of Illinois. She has two children, Adam and Sarah; a husband, John, who is also a psychologist; and an identical twin sister who is *not* a psychologist. For the past 17 years, Anne has taught courses in child development, parenting, and human development. Her research interests include fertility motivation, attitudes and social behavior, and parenting.

David M. Brodzinsky, associate professor at Rutgers University in New Brunswick, New Jersey, holds a Ph.D. in developmental psychology from the State University of New York at Buffalo. He has five children (Lara, Zachary, Shoshi, Joshua, and Adam) and a wife, Anne, who is a doctoral student in counseling psychology. For the past 15 years, David has taught courses in human development and abnormal child behavior. His research interests include issues in adoption, cognitive development, and childhood psychopathology.

Acknowledgments

Many instructors of developmental psychology contributed in-depth evaluations of the manuscript. For their thoughtful review and many suggestions, we thank Lanthan D. Camblin, Jr., University of Cincinnati; Marilyn Coleman, University of Missouri-Columbia; Vicki Dossett, Trinity Valley Community College; William L. Hoover, Suffolk County Community College; Ann Brandt, Glendale Community College; Karen H. Nelson, Austin College; Robert W. Herrmann, Christopher Newport College; Rebecca Barrionuevo, University of Northern Iowa; Rob Palkovitz, University of Delaware; Glenda S. Smith, North Harris County College; Jeanne M. Devany, Auburn University; Russell Isabella, Utah State University; Lela Joscelyn, Mount Mary College; Anisa M. Zvonkovic, Oregon State University; Duane Martin, University of Texas at Arlington; Leslie H. Ault, Eugenio Maria de Hostos Community College; Thomas P. Moeschl, Broward Community College.

Anne Gormly could not have written this text without the support and love of her husband, John, who kept the home fires burning while she wrote. Special thanks and love belong to Adam and Sarah Gormly for their "cool" ideas and inspirations. Anne's parents, Charles and Helen McLaren, deserve special mention for their contributions and encouragement early in the author's lifespan. In addition, special thanks are due Ruth Weitzenfeld for her tireless work on the keyboard.

David Brodzinsky would like to thank Anne Braff Brodzinsky, Lara Brodzinsky, and Adam, Joshua, Shoshi, and Zachary Braff for their encouragement, support, understanding, and love.

The editorial staff of Holt, Rinehart and Winston also deserve mention. For their dedication and support, our thanks to Susan Arellano and Jeanette Ninas Johnson. Thanks also go to Cheryl Mannes for finding the right photos. Very special thanks go to Jane Knetzger for her steadfast encouragement and thoughtful ideas.

BRIEF CONTENTS

x

CONTENTS

Observational Activities

Human Development in Practice

LIFESPAN HUMAN DEVELOPMENT

INTRODUCTION

You are about to begin the study of life from birth to death, an ambitious undertaking that will no doubt help raise more questions in your mind about development. Many of your questions about the changes that occur as people change will be answered as you read the following 17 chapters. You will come to appreciate the complexities of human behavior and understand more about the ways our behavior is affected by biological, psychological, social, cultural, and historical factors. You will learn that although people change throughout their lifespan, there is some consistency, and some of these changes are predictable. It is hoped that you will become more attentive to the differences among people around you and apply what you are learning to your everyday experience.

We begin in Chapter 1 with an overview of the issues involved in the study of lifespan human development and of the theories that help guide this study. The methods and techniques that psychologists use to study development are also discussed. We hope that you enjoy your study of life.

CHAPTER

1

Lifespan Development: Issues, Theories, and Methods

What a pleasure it was for Rebecca to have her family and friends with her as they celebrated her eightieth birthday. It was especially wonderful because it was the first chance she had to meet her great-grandchildren: Lara, six years of age, and Seth, only four months old. Her children, grandchildren, and great-grandchildren had come from all over the country for the event. Only her husband Samuel, deceased for three years, was absent.

What a gathering this was for Rebecca! Her daughter Karen, a grandmother now herself, and her son John, recently retired from his job, were both eager to tell Rebecca about the accomplishments and activities of *their children*. Karen's daughter Kate and her husband Michael were the proud parents of charming Lara and baby Seth. Kate was able to balance her career as a nurse with her role as parent because Michael was an active partner in the care and rearing of their children.

John's son Peter had recently become engaged to Diane. The talk of marriage plans reminded Rebecca of the time when she and Samuel courted and married. Times had certainly changed over the past 60 years. Yet the challenges and frustrations that she and Samuel met and overcame in their years together would no doubt be similar to the ones Peter and Diane would face. Rebecca smiled as she thought about her younger years.

While it was true that most of Rebecca's friends were now dead, her friendship with Clara had persisted. They warmly embraced and kidded with each other about how many candles there would be on the birthday cake. After Samuel died, they spent more time together. Most recently, they traveled together to Niagara Falls with a senior citizens' group.

As Rebecca looked around at the people she knew and loved, she thought about the many changes and events in her long life. She realized that her descendants would not be walking in her footsteps exactly, but they would continue to grow and change throughout their lives just as she had done and was still doing. It was this sense of change that added to the excitement and sense of life that characterized Rebecca and was indeed cause for celebration. For Rebecca life is change.

Lifespan Approach

Developmental Psychology The study of the physical, cognitive, personality, social, and emotional changes that occur over the lifespan.

Developmental psychology is one of many disciplines that helps people understand the nature of life. It is a relatively new field that focuses on the changes that normally occur—in body, thought, emotions, and behavior—over the course of a lifespan. Some of these changes are obvious—for example, the three inches grown by the toddler in the second year of life. Others are not so readily visible and are uncovered only by careful study and research within a given culture—for example, the emergence of gender-role behavior in early and middle childhood, or the changes in self-image that occur in middle age. This focus on change is what makes developmental psychology unique. Whereas other areas of psychology may be concerned with the way memory operates, or the nature of human social interaction, only developmental psychology is concerned with the *changes* in memory or social interaction over the course of the entire lifespan.

Let's consider the task of a lifespan developmental psychologist in more detail. Suppose that you were asked to write a biography of a person. You would probably want to describe and explain all the changes and events in that person's life. It would take you a long time and a lot of research to cover all of the major behaviors and events that characterize the subject of your biography. To simplify your task, you might decide to limit your biography to the behaviors and relevant events within a specified period of time or age—say the early childhood years. A different approach to simplifying the biography would be to look at a selected behavior and describe the way the person has changed with respect to this behavior. For example, you might limit your focus to changes in intellectual ability over the person's life. Either approach—the study of a specific age period or the in-depth study of a certain behavior over time—would produce useful information. But to capture the essence of the person and to appreciate the way behavior develops over time, the lifespan developmentalist seeks to combine both approaches. Moreover, lifespan researchers recognize that how a person behaves at any point in his or her life is influenced by what events have occurred in the person's past, by the biological and physical state of the person at the time, by the social and cultural experiences, by the person's ability to understand and comprehend, and by the person's own reactions and influence over the environment. In short, behavior occurs as a result of many factors that interact with each other.

While this lifespan approach to development is relatively new, it has provided new challenges to the way we look at and study human development. (Brim and Kagan, 1980; Featherman, 1983; Gergen, 1980; Labouvie, 1982). Researchers are now looking at the way changes can and do occur at all ages, not just during the earlier years of a life. Because development is seen as the cumulative effect of many different changes occurring at different points in time, lifespan research often involves the study of individuals over long periods of time. As a result of this type of long-range research, conclusions can be drawn about the different patterns and sequences in behavior. Yet each person's life has its own unique character, in part because individuals react differently to similar situations and in part because of the time in which people live. People who grew up in the 1940s and 1950s would be expected to have a different attitude toward sexuality than people who grew up in the 1960s, a time when sexual behavior was more openly discussed.

Contextual View The view that development and behavior must be understood in terms of the total setting or context against which it occurs.

One viewpoint that complements the lifespan perspective is the **contextual view** that proposes that behavior must be understood in terms of the total setting or context against which it occurs (Sameroff, 1983). Development is seen as a dynamic changing process in which the individual and the environment continuously interact. Thus, behavior cannot be interpreted out of context. And the contexts are many. Rebecca's life today can only be understood in light of her health and physical status (biological context), her family network and her role within her family (family context), her friendships (social context), the time during which she grew up and the current time (historical context), her financial and work status (economic context), and her abilities to deal with new challenges (intellectual context). Change in one system affects the context of other systems that in turn can have a later impact on yet other

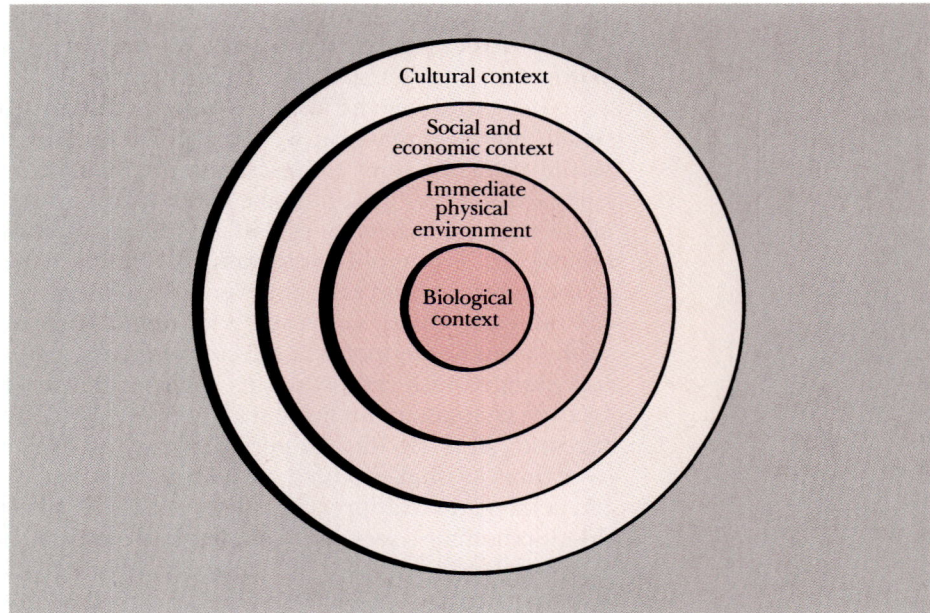

Figure 1.1
Bronfenbrenner's Model
of Developmental
Contexts. Developmental
changes occur within a
series of environments or
contexts which have
direct and indirect
influences on behavior.

systems. Should Rebecca's health suddenly fail, this would no doubt influence her contact with her family, perhaps change her financial status, and reduce her intellectual activities. One example of the contextual approach is given by Urie Bronfenbrenner (1977, 1979) who uses a series of concentric rings to represent the different contexts or environments that influence development (see Figure 1.1).

Because the lifespan approach acknowledges that change occurs all throughout life, it is also the case that behavior can be corrected or remedied in the adult years. This view is in contrast to one in which behavior is believed to be relatively fixed and unchangeable once the person has left childhood. Intervention programs have primarily been aimed at the young. But the lifespan perspective opens up the prospect of intervention programs throughout the lifespan. For example, people typically learn to read and write during childhood; however, some people reach adulthood illiterate. The belief that changes in learning occur throughout the lifespan has made possible intervention programs aimed at teaching adults how to read and write.

The Study of Human Development

In studying these many areas of human functioning, developmental psychologists ask questions that are important to all members of society. Among these questions are: Does emotional stress experienced by the pregnant woman influence the way in which the unborn child develops after birth? Or at later times in life? Does contact between mother and child within the first few hours of life lead to more effective social and emotional behavior in the two-year-old? To a reduction of child abuse? Or to no significant differences in behavior on the part of the child or mother? Does early educational intervention facilitate intellectual growth in preschool children? And if so, can educational enrichment programs be used to prevent the frequent academic failure found among lower socioeconomic children? What long-term benefits are there from enrichment programs? Are there significant differences in the development of children raised in single-parent as opposed to two-parent homes? Or differences between children raised primarily by fathers as opposed to mothers? Does the development of identity in adolescence affect intimacy relationships in young adulthood? Is there such a thing as "midlife crisis," and, if so, in what areas of life does it have an impact? How does the process of aging affect peoples' adaptation to a changing world? What type of intervention is needed and when to make it easier for people to adjust to changes in their lives.

Most of us recognize the importance of such questions to parents, and to ourselves as developing adults. In addition, these questions have a practical application for the formulation of social policy. The research of specialists in

Human Development in Practice

Nursing Care Across the Lifespan

For those of you who have selected nursing as a career, you may be reading this text as part of a course required for your major. Knowledge of human development across the lifespan is essential for people in the health-care professions. An overall awareness of the physical, cognitive, social, and personality changes associated with different stages of development can be useful to nurses for several reasons.

One reason is that nurses usually come in contact with people of all ages and stages of development. Depending on the health-care setting, nurses may care for people from selected periods of the lifespan (e.g., pediatrics and geriatrics). But even when health-care professionals specialize, they often have direct contact with other age groups. For example, pediatric nurses typically deal with children from birth through adolescence *and* with their parents. Obstetric and maternity nurses care for two patients, the fetus or newborn and the mother. For nurses who work in emergency care facilities, family practice, or general medicine, the patients they treat can span the entire lifespan.

In the day-to-day care of people, it is helpful to know what behaviors, capabilities, and issues are typical for people of different ages. This knowledge will help nurses put their patients' medical problems in perspective with their psychological development and to anticipate some of their needs. For example, adolescents often feel self-conscious about visiting the doctor's office when they have to sit in a waiting room with babies and young children (and often their par-

ents). A separate waiting room for teenagers may help make them feel more relaxed during their visit.

Often, parents who have not had the benefit of a course in human development may turn to their family doctor or nurse for guidance in dealing with their family members—young and old. The health-care professional frequently provides basic information and recommendations to parents wanting to know whether or not the behavior of their child or elderly parent is normal for that age.

It is also useful for health-care professionals to keep in mind the ways in which behavior is influenced not only by age and medical condition but by their psychological, emotional, and social condition that does change with development. A middle-aged man may find himself stressed by events that never bothered him during his young adult years and may have physical symptoms as a result.

As you read through the chapters of this text, you will learn about the many different changes that occur as people develop, and how these changes can interact to affect each individual differently. By becoming more sensitive to these developmental changes, nurses and other health-care professionals can more effectively care for their patients. Look for boxed features within each chapter that have been specially targeted for nurses. These boxes will contain information that will help you better care for people of different ages and stages of development.

human development has had an influence on such diverse social issues as child-custody planning, family law, education, media programming, occupational planning and development, retirement policy, and the care and welfare of the dying person.

Determinants of Development

Each of us is a unique individual. Our thoughts, feelings, attitudes, behavior, and even our pattern of growth is like that of no other person. But what makes us the way we are? What factors propel us along the specific developmental path that is uniquely our own?

The question of what determines development is one of the oldest controversies in the recorded history of the human race. Even the ancient Greeks speculated about this issue. In contemporary times, the controversy has centered around two major factors: heredity and environment. *Heredity* refers to the genetic program that is passed along from parents to offspring at the time of conception. *Environment* is a more broadly defined concept. Generally, it refers to the vast array of experiences to which the individual is exposed from the time of conception until death. These experiences may be biological in nature, such as exposure to disease, drugs, or inadequate nutrition, or they may be primarily social, such as the interactions one has within the family, among peers, in school, through media, and within the specific community and culture in which one lives.

Historically, the controversy over what determines development often has taken an extreme form, with one group of researchers arguing for heredity as *the* primary factor in development, and an opposing group of researchers arguing just as forcefully for the unique role of the environment. In this extreme form, however, the **heredity–environment issue** or **nature–nurture issue**, as it is frequently called, has proven not to be fruitful for understanding how development occurs. By contrast, more recent investigators have argued that development can only be understood in terms of the *interaction* between genetic and experiential forces (Anastasi, 1958). It is now realized that neither heredity nor environment alone can adequately explain the complicated way in which each of us grows and develops. At the same time, however, it is not assumed that each of these factors plays an equal role in all aspects of development. Certain behaviors, such as walking, can best be explained by the process of maturation that is guided by our genetic blueprint. Other behaviors, however, such as the type of clothes we wear or the type of games we like to play, are best explained by examining the influence of the individuals and society we encounter. Thus, the critical question concerning development is not *which* factor—heredity or environment—is responsible for our behavior, but *how* these two factors interact so as to propel us along our unique developmental paths.

The Role of Theory

During the first half of this century, most of the research in developmental psychology sought to discover and chart the course of development. Investigators often followed a specific line of inquiry, for example: When do most children produce their first word? At what age do most children learn to read?

The aim of this research approach was a *description* of the milestones of development, not an *explanation* of how the changes occurred. As developmental psychology matured as a discipline, researchers were no longer satisfied with simply describing the emergence and development of behaviors and skills. They wanted to understand the basis of development—to be able to explain why specific behaviors emerged at particular times. This shift in focus from questions of "what" and "when" to "why" and "how" heralded the emergence of formal theory in the study of human development.

A **theory** is a set of coherent interrelated statements, laws, and principles that describe, define, and predict specific aspects of some phenomenon—in our case, human behavioral development. According to Rychlak (1968), a theory serves four important functions for the researcher. The most obvious function of a theory is to describe the nature of some phenomenon. When scientists have fully described the conditions under which a particular behavior has occurred, or is likely to occur, they are said to have explained that behavior. Theories also set limits or boundaries on the phenomena for which the theorist is responsible. This is particularly important since no theory can hope to incorporate all phenomena. For example, Piaget's theory, as we shall see, is concerned primarily with the development of thinking, whereas psychoanalytic theory is concerned primarily with personality development. A third function of a theory is to generate new ideas for research by suggesting possible relations between different aspects of a theory. For example, Piaget theorized that elementary-school-age children develop the ability to consider perspectives other than their own. Based on this theoretical assumption, numerous researchers have examined how this newly developed ability influences such social skills as empathy, cooperation, altruism, and so on. In developing theoretical hunches and speculations to test out, the investigator is relying on the generative function of the theory. Finally, theories also strive to bring together existing research data into an integrated and logically consistent system. Thus, theories help us to bring together ideas, facts, and observations about behavior in a meaningful way. (See Table 1.1.)

In the study of human development, we encounter a variety of theories. Some seek to identify universal principles governing *all* of development. Others focus on only one aspect, for example, personality or intellectual development. Some theories cover the whole lifespan, whereas others are concerned with a much smaller time frame. Thus, theories of development vary considerably in their scope. They also vary in their ability both to generate

Table 1.1 ▬▬▬▬▬

Functions of Theories

Descriptive function	The description of the conditions under which the phenomena being studied occur.
Delimiting function	The setting of limits or boundaries on what particular phenomena the theory will describe and explain.
Generative function	The suggestion of possible relationships between theoretical ideas.
Integrative function	The bringing together of existing data into an integrated, logically consistent body of knowledge.

testable research ideas and to integrate data derived from research into a coherent and meaningful framework.

Developmental theories differ as well in the assumptions they make about the nature of the human organism and its development. Some theories, for example, view human beings as basically *passive,* and reactive, and ultimately responsive to the impact of environmental stimulation. Such theories place a great deal of emphasis on the influence of reward and punishment as factors shaping development. By contrast, other theories view the human organism as inherently *active.* Instead of being shaped by the environment, the individual ultimately is responsible for shaping or constructing the environment. Another area in which theories differ is in their characterization of the nature of developmental change. Some theorists, such as B. F. Skinner, believe that development is best thought of as a *continuous* process. From this perspective, the mechanisms governing development remain the same throughout life. The only difference between the younger and older individual is that the older individual is likely to know and to have experienced more in life. Thus, the focus is on *quantitative* change. Other theorists, such as Jean Piaget, believe that development is more appropriately characterized as a *discontinuous* process. The difference between the child and adult is not just a matter of degree; on the contrary, there are believed to be *qualitative* differences between these individuals. For example, young children do not think the way adults do. Adults are logical and systematic in their thinking, whereas young children are not. Thus, development, from this perspective, is described as proceeding in a *stage-like* fashion, with each stage characterized by different types of psychological organization and behavior.

It should now be evident that there is no single theory of development. On the contrary, there are numerous perspectives from which to choose, each with its own unique set of assumptions about the nature of developmental change. Our willingness to accept one or more of the existing developmental theories, even tentatively, influences the way we view people and the data we are likely to collect about them (Reese & Overton, 1970). Consequently, theories can be said to provide us with a selective view of the world around us.

Pause for Thought

If theories provide us with a selective view of the world, how would a researcher with a lifespan perspective differ from a researcher who did not hold this view in the study of play behavior? Would their views on play differ greatly? How would an historian differ from a psychologist in the study of play?

Major Contemporary Theories: An Introduction

Within the field of developmental psychology, three major theoretical perspectives have had a significant impact on the way development is viewed. These perspectives include psychoanalytic theory, cognitive theory, and behavior theory. Within each of these broad perspectives are more specific theories focusing on different aspects of behavior and development. As we consider in the chapters to follow the different changes across the lifespan, we will discuss these theories in greater detail. For now, however, a brief introduction to the three theoretical perspectives will help illustrate the various ways in which psychologists have come to understand human development.

Psychoanalytic Theories

Psychoanalytic theories of development are concerned primarily with the personality and emotional development of individuals. Their focus is on the way in which people's emotional and biological needs adapt to the requirements of the society in which they live. Traditionally, psychoanalytic theories have placed a great deal of emphasis on the role of early experience in the development of adult personality. As a result, this perspective has stimulated much research on early-childhood socialization processes. Most of this research has derived from the theories of Sigmund Freud and Erik Erikson.

Freud: Psychosexual Development

Sigmund Freud (1856–1939) was a Viennese physician who specialized in what were called "nervous" or "mental" diseases. (Today Freud would probably be called a psychiatrist.) What is important to us is that Freud was a true developmentalist when it came to the study of personality. He believed that personality grew and developed, was formed and elaborated, much as a physical structure is. He also believed that the adult personality was profoundly affected by early life experiences.

Freud's views on sexuality caused quite a sensation among his colleagues. Unlike his contemporaries, Freud did not believe that sexuality arrived full blown in adolescence. Central to this theory was the assumption that stimulation of different parts of the body is sexually arousing to children as they develop. Freud defined sexuality as any type of bodily stimulation that is pleasurable, and he proceeded to show that the sexuality of adolescence and adulthood is the end point of a long and orderly sequence of psychosexual stages.

In Freud's theory, the first stage of psychosexual development is the *oral stage*. At birth, the oral region is very sensitive to any kind of stimulation. Newborn infants will instinctively suck on any object brought to the mouth, even when they are not hungry. According to Freud, the lips and mouth are the source of sexual pleasure. At some point in the second year the anal area replaces the oral area as the primary source of gratification. This shift from the oral stage to the *anal stage* coincides with the neurological development of the anal sphincter muscles, a development that enables children to gain control over their bowel movements. The next stage of psychosexual development occurring between the ages of three to five or six years is called the *phallic stage*. It is during this stage that Freud postulated that sexual gratification is achieved through genital stimulation, or masturbation. In other words, gratification is achieved without regard to the feelings of others—it is a self-centered approach to sexuality. During the elementary-school years, the child enters the next period of psychosexual development, the *latency stage*. This is the time when much of the psychic energy formerly invested in sexual desires is displaced or channeled to other behaviors—for example, mastering culturally relevant skills, including those specifically related to school. From a psychosexual perspective, then, this period is a dormant one. Very little of the child's energy is directed toward sexual gratification. With the advent of adolescence, however, sexual desires burst forth once again, and the person enters into Freud's final psychosexual stage, the *genital stage*. In contrast to the phallic period, sexual gratification is now based on true intimacy, that is, people mutually sharing their sexual feelings with each other.

According to Freud, at every stage of psychosexual development the individual is confronted with the same basic conflict—how to give expression to one's sexual and aggressive instincts or needs in a way that is acceptable both to the self and to society. Freud's description of this conflict centered around three components of the personality structure: the id, ego, and superego. The **id** is the most primitive part of the personality and is present at birth. It is a representation of the person's most basic survival instincts—those biological and emotional urges that seek constant and immediate gratification. The problem for the individual is that direct and immediate expression of id impulses frequently conflicts with the standards, values, and mores of society, which eventually—during the preschool years—become represented within the individual's personality in the form of the **superego** (or what other theorists call the conscience or moral system). In order to resolve the conflict between the need of the id for immediate gratification and the tendency of the superego to prevent or inhibit such gratification, a third component of personality comes into play—the ego. The **ego** is the rational, planning part of personality. Although its aim is the same as the id—gratification of instinctual needs—its methods are more reality oriented. That is, the ego mediates between the id and superego so as to find reasonable, and yet satisfying, ways of gratifying one's instincts. Take, for example, the case of 10-year-old Richard who has just been hit by the boy next door. Richard's basic instinct (id) is to haul off and return the blow. However, he has been told by his parents and elders that it is more appropriate to "turn the other cheek" (superego). Besides, Richard knows that if he does hit the boy back it will only lead to further fighting and a strong reprimand from his mother. Consequently, he decides to wait until a later time and find some other way to get even with the boy (ego). For Freud, the dynamic interplay between the id, ego, and superego formed the basis for the unique personality characteristics of the individual.

Erikson: Psychosocial Development

Freud's theory has been reinterpreted by Erik Erikson (b. 1902), a Danish-born psychoanalyst who studied with the Freudian group in Germany before coming to the United States in the 1930s. In contrast to Freud, Erikson's first interest was children, and his earliest scientific observations were drawn from their play behavior. In his own psychoanalytic theory, Erikson showed that the sequence of bodily sensations Freud had identified were also reflected in a sequence of social experiences that had meaning for children within a given culture (Erikson, 1963). The stage of oral gratification, for example, is also the stage at which the infant establishes (or fails to establish) a sense of trust in the nurturing figure. The stage of anal control is also the time when the child gains control of other impulses that become the object of parental discipline. For Erikson, to move from the oral stage to the anal stage is also to move from a relationship with a nurturing parent, whom one learns to trust or mistrust, to a relationship with a disciplining (toilet-training) parent, from

Id   Within Freud's theory, an innate part of the personality system governing the expression of our most basic biological and emotional urges.

Superego   In Freud's theory, the part of the personality system encompassing our conscience and set of moral values.

Ego   In Freud's theory, the part of the personality system that is responsible for realistic adaptation to the world.

Erik Erikson (b. 1902) described development in terms of a series of psychosocial crises that occur in response to demands that society places on the developing person—demands to conform to adult expectations about self-expression and self-reliance.

whom one derives feelings of autonomy or shame. Unlike Freud, Erikson is primarily concerned with the way in which *psychosocial* rather than psychosexual forces influence the person's development. In his theory, he describes a series of crises that occur in response to demands that society places on the developing individual—that is, demands to conform to adult expectations about self-expression and self-reliance.

Erikson agrees with Freud's belief that early experience exerts a continuing influence on development. We do not simply graduate from the oral stage, with its crisis of trust completely resolved. The crisis becomes less critical but is, nevertheless, re-experienced in all later stages of development. (It is part of what we endure in developing adult intimacy, for example.) For Erikson, as for Freud, each stage of psychosocial development builds upon, and incorporates, the outcome of earlier stages—an example of what we previously referred to as the principle of hierarchic integration.

Whereas Freud believed that the final psychosexual crisis occurred in adolescence, Erikson saw additional psychosocial crises developing in adulthood. Indeed, Erikson's theory is one of the few theories of development that extend through the full lifespan. He has written extensively, not only on personality development in childhood and adolescence, but, as we shall see later in the book, on the normal changes that occur in the developing adult (see Table 1.2).

Cognitive Theories

Cognitive Development The changes in a variety of intellectual operations such as representational thought, logical reasoning, problem solving, planning, memory, and abstract thought.

When we speak of **cognitive development** we mean the orderly changes that occur in the way people intellectually understand and cope with their world. **Cognition** includes the psychology of thinking, or what we usually call intelligence. Also included in this general category of functioning are the processes involved in problem solving, memory, creativity, and the capacity for both logical and abstract thought. These cognitive processes are closely interrelated. For example, memory and creativity play an important role in problem solving.

Table 1.2

Freud, Erikson and Piaget: Stages of Development

Age	Freud		Erikson		Piaget	
	Stage	Focus	Stage	Focus	Stage	Focus
Birth–1½ years	oral	oral pleasure	trust	social support	sensorimotor	understanding through sensory physical contact
1½–3 years	anal	control of bodily functions	autonomy vs. self-doubt	establishing independence	sensorimotor/ preoperational	development of language and other symbols to guide under-standing
3–6 years	phallic	sex-role identification; moral development	initiative vs. guilt	developing self-care skills	preoperational	the use of a prelogical system of reasoning
6–12 years	latent	repression of sexuality	industry vs. inferiority	mastery of culturally relevant skills	concrete operations	systematic and logical manipula-tion of symbols with a concrete reference
12–18 years	genital	heterosexual interest	identity vs. identity confusion	definition of self	formal operations	abstract thought and hypothetical reasoning
Young adulthood	*		identity vs. isolation	establishing meaningful relationships	*	
Middle adulthood	*		generativity vs. stagnation	caring for others	*	
Older adulthood	*		integrity vs. despair	life evaluation; seeking of self-fulfillment	*	

*No specific focus for this age period. (Adpated from S. Ambron & N. Salkind, *Child Development*. New York: Holt, Rinehart and Winston, 1984.)

Constructivism A phi-losophical position that suggests that our knowl-edge of the world at any given time results from an active process of trans-forming specific stimuli (and information) in accordance with our cur-rent cognitive rules and principles.

Piaget: Cognitive Development

Until about the 1930s, children were considered to be miniature adults at least so far as intelligence was concerned. That is, children were thought to differ from adults in the *quantity* of knowledge they had managed to acquire. With the growth of cognitive research, and the revolutionary thinking of scientists such as Heinz Werner and Jean Piaget, it became clear that children think and learn in ways that are different from adults. We can understand why this is so if we accept the assumptions underlying the philosophical per-spective called **constructivism.** According to this perspective of thought, all that we know of reality is based on our mental constructions or ideas. We do not passively discover knowledge ready-made; we actively construct knowl-edge. Whatever reality is, our knowledge of it is always a function of the particular system of mental rules by which we organize information.

Jean Piaget (1896–1980) formulated a stage theory of cognitive development describing the qualitative changes that occur in thought and reasoning from infancy to adulthood.

Jean Piaget (1896–1980), a Swiss psychologist, biologist, and philosopher, developed a remarkable theory about how children think based on the philosophical assumptions of constructivism. Through his observations, Piaget showed that children construct knowledge in a way that differs from that of adults. Therefore, what children know makes a different kind of sense from what adults know. For example, if we were to ask a group of adults to tell us what makes something alive, we probably would get answers focusing on the biological processes that are found in plants and animals—cell multiplication, sensitivity to external stimulation, internal transfer of biological and/or neural information, and so on. When Piaget asked the same type of question to groups of children, however, he received quite different answers (Piaget, 1967). Preschool-age children often attribute life to anything that moves. It is common, for example, to hear five-year-olds talk about the sun and the moon following them when they are riding in the car or to describe the clouds as raining because they are "sad." Somewhat older children, in contrast, tend to restrict the concept of life to objects that move of their own accord, such as the wind or a river, as opposed to objects that are capable of movement, but only if impelled by some force—for example, a bicycle or car. It is not until early adolescence, around 11 or 12 years, that life is restricted to plants and animals—and hence is similar to adult notions of this concept.

As children develop, they replace one set of assumptions with another, thereby reorganizing and reconstructing their base of knowledge. Children undergo many developmental changes before they finally adopt adult assumptions about the world (Piaget, 1970a).

Like Freud, Piaget formulated a sequence of stages of development. These stages refer to levels of mental reasoning, showing how the child constructs knowledge differently at every stage of development (see Table 1.2).

According to Piaget, in the first stage of cognitive development, from birth to approximately two years of age, thinking is limited to immediate sensory experience and motor behaviors; hence this stage is called the **sensorimotor stage.** It is a hands-on, trial-and-error type of thinking. Infants "know" objects only in terms of their direct actions upon the objects. Thus, a nipple is known only as something to be sucked, looked at, touched, and so forth, and the only qualities of the nipple that can be known are those that are revealed by sucking on it, looking at it, and so on. Infants do not understand that nipples and other objects and events can exist somewhere else in space or time when they are not directly acting on them. Thus, the infant functions according to the principle of "out of sight, out of mind" (Piaget, 1952b). For example, if an infant under the age of nine months is playing with a rattle, and, in full view of the infant, we take the rattle away and place it under a nearby blanket, the infant will make no attempt to retrieve it. According to Piaget, from the infant's perspective, the rattle exists only as long as he or she is able to perceive and act on it directly. This is so because infants, according to Piaget, are incapable of mentally constructing a symbol to represent the object that is no longer visible. (A **symbol** is something such as a word, image, or activity that represents something else.) Without a system of symbols to represent things, infants are limited to their immediate experience.

Piaget's second stage of development, which lasts approximately from two years to seven years, is known as the stage of **preoperational thought.** During this stage children become increasingly capable of symbol formation. They master the ability to use many different kinds of symbol systems to

Sensorimotor Stage Within Piaget's theory, the first stage of cognitive development; intelligence at this time is defined primarily in terms of the infant's motor and sensory actions.

Symbol A gesture, drawing, or word that represents something else; according to Piaget, a type of mental representation that is unique to the child's experience.

Preoperational Stage Within Piaget's theory, the second stage of cognitive development that begins around two years of age and ends around six or seven years; characterized by the emergence of representational thinking but the absence of logical reasoning.

Symbolic play is a characteristic of preoperational thought. These boys are pretending to shave their "beards."

represent the objects and events they experience. For example, three-year-old Martha, through symbolic play, uses a cardboard box to represent a crib for her "baby" and calls herself "Mama." In addition to symbolic play, other symbol systems used by children at this time include language, gesturing, mental imagery, and representational drawing.

Although the ability to represent experiences mentally emerges in the second stage of development, children's representations remain limited compared to adult standards. Children can only represent states of being; they cannot conceive of something changing from one state to another. It is during Piaget's third major period of cognitive development, the stage of **concrete operations,** that children become capable of thinking about how things change—and not just how they appear at different times. This stage of development begins at about six or seven years of age and continues until early adolescence. The difference between concrete operational thinking and earlier stages of thought is illustrated in what is perhaps Piaget's most famous experiment. He presented children with two identical glasses of water and asked them if there was the same amount of water in one glass as there was in the other. The two glasses of water looked the same, so all the children agreed that there was the same amount in both glasses. Then Piaget took one glass of water and poured it into a glass of a different shape—one that was taller and thinner. Again he asked the children if there was the same amount of water in the original glass as there was now in the taller, thinner glass. Children at the preoperational stage denied that the two amounts of water were now the same. Most thought that there was more water in the tall, thin glass. Children at the concrete operational stage, however, recognized that although the appearance of the quantities of water was different, the amount of water in the glasses remained the same. Preoperational children had no way of relating the state of the quantity of water in the first glass to its transformed state in the second glass; concrete operational children, however, had developed the ability to do so.

The final stage of cognitive development in Piaget's theory is the stage of **formal operations,** or what we usually call abstract thought. According to Piaget, this stage may be attained as early as 11 or 12. However, apparently some people attain it much later in adolescence, and some people not at all—contrary to the earlier stages that are acquired by all normal children throughout the world (Piaget, 1972). The stage of formal operations differs from earlier stages in an interesting way. In the concrete operational stage, children acquire the capacity to represent transformations mentally, but only transformations of concrete objects and events—that is, things they actually experience. In other words, children master the ability to think about things. In the formal operational stage, however, adolescents master the ability to think about thoughts. By this we mean that they are able to reason not only about things that are actually experienced, but about things that have no concrete existence—for example, hypothetical events such as what life would be like in the year 2010.

Adolescents, unlike younger children, can reason about ideals and philosophy. Adolescents are, in fact, known to be idealistic and fond of talking about the meaning of justice, or love, or other abstract concepts. They are able to enter into such discussions because in the formal operational stage they acquire the capacity for *propositional reasoning* (Inhelder & Piaget, 1958).

Concrete Operations
Within Piaget's theory, the third stage of cognitive development; characterized by the development of logical thought and the ability to manipulate symbols.

Formal Operations
Within Piaget's theory, the fourth, and final, stage of cognitive development that emerges during adolescence or later; characterized by abstract, logical, and hypothetical reasoning.

They can begin with assumptions that need not have any basis in reality and then lead to conclusions that logically follow from the assumptions.

As with Freudian stages of psychosexual development, we will find that in order to understand any cognitive stage we must keep in mind the child's progress through all earlier stages. Children do not simply graduate from one stage to another; the form of reasoning most recently mastered never entirely replaces earlier forms of reasoning. (Once again, this exemplifies the concept of hierarchic integration that we discussed earlier.) Piaget has stated that people typically function at the formal operational level for only a few hours a day, and that most of the time they resort to trial-and-error forms of reasoning (Piaget, 1970a). (Most of us have had the experience of approaching some new piece of machinery with the sensorimotor skills of infancy.) In cognition, as in other areas, we are the living sum of our earlier development.

Pause for Thought

Many educators have turned to Piaget for ideas to help in developing curricula for schools. Using Piaget's stages of cognitive development as a guide, what experiences would you include in a program to teach people at different stages of cognitive development about geography? About death?

Information-Processing Theories

Information-Processing Theory A theory of thinking and cognitive development based on the workings of a computer, dealing with how people process information.

In the past 25 years or so, a relatively new approach to the study of cognitive development has emerged—one that likens human thought to the workings of a computer. Known as **information-processing theory,** this approach can be traced to scientific advances in cognitive theory, computer science, linguistics, communication, engineering, and information theory (Miller, 1983; Siegler, 1983). The focus of information-processing theory is different from that of Piaget's theory. Whereas Piaget is concerned primarily with describing the organizational patterns or structures underlying thought, information-processing theory is concerned with describing specifically how people receive, represent and process information (Kail & Bisanz, 1982). The flow of information begins with some sort of *input*—a stimulus—which is attended to, represented in some form, compared to other information in long-term memory, assigned a meaning, and which eventually leads to some sort of *output*—a response, a judgment, or decision.

Information processing is not specifically a developmental theory. The study of how people process information involves many processes—attention, perception, memory, reasoning, and problem solving. Unlike Piaget, information-processing theorists believe that many of the basic processes for registering, storing, and processing information do not change with age (Siegler, 1983). What does change is the capacity, efficiency, and speed with which people process information (Kail & Bisanz, 1982). Whereas the young child may be able to attend to a stimulus or task for a short period of time, an older child or adult can sustain interest and attention for much longer periods of time. Likewise, an adult who has developed the skill of grouping common features can remember and think about ideas more efficiently than the child who considers ideas individually.

The study of information-processing development has had its greatest impact on our understanding of memory. For this reason, we shall focus on this component of cognition as a way of highlighting the achievements of this theoretical approach. One of the more important aspects of memory development is the acquisition of memory strategies. Although even infants show a capacity for remembering things (e.g., mother's face, the sound of her voice, a favorite toy, etc.), they do not appear to engage in what has been called *deliberate memory*—that is, a planned attempt to remember something (Brown, 1975). Memory in the early years of life mostly is involuntary—it "just happens." We see something, hear something, and then recognize it later when it is re-presented. *Recognition memory* is present even in young infants and appears not to change much across the lifespan. However, some differences occur at different ages depending on the type of material that people are asked to recognize (Park, Puglisi, & Smith, 1986). What does change with development is deliberate, voluntary memory—the type of memory involved when children are asked to try to remember something. For example, if children of varying ages are read a list of groceries to buy at the store, they are likely to engage in different activities or strategies to help them remember what it is they are supposed to buy. Preschool children are unlikely to realize that they need to do anything special to remember the list; as a result many of the items will be forgotten. Somewhat older children may think to say the items aloud, often over and over again, as the list is read. This strategy, called *verbal rehearsal,* is quite effective in helping people remember things. A second deliberate strategy that is likely to emerge during the middle childhood years is *clustering,* or *categorizing,* of items. Instead of trying to remember each item individually, the 10-year-old is likely to group items into appropriate categories such as meats, dairy products, canned goods, snacks, and so on. In this way, the load on the memory system is lessened and the likelihood of remembering the individual items is increased. The important point here is that, with development, people become increasingly aware that they need to do something special in order to remember things. As Ann Brown (1975, 1979) has said, much of what we call memory development involves coming to know *when, where,* and *how* to process information so as to remember it. Information-processing theory has been in the forefront in furthering our understanding of how these processes evolve across the entire lifespan.

Behavioral Theories

Thus far, we have been discussing theories that have focused on the changes in certain behaviors over an extended period of time. The psychoanalytic theories of Freud and Erikson call attention to changes in personality and emotional behavior while the Piagetian and information-processing theories are concerned with changes in thinking and problem solving. By contrast, the theory of **behaviorism** addresses the issue of changes in a different manner. Instead of looking at changes in people's behavior as they age, behaviorists pay attention to the way in which behavior is acquired. The behavioral approach explains human development as the accumulated effects of learning. People's behavior changes as they learn new responses, as a result of experiences in new environments—the high chair, kindergarten, baseball diamond, marriage, workplace, nursing home, and so forth. The difference between children and adults is a *quantitative* one; adults have learned many more behaviors or responses to a larger number of specific people and situations than have children.

According to behaviorists, there are no developmental "stages" in the

Behaviorism A school of thought that maintains that what we call development is only what we learn.

way people learn; people at different ages do not have access to different kinds of learning mechanisms. The mechanisms of learning hold true for people of all ages, and even for animals. Behaviorists maintain that development is continuous rather than discontinuous across the entire lifespan, not just for human beings, but for all species.

Pavlov: Classical Conditioning

The first laws of learning were established by a Russian physiologist, Ivan Pavlov (1849–1936). While studying salivation in dogs, he noticed that hungry dogs would salivate not only to the sight and smell of food, but to a tone that was sounded just before food was offered. He called the learning process classical conditioning. In **classical conditioning** an automatic involuntary response (such as salivation) comes to be associated with a new stimulus (such as the tone) that does not normally result in such a response. This association usually occurs after several pairings. There are many examples of classical conditioning in human behavior. At first, baby Seth would begin to suck whenever a nipple was placed in or near his mouth. However, it was not long before he would begin to suck at the sight of his mother's breast and then at the sight of his mother. In this case, the sucking response is said to have been classically conditioned to the sight of the baby's mother.

Skinner: Operant Conditioning

Much of what we know about the second form of learning, operant conditioning, is the result of the work done by B. F. Skinner (b. 1904). *Operant conditioning* is based on the principle that a behavior that produces a pleasant or rewarding consequence for the learner will more likely be repeated. Likewise, behavior that results in unpleasant or punishing consequences is likely to be discontinued. **Reinforcement** is the term used to describe any stimulus that follows a behavior and results in that behavior being repeated.

Using rats who were placed in a specially designed box (now referred to as a Skinner box), Skinner studied the specific environmental conditions necessary for operant conditioning to occur. To begin with, the rats had to be hungry and thus motivated by the reward of food. Inside the Skinner box was a bar that, when pressed, would result in the immediate delivery of a food pellet (reinforcement). While the first few bar presses made by the rats were random hits, it soon became apparent that the rats would operate on the bar by pressing it to get more food pellets. When the food pellets were removed, the rate at which the rats hit the bar decreased sharply until they finally would no longer press the bar. In Skinner's words their behavior was *extinguished*. (Skinner, 1938).

Skinner went on to discover a series of principles regarding reinforcement and learning. For example, he found that rats retained a learned response longer if reinforcement did not follow every single bar-press during the learning process, but occurred on an intermittent schedule, so that some responses were reinforced but others were not.

Much of what we call learned behavior can be understood in terms of classical and operant conditioning. In later chapters, we shall discuss in more detail the ways in which behavior can be changed by changing the consequences of the behavior. But for now, consider the case of the charming Lara. At age six, Lara has gone to enough birthday parties to know that the surest

Classical Conditioning A form of learning in which a person learns to make a response (CR) to a conditioned stimulus (CS) that he or she has come to associate with an unconditioned stimulus (UCS) that *automatically* evokes the response (UCR).

Reinforcement The term that describes any stimulus that follows a behavior and results in that behavior being repeated.

B. F. Skinner (b. 1904) believes that changes in children's and adults' behavior across the lifespan can be explained to a great extent in terms of the rewards and punishments that follow their actions.

way to get the big candy rose on the cake is for her to smile sweetly at the grownup cutting the cake and politely say "Please may I have a rose?" Every time she had done this in the past her reward was—you guessed it! The candy rose. Her sweet, polite behavior is increased because she liked what followed it, the rose. If on the other hand, she received a reprimand, or worse yet, no response at all, she would no doubt alter her strategies.

Social Learning Theory

Social Learning Theory Based on behavioral principles, a school of thought that also recognizes that people learn by observing and imitating others; gives greater weight to cognitive processes in learning than traditional behavioral approaches.

An increasingly important variation of behaviorism is a school of psychology known as **social learning theory.** The two foremost figures in this school today are Albert Bandura and Walter Mischel. These theorists differ from the more traditional behaviorists in that they are predominantly interested in human development rather than the behavior of lower animals. They also give greater recognition to the role of social reinforcements in explaining how behaviors are learned. In addition, social learning theorists recognize the importance of certain internal processes that are not directly observable but, nevertheless, are seen as underlying much of human behavior. For example, these theorists acknowledge that a person's thoughts and feelings about a specific situation (such as the degree of danger present) can greatly influence his or her behavior in the situation (e.g., whether the person avoids the situation or not). In fact, the most recent development in social learning theory, which represents a radical break with traditional behaviorism, is the inclusion of cognitive processes as a core component for explaining behavioral development (Bandura, 1978; Zimmerman, 1981). Despite these differences, social learning theory incorporates most of the basic principles and mechanisms of learning. The social learning theorists, like the behaviorists, view development as the gradual accumulation of responses rather than as a series of qualitative changes in underlying patterns of emotional or cognitive organization.

Perhaps the greatest contribution of social learning theory is its recognition that responses can be acquired without exposure to direct reinforcement (Bandura, 1977). Much of what children learn occurs through their

Social learning theory suggests that much of what children learn occurs through their natural tendency to observe and imitate those people around them.

natural tendency to imitate or model the behavior of others. If they witness a model (such as a parent) being rewarded, their imitation of the model's behavior will increase. This is so, according to Bandura, because in imitating models, children temporarily identify with them, and consequently "share" in the pleasure of being reinforced—a phenomenon known as *vicarious reinforcement.* Social learning theorists believe that vicarious reinforcement is as strong a shaper of behavior as direct reinforcement. Parents are children's most effective models during the early periods of development. Later, as the person's world broadens, peers, co-workers, and other significant people outside the family become effective models.

Much of the research in social learning theory has sought to specify the conditions that enhance learning through imitation and modeling. For example, researchers have shown that people are more likely to imitate a model whom they hold in high regard and whom they experience as being similar to themselves than a model who is not highly regarded and who is experienced as different. In later chapters, we will encounter social learning explanations of many behavioral patterns that are important in our culture—among them, aggression and gender-role behavior.

Pause for Thought

A lifespan perspective acknowledges the influence that historical events have on changes in behavior. Theories too are viewed differently depending on the intellectual and social climate of the times. Psychoanalytic theories were more influential in the United States during the early 1950s. By the 1960s however, behaviorism was the more popular theory. What historical events or issues may have had an influence on this shift?

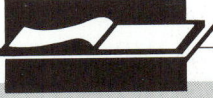

Human Development in Practice

Lifespan Approach to Education

The ultimate goal of education is to prepare people to live meaningful and productive lives. To achieve this end, educators develop curricula to teach basic skills, such as reading, writing, computing, communicating, and problem solving and to pass on the products and accumulated knowledge of a culture to their students. Educators lead their students to discover new ideas and ways of doing things and living their lives.

To be effective, teachers must have both a knowledge of the subject matter of the lessons they give *and* a knowledge of the students they teach. The study of human development across the lifespan can add to teachers' understanding of their students. Early-childhood educators are keenly aware that because children change quickly in their abilities, it is important to consider that what a child learns at age three will contribute to what a child will be able to learn at ages four and five or older. In other words, the learner is constantly changing in many different and related ways that can affect the learning process, a process that spans several years and several developmental periods.

A knowledge of the developmental changes from childhood to early adolescence or adolescence to young adulthood can help educators who teach students during transitional periods of development. For example, school boards must decide at what age children should leave elementary school and enter middle school or high school. A knowledge of the developmental needs and capabilities of students can help educators create realistic learning situations. A study of changes in behavior across the lifespan also helps

sensitize teachers to the individual differences that occur among their students. People develop at their own pace and are affected by their social and cultural environment. Individualized learning programs can be developed to accommodate students who are learning at their own pace. Teachers who are familiar with developmental changes can more easily make comparisons among their students at the same developmental level rather than using age as the criterion for comparison.

With a knowledge of lifespan changes and demands in mind, educators can more effectively develop curricula that will truly help prepare their students for life. For example, during the school years, children begin to develop the ability to consider moral issues and to reach some conclusions about which behaviors are appropriate and which are not. The ability to reason morally takes on greater significance in the adult years. Thus teachers are in a position to influence adult behavior and development by encouraging students when they are young.

Furthermore, if teachers are more familiar with developmental changes, they can teach their students about what life is like for people who are older or even younger than they are. They can help their students anticipate some of the changes that will occur and help them learn ways of dealing with these new developmental changes.

Throughout this text, you will find in each chapter boxed features that address issues of special interest to people in education. Look for these boxes and use them to help you in your preparation as a teacher.

Methods of Studying Development

It took Freud a lifetime to formulate his ideas and observations about behavior into a theory. It might take at least that amount of time to assess the usefulness of his proposals. To evaluate a theory, the researcher must design and conduct studies to test and expand the theory. Most of what you will read about in this book is based on findings from research studies. Many of these studies were designed to evaluate or test some aspect of a theory. But theories are usually stated in rather broad and general terms. In order to conduct a research study, the investigator must first define the specific question or problem to be explored. The problem, however, may be broad, for example, the nature of cognitive development; or it may be specific, such as the relationship between parental use of physical punishment and the emergence of self-control among preschoolers. Regardless of its scope, the statement of the problem, which is derived from the researcher's theoretical framework, defines the area under study.

Defining the problem, of course, is only the first step in research. Once the problem is defined it must be reformulated into a statement about the relationship between variables—for example, the relationship between physical punishment (one variable) and self-control (a second variable). In turn, the variables must be *operationalized;* that is, clearly defined in ways that will allow the researcher to observe and measure the variables. When this has been accomplished, the researcher then must consider the methods and strategies by which the phenomena in question will be studied.

Developmental researchers have many data-collection methods and research strategies from which to choose. Consider, for example, the question of the relationship between violence on television and the expression of aggression among children. Social scientists have used various strategies to gather information about this issue—from naturalistic observations of children in their home, to laboratory studies in which the amount and type of aggression children are exposed to is controlled and manipulated by the researcher; from studies that measure aggression against other human beings, to studies that examine aggression in doll play or fantasy. Some studies have investigated the effect of television violence over extended periods of time, repeatedly testing the same individuals at different ages; others have used samples of children of different ages and have tested each sample only once. Each of these studies focused on the same general problem—the relationship between television violence and childhood aggression—and yet each one took a different approach to the problem. This divergence of approaches raises several important questions: What factors determine the choice of methodology in the study of human development? Do different methods lend themselves better to some problems than to others? What are the strengths and weaknesses of the various research methodologies? In this section, we shall examine these and other questions in order to clarify how social scientists study human development.

Research Designs

Because development implies change in behavior over time, the developmental researcher must address the problem of how to study behaviors that by definition are changing. To accomplish the difficult and complex task of describing and explaining behavioral change over the lifespan, the researcher must gather information about individuals at different levels of their development. Two principal research designs are used for this task: the cross-sectional and longitudinal methods.

Cross-Sectional Design

Cross-Sectional Research A type of research design in which groups of individuals are compared at different ages on some measure at the same point in time.

In **cross-sectional research,** individuals of different ages are tested or observed at the same point in time. The findings—observed group differences in behavior at different ages—are then used to draw inferences and conclusions about the nature of development for people in general. For example, if a psychologist wants to compare the level of moral reasoning of 30- and 60-year-olds, she might interview subjects in those age categories, within the relatively short period of a week or two. If the 30-year-olds demonstrated higher levels of moral reasoning than the 60-year-olds, the researcher might conclude that young adults are morally more sensitive than older adults. She might go further and hypothesize that adults lose their ability to draw moral conclusions as they age.

Since a cross-sectional study usually can be carried out over a short period of time, it has the advantage of being quick and relatively inexpensive. Moreover, it gives the psychologist a good overview of the developmental phenomena under investigation. Yet this research is not without its limitations. For one thing, because this approach measures a person's behavior at only one point in time, it tells us little, if anything, about the historical antecedents of the behavior—that is, what earlier experiences gave rise to the behavior. And it tells us nothing about behavioral stability—whether behavior observed at one time will remain the same when observed at another time. These limitations are linked to the fact that the cross-sectional design tells us more about differences among age groups than about development within individuals (Baltes, Reese, & Nesselroade, 1977). Another problem with this approach is that people from different age groups differ not only in chronological age but also in the historical time period in which they were born and raised. In other words, age groups in cross-sectional research constitute

Back in the 1950's college students occupied their spare time by trying to break the record for the most people crammed into a phone booth. These and other shared experiences of the time often influence the development of people at different times across the lifespan.

Cohorts from the sixties may share similar characteristics because of the social and political experiences they have in common.

Cohort   A group of individuals born during the same time period who presumably were exposed to similar experiences during the socialization process.

different generations, or cohorts. A **cohort** is a group of individuals born during the same period who presumably share many general societal experiences that conceivably could influence aspects of their development. For example, think about the impact of growing up in our era of computers, computer-aided instruction, and video devices and games: People today are reaping the benefits of this "communication explosion" by being exposed to a much broader range of information than people ever have before. Compared to people born 50 or 60 years ago, we may expect to find that today's young people have a different attitude toward technology. It would be difficult, however, to know whether this difference is the result of changes due to development or simply to the differences in training and exposure to computers and other technological advances.

Longitudinal Design

Longitudinal Research A research design in which the same group of individuals is repeatedly tested over a period of time.

To overcome many of the problems inherent in cross-sectional designs, researchers sometimes adopt another strategy—**longitudinal research.** This method involves repeatedly testing the *same* group of individuals over a period of time. The span of time involved and the elapsed time between testings vary, depending on the problem being investigated. Ramsay, Campos, and Fenson (1979), for example, in their research on the development of bimanual handedness (that is, preference for the right or left hand in manual tasks), tested infants at monthly intervals from 10 months of age until a clear preference for one hand or the other was found—usually around the age of one-and-a-half. McCall, Eichorn, and Hogarty (1977), in their investigation of developmental transitions in early mental growth, needed a lengthier time frame. These researchers tested children monthly between the ages of one and 15 months, every three months thereafter until they were two-and-a-half years old, and then every six months until they were five. Other research questions require even longer periods of study, particularly when one is interested in development across the lifespan. In such cases, the time between testings usually is measured in years, and sometimes even in decades. In our example on moral reasoning, we may decide to test adults every 10 years, from 30 to 60 years of age, to see what changes have occurred in level of moral reasoning as the subjects age.

Longitudinal research has many advantages. Probably the most important one is that it provides a good picture of development within individuals and not just an overview of differences between age groups. Furthermore, in following the development of a specific behavior over a given period of time, researchers are able to answer questions about the developmental stability of that behavior. In addition, they often are able to determine what earlier conditions or experiences influenced the development of the behavior in question (Schaie & Hertzog, 1982).

For all its benefits, however, the longitudinal approach has some serious drawbacks that limit its usefulness. The most serious disadvantage is that it involves large investments of time and money. Consider, for example, the plight of the researcher who is committed to investigating the course of mental growth across the entire lifespan using a longitudinal design. The researcher faces an impossible task if he or she plans to personally collect the data. If the researcher begins testing infant subjects early in his or her research career, say at age 25, by the time the subjects are themselves 65 and entering old age the researcher most likely will be dead. Indeed, even less extreme time commitments are often prohibitive from a practical standpoint. For this reason, *short-term longitudinal* studies—usually no more than five years in length—are the rule.

Longitudinal research also has serious methodological problems. Because such research continues for months or years, some subjects invariably will drop out or be lost over the course of the experiment. It is now well known that this loss of subjects does not occur in a random fashion. Subjects who see a longitudinal project through to its conclusion are usually more cooperative, more motivated, more persistent, and more competent than those who drop out along the way. Thus, at the end of a longitudinal study the remaining subject sample may be biased, thereby making it difficult to draw valid conclusions about the more general population.

Another problem with this approach is created by the repeated testing of subjects over long periods of time. When subjects receive the same or similar tests more than once, they often become "testwise"—particularly when the time period between tests is relatively short. In such cases, subjects will perform better on later tests, not because of the effects of development but because of the effects of repeated practice.

A final, more subtle problem with the longitudinal strategy is that some changes in individuals are due to the *time of measurement* rather than development. Consider, for example, a hypothetical study that examined age-related changes in sexual attitudes during adulthood. Teenage subjects interviewed in the 1950s would have probably displayed relatively conservative attitudes regarding sexual behavior. Interviewed today, some 30 years later, these same subjects would undoubtedly be more liberal and permissive in their attitudes. This finding could be interpreted to mean that sexual attitudes become less conservative from adolescence to middle adulthood. However, times have changed since the 1950s, as society as a whole has become more permissive regarding the expression of sexuality. The observed change in this hypothetical study could well reflect a historical change in society rather than a normal developmental change occurring during adulthood. The point is, the longitudinal design in itself does not necessarily enable us to make sound generalizations about the effects of development. As with the cross-sectional design, careful interpretation is needed.

Pause for Thought

Suppose that you wanted to study how taking a course on human development affects people's ability to take care of young children. How would you go about it? What kind of design would you use?

Data Collection Techniques

Once the researcher has decided on which research design is to be used in studying a particular issue, the next step is to decide on what type of information is needed and how this information will be collected. The specific method decided upon depends on the problem under investigation, and the way in which the variables have been defined. Before choosing a technique for collecting data, therefore, researchers must be clear about what it is they wish to accomplish. This, of course, means being familiar with the strengths and weaknesses of the various data-collection methods.

Interview Techniques

Researchers often collect data by means of **interview techniques**—usually involving one-to-one interchanges between the subject and the investigator. In most interviews, the format is a flexible one. The investigator begins questioning in a relatively standard way, but then is free to follow whatever path the individual's train of thought takes.

The interview technique is one of the richest sources of data for the researcher. Its flexibility affords the chance of uncovering the person's thought processes, fantasies, dreams, and so forth — those subjective phenomena not ordinarily open to direct observation or manipulation—in an *in-depth* manner. For this reason it was used extensively by Freud and Piaget. Yet despite its obvious advantages, this approach also has some drawbacks. For one thing, the lack of standardization inherent in most interviews almost ensures that the questioning process will vary slightly from one individual to another. This problem can distort the information obtained, thereby leading the investigator to draw false conclusions. Second, reliance on language as a medium of communication limits this technique to subjects who have a well-developed language system—thus, possibly eliminating such subjects as young children, the retarded, and the deaf. Finally, because valid interviews require good rapport between subject and investigator, this technique is highly susceptible to motivational factors. Results obtained from a child who feels dominated by the researcher, for example, or an adult who is suspicious of the researcher's objectives, may be distorted and thus of questionable value.

The interview technique can be a rich source of information.

Observational Techniques

A second way of collecting data is through **observational techniques** that record the ongoing behavior of individuals with as little interaction between observer and subjects as possible. Observations may be made under naturalistic conditions or controlled conditions. By *naturalistic observation* we mean the recording of behavior under "real world" conditions, with no attempt by the researcher to impose constraints on subjects' behavior. Unobtrusively observing the daily activities of nursing-home residents would be an example of naturalistic observation. By contrast, *controlled observation* involves limiting the environmental scope under which observations are made, or imposing conditions on subjects that are not ordinarily experienced in that particular setting. Observing how children play together in the context of a university-based psychology laboratory, for example, would constitute one form of controlled observation.

In reality, the distinction between naturalistic and controlled observation is somewhat misleading. The difference between these two approaches is more a matter of degree than the traditional definitions suggest. These two categories of observation actually represent opposite poles on a single continuum—with the "naturalistic" end characterized by lower levels of investigator intervention, and the "controlled" end by higher levels of investigator intervention (Willems & Alexander, 1982).

Observational procedures are particularly useful when the goal of research is to determine exactly what individuals are *doing* in a specific setting—in other words, the focus is on behavioral description. Moreover, to the extent that researchers refrain from imposing themselves on their subjects, or the context in which the observation is taking place, this procedure also is useful for determining how children and adults function in their everyday world—a goal that often has important practical implications. By contrast, the major limitation of the observational approach is that it usually does not answer the question of cause and effect. Observational techniques provide us with information about what is happening, but not how or why it is happening. This is because observational procedures do not allow for the kind of experimental control that is necessary to determine how research variables are related causally to one another. Observational procedures also tell us little about the internal, psychological events and experiences of subjects—their thoughts, beliefs, fantasies, and so forth. Finally, observational procedures are inefficient when studying behaviors that occur infrequently or irregularly in the subject's everyday life (e.g., altruism). In such a situation, the observer would be forced to wait a long time before the behavior of interest was emitted. Despite these limitations, however, observational techniques have proven themselves to be fundamental to the study of lifespan human development.

Experimental Techniques

Consider the following hypothetical finding. A researcher who has used interview and observational techniques to obtain her data reports that children who score high in imaginative ability are more likely to come from homes that contain many storybooks and other symbolic play material. Just what does this statement imply? Has the researcher shown that the development of imagination is somehow *causally* linked to playing with certain types of toys? The answer is no. All that has been established is that children's imagination co-varies with the presence of storybooks and symbolic play material. In other words, a positive *correlation* (or association) exists between these two variables.

The data-collection methods discussed so far—interview and observational techniques—are concerned primarily with the establishment of correlational relationships between variables. They usually tell us little about cause–effect relationships. This limitation has prompted many researchers to adopt a different strategy in their study of development—**experimental techniques.**

Experimental Techniques A data-collection strategy in which one set of variables (independent variables) are manipulated and their influence observed on a second set of variables (dependent variables).

In experimental research, the investigator manipulates one set of variables—called the *independent variables*—and observes their influence on another set of variables—the *dependent variables*. To the extent that the experimental manipulation leads to changes in subjects' behavior, the experimenter is justified in assuming a cause–effect relationship between the independent and dependent variables. Take, for example, a study by Oden and Asher (1977). These investigators wanted to determine what effect coaching in social skills would have on peer acceptance and the formation of friendships in socially isolated children. Children in grades three and four who had been identified as being socially isolated were randomly assigned to one of three experimental conditions, only one of which—the coaching condition—was designed specifically to instruct children in social skills. Oden and Asher (1977) found that socially isolated children coached in social skills were better accepted by their peers than were children assigned to other conditions, thereby leading the researchers to conclude that "coaching" was a help (or causative agent) to children in forming friendships. In this experiment, the dependent variable was ability in winning peer acceptance and friendship (because it *depended* on the presence versus absence of coaching—the independent variable).

The experimental approach is clearly the most appropriate method to use when the overriding concern of the investigator is with maintaining con-

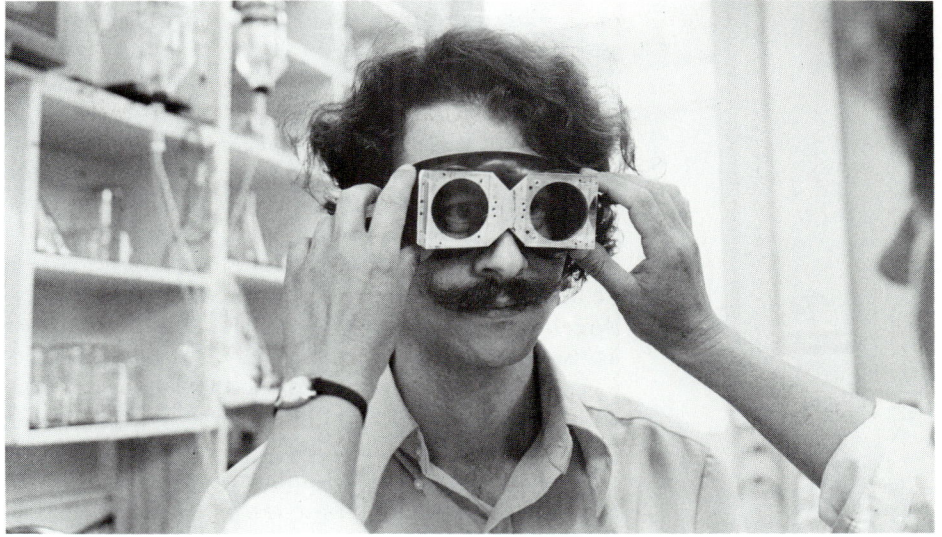

This student has agreed to participate in an experiment in which he wears a pair of glasses with distorting prisms. The experimenter varies the degree of distortion (the independent variable) and then measures the effect on the student's ability to move around in the laboratory (the dependent variable).

trol over research variables, and with establishing cause–effect relationships. In addition, this procedure is useful for studying child and adult behavior that occurs infrequently or irregularly in everyday life. In such situations, researchers can devise experiments that are more likely to bring out the behavior so that it can be studied. Certain types of behavior, however, are not open to experimental manipulation. We would not, for example, purposely expose children to abuse simply to see what effect it had on their development. Another limitation of experimental techniques is that they tell us what children can do under relatively restricted laboratory conditions, but not what they actually do in their real world. This has prompted some critics to argue that we are painting an artificial picture of development through experimental procedures. As one prominent researcher (Bronfenbrenner, 1977) has said, experimental laboratory research is the "science of the strange behavior of children in strange situations with strange adults" (p. 513). The same also could be said for the experimental study of adult development.

Standardized Tests

A final technique for gathering data is the use of standardized tests. A **standardized test** is one whose material, administration, scoring, and evaluation have been so designed that the same test can be given reliably at different times and places by different examiners (Cronbach, 1970). Standardized tests are developed by giving the test material to hundreds or thousands of individuals to establish performance levels associated with different ages— called *age norms*. When the test then is given to a subject in a research study, his or her performance is compared with the age norms derived from the original standardization sample. In this way, the researcher can tell whether the subject is performing above, below, or at about the same level as the majority of individuals of a given age.

Standardized Test A test whose material, administration, scoring, and evaluation have been so designed that it can be given reliably at different times and places by different examiners.

There are many standardized tests used to collect developmental data. Some of the most common are intelligence tests (e.g., Stanford-Binet, Wechsler Intelligence Scale for Children, Wechsler Adult Intelligence Scale, etc.), achievement tests (e.g., California Achievement Tests, Iowa Test of Basic Ability, etc.), and personality tests (e.g., Rorschach Inkblot test, Minnesota Multiphasic Personality Inventory, or MMPI, etc.). The choice of a specific test depends upon many factors, the most obvious one being the investigator's aim. One would not choose an intelligence test, for example, if the aim of the study was to examine personality. The theoretical orientation of the researcher also influences the choice of a test. For example, the Rorschach test, which is assumed to measure hidden and unconscious aspects of personality, is used almost exclusively by psychoanalytically oriented investigators.

Standardized tests are used widely in developmental research. They are also used, however, for many practical purposes—for example, grade-level tracking, clinical assessment, vocational-interest evaluation, and so forth. As we shall see later, the application of standardized tests for solving societal problems has created some rather heated controversies—the most widely recognized one being the use of intelligence tests and standardized achievement tests by school systems for assigning students to grade tracks.

Issues in Data Collection

Suppose a researcher plans to devise a questionnaire to measure test-taking anxiety. In developing this instrument and collecting research data, several important questions must be considered: Are the subjects from whom data are being collected representative of the general population? Are the subjects' responses on the questionnaire consistent from one testing to another? Does the questionnaire successfully measure test anxiety? These three questions refer to the concepts of sampling, reliability, and validity, respectively. In this section, we shall see what these components of research methodology mean and why they are so important in the practice of science.

Sampling

Random Selection A research technique by which subjects are drawn from a population in such a way that every member of the population has an equal chance of being selected.

In selecting sample subjects researchers frequently use the principles of **random selection** to ensure that every member of the population being studied has the same chance of being chosen for the study. Random sampling produces an unbiased sample of the population that may be taken to represent the entire group.

Suppose a study is planned to determine the effect of some incentive (e.g., social praise) on problem-solving behavior in older adults. If the subjects are selected through random-sampling techniques, they are likely to have the same range of problem-solving skills at the beginning of the study as the entire elderly population. Some of the subjects will be good at solving problems; others will be less successful. The randomly selected sample will have a range of skills that is in proportion to the range of skills in the population of older adults as a whole. This means that if the researchers manipulate a variable, such as social praise, to see its effect on problem solving, they can assume that the effect would be similar if measured in the larger, older-adult population. Thus, using the principles of random selection allows researchers to generalize their results beyond the relatively small subject sample employed.

Reliability and Validity

Reliability refers to the degree of consistency with which a test or scale measures something. If a researcher measures the same phenomena today, tomorrow, and again next week, and gets approximately the same results each time, then the measuring instrument is reliable. Reliability also refers to the amount of agreement between individuals who are observing the same behavior. The important question here is whether Observer A and Observer B see the same thing. Measurement instruments and data-collection procedures must be reliable if the data produced in a study are to be accurate.

Validity is the extent to which a test or scale measures what it is supposed to measure. When a variable, such as hostility, must be inferred from behavior, the researchers need to ask whether the behavior they are measuring actually demonstrates that variable. For example, suppose a four-year-old builds a tower of blocks and then knocks the tower over. Is this an expression of hostility, frustration, or the happy exuberance that comes from a feeling of control over the environment? How can the researcher determine what the behavior means? This question must be answered before research results can be applied validly to behavior outside the research situation.

It is possible for a measure to be reliable and yet be invalid. If a test for creativity is reliable, it will produce the same scores at different times if administered under the same conditions. What if the test actually measures something other than creativity, however? Although the test may produce consistent results from one time to another, the finding is of questionable value if it is measuring something other than what was intended. Good research rests on measurement instruments and procedures that are both reliable and valid.

Choosing a Research Strategy

How does one go about choosing a specific research strategy? Is one approach necessarily better than another? And why is it that some researchers consistently choose one method of studying development?

First, the choice of a research strategy is, as we noted earlier, closely tied to the investigator's theoretical orientation. As Overton and Reese (1973) suggest, "theory determines what kind of data are relevant and . . . what kind of (research) procedure is appropriate." For example, researchers who adhere to a behavioral theory of development are more likely to employ experimental or observational procedures rather than interview procedures. They also are more likely to use research instruments, which enable them to assess behavior directly, rather than instruments, such as the Rorschach test, which presumably measure internal—and hence unobservable—psychological structures. By contrast, cognitive-developmental theorists such as Piaget have made extensive use of the interview technique, primarily because this technique is well suited for studying the underlying structure of the individual's thought processes.

We have also noted that the choice of methodology is closely related to the aim or goal of the research project. If the investigator is interested in the behavior of people under real-world conditions, then the naturalistic, non-manipulative approach would be an appropriate choice. If, however, experimental control is more important to the researcher than the "naturalness" of the setting, then an experimental strategy would be preferable.

In some cases, the choice of research methods is beyond the investiga-

Reliability The extent to which measurement of the same phenomenon by the same researchers at different times, or by different researchers at the same time, will produce the same results.

Validity Degree to which a measure assesses what it is supposed to measure.

tor's control. As we have mentioned already, ethical considerations prohibit the use of certain procedures with human beings. Research on how child abuse, divorce, foster care, child-rearing practices, and so on affect subsequent development is restricted to those cases that occur spontaneously in society. Practical concerns also dictate the choice of research methods. The choice between cross-sectional and longitudinal designs is a case in point. Although most researchers agree that longitudinal designs are superior for studying development, the great majority of research studies employ cross-sectional designs because they are cheaper and less time-consuming.

Labouvie (1975) has suggested that the choice of a particular research method also is likely to be influenced by the question of how much and what kind of uncertainty the researcher is willing to tolerate. To the strict behaviorist, the laboratory-manipulative study—which minimizes uncertainty regarding the control over research variables—is the model for scientific research. Other investigators, however, worry about the meaning and generalizability of such research (Bronfenbrenner, 1977). They fear that what we are developing with such approaches is a psychology of laboratory behavior rather than a psychology of behavior in a more general sense. In essence, then, researchers such as Bronfenbrenner are more willing to live with the uncertainty that comes of relinquishing tight experimental control than they are willing to tolerate the uncertainty about the validity of the research setting.

Ethical Considerations in Research

In planning a research project, one of the most important things the investigator must keep in mind is the potential effect on the subjects participating in the experiment. Does the research design in any way expose the individuals to possible physical or psychological harm? If some risk is involved, is it worthwhile in light of the proposed goals of the project?

Ethics in psychological research have become a controversial issue in the past decade or so. In large part this is because we are now more aware of the negative consequences that sometimes result from the procedures we use in studying human beings. Consider, for example, the following hypothetical studies:

> A researcher is interested in studying the effects of punishment on children's problem-solving behavior. Punishment is operationalized as a five-volt electric shock delivered to the child's palm whenever the child makes a mistake on a test item.

> In a second experiment, a researcher decides to explore developmental trends in children's cheating behavior. The young subjects are not told that the experimental setting has been designed to facilitate their cheating on a test; nor do they know that the researcher is watching them through a one-way mirror.

> A third study is designed to evaluate the effect of environmental control on the mortality rate of nursing-home residents. Two groups of elderly adults are recruited. One group—the experimental condition—is given responsibility and control over scheduling their daily activities; the other group—the control condition—is exposed to the usual nursing-home procedure, which entails little personal responsibility and environmental control.

Table 1.3

Ethical Standards for Developmental Psychologists*

1. No matter how young the subject, the child has rights that supersede the rights of the investigator. In the conduct of their research, investigators measure each operation they propose against this principle and are prepared to justify their decision.

2. The investigator uses no research operations that may harm the child either physically or psychologically. Psychological harm, to be sure, is difficult to define: nevertheless, its definition remains a responsibility of the investigator.

3. The informed consent of parents or of those legally designated to act *in loco parentis* is obtained, preferably in writing. Informed consent requires that the parent be given accurate information on the profession and institutional affiliation of the investigator, and on the purpose and operations of the research, albeit in laymen's terms. The consent of parents is not solicited by any claim of benefit to the child. Not only is the right of parents to refuse consent respected, but parents must be given the opportunity to refuse.

4. The investigator does not coerce a child into participating in a study. The child has the right and should be given the opportunity to refuse to participate in a study.

5. When investigators are in doubt about possible harmful effects of their efforts, or when they decide that the nature of their research requires deception, they submit their plan to an *ad hoc* group of colleagues for review. It is the group's responsibility to suggest other feasible means of obtaining the information. Psychologists have a responsibility to maintain not only their own ethical standards but also those of their colleagues.

6. The child's identity is concealed in written and verbal reports of the results, as well as in informal discussions with students and colleagues.

7. Investigators do not assume the role of diagnostician or counselor in reporting their observations to parents or those *in loco parentis*. They also do not report test scores or information given by a child in confidence, although they recognize a duty to report general findings to parents and others.

8. Investigators respect the ethical standards of those who act *in loco parentis* (e.g., teachers, superintendents of institutions).

9. The same ethical standards apply to children who are control subjects, and to their parents, as to those who are experimental subjects. When the experimental treatment is believed to benefit the child, the investigator considers an alternative treatment for the control group instead of no treatment.

10. Payment in money, gifts, or services for the child's participation does not annul any of the above principles.

11. Teachers of developmental psychology present the ethical standards of conducting research on human beings to both their undergraduate and graduate students. Like the university committees on the use of human subjects, professors share responsibility for the study of children on their campuses.

*Statement of the Division of Developmental Psychology of the Americn Psychological Association, *Newsletter,* 1968, pp. 1–3. Modified to eliminate sexist language.

Each of the above examples raises a question about research ethics. In the first example, the question is obvious: Is it necessary to use electric shock to study the effect of punishment on children's learning? Clearly the answer is no. Even if one argues that a five-volt shock is mild and unlikely to cause any physical damage, one cannot ignore the potential for psychological trauma to the child in such a situation. The problems in the second example are perhaps less obvious. Observing subjects without their knowledge and without their fully understanding the nature of the experiment not only undermines interpersonal trust, but may well place these individuals at risk for psychological harm (for instance, acute embarrassment and negative self-evaluation) should they later find out that others have observed them cheating. Finally, even the intervention study described in the third experiment raises an important question about ethical research practices. If the new intervention technique proves to be successful in reducing the mortality rate of nursing-home residents (or at least postpones death for a short time), is it ethical to withhold it from the control group? If it is not, how are we to gauge the effects of the new technique without employing a control group?

Evaluating the ethics of a particular research study can be a complicated task, as the above examples suggest. While some studies (for instance, the first-described experiment) clearly violate standard ethical guidelines for research with humans, others are in an ethical "gray area." The final decision on whether or not to employ a research procedure is usually made by a research ethics peer review board. This board, which is found in virtually every research institution, reviews all research proposals involving human subjects for possible violations of standard ethical practices.

It is generally recognized that research with children and other groups who are relatively powerless (e.g., the retarded, prisoners, inmates in mental institutions, nursing-home residents, etc.) poses even greater potential ethical problems for the investigator. For children, parental consent is always required before participation in research is allowed. Yet parental consent is no guarantee that the child will participate voluntarily. Sometimes subtle pressures (from parents, peers, teachers, or researchers) are enough to coerce the child into participating when he or she really does not want to. Such coercion, whether used with children or others, is in clear violation of research ethics.

Summary

The scientific study of human development is a relatively new and growing field. Lifespan approach to development grew out of research in child development and gerontology. The focus of lifespan development is on the changes that occur in behavior over a person's life. Issues of particular concern to lifespan researchers are the cumulative effects of changes across the lifespan, the overall contexts in which change occurs, and the degree of change that can occur at any age.

Many theories of human development have been proposed during the twentieth century, and each has supporters. Scientific theories have a descriptive and explanatory role. They also serve to define the area of study, to provide a basis from which to test hypotheses, and to provide a framework for understanding the data that derive from experiments.

Sigmund Freud and Erik Erikson based their theories of development on psychosexual/psychosocial factors. Freud found that there were five stages in psychosexual development—oral, anal, phallic, latency, and genital—and that failure to develop in one stage inhibited later development. Erikson believed that social forces exert a strong influence on an individual's movement from one stage to the next. Building on Freud's stages, Erikson went on to specify psychosocial stages throughout the entire lifespan.

Jean Piaget developed a theory of cognitive or intellectual development that specified how an individual's thought processes are different at various ages. Piaget discovered four stages from birth through adolescence—sensorimotor, preoperational thought, concrete operations, and formal operations. An alternative view of cognitive development is provided by information-processing theory. This perspective is concerned with how information flows through a cognitive system, and with the developmental changes in attention, memory, and problem-solving capacities.

Behaviorism, another major theory of development, attributes primary importance to environmental factors. According to behaviorists, an organism learns behaviors that are rewarded or reinforced by the environment. B. F. Skinner and other behaviorists believe that development is comprised of what an individual learns throughout life. An increasingly significant variation of behaviorism is social learning theory, which gives greater recognition to the nature of the organism in explaining how it learns behavior.

The basic research designs available to the developmental psychologist are the cross-sectional and longitudinal designs. The cross-sectional design involves testing different age groups at a single point in time. Longitudinal designs, in contrast, test the same sample of people more than once over a longer period of time. Each method has its strengths and weaknesses, and data derived from each must be carefully interpreted.

Researchers use a variety of techniques to collect data. The most commonly used techniques include interviews, observational procedures, experimental methods, and standardized tests.

The information, or data, generated in research frequently is based on a random sample of the population under study. Two important factors in any research project are reliability—the ability to produce the same results at different times under the same conditions—and validity—the insurance that the study measures what it says it measures.

The choice of a specific research strategy is closely tied to the investigator's theoretical perspective and to the aim of the study. It also involves questions of ethics, economics, and the type of uncertainty the investigator is willing to live with. Researchers in human development must be especially aware of ethical considerations. In any studies involving children, or, indeed, any living subjects, adverse short- or long-term effects must be minimized and appropriate consent obtained.

Further Readings

Ariès, Philippe. *Centuries of childhood: A social history of family life,* Robert Baldick (trans.). New York: Vintage, 1962.
This fascinating history of childhood from early medieval to modern times includes discussions of children's games, dress, social behavior, and education. It also traces the development of the family from the fourteenth century to the present. Ariès makes extensive use of primary sources such as paintings and diaries, and his history is full of rich detail and the lives of children in early times.

Ginsburg, Herbert, and Opper, Silvia. *Piaget's theory of intellectual development* (2nd ed.). Englewood Cliffs, NJ: Prentice-Hall, 1979.
Beginning with a short biography of Piaget, this book outlines his research and theoretical work from infancy through adolescence. The authors also discuss the implication of Piaget's work in the area of education.

Irwin, D. Michelle, and Bushnell, M. Margaret. *Observational strategies of child study.* New York: Holt, Rinehart and Winston, 1980.
This practical book surveys a variety of observational techniques for studying children, with relevant applications and lab assignments.

McCain, G., and Segal, E. M. *The game of science* (4th ed.). Monterey, CA: Brooks/Cole, 1982.
An interesting, highly readable account of the role of theory and research in the behavioral sciences.

Miller, Patricia H. *Theories of developmental psychology.* San Francisco: W. H. Freeman, 1983.
This book presents a clearly written critical analysis of the major theories and issues in human development.

Skinner, B. F. *About behaviorism.* New York: Knopf, 1974.
The famous American behaviorist discusses the basic principles of human conditioning and reinforcement.

Smuts, Alice Boardman, and Hagen, John W. *History and research in child development.* Monographs of the Society of Research in Child Development, 1985, vol. 50 (4–5, serial no. 211).
This edited collection of articles includes papers by historians and developmentalists that address three major themes: the history of the family and childhood, historical approaches to child development, and the history of the Society for Research in Child Development.

Observational Activities

1.1 *Instructions for Observational Activities*
Each chapter of this new edition ends with exercises in observation designed to help you experience some of the situations about which you have just read. In most cases, the individuals you will observe will be easy to find: friends' children, children on public playgrounds, and children in campus child-care centers; people in parks, in supermarkets, shopping malls, and even in restaurants. Although you will not need to interact with your subjects, you should—out of courtesy—inform the child's caretaker, or other individuals involved, that you are engaged in observational exercises as part of a college course whenever you feel that you might be noticed.

Your procedure for the exercises will consist of the following steps, which you might want to write down on your record sheet:

1. Purpose of your observation
2. Place or location of your observation
3. Date of your observation
4. Subject(s)' age, gender, and any special characteristics you need to note
5. Length of your observation in minutes
6. If permission was granted for the observation, and if so, by whom
7. Careful record of your observation with notes describing the incident and setting in enough detail so that it can be analyzed later. Be careful to stick to the facts—what actually was done and said by the subject. Try not to interpret actions or give them emotional labels (i.e., angry, sad, confused).
8. Brief paragraph of conclusions or findings developed from your observation. Most colleges and universities have a Human Subjects Committee

to evaluate and approve of research that involves people. Your instructor will be able to help you structure your observations to meet requirements.

1.2   *Changes in Behavior across the Lifespan*
The purpose of this activity is to familiarize yourself with the degree of change in a person's life by using an informal method of collecting data. Select a friend, relative, or even yourself as the subject of your study.

Your aim is to gather information and evidence of the changes in this person's life. You can begin by collecting a series of photos of this person, perhaps from family albums or yearbooks. Baby books are also a good source of information about the early years of your subject's life. You may want to narrow your focus of study by limiting yourself to a few areas of change (e.g., physical size, interests or activities, school performance, friendships).

You can collect more information by interviewing your subject. You will need to consider what kind of questions you want answered before you actually conduct the interview.

After you have collected as much information as you can, write up a description of the type of changes that have occurred in your subject's life and when they occurred.

Now, the most interesting part of this activity is your own critique of your "study."

1. What problems did you encounter in collecting your "data"?
2. What possible biases are there in your description of your subject?
3. How would you do this "study" differently if you had the time and resources to do so?
4. What did you gain for yourself in doing this activity?

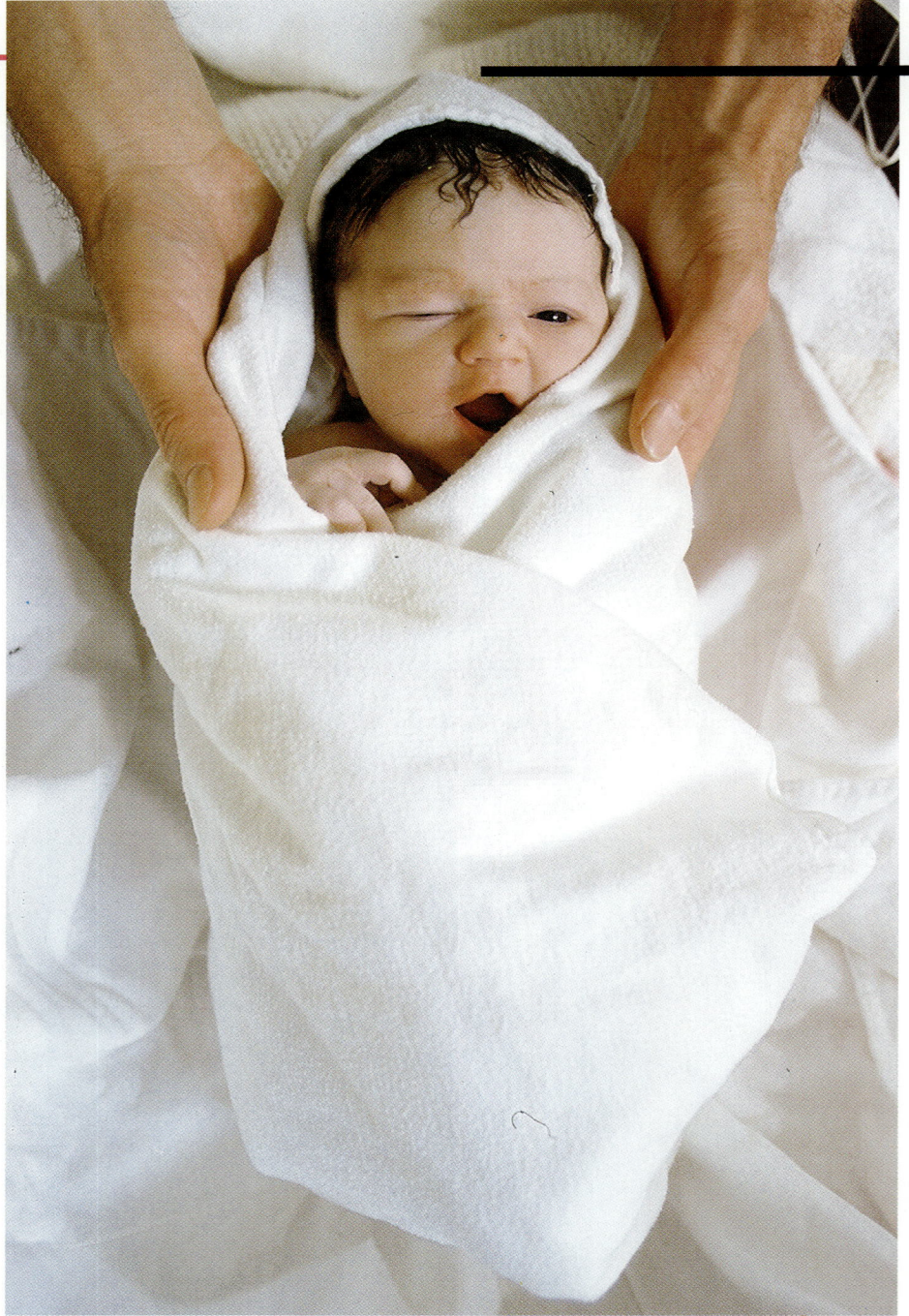

ONE

The Beginning: Conception through Infancy

Life is a process of change and at no other time does change occur so dramatically as it does during the first two years of life. Beginning at the moment of conception, development is influenced by biology and the world in which we live. How these early events and processes affect and shape later changes in behavior is the basic issue pursued by developmental researchers. While the lifespan perspective offers some challenge to the view that development is primarily limited to children, it nonetheless does not dispute the impact that early life experiences have on later development. Throughout the next three chapters, we will be examining the changes in physical, cognitive, social, and personality behavior that occur during the first two years of life. At the same time, we shall be interested in what effects these changes may have on later development.

Genetics, Pregnancy, and Birth

"*T*hat's it! One more strong push!"

"Breathe; you're doing fine!"

A sharp clear cry changed the air of tension to one of celebration as newly born Sarah made her entrance into the world.

Her happy and tired parents, Kathy and Joe, looked upon Sarah with curiosity and wonder. So here at last was the long-awaited child. After counting Sarah's fingers and toes, Kathy took delight in noticing that Sarah had red hair.

"That's from my grandmother's side of the family," she says proudly.

"But look! My dimples!" proclaims Joe, the father.

Examining their newborn child, they begin to talk about how she will change over the next months and years. They remember the nine months spent watching her grow inside her mother's body. The baby's lusty good health tells Kathy that all her attention to proper nutrition has paid off.

Kathy and Joe had been preparing for Sarah's birth even before she was conceived. Kathy made sure that she had eaten a well-balanced diet and had been cautious about not using any medications or alcohol without first consulting her doctor. Joe had even delayed painting the nursery for their new baby until Kathy went away to visit her mother. He didn't want to expose Kathy and the unborn child to the strong paint fumes. Through discussions with family members, they had discovered some possible genetic characteristics their unborn child might inherit. Several of Kathy's relatives had red hair, fair skin, and allergies. Joe's family had dimples, curly hair, and a tendency to diabetes.

It was no surprise, then, when they looked at Sarah, with her inherited red hair and dimples. But the real unknowns were: What would she be like as a child? As an adult? How would she turn out?

With her whole life ahead of her, baby Sarah's story is just beginning. However, the preface to her life story actually began with her genetic heritage and with her early days of life inside her mother's body. The factors influencing this first and important period of development in the life of a person will be the focus of this chapter. We look first at the process of conception, when the first cell of life is established. Then we turn our discussion to the mechanics of heredity and to the influence of the prenatal environment on development. In the last section, we examine the process of birth to discover answers to the question: "What factors influence growth and development in the early months of life?"

The Process of Conception

Once approximately every 28 days in the healthy mature female, a ripened egg is released from one of her ovaries into the fallopian tube to begin its route to the uterus. If the egg comes in contact with sperm cells from the

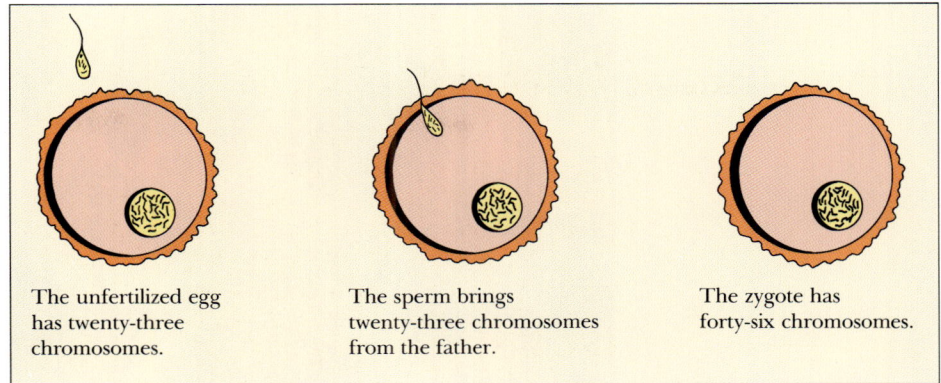

The unfertilized egg has twenty-three chromosomes.

The sperm brings twenty-three chromosomes from the father.

The zygote has forty-six chromosomes.

Figure 2.1 Conception occurs when the genetic materials from the egg and sperm unite.

Germ Cell   The egg or sperm cell.

Fertilization   During conception, the process in which the egg and sperm cell fuse their nuclei to become the first cell of life.

Zygote   The fertilized egg.

Mitosis   Process of cell reproduction in which the nucleic material is duplicated and the cell divides into two separate, identical cells.

Infertility   The inability to conceive or difficulty in conceiving a child.

Artificial Insemination A procedure for conception in which a specimen of sperm is injected into the woman's uterus.

male and one of those sperm penetrates the wall of the egg cell, conception is said to have occurred. The two **germ cells** (the egg and sperm cells) fuse their nuclei and become the first cell of life. This process is called **fertilization.** Fertilization of the egg by the sperm usually occurs in a fallopian tube, and the resulting new cell is called a **zygote.**

A few hours after fertilization, the new cell has duplicated its nucleus and divided into two identical cells. Then again, in a geometric pattern, the two cells become four, the four cells become eight, and so on. This process of cell reproduction is called **mitosis.** In mitosis, the genetic material within the cell nucleus is duplicated and then the cell splits into two genetically identical cells. By this process, cells grow and develop throughout life. As old cells wear out, they are replaced by new and identical ones, each one preserving the genetic blueprint contained in the original cell formed at conception. (See Figure 2.1.)

Alternative Methods of Conception

While most couples who want to have children are able to conceive, about one in six couples cannot conceive through normal means (Sokoloff, 1987). The reasons for **infertility,** the inability to conceive a child, are related either to problems in the man or in the woman or sometimes both. In some cases, the reasons are simply not understood. However, modern medical technology and advances in our understanding of the process of conception have resulted in the development of several alternative ways of helping couples reproduce.

Perhaps the easiest and earliest method to correct infertility has been the use of **artificial insemination.** Through this procedure, a specimen of sperm, either from the husband or from an anonymous donor, is deposited at the entrance of the woman's uterus by use of a syringe. In the case of donated sperm, attempts are made to ensure that the donor has physical and ethnic characteristics that resemble the woman's husband. Once the injected sperm fertilizes the woman's ovum, the pregnancy proceeds like any other conception produced through sexual intercourse.

In 1978, medical history was made with the birth of Louise Brown, the first child to be conceived in a test tube and successfully transplanted into her mother's uterus. *In vitro* fertilization (*in vitro* means in glass or test tube) is distinct from *in utero* fertilization because the mother's ovum has been sur-

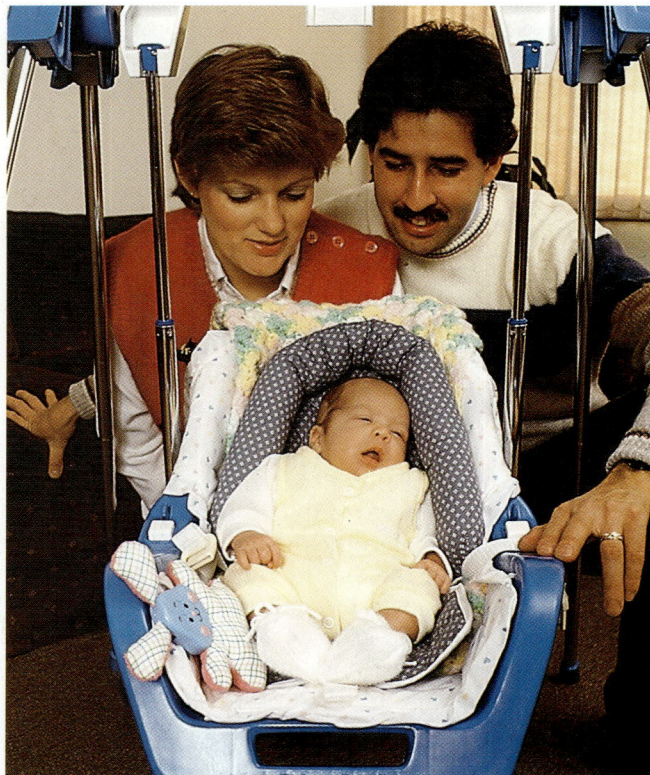

Five-week-old Matthew is a "test-tube" baby; he was conceived by means of in vitro fertilization, an alternate means of conception for couples who cannot conceive through normal means.

gically removed from her body into a special culture in a glass or plastic dish. The ovum is then fertilized with the father's sperm. When the fertilized ovum has grown in size to eight cells it is transferred back to the mother's uterus where the process of growth continues until birth.

In another milestone case, a 25-year-old Australian woman was unable to have children because her ovaries were not releasing eggs or producing hormones that would maintain a pregnancy. A team of doctors was able to help her by using an egg donated by a 29-year-old woman who had blocked Fallopian tubes. Doctors had extracted five eggs from the donor's body for *in vitro* fertilization to overcome her infertility. The donor and her husband agreed to donate one of the eggs to the 25-year-old woman. The donated ovum was fertilized *in vitro* using her husband's sperm. For two-and-a-half months before the transplant, the recipient woman had been taking daily doses of hormones designed to prepare her uterus for pregnancy. The donor and recipient were matched for hair and eye color, body build, social class, and education. After the embryo was successfully implanted in the recipient woman's uterus, she was treated with additional hormones to maintain a normal pregnancy. Thirty-eight weeks later, a healthy boy was born and became the world's first donor-egg baby. Unfortunately, the woman who donated the egg failed to become pregnant using a similar process.

In the United States, another kind of egg transfer is under experimentation. In California, a woman received an embryo fertilized not in a test tube

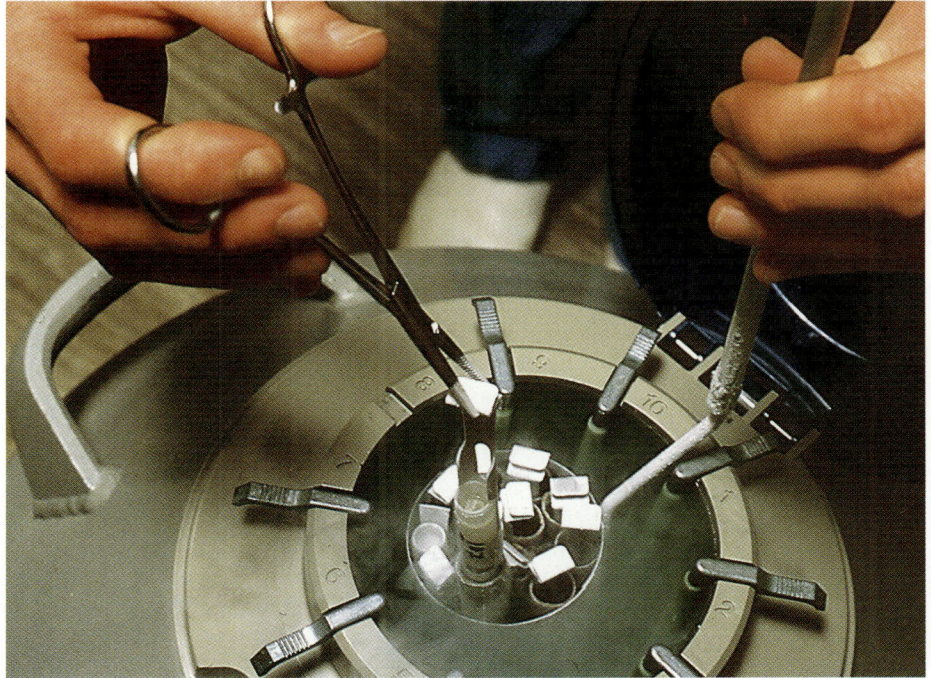

In the process of in vitro fertilization, the father's sperm is labelled and frozen, and stored until it is needed. After ova (eggs) have been removed from the mother, they are combined with the father's sperm which has been warmed to body temperature.

but in another woman's body. The donor was artificially inseminated with sperm from the recipient woman's husband. Five days after the fertilization, the donor's uterus was flushed with a special solution and the recovered ovum was re-embedded into the recipient's uterus ("Amazing Births," *Time,* 1984). Nine months later, a healthy baby was born.

Some couples seeking to have children have turned to a surrogate mother. In this situation, a couple hires a woman to become pregnant by means of artificial insemination of the man's sperm. A legal contract is drawn up in which the surrogate mother agrees to turn the child over to the couple immediately after the birth in exchange for a sum of money and paid medical expenses. This procedure of using a donated uterus has recently been the center of controversy because of the legal, ethical, and psychological issues involved. For example, the surrogate mother may decide to keep the child or the couple may not want the child.

Pause for Thought

Although turning to a surrogate mother may be a good choice for an individual couple, what are the possible consequences or moral implications for society in the use of surrogates instead of adoption as a means of having children?

Genetic Foundations

Mechanics of Heredity

Chromosomes Rodlike structures containing long segments of genes.

Genes Segments of specifically arranged molecules of deoxyribonucleic acid (DNA), which govern cell activity.

Deoxyribonucleic Acid (DNA) Found within genes, a protein molecule made up of sugar, phosphate, and bases.

Within each cell in the human body is a dark mass called a cell nucleus. Within the nucleus are rodlike structures called **chromosomes.** A chromosome is made up of long segments called **genes,** which are responsible for the formation of body proteins that affect the activity of the cell. Genes, either acting separately or in combination with other genes, are responsible for directing the physical changes in the body throughout development.

Genes are made up of specific arrangements of molecules of **deoxyribonucleic acid,** or DNA. The DNA molecule is a chain of sugar, phosphate, and four bases: adenine, thymine, cytosine, and guanine. Arranged in spiral-staircase fashion within the DNA molecule, these bases are characterized by an exact sequence to produce specific effects within the cell body. Change the arrangement of the bases, and an entirely different biochemical effect is produced. Thus, the DNA molecules arranged in gene groupings on specific chromosomes within the cell create a complex genetic code. Each arrangement directs the production of body proteins that influence growth throughout life. (See Figure 2.2.)

It is estimated that there are from 20,000 to 100,000 genes per chromosome, and within every cell except the germ cells there are 23 pairs or 46 chromosomes. Within the germ cells (the egg and sperm cells) there are only 23 chromosomes. Thus, when the egg and sperm fuse their nucleic material at conception, the 23 chromosomes within each germ-cell nucleus pair up to produce 23 pairs of chromosomes in the resulting zygote. Half of the chromosomal material from each parent combine to produce the appropriate

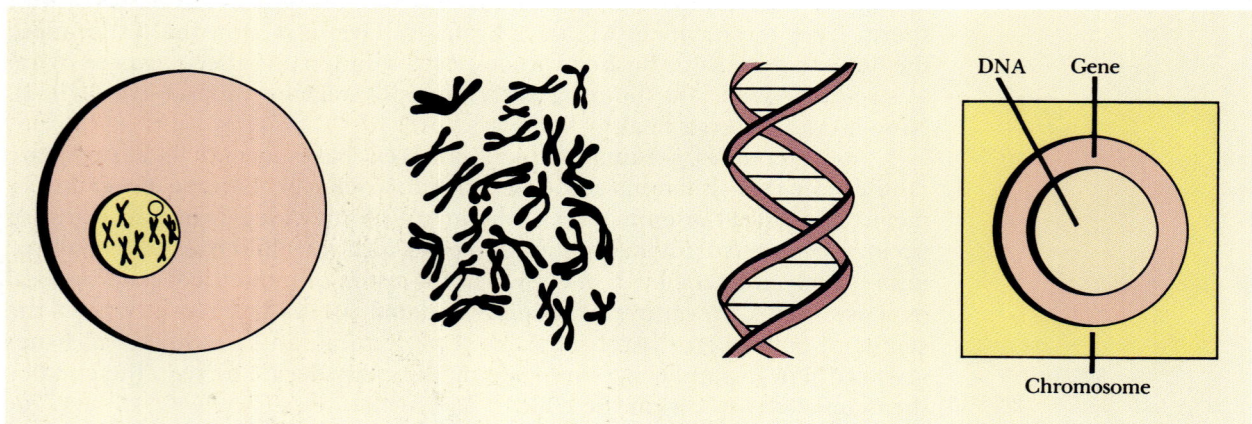

Figure 2.2 A human cell, far left. The dark mass within the cell is the nucleus containing the chromosomes. An enlargement of some chromosomes is depicted in the second figure. Chromosomes contain deoxyribonucleic acid, or DNA, the basic chemical of heredity. A portion of a DNA molecule is shown in the third figure from the left. At each level of the spiral or rungs of the ladder are particular chemical pairs. The arrangement of these pairs along the DNA molecule determines which kinds of protein will be formed in the cell. The relationship of DNA, gene, and chromosome is shown in the picture on the far right.

number of chromosomes for healthy growth (see Figure 2.1). With any more or less than 46 chromosomes, the zygote would develop with serious defects or would die.

Germ cells, like all other cells, originate from the 46-chromosome cell that began life, but germ cells are produced by a process of cell division called **meiosis.** Before meiosis begins, the germ cell has 46 chromosomes, as do other cells. In meiosis, the chromosomes duplicate themselves as the cell divides producing two new cells both of which also divide producing four cells in all. After the first division, the cells divide again, but they do not duplicate themselves as they did on the first cell division. When the second division is complete, there are *four* cells produced, each with 23 chromosomes, or half the number found in the original cell. (See Figure 2.3.) In addition, before the chromosomes separate, an exchange of DNA molecules takes place resulting in a new genetic code. The new genetic pattern within the germ cells is a mixture of the genetic contributions from each parent. Since the DNA messages have been scrambled, the genetic code in the germ cell does not match either of the parents. This is why we can say that with the exception of identical twins, no two people, even from the same family, have the exact same genetic makeup.

Identical twins, or **monozygotic twins,** are formed when the zygote is dividing in the process of mitosis and two separate cells are formed. These separate cells, identical in genetic material since they originate from the same cell, continue to grow and develop into two separate beings. Identical twins are always the same gender since their heredity is the same. Fraternal twins, or **dyzygotic twins,** are formed when the mother's body releases two egg cells, each with its own chromosomal arrangement. These two eggs are then fer-

Meiosis The process of cell division by which germ cells are formed.

Monozygotic Twins Identical twins formed from one egg that divides to form two separate beings.

Dyzygotic Twins Fraternal twins formed when two eggs are fertilized at the same time by two different sperm.

Monozygotic (identical) twins develop from a single fertilized egg and have the same genetic makeup. Dyzygotic (fraternal) twins develop from two separate fertilized eggs and have different genetic blueprints.

Step 1
Step 2
Step 3
Step 4
Step 5
Step 6

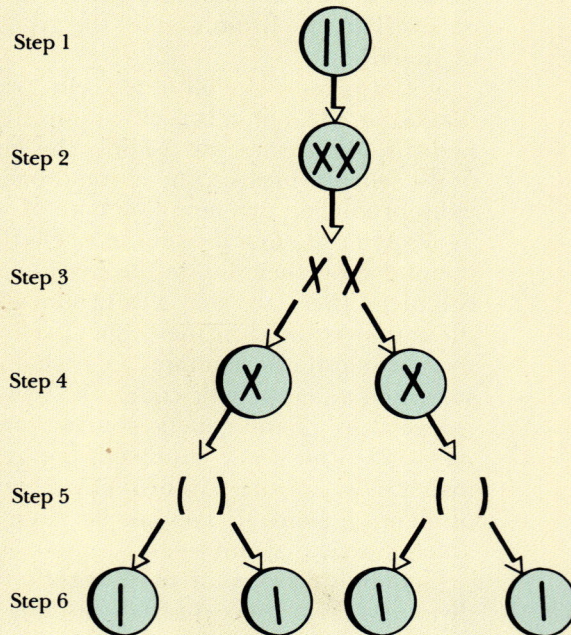

Step 1:   Shows one cell with a pair of chromosomes.
Step 2:   The chromosomes split longitudinally and begin to pair off.
Step 3:   The cell nucleus begins to divide.
Step 4:   The cell nucleus (and the cell that it occupies) has divided into two
          new nuclei, each containing a pair of chromosomes.
Step 5:   The two chromosomes in each new nucleus now begin to move
          apart as the cell and its nucleus divide.
Step 6:   A new cell and nucleus are formed, each with only one chromosome
          from the preceding cell. We can see that, from the original cell with
          a pair of chromosomes, there are four cells each with a single
          chromosome. These are the sperm cells (or eggs, if in the ovary)
          and they obviously contain 23 chromosomes, which is half of the
          original number. When a sperm with 23 chromosomes and an egg
          with 23 chromosomes meet in fertilization, a single cell is constituted
          with 46 chromosomes. We have therefore received half our
          chromosomes (and therefore genes) from our father and half from
          our mother.

Figure 2.3 Cell division by meiosis.

tilized by two different sperm cells. The result are two offspring born at the same time but with entirely different genetic codes. Fraternal twins may be the same or opposite gender. (See Figure 2.4.)

Genetic Transmission

Dominant and Recessive Genes

Within the chromosome pairs are contained the gene factors that carry the biochemical instructions that result in recognizable differences in behavior. What is inherited is not a particular trait or characteristic like intelligence or curly hair but, rather, the bodily instructions to the cell to produce or not

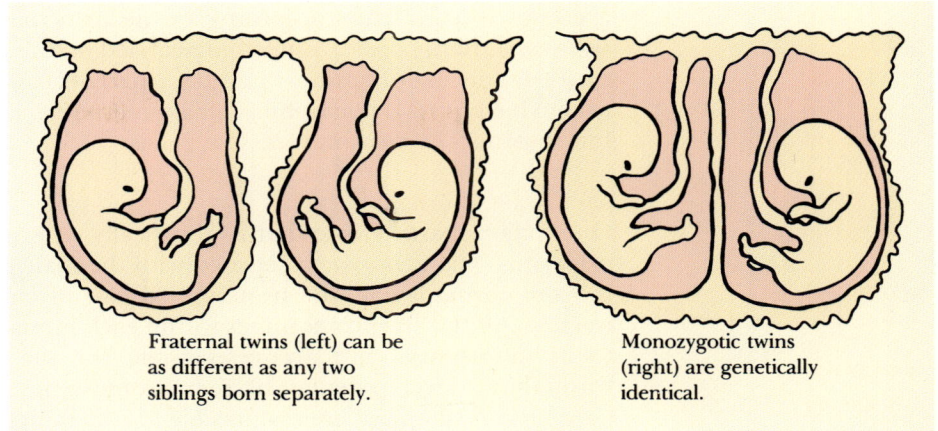

Fraternal twins (left) can be as different as any two siblings born separately.

Monozygotic twins (right) are genetically identical.

Figure 2.4 Except for monozygotic twins, it is impossible for any two people to have exactly the same genetic makeup.

Genotype The actual genetic arrangement contained in the cell; one's genetic makeup.

Phenotype The expressed and observable characteristics of a person that are the result of genotype.

Allele A single gene in a pair of genes, or alleles.

Dominant Gene A gene that is expressed when paired with the same or a different gene.

Recessive Gene A gene that is expressed only when paired with a similar recessive gene or in the absence of a dominant gene.

produce proteins that would ultimately result in intelligent actions or curly hair.

In describing the action of the genes, it is helpful to define two terms. **Genotype** refers to the actual genetic arrangement contained in the cells of an individual. **Phenotype** refers to the expressed and observable characteristics of an individual that are the result of the genotype. Often we do not know the specific genotype for the characteristics we observe in a person because we are still learning about the actions of genes. Many of the characteristics associated with personality and intelligence, for example, are complex arrangements of many behaviors, each of which may represent the action of many, many genes. For less complex traits, such as eye color or blood type, it is easier to describe the genetic code, or genotype.

The gene factors that contribute to the genotype are arranged in pairs within the chromosomes. Half of the gene pair is from the mother and the other half is from the father. These gene pairs are called **alleles.** It is possible to receive different alleles from each parent. What happens when the alleles are different can be explained by the principle of *dominance* and *recessiveness*. Some traits or characteristics are known to be the result of a single gene pair, for example, eye color.

It is possible to receive a gene from the father for brown eyes and a gene from the mother for blue eyes. These two genes, one directing blue eye color and the other brown eye color, would comprise the genotype. The actual color of your eyes would represent the phenotype. In this example, the eyes would be brown since the gene for brown eye color is known to be dominant over the blue-eye gene. A **dominant gene** is one that is expressed physically; it is the gene that, when paired with any different or subordinate gene, prevails in the phenotype. A **recessive gene** is one that is physically expressed only when it is paired with a similar recessive gene or in the absence of a dominant gene.

In our eye-color example, the brown eye gene (B) is dominant, so when a person inherits it from one parent and a blue-eye gene (b) from the other parent, the person's genotype would be Bb and the phenotype would be brown eyes. Since the blue-eye gene is recessive, the only way for a person to have blue eyes is to inherit this genetic code from both parents. Many traits are known to function according to the principle of dominance and reces-siveness. Often, physical defects are carried on the recessive gene and are only expressed in the offspring when both parents carry the recessive gene. PKU (phenylketonuria), hemophilia, sickle-cell anemia, and color blindness are a few disorders carried on recessive genes.

Sex Chromosomes

One major characteristic that is genetically determined is the gender of the offspring. The genotype associated with the male or female body is found on the **sex chromosome,** the twenty-third pair of chromosomes within the cell nucleus. Of the 46 chromosomes within each human cell, 22 pairs are referred to as **autosomes,** and are responsible for the various physical changes throughout development. The sex chromosomes represent the twenty-third chromosome pair and are responsible for the individual's sexual development.

There are two kinds of sex chromosomes. One is called the X chromo-some and the other, a much smaller one, is called the y chromosome. Females carry a sex chromosome pair of XX; males carry a chromosome pair of Xy All the cells in females are XX and all cells in males are Xy. However, the germ cell from the mother, the egg, contains only the X chromosome, whereas the germ cell from the father, the sperm, can contain either an X chromosome or a y chromosome. Thus, at conception, when the egg and sperm cell fuse and the chromosomes pair up, the offspring will be either a female (XX) or a male (Xy) depending on which sperm cell, the X or y sperm, has penetrated the egg. This means that the gender of the offspring is determined by the father, since the mother can only contribute one type of sex chromosome, the X.

Some disorders, such as hemophilia and color blindness and some forms of muscular dystrophy, are determined by genes carried on the sex chromo-

Sex Chromosome The chromosome that deter-mines the gender of the person.

Autosomes The 22 pairs of chromosomes—other than the sex chromo-somes—within a cell, that are responsible for the various physical changes throughout development.

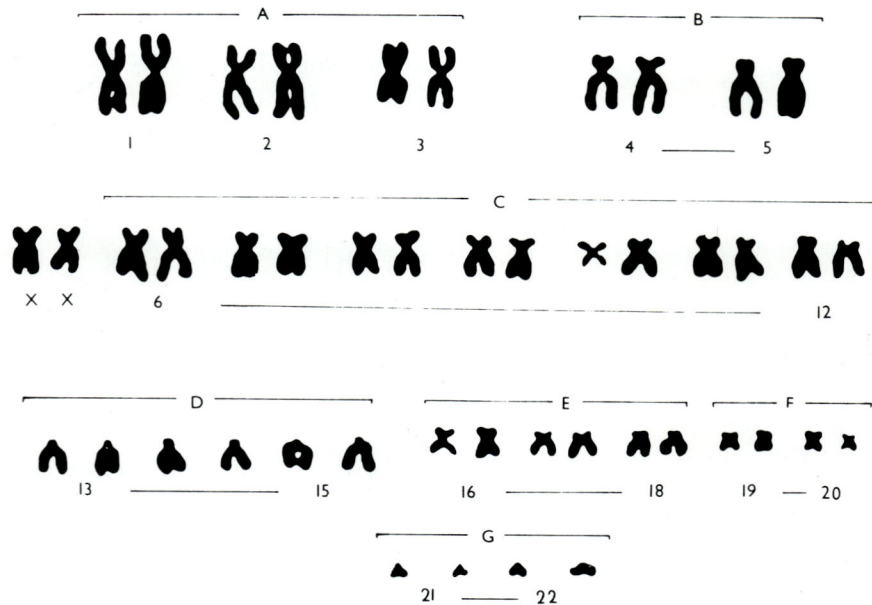

The twenty-three pairs of chromosomes within a human cell are visible in this laboratory photo-graph (known as a kary-otype). The sex chromo-some pair can be seen at the far left of the second row from the top. What is the gender of the person with this chromosome pattern?

some. In the case of the sex-linked recessive disorder hemophilia (a disorder characterized by the body's inability to form blood clots), the faulty gene is carried on the *X* chromosome. There is no corresponding dominant gene to counteract the action of the hemophilia gene. In most cases, people who have the gene for hemophilia also have a dominant gene for blood clotting so they do not display the disorder; however, they do carry the faulty gene. If the mother is a carrier, there is a 50 percent chance she will pass the hemophilia gene on to her offspring depending on which of the two *X* chromosomes is transmitted. If the offspring is a male and receives the faulty gene, he will inherit the disorder since he has no corresponding dominant blood clotting gene on the *y* chromosome to prevent the appearance of the recessive disorder. The female offspring of a mother carrying the hemophilia gene has a chance of being a carrier but not of actually inheriting the disorder. The only way the female offspring could inherit hemophilia would be if the father were afflicted with the disorder and hence contributed the recessive gene. (See Figure 2.5.)

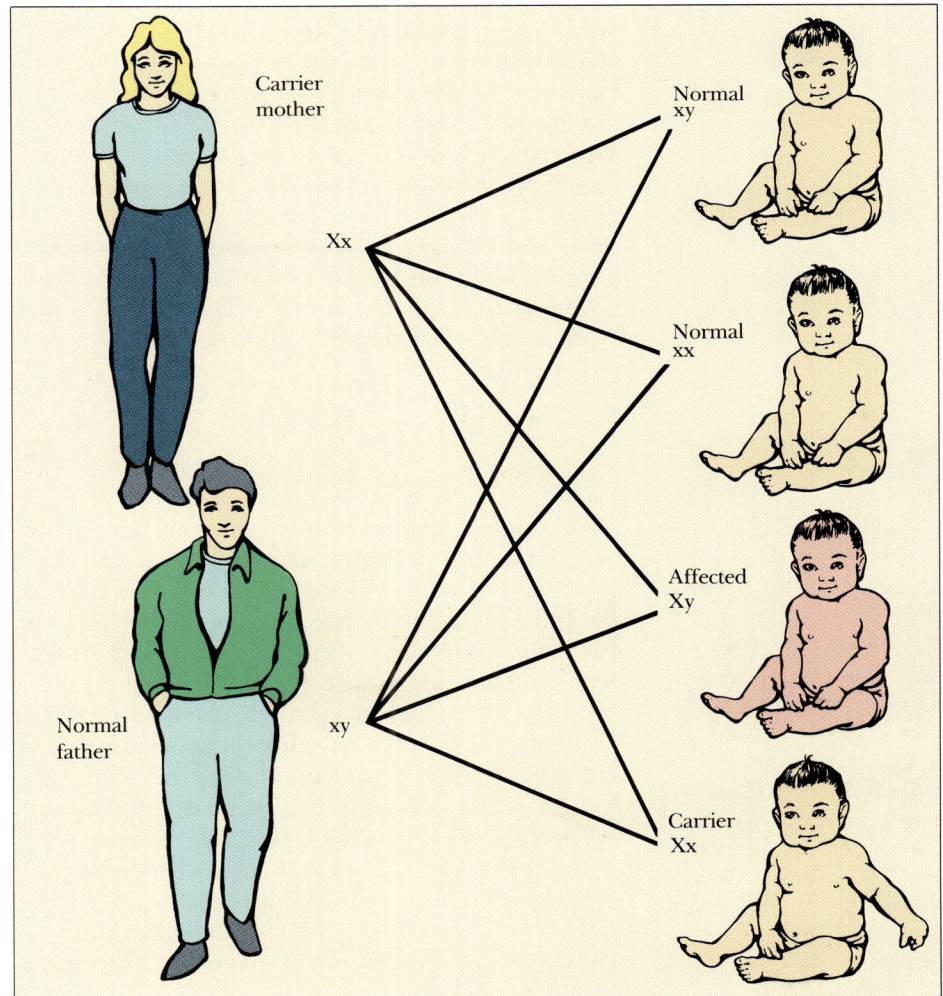

Figure 2.5 How **X**-linked inheritance works. In the most common form, the female sex chromosome of an unaffected mother carries one faulty gene (**X**) and one normal one (**x**). The father has a normal male **x** and **y** chromosome complement. The odds for each *male* child are 50/50: (1) 50% risk of inheriting the faulty **X** and the disorder; (2) 50% chance for inheriting normal **x** and **y** chromosomes. For each *female* child, the odds are: (1) 50% risk of inheriting one faulty **X,** to be a carrier like mother; (2) 50% chance of inheriting no faulty gene.

Sex-Chromosome Abnormalities

For most people, the sex-chromosome pattern is a normal *XX* or *Xy*. However, in some people a defective arrangement of the sex chromosomes results in significant abnormalities. In Turner's syndrome, the genotype is *XO*, indicating a missing sex chromosome. This defect occurs in about one in 2500 births. The person with this defect is female and is characterized by limited sexual development, short stature, and a webbed neck. Although there is no overall mental retardation, there are specific cognitive defects in spatial abilities.

Females with additional *X* chromosomes—*XXX, XXXX,* or *XXXXX*—have increasing physical and mental disabilities with each additional *X* chromosome. Klinefelter's syndrome, *XXy,* involves an additional *X* chromosome in the male genotype. Occurring in two out of 1000 births, this disorder results in tall men, with stunted sexual development, and, in some cases, mild retardation and personality disturbances.

Perhaps the most controversial and well-known sex-chromosome abnormality is the genotype *Xyy,* sometimes called "supermale" disorder. This chromosomal pattern is found in males and was originally thought to be the genetic pattern for criminality, since early studies done on men in prison found a higher incidence of the genotype in men convicted of violent and aggressive crimes. Since then, this association has been questioned because the sampling was not done on a control group of nonincarcerated males. Traits that are known to be associated with *Xyy* include tall stature, poor coordination, low intelligence, and facial acne. Witken believes that the elevated crime rate shown by *Xyy* men is not so much related to increased levels of aggression as it is to low intelligence (Plomin & DeFries, 1980, Witken et al., 1976).

Pause for Thought

Suppose that you were asked to supply expert testimony in a court that was trying to decide whether an offspring was genetically related to a person. What kinds of evidence would you look for and use before you made any statement?

Influence of Genetics on Behavior

At one time researchers asked the question: What causes certain behaviors—genetics or the environment? Now, enough is known about the action of the genes and the molecules of DNA to know that the environment is a contributing factor in the biochemical genetic coding that directs growth. The real question is: *How* does our genetic makeup interact with the environment to produce behavior?

It is the belief of many researchers in the field of *behavior genetics,* the study of the effects of heredity on behavior, that much of individual variation can be explained by genetic differences. Contrary to some beliefs, the influence of genes on behavior does not mean that nothing can be done to change the behavior. Although it is true that it is both difficult and often undesirable to change the genetic code that may direct behavior, it is possible to alter the environment in which the genes operate. The example of the genetic disorder PKU is a case in point. PKU, phenylketonuria, is a single-gene defect that when undetected and untreated results in severe retardation and then death;

these occur because the infant's body is unable to break down a body protein called phenylalanine. The phenylalanine builds up in the body and eventually damages and destroys the brain. With early detection within days of birth, afflicted infants can be placed on a low phenylalanine diet until the brain develops and is no longer in danger from the phenylalanine. Hence, the phenotype associated with the genotype for PKU is bypassed as a result of altering the nutritional environment.

Pause for Thought

Biologists studying the DNA molecule are able to experiment with this basic molecule of life. For example, the DNA molecule can be broken down and recombined to produce a different genetic code. What are the possible problems that can occur by changing the genetic code?

Unraveling the Genetic Thread

Biologists, psychologists, and counselors are teaming up to seek an answer to the long disputed question: How many differences in human behavior can be attributed to genetics and how many to the environment? The question is a complex one because the answer differs depending upon which behavior is studied. A second complication arises when researchers seek to answer the question by conducting an experiment. The simple solution would be to follow the lead of Gregor Mendel, the monk who discovered the laws of genetics by selectively crossbreeding different varieties of garden sweet peas and recording the outcomes.

However, when studying humans, it is not possible to use selective breeding for ethical and practical reasons. Thus, animal breeding is used to study the degree to which a trait or characteristic is controlled by genetics. The specific environment in which the animals are raised can be carefully controlled and compared. For example, dogs known to be even tempered by breeding can be exposed to a stressful physical environment such as one with bright lights and noise and compared with animals of the same breed in a nonstressful setting.

A second way to study the impact of genetics is to examine characteristics and traits that occur within a particular family. A family tree—a description of all the descendants within a family—must be constructed. For example, Sir Francis Galton (1869) attempted to prove that giftedness or genius was inherited by referring to the number of gifted people who were related. The study of inherited characteristics using family trees requires investigation of family records, which often are not available or accurate. Furthermore, environment may account for similar traits within families, since relatives often share similar environments as well as similar genes.

A third approach is to study monozygotic (identical) and dizygotic (fraternal) twins. Since identical twins have the same genetic makeup, any characteristics that are governed primarily by heredity would affect both identical twins. Thus, a high rate of concordance or similarity would be expected. Fraternal twins are no more alike than siblings and thus a lower rate of similarity would be expected for a genetic trait.

By comparing the degree of similarities between identical and fraternal twins on certain characteristics, researchers can identify possible hereditary contributions. The impact of the environment can be assessed by comparing the similarities between twin pairs who are raised in the same environment by the same parents (that is, reared together) with twin pairs who are raised in different environments. The difficulties with this approach are in finding sufficient numbers of twins separated at birth and in following up on the twins throughout their lives.

Yet another approach towards unraveling the contributions of genetics from the environment is to study adopted children who have no genetic connection with their adoptive parents. If adopted children are more like their biological parents than adoptive parents, the contributions of heredity are underscored. If they resemble their adoptive parents more than their biological parents, the environmental contribution is seen as stronger.

Physical Appearance and Disorders

Heredity has a strong influence on physical appearance and body shape. The color of your skin, eyes, and hair as well as blood type, bone structure, and metabolism are all guided by the genetic program contained in the DNA molecules. However, even with simple physical characteristics such as hair color, the environment can have an altering effect. The actual color of your hair, for example, can change as a result of malnutrition or exposure to excessive radiation.

Genes direct the sequence and form of physical development over a lifetime. Height, facial features, body proportion, and even the age at which your hair begins to turn grey is under genetic control. You may be able to look at your own family members and see physical resemblances that appear across generations. This observation that many physical characteristics are inherited is not new; what *is* news is that researchers are unravelling the process of genetic transmission.

A number of diseases and disorders have been tracked to their genetic origins. For example, the specific gene responsible for Huntington's disease has now been located (Kolata, 1983). Tay-Sachs, sickle-cell anemia, PKU, hemophilia, and cystic fibrosis are other diseases believed to be under the genetic influence of a single gene. Other disorders are the result of whole chromosome patterns.

One such chromosomal disorder is *Down syndrome,* or *mongolism.* In this disorder, the twenty-first chromosome pair has an additional chromosome attached to it. As a result the offspring has 47 chromosomes instead of the normal 46. The phenotypic characteristics of this disorder include short stature, flattened skull, oval-shaped eyes with an extra fold of skin over the eyelid, a large, protruding tongue, short neck, and mental and motor retardation. Occurring in approximately one baby out of every 600, Down syndrome is more frequently found in offspring of older mothers. Evidence also suggests that a defect in the father's sperm may result in the extra chromosome in the offspring (Magenis, Overton, Chamberlin, Brady, & Lovrein, 1977).

In the study of the influence of genetics on physical appearance and disorders, researchers can agree on a description of the phenotype. In the case of blood type, for example, certain laboratory tests performed on a blood sample yield results that people can use to determine whether a particular blood sample is type A+ or O+. This degree of clarity in defining the phenotype is not always possible when studying the effects of heredity on more complex characteristics such as personality and intelligence. Let's examine the evidence for the influence of genetics on these two psychological domains.

Personality

Personality is a person's unique pattern of response and adjustment to his or her environment. One of the difficulties in examining the influence of genetics on more complex arrangements of behavior such as personality and intelligence is that the environment also has a significant influence on behavior. If we examine the relationship between parent and child on a specific trait such as aggressiveness, for example, we may find that an aggressive parent has an aggressive child. This similarity cannot with confidence be attributed to heredity, however, since the same parent also teaches the child aggressive behavior through example.

Furthermore, complex traits such as personality develop and change throughout the lifespan. The genetic influence can occur at any and several points throughout this period. For example, the onset of grey hair is triggered by genetic factors at some point in mid- to late adulthood. The *pattern* of changes in adjustment and response to the environment is often the aspect of personality that reflects the influence of genetics.

The study of identical and fraternal twins is useful in distinguishing the effects of training and environment from the effects of heredity. Identical twins (called *MZ* for *monozygotic*) have the same genetic makeup and share the same environment if raised in the same family. *Dyzygotic,* or *DZ* twins, on the other hand, have different genetic makeups but share a similar environment if reared together. By comparing the degree of similarity on a given trait or behavior within MZ-twin pairs to the degree of similarity within DZ-twin pairs, certain conclusions can be drawn. If MZ twins are *more* alike on the trait than DZ twins on the same trait, then a strong heredity influence is likely. However, if the DZ twins and MZ twins show the *same* degree of similarity, this would suggest that environmental experiences are more influential for that trait.

Some behavioral traits and personality adaptations have been found to be influenced by heredity. Infant temperament, for example, which is related to the child's level of activity, sleep patterns, irritability, and sociability, has been found to be strongly influenced by genetics (Wilson & Matheny, 1983). Some studies suggest a genetic basis for the personality trait of extroversion–introversion. People who are friendly, uninhibited, and outgoing with others would be described as *extroverted,* while people who tend to be shy, withdrawn, and anxious with others would be described as *introverted.*

Psychologists at the University of Minnesota have been studying identical twins separated at birth and reared in different environments (Holden, 1980). Thomas Bouchard, one of the researchers, reports that early results from this study indicate that these twins are similar in medical histories, intelligence-test scores, temperaments, and fears. In some cases, the scores of identical twins on many psychological and ability tests were closer than would be expected for the same person taking the same test twice.

Many researchers believe that the predisposition to schizophrenia, a form of mental illness, has a genetic basis. The incidence of this disorder in the general population is about 1 percent. If one parent has schizophrenia, the percent of afflicted children is 12 percent; if both parents are diagnosed as schizophrenic, the incidence increases to 39 percent. Forty-seven percent of people with a schizophrenic identical twin also have a similar diagnosis (Kinney & Matthysse, 1978).

Although research evidence suggests that certain personality characteristics and patterns of adjustment are influenced by heredity, additional work is needed to differentiate the unique contributions of genetics and environment. In particular, we need to discover how genetic-based characteristics are modified or altered by different types of socializing environments.

Intelligence

Is intelligence inherited? Is one's ability to deal effectively with abstract problems passed along genetically? The question of the origins of intelligent behavior is one of the most widely studied and most controversial issues in psychology. Francis Galton (1869) noted that prominent public figures seemed to run in families. Bright and distinguished people seemed to produce bright and distinguished offspring. Our intuitive understanding is that there is a genetic basis for intelligence. However, what type and how much influence heredity has on intelligence is a more difficult question to answer.

Part of the difficulty in demonstrating a genetic basis for intelligence is that there are many different ideas about what intelligence actually means. Most of the studies on intelligence have used the standardized IQ test (IQ stands for intelligence quotient) as a measure of intelligence, and performance on these tests seems to be influenced by genetic factors. Twin studies have provided one basis for this conclusion.

Studies comparing the IQ scores of adopted children with their biological and adoptive parents provide further support for the influence of genetics on IQ. Overall, research has found a closer relationship in intelligence between adopted children and their biological parents than between these children and their adoptive parents (DeFries & Plomin, 1978). Later studies by the same researchers, however, point out that both heredity and the adoptive family environment contribute to the cognitive ability of adopted children. The adoptive mother's responsiveness to her child was significantly correlated with measures of infant intelligence (DeFries, Plomin, Vandenberg, & Kuse, 1981).

Genetic Counseling

Genetic Counseling
A field that provides and interprets medical information about genetics to prospective parents.

Genetic counseling is a new field that helps provide and interpret medical information to prospective parents based on the growing knowledge of human genetics. Information about the probability of their children inheriting certain genetic traits or disorders may help a couple decide when and if they want to have children. Genetic counseling is concerned with other factors in addition to genetic heritage that may produce defects in the offspring. Such factors as the quality of the prenatal environment may affect the unborn child. The aim of the genetic counselor is to provide as much information as possible to the parents to maximize the chances of giving birth to a healthy child.

Several methods exist to provide a couple with information about their genetic heritage. One involves the taking of a family history, noting any medical problems or diseases that have occurred in the parents' families. Another facet of genetic counseling includes the detection of genetic carriers of certain diseases through laboratory analysis of the parents' blood, urine, or perspi-

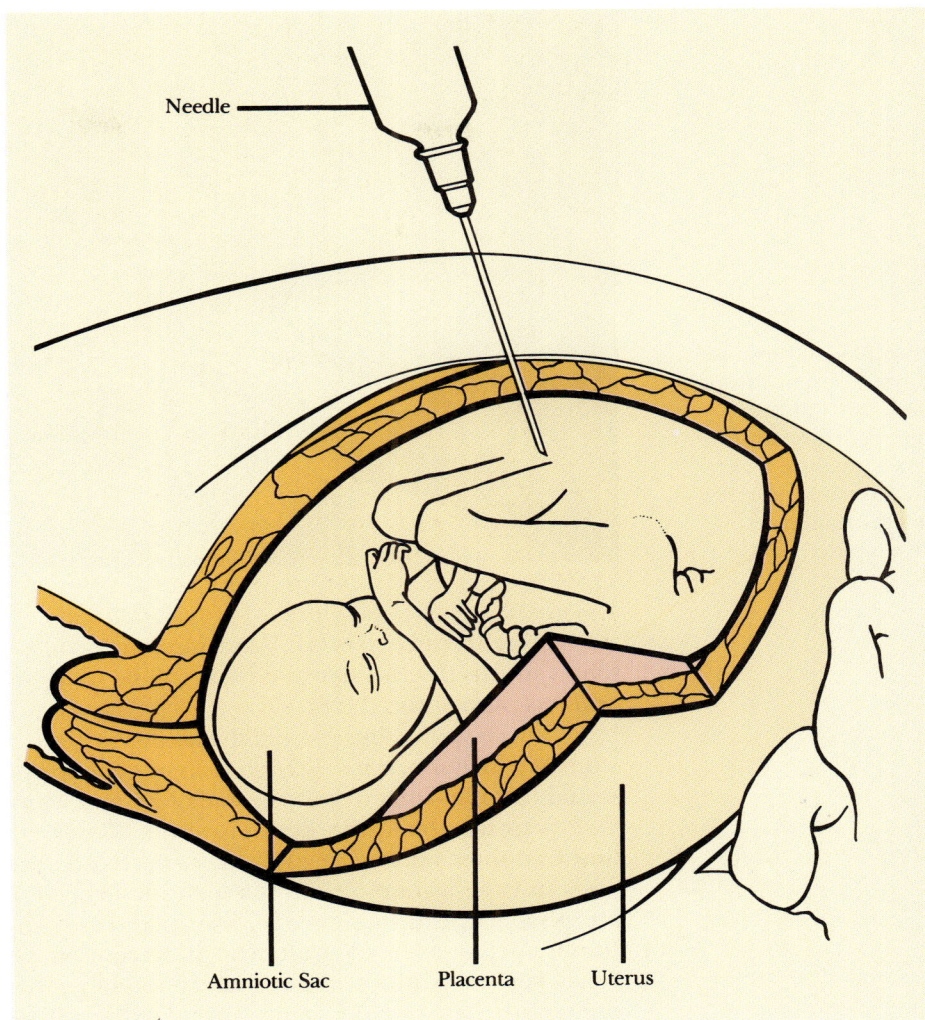

Figure 2.6
Amniocentesis. Amniotic fluid is removed from the amniotic sac and analyzed for chromosomal metabolic disorders.

Prenatal Diagnosis The use of medical techniques to provide information about the unborn child.

Amniocentesis A prenatal test of the amniotic fluid to determine the presence of defects in the unborn child.

ration. A couple may discover, for example, that one of them is a carrier of sickle-cell anemia or Tay-Sachs disease.

In the case of couples who are already expecting, methods are available to diagnose chromosomal disorders, diseases, or other defects in the developing fetus. **Prenatal diagnosis** is the name given to these new techniques that provide information about the unborn child. The possibility of prenatal diagnosis became a reality with the development of the procedure known as **amniocentesis.** (See Figure 2.6.) In this procedure, usually performed after the fourteenth week of pregnancy, a small amount of amniotic fluid surrounding the fetus is withdrawn through a long, hollow syringe inserted into the uterus through the mother's abdomen. The fluid contains the discarded skin cells from the developing fetus. After these cells have been allowed to grow in a culture, they are analyzed to learn about the chromosomal, genetic, and metabolic characteristics of the unborn child. The gender of the offspring and about 100 metabolic defects can be diagnosed. In addition, the use of *ultrasound,* or sound waves sent through the uterus, allows the physician to

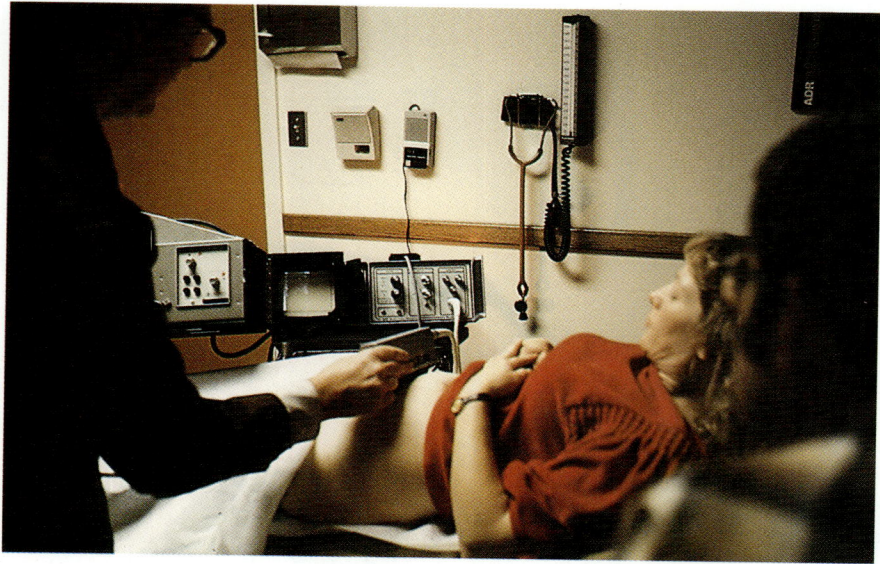

Harmless ultrasound waves are sent through the uterus of the pregnant woman to determine the size, location, and number of fetuses that are developing.

determine the size, location, and number of fetuses in the mother's uterus. This reduces the risk that the fetus will be touched by the syringe during the amniocentesis procedure.

These and other prenatal diagnostic tests are usually performed on women with comparatively high risks of genetic or chromosomal defects. This would include women over the age of 35 and women with a family history of genetic or metabolic disorders. However, 97 percent of these high-risk women find that their fetus is free of any suspected defect.

In cases where a defect is identified through early prenatal diagnosis, the physician can minimize and in some cases correct the damage through prompt action at or soon after birth. Recent advances in medical technology have even made it possible to correct a defect during the pregnancy through prenatal surgery or medicine. In any case, the prospective parents can be assisted in pregnancy and birth with early information about the child with a defect. A genetic counselor will help provide the couple with a realistic view of the choices and risks associated with the impending birth to help them deal with the ongoing problems or to plan for a future family. In some cases, when diagnostic tests reveal that the unborn child is severely defective, the genetic counselor may provide the parents with information about therapeutic abortion and help them in making the decision whether or not to terminate the pregnancy.

Pause for Thought

Through the process of amniocentesis, the gender of the offspring is detected before birth. How might knowing the gender of a child before birth have an impact on the parents? Can you think of cultures in which one gender is preferred over the other? How might this prenatal knowledge affect the parents in these cultures?

Human Development in Practice

Techniques in Prenatal Diagnosis

Once a pregnancy has begun, many couples may be concerned about whether their unborn child is developing correctly. If there is a history of genetic disorders or birth defects in one or both of the couple's families, or if the parents are older, they have greater reason for concern. Through prenatal diagnosis, the presence or absence of several congenital or genetic disorders can be confirmed.

Amniocentesis is just one of several techniques now available. Fetal cells that have been extracted from the amniotic fluid are grown in laboratory culture for two to four weeks and then studied for chromosomal or some metabolic disorders. If amniocentesis is performed later in prenatal development, the potential for diagnosing disorders is better. However, most people would prefer to know early in the pregnancy whether the fetus is developing abnormally so they can decide whether or not to terminate the pregnancy. Even if an elective abortion is ruled out, couples may still prefer to have an earlier indication of the status and well-being of their unborn child.

In the mid-1980s, a second prenatal diagnostic procedure called **chorionic villus test** was developed. One advantage of this newer technique is that it can be performed at an earlier stage of the pregnancy, between the fifth and the tenth week. Amniocentesis tests are usually performed about the fourteenth to sixteenth week of pregnancy, and results are not known for another 4 weeks after that. Terminating a pregnancy in the first trimester is much safer and easier than terminating a pregnancy at 18 to 20 weeks or 5 months. Furthermore, it is psychologically more difficult for couples to decide whether to terminate the pregnancy of a defective child when the fetus is large enough to be felt moving in the mother's uterus.

The chorionic villus test involves removing a sample of the chorionic villus from the placenta that can be reached through the mother's cervix. The chorionic villi are tiny protrusions of the chorion, the membrane that surrounds the fetus and eventually becomes part of the placenta. (See Figure 2.8.) It usually takes a short time (1 week) to completely analyze the fetal cells from the sample, although results can be obtained in a day. From the test, about 3800 diseases and disorders can be detected (Schmeck, 1983). In both amniocentesis and the chorionic villus test, ultrasound is used to locate the developing fetus and help guide obstetricians when obtaining fetal samples.

Prenatal Development

Stages

Chorionic Villus Test A prenatal diagnostic test in which fetal cell samples are obtained from the villi protruding from the chorion surrounding the fetus.

Ovum Stage The first stage of prenatal development lasting from conception to 10 to 14 days.

The normal pregnancy lasts nine months, or 266 days. The new cell, the zygote, changes in shape and size at a rapid rate during the time from conception to birth. It is helpful to break down the gestation period into three stages: the ovum, the embryo, and the fetus.

The **ovum stage,** also called the germinal stage, begins at conception in the mother's fallopian tube and ends with the implantation of the developing zygote in the uterine wall. This stage lasts approximately two weeks. During this time, the developing ovum, or fertilized egg, is rapidly growing through the process of mitosis at the same time it is traveling to the uterus. Once the mother's egg is fertilized by the sperm her body begins preparing the lining of the uterine wall with a rich blood supply to provide for the developing

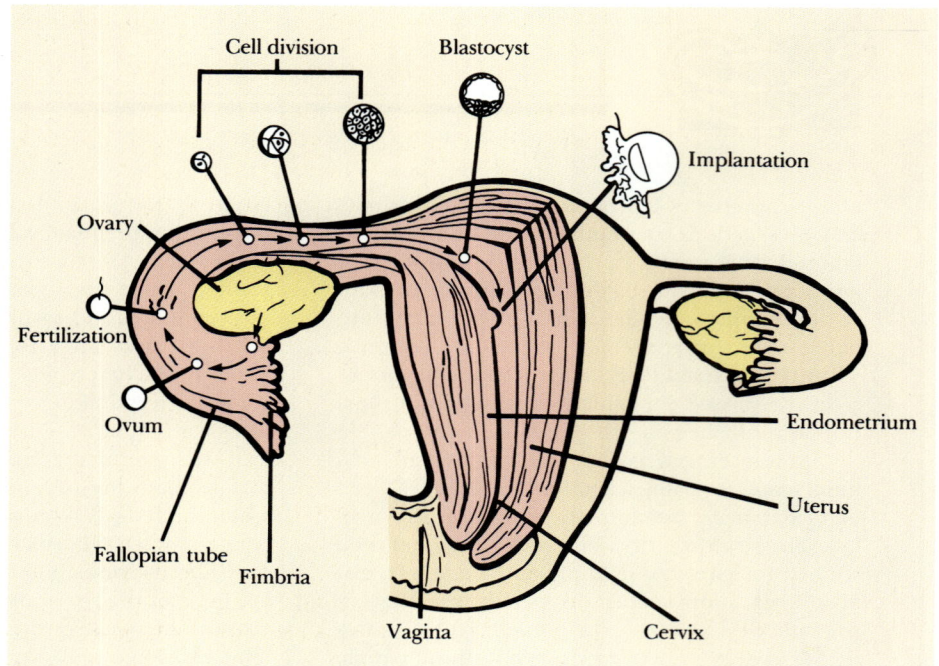

Figure 2.7 Ovulation, fertilization and implantation. The ovary releases an egg into the fallopian tube, where it is penetrated by a sperm. The zygote begins cell division as it moves down the fallopian tube toward the uterus. When the cluster of cells has formed a hollow ball, it is called a blastocyst. Six days after conception the blastocyst begins to implant itself in the wall of the uterus.

Differentiation
(1) Changes in growth and development from simple, general forms to more complex, specific forms. (2) Within two weeks after fertilization, the process in which growth of the cell becomes more specialized.

Blastocyst The hollow sphere of cells that forms within a week after fertilization.

Embryo Stage The six weeks following the implantation of the ovum into the uterine wall.

Placenta A blood-filled structure that supplies the unborn child with nutrients.

new life over the nine-month gestation period. The mother at this time may not even be aware of her pregnancy since she has yet to miss a menstrual period. By about the sixth day, the ovum has reached the uterus and the process of implantation begins. (See Figure 2.7.)

At about the time the ovum enters the uterus, the developing cells, now approximately 32 in number, start a process of **differentiation.** Through this process, the cells, triggered by genetic instructions, take on different functions. By a week after fertilization, the cells form into a hollow ball called a **blastocyst.** Some of the inner cells of the blastocyst will form the body of the baby, while the outer cells will form the placenta, umbilical cord, and amniotic sac, the structures that house and protect the developing baby during prenatal development. At this time, the cell mass is no larger than the size of the period at the end of this sentence. When the blastocyst imbeds itself into the blood-rich wall of the uterus, the ovum stage ends and the embryonic stage begins.

The **embryo stage** (from the Greek word "to swell") lasts approximately six weeks. During this time, the life-support systems—the placenta, the umbilical cord, and the amniotic sac—are refined. The part of the embryo attached to the uterine wall becomes the **placenta.** This blood-filled, spongy mass is an amazing organ that supplies the embryo with all its nutrients and carries off all its waste products. The embryo is linked to the placenta through

Umbilical Cord The structure that links the embryo to the placenta.

the **umbilical cord,** a tough hoselike structure made up of two arteries and one vein surrounded by a jellylike substance. The placenta grows in size during pregnancy and has two sets of blood vessels connected to it, one set going to the developing baby through the umbilical cord and the other set going to the mother's circulatory system. However, there is no direct link between these two blood systems. The semipermeable membrane in the vessels permits an exchange of the nutrients and other elements small enough to pass through the blood vessel walls. Through this indirect passage, the embryo receives oxygen, proteins, and other essential ingredients for growth, while exchanging waste products of carbon dioxide. The embryo is essentially a parasite to the mother's body. The remarkable thing about the placenta is that it permits the growth of a foreign body within the mother's body. Medical researchers interested in organ transplants are studying the structure of the placenta to gain new insights into improving transplants. As we will discover in later sections, the placenta is not perfect. Not only do helpful molecules pass through the placenta, but some viruses, bacteria, and harmful chemicals also pass through the placenta to affect the developing embryo. (See Figure 2.8.)

Amniotic Sac A membrane filled with a salty fluid that surrounds the embryo.

During the embryonic stage, the amniotic sac develops and encloses the embryo. The **amniotic sac** is a membrane filled with amniotic fluid, a salty solution that surrounds the embryo. Acting like a cushion for the embryo, this fluid-filled sac protects it from jolts and shocks and the effects of gravity. The fluid is maintained at a constant temperature, warmed by the mother's body. The embryo grows rapidly during this period, developing the basic

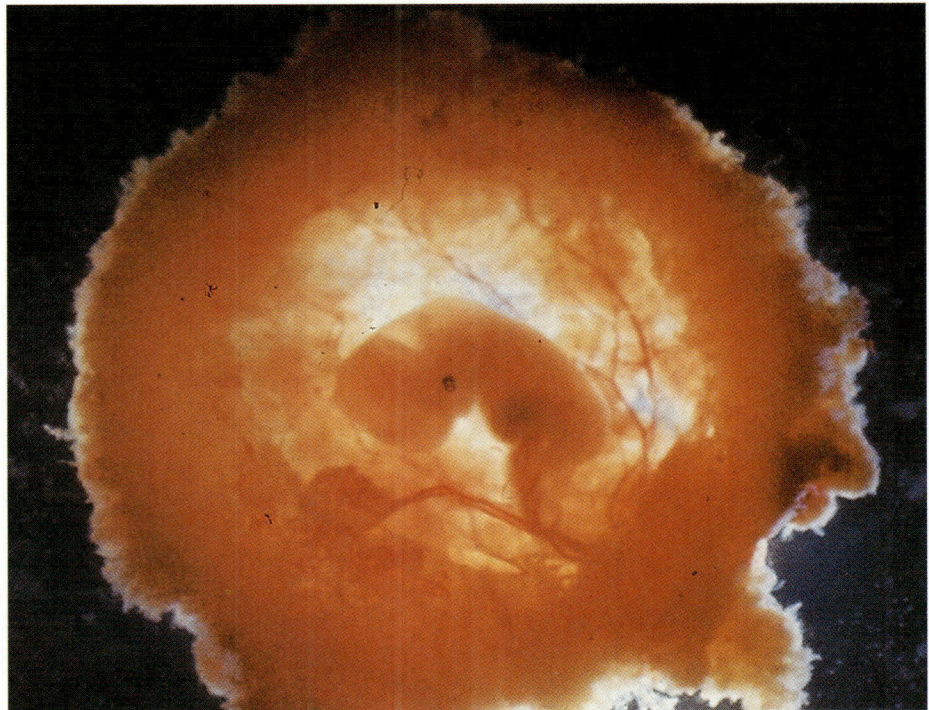

The human embryo at seven weeks of life is surrounded by the amniotic sac.

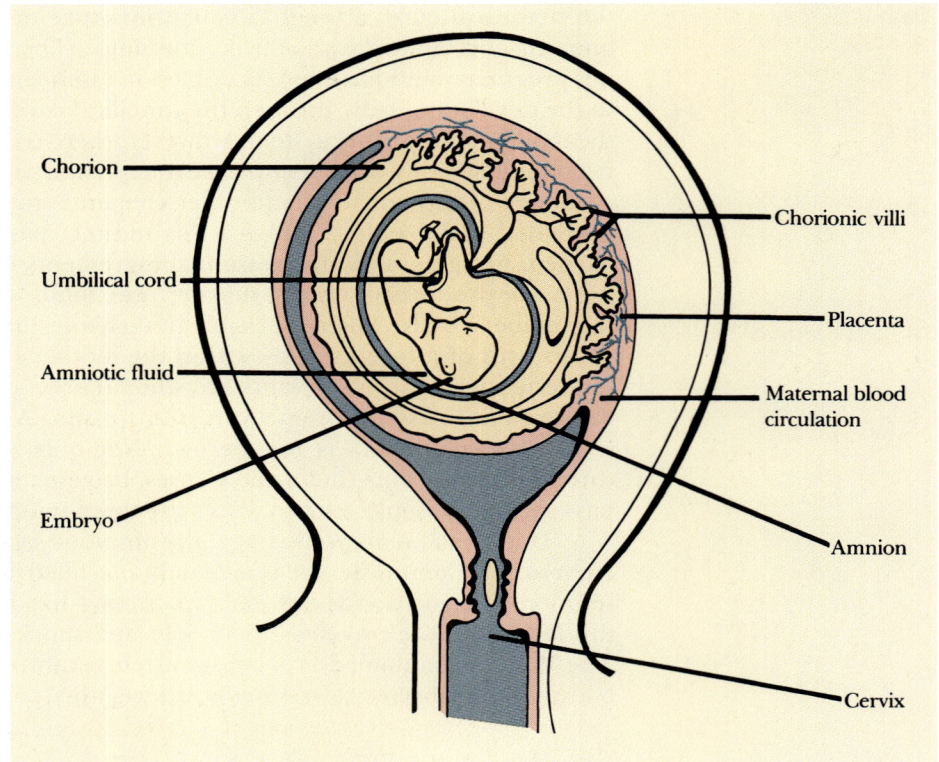

Figure 2.8 The embryo. As the embryo's blood circulates through the placenta it picks up oxygen and nutrients and discharges wastes into the mother's blood without actually mixing with it. The amniotic fluid protects the embryo from shock and helps regulate its temperature.

Ectoderm   The outer layer of the embryo from which the skin, sense organs, and nervous system develop.

Mesoderm   The middle layer of the embryo from which the circulatory, excretory, and musculatory systems develop.

Endoderm   The inner layer of the embryo from which the digestive, respiratory, and glandular systems develop.

structures of most of the body parts. Through differentiation, the different cells within the blastocyst take on distinct form and function. The head, heart, arms, legs, and nervous system are but a few of the systems that are developing.

By the end of the first month, three distinct layers are formed in the embryo: the **ectoderm,** or outer layer from which the skin, sense organs, and nervous system develop; the **mesoderm,** the middle layer from which the circulatory, excretory, and musculatory systems will develop; and the **endoderm,** the inner layer from which the digestive, respiratory, and glandular systems emerge. The heart has begun to beat; a simple brain is functioning; and liver, digestive tract, and kidneys have emerged. The embryo at this point is only ¼ inch in length. The mother may still be unaware of the new life within her body.

By the end of the second month, almost all of the structures of the baby have been formed and a few, such as the heart, are functioning. The embryo is about 1¼ inches in length. Most of this length is the embryonic head, which is clearly distinct. A primitive tail, believed to be an ancestral genetic relic, emerges during this stage, only to disappear as the spinal cord develops.

Because of the rapid changes in the physiological structures and because of the primitive nature of the developing organs, the embryo is in a most vulnerable state. A slight environmental insult at this stage of growth can have a gross effect on later development. For this reason, the embryonic stage

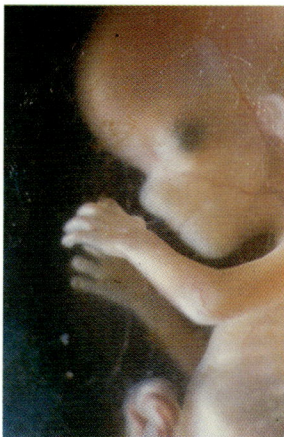

In this photo of a human fetus at four and a half months you can see the appearance of bones. It is during the fetal period that body structures develop in size.

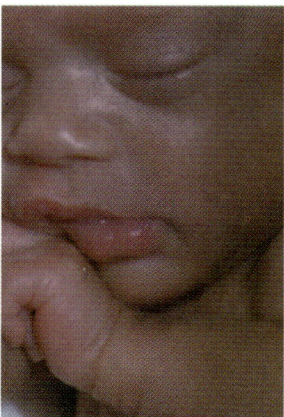

During the fifth month of prenatal life, the face and hands take on human characteristics. The maturation of the nervous and muscular system allows the fetus to perform simple reflex actions such as sucking its thumb.

is viewed as a **critical period** in development. A critical period is a time in which the organism's parts are emerging or changing and hence are most sensitive to outside environmental stimuli. For example, during the time when the sense organs are forming, the embryo is most vulnerable to the rubella, or German measles, virus. If the virus is transmitted to the embryo by way of the placenta at this stage of development, severe defects in the eyes or ears may result. If the same virus were transmitted at a later time in development when the sense organs were already formed, then no defects would be seen in the baby's sensory systems. In conclusion, the embryonic stage, lasting from the second to the eighth week after conception, is the most vulnerable and sensitive period for the developing unborn child. We will discuss other environmental hazards in the next section.

The **fetal stage** begins technically with the appearance of the first real bone cells that replace the embryonic cartilage. During this time, completion of bodily structures takes place. The primitive organs and systems of the body take on form and grow in size. This stage begins at approximately the eighth week and lasts until birth at about 38 to 40 weeks after conception. By the third month of pregnancy the fetus is three inches in length and weighs about three-and-a-quarter ounces. It can make primitive breathing movements, and when stimulated, will even suck. Despite this activity, the mother does not yet feel the fetus inside her body.

Up to this point in development, it would be impossible to detect the gender of the baby by examining the genitals, for both male and female fetuses develop genitals from the same type of gonadal tissue. During the third month, the genitals emerge as a result of a biochemical sequence initiated by the genetic messages on the sex chromosomes. If the fetus is female, or *XX* genotype, no hormones are released into the uterine environment, and the primitive gonadal tissue develops into ovaries. If the fetus is male, with an *Xy* genotype, then the genes on the *y* chromosome trigger the release of male hormones that cause the development of the testicles and penis from the primitive gonadal tissue.

By the fourth month, the fetus is six inches in length and weighs six ounces. Looking much like an astronaut in space, the fetus moves about, swimming and floating in the amniotic fluid attached to the placenta by the umbilical cord. It is during this month that many mothers begin to feel the fetus's movement within them. This sensation, called **quickening,** is hard to detect at first because it feels like a mere flicker, but later the suspicion of fetal movement is confirmed by the mother by strong and hard kicks from the fetus. During the fifth and sixth months of pregnancy, fetal activity increases. It is known that fetuses suck their thumbs and respond to loud extrauterine noises with a startle. The fetus goes through sleep and wakefulness and even has a favorite position in which it lies when asleep. Although the fetus receives oxygen from the placenta, it does occasionally make irregular breathing movements. Sometimes the fetus even develops hiccups, much to the amazement of the mother.

By the seventh month, the fetus, if born prematurely, has a chance at survival outside of the womb. The fetus is said to be viable at this age, although it has been possible to sustain fetuses born as early as 23 weeks of gestation. Even at 28 weeks, however, the risks associated with premature

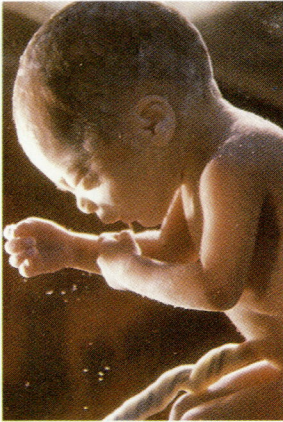

At seven months the fetus has a chance of surviving outside the uterus if born prematurely.

birth are high, and special environments are necessary to protect the prematurely born infant while it continues to grow outside of the uterus (Kleiman, 1984).

From the eighth month until birth the fetus gains weight rapidly. The skin, previously red and wrinkled, fills out with fat as the fetus increases in size at the rate of a half-pound a week. The fetus is now so large that its once comfortable amniotic sac provides very cramped living quarters. By the end of this period, the fetus will weigh an average of seven pounds and will be about 20 inches in length. The fetus is ready now for birth. Before discussing labor and delivery, let's take a look at some of the ways that the environment may influence the developing child during the mother's pregnancy.

Effects of the Prenatal Environment

How does the world outside of the uterus affect the developing child? About 30 years ago, this question would have been answered by "it doesn't" on the erroneous assumption that the unborn child was cut off from its outside world, and thus safe from harm within the mother's body. But, in the early 1960s, this belief was shattered by medical research that linked the birth of grossly deformed babies to a drug taken by mothers. These babies were born either without limbs or with embryonic-like flippers. The cause of these defects was ultimately traced to the drug thalidomide, which had been prescribed to alleviate morning sickness, a typical symptom in early pregnancy. When taken during the critical period of limb formation (27 to 40 days after conception), the drug drastically altered the normal course of limb development (Taussig, 1962). When taken much later in pregnancy, little or no effects were found in the newborn.

The thalidomide crisis caused researchers and obstetricians to take a closer and more conservative look at the substances the developing unborn child might be exposed to in the uterus. No longer could one assume that the substances crossing the placenta would only be beneficial to the offspring. The question became, "What substances cross the placental barrier and what is the impact of these substances on development?" The answer to this question may take a lifetime's worth of research to achieve. This is especially the case for substances that pass the placental barrier but do not display an effect until the offspring has reached maturity. Longitudinal studies specifically aimed at the effects of the prenatal environment are few and rather recent. Thus, most of what is known about the effects of the prenatal environment on development is concerned with the more immediate effects on the infant or young child. Let's examine some of the prenatal environmental influences.

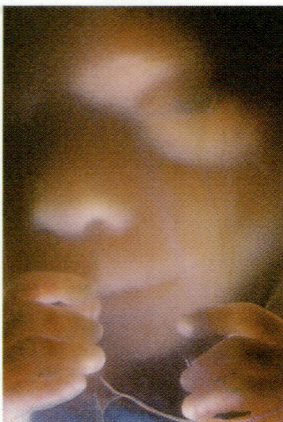

At eight months, the fetus gains weight rapidly at a rate of a half pound a week.

Maternal Condition

The most obvious source of outside influence is the mother herself. The health, age, and nutritional status of the mother affect the status and condition of the baby. Between 20 and 35 years of age is considered the optimal time to bear children (Rugh & Shettles, 1971). Women in this age category have fewer complications in pregnancy and easier labors and deliveries than either older or younger mothers. For teenage mothers, those under 20 years of age, the risk of infant death is twice as high when compared to mothers in their twenties. This is mostly because teenage mothers are still developing

Table 2.2 ▬▬▬▬▬

Relationship of Down Syndrome to Maternal Age

Mother's Age	Incidence of Down Syndrome
20	1 in 2000
30	1 in 900
35	1 in 400
36	1 in 300
37	1 in 230
38	1 in 180
39	1 in 135
40	1 in 105
42	1 in 60
44	1 in 35
46	1 in 20
48	1 in 12

Critical Period   A time of growth and development during which the organism is changing and is most vulnerable to outside influence.

Fetal Stage   The last stage of prenatal development when all major bodily systems are completed.

Quickening   The experience of feeling the fetus's movement in the uterus.

physically and their bodies are not yet hormonally ready for the task of carrying a baby. Teenage mothers are more likely to give birth to low-birthweight infants (Brown, 1983). At the other end of the age continuum, women older than 35 years of age have a greater proportion of defective children, stillborns, low-birthweight, or short-gestation period infants. One view is that the reproductive system in the older women is deteriorating and thus the woman cannot adequately nourish and protect the developing fetus. With older women, the risks of giving birth to a child with Down syndrome increase dramatically with each year after the age of 35. (See Table 2.1.) One theory is that a woman is born with all the eggs that are necessary for bearing children. By the time she is 35, her eggs are also 35 years old. The chances are greater that the older the egg, the more likely it is that it has been exposed to physical or chemical agents that may damage the chromosomal material in the egg. Recently, it has been found that the condition of the father's sperm is also a factor in producing a Down syndrome baby. Research has shown that as many as 24 percent of all Down syndrome babies were attributable to a faulty sperm fertilizing a healthy egg (Holmes, 1978). Other difficulties associated with older mothers include longer and more difficult labors, a greater chance of multiple pregnancies (fraternal twins) and higher incidence of congenital hydrocephalus (Annis, 1978).

The Mother's Nutrition   The developing fetus receives its nutrients through the mother's body and thus is dependent on her for an adequate prenatal diet. Research has linked the mother's diet with the health of the newborn (Cravioto, DeLicardie, & Birch, 1966; Drillien & Ellis, 1964; Lester, Garcia-Coll, Valcarcel, Hoffman, & Brazelton, 1986; Vore, 1973). It is now believed that inadequate nutrition poses the greatest potential threat to the development of the unborn child. Since the critical period for the development of brain cells is during much of the prenatal period, insufficient nutrients at this time can affect the entire nervous system.

The importance of prenatal nutrition has not always been recognized. However, it used to be believed that the developing baby's needs would take priority over the dietary needs of the mother and hence a mother did not have to worry about what nutrition her baby was getting. However, this misconception was corrected after studies done during World War II revealed that babies born in European countries where food shortages were most severe were of lower birthweights. Also, the incidence of stillbirths and short-gestation period births increased. These early studies triggered more extensive research on the effects of inadequate diets on the developing fetus.

We now know that severe maternal malnutrition can have a profound effect on the development of the baby's nervous system. Lower levels of intellectual functioning are frequently found in babies born to poorly nourished mothers (Winick, 1976). In particular, animal proteins usually found in meat and egg products appear to be essential to adequate brain development. Often these proteins are missing in the diets of mothers in low-income families primarily because they are a relatively expensive food source. Women in low-socioeconomic families have a greater number of low-birthweight and short-gestation period infants.

Also of concern are mothers who go on crash diets during pregnancy, thereby starving their babies. Likewise, the teenage mother poses an additional threat to the health of her baby when she eats a diet of snack and junk foods that are high in fats and carbohydrates and low in protein. Optimal weight gains during pregnancy have increased from the once-recommended 15 to 20 pounds to 25 to 30 pounds—although the optimal weight gain will vary considerably depending upon the size and normal weight gain of the mother. Physicians now recognize the hazards to mother and child of a restricted dietary regimen.

Just as developmental changes occur over time, so too an adequately nourished baby during pregnancy occurs as a result of earlier years of eating a nutritious diet. The mother's ability to nourish her unborn child began to develop in the mother's early teens and twenties. It takes time for her body to build up the necessary nutritional reserves for pregnancy. Thus, the pre-pregnancy diet can be as important to the fetus's development and survival as the diet during pregnancy (Wyden, 1971).

Mother's Emotional State

One myth about pregnancy is the belief that whatever the mother is feeling will be experienced by the unborn child and will have a lasting effect. Research has discounted this belief. We know that there is no direct neural connection between the mother and fetus that would directly communicate the mother's emotional state to the fetus. However, a woman under emotional stress does experience hormonal changes in her body. Under states of high emotional arousal, the adrenal glands secrete hormones into the blood and these hormones can pass through the placenta. Thus, indirectly, the mother's emotional state does register in the intrauterine environment.

In early studies by Sontag (1966), it was found that when mothers were emotionally upset there was a large increase in fetal activity. Even though maternal distress may have been of short duration, the fetal activity lasted for several hours. One consequence of prolonged maternal distress is low birth-weight in the infants.

Most maternity nurses have recognized that the more relaxed the mother is during labor and delivery, the easier and shorter the process of giving birth will be. Highly anxious mothers who are sensitive to pain and fearful about the delivery process, in fact, do have more difficult deliveries and also have more irritable babies. In an extensive study, Stott and Latchford (1976) found a greater increase in behavior disorders and chronic illness in children of mothers under stress during pregnancy. Other studies have linked mothers' excessive emotional stress during the time when the upper jaw and mouth are forming in the fetus to the development of a cleft palate and harelip.

It is difficult to attribute all of these disorders solely to the effects of prenatal emotional stress in the mother, since the same stress may be present postnatally to affect the social and emotional environment of the baby. The presence of an emotionally supportive person during labor and delivery has been shown to significantly reduce the length of labor and signs of fetal distress (Sosa, Kennel, Klaus, Robertson, & Urrutia, 1980). In the case of an already anxious mother, then, the presence of a reassuring spouse or family member will help reduce the negative consequences of emotional stress on the newborn.

Rh-Factor Incompatibility

The Rh factor is an inherited, genetically dominant trait in the blood. Most people have this Rh factor (Rh+). When no factor is present, however, the person is said to be Rh−. When the blood of an Rh+ person is mixed with the blood of an Rh− person, the Rh− person's body reacts by producing antibodies. These antibodies can pass through the placenta into the fetal bloodstream to destroy any Rh+ red blood cells. If an Rh− woman is carrying an Rh+ offspring, it is possible for some fetal blood to escape the placenta and enter her bloodstream. Her body will then produce Rh antibodies. The production of these antibodies does not pose a threat to the current baby because of the low level of antibodies produced. However, over time, the mother's body produces more Rh antibodies, and the child of a subsequent pregnancy may be affected with *fetal erythroblastosis,* a condition in which the maternal antibodies cross the placenta and attack the fetal red blood cells thus leading to brain damage. Out of 3.3 million births in the United States each year, 260,000 result in the birth of an Rh+ child to an Rh− mother. Of these, 10 percent are afflicted with some degree of Rh disease. (See Figure 2.9.)

Genetic counseling can alert the parents to the possibility of this disease. Treatment includes the injection of an Rh-immune globulin to the mother directly after the birth of her first child to prevent the deadly buildup of antibodies in her body. In some cases, it may be necessary to totally replace the damaged infant's blood supply by an exchange transfusion. New prenatal techniques have even permitted a fetal blood exchange transfusion.

Teratogens

Earlier, we mentioned the effect of the drug thalidomide on the developing fetus as an example of how the unborn child is influenced by the environment.

How Rh disease develops...

| Rh–positive father | Rh–negative mother | During Pregnancy Rh–negative mother with Rh–positive baby | At Delivery Rh–positive baby's blood cells enter mother's bloodstream | Invading Rh–positive blood cells cause the production of Rh antibodies | Months Later Rh antibodies remain in mother's bloodstream | Later Pregnancy The Rh antibodies attack the baby's blood cells, causing Rh disease |

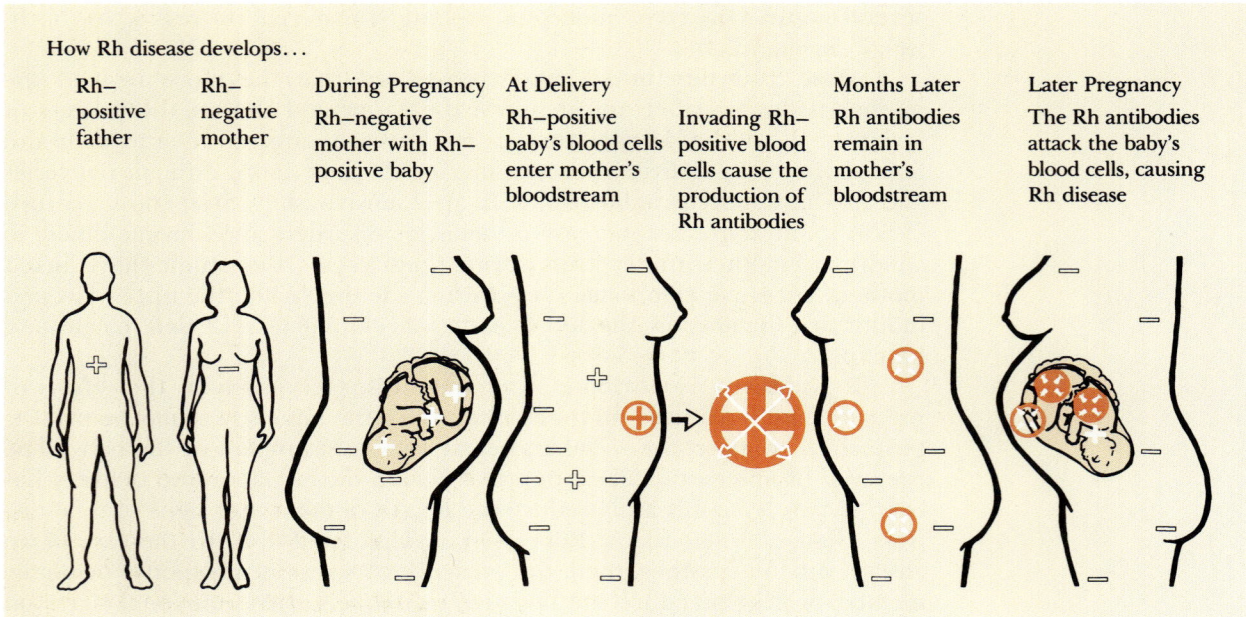

Figure 2.9 How Rh disease develops.

Teratogens Specific environmental agents that cause abnormalities in the developing fetus.

The scientific study of defects or deformities in newborns caused by the influence of the environment during pregnancy is called *teratology*. The specific environmental agents that cause the abnormalities are called **teratogens.** Teratogens may take the form of drugs, diseases, chemicals, or radiation. The effect of teratogens will depend upon the substance and the timing of prenatal exposure. Generally, the first three months of prenatal development (called *the first trimester*) are the most critical time for development and hence the period of greatest vulnerability for the developing child. Let's examine some of the known teratogens.

Drugs Montagu (1962) points to two potential dangers to the fetus from maternal drug use. First, the drug dose is prescribed for an adult body. Even when filtered through the mother's body, the dose nonetheless crosses the placenta to the fetus and may be too high for the unborn child. Secondly, the fetal liver cannot break down the drug in the same way that the mother's liver does and hence the chemical action of the drug may be different on the fetus. Adults, believing them to be safe, often take prescribed and over-the-counter drugs. One national estimate suggests, however, that there is an *increase* in the average number of drugs taken by a person when pregnant (Niswander & Gordon, 1972). These drugs include aspirin, antihistamines, antibiotics, barbiturates, and caffeine, to name just a few. While most drugs taken during pregnancy have no defects associated with them, when taken in large amounts or in conjunction with other drugs, teratogenic effects may occur. For example, a woman taking 10 to 15 aspirins daily while also smoking one-and-a-half packs of cigarettes a day gave birth to a grossly deformed infant that lived only one-and-a-half hours (Benawra, Mangurten, & Duffell, 1980).

Antibiotics, particularly streptomycin and tetracycline have been associated with minor defects in the infant's teeth and bones. The United States

Food and Drug Administration has warned against the use of popular tranquilizers during the first months of pregnancy, saying they may cause cleft palate and other defects. While drug manufacturers dispute some of these claims, a conservative strategy is usually taken by physicians, who recommend little or no prescribed or over-the-counter medication during the early months of pregnancy.

Heroin and morphine are addictive drugs, and habitual maternal use during pregnancy often produce newborns who exhibit withdrawal symptoms from the drugs. These babies display symptoms of hyperactivity, tremors, vomiting, fever, a shrill cry, and low birthweights (Zelson, 1973). Similar withdrawal symptoms have been found with babies whose mothers are taking methadone (Zelson, Lee, & Casalino, 1973).

In addition to these physiological symptoms, early mother–child interaction is greatly disrupted by the effects of these drugs. Irritable babies are harder to care for, and the addicted mothers often have difficulty establishing a bond with them. These mothers often have had poor prenatal care and nutrition, which further add to the difficulties of the newborn.

The long-suspected connection between heavy alcohol consumption during pregnancy and faulty development in the unborn child has been scientifically substantiated (Jones & Smith, 1973). The researchers noted a pattern of abnormal growth and development in the children of chronic alcoholic mothers. This pattern, called **fetal alcohol syndrome,** or FAS, has been the subject of much research (see Clarren & Smith, 1978). FAS includes four basic kinds of abnormalities: (1) growth deficiencies both pre- and postnatally, (2) facial malformations, (3) central nervous system dysfunctions, and (4) certain malformations of the eyes, ears, mouth, and heart. It is believed that alcohol passes directly to the fetus and adversely affects the fast-growing tissues, either killing the fetal cells or slowing their growth. Not surprisingly, the brain, which grows throughout pregnancy, is the most affected organ. Some FAS infants are even born with the odor of alcohol on their breaths.

Even moderate drinking can produce symptoms similar to FAS. As with drug use, the dangers of excessive alcohol use to the unborn child are increased by poor nutrition and prenatal care. A recent study (Sokol, Miller, & Reed, 1980) reported that the risks of a growth-retarded infant are doubled if the woman drinks or smokes and are quadrupled if she does both. The growth retardation accompanying FAS lasts through life, with significant above-average deficiencies in height and weight (Luke, 1977). Alcohol consumption during pregnancy has also been found to have an affect on attention and reaction time in preschool age children (Streissguth, Martin, Barr, Sandman, Kirchner, & Darby, 1984). Four-year-olds whose mothers were moderate drinkers (that is, who drank an average of two drinks per day before realizing they were pregnant and an average of five drinks per week during pregnancy) performed slower and with poorer attention on a task that required them to press a key whenever the figure of a cat appeared on a display board. Research on the effects of alcohol on the unborn child continues; the best recommendation is that pregnant women abstain from alcohol to ensure a healthy start for their children.

What about the effects of smoking on the unborn? Aside from the obvious health hazard smoking presents to the mother, there are additional hazards to the unborn child. One of the earlier effects noted is that fetal heart-rate activity increases when mothers smoke (Sontag & Wallace, 1935).

Fetal Alcohol Syndrome (FAS)   A pattern of abnormal growth and development in children of chronic alcoholic mothers.

Cigarette smoke contains carbon monoxide and nicotine, the latter's effects being first, to stimulate and then depress the body's functioning. The effect on mother and fetus is an increase in blood pressure and a decrease in amount of oxygen available in the placenta. Carbon monoxide also reduces the amount of placental oxygen. Since the oxygen demands of the fetus increase as it grows, the latter months of pregnancy are the time when oxygen deprivation has its most severe effect on the fetus. For this reason, mothers who smoke are urged to give up smoking, especially during the second half of pregnancy (March of Dimes Birth Defects Foundation, 1983).

The effects of maternal smoking include low-birthweight babies, a higher rate of miscarriage or spontaneous abortion, and a greater risk of premature delivery. The more the mother smokes, the less the baby's birthweight. Women who smoke heavily are twice as likely to deliver low-birthweight babies as nonsmoking mothers, regardless of the length of pregnancy (Frazier, Davis, Goldstein, & Goldberg, 1961).

Caffeine is a drug contained in coffee, tea, chocolate, and cola drinks and is another substance under scrutiny as a teratogen. Although animal studies are still being done on the effects of caffeine on prenatal development, results so far show an increase in birth defects in litters of animals given large doses of caffeine. So far, the evidence for the effects on human infants is inconclusive. Acting as a stimulant to the central nervous system, caffeine can cause sleeplessness, irritability, anxiety, and disturbances in heart rhythm and rate. The United States Department of Health and Human Services has cautioned pregnant women to watch their consumption of foods and drugs containing caffeine (U.S. Department of Health and Human Services, Publication #80, 1979).

Diseases   Some viruses and bacteria that cause diseases in the mature adult can cross the placenta and invade the developing body. Depending on the time during pregnancy, maternal diseases can cause varying degrees of birth defects.

In 1964–1965, more than 20,000 babies were born with birth defects during an outbreak of rubella, or German measles. The pregnant mothers may have experienced mild flu-like symptoms and a rash from this highly contagious disease. The affected offspring exposed prenatally to rubella during the first three months of development were born with such defects as blindness; deafness; heart, nerve, and brain defects; and mental retardation. Fortunately, a vaccine against the rubella virus was discovered in 1969, the use of which caused a decline in the number of children and adults contracting the disease. However, pregnant women cannot be vaccinated since the fetus would be directly affected. Only when a woman is sure she will not get pregnant for at least three months is the vaccination recommended during the childbearing years.

Toxoplasmosis is a parasitic infection that can result in damage to the fetal eyes, ears, and brain while the mother is unaware of the infection in her body. The parasites carrying toxoplasmosis enter the mother's body through red meat or exposure to fecal matter of cats (for example, through handling cat litter). The best protection for the unborn child is for the mother to avoid contracting the infection while pregnant. Chicken pox, mumps, measles, and infectious hepatitis also had at one time been linked with birth defects. However, a thorough study (Siegel, 1973) comparing 409 pregnant women infected with one of these viral diseases to a matched sample of uninfected women found no differences between their offspring in birth defects. However, maternal infection is likely to increase the chances of an early delivery.

Untreated maternal syphilis also may cross the placenta and cause deformities in the developing child. Gonorrhea and active genital herpes can be passed on to the baby during delivery and result in blindness or severe brain damage. More recently, the newly diagnosed disease AIDS (acquired immune deficiency syndrome) has been found to cross the placenta and infect the inborn child. If the mother has the disease or is even a carrier of the virus, her unborn child is at risk for being born with this incurable disease. In fact, 80 percent of all children with AIDS were infected during pregnancy (The Health Information Network, 1987).

Hormones   Between 1945 and 1970, a synthetic hormone called *diethylstilbestrol,* or DES, was used to maintain pregnancies in women who showed signs of miscarrying. The effects of DES on the offspring were not apparent at birth or even shortly thereafter. It was not until years later when the female offspring of women who had taken DES during pregnancy had reached puberty that the teratogenic effects of the hormone were apparent. Some developed rare forms of vaginal and cervical cancer. While this hormone is no longer being used for pregnant women, the question remains about the effects of other hormones taken during pregnancy.

The development of male and female characteristics during the third month of pregnancy is dependent on a specific hormonal intrauterine environment. A pregnant woman taking hormones for medical reasons may be disturbing the hormonal balance *in utero.* For example, Reinisch (1981) reports that women who received male hormones during the first three months of pregnancy had children who were rated as more aggressive when compared to women who did not take any hormones.

Radiation and Environmental Hazards   During early pregnancy, repeated exposure to X-rays, especially in the pelvic region, may endanger the fetus. The fact that radiation can destroy sensitive growing cells was tragically demonstrated in the survivors of the atomic bombings of Hiroshima and Nagasaki, Japan, when great increases in stillborns, miscarriages, and gross deformities were found. While X-rays used in medical diagnosis contain a far lower dose of radiation, the effects of exposure are cumulative.

Another source of danger to the unborn child are the environmental pollutants or toxic wastes of industry. Various wastes and pesticides have been shown to cause defects in animals exposed to high doses of these pollutants. Some, such as methyl mercury, have been shown to cause defects in the nervous system of the fetus (Snyder, 1971). Hexachlorophene, a chemical once widely used in disinfectant soaps, has been associated with high rates of severe congenital malformations when pregnant women washed their hands frequently with it (Halling, 1979).

Researchers have found that mothers who had eaten fish contaminated with the industrial chemical PCB (polychlorinated biphenyl) gave birth to children with lower birthweights, smaller heads, and shorter gestations (Fein, Jacobson, Jacobson, Schwartz, & Dowler, 1984). Furthermore, children who were exposed to PCBs while in utero and who appeared normal at birth, when tested at seven months of age showed less preference for novel stimuli when compared to children who had not been exposed prenatally to the chemicals (Jacobson, Fein, Jacobson, Schwartz, & Dowler, 1985).

It is difficult for a person to know whether fish or other foods, air, water, or soil have been contaminated by industrial toxins. While people in the child-bearing years cannot possibly avoid all possible environmental toxins, they can become more aware of reports of toxic wastes and take precautions to avoid contact. Just as Joe and Kathy had done during their months in preparation for Sarah's birth, couples can make simple changes in their daily habits to maximize the expectation of a healthy birth.

A Note of Reassurance

After reading about all the many possible side effects of chemicals, diseases, and other substances on the developing fetus, you may find yourself becoming alarmed, particularly if you are already pregnant. You can relax a bit by putting the information about teratogens into perspective. Although there are many possible causes for abnormality in children from teratogens, genetic disorders, and mother's health, it should be noted that 95 percent of all live births are healthy and well formed. Furthermore, not all birth defects are serious ones. Education of parents and caution during pregnancy help to keep this live-birth success rate high.

Pause for Thought

Do you think that high schools should include in their curriculum information on the prenatal environment and its effect on unborn children? Should the information be presented in biology classes or health classes? Why?

Birth

After an average of 266 days in the mother's uterus, the baby is ready to be expelled into the world. Birth is the process in which the fetus makes the transition from the intrauterine home to the extrauterine world.

The Birth Process

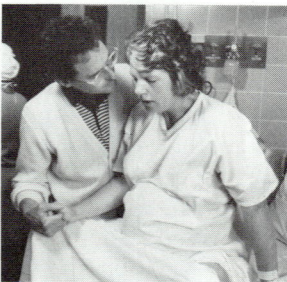

This husband is encouraging his wife during a uterine contraction in the second stage of labor.

The onset of the birth process is signalled by several physical changes in the mother. The uterus begins to contract regularly and these contractions increase in strength. The mother may have a slight bloody "show" or may discharge some amniotic fluid. At this point, **labor,** the process of expelling the baby, has begun. Labor is divided into three stages. During the first stage the **cervix,** or opening to the uterus, is dilated by the action of the increasingly stronger uterine contractions. This stage, averaging from two to 24 hours, is the longest and most difficult stage of labor. Mothers who have had previous deliveries have shorter labors than first-time mothers.

At the beginning of the second stage of labor, the cervix is completely open, and the baby is ready to be expelled through the vaginal birth canal into the world. An alert and unanesthetized mother helps the passage along by pushing down with her abdominal muscles. This stage lasts an average of two hours. The baby's head appears first at the opening of the vagina; this is

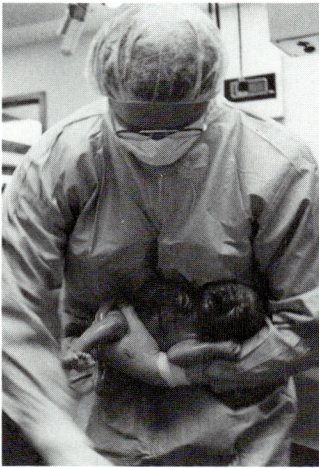

Seconds after birth, the newborn's cry announces its arrival.

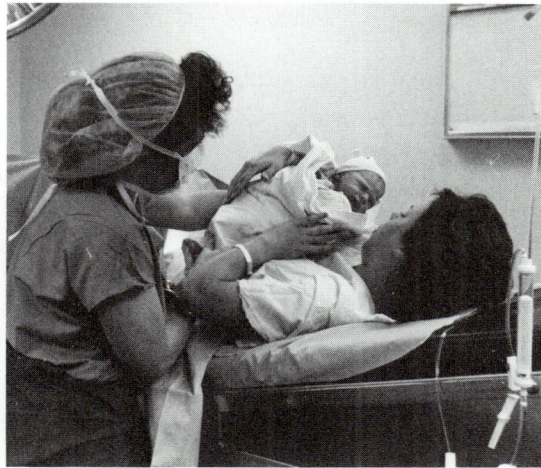

The new parents' initial contact with their newborn is likely to be a very special and tender moment.

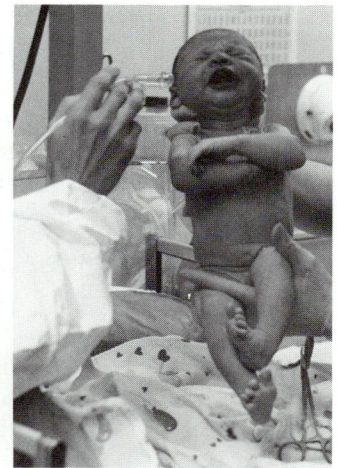

Within minutes after delivery, the attending physician examines the newborn and assigns an Apgar rating.

Labor The process of expelling the baby from the uterus.

Cervix The opening to the uterus.

Crowning During the birth process, the moment at which the baby's head first appears at the opening of the vagina.

Episiotomy A surgical slit made in the skin around the vaginal opening to ease delivery of the baby.

called **crowning.** At this point an **episiotomy,** or surgical slit in the skin around the vaginal opening, may be performed to ease the baby's passage. The baby's head is then delivered, usually face down, and the baby's airways are cleared. The shoulders and the rest of the body quickly follow the head. The umbilical cord, still attached to the placenta, is now clamped and cut. As soon as the newborn's lungs receive air through the unclogged nasal passages, the umbilical cord's function of delivering oxygen from the placenta ends. A jellylike substance inside the cord closes off the oxygen supply line. At this point in delivery, the newborn's condition is evaluated using the *Apgar scale.* Developed in 1953 by Virginia Apgar to assess the newborn's physical condition, this scoring system is now routinely used in most hospitals in the United States. The newborn is rated at 60 seconds after birth, and then again at 5 and 10 minutes after birth. The Apgar scale involves rating the newborn on five signs: heart rate, respiratory effort, reflex irritability, muscle tone, and color. Each sign is given a score of 0, 1, or 2 depending on the condition of the infant. A score of 2 is given if the infant is in the best possible condition for the particular sign. A zero score is given if the sign is not present and a 1 is given for all conditions between 0 and 2. The best score is then a 10 and a score of 0 indicates a serious life-threatening condition in the infant.

Within 20 minutes after the delivery of the baby, the mother may experience another strong contraction. This begins the third stage of labor, the delivery of the placenta, umbilical cord, and membranes. With the delivery of the placenta, the birth process is complete.

Complications

Breech Birth A delivery in which the baby appears in a bottom-first position.

Although most deliveries are normally head-first vaginal deliveries, sometimes **breech birth** occurs, when the baby appears at the vagina in a breech, or bottom-first, position. This position presents difficulties for the mother and child since the opening may not be wide enough to accommodate the baby without damage to the spinal cord. Unlike the brain, which is well protected by the skull during the birth passage, the spinal cord may be damaged in the tight passage to birth.

73

Cesarean Section   A surgical procedure used to deliver a baby by making an opening in the uterus.

When it looks like there may be danger to the baby, the physician may use a surgical procedure, called a **cesarean section.** In this procedure, a surgical incision is made through the mother's abdominal wall into the uterus, and the newborn is extracted. The cesarean newborn looks better than a vaginally delivered baby since it has not had to make the journey through the tight vaginal passage. Although safe, the procedure presents additional stresses and risks to the mother and consequently to the baby. Infection and a prolonged convalescence for the mother are the two biggest disadvantages.

Another complication in delivery can occur as the result of the use of drugs during labor and delivery. Since the drugs administered to the mother pass through the placenta, the newborn may also experience the effects of the drugs at birth. Further, a mother who is totally anesthetized during delivery cannot aid the delivery by pushing down with her muscles. The delivery, therefore, may take longer or require the use of forceps, a clamplike set of tongs used to extract the baby. Another disadvantage to an overly drugged mother is that she often does not experience the early contact and joy associated with the birth of the baby. This first contact between mother and child is considered by some professionals to facilitate an affectionate bond between mother and child that endures during the early years of life (Klaus and Kennell, 1982). Modern obstetric practices are limiting the use of drugs during delivery in favor of other means of pain control such as hypnosis or relaxation training.

Anoxia   Lack of oxygen to the baby at birth.

One final complication that may occur is when the newborn doesn't readily make the transition to breathing on its own. **Anoxia,** or lack of oxygen, can cause severe brain damage resulting in impaired motor and mental development. The longer the brain is deprived of oxygen the more severe the damage. The immediate effects of mild anoxia are a greater irritability and tenseness in the baby's body. Decreased sensitivity to pain and visual stimulation have also been reported. Long-term effects include lowered mental functioning and learning disabilities (Epstein, Cullinan, Lessen, & Lloyd, 1980). Follow-up studies on anoxic children at ages three and seven indicate a deficit in cognitive skills at age three and slight cognitive deficits at age seven (Corah, Anthony, Painter, Stern, & Thurston, 1965; Graham, Ernhart, Thurston, & Craft, 1962). Behavioral problems were also found in the seven-year-old children who had been anoxic at birth.

Low-Birthweight Infants

Short-Gestation-Period Babies   Infants born before the full 38 weeks of development; also referred to as preterm babies.

Low birthweight is the most common problem affecting one in every 12 babies born each year in the United States. Seventy percent of infant deaths are attributable to a birthweight under 2500 grams, or five lbs, eight oz. Very low-birthweight infants are those weighing less than three pounds, five ounces.

There are two categories of low birthweight. **Short-gestation period babies,** or preterm babies, are born before the full 38 weeks. Babies as early as 23 weeks of gestation have been known to survive birth. Most of the low-birthweight infants fall into this category.

Small-for-Date Babies   Infants born after the full period of gestation but who are under 2500 grams or 5 lbs. 8 oz. in weight; also referred to as growth-retarded babies.

Small-for-date babies, or growth-retarded babies, are born after the full nine months of gestation but are too small either because of a slowdown or

Human Development in Practice

Where Do Babies Come from? Teaching Children about Conception and Birth

Eventually children ask: Where do babies come from? How does the baby get inside the Mommy? and How does it get out? Parents and teachers, when asked these questions, may be a bit uncertain about how and what to tell young children about conception and birth. Some people feel awkward about introducing the topic of sex education to young children even though most people believe it is important for children to understand the facts of life.

One difficulty with teaching children about conception and birth is that children of different ages vary in their ability to comprehend the facts of life. For example, in a study of 60 children of varying ages, Anne Bernstein and Phillip Cowan (1975) found that no matter what information is given to very young children (three- to four-year-olds) about where babies come from, they distort it to fit their own level of thinking. Some three-year-olds said that babies were bought at a baby store or that they just appear in the mother's

The birth of a child provides an opportunity to teach older siblings about conception and birth.

tummy. Older children (seven- to ten-year-olds) may take explanations about conception quite literally (e.g., "the daddy plants the seed like a flower, except you don't need dirt"). For this reason, it is important for teachers and parents to be aware of children's abilities to make sense out of the information they give them about how babies are made. Generally, children use their immediate experiences to make sense out of what they are told. If children have witnessed the birth of animal babies (e.g., watched chickens hatch or seen a litter of kittens being born) they may be better able to understand an explanation about human birth. When talking about conception it is important to teach children the correct terms (such as egg, sperm, vagina, penis, and womb or uterus) rather than use made-up terms or allow children to create their own. Preschool children usually don't know enough about the human body to be able to distinguish the stomach from the uterus and may persist in saying that babies grow in the mother's stomach even when they are told differently. There are numerous picture books available that teachers and parents can use to tell children about how babies are made, how they grow in utero, and how they are born. Some examples are *Where Did I Come From?* by Peter Mayle (Secaucus, N.J.: Lyle Stuart, 1973), *Where Do Babies Come From?* by M. Sheffield (New York: Knopf, 1972), and *Making Babies* by S. B. Stein (New York: Walker, 1974).

Teachers and parents may supply children with correct information about conception and birth but it may take a while before they actually fully comprehend the process. Nonetheless, it is important to expose children to the facts of life. In a study of 838 children from Australia, England, Sweden, the United States, and Canada (Goldman & Goldman, 1982) it was found that Swedish children had a much earlier and better understanding of the facts of life than did children from other countries. In Sweden, children from age eight on are routinely taught sex education in the classroom.

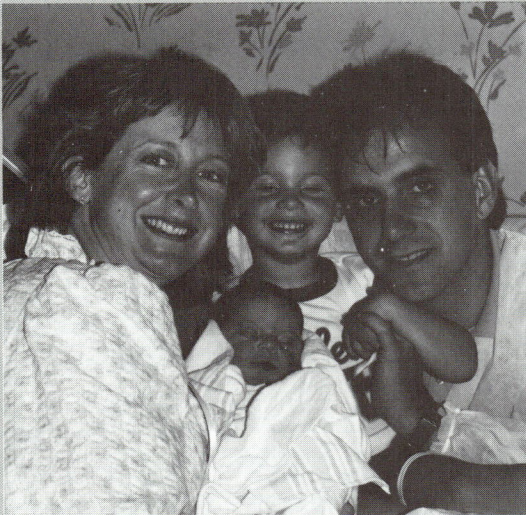

halt of prenatal growth. Maternal malnutrition, poor prenatal care, overuse of drugs, alcohol, smoking, and exposure to certain diseases have all been suggested as causes of low birthweight. The risks to the infants are great since they are more susceptible to illness early in life and often experience difficulties in breathing. Some preterm babies do not have enough fat to keep them warm so they must be kept in heated incubators. The lower the birthweight, the greater the complications to the infant. Research suggests that long-term effects of low birthweight exist in areas of motor, mental, social, and emotional development. A fuller discussion of low-birthweight infants will be presented in the next chapter.

Childbirth Methods

Prepared Childbirth
Method of childbirth in which both parents are prepared to deal with the various aspects of labor and delivery.

Lamaze Method A type of prepared childbirth involving lectures and specific exercises and routines.

Birthing Rooms
Homelike settings in hospitals designed for both labor and delivery.

Today, couples who are expecting a baby are presented with a variety of ways to have their children. One such choice is called **prepared childbirth** because the parents are prepared for the birth by going to classes about six weeks before the expected delivery date. In these classes, the parents learn about the stages of labor, hospital obstetric routines, and specific exercises and routines to use during the labor. The most popular method of prepared childbirth is the **Lamaze method,** named after the physician Fernand Lamaze (1981). One advantage of the Lamaze method is that women require lower dosages of medication during labor and delivery and hence they are more active and alert in the birth process.

Some couples would prefer a more homelike setting to the standard sickroom atmosphere of a hospital. **Birthing rooms** are homelike settings in hospitals that are medically equipped but casually decorated to create a relaxed atmosphere. Unlike the traditional hospital setting, where labor and delivery are in separate rooms, the birthing room serves both functions. A similar arrangement to a birthing room can be found in Alternate Birthing Centers, which are located in separate settings from hospitals. These centers are focused on the needs of prospective parents and provide complete prenatal and delivery services to families.

Pause for Thought

Childbirth practices are influenced by the traditions and resources within a culture and within a specific time frame. Having a baby at home was once standard practice in the United States and still is the norm in other cultures. Does the change to modern technology represent progress?

Summary

Conception is the process by which the egg and sperm unite to form the zygote. Alternative methods of conception involve use of donated egg and sperm. The new cell grows by a process known as mitosis.

The growth and development of the fertilized egg is guided by its unique genetic programming. The genes, which are made up of molecules of DNA, are specifically arranged on the chromosomes, which are found in the nucleus of every living cell.

Sex chromosomes determine gender and other sex-linked characteristics. Other physical features such as eye and skin color, height, body proportion, and certain diseases are inherited through the genes and chromosomes. Evidence from studies on personality and intelligence suggests a genetic influence. The environment and genetic code interact to produce most of the characteristics of human behavior.

Prenatal diagnosis using amniocentesis is one aspect of genetic counseling, which provides information to parents about the possible characteristics or defects in the offspring.

Prenatal development involves three stages of growth. In the ovum stage, the growing zygote enters the uterus and imbeds itself into the uterine wall. In the embryo stage, the cells differentiate into different systems and organs. In the fetal stage, the baby grows in size until birth occurs.

The prenatal period is a critical period in development in which the unborn child is vulnerable to environmental influences. The physical condition of the mother is one source of environmental influence on the baby. Teratogens are specific environmental agents such as drugs, bacteria, viruses, chemicals, and radiation that affect the physical prenatal development. Many agents are known to cross the placenta and adversely affect the unborn child.

The birth process involves three stages, beginning with the dilation of the cervix. The second stage is the delivery of the baby. During the third stage the placenta and umbilical cord are delivered. Birth complications include breech birth, cesarean section, anoxia, and low birthweight. Drugs used in labor and delivery affect the alertness of the newborn.

Prepared childbirth classes and other new methods of delivery help the parents to be more relaxed during birth and to be prepared to establish contact with their newborn.

Further Readings

Annis, Linda Ferrill. *The child before birth.* **Ithaca, NY: Cornell University Press, 1978.**
A clear and easy-to-read account of the factors influencing the unborn child's development. Authoritative and complete with color photographs and drawings.

Donovan, Bonnie. *The caesarean birth experience.* **Boston: Beacon Press, 1978.**
A practical and sensitive guide for expectant parents describing the physical and psychological aspects of caesarean delivery.

Farber, Susan. *Identical twins reared apart: A reanalysis.* **New York: Basic Books, 1981.**
A review and analysis of all the studies done on identical twins reared apart. The influence of genetic and environmental factors on personality and intelligence is considered.

Jimenez, Sherry Lynn Mims. *Childbearing: A guide for pregnant parents.* **Englewood Cliffs, NJ: Prentice-Hall, 1980.**
An illustrated handbook for the expecting man and woman prepared by a childbirth educator. The physical, psychological, sexual, and social aspects of childbearing from conception to postpartum depression are discussed.

Korte, Diane, and Scaer, Roberta. *A good birth, a safe birth.* **New York: Bantam Books, 1984.**
With a focus on natural childbirth, this book discusses the various options for delivery and critically evaluates the methods of delivery and their effects on the infant.

Lamaze, Fernand. *Painless childbirth: The Lamaze method.* **New York: Pocket Books, 1981.**
The most popular type of prepared childbirth is described by the physician who developed the technique. Breathing, relaxation, and muscle exercises are explained.

McCauley, C. S. *Pregnancy after 35.* **New York: Pocket Books, 1976.**
The risks, advantages, and difficulties in having a child after the age of 35 are discussed through case studies.

Sumner, Phillip, and Phillips, Celeste. *Birthing rooms: Concept and reality.* **St. Louis: C. V. Mosby, 1981.**
A descriptive account of the different aspects of birthing rooms based on the experiences of 13 couples. This well-documented book written by a physician and nurse offers guidelines for the use of birthing rooms.

Observational Activities

2.1 *A Family Pedigree: The Influence of Genetics*
One way to identify the genetic contribution to behavior is to look at the traits or characteristics appearing and reappearing in the same family over generations. *Pedigree analysis* is the name given to the process of examining the incidence of a particular trait in the various branches of a family.

To illustrate the impact of genetics in your own family you will have to develop a family tree. Start with your parents and work forward to their children, including yourself, and backward to include aunts, uncles, cousins, and your grandparents. Include only blood relatives. Use the chart below as a model to set up your family tree. If you have more siblings or aunts and uncles you will need to add more branches. Use a circle to indicate a female and a square to indicate a male.

Once you have outlined your family tree, select a physical characteristic known to have a genetic basis, such as eye color, hair color, curly hair, facial

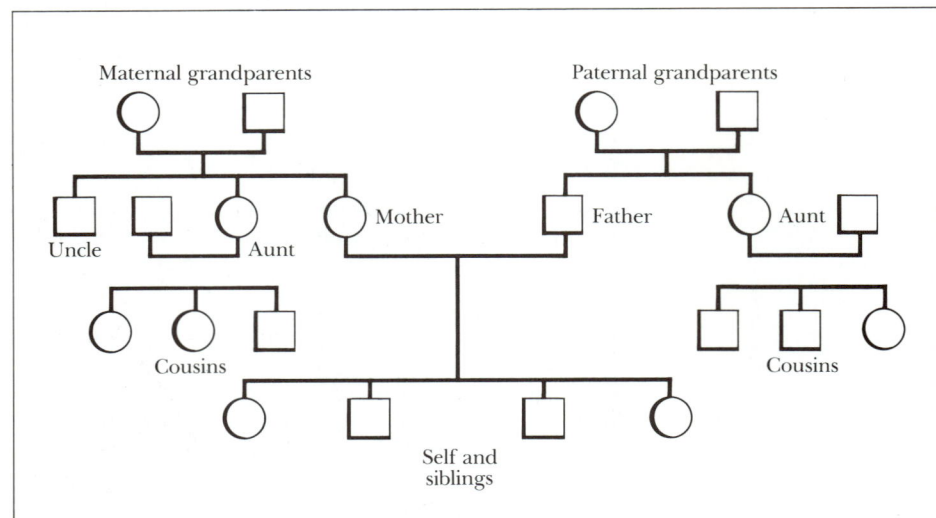

dimples, attached earlobes, poor eyesight, baldness, or color blindness. For each member in the family tree put a check next to the person who *has* the particular trait or an X if that trait is *not* present in the family member. You can ask your parents or grandparents if you do not know whether a relative has the trait or not.

Now examine the incidence of the chosen trait within your family. Compare your pedigree analysis with those of other classmates. What observations can you make about the influence of genetics on the trait?

You may want to try the analysis again using different traits or characteristics. Certain illnesses such as diabetes, asthma and allergies, and hypertension occur more frequently in some families than in others. Identifying your genetic heritage is one way to provide early diagnosis and treatment.

2.2 *Changes in Obstetrical Care: A Generation Gap*

Over the past 20 years, there has been considerable change in obstetric care. Attitudes toward pregnancy have changed as well as hospital procedure during labor and delivery. To become aware of these changes in prenatal care and methods of childbirth you will need to locate two or more mothers who are willing to be interviewed by you. Locate at least one mother who gave birth 20 or more years ago. Your own mother or an aunt may be a good choice. Also locate a mother who has given birth within the past five years. A relative or friend would be more likely to cooperate with your interview.

Explain to each mother that you would like to learn about the changes that have occurred over the years in attitude and treatment during pregnancy and delivery. If you can, tape the interview so that you can listen more attentively to what their responses are during the interview instead of taking notes. After eliciting their cooperation, ask them the following questions (you may want to ask other questions in addition to these):

1. When you were pregnant what recommendations did your doctor give you about your pregnancy?
2. Did you change your eating habits during pregnancy? If so, why?
3. Were there some things you didn't do when you were pregnant? For example, did you stop smoking or physical activity?
4. What special plans did you and your husband make in preparation for the birth of the baby?
5. What was your husband doing during labor? Was he with you? Did you want him there?
6. What do you remember about the way you were treated by the nurses and hospital staff during labor?
7. Did you receive medication while in labor?
8. Were you able to see the birth of the baby?
9. After the birth, how much contact did you have with your baby while you were in the hospital?

After collecting this information from the mothers, compare and contrast their responses. What changes can you identify? What new insight or information did you gain for yourself in doing this activity?

CHAPTER

3

Infancy: Physical, Perceptual, and Cognitive Development

Little Adam seemed so tiny and helpless in his bassinet. His scrawny legs and wrinkled arms seemed to move without control as he gazed out onto his new world, the nursery. Yet despite his tiny beginnings, Adam soon was busily learning about his physical world.

Over the crib, his mother had hung a colorful mobile of animal shapes. Although as a two-week-old infant he could not yet reach the yellow dog and blue cat figures, he seemed to look at them intently. One day, he actually succeeded in reaching up and grabbing the blue cat, only to be outwitted when his mother moved the mobile to a safer height.

Friends and relatives knew that Adam was a bright child. He was so attentive to people and objects around him. Whenever his father came into the house, Adam seemed to know it right away simply by the sound of his father's keys hitting the table by the front door. Every day brought yet another example of the ways in which Adam was taking in and adapting to his world.

As the months went on, Adam gradually acquired many new skills. He learned how to roll over, to sit and stand up, and then later to climb out of his crib. He learned how to tell his parents what he wanted and didn't want. He learned how to use the toys and other objects he found in his travels about the house. In just two short years, Adam had emerged as a capable, inquisitive, and active child.

Infancy, the period of development from birth to two years of age, is an exciting time. Change occurs in many aspects of development. During this time, the young child establishes him- or herself in a physical and social world. Without the benefit yet of language skills, the infant nonetheless learns to both adapt to and manipulate objects and people. Infants become more aware of their world and acquire new ways of taking in the many aspects of their expanding world. It is a time to lay down the foundations for a long life ahead.

Our focus in this chapter will be to explore the way the infant changes physically. We will also examine how the infant perceives and comes to know or think about the world. We begin with the neonate, the term for the infant during the first few weeks of life. Next we turn to the infant's physical development. Finally, we consider the ways in which the infant learns about the world and describe the cognitive skills of the infant.

The Neonate

Neonate The infant during the first few weeks of life.

The infant during the early weeks of life is referred to as a **neonate,** and its entry into the world represents a major life transition. While in its mother's uterus, the fetus acquired nutrition and oxygen through the placenta. At birth, the newborn's own respiratory and digestive systems take over the function performed by the mother. The newborn's body, once warmed by the mother's body, now must rely on active movement and crying to maintain an adequate body temperature. Even the newborn's body movements, which were held in check by the limited space in the mother's uterus, must now be controlled by the baby's developing nervous system.

These major transitions from intrauterine to extrauterine life occur over a period of several weeks. The first few hours, days, and weeks of life are a vulnerable time, especially since the newborn's nervous system, which regulates these transitional events, is still growing. In the case of infants born prematurely, this transitional period lasts even longer.

Physical Appearance

Most new mothers, when they look at their newborns, exclaim how beautiful the child is. However, to any objective viewer (that is, someone who is not related to the newcomer) the newborn is often anything but beautiful. Take a peek through a newborn nursery window and you will see a variety of funny-looking infants—none of which resemble the famous Gerber baby.

The baby's skin, while soft, is also relatively free of fat, giving the skin a certain looseness. It seems to hang off the bones, sometimes folded over. The baby's body may be covered with fine hair, called **lanugo.** Sometimes the baby's body is also covered in a cheeselike substance, called **vernix caseosa.** This substance, secreted by the hair follicles on the body, helped to protect the infant's thin skin while in the amniotic sac. The skin is often blotchy red in color because the capillaries are visible through the thin, unfatted layer of skin.

Similarly, the head and face of the newborn are not particularly attractive. The neonate's eyes are puffy because of the accumulated fluid from being in the head-down position during the birth process. The bones of the skull may have come together, or **molded,** during the neonate's tight squeeze through the mother's pelvis. The head may be misshapen, pointed, or lopsided, as the open spaces in the skull—the **fontanelles**—come together to

Lanugo   Fine hair covering a newborn's body.

Vernix Caseosa   A cheeselike substance covering the newborn's skin.

Molding   The coming together of the bones of the newborn's skull during the birth process.

Fontanelles   Open spaces in a neonate's skull.

To an objective viewer, the newborn is often anything but beautiful.

protect the brain during the birth passage. Some infants have flattened noses or ears that are pressed close to the skull as evidence of the tight passage.

The neonate's irises appear to be a grey-blue in caucasian infants and brown in noncaucasian newborns. By about 12 months the genetically coded color of the iris emerges. The neonate may sometimes appear cross-eyed because the eye muscles are not yet strong enough to maintain coordination. The tear ducts are not fully functional, so although the neonate cries, there are no tears. The eyes have a glassy look to them.

The head is proportionately the largest part of the baby's body. It is so large, the newborn seems to have trouble holding it on its own body. In addition, the neck muscles are not strong enough to support the head for any long period of time. The tiny arms and legs and minuscule buttocks add to the top-heavy look of the neonate.

The average newborn weighs seven-and-a-half pounds and is about 20 inches in length. Within the first four days of life, the neonate loses an average of 6 to 9 percent of its birthweight mainly due to loss of body fluids. It takes about 10 days for the infant to regain this loss. By that time, the neonate's digestive system is functioning regularly, and the mother and infant are on regular feeding schedules.

When the neonate is born, the spinal cord may still be curled from the fetal position in the mother's womb. Within a few days after birth, the backbone stretches out, resulting in an increase in length since birth.

Pause for Thought

Alright, you get the point. The newborn is not always good looking. Why is it then that many people describe babies as beautiful? Is their judgment clouded by advertising and marketing campaigns that use only beautiful babies as models? Is there something about babies that makes them appear beautiful? Offer an explanation for this phenomenon.

Physiological Functioning

Respiration and Circulation

As soon as the infant is born and air fills its lungs, the artery that has carried oxygen from the placenta to the fetus closes off. The neonate's breathing during the first weeks of life is often irregular. The rapid, shallow, regular breaths often observed in newborns may stop suddenly, a condition called **apnea.** This brief halt in breathing results in a buildup of carbon dioxide in the blood, causing the brain to stimulate breathing. Sometimes the neonate breathes deep, irregular breaths. Coughs, sneezes, and wheezes are not uncommon and help to clear any mucus in the nasal or throat passages.

A healthy heart rate for the newborn is between 120 to 150 beats per minute. The new circulatory system primed by the action of the lungs replaces the umbilical circulation system. As a result of the oxygen now delivered through the lungs, the infant has more red blood cells than are needed. As the neonate's body destroys the surplus red blood cells, a byproduct of bilirubin accumulates in its body. The newborn's liver cannot break down the accumulated bilirubin fast enough, and the result is a condition called **physiological neonatal jaundice.** In about 55 to 70 percent of newborns who have

Apnea   A condition in which regular breathing suddenly stops.

Physiological Neonatal Jaundice   A condition frequently found in neonates in which the baby's skin appears yellow.

this condition, their skin appears yellow. Usually this condition disappears after a few days of exposure to fluorescent light, the rays of which help to break down the bilirubin.

Digestion

For the neonate, digestion of food does not begin immediately. For one reason, many newborns have difficulty sucking in nourishment right away because of the mucus remaining in the throat after birth passage. Second, it generally takes about two to three days before the mother's breasts secrete milk. In the interim, a thin, watery, yellowish substance called **colostrum** is secreted by the mother's breasts. Newborns are encouraged to ingest the colostrum because it is a high-protein food source and contains antibodies that help the newborn resist infections.

Colostrum   A thin, watery, yellowish substance secreted from a new mother's breasts.

Temperature Regulation

The newborn's ability to maintain a constant body temperature is not stable during the first week of life. In addition, the neonate's thin skin lacks a layer of insulating fat so heat is more readily lost. Newborns lose heat four times as fast as an adult does (Bruck, 1961). One way the infant regulates its body temperature is through activity and crying. Temperature regulation in a heated incubator is essential for survival for prematurely born infants since they have greater difficulty maintaining an even body temperature.

States of Consciousness

In 1959, Peter Wolff presented data documenting the fact that newborns experienced six separate states of consciousness. This was a landmark discovery in one sense because his findings contradicted the then-popular belief that the newborn was not attentive or alert to the objects or people in its environment. By maintaining an 18-hour vigil over newborn babies and by carefully recording their activities, Wolff was able to detect different states of alertness and activity. In *regular sleep* the infant breathes smoothly and evenly, and there is little motor activity. The face and eyes are still and the infant is at full rest. About one-third of the infant's day is spent in regular sleep. During *irregular sleep*, the infant's breathing is uneven and there is periodic body movement. The infant frequently smiles, frowns, and pouts. The eyes move rapidly under the eyelids in a pattern called **rapid eye movement,** or **REM.** Fifty percent of the infant's sleep and one-third of its day are spent in REM sleep (Parmelee & Stern, 1972). As the newborn's brain develops, the proportion of time spent in this REM-sleep state diminishes from 50 percent at birth to 20 to 25 percent in adulthood.

Rapid Eye Movement (REM)   A phase of sleep characterized by rapid eye movements.

In the third state, *drowsiness,* the infant's eyelids are heavy, and the eyes open and close intermittently and appear glazed. There is less motor activity than in the irregular-sleep state and the infant breathes regularly and faster than in regular sleep. In the state of *alert inactivity* the infant is awake with open eyes, and has a relaxed face with a bright, shining appearance. Respiration is regular. During this period of alert inactivity, the newborn is able to learn and interact with parents and siblings. Although newborn infants differ widely in the amount of time spent in this state, it usually lasts no longer than 15 minutes at a time and occurs only a few times in a day. As the infant matures, it spends increasingly longer periods of time in this state.

In *waking activity* the infant is awake and shows spurts of diffuse motor activity, moving arms, legs, head, and trunk. Breathing is irregular, and the infant often displays fretful facial expressions but does not cry for a sustained period of time. The face at other times appears relaxed but the eyes are not shiny. The defining behaviors in the *crying state* are crying vocalizations, accompanied by motor activity and a facial grimace. Infants spend about 5 percent of their time in this state.

Neonates differ widely in their attentiveness to stimuli within the first five days of life. Birns (1973) found that individual newborns were rather consistent in their reactions. Babies who responded vigorously to one stimulus responded vigorously to all stimuli and did so consistently over five days of testing.

Sensory and Perceptual Systems of the Neonate

Discovering Infant Capabilities

Sensation refers to the ability to respond to and be aware of stimuli. If you wanted to discover how well adults or children could see, hear, or respond to different stimuli, you would probably present different sights, sounds, or objects to them and ask them to describe their experience. But newborns and infants cannot directly tell us what they see, hear, or feel because they have not yet acquired the language skills to do so. Other more indirect methods of studying infants' sensory and perceptual systems have been developed. One way to indirectly measure the extent to which newborns are capable of responding to light, sound, or odors is to measure their physiological reactions when different stimuli are presented. Heart rate, rate of breathing, and muscular movements are some of the physiological measures typically used by researchers. First, the researchers must find out what the physiological rates are when the newborn is unstimulated by sight or sound. Typically, this is done by monitoring the heart rate and breathing while the newborn is sleeping—which as you recall is most of the time. Then a tone or sound is presented and the newborn's physiological reactions are recorded. If there is a noticeable change in the physiological rate of responding, then it is inferred that the newborn must have heard or seen the stimulus.

Robert Fantz (1958, 1961, 1965) used a different method of studying infants' reactions to visual stimuli. He placed the infant in a specially designed booth that allowed him to watch the infant's eyes and measure how long the infant would look at different pictures. The method Fantz used is called the *preferential looking technique*. In recent years, this technique has been improved by using infrared lights that enable researchers to tell not only how long a picture is viewed but also what specific aspects or features of a picture newborns look at (Maurer & Salapatek, 1976).

Yet another way to determine the extent to which newborns can see or hear is to measure whether they reach out for objects presented to them or if they turn their heads in response to sound. In some studies, the newborns' sucking response is used as a measure of their attentiveness to stimuli. Using a pacifier that is rigged to the focussing apparatus of a slide projector, researchers have found that newborns will suck harder and faster to bring specific pictures into focus.

Habituation The process by which a person becomes familiar with a stimulus and decreasingly reacts to it.

To help them interpret the measures of attentiveness to various physical stimuli, researchers rely on **habituation,** the process by which someone becomes familiar with a stimulus and also less sensitive to it. The principle can be demonstrated by a two-step testing procedure. In the first step, the sound of a buzzer, for example, is presented several times, and the baby's startle reaction, breathing, and heart rate are recorded. Over repeated presentations, the baby's reactions change and diminish as if the baby grows bored by the noise. Heart rate and respiration may slow down and eventually after several presentations the startle reaction disappears. If, however, a new sound, say a ringing bell, is presented, the baby perks up and responds with a startle and a change in heart rate and respiration. By using ultrasound to measure fetal movements, researchers have demonstrated that habituation also occurs during the prenatal period (Madison, Madison, & Adubato, 1986).

Vision

At one time, it was thought that the newborn was unable to see at birth. As researchers developed new ways to measure visual behavior in the neonate, this belief was proven false. Wolff's (1959) study of newborn states illustrated that these young infants could indeed focus on an object held before their faces. If that object is moved, the infant can also visually follow it by moving its eyes and head (Brazelton, 1973).

Pupillary Reflex The automatic opening or closing of the iris in response to light.

When bright light is presented, the iris constricts. In dim light, the iris widens to let in more light. This automatic reaction of the iris to light is called the **pupillary reflex.** The neonate has a primitive pupillary reflex responding to gross changes in light. While researchers have discovered that newborns can tell the difference between the brightness or darkness of light, what is not known is whether newborns can see and distinguish between colors. Although clearly by a few months of age this capacity has developed (Bornstein, 1985).

Binocular Fixation The ability to simultaneously use both eyes to focus on an object.

Binocular fixation, the ability to simultaneously use both eyes to focus on an object, is present in some newborns at birth. By two months of age, the infant readily uses both eyes to look at an object.

Visual Accommodation The eye's ability to change the shape of the lens to obtain a clear focus.

The range within which a newborn can see an object clearly is limited to between about 7 to 15 inches at birth. This occurs because the newborn lacks **visual accommodation,** that is, the eye's ability to change the shape of the lens to bring objects at varying distances into clear focus. By about four months of age, the infant is capable of visual accommodation (Haynes, White, & Held, 1965). The ability to distinguish between different features of an object is called *visual acuity*. At birth newborns have poor visual acuity. The normal adult measure of acuity is 20/20; reports of newborn acuity have ranged from 20/150 to 20/800 (Banks & Salapatek, 1983).

Researchers are also asking the question: "What do newborns like to look at?" The most common answer to this question is "The human face." For example, newborns can tell the difference between different facial expressions (Field, Woodson, Greenberg, & Cohen, 1982) and can even match some facial expressions with their own facial expressions (Field et al., 1982; Meltzoff & Moore, 1977, 1983).

Researchers have also discovered that newborns prefer to look at figures with strong contrasts and complex designs (Fantz, 1961). Infants prefer to look at visual patterns that are irregular rather than regular, curved rather than straight lined, symmetrical rather than nonsymmetrical, and concentric rather than nonconcentric (Olson & Sherman, 1983). By measuring eye movements, Haith (1980) demonstrated that newborns prefer to scan the edges and contours of complex shapes. Even when they are in the dark, newborns scan their visual environment. In fact, newborns seem to use a set of "rules" to guide them as they visually scan objects in their environment (Haith, 1980). These rules include:

Rule 1: When awake and alert and in a setting that is not too bright, open eyes.
Rule 2: In dark settings, do a detailed search.
Rule 3: In lightened settings, search the edges of an object using broad visual sweeps.
Rule 4: When an edge of an object is found, concentrate the visual search on or about the contours.

Pause for Thought

Perhaps your grandparents and certainly your great-grandparents believed that newborns were blind at birth. Now we believe differently. How do people today differ in the way they treat newborns as a result of this changed belief? Do you think that the way we treat newborns has an effect on their later development?

Hearing

Research on fetal and prematurely born infants has provided evidence that the ability to hear develops several weeks before full-term birth (Aslin, Pisoni, & Jusczyk, 1983). After birth, the study of newborn capability to hear is limited by the ways researchers can assess how and what neonates hear. Using habituation responses, researchers have learned that newborns can distinguish between high- and low-pitch tones and loud and soft sounds. They can also locate a sound in space and turn their heads in the direction of the noise (Brody, Zelago, & Chaika, 1984). They can discriminate the sound of their mother's voices from unfamiliar ones within 12 hours of birth (DeCasper & Fifer, 1980). Infants are more sensitive to higher pitched sounds (Aslin, Pisoni, & Jusczyk, 1983).

Using heart-rate changes, researchers have found that neonates respond more to complex patterns of vowel sounds than to continuous presentations of the same sound (Clarkson & Berg, 1983). This finding suggests that infants may be primed from the beginning of life to attend to the complexity of human speech (Aslin Pisoni, & Jusczyk, 1983), which is probably of no surprise to parents of a newborn. One way parents learn to calm a crying infant is by talking quietly but steadily to it.

Smell, Taste, and Touch

Newborns react to strong odors, such as ammonia and fresh onion. Infants are able to detect the smell of their mothers' breast as early as six to 10 days of life (MacFarlane, 1978).

Newborns can distinguish between different tastes such as sugar, lemon, salt, and quinine. They have a preference for sweet tastes and will suck longer and slower at fluids laced with sucrose (Lipsitt, 1975). Because the taste buds of newborns are more widely distributed on the tongue than are those of older infants, they are more sensitive to strong tastes.

Another well-developed newborn sensitivity is touch. Many of the early behaviors of neonates are triggered by a touch to the skin. For example, stroking the cheek of a newborn will result in the baby turning its head in the direction of the stroked cheek. The newborn's skin is soft and pleasant to touch. Hence, tactile stimulation is frequent during the early weeks and months of life. Some researchers maintain that touching the newborn immediately after birth triggers an affectionate caretaking response in adults (Klaus & Kennell, 1982).

One commonly asked question about newborns is "How sensitive are they to pain?" At one time it was thought that newborns were not particularly sensitive to pain. In fact, infant boys are still circumcised without the benefit of anesthesia. However, more recent studies suggest a greater pain sensitivity exists in newborns.

Behavioral Responses—The Reflexes

Reflexes Automatic and unlearned responses to particular stimuli in the environment.

Not only are infants capable of detecting stimuli in their new world, but also they are capable of responding to certain stimuli in a specific way. **Reflexes** are automatic and unlearned responses to particular stimuli in the environment. The newborn's pupillary reaction to bright light is one example. Other reflexes that are present at birth and continue to be present throughout development include the knee jerk, eye blink, gagging, and sneezing reflexes. Controlled by the central nervous system, reflexes are often used to assess the status and development of the nervous system. An absent knee jerk or pupillary reflex would suggest some damage to the nervous system.

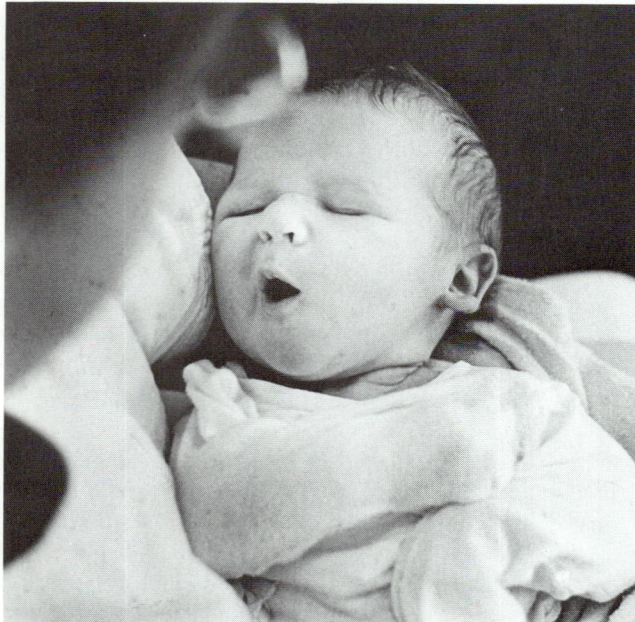

The rooting reflex helps the newborn locate the mother's breast. The newborn will turn its head in the direction of whatever touches its cheek.

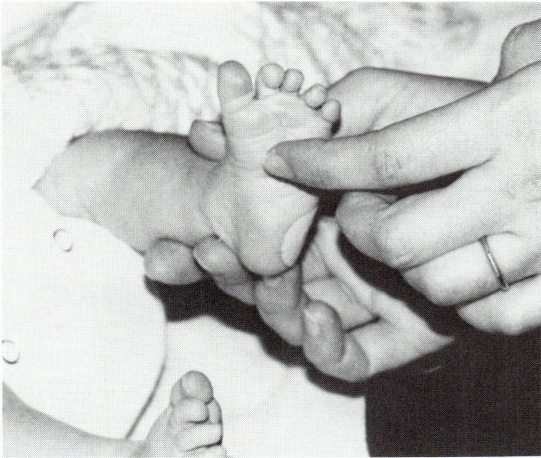

The Babinski reflex causes the newborn's toes to fan outward when its sole is stimulated.

The Moro reflex is released by a loud noise or sudden loss of support.

Neonatal Reflexes
Automatic responses that are present in the early weeks and months of life.

In addition to the essential physiological reflexes, the infant possesses a variety of **neonatal reflexes,** automatic responses that are present only in the early weeks and months of life. These neonatal reflexes help the infant adapt to the physical environment and disappear quickly as the newborn's brain matures. Some appear to have an adaptive function, including the *sucking reflex,* which is elicited in the newborn whenever an object touches the lips. Whether the object be the mother's nipple, a bottle nipple, or a finger, the infant will respond to this stimulus by sucking. The *rooting reflex,* in which a stroke to the baby's cheek causes the baby to turn its head in the direction of the cheek, often occurs in conjunction with the sucking reflex. These two reflexes, sucking and rooting, have a survival value because they enable the infant to locate and receive food. By about three months of age, these reflexes are replaced by more deliberate and voluntary actions of the baby.

Other neonatal reflexes do not have such an obvious adaptive function. The *Moro reflex* occurs when the infant is stimulated by a loud noise or a sudden loss of support. The infant responds by first throwing out its arms and fingers and then bringing them back to the body midline. By about three to five months of age, this reflex disappears in neurologically healthy infants. Place an object—a rattle or toy, for example, in the palm of the newborn's hand and the infant will automatically grasp the object. This *palmar grasp reflex* is so strong that an infant can be lifted to a standing position while grasping onto an object. Starting to weaken at three months of age, this reflex is absent by the infant's first birthday. The *Babinski reflex* occurs when the sole of the foot is stimulated and the infant's toes fan out and upward. By about six months of age, the infant's nervous system has matured somewhat and the infant's response to the same stimulation is to curl its toes downward. The *Babkin reflex* can be demonstrated by pressing the palms of the infant's two hands. The reflexive response is that the infant turns its head to the side and opens its mouth. Perhaps *the stepping reflex* is a precursor of later walking behavior. Hold the infant upright and it will make stepping movement. How-

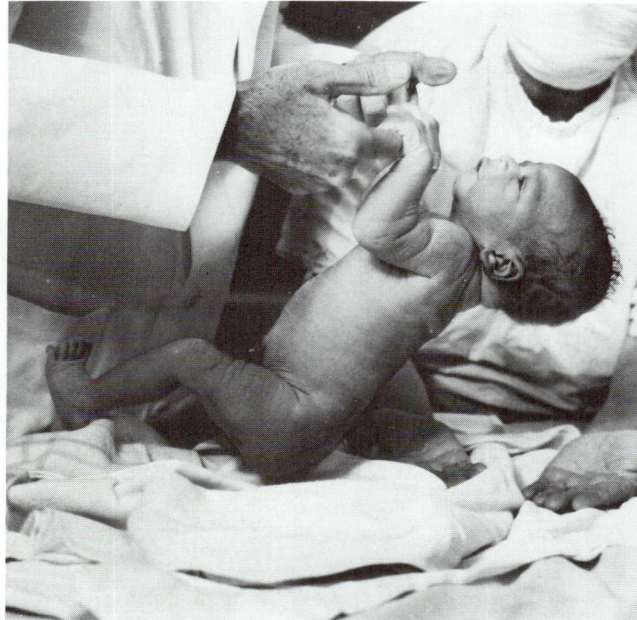

The palmar grasp reflex is so strong that this newborn can be lifted to a standing position by the strength of its hold on the physician's fingers.

ever, these coordinated movements disappear by three months of age, long before actual walking movements appear.

The Premature Infant: A Special Case

Although most infants are born after 38 to 40 weeks of prenatal development, some infants are born before they are fully ready. At one time, these infants were referred to as *premature babies*. However, this term is misleading since some babies are born after a full nine months of gestation but are small in size. Today the term *low birthweight* is used to describe infants who are born weighing less than 2500 grams (approximately 5½ pounds). Infants born before 37 weeks of gestation have past are referred to as *preterm*. In years past, the chances of survival for an infant born prematurely were low. However, with newer methods of caring for the neonate has come a much higher survival rate. Henig (1981) reports that in the early 1980s, 80 to 85 percent of preterm infants with birthweights between 1000 to 1500 grams (2¼ to 3¼ pounds) are surviving. Fifty to 60 percent of preterm infants with very low birthweights of 750 to 1000 grams (1½ to 2¼ pounds) are also surviving, although 11 percent of this group have serious problems such as mental retardation, blindness, or cerebral palsy.

Preterm infants are more vulnerable to complications and delays in development. Furthermore, boys are more vulnerable than girls to delays in both mental and motor development as a result of their premature birth (Braine, Heimer, Wortis, & Freedman, 1966).

The younger and smaller the infant at birth, the more problems there are in later development. These problems occur because many of the infants' physical systems are not yet developed or functioning and because the infant

Human Development in Practice

Caring for Tiny Babies

Years ago, a baby born earlier than the average 38 to 40 weeks of gestation probably would not have survived. Infant mortality rates for preterm births have diminished primarily because of the development of highly specialized neonatal intensive-care units (NICUs). These NICUs take over for the physiological systems in the tiny infant that are not yet developed or functioning adequately enough for survival.

The NICU looks like a conglomerate of blinking, beeping monitors, catheters, electrodes, and lights, all connected to the tiny infant. While these units have increased preterm and low-

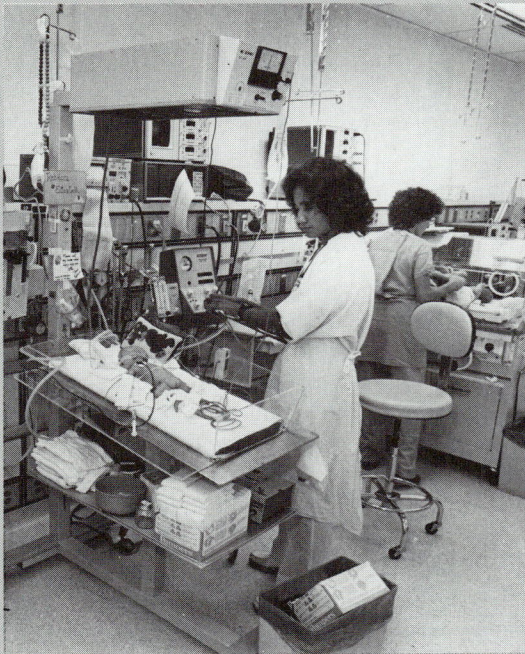

birthweight infants' chances of survival, they also have presented other problems for the parents and nurses who care for these infants. For one thing, it is often awkward and difficult to hold and cuddle a newborn who is attached to medical monitors. Even nurses who are trained in the medical procedures and care of preterm infants may be reluctant to handle their tiny patients. Yet holding, cuddling, rocking, and generally stimulating preterm infants promotes their growth. Unfortunately, the kind of stimulation an infant in a NICU often receives is aversive and stressful since it involves drawing blood samples and inserting catheters.

A second and related problem in preterm infant care is that the parents often have difficulty establishing contact with their newborns. Many neonatal care nurses are recognizing the benefits to parents and infant in establishing early contact and are encouraging new parents to spend time with their preterm or low-birthweight baby; to hold, talk to, and care for the infant in every possible way. Hospitals have tried to stimulate a normal home environment by involving family members in the regular care of the infant and by placing colorful mobiles over the NICU.

Parents, nurses, and other caregivers may unintentionally contribute to the newborn's difficulties. Researchers Marilyn Stern and Katherine Hildebrandt (1986) labeled full-term infants as either "premature" or "full term" and observed the reactions of caregivers to these babies. Infants who were described as "premature" were touched less, described as smaller, finer featured, and less cute and were liked less than infants who were labeled "full term." And the full-term infants labeled as "premature" were less active with the caregivers as a result of what the researchers believe is a self-fulfilling prophecy.

The care of a tiny infant does present additional problems. However, when caregivers recognize the importance of caring contact in the early days of a newborn's life, many of the difficulties can be reduced.

The special environment of the preterm and low birthweight infant results in higher rates of survival. One problem with this environment is that it makes it more difficult for parents to have direct contact with their newborn.

may have additional medical problems resulting from the neonatal care given while developing outside the mother's womb. (See Box, Caring for Tiny Babies.)

Although there are wide individual differences among both full-term and preterm infants in their capacity to respond to their environment, striking differences exist in the way the preterm infants react to their physical extrauterine environment. For example, preterm infants spend less time in the state of alertness. They sleep more than full-term infants, and when they are alert, it is difficult to keep them in this state (Goldberg, Brachfield, & DiVitto, 1980). They are also less responsive to sights and sounds around them (Friedman, Jacobs, & Werthmann, 1981; Hernandez, 1981). Motor development in preterm babies is somewhat delayed, especially during the second half of the first year when noticeable changes in an infant's motor development occur (Hunt & Rhodes, 1977). Many of these differences between full-term and preterm infants diminish or disappear with age. Some researchers have argued that preterm infants should not be compared to full-term infants on developmental status. Goldberg and DiVitto (1983), for example, cite the following example:

> Amy, a prematurely born infant, spent only 30 weeks in the uterus. She was born 10 weeks earlier than most full-term infants at birth. If we were to evaluate Amy's development, would it make any sense to use, as the standard, babies who were 40 weeks from conception plus 1 month from birth when they were tested? Development really begins at conception rather than at birth, and we would not expect Amy, born after 30 weeks, to look or behave like average 1-month-olds a month after her birth. A 34-week-old fetus? Other preterm babies at 34 weeks from conception? Probably the latter would be most appropriate. (p. 52)

When age is measured from conception rather than from birth, the early developmental differences in motor behavior between preterm and full-term infants are diminished.

One interesting finding is that preterm infants who were stimulated either by rocking or visual/auditory stimulation showed greater gains in weight and overall development than did preterm infants who did not receive such treatment (Goldberg, 1979). The effects of early environment on preterm infant development are currently under study by many researchers (Barrera, Rosenbaum, & Cunningham, 1986; Beckwith & Parmelee, 1986). It is clear that the special environment of the preterm and low birthweight infant results in different social interactions between the infant and its caregiver. We will discuss the impact of preterm birth on emotional and social development in the next chapter.

Pause for Thought

Recall that a lifespan developmentalist is interested in how different factors affect development. In what ways would the culture affect newborn development? For example, would you expect an infant born in China, Saudi Arabia, or Chile to develop differently than an infant born in the United States? What information would you need to know about a culture to be able to answer this question?

The Infant

Physical Growth

General Principles

Infancy covers the period from several weeks after birth to about two years of age. During this relatively short period of time, physical growth and motor development are most evident. The infant seems to change from week to week in physical and motor capabilities with such regularity that a careful observer can accurately guess an infant's age by noting the degree of physical and motor development of the baby (Alley, 1983a). Similar to Adam described at the beginning of this chapter, as infants grow physically, they also gain increasing control over their bodies. The order of both physical and motor development follows two basic patterns: **cephalocaudal** (head to foot) and **proximodistal** (inner to outer) (Gesell, 1954).

In the cephalocaudal pattern, development occurs first and more rapidly in the head and upper parts of the body than in lower parts of the body. The proportionately large head of the newborn is an example of cephalocaudal development. Proximodistal growth, on the other hand, occurs earlier and more rapidly in the center of the body than in the extremities. For example, infants will gain control over their arms before they can use their fingers reliably. Before Adam could grab the figures on his crib mobile, he could hit them with his forearm and hand. These general patterns of growth continue throughout development but are more apparent during infancy because physical change is more frequent. Individual infants, of course, may differ greatly from one another in rate of growth and onset of motor skills during the early years of growth. These general growth patterns are derived from observing growth changes in many infants from different environmental experiences over time.

A third characteristic of development is that children develop from general, less specific reactions to more controlled, specific reactions. This process is called *differentiation* and can be seen in the infant's changing reactions to a visual stimulus. The newborn may respond to a colorful toy with global body movements; the same infant when older may specifically reach for the toy. Differentiation means the child has increasing voluntary control over its body, and this control is regulated by the central nervous system, the brain. So with the maturity of the brain comes greater control over voluntary movement and hence a more specific response to stimuli.

While it is generally accepted that physical growth and motor development are guided primarily by genetic or biological factors, the specific environment that the child is in does have an impact on growth. For example, Dennis (1973) found that infants in a nonstimulating physical and social–emotional environment developed motor skills and physical size at a much slower rate than did children in a more responsive early environment.

Changes in Size and Proportion

By the fourth or fifth month of life, the infant has doubled its birthweight; by a year, the weight has tripled. Because height is slower to change, it is not until age four that the birth length has doubled. The result is that children appear round and plump-looking during infancy. Furthermore, infant boys are generally taller and heavier than infant girls during this period of growth

Cephalocaudal Pertaining to the pattern of growth that proceeds in a head-to-toe direction.

Proximodistal Pertaining to the pattern of growth that proceeds from the center to the outer or peripheral parts of the body.

because they have more muscle and bone. At birth, the infant's skeletal system is made up mostly of soft cartilage, so the bones are more flexible. This skeletal flexibility makes the birth passage easier for mother and child. During infancy, the bones harden, or ossify, at different rates for different bones in the body. The age at which the cartilage turns into bone is used to determine the maturity of the child. By comparing the rate of ossification between boys and girls, we see that even though boys are heavier and taller than girls in infancy, the girls actually mature faster. At birth, girl babies are four weeks ahead of boy babies in terms of skeletal development (Tanner, 1970).

Pause for Thought

Do you think that this difference in skeletal maturity between girls and boys would have an influence on the way infants are treated by adult caregivers? How would girls and boys be treated differently?

Brain Development

During infancy, the brain is growing rapidly. At birth, the brain is about 25 percent of adult weight; by three months of age, it is 40 percent; by six months, it is 50 percent; and by two years of age, it is 75 percent of its adult size. The neurons increase in size and density and develop a protective sheath called **myelin.** The myelin sheath around the neurons permits a faster transmission of neural messages, which makes it easier for the infant to control its behavior.

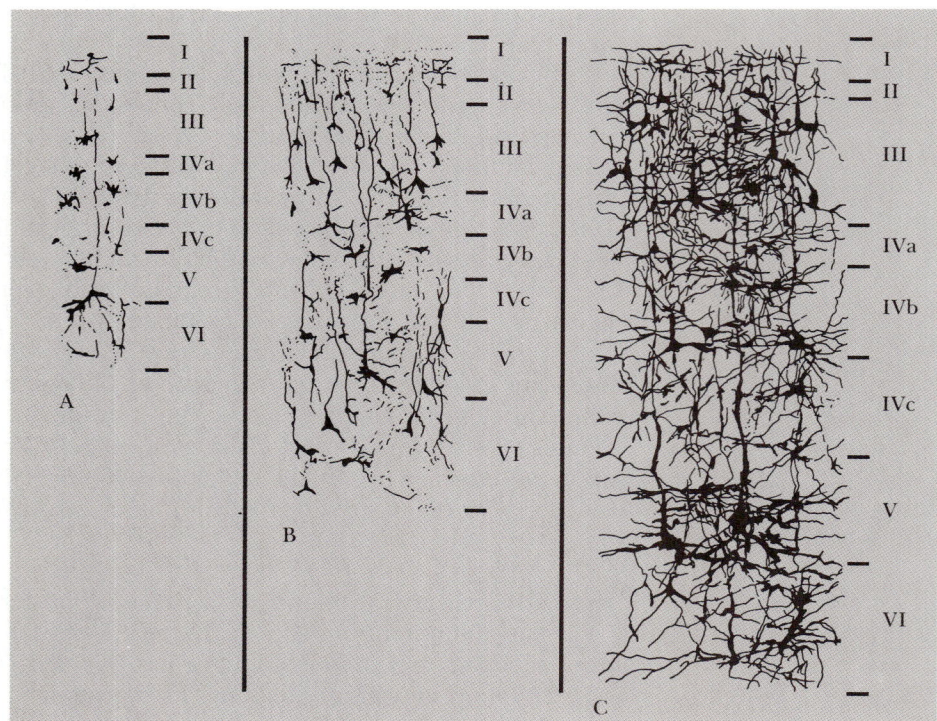

Figure 3.1 The development of dendrites in the human occipital cortex: (A) the newborn; (B) the three-month-old; (C) the two-year-old.

The cerebral cortex, the portion of the brain responsible for voluntary control and thought, develops during infancy. By the first month of life, the section of the cortex controlling motor development begins to function; by three months of age, the sensory areas of the cortex are more fully developed. This neurological development allows infants to coordinate responses controlled by their motor cortex with their visual responses. Thus, the infant can now look and touch an object at the same time, although precise eye–hand coordination will develop somewhat later (see Figure 3.1). The onset and refinement of sensory and motor events in infancy are correlated with growth and changes in the nervous system. Researchers are even suggesting that spurts in brain growth are correlated with spurts in cognitive development (Fischer, 1987; Kagan, 1982)

Sudden Infant Death Syndrome (SIDS)

Sudden Infant Death Syndrome (SIDS) is the name given to the sudden and unexpected death of seemingly healthy babies between the ages of three weeks and one year. It is the major cause of death of infants between the ages of one month and a year. In the United States, SIDS, or crib death, as it was formerly called, is responsible for 7000 deaths a year. The tragedy of SIDS is that the syndrome is neither predictable nor preventable.

In the typical case, the baby, usually between two and four months of age, when put to bed appears healthy or may have signs of a slight cold. Sometime later, the baby is found dead, usually with no signs of a struggle or discomfort. An autopsy may reveal at most a minor upper respiratory inflammation but nothing so serious as to cause death.

Who are the SIDS victims? Many are boys, especially those who had been born prematurely. The rate of incidence of SIDS is also higher among the poor than among the well-to-do, and the rate is higher among minority nonwhites (predominantly blacks) than among whites (Valdes-Dapena, 1980). Many of the SIDS victims die during the winter months, suggesting that cold, wet weather may be an influencing factor.

Infants of young mothers are most susceptible to SIDS. Related to the age of the mother is the fact that the rate of death among illegitimate infants is twice as high as that for babies considered to be legitimate. Further, the incidence of SIDS is higher among infants whose mothers smoke.

What causes the syndrome? Researchers now believe that SIDS probably has more than one cause, even though the actual process of death may be similar. It is now believed that SIDS victims are not as normal or healthy a group as was previously thought. Many have subtle physiological defects that are detectable only after death. A sizable number of the infants are found to have abnormalities in the central nervous system that had caused the infants difficulty from birth. Other studies point to the possibility of lesions in the respiratory area of the brain stem as a factor in SIDS.

The apnea (cessation of breathing) hypothesis as a cause of SIDS has received much attention in the news, and many people have erroneously concluded that apnea is the cause of most SIDS cases. Many, but not all, SIDS babies had episodes of *apnea* while they were asleep. When apnea episodes are prolonged (10 to 20 seconds in duration) this condition may lead to anoxia, cardiac arrest, and death. However, only about 5 percent of SIDS victims seem to have had a history of severe apneic episodes (Valdes-Dapena, 1980).

Digestion, Diet, and Feeding

In Chapter 2, we discussed the importance of adequate maternal nutrition for the development of the prenatal nervous system. Since neurological growth continues after birth, the importance of adequate nutrition during infancy is equally important. As the infant's body grows, so does its need for nutrients, particularly protein. Milk is the primary source of protein for the infant during the first year of life. In the United States, most infants are either breast-fed milk from their mother's body or receive a cows' milk formula from a bottle. From a purely physiological viewpoint, breast milk is the ideal food for the baby. For one reason, it is more readily digested by the infant than cows' milk. In addition, the child is less likely to be allergic to the milk produced by its mother. Breast milk also contains the mother's antibodies and immunities, which help provide the infant with protection from diseases. Research has discovered that breast milk contains a factor that seems to promote growth by increasing the absorption of folic acid by the infant's body (Colman, Helliarachy, & Herbert, 1981).

Breast feeding has advantages for the mother. First, the infant's sucking stimulates her uterus, which promotes a quicker return to its normal prepregnancy size. Breast feeding is more convenient, as there is no preparation required; no bottles, no need to heat the milk, no need to carry extra bottles while traveling. As nutritional needs increase, the infant sucks harder and longer, the mother's body compensates by producing greater quantities of milk, free of charge. During nursing many women report great satisfaction from the intimate skin-to-skin, eye-to-eye contact. A similar degree of contact can, of course, be achieved in bottle feeding. In a study by Richards and Bernal (1971), however, it was found that breast-fed babies were held, touched, and talked to more during feeding than bottle-fed infants. This difference may reflect personality differences between mothers who decide to breast-feed and mothers who choose bottle feeding.

Not all women share the pleasures of breast feeding, however. Some are unable to nurse because it is too painful or fatiguing. Others may feel embarrassed or too tied to the baby for their own comfort. Career commitments may conflict with the need to be physically available to the child. Other mothers may want to share the care and feeding of the infant with the fathers and prefer to bottle-feed. Obviously, there are many factors that influence the choice of bottle or breast as a source of nutrition. New parents, therefore, must balance the benefits and restrictions in light of their own situation. The long-term psychological benefits of breast or bottle feeding are not known.

Whether the infant is breast- or bottle-fed, by about six to eight months most mothers usually begin to wean the child from sucking to drinking from a cup. By eight months, the first tooth has appeared, and the mother and infant may both be ready for a change in the feeding pattern. By this age, the infant is showing increasingly greater interest and curiosity in its physical world. The baby is ready to try new foods and new eating skills. The best approach to weaning is a gradual one in which the child is offered a cup instead of the breast or bottle. Toward the end of the first year, most infants are avid self-feeders.

The average one-year-old has six to eight teeth and sufficient hand–eye coordination to self-feed. Because growth is rapid during infancy, the amount of food infants eat is more than their actual bodily size would suggest. Studies on the long-term consequences of an inadequate diet emphasize the effects of malnutrition and starvation on physical and mental functioning. An equally serious problem occurs when a child is overfed and encouraged to overeat by being offered foods with lots of sugar and fats. During the first year of life, the number of fat cells in a baby's body is determined by how much it eats. After the first year, this number remains the same no matter how much a person eats. In later development, as a person consumes an excess of calories, the fat cells expand, resulting in overweight. Thus, the number of fat cells developed during the first year of life theoretically can influence later tendencies toward obesity. Chubby babies are more likely than average weight babies to become overweight adults. However, the connection between obesity and overfed babies is not a direct one. Not all fat babies grow up to be obese adults. Nonetheless, most pediatricians recommend diets that are not loaded with sugar during infancy.

Motor Development

Friends and relatives who have watched an infant grow from birth are likely to use the ages that the baby rolls over, sits up, or takes its first step as an index of the child's overall development. Changes in the child's ability to use its body are numerous and obvious, but they are not related to other types of development. Children who sit up and walk at early ages are not necessarily early in language development or other cognitive skills. Motor skills seem to occur in a regular progression in development.

The two major motor skills that develop in infancy are *prehension,* the ability to grasp and hold an object, and *locomotion,* the ability to move from one place to another. These skills emerge in an orderly sequence that follows

Infant motor development proceeds more rapidly in the upper parts of the body than in the lower parts. This baby has greater control over his head than he does over his legs and lower body.

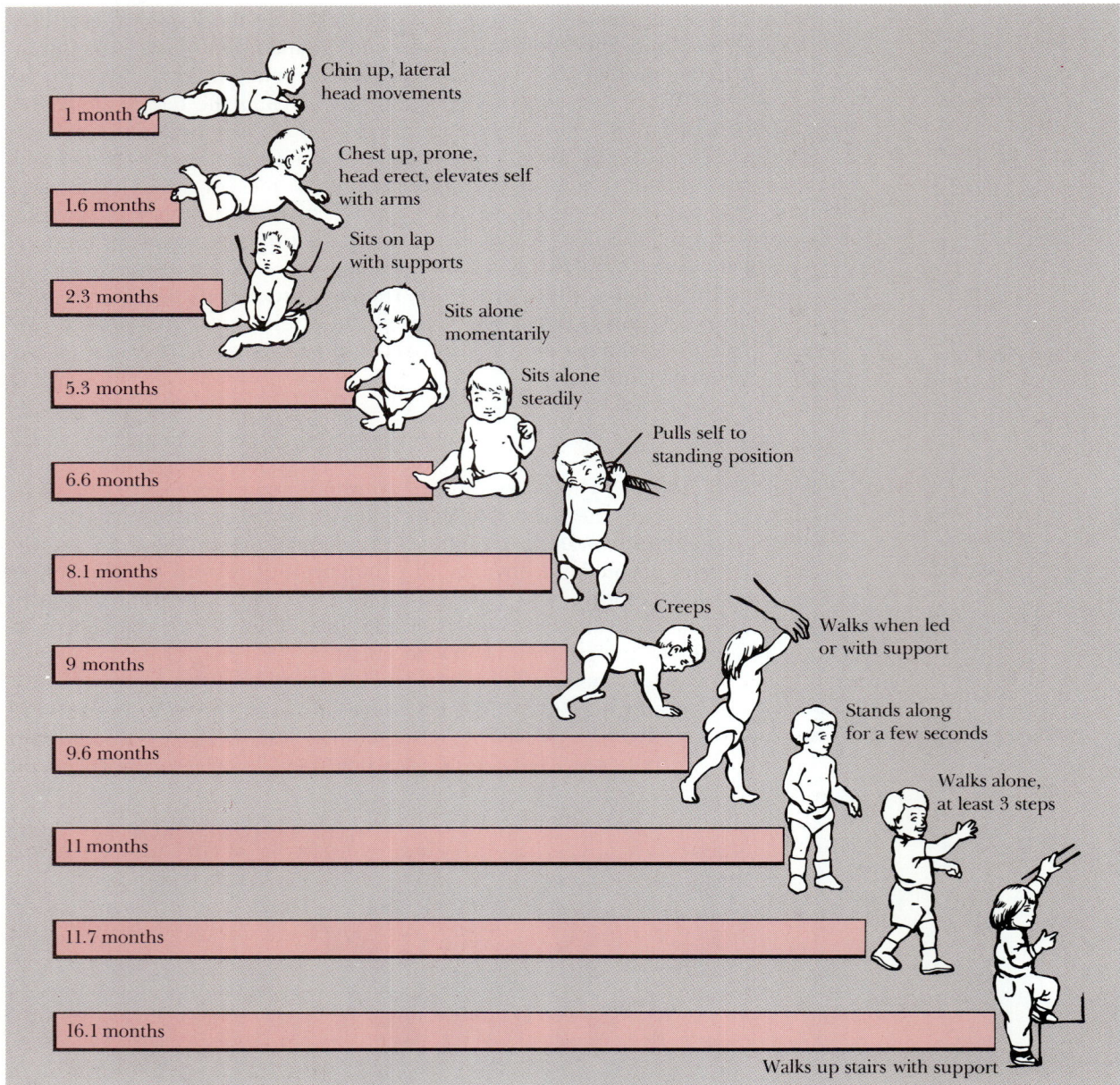

Figure 3.2 The development of locomotion in infants.

cephalocaudal and proximodistal growth patterns. In the case of reaching and grasping, the infant progresses from the gross hand control of the *palmar grasp* to a more refined grasp of smaller objects using its thumb and forefingers in a *pincer grasp.* In getting from one place to the next, the infant first sits up, then stands, followed by creeping, assisted walking, and then finally unassisted walking. These sequences of locomotor and prehension development are illustrated in Figures 3.2 and 3.3.

The order of motor events is believed to be the result of maturational factors. The growth of the nervous system, in particular the network of neu-

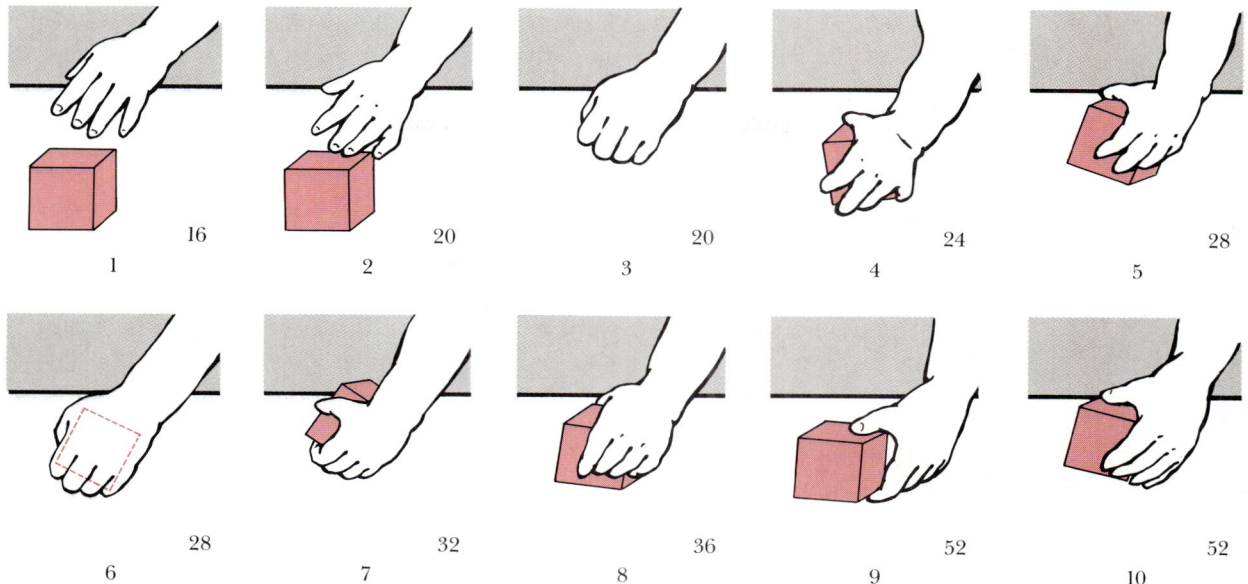

Figure 3.3 Ten types of grasping behavior: (1) no contact; (2) contact only; (3) primitive squeeze; (4) squeeze grasp; (5) hand grasp; (6) palm grasp; (7) superior palm grasp; (8) inferior forefinger grasp; (9) forefinger grasp; (10) superior forefinger grasp. The number in the lower right indicates the child's age in weeks at which these stages normally appear.

rons, permits greater control over the large and small muscles controlling body movement. The center in the brain that integrates neural messages from the parts of the body also develops so that the infant can coordinate its control over specific body parts.

The role of experience in the onset of motor skills has been the subject of many studies. Dennis (1940), for example, reported on Hopi Indian babies, who are bound to a cradle board during the first nine months of life. As a result, they cannot roll over, move their hands or feet, or otherwise practice motor skills. This restricted early motor experience, Dennis observed, did *not* affect their motor development. The cradled infants also did not differ in age of walking when compared to nonrestricted infants. In another study, Gesell and Thompson (1929) used identical-twin girls and gave one twin specific training and practice in stair climbing for 6 weeks beginning at age 46 weeks. The other twin received no practice. At 53 weeks, both twins could climb the stairs but the practiced twin could climb them faster. After only two weeks' practice, the untrained twin was climbing at the same rate as the twin who had practiced climbing. Practice and training, therefore, seemed not to affect overall motor development. One criticism of this early study, however, was that because the experimental twin was trained in stair climbing by being passively lifted from one tread to the next, this type of practice would not be expected to give the trained infant an edge on stair climbing (Bower, 1982).

Later studies by White (1971) have emphasized the role of the environment in the development of reaching. In order for the infant to be able to reach and grasp an object, it must first develop eye–hand coordination. For such coordination to occur, the infant must first look at its hand, then the object, and then, after repeated object and hand viewings, coordinate its actions to reach and locate the object. Only then can the infant successfully grasp the object. When the physical–visual environment was made more stimulating by introducing colorful objects, White found that infants reached for these objects at an earlier age than infants in a less enriched visual environment.

We can conclude that the sequence of motor development is broadly guided by maturational factors and refined by the specific experiences of the infant in its physical environment.

Pause for Thought

Suppose that you are an ambitious and creative designer of infant toys. On the basis of what you now know about newborn and infant physical development, what features would you include in the design of your toys to encourage infants to play with your toys? What would you tell parents about these toys?

Perceptual Development

Adam's mother loved to watch him in his crib because he seemed to be carefully studying the animal mobile suspended above him. There was no doubt in her mind that at two months of age he could see the figures, but what was he thinking about as he watched the shapes move? She could tell that he recognized the figures by the way he would move excitedly in his crib while watching the yellow dog bob around. The question that Adam's mother considered—how does an infant interpret information gathered from the senses—is one that has stimulated a great deal of infant research.

Perception involves the interpretation of sensory information that is gathered. Perceptual capabilities of infants and newborns develop rapidly during the early months of life. Infants as young as one to two months selectively attend to shapes, contours, patterns, and colors. At three months, infants prefer to look at familiar sights. By six months, infants scan, touch, and manipulate objects, actively acquiring information about the properties of these objects. For example, in one study researchers found that six-month-old infants could distinguish an unfamiliar object from a familiar one by touching it and detecting whether it was hot or cold (Bushnell, Shaw, & Strauss, 1985).

Face Perception

Perhaps the earliest thing a newborn sees is a face. Doctors, nurses, eager parents, and later family members are likely to present themselves face-to-face to the infant early in life. Research (Meltzoff & Moore, 1983, 1977) has demonstrated that infants as young as 12 to 21 days of age are able to imitate simple facial responses modeled by adults. In another study (Carpenter, 1975), infants as young as two weeks of age looked longest at their mothers when they were talking to them and preferred to look at the mothers' faces than at either strangers' faces or the mothers' faces while listening to strangers' voices. These ages for facial perception are younger than earlier studies on infant perception would suggest (Maurer & Salapatek, 1976; Caron, Caron, Caldwell, & Weiss, 1973). By the age of three months, the infant is able to distinguish the familiar mother's face from other facial patterns. By four months of age, infants perceived differences in facial expression, particularly

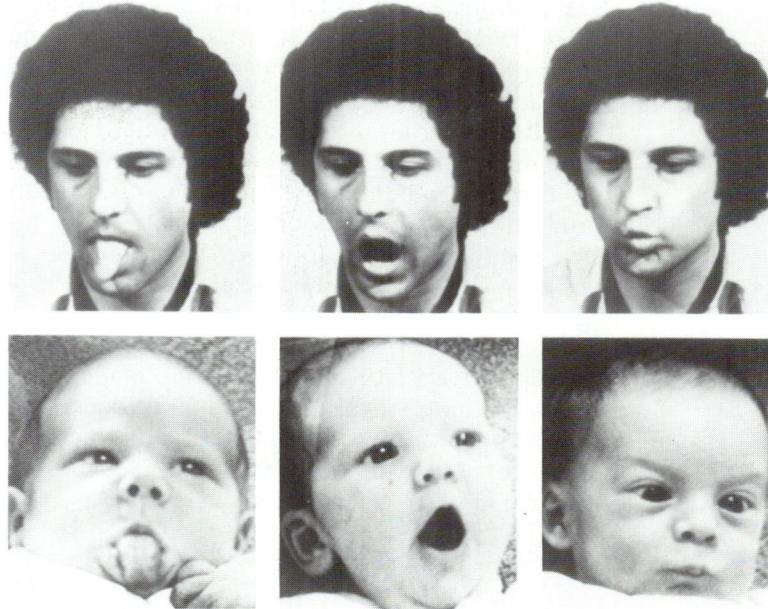

Researchers have discovered that newborns will imitate the facial expressions of adults.

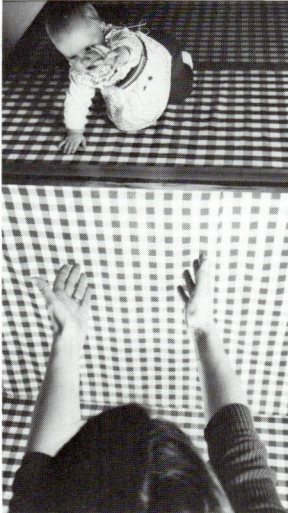

Gibson and Walk (1960) used the "visual cliff" apparatus to assess the depth perception of infants. Even though crawling infants can feel solid glass underneath them, they do not cross over the edge to reach their mother.

when the face they were looking at was smiling (Kuchuk, Vibbert, & Bornstein, 1986). By seven months of age, infants can tell the difference between a happy face and a fearful one (Nelson & Dolgin, 1985).

Depth Perception

The answer to the question, "When can the infant perceive that an object has depth or solidity?" depends on what response in the infant is used to assess depth perception. In a classic study by Gibson and Walk (1960), infants six to 14 months of age were placed on an apparatus called the *visual cliff*. The apparatus was a raised table with a shallow side and a side that appeared to drop off. In fact, the deep side was covered with glass and presented no danger of a fall to the infant. The infant's mother was stationed on the deep end of the apparatus and tried to coax the infant to cross over into the deep area. Even though infants felt the solid glass under them they would not cross over the "cliff," indicating that the infants perceived depth. By using a decrease in the infant's heart rate as an index of attention, Campos, Bertenthal, & Caplovitz (1982) discovered that infants begin to focus their attention on the deep side of the apparatus by about three months of age but they do not appear to fear falling. It is not until eight months of age, after the infant has had experiences with locomoting and with falls and spills, that the infant shows fear when on the deep side. However, this conclusion has been challenged by research by Nancy Rader and her associates (Rader, Bausano, & Richards, 1980). Twenty-two infants between four and eight-and-a-half months of age who were trained to use a walker and who could crawl to their mothers upon request were tested on the visual-cliff apparatus. When infants were tested in their walkers, they were as likely to move into the deep end as they were to move into the shallow end of the visual cliff. However, infants who had been crawling at an early age (before six-and-a-half months), were more likely to cross over into the deep end, while those who learned to crawl at or after six-and-a-half months were more likely to avoid the deep end. Infants who learn to crawl before six-and-a-half months do so by using tactile cues (how the floor feels) rather than visual cues (how the floor looks). Infants who learn to crawl at six-and-a-half months or later rely more on visual cues. Thus, Rader argues that depth perception is less influenced by motor experience than Campos and his associates suggest.

It may also be that the infant's mother is communicating her emotions to the infant. Using a modified version of the visual cliff apparatus, James Sorce and his associates found that if a mother's emotional response was joy or interest, infants were more likely to cross over the visual cliff. If the mother expressed fear or anger, the 12-month-old infants did not cross (Sorce, Emde, Campo, & Klinnert, 1985).

Closely related to the perception of depth is the ability to tell how far away something is from you. Infants between five-and-a-half and seven months appear to use the relative size of objects as a cue for distance. When objects were large, infants were more likely to reach for them assuming that they were closer to them than smaller objects (Yonas, Granrud, & Petterson, 1985).

Cognitive Development

So far, we have learned that the infant is quite skilled at collecting information about its world. Through its sensory systems, the infant tastes, smells, sees, touches, and hears its world. Growing motor skills gives the baby greater access to people and objects. But how does the infant put all the information together? How does the infant make sense out of its world? Such questions focus on the infant's *cognitive skills*. **Cognition** is the process by which a person acquires and organizes information and knowledge about the world. It is the process by which we learn. The perceptual skills of the infant are just one example of an infant's attempt to organize the information about the physical world.

Cognition The process by which a person acquires and organizes information and knowledge.

Infant Memory

Researchers now recognize that young infants are active processors of information (Olson & Sherman, 1983). They attend, select, perceive, and remember hundreds of pieces of information from their everyday world. Researchers became interested in the memory capabilities of infants as a result of habituation studies. Recall that infants (and adults) will grow bored with and appear uninterested in an object that is frequently presented to them. If that same object is presented again at a later time, infants will often become excited again as if they recognized the object. In order to have recognized the objects, infants must have encoded or stored in memory the important features of the objects.

Being able to recognize a familiar object is just one indication of memory. Recalling previously learned responses is another. In a cleverly designed experiment, researchers taught three-month-old infants to turn a mobile overhanging their cribs by kicking their feet (Rovee-Collier, 1984). After a few 10-minute training sessions, the infants learned that the way to watch their mobiles was to kick. Several weeks later, after not having had any practice with their kick-start mobile, the infants quickly remembered how to get them spinning. Infants who had not had the training sessions could not make the mobile turn. Even infants as young as eight weeks are capable of retaining the mobile training over a period of two weeks (Vander Linde, Morrongiello, & Rovee-Collier, 1985).

Pause for Thought

How much you remember is influenced by the amount of information you receive. Too much information at one time can be confusing, however. What skills do you think infants have to help control the amount of information they receive?

Piaget's Theory

Perhaps one of the most challenging views about how infants and young children make sense of their world has been that of Jean Piaget. Central to Piaget's theory of cognitive development is the idea that knowledge is constructed as people interact with their environment. The basic structures necessary for acquiring information about the world—for example, the sensory and motor systems—are present at birth in a primitive fashion. As the infant uses these structures, they grow and make it possible for the infant to gain more knowledge about its world. Thus Piaget's theory stresses the contribution of both biological and environmental factors as the infant's own actions set the stage for further knowledge and learning. Piaget postulated two processes to explain how knowledge is acquired through interaction with the environment. **Assimilation** is the process by which the person, using existing knowledge, or *schemes*, takes in new information about the environment. **Scheme** was the term Piaget used to describe an action sequence. For example, a baby presented with a rattle may look at it and then grasp it; this action sequence could be labeled the "look and grasp" scheme. When presented with an object other than a rattle—say a rubber ring—the infant, using the existing "look and grasp" scheme, would assimilate the new object. As soon as the infant applies the "look and grasp" scheme to the rubber ring, however, it may notice some differences. For example, the ring doesn't make a noise like the rattle, and it has a different shape as well. Through its experience of interacting with the rubber ring, the infant will modify its existing "look and grasp" scheme to include a "look, grasp, and listen" scheme. Changing existing schemes as a result of new experiences is called **accommodation.**

According to Piaget, assimilation and accommodation occur simultaneously. When the infant reaches for the rubber ring, it is using the existing scheme and at the moment of contact with the ring is changing that scheme in light of the information gathered by its senses. Together, accommodation and assimilation help infants develop increasingly complex schemes that enable them to adapt to the world.

As physical structures grow—for example, the nervous, muscular, and skeletal systems—infants progress through different stages in which they use increasingly symbolic or conceptual schemes to guide their actions. The first stage, the sensorimotor stage, begins at birth and continues to two years of age. The infant interacts with its world primarily using sensory and motor schemes. Since Piaget viewed cognitive growth as a process, he placed a great deal of emphasis on the sensorimotor stage as the foundation for later sym-

Assimilation The process by which a person, using existing knowledge, takes in new information about the environment.

Scheme According to Piaget, an action sequence.

Accommodation The process of changing existing schemes as a result of new experiences.

Table 3.1 ■■■■■■■

Piaget's Stages of Cognitive Growth—The Sensorimotor Period

Substage	Approximate Age	Characteristics
1. Reflex	0–1 month	Ready-made schemes are used; reflexes are initiated both internally and environmentally.
2. Primary circular reactions	1–4 months	Goal-directed behavior is present, but internal goals are prevalent; infant repeats learned schemes.
3. Secondary circular reactions	4–8 months	Goals are more involved with environment; infant uses trial-and-error more, still depends on chance to learn responses, and develops a primitive concept of objects.
4. Coordination of secondary schemes	8–12 months	Orientation to environment increases; infant distinguishes between goals and methods for achieving them; shows originality in combining two or more learned schemes.
5. Tertiary circular reactions	12–18 months	Curiosity begins, and novel stimuli are important; infant experiments with environment, systematic with trial and error.
6. Invention of new means through mental combinations	18–24 months	Problem solving begins; infant begins to develop insights; can think without action.

bolic thought. The changes he described in the sensorimotor substages reflect qualitative differences that children demonstrate in how they understand their world at different ages. Age alone, however, does not determine which substage characterizes the child. One 12-month-old infant may be functioning at the fourth substage (coordination of secondary schemes, 8–12 mos.) while another infant the same age may be at substage 5 (tertiary circular reactions, 12–18 mos.). However, Piaget believed that the *sequence* of the stages and substages was the same for all people even though the speed with which they go through the stages may vary from person to person. Table 3.1 lists the six distinct substages within the sensorimotor period; the ages for each substage are only approximate. By the end of the sensorimotor period at age two, the infant has accomplished several major cognitive tasks: (1) It has become familiar with its own body; (2) the infant has learned that events are preceded by some cause; (3) the infant has acquired **object permanence,** the knowledge that objects still exist even when not in sight; and (4) the infant is now capable of using symbols in language and thought. Let's examine in detail the progressive changes in the infant's structures, or schemes, during this period of cognitive growth.

Object Permanence
The knowledge that objects still exist even when they are not in sight.

Substage 1: Reflex (0–1 month)   The reflex stage was originally called "Exercising the ready-made sensorimotor schemes" because the infant reacts to environmental stimuli using simple reflexes, or schemes that are present at birth and even prenatally. The neonatal reflexes of sucking, grasping, and rooting are but a few of the ready-made ways of responding available to the newborn. By using or assimilating ready-made schemes, the infant also changes or accommodates them with experience. For example, at birth the infant will suck on any object placed in its mouth. By the end of this substage, however, the infant may refuse to suck on anything but the nipple it has had the most practice using. For this reason, mothers who plan to supplement breast feeding with a bottle are advised to introduce the bottle nipple to the infant in the early days of life to ensure that the baby will accept the bottle in the third or fourth week.

Substage 2: Primary Circular Reactions (1–4 months)   The term *circular* refers to the infant's tendency to repeat activities or schemes that create a desirable action. In effect, the infant's reactions are maintained by the behavior action. The action creates an event that triggers a repeated action, thereby creating the event again. These circular reactions are first noticed with the infant's own body rather than with objects in the environment; hence they are called *primary*. The young infant in its crib, who watches its hand move, is one example Piaget gave of primary circular reaction. The infant's random movements of its limbs results in its hand coming into view. This action of moving the hand over the body into the visual range is repeated often in the infant's day.

The child in this substage will not look for an object that has been taken from its sight, but will stare at the place where the object was last seen. While this action reflects a primitive visual attempt to locate an object, it does not reflect object permanence.

Substage 3: Secondary Circular Reactions (4–8 months)   The circular actions in this substage seem to be focused more on objects and events *outside* of the infant's own body and hence is labeled *secondary*. The infant at this stage perhaps has discovered the mobile hanging over its head in the crib. After months of watching, foot kicking, and organizing his motor schemes, young Adam accidentally discovered that the animal shapes on the mobile would move when he moved his arms and legs, causing the crib to shake. This event caused pleasure, so Adam would repeat the action of moving his arms and legs and watching the mobile figures shake. His own activity is a means to an end. Piaget used the term *motor meaning* to describe the infant's first understanding of objects through the specific motor actions it uses in the presence of objects. Modifications in the object permanence scheme are also made in this substage. When an object is only partially hidden, the infant will search for it. When the object is completely hidden, however, the infant will not search even if it has seen the toy being hidden.

Substage 4: Coordination of Secondary Schemes (8–12 months)   Infants at the substage of coordination of secondary schemes are much more intentional in their actions. No longer are they content to repeat schemes, for they now use their accumulated knowledge and schemes to produce an effect. For example, Piaget's son Laurent at age seven months had perfected his "hitting at things" scheme to the point where he would hit objects to remove them as

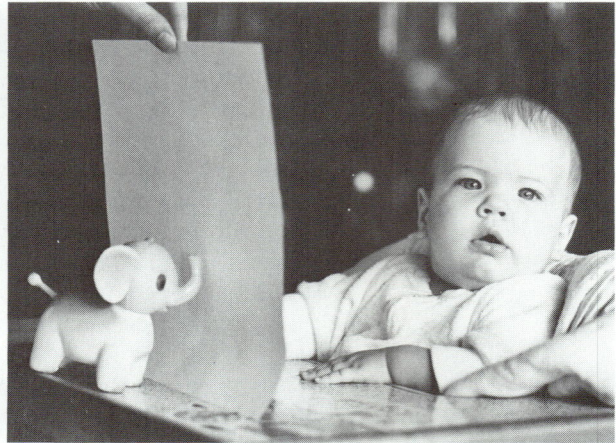

During the secondary circular reaction substage (4 to 8 months), infants may recognize a favorite toy so long as it is in full view. However, when the toy is hidden from sight, infants may act as if the toy never existed.

an obstacle. In trying to reach a matchbox that was obstructed by a pillow (placed in front of the matchbox by Piaget), Laurent hit the pillow until it was out of his way (Piaget, 1952b). Several schemes were thus coordinated to accomplish this goal: the looking, hitting, reaching, and grasping schemes culminate in Laurent getting the matchbox. No longer is some point achieved by chance and then simply repeated. For the first time, the young child is capable of using well-practiced schemes to achieve aims that have been conceived *ahead of time*. Should these well-practiced behaviors fail to achieve the desired goal, however, the child at this substage still is unable to alter its routine to increase the chances of success.

Object permanence emerges in this substage in a specific form called *contextually bound object permanence*. If the infant sees an object being hidden, it will search where it saw the object hidden. If the object is moved from one hiding place to another, the infant will continue to look in the original hiding place even though it had seen the object being placed in the new hiding place.

AB̄ Error The infant's inability to locate an object that has been visibly put in a different hiding place.

Psychologists refer to the infant's inability to locate the displaced object as the **AB̄ error.** Piaget used the AB̄ error as evidence for the development of object permanence. He believed that eight- to 12-month-old infants must rely on their sensorimotor actions to define an object since they have not yet developed the capacity to symbolically represent objects. However, other researchers explain the AB̄ error in terms of infants' limited memory skills. Infants look for the toy under the first pillow (A) and not the second pillow (B) because they do not remember the second hiding place (Bjork & Cummings, 1984; Cummings & Bjork, 1983). As infants develop, their capability for holding items in short-term memory increases so that 14- to 16-month-old infants can remember hiding places longer than do younger infants (Schacter & Moscovitch, 1984). One study compared the performance of adult amnesic patients who were asked to locate an object that had been changed to a new hiding place with the performance of eight- to 10-month-old infants who were given a similar task of locating a hidden object (Schacter, Moscovitch, Tulving, McLachlan, & Freedman, 1986). The adults had significant memory deficits, yet were able to symbolically represent objects and recognized the permanence of objects. The infants had not yet acquired object permanence and had limited memory capabilities. The performance of the amnesic adults on the object search tasks was similar to the performance of the eight- to 10-month-old infants. The researchers concluded that the AB̄ error in infants may not reflect an immature object concept but rather reflects a memory deficit.

The infant also advances in its understanding of meaning. Instead of acknowledging an object or event by simple motor activity (as was the case in the earlier substage), the infant now activates more specific schemes in response to a signal event. For example, the sound of the refrigerator door opening may signal the baby that mealtime is at hand, and the infant activates the schemes associated with eating, such as crawling to the mother or reaching for the food, even though food has not yet been presented. This type of understanding of objects and events by the infant is called *signal meaning*.

Substage 5: Tertiary Circular Reactions (12–18 months) Infants during the tertiary circular reaction stage are exciting to watch because they are curious and actively engaged in trying out new ways to accomplish their goals. The physical structures have matured to the point that the infant is capable of moving about on foot as well as climbing. New schemes are created to achieve desired aims by active exploration and experimentation. The infant seated in its high chair can be observed experimenting with what happens to objects dropped from the high-chair tray. One-year-old Adam would bang various toys, foods, and utensils on his metal high-chair tray, and note the sound. Then he would systematically drop each object while waiting to hear the sound it made as it hit the floor. He soon discovered that different shapes had different sounds. The infant may even incorporate its parents in the experimentation—the child will note and even wait for their reactions as it drops objects from the high chair.

By this substage, object permanence improves to the point that the baby will look for an object in the last place it was found and search for it in other hiding places it has observed. If the infant cannot see the object being changed from one hiding place to the next, however, the infant cannot find it. For example, if the mother pretends to have a ball in her right hand but switches it to the left hand behind her back, the infant will look in the right hand for the ball. Not finding it, the infant will be at a loss. Its inability to form a mental representation of the ball being transferred from one hand to the other prevents it from successfully solving this problem.

Substage 6: Invention of New Means through Mental Combinations (18–24 months) This substage of invention of new means through mental combinations represents the transition to symbolic thought. The ability to represent internally certain events that are not currently impinging on the child's sense organs is called *symbolic thought*. The infant now applies symbolic meaning to the objects and events in its world. The infant can now think about properties of events or objects not by engaging in sensory or motor actions but by forming a mental picture or image to help achieve a desired outcome. For example, Laurent at this stage was able to figure out how to reach a piece of bread that was out of his reach by mentally combining the action of reaching with the action of using a stick as an extension of his arm. Then he picked up the stick and used it to draw the bread toward him.

Although younger infants have demonstrated that they can imitate the actions of others, it is not until this last stage of sensorimotor development that infants exhibit *deferred imitation*—the ability to imitate an action in the absence of the model demonstrating that action. In order for infants to copy a model's actions, they must have some representational image of the model's actions to guide their response. Older siblings provide a rich source of novel behaviors for the active two-year-old to copy, sometimes resulting in unwanted behaviors such as spitting or hitting.

Object permanence is complete at this substage, as evidenced by the infant's continued search for objects that have been secretly hidden. Language skills emerge during this time as the infant associates both the verbal responses of others and its own verbalizations with the objects and people in its world. By the age of two, the child has replaced many of its infant sensory motor reactions with symbolic verbal actions.

When Piaget began his study of young children, much of what we know today about infant memory and perceptual abilities was not yet known. Piaget was truly a pioneer in the field of cognitive development. However, not all researchers who have tested some of Piaget's ideas using experimental studies have supported his views. For example, Piaget maintained that the ability to

Human Development in Practice

The Same Old Story: Infants Repeating Themselves

Anyone who has spent time caring for infants or young children has probably had this experience: An infant shoves a story/picture book into your hand and says the equivalent of "Book?" to you—meaning "Will you read this book to me.?" Of course, you read the child the story of *Cat in the Hat* or *The Pokey Little Puppy*. No sooner have you come to the end of the book when the infant turns the pages back to the first page and says "Book?," as if you had not already just read it. You could read the story several times before the infant was either asleep or until you have memorized the story!

Early-child-care and day-care workers, or parents and relatives who are around children between one and two years of age may at first be a bit confused by infants' persistence in repeating an action just completed such as hearing the same old story or throwing toys out of the crib or playpen. Yet, according to Piaget, these behaviors are part of infants' attempts to understand and master their world. The repetition of an action helps infants to refine schemes that

they use to adapt to the environment. Thus the infant who says "Book?" and turns to the first page is in the process of acquiring a scheme that could be labeled "Let's get this adult to read me this book." Every time the action sequence of verbalization ("Book") plus motor behaviors (turning pages, shoving book into adult hands) is repeated, the infant becomes more proficient at making his or her intentions known. Depending on whether the child is successful, the end result could be either a sense of mastery or manipulation (and a nice story) or a sense of frustration. The scheme that does not work will be changed or accommodated until it does work. The scheme that does result in another reading of the book will also be used to hear a different story—perhaps this time *Pat the Bunny*.

So, if you find yourself in a similar situation where an infant is practicing repetitive behavior with you, look at it this way, you are probably helping the infant to become more competent. Go ahead then; read the story one more time.

imitate develops with age, yet Meltzoff and Moore (1983, 1977) found that two-week-old infants could imitate facial expressions. Further research (Abravanel & Gingold, 1985; Meltzoff, 1988, 1985) has found that under certain conditions 9–, 12–, and 14–month-old infants will imitate actions after a delay of time. For example, in one study (Meltzoff, 1988), infants observed an adult engage in novel behaviors (rattle an orange plastic egg, push a button that produced a beeping noise, and fold down a wooden hinge). The infants not only imitated the novel actions immediately after watching the adult, but they were able to reproduce the novel actions after a 24-hour delay. Although Piaget may have underestimated the abilities infants have to make sense out of their world, he nonetheless has presented developmental psychology with a rich theory to stimulate further research.

Learning Theories

According to learning theories, developmental changes in infants' reactions to their world occur as a result of the infant's learning experiences. The central theme in the theories presented by Skinner, Watson, and Bandura is that behaviors or actions are acquired and maintained by the consequences of those actions. The person's ability to make sense of and cope with the circumstances in the world is dependent on what behaviors the person has acquired, or learned, in life. *Learning* is defined as a relatively permanent change in behavior as a result of reinforced practice. This definition excludes any changes in behavior resulting from injury, disease, or maturation. In Chapter 1, we described three models that have been used by learning theorists to describe how behaviors are changed or new ones acquired. Let's consider learning in infancy using these models.

Classical Conditioning In a classic study, Watson and Raynor (1920) demonstrated how emotional behavior could be explained by a classical conditioning model when a young infant named Albert was conditioned to be

Children's fear or lack of fear of animals is a learned behavior which can be classically conditioned.

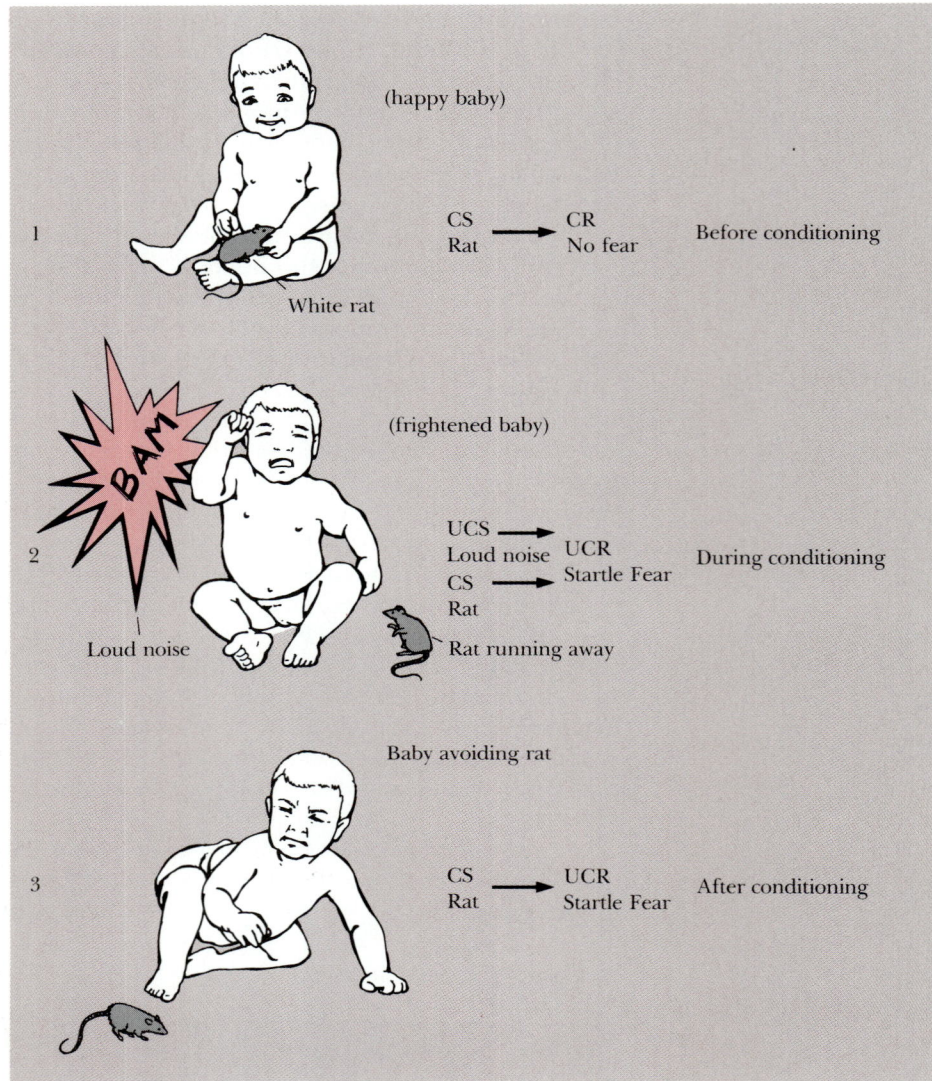

Figure 3.4 The classical conditioning of a fear response to a rat. In Watson and Raynor's experiment, a baby who was not afraid of a rat was conditioned to fear the rat by pairing the presence of the rat with a sudden loud noise which produced a startle and fear response.

fearful of a white rat. The UCS was a sudden, loud noise, which resulted automatically in the UCR, a startle response. The white rat was used as the neutral stimulus—"neutral" in the sense that little Albert did not react to it with a startle at the onset of the experiment. The rat (the CS) was presented to Albert while the loud noise was sounded—Albert naturally reacted with a startle and a cry. After several similar pairings, the white rat was presented *without* the noise, yet Albert reacted to the rat with a conditioned startle response (see Figure 3.4). Little Albert was not only conditioned to be afraid of the white rat, but he displayed a similar fear of other, white, furry animals. Although Watson and Raynor's (1920) experiment illustrated the potency of the classical conditioning process for changing behavior, most researchers today would not conduct such an experiment with children because of the potential risks of psychological damage to the subjects in the study.

In another classic study, Jones (1924) illustrated how children's fears could be eliminated by using a classical conditioning model. In a more contemporary study, Lipsitt and Kaye (1964) conditioned infants to suck whenever they heard a pure tone. For the most part, classically conditioned responses have been demonstrated using reflexive responses that are automatically evoked by specific stimuli. Such responses include eye blink, startle, and sucking.

It has been difficult to clearly establish how readily neonates learn behaviors through classical conditioning (Sameroff & Cavanagh, 1979), for the experiments performed have used small samples of infants. A second difficulty is that the experiments must be conducted on alert, awake infants during the early months of life—the period when infants usually spend much of their time asleep or drowsy.

Operant Conditioning
A form of learning in which the learner acquires a behavior as a result of the consequences of the behavior.

Reinforcement The term that describes any stimulus that follows a behavior and results in that behavior being repeated.

Negative Reinforcement A process whereby the removal of an aversive stimulus results in an increase in behavior.

Punishment A process whereby the application of an aversive stimulus after a response has been made decreases the frequency of the response.

Operant Conditioning **Operant conditioning** is a learning process described by B. F. Skinner in which the learner repeats behaviors that have resulted in a positive outcome and eliminates behaviors that have resulted in a negative outcome. **Reinforcement** is the term used to describe a stimulus that follows a behavior and that results in that behavior being repeated. The term *positive reinforcement* refers to a pleasant stimulus that follows a behavior and that increases the frequency of that behavior. For example, a dose of sugared water given to an infant when it turns its head to the left will result in the infant turning its head more frequently to the left; the sugared water is the positive reinforcement. A **negative reinforcement** is the process whereby an aversive (unpleasant) stimulus is *removed* after a behavior has occurred and results in an increase in frequency of that behavior. For example, if a rat is in a box with an electrified floor grid that delivers a shock, it will increase its response of lever pressing if that response is followed by a cessation in the shocks. **Punishment** is the process whereby an aversive stimulus is applied after a response has been made and the response decreases in frequency. For example, if every time a child spits she is sent to her room, one would expect to see a reduction in spitting—assuming that being sent away is unpleasant to the child.

In the Rovee-Collier (1984) study mentioned earlier in which eight-week and three-month-old infants were trained to turn a mobile, operant conditioning was the type of learning involved. The infant's behavior of kicking resulted in a positive reinforcement—the mobile turning—which increased the infant's behavior of kicking. The success of operant conditioning in changing behavior also depends upon the nature and complexity of the infant behavior you wish to change and on the ability of the infant to perform the behavior. Kicking is a simple response that even very young infants can make. If infants had been required to grasp the mobile to make it turn, then the three-month-old infants would most likely not be able to make the mobile work.

Observational Learning
A form of learning in which behavior change occurs as a result of watching others engage in specific behaviors.

Observational Learning **Observational learning** refers to a change in behavior as a result of watching others engage in specific behaviors. Kaye and Marcus (1978) point out that as infants become older they become more skillful at imitating models because they have greater voluntary control. The behaviors an infant imitates parallel their developing motor skills. They also are capable of representing what they have seen symbolically and hence are better able to recall and match the model at a later date. We shall see in later chapters that children acquire many of their social behaviors by observing others. The impact of other people's actions further depends on the infant's attention to these people as models.

Summary

The neonate's physical appearance may not be attractive because of the birth experience. The skin may be wrinkled and the head misshapen.

The newborn's physiological systems must adjust to the extrauterine life. Respiration and circulation of oxygen from the lungs to the heart and brain begin when the umbilical cord is cut. It may take several days for the digestive system to function smoothly.

Newborns experience six separate states of consciousness. During the alert inactivity state, the infant is most attentive to its environment.

Methods for studying infant capabilities include measuring physiological responses, habituation changes, preferential looking, and other behaviors that signal infants' interest in objects.

Although there are limits to the newborn's visual skills, infants can see at birth and they prefer to look at complex, symmetrical, high-contrast designs.

The newborn's behavioral responses include neonatal reflexes, which are responses triggered by specific stimuli in the environment. These neonatal reflexes disappear with the maturation of the nervous system.

Premature babies are not fully developed and require special environments for survival. Because of newer medical technology, more premature infants are surviving than in the past.

Physical growth in infancy follows a cephalocaudal and proximodistal pattern. The infant develops more specific, controlled behaviors as the nervous system matures. Sudden infant death syndrome is a disorder that seems to be related to the central nervous system development.

Adequate diet is important in infancy to ensure physical and neurological growth. Breast feeding has many physiological advantages over bottle feeding, but many mothers prefer to bottle-feed.

Motor development is guided by maturation and follows a predictable sequence. Prehension and locomotion are two major motor skills acquired during infancy. The environment can influence an infant's interest in exercising motor skills.

Perception involves the interpretation of sensory information. Infants recognize faces at a young age and are able to imitate facial gestures. Infants also perceive depth at an early age.

Infants are capable of visually recognizing objects because they have encoded features of the objects into memory. Memory is evident in infants as young as eight weeks.

According to Piaget, during the sensorimotor period, the infant acquires object permanence; learns to control its body and to understand cause and effect; and begins to think in images. Schemes are assimilated and accommodated by the infant to adapt to the environment.

Learning theories explain cognitive development as changes in learned behaviors. Behaviors are acquired through classical and operant conditioning and through observational learning. Reinforcement is any stimulus that increases the frequency of a behavior. Punishment reduces the frequency of a behavior.

Further Readings

Ault, R. *Children's cognitive development*, (2nd Ed.). New York: Oxford University Press, 1983.
A simple and readable account of Piaget's basic principles and findings. Special attention is given to perception, memory, and hypothesis in this updated edition.

Bower, T. G. R. *A primer of infant development*. San Francisco: W. H. Freeman, 1977.
A vivid and authoritative account of the physical, perceptual, cognitive, social, and emotional development of the infant. The author, a noted infant researcher, describes the outcome of infant research in a simple and easy-to-comprehend style.

Brazelton, T. B. *Infants and mothers*. (Rev. Ed.). New York: Delta/Seymour Lawrence, 1983.
This book describes the first year of an infant's life, providing a month-by-month description of the average, quiet, and active baby. The influence of family members and special difficulties with infants are also addressed.

Caplan, F. *The first 12 months of life*. New York: Grosset & Dunlap, 1973.

Caplan, F. *The second 12 months of life*. New York: Grosset & Dunlap, 1979.
These two books combine to give the reader a detailed and well-illustrated account of growth and development during the first two years of life.

Goldberg, S., and DiVitto, B. *Born too soon*. San Francisco, W. H. Freeman, 1983.
This book presents the reader with an up-to-date discussion of the significant aspects of preterm infant development. Topics in this readable book include intensive-care and intervention programs, parent adjustments, and new methods for studying preterm capabilities.

White, B. L. *The first three years of life*. Englewood Cliffs, NJ: Prentice-Hall, 1975.
A detailed guide to the intellectual and emotional development of the young child. The 36 months are divided into seven developmental categories with particular attention given to the periods covering 8 to 24 months. This book is both comprehensive and practical.

Observational Activities

3.1   *Physical Characteristics and Behavior of the Newborn*

Newborns are fascinating to watch, particularly after you have learned about their growing sensory capabilities. In order to have a better understanding of newborn behavior, visit a local hospital's maternity ward during the public visiting hours. You may need to ask special permission to visit the nursery. If so, your instructor may be able to assist you.

Look at the newborns in the nursery and note their weights and lengths, date of birth, and sex from the identifying cards on the infant cribs. Notice the infants' appearance and any behaviors. For the purposes of this assignment, select one particular infant and describe your selected infant according to eight categories:

1. *Size:* include length and weight.
2. *Head:* include shape, size, and amount of hair.
3. *Skin:* include color, texture, birthmarks, wrinkles, and hair.
4. *Eyes:* include color and degree of coordination.
5. *Activity:* include the infant's alertness, drowsiness, sleeping, and crying.
6. *Motor activity:* include hand and leg activity.
7. *Sensory activity:* include reactions to light, noise, and touch.
8. *Reflexes:* include sucking, blinking, rooting, pupillary reflex, Moro.

Stay long enough to collect the information you need to be able to describe your neonate. Share your observations with your classmates. What did you gain for yourself in doing this activity? How will you be able to apply what you have learned from this activity in nursing?

3.2 *The Child's Understanding of Object Permanence*

Piaget has detailed the progression of the acquisition of object permanence in his theory of cognitive development. With each substage, the child demonstrates a more thorough understanding of the idea that objects exist even when they are not visible. In this activity, you will be asked to observe a young infant between the ages of six months and two years. You may be able to find a baby in this age range from among the children of your friends and relatives. Try a local infant day-care center or nursery. (Your school may offer a day-care service for students and staff.) Be sure to obtain permission from the day-care center director before you begin your observation. Try to find out the chronological age of the infant you are observing.

Once you have selected an infant, observe that infant while the baby is playing with toys in the playpen or on the floor. Using the following questions as a guide, notice the infant's reactions to the objects.

1. Does the infant notice the toys? How does it react?
2. Does the infant pick up any of the toys?
3. Does the infant repeat any actions with its body and the toy?

Now, cover the toys with a cloth or blanket and observe the baby's reaction. Does the infant know that the toys are still there? Does the infant search for the toys? Describe the infant's attempts to locate the toys.

On the basis of your observations, identify which substage in the sensorimotor period best describes your infant's behavior. Summarize your findings and describe what you have learned in doing this activity. Share this with your classmates. How might an awareness of infants' development of object permanence help an early-child-care teacher?

CHAPTER
4

Infancy: Social and Personality Development

*E*ven as a three-month-old infant, Benjamin was already charming his parents and visitors with his flashing eyes and quick smile. He seemed to love to be held, touched, and stimulated by anyone. Because he seemed so receptive to people, his aunts, uncles, and older cousins all welcomed the chance to talk to and play with him.

Ben's mother and father had been watching his reactions to them and the many toys he'd received in three months. An observer watching all of them interact would have noticed right away that Ben was having quite an effect on his parents! Not only was Ben learning about the people and objects around him, but he was also influencing the way the people in his world responded to him. When he smiled and enthusiastically moved his body, his parents smiled back. And little Ben? He'd smile again and repeat the exchange.

By nine months of age, he clearly preferred his mother's company but still continued to be receptive to others. With his smile now came a delightful cooing and babbling response that, miracle of miracles, invited even *more* attention! And the fun continued—as he explored his environment, his interest in toys and other objects grew. As he'd find new things to bring to his mother, she would smile and encourage his curiosity.

Over the months since his birth, Ben was interacting with people and objects in his unique way. His style of interacting was becoming integral to his emerging personality.

One of the challenges in describing development from a lifespan perspective is to capture the essence of multidirectional and multidetermined changes and convey this notion to you the reader. One way would be to require students to observe an infant daily for the course of the infant's life! Then you would see how changes in one system such as the perceptual system are related to and affect the changes in other behaviors such as cognitive or social skills. But you would be very old yourself by the time you completed the course requirement.

In the last chapter, you read about the changes that occur in infants' capacity to take in, interpret, and respond physically and psychologically to events and stimuli. But that was really only half the story. Like Ben, infants display their own unique reactions to people and objects—they interact with people in different ways and with different consequences. Thus, to get a true picture of the emerging infant, we must consider the social–emotional changes that occur. These changes in social and emotional responding are both influenced by and influential in the physical, perceptual, and cognitive changes you read about in Chapter 3. Furthermore, infants' social, emotional, and personality development is affected by the social context in which they are developing.

In this chapter, we begin with a discussion of the ways an infant and its parents influence each other in the first two years. Then we turn our attention to the development of attachment and the problems that can occur in the establishment of the first primary relationship with another human being. We also examine the child's developing view of self. In the final section of this chapter, we examine the way in which infants communicate with their parents.

Early Social Interactions: Bidirectional Influence

Up until the late 1950s, most of the studies on infant behavior focused primarily on the effects of different child-rearing practices. Most of the changes in infant behavior were considered to be the result of either maturation or the result of the way the parents treated the child. This view of development, in which the child was seen as a passive recipient of the parents' actions, was based on a **unidirectional view.** In the 1950s, however, Piaget's theory and research began to have an impact on the way developmental psychologists viewed the infant. As we saw in the last chapter, Piaget saw the infant as an active and involved participant in its own development. Later research focused on the infant's abilities to respond selectively to experiences. As we learned in Chapter 3, the infant is capable of responding to its physical and social world through its growing sensorimotor actions.

With this new view of the infant as an active agent in the parent–child interaction came a need for a different model of development, however. Richard Bell (1968; Bell & Harper, 1980) views the unidirectional model as too simplistic and has emphasized the ways in which the child's actions affect the parent's caregiving behavior. In the **bidirectional view** of development, the parent and child are seen as having an active influence on each other. The infant's behavior is seen as one factor in the parent's response to the child. For example, the infant who squirms and protests when restrained on the parent's lap is likely to discourage the parent's future attempts at holding the child in the lap. Rather than simply focusing on the parental dimension of the interaction, attention is now given to both participants, and to the sequential nature of their interactions.

The view that infants are capable of engaging in a dynamic, reciprocal social exchange comes as no surprise to many parents of a young infant. Most parents would readily acknowledge the degree of control and influence their so-called helpless infant has over them. A cry or protest from the baby can send parents into a predictable flurry of activities designed to quiet the infant.

Pause for Thought
The bidirectional view of development is a concept stemming from studies done mainly with American families. What specific characteristics of American families might have influenced the view that children actively influence their parents' behavior toward them? Can you think of cultures in which children may not be seen as so influential? At other times in history, would children have had less influence on their parents' behavior?

The Infant's Contribution

Physical Characteristics
Beginning at the moment of birth, the newborn infant and its parents are primed to form a powerful affectional bond. Klaus and Kennell (1982) maintain that the timing for the formation of this bond is critical. They suggest

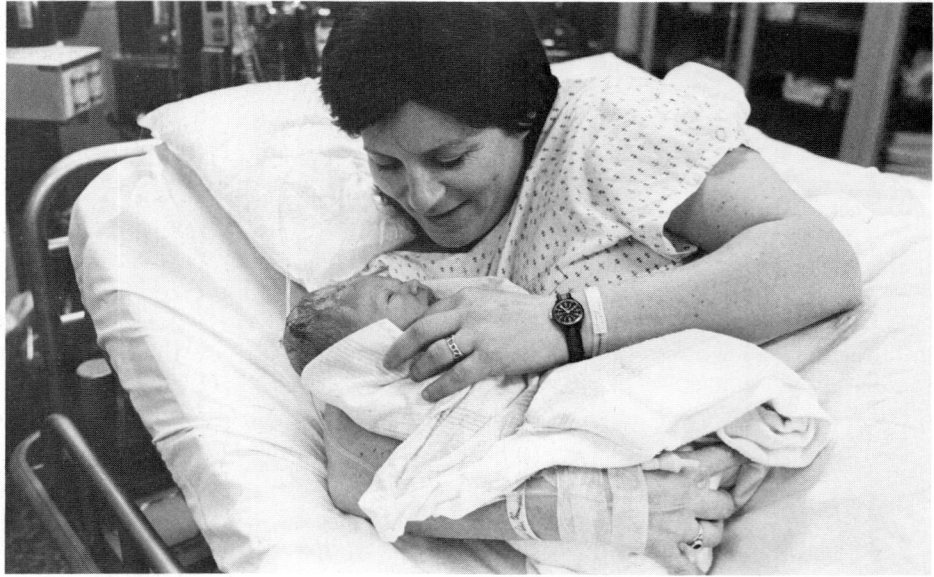

Physical contact within the early days of this infant's life helps establish an affectional bond between the new parent and child.

that a sensitive period exists in the first hours after birth in which the mother or father is most likely to "fall in love with" the infant. Other researchers (Palkovitz, 1985; Svejda, Campos, & Emde, 1980) dispute this view that early and sustained physical contact between parent and child is necessary for the formation of an affectional bond. Research with adopted infants and their mothers, for example, supports the view that immediate postdelivery contact between mother and infant is not necessary for the development of secure attachment relationships (Singer, Brodzinsky, Ramsay, Stein, & Waters, 1985).

Even though there is not agreement about when the bond between parent and infant is best formed, most researchers agree that many of the infant's actions are instrumental to the formation of the bond. Studies by Condon and Sander (1974) have shown that newborns in the first hours of life engage in behaviors that complement the parent's actions. In particular, the infants were shown to move in rhythm to their mother's voice, creating a beautiful synchronized "dance" with her. Infants engage in eye-to-eye contact with their caregivers, once the caregiver's face falls within eight to nine inches from the infant's face, the distance at which newborns can best focus on an object. The feeding position provides many opportunities for parents and infants to gaze into each other's eyes. In addition, the infant sucking at the mother's breast triggers the release of the hormones oxytocin and prolactin, which some researchers believe act as a chemical releaser of affectionate maternal behavior. The cry and voice of the infant affect the nursing mother by stimulating the blood flow to her breasts. Further, mothers have been known to be able to distinguish their own babies from among several by the unique smell of their own infants. Parents also quickly learn to distinguish the cries of their own babies from those of other babies.

Brazelton (1981) suggests that the very shape of the infant evokes a more nurturant response in adults. The large head and small, soft body of the newborn produce protective and cuddling behaviors in humans. One study examined how the shape of the infant's body influenced adult's willing-

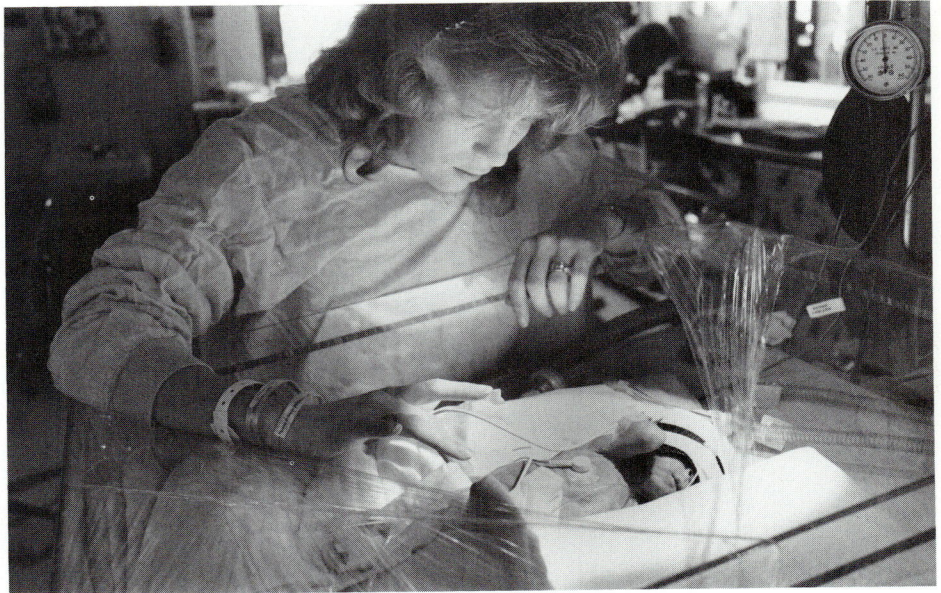

Parents of high-risk preterm infants need special encouragement and instructions on how to handle and stimulate their infants in the early days of life.

ness to care for children (Alley, 1983b). The study found that caretaking responses decreased as the proportion of head to body decreased; that is, as the shape of the child lost its "babyish" look, adults were less likely to engage in caregiving behavior.

Health and Maturity

The health and maturity of the newborn seem to have an influence on the parents' attitudes and behavior. Several studies have found that mothers of preterm infants spend more time stimulating their infants than do mothers of full-term infants (Brachfeld, Goldberg, & Sloman, 1980; DiVitto & Goldberg, 1979; Stern & Hildebrandt, 1986). Other research (Greene, Fox, & Lewis, 1983) has found that mothers of full-term newborns who were ill spent less time in social interactions and more time in caregiving behavior than did mothers of healthy infants. The sick infants were also less responsive and attentive than healthy infants. Furthermore, the mothers' behavior seemed to be influenced by the sick infants' behavior, even after the illness had subsided. At three months of age, the infants were no longer ill or unresponsive, and yet the mothers continued to compensate or be affected by the neonatal behavior of their infants. The long-term consequences of these early parent–child interactions could be a restrictive or overprotective style of parenting. In a different study (Lasky, Tyson, Rosenfeld, & Gant, 1984), infants who required neonatal intensive care were observed interacting with their mothers at one year of age; a similar observation was made of infants with normal neonatal experiences. Mothers of the normal infants were more likely to look directly at their infants in a face-to-face position, play with, talk to, comfort, and smile at their infants than were mothers of the high-risk infants. The normal infants were also more likely to smile back at their mothers.

The conclusion from studies on high-risk infants and their interactions with their parents is that special attention and encouragement may be needed for the parents of ill newborns in order to promote a healthy parent–infant

Table 4.1

Characteristics of Infant Temperament

1. Level of activity

2. Rhythmicity or regularity of biological functions such as sleep, activity, eating, and elimination

3. Approach or withdrawal, based on the child's initial reaction to new stimulation

4. Adaptability, referring to the child's flexibility of behavior following its initial reaction to a new stimulus

5. Intensity of reaction

6. Threshold of responsiveness, or the level of stimulation necessary to evoke a response

7. Quality of mood, or the amount of pleasant behavior compared to unpleasant behavior

8. Distractibility, or the degree to which extraneous stimulation disrupts ongoing behavior

9. Attention span and persistence, or the length of time the infant maintains its activity and tolerates difficulty

bond, as well as to encourage infant development (Barrera, Rosenbaum, & Cunningham, 1986; Goldberg, Perrotta, Minde, & Corter, 1986).

Temperament

Temperament A person's inborn, characteristic way of responding to stimuli.

Ben's way of interacting with people was evident early on—he was easygoing. For years, maybe even centuries, parents have described their newborns in terms of their temperament. Recently, one of the most popular areas of research has been the study of infant temperament. **Temperament** refers to a person's inborn, characteristic way of responding to stimuli. Temperament is believed to be the first manifestation of what will later be called "personality." Temperament is the result of the interaction of one's genetic or biological heritage with one's experiences. Because newborns have not been exposed to the many social experiences that influence personality, whatever individual differences that exist must be the result of inborn genetic factors and/or neonatal experiences.

The current interest in infant temperament was triggered both by Bell's (1968) research on the infant's contribution to the parent–child relationship, and by the research results from the New York Longitudinal Study (NYLS) reported by Thomas and Chess (1977). In this 20-year study, Thomas and Chess observed the temperament and behavior of 136 people from early infancy into adolescence. Parents of the infants were asked to describe precisely how their infants reacted during specific routines of daily living such as feeding, bathing, sleeping, and responding to people. The infants were also observed in the home. The researchers found that newborns differed on nine qualities of behaving and reacting and that these differences sometimes continued into childhood. The nine characteristics are described in Table 4.1.

Thomas and Chess (1977) found that certain of these qualities tended to occur together. Clusters of characteristics fell into three types: *the easy baby, the difficult baby,* and *the slow-to-warm baby.* The easy baby has regular patterns of eating and sleeping, easily approaches new people and objects, adapts readily to changes in the environment, reacts with moderate to low intensity, and typically is in a good mood. The difficult baby has irregular patterns of eating and sleeping, withdraws from new people and objects, adapts slowly to changes, has intense reactions, and is often irritable. The slow-to-warm baby has a low activity level, tends to withdraw when presented with an unfamiliar object, reacts with a low level of intensity, and slowly adapts to changes. Easy babies represented 40 percent of the total sample, difficult children, 10 percent, and slow-to-warm babies, 15 percent of the sample. The remaining 35 percent did not fit easily into one of the patterns and showed a mixture of behavioral patterns.

Most of the data from the Thomas and Chess study come from parents' reports about the infants' behavior. More recently, data from the Louisville Twin Study, a longitudinal study of young twins, suggests that infant temperament can be readily detected by observers as well as by parents (Matheny, Riese, & Wilson, 1985; Wilson & Matheny, 1983). By observing and videotaping the infants in the laboratory during a standardized set of interactions with strangers, Wilson and Matheny found infants differed in their emotional reaction, attention, and receptivity to the strangers and that these differences paralleled differences reported by the parents in describing their infants' reaction at home. In a later study, Matheny and his associates (1985) found that measurements of a newborn's temperament could be used to predict whether that infant would have a strong emotional reaction to stimuli presented at age nine months. They discovered that irritable, difficult-to-soothe newborns were likely to be fussier and distressed in the laboratory test than were newborns who were more easygoing. Another study found a relationship with newborn physical activity and later measures of activity at four to eight years of age. (Korner, Zeanah, Linden, Berkowitz, Kraemer, & Agras, 1985). The most active neonates became the children who were more active and who were perceived by their parents as being more likely to approach new experiences.

Thomas and Chess found that parents were influenced by whether a child was easy, difficult, or slow to warm in infancy. An easy child more often than not made parents feel competent in their role, whereas the difficult, irritable child caused some parents to doubt their ability to care for their infant. The degree of "fit" between parents' expectations regarding their infant's behavior and the actual behavior of the infant also plays an important role in the family's adjustment. Difficult behavior on the baby's part is less of a problem for parents when, for whatever reason, they expected such behavior to emerge. It is the disconfirmation of expectations—such as when a baby who manifests difficult behavior is born to parents who expect an "easy" baby—that produces problems in the ongoing social interaction between parent and child.

Many questions about temperament have yet to be adequately answered (Lerner & Lerner, 1983). For example, how stable are measures of temperament? How does the social context and setting influence temperamental behavior? Different researchers studying infant temperament have focused their attention on somewhat different aspects of the infant's behavior (Goldsmith & Campos, 1982). One dimension of temperament that seems to be commonly studied, however, is the emotional reactions of infants.

Pause for Thought

The characteristics that are used to describe a difficult or easy baby are recognizable and accessible. So that we can say that an infant is a "difficult" baby or an "easy" baby. What similarities are there between a "difficult" baby and a "difficult" child? A "difficult" adult? Are the labels referring to the same set of stylistic behaviors?

Emotions

A growing number of infant research studies reveal that infants have a much more complex emotional life than was previously thought. By carefully observing infants' reactions to people and situations in early life, researchers are discovering that infants go through stages in their emotional development in much the same way as in physical and cognitive growth (Greenspan, 1984). In fact, most researchers see emotional development and cognitive development as closely linked (Sroufe, 1979). Experiencing its world, the infant not only understands it, but reacts to it emotionally with joy, anger, and even anxiety.

Stages of Emotional Development   For a developmental theory of emotions to be meaningful from a lifespan perspective, it must relate the emergence of affect (emotion) with concurrent changes in social and cognitive development. Sroufe (1979) has combined the results of several empirical studies on infant social, emotional, and cognitive development in his stages of affective

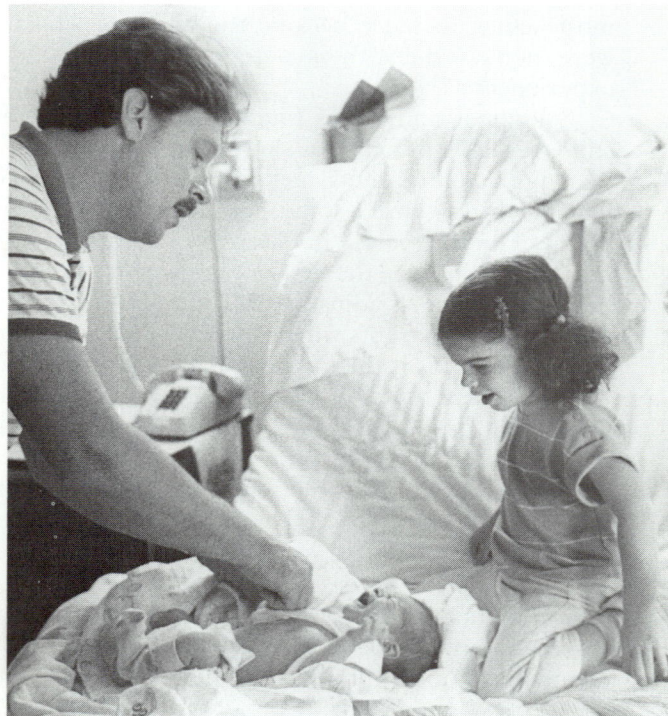

In the first month of life infants are likely to cry in response to physical stimulation. This newborn is probably crying in response to having its diaper changed.

Table 4.2

The Ontogenesis of Some Basic Human Emotions[a]

Month	Pleasure–Joy	Wariness–Fear	Rage–Anger	Periods of Emotional Development
0	endogenous smile	startle/pain	distress due to: covering the face, physical restraint, extreme discomfort	absolute stimulus barrier
1	turning toward	obligatory attention		turning toward
2				
3	pleasure		rage (disappointment)	positive affect
4	delight, active laughter	wariness		
5				
6				active participation
7	joy	anger		
8				
9		fear (stranger aversion)		attachment
10				
11				
12	elation	anxiety, immediate fear	angry mood; petulance	practicing
18	positive valuation of self-affection	shame	defiance	emergence of self
24			intentional hurting	
36	pride, love		guilt	play and fantasy

[a] The age specified is neither the first appearance of the affect in question nor its peak occurrence; it is the age when the literature suggests that the reaction is common.

Source: From "Socioemotional Development" by L. A. Sroufe. In J. Osofsky (Ed.), *Handbook of infant development*, New York: Wiley, 1979.

development (see Table 4.2). In *Stage 1,* during the first month of life, the infant is relatively vulnerable to external, physical stimulation and shows no true emotions. In *Stage 2,* labeled the period of turning toward, the infant starts to react emotionally with a reliable social smile. The infant shows an interest in the outside world and through its smile usually generates a social response.

In *Stage 3,* beginning at age three months, the infant shows positive and negative emotion. The infant also displays anticipation, disappointment, and frustration. Wariness and rage may be expressed as the infant experiences more contact with the environment. The infant laughs and generally displays excitement with vocalizations and cooing while interacting with its caregiver. By this period, a reciprocal social exchange between parent and child is well under way. In *Stage 4,* from seven to nine months of age, infants are active participants in social games with their parents. The baby makes persistent efforts to elicit social responses even from other infants. The infant at this stage uses developing motor and vocal skills to initiate contact with people and toys. During *Stage 5,* lasting from nine to 12 months, infants display an exclusive preoccupation with their caregiver, a phenomenon known as **attachment.** The baby not only shows strong positive feeling toward the mother or father or other primary caregivers, but displays more subtle emotions of ambivalence and fear toward strangers. In *Stage 6,* from 12 to 18 months, infants actively explore and master their inanimate environment. This is the stage when infants are likely to show strong emotions of joy and anger, when their moods fluctuate depending on the specific task in which they are engaged. By *Stage 7,* from 18 to 36 months, infants are well into forming a view of themselves. In separating themselves from their caregiver, infants are likely to experience anxiety. Frustration and anger are other common emotions observed as infants experience their newfound sense of autonomy. We will examine other aspects of self-awareness shortly.

Finally, *Stage 8* begins at three years of age when children have formed a view of themselves as seen by others, namely parents. Emotions are experienced as they engage in role playing and fantasy. The child experiences pride and guilt as by-products of a natural inclination to practice newly developing skills and to evaluate performance of these skills using other peoples' standards (Stipek, 1983).

Assessing Infant Emotions   As with most age-related sequences, it is important to keep in mind that infants may vary in their emotional reactions. Furthermore, the assessment of infant emotional reactions is complicated by the fact that infants cannot tell us what they are feeling—their reactions must be inferred from their behavior. Several researchers have been using facial expression as a measure of emotional experience. Psychologist Carroll Izard (1979), for example, has been studying videotapes of infants reacting to a wide variety of situations such as being given an ice cube, or having a favorite toy taken from them. On the basis of these observations, he and his colleagues have developed a code to identify different emotions by rating different facial responses. For example, anger is indicated when the eyebrows are lowered sharply and drawn together, the eyes are narrowed or squinted, and the mouth is open in an angular, squarish shape.

Using a similar coding system for facial expressions, Stenberg, Campos, and Emde (1983) demonstrated that specific facial expressions of anger could be reliably detected in seven-month-old infants. In this study, infants were given a teething biscuit. Once the infant began to suck on the biscuit, the biscuit was removed and held just beyond the child's reach. This sequence was repeated several times. Since only the infant's face was videotaped, raters had no contextual cues as to what specific emotion the infant might have been experiencing. Using only the eyes, mouth, and eyebrows for facial cues, raters

Attachment   An affectionate emotional bond between parent (or caregiver) and child.

Human Development in Practice

Infant Psychiatry

Several years ago, the idea of consulting a psychiatrist for help with a difficult infant would have seemed far-fetched. However, over the past 20 years, professionals have been learning more about the infant's complex emotional life. By examining the early stages of emotional development, many researchers hope that pediatricians will be able to monitor an infant's emotional growth in much the same way that they monitor its physical and mental growth. In doing so, they may be able to detect emotional disturbances before they become more serious psychological problems (Crittenden, 1983).

Infants are born with differing temperaments and sensitivities to their physical and social environment. By observing parents interacting with their babies, pediatric specialists can identify disruptive parent–child patterns in the making and help parents develop new ways of responding to their infants. For example, an irritable baby may be hypersensitive to noise or touch. The parent who is unaware of the infant's temperament may actually aggravate the infant by frequently picking up the infant or by placing the infant in a noisy setting. A pediatric therapist can provide parents with new ways of caring for their infant to promote a more satisfactory relationship. Another example is the severely depressed parent, who may pick up inappropriate emotional cues from the infant or misinterpret the infant's fussiness or lack of smiling as rejection.

While therapy may change the parent's depression, the infant still requires an emotionally responsive caregiver to help it develop affectionate social behaviors. While the parent is experiencing depression, the young infant especially requires contact with a sensitive, nurturing, and affectionate caregiver. A pediatric specialist who was familiar with infant emotional behavior would be able to train caregivers how to care for infants at risk for emotional disturbances so as to reduce their risks.

Although researchers agree that it is much harder to alter maladaptive patterns after the age of three, there currently are only a few mental-health and university-based facilities that provide pediatric psychiatry services. The idea of providing such psychological care to young infants is still new, and additional programs are likely to emerge soon. The American Academy of Pediatrics is currently developing a set of guidelines to help pediatricians assess the emotional well-being of infants.

were able to reliably assess the angry emotional reactions. Infants not only imitate facial expressions of emotion, they also learn where and when to express their feelings. The learning process occurs daily through countless face to face interactions with their parents (Malatesta, Grigoryev, Lamb, Albin, & Culver, 1986; Malatesta & Haviland, 1982). As was the case with our little friend Ben, whenever he would smile, he would be rewarded with a returned smile from his parents and a happy lesson was learned. Ben's parents would also be encouraged to continue the pleasant exchange.

Pause for Thought

During parent–infant face-to-face interactions, both modeling and operant conditioning are used to teach emotional reactions. What predictions would you make about the emotional development of infants blind from birth? What predictions would you make for infants whose parents are chronically depressed? What sort of changes in care would you make for these infants to promote their emotional development?

Parents' Contribution

Freud's Oral Stage

Much has been written about the early influence that parents have on the developing child's personality. Freud first called attention to the importance of the first five years of a child's life in his psychosexual stages of personality development. As we noted in Chapter 1, Freud was particularly interested in personality development during the first five years of a child's life. Personality develops during the *oral stage* when the young infant's needs are met through the gratification of its oral needs. The infant's mouth is the source of food and sensual sucking, gumming, and biting. Freud believed that infants who are allowed to gratify their psychosexual needs will develop an optimistic view of self and the world. Those infants whose oral needs are frustrated, are likely to become fixated on these needs in later life.

Erikson's Stage 1: Basic Trust vs. Mistrust

Freud's theory was later elaborated upon and reinterpreted by Erik Erikson (1963, 1968), who suggested that the "cornerstone of a vital personality" is laid down in infancy as the child interacts with parents. The early social interactions between parent and child form the basis for the first psychosocial "crisis" in development, which Erikson labeled *Basic Trust* vs. *Mistrust*. The term *crisis* refers to a turning point, a time of increased vulnerability, as well as a time for potential growth. During the first stage of basic trust, the infant learns to trust or mistrust that other people will meet its needs. If the baby's physical needs are met in a consistent and affectionate manner by the caregiver or mother, then the baby comes to interpret the world as a safe place. The infant trusts its caregivers, and this positive orientation applies to itself as well as to others. A certain amount of frustration of needs by others can help infants develop greater trust in themselves as they figure out new ways of meeting their own needs. If, however, the infant is less fortunate and experiences inconsistent or abusive treatment at the hands of parents, then the infant is likely to acquire a mistrustful outlook toward others. If cries are ignored, or needs for touching and cuddling are not recognized, then the infant may interpret its world as a neglectful and unfriendly place. The mistrustful infant will also lack confidence in itself as a person worthy of attention. In Erikson's theory, a healthy resolution of the trust-vs.-mistrust conflict is represented by the infant's learning to trust itself and others in the world. A certain amount of mistrust, however, is seen as healthy since the child has discovered that not everyone or everything responds in a predictable manner. Overall, however, the child's basic trust encourages continued interaction with people and surroundings.

Parental Characteristics

Parents play a particularly important role in the child's acquisition of basic trust or mistrust. Since parents structure the physical and social environment for the young child, the characteristic manner in which parents interact with the infant can strongly affect the infant's early experiences. What characteristics are associated with being a good parent? How does an effective caregiver behave toward his or her child? These questions are useful but difficult to answer specifically because we know that parental behavior is influenced by the child's characteristics as well as by their parents' own personality and personal history. Data from studies on parent–child interactions are also difficult to interpret because of the way in which the data are collected. If you ask parents in an interview or questionnaire to describe their behavior with their children, their answers may reflect how they think they *should* respond rather than how they actually do respond. The very act of observing parent–child interaction in the home or in a laboratory may alter it. The best approach for such study is to combine observational data with interview or questionnaire data (Wachs & Gruen, 1982).

By observing parents and children interacting in the home and in the laboratory and by assessing the child's social and cognitive development, some broad conclusions about the parent's influence in the child's development have been drawn. Parents who stimulate their infants—who talk to, cuddle, and express warm positive emotions with their babies—generally have more responsive and socially competent children (Belsky, Lerner, & Spanier, 1984; Clarke-Stewart, 1973; Crockenberg, 1983). Furthermore, the more sensitive attention and stimulation the infant receives, the earlier and more accelerated will be its performance on tests of cognitive development (Yarrow, Rubenstein, & Pedersen, 1975).

In earlier studies on parent behaviors mothers were often the primary caregivers during children's first two years of life and thus were more frequently studied than fathers. Schaffer (1977) examined the mother's sensitivity to her child's particular needs and suggested that insensitivity is the greatest obstacle to a child's development. Data from a study of 30 mothers

Parents who stimulate their infants are more likely to have responsive and competent children.

and their one-year-old infants suggest that the less child-centered the mother's actions are, the more the infant displays negative behaviors such as hostility, impulsiveness, and irritability (Stern, Caldwell, Hersher, Lipton, & Richmond, 1969).

Additional information about the effects of parental interactions on the child comes from studies of parents known to have personality disturbances or difficulties. In particular, mothers who are depressed are likely to interact with their infants in an inconsistent and nonresponsive manner. Research by Zahn-Waxler, Cummings, McKnew, and Radke-Yarrow (1984) has found that children with a bipolar (manic-depressive) parent display problems in social interactions as early as 18 months of age. However, children of parents with bipolar disorder may themselves have an inherited tendency toward emotional difficulties and thus may contribute to the problems in social interactions. In a different study, Cohn and Tronick (1983) demonstrated that infants as young as three months of age respond to the affective quality of the parent's interaction. Infants were exposed to two experimental conditions: (1) *normal mother condition,* in which the mother responded to the infant in her usual way, and (2) *depressed mother condition,* in which the mother made no facial emotional expressions while interacting with her child. Compared to the normal mother condition, infants in the depressed mother condition spent more time in a state of distress and less time in positive emotional states. Clearly, the reciprocal impact of the parent and child on each other works to maintain and enhance the quality of the interaction. If the initial parent–child interaction is negative, regardless of the origin, then a negative cycle may be established. An anxious parent may be giving facial emotional cues to the infant, who responds in a negative way such as crying. The anxious parent, in turn, interprets this response as further evidence of his or her inability to cope or care for the infant and continues to react in an uncertain and negative manner toward the baby.

Whether the caregiver is satisfied with his or her role can also influence the quality of the parent–child interaction. Lerner and Galambos (1985) found that mothers who were satisfied with their roles displayed more warmth and acceptance of their children than did mothers who were dissatisfied with their roles. We know that infants are affected by the emotional behavior of their parents both directly and indirectly. Directly, parents model specific emotional reactions and selectively reinforce their infant's emotional responses. Indirectly, young children are affected by angry exchanges that they witness even though the emotion is not directed toward them (Cummings, Iannotti, Zahn-Waxler, 1985). Thus parents who argue and fight with each other may contribute to the distress of their young children.

Effects of Social Support

Additional social support and information about infants and their care seem to help parents establish a more positive style of interacting with their children. As we shall learn in Chapter 6, parents who physically abuse or neglect their children often have both unrealistic expectations of children and inappropriate ideas about proper care. A large number of child-abuse victims are preterm births, a fact suggesting that disturbance in the parent–child interaction may have had an early origin. In a study comparing the effects of stress and social support on mothers of preterm and full-term infants, it was found that mothers with greater stress were less positive in their attitudes and behavior, while mothers with greater support from the father, family members, and community were significantly more positive in their attitude toward their infants (Crnic, Greenberg, Ragozin, Robinson, & Basham, 1983).

Parents who receive social support are likely to be more sensitive to their infant's needs and thus provide a more secure and stable emotional atmosphere for their children (Crockenberg & McCluskey, 1986; Crittenden, 1985). The most helpful types of social support come from close friends and relatives who provide the parents with empathy and understanding. However, neighbors and community workers are also important as support because they can provide assistance and needed information on how best to care for their children. Through early intervention, potentially negative parent–child interactions can be altered to promote a more satisfactory relationship for both.

Pause for Thought

Taking care of and raising children is perhaps the most important occupation in a culture since it guarantees the future of the society. Yet, very few parents receive any formal training in the care and nurturance of children. What explanations can you offer for this inconsistency?

The First Social Relationship: Parent–Child Attachment

Many theorists and researchers agree that social contact early in the child's life is important for healthy personality development. Through their interactions with parents, infants come to define themselves. Through physical touching and handling, the growing infant learns limits, such as where its own body ends off and another person begins. Through frequent social and emotional exchanges with parents, the infant acquires a particular style or orientation that some researchers believe carries over into later childhood (Sroufe, 1978). Let's take a closer look at this important first social relationship.

Attachment

Suppose that you entered a playroom in which young infants between the ages of eight months to a year were gathered. Then suppose the parents of these infants entered the room. Without even waiting to see which parent paired up with which infant, you could probably accurately match the parents and infants simply by noticing the reactions of the babies and mothers or fathers. What you would be noticing is the affectionate emotional bond between parent and child that we call *attachment*. Virtually all infants form an attachment to their caregiver, although the quality of the attachment may vary widely.

John Bowlby (1969) was one of the earliest writers to call attention to this special relationship, which he described as an affectional tie that the infant forms with another specific person, bonding them together in space, enduring over time, and having survival benefits. Physically immature and unable to care for itself at birth, the human infant without an adult to feed and protect it would surely die. Unlike other mammals that are physically more mature at birth, the human infant is particularly dependent on its parents during the first two years of life.

The affectional tie exists for both baby and parents. This means that the parents are very much interested in being with or close to their infant, a state that ensures care and protection during the most vulnerable period of development. Attachments are believed to be universal not only for humans but for all species. Early and frequent contact and familiarity with the caregiver create an affectionate relationship.

At one time, it was assumed that feeding, not the contact itself, provided the essential basis for the development of attachment. In several classic experiments with infant monkeys conducted by Harry Harlow and his colleagues (1962; Harlow & Harlow, 1966), this belief was confronted. The experimenters constructed two surrogate monkey mothers. One of the substitute mothers was made out of wire mesh and the other was covered with a terrycloth fabric. In the center of each figure was a slot to attach a feeding bottle. Separated from their biological mothers at birth, the baby monkeys were reared by both types of surrogate mothers. Some were fed only by the wire-mesh mother, and others were fed by the terrycloth mother. Harlow found that all the monkeys developed a clinging attachment to the terrycloth mother even when they were not fed by her. The baby monkeys preferred to spend their time between feedings close to or clinging to this soft, cloth mother. The wire-mesh mothers were ignored by the baby monkeys except at feeding time.

Harlow's studies demonstrate the importance of physical contact for the attachment bond. His study of infant monkeys produced an additional striking finding: He found that as these baby monkeys, who were essentially raised from birth in the laboratory, matured, they displayed inappropriate sexual and maternal behavior. They did not engage in typical mating behavior, and, once impregnated, the female monkeys proved to be neglectful and abusive mothers. They would not feed or cuddle their young, and some even attacked their babies. Harlow attributed this highly disruptive behavior to the lack of social contact with other monkeys during development. It seems that the laboratory-raised monkeys did not have the opportunity to establish healthy social behaviors.

Attachment Behaviors

Seeking the contact and closeness of the parent or caregiver is one set of behaviors that indicates an attachment. Other attachment behaviors include the infant showing distress when separated from their attachment figures and showing relief or joy upon reunion. Even if there is no physical contact, the infant displays a clear preference for the caregiver by seeking eye contact or by being especially attentive to the sound of the mother's or father's voice.

In our example of a room full of babies, you would most likely use these behaviors of the infant to identify their parents. You would also probably notice that the parents would display a similar, though more subtle, set of attachment behaviors. They most likely would seek and establish, first, eye contact and, then, physical contact. Not immediately locating the infant, the parent would have a worried or concerned look and would then smile when the baby was found. The bond is, therefore, a reciprocal process, for both are interested in maintaining closeness to each other.

Another characteristic of attachment behavior is the extent to which the infant uses attachment figures as a secure base from which to explore the physical and social environment. The toddler in a new situation may stick close to its parent until feeling secure enough to venture out to explore it. Visual contact with the parent may be sufficient to ensure comfort. Becoming afraid or upset during exploration, the toddler will return to the mother's or father's side for comfort. Infants vary in the extent to which they use their parents as a secure base and source of comfort.

Development of Attachment

Attachment refers to an organized system of parental and child behaviors that have an emotional quality. When psychologists speak about attachment, they refer not to a specific set of behaviors, but to the way a parent and child respond to each other. The specific behaviors change as the child's cognitive, social, and emotional skills develop. Because it is a process, attachment is not immediately present at birth, but rather, develops gradually from the first moment of contact.

Bowlby (1969) detailed four phases during the first few years of life during which the infant gradually directs more of its attention and efforts toward being physically close to its caregiver. In the first, *preattachment phase* (0–3 months), the infant appears to be interested in anyone. It does not distinguish the primary caregiver from others. It is not until about two to three months of age that the infant consistently visually and auditorally discriminates its caregiver from other people. During the *attachment-in-the-making phase* (3–6 months of age), a unique relationship is forming between the baby and its primary caregiver. The infant smiles and vocalizes more frequently and intensely to the caregiver. Although the infant may be relatively receptive to strangers, the baby clearly is able to discriminate the mother figure.

The *clearcut attachment phase* emerges between six and 12 months of age. At this age, the infant is able to physically get around by crawling, creeping, and walking. These locomotor skills allow the infant to actively seek out and become physically close to its parent. During this time, infants also generally acquire object or, in this case, person permanence; that is, the infant can now keep someone in mind even when he or she is absent. The infant has also learned how to hold its parent's attention through vocalization and crying. At this point, the caregiver is well under the control of an expanding repertoire of behaviors designed to keep the parents close at hand. When the mother and father leave the room or go out for an evening, the infant is likely to show signs of distress or to protest by crying. This reaction is called **separation distress** and usually peaks in intensity around 12 months. A similar wariness is present when a stranger approaches or interacts with the infant. **Stranger anxiety** refers to the infant's general wariness of unfamiliar people. This type of wariness usually peaks in intensity around eight to 10 months of age. Stranger anxiety can occur in response to people who are not necessarily strangers, but who merely appear to the infant to be different from the attachment figure. If Mother is a light-skinned, blonde woman who speaks softly to the baby, then a dark-haired, dark-skinned uncle who smells of aftershave and speaks in a deep voice may well trigger a wariness reaction from the baby. The discrepancy between the infant's scheme of Mother and Uncle is too

Separation Distress The infant's protest or crying when mother and infant are separated.

Stranger Anxiety An infant's general wariness of unfamiliar people.

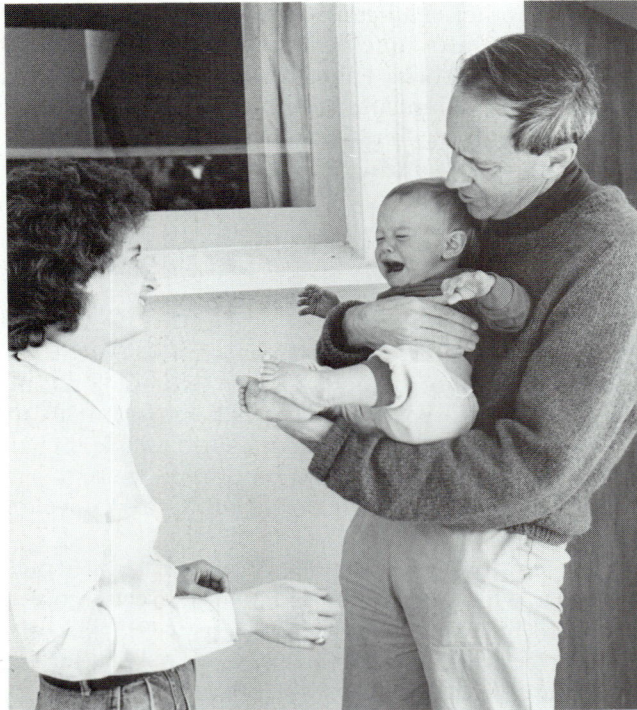

Infants between eight to ten months of age frequently display upset when left in the care of an unfamiliar babysitter.

great. The different reaction to the stranger tells us that the infant has made a conceptual distinction between its caregiver and other people.

The last phase according to Bowlby (1969) is the *goal-corrected partnership phase* (12–24 months), which represents a more complex interplay of cognitive, social, and emotional behavior. The attachment between the infant and caregiver becomes much more complicated. The infant may initiate attempts to influence the attachment figure in fairly sophisticated ways. The infant may try to figure out the parent's actions and influence his or her behavior. An example is the infant who protests by crying and holding onto the father when the babysitter arrives. The infant has figured out that the father and mother will leave when the babysitter arrives; it also has learned that by crying and holding onto the father, he may change his plans about leaving.

The Father and Other Attachment Figures

Until recently, the father's involvement with the care of the infant was assumed to be minimal. However, there have been growing changes in the degree to which men are caring for their young infants (Cordes, 1983). More men are participating in the birth of their babies, and this early contact with their infants seems to be important for later involvement (Lamb, 1976).

Are there differences in the way infants respond to each parent? Studies of infants observed in the laboratory and at home indicate that infants react positively to both mothers and fathers, but the quality of the father's involvement seems to be an important determinant of the infant's reaction (Parke, 1979). With the exception of breast feeding, fathers are capable of performing

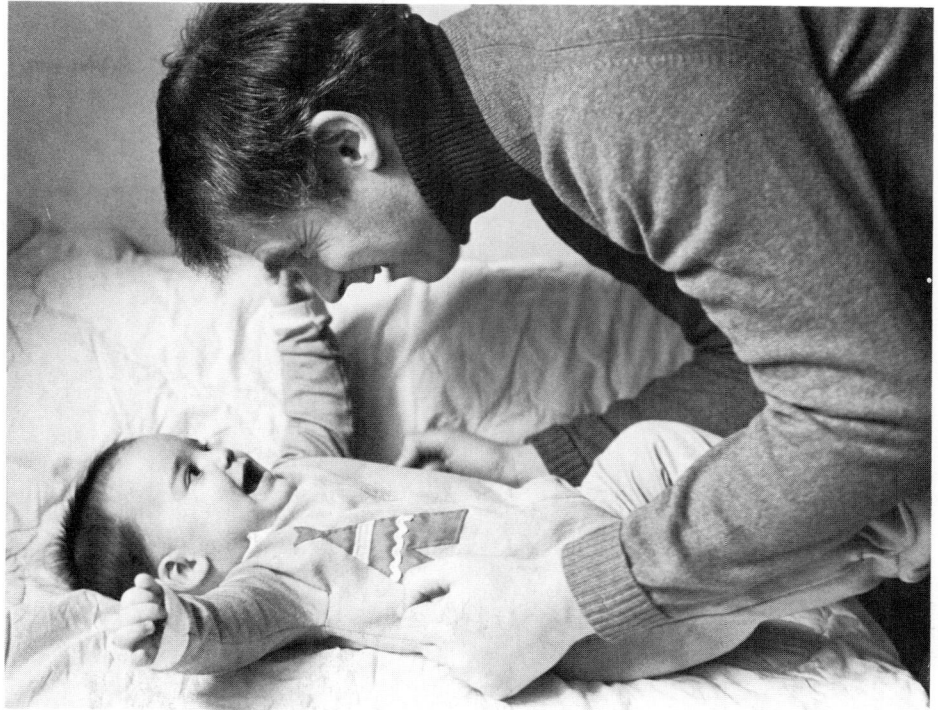

Today, many fathers participate in the active care and enjoyment of their young children.

most child-care routines and of being responsive to infant cues that signal the need for care (Parke, 1979). There are noted differences, however, between the ways mothers and fathers interact with their babies. Parke and Sawin (1980) observed new mothers and fathers with their infants in the hospital. Fathers were just as likely as mothers to hold, rock, cuddle, smile, and talk to their babies, and look directly into their babies' faces. When the infants were older, the same parents were observed at home, and the parents' style of interacting with the infants was noticeably different. Mothers were more involved in routine child care, while fathers more often were engaged in playful stimulation of the infant. Fathers tended to take more interest in their infant sons than in their daughters. This may have been because the father's style tended to be more physical, involving playful wrestling. Mothers were more likely to use a toy in playing with their infants. In a study examining how new mothers and fathers use toys with their eight-month-old infants, Power and Parke (1983) found that fathers were more physical in their use of toys, while mothers paid more attention to the infant's cues of interest in a particular toy.

These differences in style may be related to the father's less frequent contact with the infant, which, in turn, could affect his ability to interpret the baby's nonverbal messages. In examining families where the role of caregiver was assumed by the father rather than the mother, researchers have found that fathers who are the primary caregivers act more like traditional mothers—they are responsive to their infants' subtle cues, and imitate their infants' facial expressions and vocalizations (Field, 1978). In a similar study of Swedish fathers, Lamb and his associates found that fathers who were primary care-

Four-year old Danielle and her six-month-old sister Ashley are well on their way toward establishing a strong sibling attachment.

givers interacted more with their daughters, whereas fathers who were secondary caregivers interacted more with their sons (Lamb, Frodi, Hwang, Frodi, & Steinberg, 1982).

Young children receive care not only from their parents but from older siblings as well. In some cultures and even in subcultures within our own society, infants and toddlers are predominantly cared for by siblings or older children. Does the infant form a similar attachment to the caregiver when that person is also a child?

A study by Robert Stewart (1983) suggests that infants, in fact, do become attached to their older siblings, and display prominent attachment behaviors toward the siblings when the parents are not present. Stewart observed 54 mothers of infants aged 10 to 20 months and their older siblings, who ranged in age from 30 to 58 months. He used a modified version of Ainsworth's "strange situation" (described in the next section) in which the older sibling was also introduced when the infant was separated from the mother. Over half of the four-year-old children were both active and effective in caring for their younger siblings who were distressed by the mother's absence. The older sibling comforted the infant and reassured the baby of the mother's eventual return. The infant was calmed by the sibling's efforts and returned to play activities. When a stranger entered, the infant used the sibling as a secure base for exploration. Even though the infants responded to the siblings in a manner similar to the way they responded to the mothers, Stewart claims the sibling attachment does not replace the parent attachment.

Patterns of Attachment

In order to gain a better understanding of the attachment process, Ainsworth, Bell, & Stayton (1971) developed a method of studying attachment behaviors by observing the child with its parent, usually the mother, in specific situations. The "strange situation" procedure has been used by Ainsworth and her associates to study hundreds of children at varying ages. In this procedure, the caregiver and baby are brought into an observation room that is well supplied with toys. The parent puts the baby down and sits on a chair. After three minutes, a female stranger enters and begins a conversation with the mother. The stranger then tries to play with the baby, and the mother quietly leaves the room but leaves her handbag on the chair to signal that she will return. The mother is gone for three minutes, and during this time the stranger reacts to the infant either by giving comfort if it is protesting the parent's absence or by engaging it in play with the toys. Then the parent returns and the stranger leaves. After three minutes the parent leaves again; this time the infant is left alone in the observation room. In the last six minutes of this standardized observation the stranger returns and again attempts to interact with the infant, after which the parent returns and the stranger departs. Throughout the 20-minute testing period, the infant's behaviors are observed and recorded by trained researchers. On the basis of the quality and pattern of infant behavior, Ainsworth and her associates (1978) have identified three categories of attachment behavior: *secure attachment* (Type B) and two varieties of *insecure attachment*: avoidant (Type A) and resistant (Type C).

The securely attached infant (Type B) uses the parent as a base of security in the strange situation. During the parent's absence and/or in the presence of the stranger, the infant may or may not reduce play and exploration, and may or may not show signs of distress such as crying. Upon the parent's return, though, securely attached babies generally make contact with their parents either by looking at and vocalizing to them or, in the case of those who have experienced distress, by seeking contact and comfort from them. The hallmark of securely attached infants is their ability to use their attachment figures to regain their source of security when stressed; this allows them to move forth into the world once again through exploration and play. Most of the children observed by Ainsworth and her colleagues displayed the securely attached pattern.

The resistant, insecurely attached infant (Type C) is more likely to seem anxious or distressed even when its parent is present in the room. This type of infant has trouble using the parent as a secure base for exploration. Upon reunion after separation, the infant, while seeking contact with the parent, in the next moment may resist contact or act angry. The avoidant, insecure attachment pattern (Type A) also reflects some difficulty between parent and child. The infant seems to ignore the parent much of the time and does not use the parent as a secure base for exploration. There is little distress or protest when the parent leaves, and the infant usually ignores the parent when she or he returns. This type of infant is as easily comforted by a stranger as by its parent.

Individual Differences in Attachment Patterns

Back in the late 1940s and early 1950s, researchers who were interested in infant personality development were interested in the question: What happens to infants who do not establish an attachment? This question triggered a series of studies involving institutionalized orphaned infants and children.

These infants suffered in several ways. Not only did they not form an emotional bond with a consistent and caring adult, but they also were deprived of a normal level of social and physical stimulation that is now recognized to be an important ingredient for infant cognitive and social development.

Today, researchers continue to be intrigued by the attachment process. The question that is asked now is: Why is it that some infants are securely attached to one or more caregivers and other infants are insecurely attached? Some researchers believe that the differences in attachment patterns among infants can be explained in terms of the differences in infant temperament (Kagan; 1982, 1984). For example, from this view you would expect to find that infants with a difficult temperament would be more likely to have difficulty establishing a secure attachment. Even in secure attachments, infants with difficult temperaments are likely to react differently than easy-temperament infants to their caregivers. Other researchers (Sroufe, 1985) argue that temperament is not a factor at all in attachment patterns.

Perhaps attachment differences can be explained by examining differences in the parents' behavior. In one study (Weber, Levitt, & Clark, 1986), researchers found that mothers' temperament was linked to the attachment patterns of their infants. For example, infants whose mothers rated themselves as less adaptable cried more often during the separation and reunion phases of the strange situation procedure. Other studies have found that mothers of avoidant infants did not like to have physical contact with their babies (Egeland & Farber, 1984) and that mothers of insecurely attached infants expressed more negative and less positive emotion (Radke-Yarrow, Cummings, Kuczynski, & Chapman, 1985).

Ainsworth and her colleagues (1978) report that the type of attachment an infant forms is influenced by the quality of the caregiver–child interaction. Caregivers who sensitively responded to their infants during the first year of life were likely to have securely attached infants. When the caregivers were insensitive, insecure relationships more often resulted. These studies and others suggest that the nature of the attachment relationship is jointly influenced by both the infant and the caregiver.

What are the long-term consequences of the different patterns in attachment? From the descriptions you have read of securely and insecurely attached infants, you might predict that securely attached infants would be more trusting of others and hence have more success in later relationships. This prediction has received much support by researchers (Bretherton & Waters, 1985). Furthermore, securely attached infants engage in more autonomous exploration and problem solving that may contribute to their persistence and increased attention span when dealing with tasks. Compared to insecurely attached children, the securely attached children get along better with peers and preschool teachers. On the other hand, insecurely attached children have been found to avoid contact with their preschool peers. Generally, the securely attached infant seems more likely to emerge in the preschool years as more self-reliant and having a more positive view of self.

Margaret Ricks (1985) has suggested an even longer-term consequence of attachment patterns. She maintains that when adults serve as parents to their own children, they use as their model the type of attachment relationship they shared with their parents. For example, mothers of securely attached infants had more positive recollections of their childhood relationships with their mothers, fathers, and peers than did mothers of infants who were judged to be anxiously attached. Thus, the prospect remains that during the first few years of life the infant is acquiring attitudes, emotions, and behaviors that may extend their influence well into adulthood and into the next generation.

Issues in Foster Care

During World War II, when Hitler's bombs were showering the major cities in Great Britain, people were concerned about the health and welfare of the children living in these cities. So, as a measure of precaution, a national scale program was instituted in which children were relocated to the country villages and towns that were out of danger from bombing. This meant that children were often separated from their parents and placed in the care of other unfamiliar adults. Because of the extreme circumstances involved, the separation of infants from their caregivers was considered to be the lesser of two evils. After the danger of attack was over, the relocated children were reunited with their parents so the separation was, for most children, only temporary.

Today, a similar forced separation exists for some children when they are placed in foster care. Although there is a strong value within our country and many other cultures that it is best to preserve the integrity of a family, to help keep a family together, in some circumstances it may be necessary to remove a child from its parents. When a parent is severely depressed or physically incapable of providing appropriate care for a child or in some cases when a parent is physically abusive or neglectful, the child may be temporarily removed from the family for its own protection. Rather than place a child in an institutional setting that may be too impersonal and understaffed to meet the child's developmental needs, the social welfare agency involved may seek a foster home for the child. Foster parents are screened by social welfare agencies and receive payment for their care of a child. The placement in a foster home is intended to be a temporary situation, but unfortunately many children often remain in foster care for several years rather than weeks or months. Often there may be several different foster parents who care for the child.

One of the major issues in foster care concerns the effect that the disruption in care has on the infant's social and emotional development. It takes time and a continuous caring relationship for an infant to establish an emotional attachment with its caregiver. In the case of foster care, the infant may be abruptly removed from the parents' care and thrust into the arms of a total stranger—at an age when the infant cannot comprehend the reasons for the loss of its original caregivers. This event alone could be distressing to both parents and child. Furthermore, because a foster-care placement is temporary, the foster parent may be urged *not* to establish a close emotional bond with the child. The argument made is that it is too difficult for an infant to separate from a caregiver to whom it has established an attachment. Since most foster parents do not receive specialized training or supervision in their special role, it may be too much to expect that they could be aware of and respond to the need to be caring, stimulating, and consistent in the care of an infant they will soon return.

Recent legislation in the United States has been directed at reducing the number and duration of foster-care placements. The issue is one of providing adequate and continuous care to infants and children who are in difficult family settings. An alternative arrangement to foster care might be to foster improved parenting from the infant's parents within the home. The benefits of providing stressed families with social and informational support have been demonstrated in social welfare programs directed at preventing child abuse and neglect.

Pause for Thought

Attachment to a sensitive and caring caregiver leads to a greater sense of security and self-confidence in the baby. What would you expect to happen to securely attached infants who were separated from their mothers or caregivers for a long time or even forever? What recommendations would you make to a parent whose eight-month-old was to be hospitalized for an extended period of time—to reduce the negative consequences of this experience?

Development of Self

Does a young infant have a view of itself? When does this view develop and how? These questions, while intriguing, have not generated as much research as they have speculation and theory. The sense of self involves a recognition of one's separateness from others as well as a conceptual image of one's characteristic behaviors. Many psychologists view the development of self as a process occurring throughout development and one that closely parallels cognitive, social, and emotional development (Lewis & Brooks-Gunn, 1979; Maccoby, 1980). The development of self-awareness is tied to the child's early attachment with its parents. With the security so provided, the one-year-old explores more and more aspects of its physical and social world. Trying new toys and meeting new people in different settings, the infant learns something new about how it can and does function in the world with each new adventure.

Freud's Anal Stage

Beginning about the age of 18 months, children enter what Freud called *the anal stage* of personality development. During this stage, the bodily focus for sensual stimulation and gratification shifts from the infant's mouth to its anal region. This shift corresponds with infants' interest in releasing and controlling its bowels. Toilet training is typically the event that highlights the child's active attempts to gratify its need for anal stimulation. During the anal stage, children learn how to delay gratification of their sensual anal needs until there is a suitable opportunity (that is, until they are on the toilet). If parents or caregivers are too harsh or rigid in their toilet training attempts, Freud believed that children will become stuck at the anal stage of personality development and display traits such as stubbornness, extreme orderliness, or defiant messiness in later adult life.

Erikson's Stage 2: Autonomy vs. Shame and Doubt

Erik Erikson (1968) described the period from one-and-a-half to three years of age as being critical for the child's development of a sense of self. The psychosocial crisis of this period centers on the child's attempts at self-control.

Human Development in Practice

Creating an Environment for Autonomy

The home is not the only setting in which young children learn about what they can do. Many two- and three-year-olds acquire a sense of mastery and autonomy in nursery schools and day-care centers. What can preschool teachers do to help encourage young children to develop a sense of self-worth and mastery?

First of all, the physical environment must be a safe one for the actively exploring toddler. This means that bathrooms, playrooms, and playgrounds must be free of hazards such as un-guarded stairs, sharp-edged corners, exposed cleaning chemicals, or glassed doors that can be shattered by an inattentive running child. In most states, preschool and day-care facilities must meet licensing requirements that include fire and health inspections. Children must not only be in a safe environment, they must feel safe. By showing children how to walk a safe distance in front of a slide or swing or how to use safety scissors, teachers encourage children to be more adventuresome.

Children who have a limited and safe environment are more likely to explore and experiment. Teachers can encourage mastery by providing their young students with opportunities to experiment with different surfaces, objects of different sizes, shapes, and weights, different tastes in food, different sounds. Let them play with objects that have some safe consequences to them—like a keyboard, or computer, or a slinky toy.

Giving children a choice of activities helps them become more autonomous and they are less likely to say "No" when you ask them which activity they would like to do. Ask children whether they would like to listen to a story, look at picture books, or build with blocks rather than tell them what they will do. Furthermore, while giving children a choice, teachers also encourage them to structure some of their own time. Free play time is a chance for children to define themselves through their choice of activities.

Most preschool teachers have a vested interest in teaching young children how to dress and undress themselves. It makes the teacher's job much easier *and* it encourages a sense of mastery in the child. ("I can put on my own coat!") In a day-care center, the teacher may be the one who teaches the child how to use the toilet and how to safely use eating utensils, activities that greatly increase a child's sense of mastery and self-worth.

Part of knowing what you can do is also knowing what you cannot do. By making clear rules about what is not acceptable in the preschool—such as no toy guns or candy may be brought to school, only one child on a swing seat at a time, and no making noise during nap time—teachers help children avoid situations that could result in unpleasant consequences and a sense of shame and doubt.

Most importantly, preschool educators contribute to children's sense of competence by encouraging them to try new skills, to be aware of what they *can* do, and by applauding their growing independence. Let children show you and others what they *do* know and provide a safe setting in which to learn more about the world and you have a pretty good blueprint for autonomy.

A successful resolution of this crisis leads the toddler to develop a sense of its own autonomy, including a realistic view of what it is capable of performing. In establishing basic competency, the infant begins to see itself as distinct from its caregiver. At the same time, the toddler is learning to comply with social constraints or rules laid down by parents and other adults. The child's sense of autonomy is very much influenced by parental demands, which, if in keeping with the child's capabilities to comply, cause the child to acquire a sense of self-worth.

If, however, the parents have placed unrealistic or overly rigid demands on the young child, it may fail to comply and consequently may acquire a sense of shame and doubt about its own competence to deal effectively with people and objects. According to Erikson, a successful resolution of this crisis requires a balance between what the child can and should do (autonomy), and what the child cannot and should not do (shame and doubt). Healthy limits imposed on the child during this period allow the child to gain positive experience with people and objects that add to its sense of self. With a healthy sense of autonomy, the infant then is able to regulate its own body and actions with increasingly greater ease. Often the two-year-old who has acquired language will assert a new-found sense of self by saying "No!" and resisting the caregiver's attempts to regulate its activities. By saying "No!" the child is expressing its desire to be separate from the caregiver. Parents who allow their toddlers a certain amount of self-expression and choice encourage their children's development of a sense of autonomy.

Mahler's Theory of Separation and Individuation

Other psychoanalytic researchers have focused more exclusively on the influence of the mother–child relationship on personality development (Mahler, Pine, & Bergman, 1975). While Freud believed that the mother–child relationship is the most important one in an infant's life, he did not actually study it. However, Margaret Mahler, a clinical psychoanalyst, has studied the changing characteristics of the mother–infant relationship through clinical observations. She offers a three-phase theory of the process by which children separate from their mothers and establish themselves as individuals.

In the first phase, *the autistic phase* (birth to two months), the newborns are preoccupied with their own internal sensations and are pretty much oblivious to events and people around them. Infants spend most of their time sleeping and eating. Their only awareness of their mother is as an agent who helps them meet their basic needs. From two to five months infants enter the second phase, *symbiosis*, and establish a mutual dependency on their mother. It is as if the child becomes part of the mother. The infant acts as if the mother's primary function is to minister to its need. Through numerous experiences of depending upon its mother, the infant builds a solid foundation for later growth and exploration. Mothers who are sensitive and responsive to their infants unspoken needs are likely to encourage a secure symbiotic relationship with their infants. Those who are not, will frustrate their infant's attempts to fuse with her.

The last phase is the longest (five months to 36 months) and is called the *separation–individuation* phase because infants begin to recognize that they are separate from their mothers and that they themselves are autonomous individuals. Infants see themselves as different from their mothers. Mahler refers to this awareness of self as a "second birth experience." The infant's dependency on its mother is reduced by the infant's growing independence and exploration; yet the infant still requires the reassurance that its mother will be available in times of stress or fatigue. Sometime during the period between 15 and 22 months, Mahler observed that infants who had established their independence from their mothers seem to become more attached and dependent on them. This seeming regression is viewed as a normal part of separation. With a caring and responsive mother, the child learns to balance its conflicting needs for independence and dependence.

Infancy: Social and Personality Development

Research on Self-Awareness

One of the problems with doing research on the issue of self-awareness in infancy is assessing self-awareness. Since the young infant has not yet acquired language, indirect measures of self-awareness must be used. One technique initially used with animals (e.g., Gallup, 1977) measured the infant's recognition of its image in a mirror. The infant's mother surreptitiously put an orange dot on the child's nose. During a pretest, the observer rated how often the infant touched its nose. In the test, the infant was placed in front of a mirror, and observers recorded the frequency of nose touching. In studies using this technique (Bertenthal & Fischer, 1978; Lewis & Brooks-Gunn, 1979) it was found that by 18 months of age infants touched their noses significantly more frequently when in front of the mirror. In contrast, younger infants did not try to locate the distinctive orange dot on their own body, although they often pointed to the dot in the mirror as if it existed on another person. For the infant to realize that the dot was on its own nose, it must have possessed a primitive scheme of what it looked like, knowledge that allowed it to recognize the discrepancy between the mirror image and self-concept.

Another way of measuring self-awareness is to assess the child's use of self-referent words, such as the personal pronouns "I," "my," or "mine." By observing young infants between the ages of 13 to 24 months of age, Kagan (1981) discovered a significant increase in 19- to 24-month-olds in the use of

One way to measure self-awareness in infants is to observe their reactions to a dot placed on their nose. If this infant touches her nose and not the mirror-image of her nose, this may indicate that she recognizes herself in the mirror.

both these self-referent words and words that occur while the child is engaging in an action. For example, as a little girl was climbing up on a chair, she might describe her actions by saying "up." In a recent study by Levine (1983), two-year-old boys who had a more advanced sense of self, as measured by pronoun use and by mirror recognition, claimed toys as their own and were able to interact more positively with other two-year-olds than were boys who had a less mature view of themselves. Levine concluded that the possessiveness of a two-year-old actually may reflect the child's attempt to interact socially with another child, and thus, a greater self-awareness.

The sense of self begins in infancy but develops in complexity with cognitive and social maturity. We will explore other aspects of the child's self-concept in Chapter 6.

Parent–Child Communication: Prelanguage Skills

Infancy stems from the word *infans,* meaning "without language." Many developmental psychologists mark the end of the infancy period with the emergence of language acquisition. Even though young infants may not have acquired formal aspects of their native language, they are capable of getting messages across to parents. From birth, we have seen that the infant is able to communicate its needs and preferences in a variety of ways. These early patterns of communication through sound and body movement are believed to be important precursors to language acquisition. Jerome Bruner (1978) sees language mastery as involving the parent as much as the child. At the least, in order to develop speech, the child must hear the native language spoken in social interactions with the parents (Slobin, 1982).

Prelanguage Behavior

During the first six months of life, the young infant gradually practices and expands a growing repertoire of sounds and gestures. By engaging in a synchronous exchange of body movement with its parents, the infant communicates awareness and interest. At birth, the most prominent vocalizations are in the form of crying. By two months of age, the infant makes cooing sounds that contain many of the basic sounds of languages, not just those of its native language.

By four to five months of age, the infant produces more sounds and strings them together to produce babbling. Gesturing by pointing to a desired person or object is added to the infant's prespeech behavior. The babbling sounds have no special meaning, but the infant appears to enjoy such vocalizations by playfully repeating sounds such as "la-la-la," or "ba-ba-ba." At first, the infant engages in language play only when alone, but as the infant gets older it involves parents and familiar adults in a playful exchange of sounds (Kuczaj, 1982). A child's activity during the babbling stage has no clear connection to later language development. Early babblers do not become early or more fluent speakers.

By about six months, the infant gradually produces only the sounds contained in the language it hears (Lenneberg, 1967). For the child with English-speaking parents, numerous social interactions encourage the child to acquire and produce the sounds specific to English and to drop the sounds

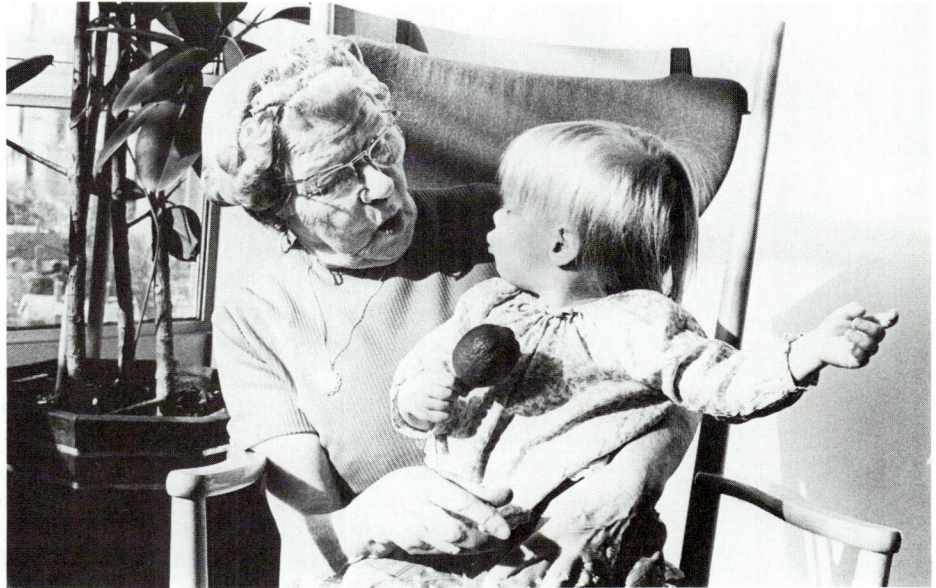

This grandmother enjoys the playful exchange of words and sounds with her grandchild. Some researchers believe that these early verbal interactions encourage language development in children.

suitable for other languages. If the child has no verbal interactions by this age (for example, the deaf child), then it gradually loses the capability to communicate verbally. Between six months and one year, infants engage in a speech pattern that sounds like adult conversation; this is termed *expressive jargon* because it resembles the intonation and sounds of adult speech, yet is meaningless in content. The infant engaging in expressive jargon is learning to control speech and to use sound patterns to engage parents in social interaction. Often, the child will vocalize while smiling or laughing with its parents. By one year of age, the infant's first words emerge. These one-word utterances such as "mama" or "dada" are usually associated with objects or people or with specific actions of the child such as "bye-bye." The words are typically concrete nouns that are spoken by the child in the actual presence of the objects.

By 15 to 18 months of age, the infant's use of one-word utterances carries additional meaning. Linguists have debated whether the use of one word to convey meaning implies the acquisition of true language. The infant who says to its mother "more!" conveys the meaning "I want more milk" by the emphasis and intonation of the word and by the context. The mother interprets the meaning for the child and responds. By the age of two years, children generally are creating two-word combinations. The child at this stage is combining words into a primitive sentence, which reflects the beginning of true language behavior. The meaning of the sentence is less tied to the mother's interpretation. Other adults are now able to understand the infant's use of words. As adults use language in their interactions with the infant, they facilitate the infant's learning and later production of the language by the model they present to the infant (Snow, 1981). The more experience the infant has with the language, the greater the child's fluency. Let's examine the parent's influence on the infant's acquisition of language.

Parent–Child Speech

Most of the studies on early parent–infant language behavior have focused on the quality of the mother's speech to her baby. This interest was partially a result of observations of mothers while they were interacting with their infants (Bruner, 1978). Through a myriad of verbal and nonverbal interactions, mothers help infants fine-tune their language skills. The initial nonverbal dialogue between parent and child requires that the parent interpret the meaning of the infant's motor actions and vocalizations. With the parent's involvement and encouragement, the infant increases its efforts at communication.

Parents respond differently when talking to their infants than they do to older children and adults. The term *motherese* has been used to refer to the short, grammatically simple, baby talk that mothers and other caregivers use when talking with their infants. The parent repeats and expands the utterances that the baby makes. Let's return to Ben, whom we met at the beginning of this chapter. When he says "bah-bah," his mother replies "Where is your bottle?" Often the caregiver uses more commands and questions and fewer pronouns, verbs, and modifiers when talking to the infant. As the child's capacity for language advances, the parent increases the complexity of verbal exchanges (Furrow, Nelson, & Benedict, 1979; Slobin, 1975).

The more recent studies on motherese have focused on the function of verbal exchanges in promoting social interactions between the parent and child. When parents talk to their infants, they are not trying to teach them how to speak the language so much as using language to make contact and playfully communicate with them (Molfese, Molfese, & Carrell, 1982). Furthermore, the infant's verbal responses seem to elicit the parent's verbal interactions. The parent and child appear to take turns "talking" to each other. What the parent talks about is influenced by the child's linguistic and cognitive level and most importantly by the child's interests. Parents of a toddler, for example, learn to make the "rrrring" sound of trucks if their child shows particular interest in them.

Mothers vary in the amount of talking they do with their infants. Middle-class mothers engage in more verbal conversations with their babies than do mothers from lower socioeconomic groups. However, it is not certain whether more frequent exposure to child-directed language leads to greater ease or early fluency with the language (Gleitman, Newport, & Gleitman, 1984). It is known, however, that early language exchanges have an effect on the child's social skills and help to establish an affectionate bond between parent and child.

Summary

The infant's earliest social interactions are with parents, who not only care for the child but are affected by the child's behavior. Parenting behavior is determined by the parents' personality, the child's characteristics, and the social context in which the parent–child relationship occurs.

The child's physical appearance, health, and maturity may influence a parent's initial reaction and bonding with the infant. The child's temperament may be described as easy, difficult, or slow-to-warm. Different temperaments elicit differing reactions from the caregiver.

The young infant is capable of expressing a progressively greater variety of emotions during the first two years of life. The infant's emotional development is closely related to cognitive development. One way to assess infant emotions is to rate the changes in facial expressions for different emotional experiences.

The early social interactions between parent and child form the basis for Erikson's first psychosocial crisis of basic trust vs. mistrust. A consistent and affectionate caregiver helps the child acquire a basic trust in itself and others. Abusive, inconsistent, or neglectful parents may foster a sense of mistrust in the infant.

Since the parent's behavior toward the child is influenced by the child itself, it is difficult to specify precisely what parental characteristics are necessary to promote a healthy personality in the child. However, research on parent–child interactions suggests that parents who stimulate, touch, and hold their infants and express warm, positive emotions are likely to have more responsive and socially competent infants. Social support given to parents under times of stress is likely to help foster a positive parent–child relationship.

The attachment between parent and child begins at birth but is clearly established by the age of six to 12 months. Attachment is indicated by the child's seeking contact with the caregiver, by the degree of comfort and affection displayed in parent–child interactions, by the degree of distress when they are separated or when a stranger is present, and by the extent to which a child can use the parent to recover from stress and begin to explore the environment once again.

Children may have more than one attachment figure, including the father. Fathers and mothers tend to interact with their infants in different ways.

Three patterns of attachment have been observed: securely attached, insecure-resistant, and insecure-avoidant attachment. Most children are securely attached and use the attachment figure as a base of security from which to explore the world.

Individual differences in patterns of attachment occur as a result of developmental and temperamental differences among infants. Differences in maternal behavior also result in different attachment patterns. The long term consequences of attachment have been found in cognitive, social, and emotional development.

The toddler begins to separate from the parent and to develop a sense of autonomy. If the demands on the child for self-control are too rigid, it may develop a feeling of shame and self-doubt. By 18 months of age, infants are able to recognize their images in a mirror. The sense of self begins in later infancy and continues to develop throughout childhood.

Prelanguage behavior begins in infancy as the child communicates by crying, cooing, and gesturing. Mothers have a particular way of talking to their babies to maintain social contact with them.

Further Readings

Arnstein, H. *The roots of love.* New York: Bantam Books, 1975.
This book translates the psychological knowledge of how to raise healthy, loving children in a way that benefits parents and children alike. The author focuses on the first

years of love and discusses such topics as attachment, separations, impulse control, and temper tantrums.

Bell, R. Q., and Harper, L. V. *Child effects on adults.* **Lincoln, NB: University of Nebraska Press, 1980.**
Documenting the ways in which children are both architects and products of the child-rearing process, this book has a bidirectional approach to the study of child rearing that is supported by research and theoretical viewpoints. This book is readable and thought provoking.

Brazelton, T. B. *On becoming a family: The growth of attachment.* **New York: Delacorte Press/Seymour Lawrence, 1981.**
A noted pediatrician and researcher discusses the way a new baby establishes a bond with its parents. Beginning with the feelings of expectant couples and tracing the process of early attachment, Brazelton discusses the adjustments parents and child make to each other. Special attention is given to the father's relationship with his baby. Personal anecdotes highlight this sensitive and readable book.

Klaus, M. H., and Kennell, J. H. *Parent–infant bonding* **(2nd Ed.). St. Louis: C. V. Mosby, 1982.**
In this updated version, the authors present research and clinical data to support their view that the early hours of contact between parents and their infant is critical for the formation of an affectional bond. The book is a blend of scientific data and humanistic concern and insight into parent and infant behaviors.

Parke, R. *Fathers.* **Cambridge, MA: Harvard University Press, 1977.**
The father's role in child development beginning at birth is presented by a noted researcher. The effects of fathers on children, how fathers differ from mothers in the care of children, and the changing role of fathers are described in this easy-to-read book.

Schaffer, R. *Mothering.* **Cambridge, MA: Harvard University Press, 1977.**
The essential ingredients of "mothering" are explored in this book. Schaffer emphasizes the importance of the mother's sensitivity as she stimulates and enters into verbal and nonverbal dialogue with her child.

Observational Activities

4.1   *Attachment Behaviors*

The purpose of this observation is for you to gain a better understanding of the behaviors that signal the infant's development of an attachment to its caregiver. You will need to observe a mother and her infant between one and two years of age in a setting for about a half hour. An infant day-care center, a church nursery, a pediatrician's waiting room, or a play area in a shopping mall are good places to locate a mother–child pair. Ideally, you want to find a place where the toddler is allowed some freedom to move about while in the presence of the mother.

While observing the mother and child, take notice of the following behaviors:

1. *Physical contact.* How often does the child touch or hold the mother? Who initiates the contact? Under what circumstances do the mother and child make contact with each other?
2. *Exploration behavior.* Does the child move away from the mother and examine toys, people, or objects in the room? Does the mother encourage the child's exploration?

3. *Use of mother as a secure base.* Does the child make eye contact or verbal contact with the mother while playing with toys? What is the mother's reaction?

4. *Stranger reactions.* How does the infant respond to unfamiliar people who make contact with it? What emotional reaction can you see in the infant's face? Does the infant return to the mother?

5. *Separation distress.* If the mother leaves the immediate area, observe the infant's reaction. Does the infant protest or cry? What is the infant's reaction when the mother returns?

Stay long enough in the setting to collect the information you need to describe the attachment behavior. Summarize your observations and share it with your class. What insight did you gain for yourself in doing this activity?

4.2 *Parent–Child Communication*

During the first year of life, parents and infants communicate with each other through verbal and nonverbal behaviors. In this activity, you will be asked to observe the parent–child communication process in action. You will need to locate a couple with a young infant, between the ages of six months to a year. You may have a relative or friend who has a young child that you can visit to complete this activity. Or you may be able to locate a couple at a pediatrician's office or at a public outdoor park on a Sunday afternoon.

Once you have selected a family, observe the ways that the father and mother interact and communicate with the baby. Note the gender and approximate age of the child. Use the following questions to guide your observations:

1. What does the parent say to the baby? Record what each parent actually says to the child.

2. What sounds does the baby make? Does the parent repeat the baby's sounds or babbling?

3. Does the baby respond to the parent's talking by body movement or facial expressions?

4. How does the parent make contact with the child nonverbally? By touch or by eye contact?

5. Do the parents interact differently with the baby? How does the baby respond to each parent?

Summarize your findings; compare and contrast the mother's and the father's style of communication. What did you learn about how babies communicate with their parents? What new insight did you gain for yourself from doing this activity?

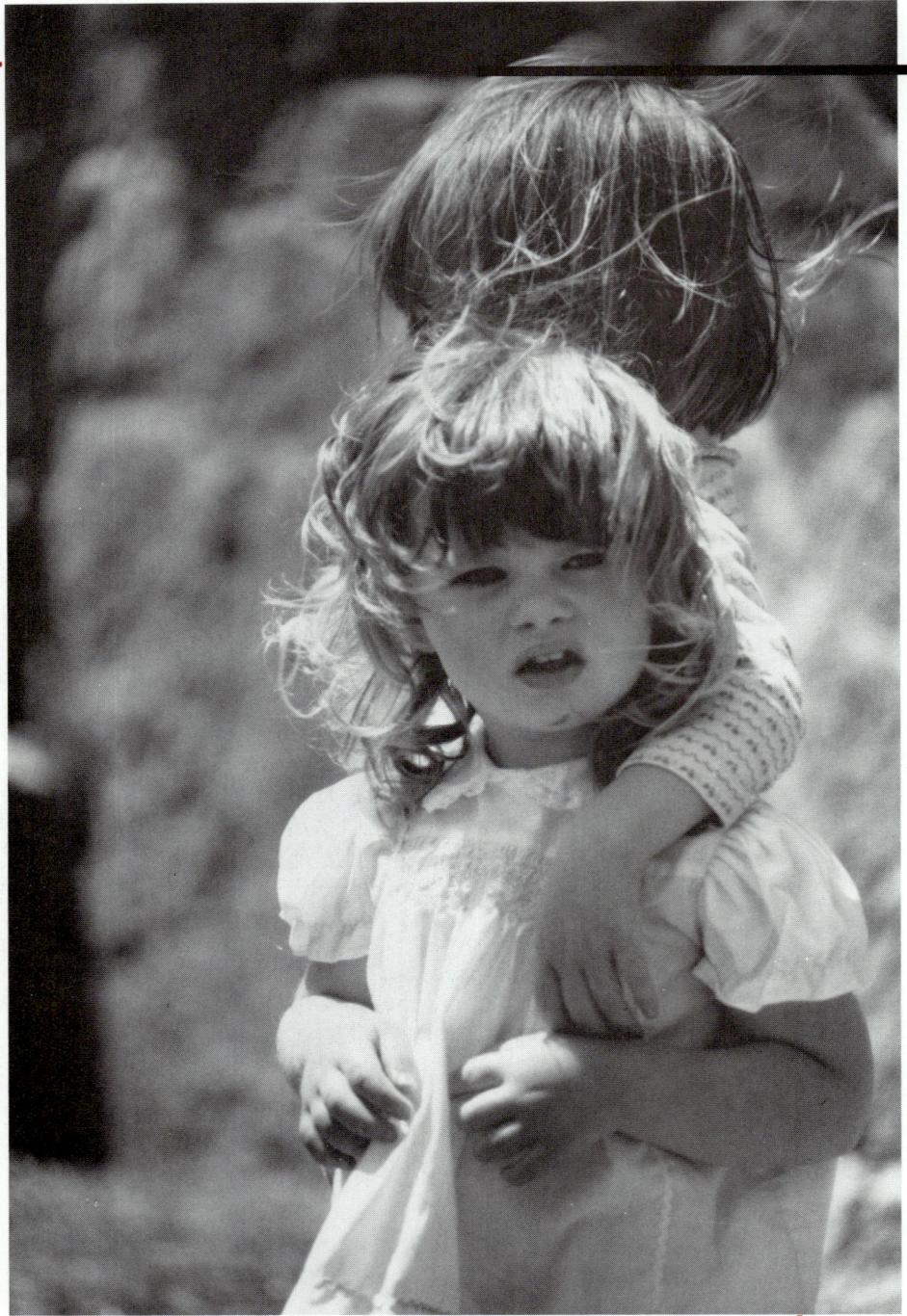

PART

TWO

Preschool Years

*T*he period of development from two to six years is a time from which most of us can recall some of our childhood experiences. It is a time when children acquire new social skills, when they learn to express themselves clearly, and a time when they discover their world and themselves. For many developmental theorists and researchers, the preschool years are seen as the time when the basic foundations for learning and personality are established. In the next two chapters, we will be examining the physical, cognitive, social, and personality changes that occur during the preschool years from two perspectives: What are the changes that typically occur, and how do these changes relate to overall development throughout the lifespan?

CHAPTER
5

Preschool Years: Physical, Cognitive, and Language Development

When Rachel was two-and-a-half years old, her parents decided that she was ready for nursery school. She was toilet-trained and seemed to have lots of energy that her mother thought would best be shared with other preschoolers.

Her nursery school teacher, Mrs. Riddering, was a kind and wise grandmother who had a basic rule for the children in the play yard: Before a child could use the swing set, she had to be able to get herself on the swing seat unassisted. By her third birthday, Rachel prided herself on the fact that she could indeed get herself on the swing.

Now, at age five, she was a delight to watch as she moved easily about the playground. Jumping on the swing, she pumped her way toward the sky, pretending she was in an airplane soaring into the clouds. Quickly getting bored, she thought, What can I do now?? Play on the jungle gym!! Using hands, arms, and legs, she climbed to the top of her make-believe mountain. When she got there, she called out to her friends, "Look at me! I want to sing my favorite song!!" Rachel, it seemed, atop her jungle gym, had gained new skills to broaden her understanding of the world and even herself.

In this chapter, we will learn about the physical, cognitive, and language skills that children acquire during the period of growth covering two to six years of age—the preschool years. We begin by describing the physical changes that punctuate the child's growth, including gross and fine motor skills. Then we turn our attention to how children understand their world, and the cognitive and linguistic skills they develop during this period. In the final section, we examine different types of preschool day-care programs and their influence on children's development.

Physical Development

Size and Proportion

Compared to the rapid growth in height and weight during the first two years of life, growth during the next four years appears to have leveled off. At two years of age, the average child has quadrupled its birthweight and increased its height by two-thirds. From age two to three, the average child increases by 4 pounds and three-and-a-half inches a year. Between four to six years of age the rate of growth has slowed down to two-and-half inches in height a year, while body weight increases to five to seven pounds a year. By age six, the average child weighs 48 pounds and is 46 inches tall (Watson & Lowrey, 1967). By age two-and-a-half for boys and one year, nine months, for girls, they have achieved one-half of their predicted adult height. This gender difference reflects a difference in predicted adult heights; for the most part, boys

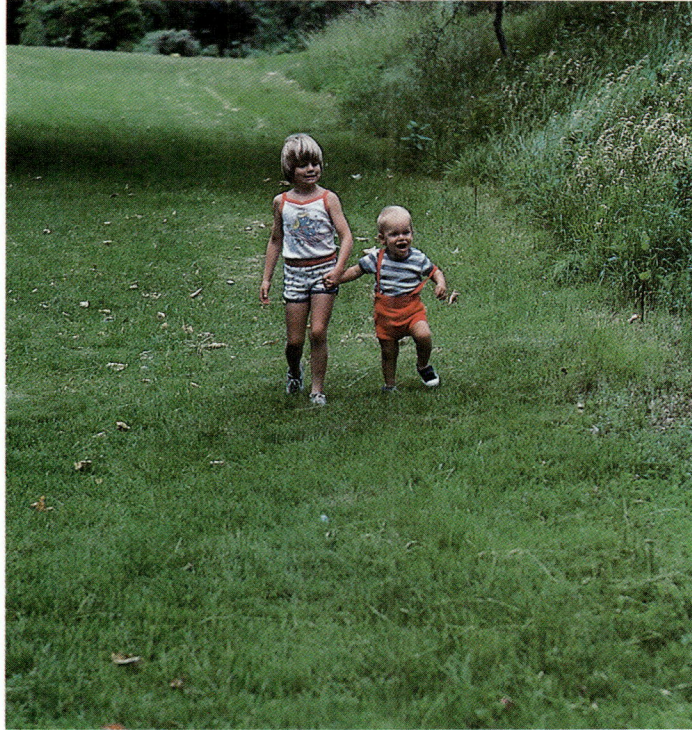

The difference in size and shape between the two-year-old and five-year-old reflects the physical changes that occur during the preschool years.

and girls are similar in their physical development (during the preschool years.) (See Table 5.1.)

Of course, there is considerable variation among children in their physical growth. After reviewing more than 200 studies of preschool-aged children around the world, Meredith (1978) concluded that much of this variation is tied to ethnic origin or nutrition. In the United States, black children are taller than Caucasian children, who are, in turn, taller than Asian–American children. Urban middle-class and first-born children are taller than rural

Table 5.1

Physical Growth, Ages 3 to 6 (Fiftieth Percentile)

Age	Height (Inches)		Weight (Pounds)	
	Boys	Girls	Boys	Girls
3	38	37¾	32¼	31¾
3½	39¼	39¼	34¼	34
4	40¾	40½	36½	36¼
4½	42	42	38½	38½
5	43¼	43	41½	41
5½	45	44½	45½	44
6	46	46	48	47

Human Development in Practice

Psychosocial Dwarfism

The little child was actually three years old, but to look at his size you would guess his age to be about one year. The boy's parents did not get along, and shortly after the boy had his first birthday, his father left. The tension and resentment the mother felt toward the father were now directed at the boy. She would scream at him, and verbally and physically abuse him without warning. The little boy was not only denied the love and care we normally expect a child to receive from its mother, but he was hated as well.

His small size and retardation in growth might suggest that he was malnourished or suffering from a disease. Hospital tests, however, suggested otherwise. This child was the victim of growth retardation as a result of severe psychological stress, a condition known as **psychosocial dwarfism** or **deprivation dwarfism** (Gardner, 1972; Green, Campbell, & David, 1984).

The relationship between children's emotional environment and their physical well-being has been known for many years. Infants removed from or deprived of adequate mothering sometimes fail to thrive. Early studies of institutionalized and hospitalized infants, for example, yield several cases in which infants did not grow despite an adequate diet and hygiene.

Deprivation dwarfism results when the caregiver–child relationship is so seriously disturbed that the child's growth is retarded. The quality of the psychosocial environment can be described as a combination of two factors: (1) the lack of warm, positive nurturing from the caregiver and, at the same time (2) the presence of negative, hostile, and highly stressful caretaking (Green, Campbell, & David, 1984).

Psychosocial growth retardation is believed to be mediated by activity in the brain (Gardner, 1972). Extreme emotional deprivation and high levels of stress are registered in the higher centers of the brain. Messages are sent from the brain to the hypothalamus, which, in turn, regulates the pituitary gland. The pituitary gland regulates the release of somatotropin, a growth hormone (GH) that causes the body to grow. In some children, severe psychological stress stops the production of GH, thereby resulting in a slowdown or stoppage in growth.

The child who is a victim of deprivation dwarfism often begins to gain weight as soon as he or she is removed from the stressful environment. Usually the child is first hospitalized and tested to eliminate the possibility that the small size is the result of malnutrition or disease. Once in the new environment, without any medical, hormonal, or psychiatric treatment, the child promptly gains weight and often catches up to the normal size and weight appropriate to age and genetic background. If the child is returned to the stressful home environment, however, a rapid decline in growth rate usually occurs. In some cases, the treatment of deprivation dwarfism may involve permanently removing the child from the stressful home environment.

The occurrence of deprivation dwarfism emphasizes the impact that stress can have on a child's development. The rate of growth in children is influenced not only by the food and physical care they receive, but also by the emotional atmosphere in the home.

Psychosocial Dwarfism Failure to grow as a result of an impoverished social environment; also referred to as Deprivation Dwarfism.

lower-class and later-born children. Furthermore, Meredith found that children whose mothers smoked during pregnancy are on the average one-half inch shorter at age five than are children whose mothers did not smoke. A poorly nourished child can be expected to be smaller and to develop at a slower rate. It is also possible that a child who is experiencing extreme emotional stress may have growth retardation. (See Box, Psychosocial Dwarfism.)

Motor Coordination

Gross Motor Coordination

Although the changes in the child's motor development may not appear to be as dramatic as the changes in the first two years of life, the preschool-age period from two to six years is highlighted by increasingly more coordinated neuromuscular development. The child's large muscles and leg and arm joints are growing during this period, thus increasing their susceptibility to injury. Throughout the sensorimotor period of infancy, the child has been using its body and practicing body motions so that by age two and thereafter it has increasing skill and mastery of its body. Instead of walking with the side-to-side gait characteristic of the toddler, the preschooler walks more steadily and

Figure 5.1 Running styles of 18- and 36-month-old youngsters. Changes in body proportion as well as changes in coordination help account for the difference in styles.

Table 5.2

Motor and Manipulative Skills in Preschool-Age Children

General Ability	Specific Ability	Approximate Age of Onset
Running Running involves a brief period of no contact with the supporting surface	First run	2–3 years
	Efficient and refined run	4–5 years
	Speed of run increases	5 years
Jumping Jumping takes three forms: (1) jumping for distance; (2) jumping for height; (3) jumping from a height. It involves a one- or two-foot takeoff with a landing on both feet.	Jumps down from low object with both feet	2 years
	Jumps off floor with both feet	28 months
	Jumps for distance (about 3 feet)	5 years
	Jumps for height (about 1 foot)	5 years
Hopping Hopping involves a one-foot takeoff with a landing on the same foot.	Hops up to three times on preferred foot	3 years
	Hops from four to six times on same foot	4 years
	Hops from eight to ten times on same foot	5 years
	Hops distance of 50 feet in about 11 seconds	5 years
	Hops skillfully with rhythmical alteration	6 years
Galloping The gallop combines a walk and a leap with the same foot leading throughout.	Basic but inefficient gallop	4 years
	Gallops skillfully	6 years
Skipping Skipping combines a step and a hop in rhythmic alteration.	One-footed skip	4 years
	Skillful skipping (about 20 percent)	5 years
	Skillful skipping for most	6 years
Throwing Throwing involves imparting force to an object in the general direction of intent.	Body faces target, feet remain stationary, ball thrown with forearm extension only	2–3 years
	Same as above, but with body rotation added	3.6–5 years
	Steps forward with leg on same side as the throwing arm	5–6 years
	Mature throwing pattern	6.6 years
	Boys exhibit more mature pattern than girls	6 years and over
Catching Catching involves receiving force from an object with the hands, moving from large to progressively smaller balls.	Chases ball; does not respond to aerial ball;	2 years
	responds to aerial ball with delayed arm movements	2–3 years
	Needs to be told how to position arms	2–3 years

Table 5.2

Motor and Manipulative Skills in Preschool-Age Children (cont.)

General Ability	Specific Ability	Approximate Age of Onset
	Fear reaction (turns head away)	3–4 years
	Basket catch using the body	3 years
	Catches using the hands only with a small ball	5 years
Kicking Kicking involves imparting force to an object with the foot.	Kicks with leg straight and little body movement (kicks *at* the ball)	2–3 years
	Flexes lower leg on backward lift	3–4 years
	Greater backward and forward swing with definite arm opposition	4–5 years
	Mature pattern (kicks *through* the ball)	5–6 years
Striking Striking involves imparting force to objects in an overarm, sidearm, or underhand pattern.	Faces object and swings in a vertical plane	2–3 years
	Swings in a horizontal plane and stands to the side of the object	4–5 years
	Rotates the trunk and hips and shifts body weight forward; mature horizontal patterns	6–7 years

Adapted from: *Motor development experiences for young children* by D. L. Gallahue. New York: John Wiley & Sons, 1976, pp. 65–66.

is able to start and stop movements with ease. The two-year-old is likely to be clumsy, and spills and falls are a common occurrence. However, by five years of age, the child walks, runs, climbs, and jumps with grace. Skipping, walking a balance beam, and hopping on either foot are other milestones achieved by the end of this period (Figure 5.1). With practice in play, the preschool-age child masters the skill of throwing and catching a ball with increasing poise and accuracy. Even though preschoolers learn to control the movement of their large arm and shoulder muscles, they may not be able to throw a ball with a lot of strength or accuracy. This skill develops later in childhood. Overall, the preschooler's degree of mastery over his or her body is impressive.

Fine Motor Coordination

Fine motor skills involve the use and control of smaller muscles in the fingers and are harder for the preschooler to master than gross motor skills involving larger muscles. Imagine the difficulty you might have if you were asked to tie a shoe or write your name while wearing thick gloves. You probably would not be able to hold the pen or grasp the shoelace easily and would not be coordinated in your actions. The two-year-old has fat fingers, and the neurons in the fingers are not yet fully covered by myelin, the protective sheath. The result is that children have less neurological control over the fine muscles that help move the fingers. By four years of age, this myelinization is complete, and the result can be seen in the ease with which a four-year-old can use a crayon or pencil to copy a figure or write on the walls.

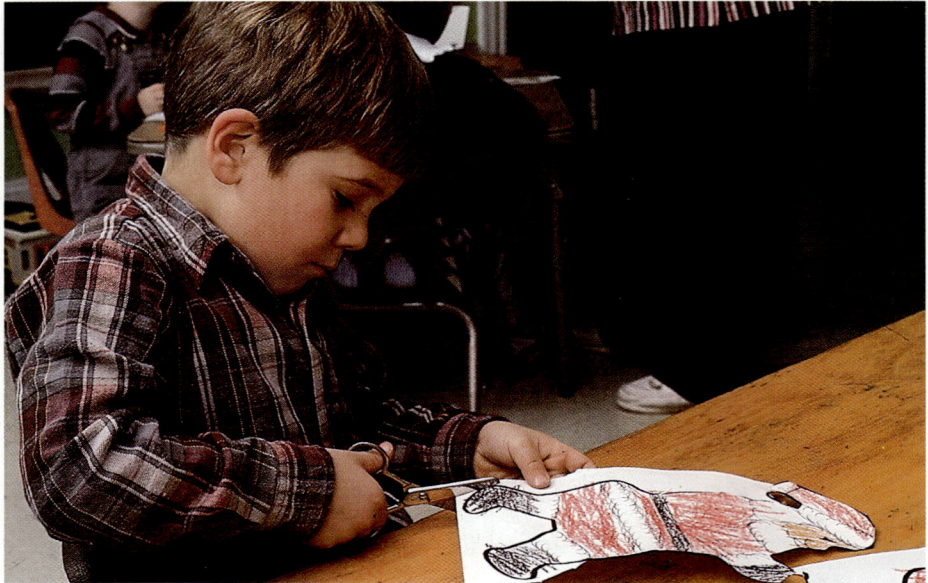

The use of scissors requires fine motor control and coordination which improves with growth and practice.

By age four, children can use child-size scissors, put together puzzle pieces, and make paintings with a brush. By age five, they can manage buttons and zippers, use a fork, spoon, and knife while eating; some may even be able to tie shoelaces. Much of the preschooler's skill in fine motor activities is a result of everyday practice in play. While maturation of the nervous system is necessary for the development of fine motor coordination, experience ma-

The preschool years are highlighted by increasingly more coordinated movement, especially seen in children's play activity.

nipulating objects helps children develop fine motor skills. The more opportunity children have to use utensils, crayons, brushes, and scissors, the greater the ease and proficiency they will have with these tools.

Handedness, the basic preference for the use of one hand over the other for manipulating develops during the preschool period. While most preschoolers develop a consistent preference for one hand by the age of five (Goodall, 1980), some children begin to rely on the use of one hand as young as eighteen months (Gottfried & Bathurst, 1983). Furthermore, girls who showed a consistent hand preference also tested higher on measures of intellectual development; this finding did not hold true for boys. About one in every 10 children is left-handed (Hardyck & Petronovick, 1977). Handedness appears to be under the influence of genetics or the prenatal environment rather than training. Thus, attempts to alter the child's natural preference may be frustrating and futile. The obvious difficulties for the left-handed child in writing and manipulating right-handed objects may be offset by the greater ambidexterity often found in left-handed children (Fischer, 1987).

Pause for Thought

It's one thing to recommend that two- and three-year-olds be given more opportunity to use utensils, crayons, paints, and scissors; it's another thing to put this recommendation into practice. What conditions would have to be met to ensure the safety and well-being of the child? How much adult supervision and instruction would be needed? Would all parents be able to provide their children with the opportunity to practice fine motor skills?

Cognitive Development

Piaget's Theory: The Preoperational Child

Even before the second birthday, children show signs of increased ability to adapt to the many different features of their world. Piaget's first stage of cognitive growth, the sensorimotor stage, describes how children understand their world through sensory and motor actions, or schemes. Their knowledge is limited to a here-and-now understanding of the objects and people with whom they interact. Toward the end of the sensorimotor stage, however, children begin to break out of their restricted view of the world by mentally representing these people and objects. *Deferred imitation,* imitation of actions in the absence of a model, signals the beginning of **symbolic representation.** In order for children to imitate a model's actions without a concrete example directly in front of them, they must be able to represent the model's action in some form of mental picture or image.

When children are capable of mentally representing events, objects, or people, they can think about these things without having to act on them using their senses or body. Mental representation, or **symbolic function,** is one distinguishing characteristic of the **preoperational stage of cognitive development,** the second major stage in Piaget's theory of cognitive development. This stage is called *preoperational* because it describes thought that occurs before children are capable of *operations*—the logical mental manipulation and transformation of information. The preoperational child can mentally rep-

Handedness A person's basic preference for the use of one hand over the other.

Symbolic Representation or Symbolic Function The ability to create and use symbols or images to represent something that is not present.

Preoperational Stage Within Piaget's theory, the second stage of cognitive development that begins around two years of age and ends around six or seven years; characterized by the emergence of representational thinking but the absence of logical reasoning.

resent information gathered through the senses, but does not yet integrate this information with other information in a logical manner. True symbolic thought involves both representation and operations (Piaget, 1952a).

Symbolic Function

The ability to mentally represent an event, referred to as *symbolic functioning,* enables children to increase their sphere of activity to include past and future events as well as present ones. The degree of correspondence between the children's mental representation and the real object or event can vary from a highly concrete mental picture of an object to a highly abstract representation in the form of a word. According to Piaget, children use two types of mental representation, or *signifiers.* **Symbols,** the first type, refer to mental representations that are unique, or idiosyncratic, to the child's own personal experiences; **signs,** however, refer to mental representations that are conventional, or socially defined and accepted by other people. At the beginning of this chapter, we met Rachel. When she climbed the jungle gym, for example, this action *symbolized* for her climbing a mountain. To someone else, her actions could have meant that she was climbing stairs or pretending to be a monkey. The most common *signs,* however, are words, that is letters and sounds accepted and understood by people who speak the language. When you read the words *jungle gym* you understand these signs to refer to a metal or wooden structure used by children for climbing and exercising. Other signs may include musical notations or mathematical symbols. The range of idiosyncratic symbols that children use is limited only by their imagination and experience. Symbols also bear some resemblance to the event or object they represent, such as a toy car that symbolizes a real car, or a shoulder shrug that says "I don't know."

Children readily acquire and use more and more complex symbols throughout the preoperational period. As we shall soon learn, children's use of words to represent thoughts about the past and future also increases with age. In fact, it was Piaget's view that the ability to mentally represent events precedes language development. Before children can learn to use words, Piaget believed they must first acquire their own symbol to represent a favorite toy or object.

Symbolic Play and Imitation

Many examples of the child's use of symbols to represent reality can be seen in children's play. Preschool-age children gradually spend more of their time in **symbolic play,** by pretending and engaging in make-believe. When Rachel and her sister play together, for example, they often pretend that they are mother and baby and use such props as a pillow to represent a bed and a cup to represent dinner. In this game of make-believe, the two children are imitating the actions of their parents. Again, mental representation allows them to imitate actions they observed sometime in the past. For example, when Rachel puts her hand on her hip and points her finger at her sister while saying "Now go to sleep, baby!" she is imitating the previous actions of her parents.

In symbolic play, the child can often work out conflicts encountered in the real world. By pretending to be "mother," Rachel is able to express some of her displeasure at the way people, namely the "baby," respond to her. She

Symbol   A gesture, drawing, or word that represents something else; according to Piaget, a type of mental representation that is unique to the child's experience.

Sign   A type of mental representation that is socially defined and accepted by other people.

In symbolic play children imitate actions and gestures they have seen in others. This young man is pretending to be a knight in shining armor!

Symbolic Play Play involving the use of symbols to represent reality such as make-believe or pretend games.

can structure her time as the "mother" in whatever way she chooses, which may not be so easy for her to do in reality. The use of pretense and fantasy in play increases with children's age so that by four years of age children not only incorporate fantasy into much of their play but they share their pretense in play with other children (Howes, 1985). Social pretend play requires greater cognitive skill because the child must simultaneously coordinate his or her actions with those of another child *and* keep up the action that maintains the pretence. Thus, Rachel must be aware of her sister's pretend role of "baby" and adjust her pretend role of "mother" to her sister's actions.

What Is Real?

When Rachel referred to the jungle gym as a mountain, it was clear to her that it was not *really* a mountain. But do preschoolers typically make the distinction between what is real and their mental representations? This is a question that has puzzled both parents and researchers.

Consider this example. Four-year-old Ben ran to his father and said "There's a baby dinosaur sleeping in my toy box!" His father thought he was telling a tall tale but Ben persisted: "I *really* did see a baby dinosaur!" The next day when his father was cleaning Ben's toy box he discovered a very large, dead June-bug beetle! What Ben actually saw was a dead bug; his mental representation was that it was a sleeping dinosaur.

Animism The tendency of young children to attribute animate characteristics to inanimate objects.

Realism The tendency to attribute real physical properties to mental entities.

Piaget (1929) claimed that children do not make a distinction between real and mental entities. Children will attribute feelings and intentions to objects that are not alive. Piaget referred to this characteristic as **animism**. For example, three-year-olds might say that the ocean is asleep or that a flower is bad when it wilts. **Realism** refers to children's tendency to attribute real physical properties to mental events. For example, a three-year-old believes that a dream is tangible and real like a picture in a book is real.

More recent researchers have challenged Piaget's views on childhood realism. Henry Wellman and David Estes (1986) tested the ability of three-to-five-year-olds to distinguish real objects (like a cookie) from a mental representation of the object (like thinking about a cookie). They found that children as young as three years old could make the distinction between real and mental entities. In a different study in which three- and four-year-olds were questioned about the differences between a rock, a person, and a doll, it was found that the children understood that people are alive but rocks are not (Gelman, Spelke, & Meck, 1983).

Children are also able to distinguish between appearances and reality. Three-year-old children understand the difference between the apparent identity of an object (e.g., a rock) and its real identity (e.g., a sponge shaped like a rock) (Flavell, Green, & Flavell, 1986). Although young children may sometimes be fooled by appearances, they have the ability to be able to tell the difference between reality and its appearance.

Pause for Thought

Some of the best read and loved children's books have an animal as their main character (e.g., Peter Rabbit, Paddington Bear, and Winnie-The-Pooh). Do you think that these books might add confusion to the preschooler's ideas about what is real and what is not? What advantages are there for children in fantasy stories?

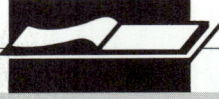

Human Development in Practice

Children's Drawings: What Do They Mean?

At age four, Sarah, the daughter of one of your authors, loved to draw. Her favorite pastime was to use her crayons and magic markers. One morning her mother noticed a face on the wall directly next to her bed. It was a happy face and was partially hidden by Sarah's bed pillow. When asked about her "mural," Sarah replied simply and sweetly, "Oh, that is my friend Molly."

Sarah had drawn a circle with a curved line, two smaller circles and several other lines. To her, these shapes and lines represented a face. The picture of the face is a symbol she used to represent her mental image of her friend Molly.

Young children love to draw—even on the walls. Drawing is an activity that children spontaneously initiate. People have long been fascinated by the way children busy themselves with a crayon. Does the drawing mean anything to the child? Why does the child draw? Psychologists have used children's artwork to gain insight into their mental world. Clinical psychologists and therapists use children's drawings, especially pictures they draw of themselves, to indicate children's emotional reactions and view of themselves.

Cognitive and developmental psychologists consider children's drawing to be an example of their mastery and use of graphic symbols to communicate their view of the world. For example, preschoolers typically draw objects and people in proportion to how important they are to them. The more important the object or person is to the child, the larger it is drawn. This character-istic is understood as an example of their ego-centric perspective.

At first, children's drawings look like scribbles, in the same away that their early attempts at language sound like babbling or gibberish. But with practice and greater fine motor control, they perfect their use of lines and shapes and use them to stand for things. If you ask a four-year-old, the child will usually tell you what the picture shows. By age five or six, a child will be able to draw a body showing head, arms, legs, hands, feet, face, hair, and clothes. Their drawings become more complex and detailed, paralleling their increasingly more complex cognitive skills.

Young children tend to draw what they know rather than what they actually see. Up to about the age of seven or eight years, children rely on mental images to guide their drawings. In one study (Freeman & Janikoun, 1972), children ranging in age from five to nine years were shown a cup that had a flower painted on it. The cup was positioned so that the children could not see the handle of the cup. When asked to draw what they saw, children under seven drew the cup with a handle and without a flower. Eight-and-nine-year olds, however, drew what they had actually seen—the cup with a flower, without a handle.

At age seven or eight, children can draw in perspective, with nearer objects being larger and objects in the background smaller. An important acquisition for children is the ability to see the

Limitations of the Preoperational Thinker

In many ways, preschoolers seem to be well along in their ability to think about things. However, preoperational children are somewhat of a puzzle to those who listen to their ideas. The way in which they combine ideas and draw conclusions is difficult for adults to understand because their thinking is not logical. Anyone familiar with Winnie-The-Pooh, a character from a children's book by A. A. Milne (1926), will recognize how Pooh's thinking is that of a preoperational child.

> One day when he was out walking, he came to an open place in the middle of the forest, and in the middle of this place was a large oak-tree, and, from the top of the tree, there came a loud buzzing-noise. Winnie-the-Pooh sat down at the foot of the tree, put his head between his paws and began to think.

Children's drawings improve with practice and with the development of fine motor skills. Children draw things as they know them rather than as they are seen, as is shown in a six-year-old's self-portrait and another six-year-old's drawing of family.

same scene from several points of view. At nine or 10, children can draw an object not only as they see it, but as it would be seen by someone on the opposite side of the object and to someone to their right or left.

Children's drawings can be used by teachers and parents as a way to understand the child's view of the world. By encouraging children to put their ideas onto paper, they may be able to discover characteristics of children that otherwise may be hidden. If, in fact, a picture holds a thousand words, then preschool children's drawings have quite a bit to tell us.

First of all he said to himself: "That buzzing-noise means something. You don't get a buzzing-noise like that, just buzzing and buzzing, without its meaning something. If there's a buzzing-noise, somebody's making a buzzing-noise, and the only reason for making a buzzing-noise that I know of is because you're a bee."

Then he thought another long time, and said: "And the only reason for being a bee that I know of is making honey." And then he got up, and said: "And the only reason for making honey is so as I can eat it." So he began to climb the tree. (pp. 5–6)

Pooh's thinking bears a resemblance to a rational thinker even though the scope of his thinking is limited to what he wants to accomplish.

Egocentrism The inability to distinguish easily between one's own perspective and any other perspective.

Egocentrism

One of the limitations of the preoperational child's thought processes is called **egocentrism,** the inability to distinguish easily between one's own perspective and other perspectives. Pooh cannot conceive of any reason for bees to make honey other than for him to eat it. The young child often acts as if other people see the child's world in the same way as he or she does. Four-year-old Molly would delight her parents by covering her eyes and saying, "You can't see me!" If she cannot see them, she assumes that their perspective is the same. Another common example of egocentrism is when children report that the sun or moon follows them when they walk. According to Piaget, preschool children are unable to take another person's viewpoint and hence are limited in their ability to display empathy toward another person's experiences. However, more recent research on empathy and altruism (Zahn-Waxler, Cummings, McKnew, & Radke-Yarrow, 1984), suggests that children as young as two years of age are able to show some sympathy toward a hurt or upset child. Furthermore, Lempers, Flavell, and Flavell (1977) reported that young children know that people have their own perceptions. When presenting a picture to another person, children as young as two-and-a-half years of age would turn the picture so that it faced the viewer rather than themselves.

Egocentric Speech Speech that is uttered when the child is alone or not making an attempt to communicate.

Young children also engage in **egocentric speech;** that is, speech uttered either when children are alone, or when they are with others but making no attempt to communicate their views to them (Piaget, 1926). Piaget observed that the proportion of egocentric utterances in a preschooler's speech decreases with increased social interactions. By the age of seven, the child is aware of the listener and adjusts speech so that the listener will be able to understand. Piaget interprets this change from egocentric speech to a socialized speech as evidence of the child's growing intellectual ability to mentally consider more than one viewpoint at a time.

Concreteness

A second limitation found in the preoperational child's thinking is the degree of reliance the child has on physical objects or events. Most of children's mental representations—symbols and signs—refer to concrete objects and events that they can mentally manipulate. For example, children may use a stick as a symbol in the same way they would a real gun. An older child or adult may use a word to symbolize the process of aggression, a more abstract event without any single physical referent.

Centration Piaget's term for the process of focusing attention on one detail or aspect of an object or event.

Centration

Children in the preoperational period also have a tendency to focus their attention on one detail or aspect of an event. This process is called **centration.** Because of centering on a particular perceptual aspect, preschoolers are often unable to accurately process information about an event. Piaget illustrated this characteristic of centering in his famous water-jar task, in which the child is presented with two identical glasses that have been filled with juice to exactly the same level. One is identified as the child's glass, the other as the experimenter's. After the child acknowledges that the two glasses contain the same amount of juice, the experimenter pours the contents of his or her glass into a tall, thin glass. When asked "Who has more juice to drink, or do we have the same amount?" the preoperational child will usually respond that the tall, thin container holds more juice because the child is centering its attention on

In Piaget's conservation of liquid task, the preoperational child confuses the height of the liquid with the amount of liquid and does not see the two amounts as the same.

the *height* of the juice in the glass. Another child may be centered on the *width* of the glass and respond that the shorter, fatter glass has more juice. In both cases, the children base their judgment on one dimension and not both height and width. If such children could *decenter,* that is, shift attention from one aspect of this problem (height of the liquid) to another (width of the glass), then they would be able to think the problem through and come to the conclusion that the glasses contain the same amount of juice. This knowledge—that so long as nothing has been added or subtracted, the amount of liquid in the jars remains the same—is referred to as *conservation of liquid.*

There is a practical application to be abstracted from Piaget's principle of conservation of liquid. Suppose you are giving a birthday party for your three-year-old and you do not have enough of the same sized clear plastic glasses for all the children. You supplement your supply of glasses with several different sized clear glasses. To insure that each child believes that the amount of juice in each glass is the same, be sure to have the same level of juice in each glass. However, if there is a seven- or eight-year-old at the party, you can be certain that he or she will grab the shortest and widest glass!

Irreversibility

Irreversibility The child's inability to mentally reverse his or her thinking.

Another limitation in the preschooler's thought processes is called **irreversibility,** the child's inability to mentally reverse its thinking, to go back to the point of origin. Older children and adults are able to solve the water-level problem described above because they can mentally go back through the steps and return to the point when both glasses contained the same amount of juice. They know that so long as no juice was added or subtracted, the glasses would contain the same amount. This knowledge is called **conservation.** In the water-jar task, preoperational children do not demonstrate conservation of liquid, partly because they center their attention on one perceptual attribute and partly because they do not reverse their thinking.

Conservation The recognition that characteristics of objects remain the same so long as nothing is added or subtracted.

Transductive Reasoning

Transductive Reasoning
Reasoning from the particular to the particular.

A final limitation of preoperational thinking can be seen in the way the child reasons. Instead of reasoning from the particular to the general (inductive reasoning) or from the general to the particular (deductive reasoning) as adults do, the preschooler engages in what Piaget called **transductive reasoning,** that is, reasoning from the particular to the particular. For example, Rachel has a dog named JoJo who is exceptionally friendly with children. However, Brutus, the dog down the street, is not so friendly. Using transductive reasoning, however, Rachel may think otherwise:

> JoJo is a dog (particular). JoJo is friendly (particular).
> Brutus is a dog (particular). Therefore, Brutus is friendly.

The preoperational child may be just as convinced of the soundness of its logic as an adult using deductive or inductive reasoning, even though such conclusions may be obviously inaccurate. In our quote from *Winnie-The-Pooh,* "the only reason for making honey is so as I can eat it" is another example of a conclusion reached by transductive reasoning. Because two events occur together, the preschooler thinks they are connected. That some events occur by chance is incomprehensible to the preoperational child. "Why does the moon shine?" "To light my bedroom at night when I am in it," may be a typical response. This type of thinking is both amusing and confusing to people far removed from the preoperational child's level of transductive reasoning.

While there are numerous examples of transductive reasoning in preschool-aged children, more recent research has demonstrated that when the problem was purely fictional and was not based on any practical world knowledge, four-year-olds could reason deductively (Hawkins, Pea, Glick, & Scribner, 1984). For example, four-year-old children could solve this problem:

Merds laugh when they are happy.
All animals that laugh don't like mushrooms.
Do merds like mushrooms? (No)

They could not, however, solve the following problem because the conclusion contradicts their daily experience with glasses:

Glasses bounce when they fall.
Everything that bounces is made of rubber.
Are glasses made of rubber? (Yes)

Pause for Thought ▬▬▬▬▬▬▬▬▬▬▬▬
Egocentrism, irreversibility of thought, centration and illogical reasoning are characteristics that are typically associated with preschoolers. Under what circumstances might these characteristics be used to describe an older child or an adult?

Conceptual Understanding

By the age of four, the child seems to be able to think about things beyond its own experience. The way the preschooler understands its world, however, is different from the way older children and adults conceptualize the world.

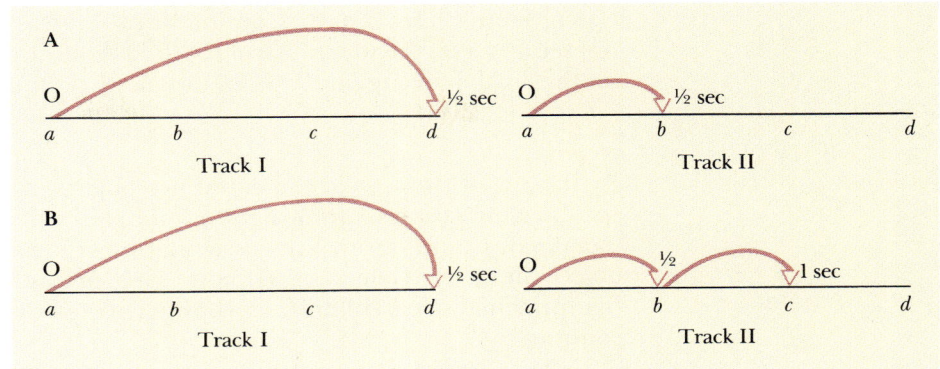

Figure 5.2 Understanding time. In A an object is moved from point *a* to point *d* in ½ second while a second object is moved from point *a* to point *b* in the same amount of time. Preoperational children describe the object that moved from *a* to *d* as taking longer. In B an object moved from *a* to *d* in ½ second is still judged to take longer when compared to an object moved from *a* to *b* to *c* in 1 second.

Gradually, over the period of time from two to six, the child develops a fuller understanding of the more abstract concepts such as time, number, and groupings.

Time

Although preschool-age children may use words reflecting an understanding of time, such as minute, hour, day, or week, their understanding of time is not yet complete because they often confuse the concept of time with the concept of space. Piaget (1927/1971) illustrated this confusion by using the following task. Two tracks are presented to the child. On Track I, a car is moved from Point A to Point D while simultaneously a second car is moved on Track II from Point A to Point B (see Figure 5.2a). Both cars travel for the same duration of time (.5 second), yet preoperational children are distracted by their perception of space and describe the car on Track I as "taking longer." Even when the car on Track II is moved twice (see Figure 5.2b), children still maintain that the car on Track I took longer than the car on Track II. Their perception that the first car is ahead of the second car influences their judgment of duration.

It is not until age 10 that the child understands that movements that begin and end at the same moment take the same amount of time, and that the objects can move over unequal distances in the same amount of time by varying the speed at which they travel.

Usually children comprehend time by referring to the movement of a clock's hands. In fact, many preschool and kindergarten teachers instruct children on time telling by calling their attention to the movement of the big hand and the little hand of the clock. For example, five-year-old Ray had asked his friend's mother to tell him when it was 5 o'clock since he had to go home at that time. Noticing that he was wearing a new and rather spectacular digital watch that displayed the hour clearly, the mother asked Ray why he did not just look at his own watch for the time. He replied quite simply, "My watch doesn't have 5 o'clock on it." In fact, it was only 4 o'clock, and he did not see any 5 on the watch! An older child or an adult would not be dependent on the spatial arrangement of the numbers on the clock to determine time.

Number

By the age of two a child can count two objects; by age four, four objects. By six, the child's capacity for assigning a number to a series of objects has greatly increased. Counting involves assigning objects a number and placing these objects in order. Gelman (1979) and Gelman and Gallistel (1978) identified five principles that children as young as two-and-a-half years of age use in counting.

1. *One-to-one correspondence.* Each item must be given one unique tag.
2. *Stable order.* The tags given must be from a stably ordered list.
3. *Cardinal principle.* The last tag given designates the number of items in the array counted.
4. *Abstraction.* Any set of items can be counted.
5. *Order-irrelevance.* The items to be counted can be tagged in any order, as long as each is tagged once and only once.

Even though young children use these principles, they may not apply them correctly or be able specifically to use these principles to justify their numerical actions. According to Gelman and Gallistel (1978), once these principles are acquired, children learn to skillfully count through practice. However, the development of skilled counting is dependent on the child not only acquiring but coordinating separate skills such as knowing how to tag items, how to group items, and when to stop counting (Wilkinson, 1984). These component skills are first acquired as separate skills and later coordinated to achieve accurate counting. In a series of studies in which preschool children were given counting tasks, it was found that when a task required few component skills, children performed well. When many skills were involved, their performance was lower and more variable (Wilkinson, 1984).

Piaget (1952a) explained the child's understanding of number concepts as a special type of conservation. Conservation, encountered earlier in the water-jar task, now occurs in a different form—when the child recognizes that characteristics of objects, such as number, remain the same so long as nothing is added or subtracted. In order to test the child's ability to conserve *number,* Piaget constructed a series of tests involving two parallel rows of objects, such as pennies (see Figure 5.3). At first, the two rows are the same length and have the same number of coins. After the child has examined the rows, the examiner shortens or lengthens one of them and asks the child, first, which has more coins in it and, second, explain why one row has more coins than another row. Preschool-age children appear to acquire conservation of number in stages (Brainerd, 1978). In Stage I, children's numerical judgments are dominated by the relative length of the two rows. For Rows A through D in Figure 5.3 children under five years of age report that the longer line has more coins. Children judging Lines E and F describe them as having the same number. By about age five or six, children enter Stage II, in which they now consider the density of the coins as well as the length of the rows in making a number judgment. The child in Stage II recognizes that denser means more and so judges denser lines in E and F to be more numerous. However, the

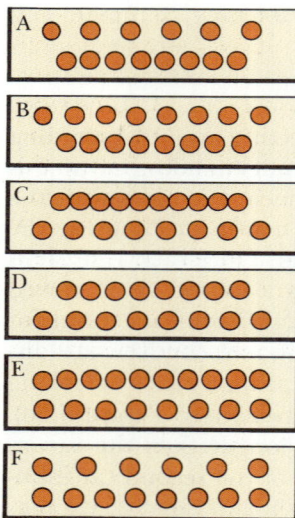

Figure 5.3 Children under five years of age generally judge the longer lines in Rows A through D to have more objects. Rows E and F are judged to have the same number by children five years of age. By age five or six, children are able to use both the length and density of the line to make a number judgment.

Stage II child does not coordinate density and length and thus judges Lines A through D on length alone. It is not until age six or seven that true number conservation is attained and children use both density and length to accurately judge and explain which lines have more coins.

If an older child or adult were given a similar task of judging Rows A through F, they would most likely count and or match the coins one-to-one in each row to determine which has more. Preschoolers do not spontaneously use matching and counting to judge number. Rather, they rely more on the gross perceptual features such as the length of the row. However, if the child is encouraged to use matching or counting to determine how many coins there are, the child can do so (Fuson, Secada, & Hall, 1983). Recent research has questioned Piaget's view that young children are limited to gross perceptual information in determining number. By altering the instructions on the Piaget number-conservation tasks, kindergarten-aged children were able to use counting and matching and not just the length of the line to determine number (Hudson, 1983).

Classification

Imagine that you entered your bedroom and found that all of the contents of your drawers had been emptied onto the floor. Immediately (after you got over the shock), you would probably begin to restore order by grouping different items together—the socks in one pile, shirts in another, underwear in a third pile, and so forth. Once you had separated the clothes, you might sort them even further by color—light colors in one pile, dark colors in another. The useful process of sorting objects into categories is called **classification** (Inhelder & Piaget, 1970). True classes have four properties: (1) Classes are mutually exclusive: No article of clothing can belong to the sock pile *and* the shirt pile. (2) The class is defined by its *intention;* that is, by the characteristics held in common by the members of the class, for example, "sockness." (3) A class is also determined by *extension;* that is, by the sum of all the members that meet the definition of the class. (4) *Intention must define extension,* meaning that the defining characteristics of a class determines what objects may be included within it. If only dark socks are included in one pile, then white socks would not be considered part of that class.

When young children are given a similar task of sorting a collection of objects into piles of objects that are alike or go together, they typically do not form true classes. Often, in sorting the objects, the child will begin by sorting on the basis of one characteristic, such as the color of the object, and then switch to a different criterion, such as shape, to finish. At other times, the child may put a collection of red things together but fail to include all the objects that share this color. When more meaningful objects are used in a classification task, preschool-age children will often group objects together on a thematic basis, by grouping together objects that are associated by events. For example, a man and a car may be grouped together because the man drives the car.

Children over seven years of age are more likely to form classes on the basis of truly defined, or *taxonomic*, categories. For example, a car and truck would be grouped together as both being vehicles (Markman & Hutchinson, 1984). Gradually, during the preschool period, children acquire the ability to group and even subdivide groups. However, it is not until the end of the preschool period that children are able to form true classes.

Classification The ability to sort objects into categories.

Pause for Thought

Suppose that you wanted to make sure that preschool-aged children had a better grasp on the concept of time. How would you do it? What type of activities would you plan for them to help them understand that time changes? Would children have to understand numbers before they could understand time?

Information Processing

Piaget's theory of cognitive development has underscored the limitations in the way young children make sense out of their world. While Piagetian theory has made significant contributions to our understanding of the stages in cognitive functioning, modern developmental psychologists are taking a different and more positive look at cognitive processes in children. Instead of seeking to identify the child's limitations, some researchers are asking the question: What capacities do young children have to process information? In seeking answers to this question, psychologists have been studying how children attend to information around them and how children remember this information.

Attention

As any parent or preschool teacher will tell you, as children grow, their ability to pay attention increases. Whereas three-year-olds are easily distracted by other events, six-year-olds can focus their attention on a game or book for 20 minutes to a half hour. Not only are older children able to look longer at something, the way they look becomes more efficient. Older children learn to focus on relevant or important features of a task and to ignore the irrelevant ones. As a result, older children generally need less time to select out important information. Furthermore, older children are better at selecting information because they seem to have developed strategies to guide their selections. In one study by Elaine Vurpillot (1968), children were given pictures of house windows to compare. A sample of these windows is found in Figure 5.4. As you can see, some of the windows in each house were the same, and some pairs of windows were different. The children were asked to say whether the pairs of houses were the same or different. What Vurpillot measured was the way in which the children came to their answers. By measuring the reflections in their eyes, she could tell what they were looking at, how long, and in what sequence. She found that children under the age of six years were not efficient or accurate in the scanning of the windows. They did not examine all features of the windows, whereas older children were more complete and systematic in their visual scanning.

Memory

Infants and young children are active processors of information. Their skill and efficiency in selecting what information to attend increases with age. So too does their ability to remember the information they have acquired. Memory is an important cognitive skill that actually involves two different types of memory. *Short term memory* (STM) refers to the temporary storage of information that is available for about 30 seconds. For example, telephone numbers are usually only remembered for the short time it takes to dial the num-

Children's attention is influenced by their interest in the material. As a result, most children's books are colorfully designed to capture children's interest and attention.

Figure 5.4 A pair of different houses (top row) and a pair of identical houses (bottom row) used in Vurpillot's study of children's attention.

ber. *Long-term memory* (LTM) accommodates a more permanent storage of information, and includes items that have been transferred from short-term memory. There are several ways to assess a person's memory. One way is to present various stimuli and ask the child to pick out the ones they have seen before. This process is called *recognition* memory. The second way to assess memory is to ask the child to *recall* specific information such as the name of a nursery school teacher. A recall memory task is much more difficult than a recognition task. For an item to be recalled, it must be first stored in long-term memory and then later retrieved. This process is a more complex process than recognition, which simply requires a match between what you've seen or known before and what is presented.

Infants and young children are fairly good at recognizing familiar stimuli especially visual stimuli (Fagan, 1982). On recognition tasks, two-year-olds average 81 percent correct and four-year-olds average 92 percent correct. However, on a recall task, two-year-olds only remembered an average 23 percent of the items in recall and four-year-olds recalled an average 35 percent of items (Myers & Perlmutter, 1978). Recall memory is harder than recognition memory at all ages. For the preschooler, part of their difficulty is due to the fact that they do not classify items for memory storage, thus making it more difficult to remember. Older children and adults realize that in order to remember a lot of information, you have to group items and then develop a way to rehearse and memorize these groups. Younger children have more trouble because they are not as efficient in processing material for memory.

Language Development

If you have ever tried to learn a foreign language you can probably appreciate the ease with which young children seem to acquire their first language. As an adult language learner, you would, no doubt, thrust yourself into the task of learning as many words as you could, while at the same time you would try to learn the rules for putting the words together in a sentence. You might also tackle pronunciation and comprehension of the spoken version of the language. The mastery of language opens many conceptual doors. For young children, the acquisition of language allows them to deal with objects, people, and events beyond their immediate experience. In fact, the onset of language skills marks the end of infancy and the beginning of early childhood.

Structure of Language

Phoneme   The basic unit of sound in a given language.

Language involves five components. The first component involves the production of the basic units of sound, or **phonemes.** Human beings are capable of producing sounds with their mouth and vocal cords and of discriminating these sounds through hearing. Each language is produced by a combination of a specific set of phonemes. In the English language, there are 45 phonemes; other languages use either more or less phonemes to produce the sounds specific to the language.

Morpheme   The smallest unit of meaningful sound in a given language.

Second, within each language community, these basic sounds or phonemes are combined and arbitrarily assigned meaning by the users of the language. The smallest unit of meaningful sound is called a **morpheme.** Thus the sound "Ma" when repeated becomes "MaMa," which means Mother in English and several other languages as well. A word is an example of a morpheme although endings and prefixes such as *s, ed, ing, pre,* and *un* are also examples of morphemes, since they add meaning to the root word. Many words are composed of more than one morpheme. The word *breakfast,* for example, is composed of two morphemes, *break* and *fast,* each of which carries a separate meaning. The meanings of the utterances of a language have to be learned.

Syntax   The rules of a language by which words and morphemes are combined to form larger clauses and sentences.

Semantics   The study of meanings of words and sentences within a language.

Pragmatics   The rules for using the language in a social context.

The third component of language involves the **syntax,** or rules by which words and morphemes are combined to form larger clauses and sentences. Syntax is sometimes referred to as the *grammar* of the language. Each language has it own set of rules that a person must master in order to understand and be able to produce the language.

The fourth component of language, **semantics**, refers to the rules governing the meaning of words and sentences. Often when people are stuck for the right word to use to convey their intended meaning they are struggling to find the semantically correct term. For example, consider the two sentences: "The writer dragged the pen across the paper," and "The writer glided the pen across the paper." Both of these sentences are syntactically similar and correct, yet they convey different meanings. Likewise, the sentence "The elephant spoke softly and carried a big stick" would be interpreted either as a joke or as a misprint because the meaning is not clear. As far as we know, elephants do not speak.

A last component of language involves **pragmatics,** the rules for using the language in a social context. This would include learning how to interpret the intended meaning of a grammatical statement through the intonation and gestures of the speaker. For example, "Have you washed your hands?" grammatically is a question that requires either a "yes" or "no" response. The *intended* meaning, however, is really a demand—"Wash your hands."

Language Acquisition

The beginnings of language acquisition are rooted in infancy through the many verbal and nonverbal exchanges infants have with their caregiver. Early cooing and babbling is replaced by one-word utterances at one year of age. In just a short period of time between ages two and six, remarkable events occur: Children not only increase their vocabulary to an average of between 8000 and 14,000 words (Carey, 1977), but they also master the basic grammatical rules or syntax of their native language. All children in different language communities around the world appear to go through identifiable stages in their acquisition of language skills. Table 5.3 lists the major language-development milestones in the first three years of life.

Semantic Development

One day the toddler is delighting relatives with one-word recitations, usually "Mama," "Dada," or "bye-bye" and before long, the size of the child's vocabulary has grown to hundreds of words. The rate at which children understand word and sentence meaning varies during the preschool period. Early in their semantic development, children slowly add new words to their vocabularies, but by the age of three, they rapidly acquire new words. (See Table 5.3.) *Active vocabulary* refers to the words the child can actually say and use, while *passive* or *receptive vocabulary* refers to the words that are understood, as indicated by the child's actions in response to the words. Passive vocabularies are usually larger than active vocabularies, even for adults, since recognition occurs earlier than production.

The first words children learn are largely used to represent people, objects (nouns), actions (verbs) such as "jump," "eat," "go," and states (modifiers) such as "fat," "dirty," and "there." Usually concrete, the words refer to immediate actions or objects in the child's experience. Later, prepositions,

Table 5.3

Language Development Milestones During the First Three Years

Birth	3 mos.	6 mos.	9 mos.	1 yr.	15 mos.	18 mos.	21 mos.	2 yrs.	27 mos.	30 mos.	33 mos.	3 yrs.

Startles to sharp noises

Interest in sounds, plays with saliva, responds to voices

First words understood

Birth	3 mos.	6 mos.	9 mos.	1 yr.	15 mos.	18 mos.	21 mos.	2 yrs.	27 mos.	30 mos.	33 mos.	3 yrs.
			(3)	(12)	(50)	(100)		(>300)		(>750)		(>1000)

Growth of receptive vocabulary (average no. of words understood)

First instructions understood ("wave bye bye," etc.)

First words spoken

Birth	3 mos.	6 mos.	9 mos.	1 yr.	15 mos.	18 mos.	21 mos.	2 yrs.	27 mos.	30 mos.	33 mos.	3 yrs.
					(0–5)	(10–15)	(20–25)	(200–275)		(400–450)		(800–900)

Growth of spoken vocabulary (average no. of words)

Birth	3 mos.	6 mos.	9 mos.	1 yr.	15 mos.	18 mos.	21 mos.	2 yrs.	27 mos.	30 mos.	33 mos.	3 yrs.
						(1)		(2)		(3)		

Length of spoken sentences (average no. of words)

such as "in" and "on," emerge to indicate locations. Personal, possessive pronouns such as "I," "me," or "mine" also appear at age two.

Gradually, with practice and exposure to new words, children enlarge on the types of words used. Sometimes the words are used to label different classes of objects children have mentally created. For example, when Rachel was two she referred to all grey-haired men as "Grampa." This use of one word to symbolize a larger class of objects than what adults normally intend with a word is called *overextension;* this may be the result of the child limiting the number of properties used to define the class (e.g., grey hair and male) as opposed to the large number used by adults. Other researchers believe that many overextensions may represent the child's early use of metaphors; that is, describing an object in terms of another object (Gardner, 1974; Mendelson, Robinson, Gardner, & Winner, 1984).

Young children also use words in overrestrictive fashion when they refer to a smaller set of properties than adults would use for the same word. This phenomenon is called *underextension.* For example, Rachel uses the word *blanket* to refer to the small, yellow blanket she regularly takes to bed with her. However, she does not use the word *blanket* to refer to any other blanket.

Table 5.4 ▰

Meanings Conveyed in Two-Word Utterances

Meaning	Example
Identification	"See doggie"
Location	"House there"
Repetition	"More milk"
Nonexistence	"Allgone cookie"
Negation	"Not doggie"
Possession	"Mommy hat"
Attribution	"BIG ball"
Agent action	"Baby run"
Agent object	"Daddy book"
Action location	"Sit chair"
Action object	"Put cup"
Question	"Where doll?"

Often a child will use one word to refer to a whole sentence or several thoughts. *Holophrases* are single words that convey whole thoughts. For example, when Rachel says "Dinner!", she is really saying "I'm hungry and want my dinner." The meaning of the one-word sentence is conveyed through intonation and accompanying gesture. Usually, the child's parents serve as translators of these holophrases for relatives or babysitters who do not understand the context of the child's remarks. Holophrases represent a gap between children's ability to formulate thoughts and their ability to put their thoughts into words and sentences.

By about two years of age, children communicate by combining two words. Linguists and psychologists debate whether the production of two-word strings represents the child's first sentence. By combining two words, children are able to express a much wider variety of thoughts. (See Table 5.4.) For example, "Dada byebye" may represent a shortened version of "Daddy has gone away." Two-word utterances such as this are examples of **telegraphic speech** since they resemble the abbreviated form used when sending a telegram. Even though two-word utterances carry much meaning, they do not conform to the grammatical rules that apply to sentences. Thus, it is difficult to determine whether children have acquired the rules of syntax from their two-word productions. They seem to appreciate the importance of word order (as in "Dada byebye" to mean "Daddy has gone" and "Byebye Dada" to mean "Goodbye Daddy"), however, children are not consistent in their use of word order. Furthermore, depending on the context, the same two-word utterance can have entirely different meanings. For example, "mommy's sock" was used by a child to refer to the mother's sock and in another context to refer to the mother putting the sock on the child (Bloom, 1970).

Telegraphic Speech Abbreviated speech containing only the most informative words (similar to the sentence structure used in sending a telegram).

Syntactical Development

As children move beyond two-word utterances to produce longer strings of words, they display a growing mastery of the grammatical rule within a language. Most children (and adults) acquire rules of syntax without actually being able to state the rule. For example, the four-year-old may be able to invert the auxillary verb in the sentence "Daddy is sleeping" to produce the question "Is Daddy sleeping?," yet not be able to actually state the grammatical rule.

As children learn the rules that govern the production of sentences, they tend to overuse these rules. They frequently produce new combinations of words, a process called **overregulation** because the child is attempting to make language more regular than it actually is. For example, Rachel has learned the rule to add *-s* to the end of a word to indicate more than one. She engages in overregulation when she pluralizes "mouse" and "foot" to produce "mouses" and "foots." The "errors" indicate that the child is learning the grammatical rules; the exceptions to the rules take longer for the child to acquire. Even though children may have demonstrated correct usage of a rule (such as creating plural words) in the past, they seem to regress to nongrammatical usage when they learn the rule for producing words. Thus, before Rachel learned the plural rule of adding "s" she would use the words "mice" and "feet" correctly. Parents and preschool teachers may be concerned about their children's seeming regression in language development. However, the loss in grammatical fluency is a short term one and seems to be a part of the process by which children acquire more sophisticated skill with their language. By about age seven, most children have learned the rules of their language *and* the exceptions to these rules and no longer overregularize

Around the age of three-and-a-half years, children are able to reorder the words of a sentence to express a new idea. Children now develop longer sentences, and they now can construct a negative sentence by rearranging the order of the words in a sentence (e.g., "Daddy is not eating" or "Why is the baby eating?"). In the earlier stages of sentence construction, the child conveyed a question or negation by intonation or by adding a word to the front or end of the sentence, as in "No daddy eat" or "Baby eat?"

In order to construct negations and questions, the child must use **transformational rules,** which allow the child to translate the basic meaning of a sentence into a grammatically correct sentence. For example, the rule for negation involves moving a negative word such as "no" or "not" to a position in front of the verb. Yes/no questions are created by either moving the first auxiliary verb of a sentence to the initial position or, if there is no auxiliary verb, adding one. For example, "Baby is sleeping" becomes "Is baby sleeping?" or "Anne runs" becomes "Does Anne run?" "Wh" questions such as why, what, where, or when are formed by adding a "wh" word to a yes/no question—for example, "Why does Anne run?" and "Where is baby sleeping?" Children learn the transformational rule for yes/no questions before they learn the rule for "wh" questions.

Children also learn how to use the active and passive voices. They have learned the basic subject-verb-object (SVO) order of an active sentence but have difficulty interpreting a passive-voice sentence. For example, consider the following two sentences.

1. The dog chased the cat. (*active voice*)
2. The cat was chased by the dog. (*passive voice*)

Overregulation The child's tendency to over-use the rules of a language to produce new and non-grammatical combinations of words.

Transformational Rules Rules that allow the child to translate the basic meaning of a sentence into a grammatically correct sentence.

Three-year-olds, when asked to select a picture that depicted sentence 2, selected the picture of a cat chasing the dog. The passive voice violates the normal S-V-O order in a sentence, and hence the children are confused. By five years of age, children are able to interpret passive-voice sentences (Bellugi, 1970).

Language skills increase when children learn to deal with increasingly more complex and sophisticated sentence structures. As they get older, children increase the length of their utterances and are able to combine sentences together and embed parts of sentences in other sentences. For example, a child may say "My teddy that Nana gave me is brown and fat," thus constructing a sentence containing two ideas: (1) My Nana gave me a teddy, and (2) My teddy is brown and fat. By about age six, children are able to construct simple compound sentences using the conjunction *and*—"Mary hit the ball and Johnny ran."

Theories of Language Acquisition

Psychologists and psycholinguists have long debated the question "How does language develop?" One answer to this question, *the empirical approach,* emphasizes reinforcement and imitation as the basic processes for acquiring language skills. B. F. Skinner (1957) believes that language is a verbal behavior and is acquired in the same way that all new behavior is acquired, by its consequences (reward and punishment). If a little girl accidentally says something approximating the word "cookie" and receives a cookie, or says "dada" and receives a warm welcome from her father, she is more likely to continue her language efforts. By imitating her parents' speech, she receives further encouragement.

Although the quality of the language environment surrounding the child is an important factor in language development, it does not explain how children can and do say things they have never heard before. The two-and-a-half-year-old is likely to make up sentences such as "Daddy hurted self" and "Kitty goed home," which are clearly not the result of pure imitation, but instead, reflect overregularization. Furthermore, most parents reward children for the truthfulness of their statements rather than their grammatical correctness (Brown, 1970). In response to "Kitty goed home," the parent is likely to respond with agreement if, in fact, the cat went home.

Another approach, *the nativist,* or *rationalist, approach,* views language development as a natural, biological consequence of physical maturation. One advocate of this view is Noam Chomsky (1968), who maintains that humans are born with an innate tendency to acquire language, just as they possess an innate capacity to learn to walk. Chomsky believes that all languages share certain basic structural characteristics. Even though languages differ on the surface (different words, word orders) they have a common universal grammar that consists of rules and principles for generating sentences and meaning. Likewise, people have inherited the biological structures (namely the central nervous system) to process these common linguistic features. Chomsky called the mental blueprint for acquiring language the *language acquisition device,* or LAD. A little boy, for example, hears language spoken and, as he does, the LAD processes the information and helps him gain an understanding of the vocabulary and rules of spoken language. Chomsky argues that without this inborn capability, the child would be unable to process the sentences heard. The LAD permits the acquisition of grammatical rules that allow the child to translate and later produce sentences. As the brain matures, children acquire greater skill in understanding and producing language.

The view that the capacity for language is innate has been supported by Eric Lenneberg (1967), who suggests that language development parallels neurological changes that occur as a result of maturation. He points to the fact that children of all cultures learn language at about the same age and make the same kinds of errors in their language production. Lenneberg points to the changes in the organization of the brain around three years of age that aid the child in its ability to understand as well as produce the language heard. The rapidness with which children master their language between two and three years of age is hard to explain without reference to changes in children's overall neurological capacity to process information. *Interactionists* (Berko, 1958; Brown, 1973; Ervin, 1964) have accepted the nativist view of language development but have focused on the ways in which children learn the rules of the language. These theorists reject the empirical view that the child acquires language simply by imitation and practice. They argue that the child who correctly imitates an adult by saying "The kitty went home" does not necessarily display a comprehension of grammatical rules. However, when saying "Kitty goed home," the child has demonstrated mastery of the specific grammatical rule: Add *-ed* to form a past tense of the verb. Interactionists focus their study of language development on the way children acquire concepts and meanings attached to words. Although innate biological mechanisms such as LAD may guide language development, interactionists place equal importance on the role of experience.

A fourth view of language acquisition is called the *cognitive approach* because it is believed that language is a direct result of cognitive development. Piaget (1926) viewed the child's ability to mentally represent actions as the necessary foundation for language. Once having formed a mental scheme, the child can apply a linguistic label to it. This ability to symbolically represent events emerges at the end of the sensorimotor period at age one-and-a-half to two years, just the age at which children begin to master language. Vygotsky (1962) presented a different view from Piaget. He believed that thought and language and speech originate from two separate roots, a *preintellectual stage* and a *prelinguistic stage*. At about age two, these two lines of development meet, and language and thought merge. At this point, what children think influences what they want to say. Further, language helps them to pull together and communicate their thoughts. This union of language and thought helps to explain the child's rapid use of new words at a time when curiosity about people and things is so intense. Overnight, it seems that a child has learned to talk *and* has so much to say. While Piaget believed that language is a manifestation of cognitive development, Vygotsky believed that they develop separately.

Pause for Thought

What aspects of a culture or community would be changed if the primary language of that culture were to change? Can a language be imposed on people or do people create their own language?

Bilingualism: Are Two Languages Better than One?

Today, many children grow up in families and communities in which two languages are spoken. In the United States, English is the major language, but children may also hear Spanish, Chinese, Hebrew, Italian, Polish, French, Vietnamese, or Arabic. Children may be exposed to Spanish or French on television. In Rachel's nursery school, she was taught to count in Spanish and to name colors in French.

Before 1962, parents, teachers, and researchers thought that exposing children to two languages would only confuse them and delay their language acquisition. But research by Peal and Lambert (1962) shifted the view of bilingualism from a negative to a positive one. While previous studies had shown that children who could speak two languages did not perform as well on intelligence tests as children who spoke one language, Peal and Lambert found just the reverse to be the case. Bilingual children had higher cognitive abilities than monolingual children. Their sample included bilingual children who were "balanced," that is, children who knew two languages equally well. Earlier studies compared monolingual children with bilingual children who knew little English but had greater familiarity with a second language. Monolinguals and bilinguals differ not only in the degree of familiarity with their languages, they differ in the socioeconomic and educational level of their parents. Differences in cognitive abilities between monolinguals and bilinguals may reflect differences in these social variables as well as differences in language learning.

What are the cognitive advantages to young children in learning two languages? Bilingual children who acquired their second language from an early age were more flexible in their use of labels for words (Oren, 1981). They were more familiar with coding by stems and could easily switch from one coding system to a different one. Compared to monolingual children, bilingual children are more creative storytellers but have smaller vocabularies in both languages (Doyle, Champagne, & Segalowitz, 1978). Some researchers (Diaz, 1985; Hakuta, 1987) believe that learning two languages helps children learn *about* languages. They become more flexible in thinking because they learn to see the world from two different perspectives and from two different cultures. They learn that language is arbitrary, that the name of an object can be changed so long as other people agree to rename the object. For some children, learning two languages may also add to their sense of self-esteem and help them learn about their cultural heritage. Thus, it appears that learning two languages is not a liability, and for children who learn two languages simultaneously, it could prove to be an asset.

Preschool and Day-Care Programs

In 1982, 48 percent of children under the age of six were enrolled in some type of preschool or day-care program (Clarke-Stewart, 1982). Part of the reason for this large enrollment is because more than half of the mothers with preschool-age children are working either part- or full-time. Economic changes in the family, divorce, and separation have resulted in more parents leaving the day-to-day care of their children to other people. Twenty years ago a parent would have few alternatives for child care or preschool educa-

With an increase in the number of mothers in the workforce, more preschool-age children attend some type of nursery or daycare program.

tion. Today, however, preschool and day-care programs are more abundant. Many large cities now offer franchised day-care centers to accommodate the working parents. Other nonworking parents have found a growing variety of preschool programs that offer different services and are designed to accomplish a variety of aims. The impact of these various preschool programs on the child's immediate and long-term development is an issue of concern, research, and debate (Belsky & Rovine, 1988; Belsky, Lerner, & Spanier, 1984; Blum, 1983; Etaugh, 1980; Fraiberg, 1977; Kagan, Kearsley, & Zelazo, 1978; Ruopp, Travers, Glántz, & Coelen, 1979; Scarr, 1984; Zigler & Gorden, 1982).

Types of Programs

Preschool programs can be divided into two broad categories: nursery school and day care. The choice of preschool program is an important one for parents and children and depends upon the individual needs of the family and the availability of programs in the community.

Nursery Schools

Most nursery schools generally offer a program of educational enrichment on a basis usually limited to three to five half-days a week. Children typically attend nursery school after they have reached age three and have been toilet-trained. While the aims of nursery school vary depending on the philosophy of the school, most nursery schools include preparation for kindergarten and elementary school as part of their curricula. There is an emphasis on teaching appropriate social skills and enriching the child's intellectual experiences.

In the United States today, over a million preschool children attend some form of nursery school (Clarke-Stewart & Gruber, 1984). Most nursery school teachers are college educated and specifically trained in child development. Some nursery school programs, called cooperative nursery schools, are operated by parents who organize and assist in the operation of the school. Parents take turns working in the school either as an assistant to the teacher or by building or repairing school equipment or facilities.

For parents who work, a half-day, part-time, or cooperative nursery-school schedule may be practically impossible for them to manage. As an alternative to nursery schools, many parents turn to day care for their preschool-age children.

Day Care

Day-care programs are designed to provide daylong care on a year-round basis. Three types of day care are typical. In *home day care*, children receive care in their own home by someone other than a relative. Typically, the home day-care setting is not child oriented. There are no special activity areas and few planned activities or little, if any, structured program. The daily activities are informal and vary from day to day. Usually there is an older adult sitter who takes care of one or two children so the adult-to-child ratio is high. As a result, the child in this type of day care has limited experience interacting with other children. Most of the children whose parents work receive care in their own home (Clarke-Stewart, 1982).

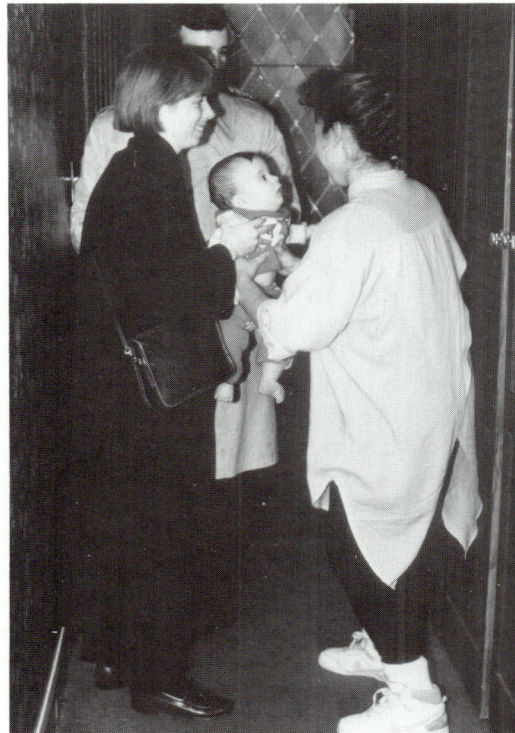

Most of the children whose parents both work are cared for by a babysitter who comes to their home.

In *family day care*, children are cared for in small groups of up to six children in the private home of another person. The women who run family day-care centers are usually younger than the home-care sitters and usually have not had any professional experience in child care (Clarke-Stewart & Gruber, 1984). Nationally, about 35 percent of all employed women use family day care to provide for their children's care. Typically, the center is a home that has been rearranged to accommodate children (e.g., extra playrooms). Children have contact with other children, who usually are of similar ethnic and socioeconomic background.

The third type of care is the *day-care center*, a licensed facility providing care to 13 or more children on an all-day basis, five or more days a week, year-round. In all types of day care, children's ages range from birth to 13 years of age, with most of the children preschool age. Day-care centers are used by about 13 percent of working mothers with preschool children in the United States (Clarke-Stewart & Gruber, 1984). The day-care center is child oriented both in its activities and physical facilities. In many ways, day-care centers are similar to nursery schools. The teachers are usually trained in child care, there are several children and more than one adult is involved in the care of the children. The major difference between nursery schools and day care is the time that children spend in the center. Children in day care spend on average eight hours every day, while nursery schoolers spend fewer than three hours a day in the center.

Pause for Thought

When most of you were babies (in the 1970s), most preschoolers were cared for in their homes by their mothers. Today, the situation has dramatically changed. Preschool programs and day care are no longer seen as unusual or a last resort for working mothers. What impact does this shift in attitude and behavior have on the quality of preschool and day-care programs? What are the possible long-term effects you might expect from extensive preschool experiences?

Evaluating Preschool Programs

Researchers began to focus their attention on preschool and day-care programs in the mid-1970s when the number of preschoolers enrolled in out-of-home care increased dramatically. Initially, the research focused on one issue: Is day care bad for children? (Belsky, 1984). To answer this question, researchers studied the effects of rearing outside the family on children's intellectual, social, and emotional development. The popular belief at the time was that the home was the best place to raise young children and the mother was the best person to do it. So the research studies were designed to find out what negative effects there were from day-care and preschool programs.

According to Jay Belsky (1984), current research on day care is directed toward answering the question: Under what conditions do children fare best in day care? This focus is built on a number of studies supporting the conclusion that day care is *not* bad for children. Instead, a more detailed examination is made into what specifically is *good* about day care and under what conditions.

Head Start programs provide preschool-age children with skills that they will need to do well in school.

Both the issue of the effects of day care on development and the issue of the conditions needed for quality day care present some difficulties. Most of the studies conducted on preschool programs have been conducted using children enrolled in day-care rather than nursery school. This occurs because children in day care attend on a more regular basis and because researchers generally have easier access to day-care centers for research purposes due to the fact that many of these centers are located in or sponsored by universities. The conclusions drawn from studying children of college-educated parents, however, may not apply to all children.

Another problem with studying the effects of preschool programs is deciding what behaviors to look at and when. Most of the studies look at the immediate or short-term impact of preschool and not the long-term effects. Yet the impact of preschool programs may not be felt immediately. Consider the example of the Head Start program.

Begun in the 1960s to enrich the disadvantaged child's knowledge of basic skills before enrollment in public school, Head Start programs provided preschool-age children with experiences they were deprived of in their home environments—being read stories, using scissors, playing with blocks, puzzles, and shapes, writing with pencils, playing pretend games, learning songs, and so on. Most of the evaluative studies that compared Head Start children with neighborhood children who were not enrolled in the program found some immediate gains in IQ and other school-related skills. However, these initial gains did not persist when the children entered school. In a large-scale follow-up study, the long-term effects of 14 different programs similar to Head Start were examined. Even though the programs varied in the way they were implemented (e.g., degree of parental involvement, amount of contact with the child), they all had positive long-term effects, some lasting as long as high school (Lazar & Darlington, 1982). Apparently, the impact of Head Start incubated over the intervening years.

Effects on Development

Prior to 1980, most of the research on the developmental effects of preschool programs had used high quality university-sponsored demonstration programs (Etaugh, 1980). More recently, researchers have extended their study of preschool effects by studying infants in a variety of nonmaternal care programs (Belsky & Rovine, 1988). The major concerns have been the effects of day care on (1) the emotional bond to the mother, (2) the child's cognitive skills, and (3) the development of social skills.

Emotional Bonds

Several studies have examined the attachment behavior of children reared at home with those of children reared in day-care centers. Most of these studies have found that day care does not disrupt the child's emotional bond to the mother (Belsky & Steinberg, 1978). Jerome Kagan and his associates (1978) created a high-quality day-care center to service 33 infants who enrolled in the program as infants between the ages of three to five months. These infants were studied over a period of two-and-a-half years. The authors concluded on the basis of data collected on these infants that: "Day care and homereared infants did not differ in their emotional responses to their mothers. Although some children may display some distress at being separated from their mothers at nursery school or at the day-care center, this reaction appears to be transient and not different from the distress reaction of homereared children." When the supplementary child-care arrangements are stable and of a reasonable quality, infants and young children's emotional ties to their mothers are not disturbed, or diminished (Belsky, 1984). However, in a more recent longitudinal study of one-year-old infants and their attachment behavior toward their mothers and fathers, Belsky and Rovine (1988) found that extensive nonmaternal and nonpaternal care in the first year resulted in insecure attachment patterns. The researchers used Ainsworth's Strange Situation to measure the infants' reactions to their fathers and mothers upon reunion. They found that infants who received 20 or more hours of care per week displayed more avoidance of their mothers on reunion. Sons whose mothers were employed on a full-time basis were more likely to be insecurely attached to both parents.

Cognitive Skills

Two secondary aims of some day-care programs are to enrich or enhance the child's awareness of the world and to stimulate the development of the child's cognitive skills. Most of the studies on day care indicate that for middle-class children good-quality nonmaternal care does *not* appear to have either an adverse or beneficial effect on the child's intellectual or cognitive functioning (Belsky & Steinberg, 1978; Etaugh, 1980).

In a study using a sample of day-care centers more representative than the overused high-quality, university-based programs, McCartney (1984) found that verbal interactions with day-care workers enhanced children's language skills. Other studies (Ramey & Mills, 1977; Ramey & Smith, 1977) have found that high-quality, educationally oriented day-care programs offered to children from low-income families prevent the decline in intellectual performance frequently found in home-reared children from poor families. Further, there is evidence that community-run as well as university-based day-care programs may also help prevent intellectual deterioration among poor children (Golden, Rosenbluth, Grossi, Policare, Freeman, & Brownlee, 1978).

Social Skills

Most of the programs for preschool-age children have the development of social skills as one of their major aims. The results of many studies show that day-care children interact more with their peers than do home-raised children. These interactions include both positive and negative aspects (Belsky, 1984; Belsky & Steinberg, 1979). This is especially true for children who begin day care before the age of two. While the day-care children were more likely to share their toys, they also engaged in more fights than home-reared children. In fact, children who enter day care before the age of two are reported to be more aggressive and less cooperative with adults than later-entering children (Haskins, 1985; Largman, 1976). These behaviors may be the result of several factors, such as the length of stay in the center, the quality of the home environment, and the cultural context.

Conditions for Quality Day Care

Research on day care indicates that it is not bad for children. But not all day-care programs are the same. There are considerable differences in quality among the many preschool programs available today.

High quality day-care programs are characterized by the following:

1. Low child-to-adult ratio. Four to six infants and toddlers per adult and eight to 10 three- to five-year-olds per adult (Ruopp & Travers, 1982).
2. Day-care workers who are trained in childhood education (Ruopp & Travers, 1982).
3. Responsive, affectionate, and stimulating day-care workers (Howes & Rubenstein, 1985).

In one study (Howes & Olenick, 1986), children who attended high-quality day-care centers have been found to be more compliant than children enrolled in low-quality day care. Researchers also found that parents who placed their children in low-quality day-care centers were less involved and interested in their children being compliant when compared to the parents of children enrolled in high quality day care centers. This finding suggests that the quality of care a child receives in the home may indirectly affect the quality of care the child receives in day care. After reviewing the research on the developmental effects of day care and the conditions for quality day care, Jay Belsky (1984) concluded that it is not where the child is reared that is so important but how the child is treated. The day-to-day experiences provide the key influences on development.

Summary

The rate of growth levels off during the preschool years as the child's body approximates the shape and proportion of an adult. The child's body grows in length, most of which is growth of the legs.

The gross motor skills become more coordinated, allowing the child to run, hop, skip, and jump. Taking longer than the gross motor skills to develop, fine motor skills involve the use of the fingers and small muscles. By four years of age most children are able to handle tools and toys requiring fine motor precision.

One of the major differences between Piaget's sensorimotor period and the preoperational period is the development of the symbolic function. Preschool-age children are able to mentally represent their experience by means of language, gestures, deferred imitation, drawing, and symbolic play.

Preschoolers are able to make the distinction between physical reality and mental reality. They can distinguish between what an object actually is and how it appears.

Preoperational thought is characterized by several limitations. The child is egocentric (unable to take a point of view other than its own), centers its attention on one perceptual attribute at a time, and is unable to use abstract symbols. Also, the child cannot mentally reverse its thinking and engages in transductive reasoning.

Preoperational children equate time with space and distance. Although most children can count by age five, they have difficulty mastering conservation of number because they understand number in terms of gross perceptual cues such as density or length. Although preschool children can group objects together, they do not form true classes based upon logical properties.

Preschoolers attend to information in a haphazard manner and are distracted by irrelevant stimuli. They are not selective about what they notice.

Young children's memory is limited by their inability to group items together and to use rehearsal to process the information.

Language development involves the acquisition of sounds or phonemes, learning the meanings of words, and acquiring syntax or the rules for combining words into sentences. Children begin to acquire language at age two, and by six have mastered the essentials of their native language. Psychologists and linguists have developed several different theoretical approaches to understanding language acquisition.

Preschool and day care are increasingly common experiences for young children. Overall, research on day care indicates no adverse effects on development, although more recent studies suggest that infants' attachment to parents may be adversely affected. High-quality day-care programs are staffed with trained caregivers who interact positively and frequently with the children.

Further Readings

Caplan, J., and Caplan F. *The early childhood years: The 2 to 6 year old.* New York: Putnam, 1983.
This book is a comprehensive guide to children's physical, cognitive, social, and emotional growth during the period from two to six years. The authors present an updated account of the capabilities of young children and offer practical suggestions for enhancing the child's development. Numerous photographs and charts are included.

deVilliers, P., and deVilliers, J. *Early language.* Cambridge, MA: Harvard University Press, 1979.

Language acquisition from birth to six years of age is detailed by this husband-and-wife team who are experts in the field of child language. Numerous examples of children's speech highlight this authoritative text.

Donaldson, M. *Children's minds.* New York: Norton, 1978.
The preschool-age child is capable of more rational thought than educators had previously thought possible. The author supports this thesis with examples of how the preschool child learns in a real-life context. A critical view of the transition to the classroom is supplemented with strategies that parents and schools can use to help children.

Phillips, J. *Piaget's theory: A primer.* San Francisco: Freeman, 1981.
A clear, concise account of Piaget's theory of intelligence. Chapters on each period of cognitive development from birth to adolescence are highlighted by examples of children's thought. An extensive bibliography and notes are included.

Scarr, S. *Mother Care/Other Care.* New York: Basic Books, 1984.
Written by a mother and psychologist, this book examines various child-care options in light of child development. Results from child-development research studies are translated into every-day language. The author addresses the common concerns of working mothers who want to provide their children with adequate child care.

Observational Activities

5.1 *Preschool Toys*

During the period from two to six years of age, the most frequent activity children engage in is play. They spend hours building with blocks, pretending with dolls and trucks, and coloring with crayons. Toys can stimulate a child's creativity and fantasy. They can be used to practice sensorimotor skills as in riding a tricycle, throwing a ball, or painting with a brush. Toys can supplement and encourage the imagination of the four-year-old in a game of pretend. Many toys are designed to promote some aspect of the child's physical, cognitive, and social development.

The purpose of this activity is for you to become aware of the diversity and function of toys available and recommended for children between the ages of two and six. Although toys must be tested for safety before being marketed, not all toys available for purchase are safe when placed in the hands of a curious and determined preschooler. A second purpose of this activity is for you to discover potential safety hazards in toys on the market.

In order to complete this activity, you will need to locate a toy store, preferably a large supermarket-type store that offers a large selection of toys. Once you are in the store, study the arrangement of toys in the store. They are usually grouped according to age of child and type of toy (e.g., dolls, trucks, puzzles). For each of the categories listed below, locate a toy that would stimulate or encourage the child's mastery of each skill listed. Select at least one toy in each category for a two- to four-year-old and at least one toy for a four- to six-year-old. Read the description of the toy supplied by the manufacturer to help you in your selection. Then assess the possible safety hazard of each toy. Consider the use and abuse the toy will receive when used by a young child.

1. Sensory gross motor skills
2. Sensory fine motor skills

3. Sorting, classifying
4. Numbers, counting, and matching
5. Time, duration
6. Language, vocabulary, labels, letters

Compile your observations and share your discoveries with your class-mates. What did you learn about toys? What did you gain from doing this activity? How might you apply what you have learned in a preschool-education setting?

5.2 *Piagetian Tasks*

In this chapter, you learned of several limitations in the child's understanding. This activity focuses on classification and number. You will need to locate a four-year-old who is willing to "play some games" with you. Be sure to get permission of the child's parent before you ask the child to play your games.

1. *Classification task:* You will need to cut out of construction paper an as-sortment of shapes (circles, squares, and triangles) of different sizes (small, medium, and large) and of different colors (red, yellow, and blue). Mix up the different shapes in a pile in front of the child and ask the child to make piles of the pieces that go together. You may want to illustrate the task for the child. As the child makes the different classes, note the di-mension the child uses to sort the pieces. After finishing, ask the child to name the piles. Then ask the child if there is any other way the shapes can be rearranged and if so to go ahead and make new piles. Continue with the task so long as the child has different ways of classifying the objects.

2. *Number:* Reread the section on conservation of number in this chapter and refer to Figure 5.3 for the arrangement of the coins. Ask the child to tell you whether the rows have the same number of coins, and, if not, which row has more. Note the answer for each arrangement depicted in Figure 5.3 Ask the child to tell you why he or she thinks the row selected has more coins.

Compile the answer to the two tasks and describe the child's level of understanding. Share your observations with your classmates. What did you learn from doing this activity?

Preschool Years: Personality and Social Development

At age three, Andrew had spent his entire life at home with his parents and older brother. Learning how to interpret his grunts and gestures and how to anticipate his needs, his family now knew how to get along with *him*.

When he turned three, however, his parents decided that it was time for Andrew to learn how to get along with other people. Fully toilet-trained, equipped with early language skills and a fairly coordinated body, little Andrew entered the local nursery school and immediately began his new education.

It was a rude awakening. Much to Andrew's surprise, the other children in the classroom did not immediately acknowledge his presence, as had been the case at home. Undaunted, he approached a table where several children were putting together puzzles. Cautiously picking up one of the pieces that a boy named Jonathan was using, he suddenly found Jonathan grabbing it out of his hand! Andrew began to cry, as much in surprise as in indignation over the lost puzzle piece. The teacher, noticing the crisis, interceded by introducing Andrew to the other children, who by now were regarding intently the crying newcomer. "Let's all welcome Andrew, boys and girls!" coached the teacher.

By the end of the first day at nursery school Andrew had made friends with Jonathan, enjoyed a pretend game in which he got to wear the firefighter's hat, and had a fight with Amy because she insisted that *her* Daddy was stronger than *his* Daddy. This was a very busy day for Andrew!

Gradually, over the days, weeks, and months that followed, Andrew expanded his understanding of the world to include an awareness of himself and other people. He was learning how to get along with others and how to get others to notice him. He was learning how a "good boy" acts and how to ask for what he wanted. He even learned how to wait his turn and one day reprimanded his older brother by telling him "That's not nice!" when the boy had grabbed a toy from his hands.

At the same time that preschoolers are changing physically and developing their cognitive skills, they are also acquiring new views of themselves as persons. During the developmental period from two to six years, children learn behaviors that allow them to become members of a group—their family, a neighborhood play group, or a preschool program. In short, children are exposed to the life-long process of **socialization**—learning how to get along with other groups of people. Through their interactions with family members and with significant people outside the home, young children learn the socially expected attitudes, behaviors, and emotional responses that are valued by their culture and community. In doing so, children add new dimensions to their emerging personalities. Some of these newly acquired personal and

Socialization The process by which a child learns the expected behaviors of a culture or group.

social skills have enduring qualities that influence later childhood and adulthood adjustments. Other characteristics are unique to the preschool period and have little obvious or direct influence on development across the lifespan. Preschool play activities, for example, provide rich opportunities for children to practice cognitive and social behaviors, but they do not have a direct correspondence in adult development.

In this chapter, we consider the ways in which children acquire new social and personal behaviors and refine and build on earlier skills. We begin with the child's emerging sense of self and awareness of gender. Then we examine the ways in which parents and the family influence children's social and personality development. We end with a discussion of the ways children actively influence their own development by way of social behaviors.

The Development of Self

As we learned in Chapter 4, children as young as 18 months show signs of having a conception of themselves. Although primitive, these early behaviors mark the beginning of development of self. By the end of the preschool period, the child has acquired the ability to stand apart and view the self from another person's perspective. They are able to describe themselves as different from other children by listing their unique characteristics, especially the fact that their names are different. Young children first define themselves in terms of their activities, such as "I sleep in a bunk bed," "I go to nursery school," and "I ride a tricycle" (Keller, Ford, & Meachem, 1978). Later, after five years of age, children employ more psychological descriptions of themselves—for example, "I am smart" or "I am happy."

How does the child come to form a view of him- or herself? What factors influence the child's self-concept? Are there similarities in the way children describe themselves? And what effect does this early-childhood self-concept have on later development?

Self-Concept Defined

Personality generally refers to the characteristic way that a person behaves, the pattern of beliefs, actions, and feelings that distinguishes one person from another. Part of one's personality includes the way a person views him- or herself, or the **self-concept.** The process of discovering one's personal picture of self is a gradual one. A child does not wake up suddenly and discover who he or she really is. In fact, although a person's self-concept begins in the preschool years, the process of self-discovery is one that continues throughout the lifespan.

Self-Concept A person's sense of his or her identity, including physical and psychological traits; the way a person views self.

The development of self-concept is closely related to the child's growing cognitive, emotional, and social skills (Lewis & Brooks-Gunn, 1979; Maccoby, 1980, 1984). Jerome Bruner (1984) asserts that the child's view of self develops through the many verbal and nonverbal interactions with caregivers, especially the mother. Other theorists, such as Freud (1924) and Erikson (1963), however, view personality and the child's concept of self as a product of a broader socialization process. Through the various interactions with parents, peers, and other adults, children learn to relate to people in ways that are appropriate to the family in particular and the culture in general.

Erikson's Stage of Initiative vs. Guilt

The two- to three-year-old is exciting to watch because the child brings together growing perceptual, motor, cognitive, and language skills to make things happen. Nothing seems to deter the active, inquisitive child who, by age four, has mastered the mighty question "Why?" Like Andrew, preschoolers insert themselves in the middle of social exchanges. A common example of this boundless yet intrusive enthusiasm is the child who interrupts her mother in the middle of a telephone conversation. The egocentric child cannot yet conceptualize that her mother might not be as eager to talk to her as *she* is to talk to her mother.

Erik Erikson (1963) theorized that children develop their personality by resolving various developmental crises at different stages in life. These crises focus on the conflicts between the child and the social environment, which places demands and restrictions upon the child's behavior. As we learned in Chapter 4, Erikson suggests that children first learn to either trust or mistrust themselves and others; then they move on to resolve issues related to their own sense of autonomy vs. shame and doubt.

Once children have resolved the second crisis and are convinced of their ability to be separate—to be their own persons—they start to be more assertive in their activities. On their own initiative, children engage in play with other children; they pursue their own interests in the family by asking to help. In this stage of Erikson's theory, which lasts from three to six years of age, children are eager and ready to learn to cooperate in working with others to make things happen. They welcome the guidance and assistance that grown-ups offer them to help them demonstrate what they can do. Because of their exuberance, this is the perfect time for parents to begin to teach children more about social rules and expected behaviors. For example, while Andrew was taking great pleasure in being asked to be the child in charge of returning the puzzles to the toy box, the teacher also was encouraging appropriate social behavior.

At the same time, children's enthusiasm and initiative may result in actions that earn them reprimands instead of praise. Consequently, they may experience a sense of guilt for their transgressions. In part, this guilt may be the result of the child's limited cognitive skills. For example, not long after Andrew's mother had expressed delight at the painting he made in nursery school, he duplicated the design on his bedroom wall. His mother, however, was not at all amused. "Don't you know you are not supposed to draw on the walls?" she demanded. Clearly, Andrew did not understand this rule. Having been praised for his previous design, he naively copied it on his bedroom wall in the hope of additional praise. His mother's response, however, would more likely result in feelings of guilt than a positive sense of initiative and accomplishment.

In Erikson's view, a small amount of guilt over transgressions is normal and helps the child gain self-control over future actions. However, if parents consistently overreact to the child's activities, the child may be overburdened with a sense of guilt and lose the sense of initiative. By clearly setting some

This three-year-old wants his mother's attention, especially when she is on the telephone. The egocentric child cannot imagine that its mother is talking to another person and does not want to talk to the child.

Sometimes children's enthusiasm and initiative may earn them a scolding or reprimand.

limits and rules for self-expression, parents and teachers can help the child achieve a healthy resolution of the crisis of initiative vs. guilt.

Pause for Thought

Erikson's theory of psychosocial development is one of the few personality theories to incorporate a lifespan approach. He maintains that conflicts or issues that are not resolved at their developmentally appropriate time can be resolved at a later time in a person's life. What adult characteristics might you expect to find in a person who is seeking to resolve the crisis of initiative versus guilt during his or her early twenties or thirties?

Identification

By the time Andrew was four, his relatives had noticed the way he seemed to act like his father. He echoed his father's opinions about the Boston Red Sox and scolded his brother using a similar tone and gesture that his dad used.

One way to explain this observed similarity between children and their parents is by **identification,** a process by which the child takes on the beliefs, desires, and values of another person as his or her own. Freud was one of the earlier theorists to emphasize the important role that identification plays in the child's developing personality. By assuming characteristics of the parents, children are able to reduce their fears of losing their parents' love or experiencing their retaliation as a result of their errors or social transgressions

Identification The process by which a child takes on the beliefs, behaviors, desires, or values of another person as his or her own.

Young children often will take on prominent characteristics of their parents. This boy has copied his father's dress and behavior.

(see Bronfenbrenner, 1960). By aligning themselves with a parent, usually of the same gender, children acquire such characteristics as gender-appropriate behaviors, self-control, prosocial forms of aggression, guilt feelings, and adult standards for assessing the goodness or badness of an act (Mischel, 1970; Sears, Rau, & Alpert, 1965).

The process of identification includes two subprocesses: (1) imitation of parental actions, and (2) incorporation of these behaviors into the child's view of the self. The child is not just copying parental actions, but uses the parental characteristics to describe him- or herself. Although there is not clear agreement about what motivates children to identify with their parents (Mischel, 1970), there has been much research on what parental characteristics foster the identification process.

Children are more likely to identify with the parent who is similar to them in physical or psychological characteristics. Parents who are nurturant and warm, while at the same time seen as powerful by the child, are more likely to function as models.

Gender-Role Typing

Gender refers to whether a person is male or female and is based on the physical and chromosomal make-up of the person. Although gender is an obvious characteristic, it usually is not until ages two or three years that young children become aware of and use gender as a dimension on which to classify people (Serbin & Sprafkin, 1986). Once children become aware of gender, they quickly learn to label themselves as boy or girl. Gender awareness and **gender identity**, the recognition and acceptance of one's own gender, are considered to be important cognitive events. Knowing about gender helps children learn which behaviors are considered to be appropriate and expected

Gender Identity The recognition and acceptance of one's own gender.

Gender Typing   The process by which children acquire the culturally expected behaviors for their gender.

of males and females. These gender expectations vary according to the culture and time period in which children are reared. **Gender typing** refers to the process by which children acquire the culturally expected attitudes and behaviors for their gender. They learn how males and females should act. Identification with the parent of the same gender helps children identify what it means to be a male or female in their culture. These characteristics in turn become part of a child's self-concept.

Gender Identity

Gender identity develops in stages. First, the child recognizes his or her own gender but may not yet understand that it is a characteristic that does not change. **Gender constancy** is only achieved when the child comes to believe that boys always grow up to be men and girls always grow up to be women. A typical question from a three-year-old who has not yet achieved gender constancy might be, "When you grow up, Mommy, will you be a man?" The concept that gender does not change with growing up is difficult for the preschooler to master. One reason for this difficulty may be because children are familiar with many physical characteristics that *do* change with age, such as size or strength, so the possibility of changing gender does not seem unusual to them.

Gender Constancy   The recognition that one's gender does not change.

Children learn the culturally expected behaviors for their gender through their play activities.

By three years of age children have established gender identity. By five years of age they know what behaviors are expected from boys, what behaviors are expected from girls.

The way researchers measure gender constancy is by asking children to match gender properties (such as "plays with trucks and does boy things" or "plays with dolls, wears dresses, and does girl things") with a gender category of male or female. A four-year-old may be asked the question: "If a boy wears a dress will he be a boy?" The answer is likely to be "No." But if you ask children to go from the category (male or female) to the properties, they are able to answer appropriately. They recognize that boys play with trucks and do not wear dresses, and girls play mommy and do wear dresses. (Gelman, Collman, & Maccoby, 1986). Thus, the age of gender constancy may vary depending on how the question is asked.

Children develop an awareness that their own gender does not change before they realize that the same gender constancy applies to other children (Gouze & Nadelman, 1980; Marcus & Overton, 1978). According to Kohlberg (1966), gender constancy is a byproduct of the child's cognitive development, and by age six, most children have accepted the notion that one's gender does not change. Gender constancy may not be necessary, however, for a child to acquire a sense of gender identity (Martin & Halverson, 1981). Since young children are typically oriented to the present, when you ask them "What sex are you?" they are able to respond quite readily "I am a boy" or "I am a girl."

Gender Roles

Even though by three years of age the child has acquired gender identity, it is not until age four or five that the child can reliably identify the gender of other people. Usually this distinction is made on the basis of clothing, hairstyle, and behaviors they have come to associate with one gender in particular. For example, if you ask a four- or five-year-old to explain how she knows that a particular child is a girl, she might reply "Because she has long hair and is playing with dolls." This response reflects the fact that children not only have learned that there are two genders, but that boys and girls differ in the way they act. These attributed differences form the basis of **gender roles,** the

Gender Role The pattern of behaviors considered to be appropriate for the male and female within the culture.

pattern of behaviors considered to be appropriate for males and females within a particular culture. Every culture defines the gender roles of men and women somewhat differently, and attempts to socialize their young to fit these roles at an early age.

In a study (Kuhn, Nash, & Brucken, 1978) that asked two- and three-year-old children to describe "masculine" and "feminine" behaviors, it was found that boys and girls did not necessarily agree on what was appropriate gender behavior. However, both boys and girls agreed that girls like to play with dolls, help their mothers, talk a lot, say "I need some help," never hit, and clean the house. Both boys and girls believed that boys like to help their fathers, say "I can hit you," play with cars, and mow the lawn. Boys, but not girls, thought that girls are likely to cook the dinner, cry, be slow, and say "You hurt my feelings," and "You're not letting me have my turn." Girls, but not boys, thought that girls are likely to look nice, give kisses, say "I can do it best," take care of babies, and like to sew. Boys, but not girls, thought that boys work hard, are loud, naughty, and could make you cry. Girls, but not boys, thought that boys liked to fight, be mean, and climb trees.

Children's knowledge of gender stereotypes increases with age, although children as young as two years of age appear to adopt gender stereotypes (Smith & Daglish, 1977; Weinraub, Clemens, Sockoloff, Ethridge, Gracely, & Myers, 1984). Preschoolers not only learn what behaviors are appropriate for girls and boys, they are also not very accepting of other children who do not conform to these expected behaviors (Stoddart & Turiel, 1985). When you ask five-to-seven-year-olds if it is alright for a boy to wear a barrette while playing football or for a girl to wear a boy's suit, they will probably answer "No."

The child's understanding of appropriate gender behaviors is strongly influenced by the cultural stereotypes to which he or she is exposed. These stereotypes are based on a shared set of beliefs about the differences between men and women. Gender-role expectations change according to the circumstances within the particular culture. For example, at one time, the gender-role stereotype for girls in the United States included the expectation that little girls did not play baseball. Today, that expectation has changed; Little Leagues now include girls as well as boys. In the United States, a wide range of behaviors is accepted as appropriate to either gender. Even though gender roles still exist in all modern cultures, they are becoming more flexible to allow for greater individual differences (Tavris & Wade, 1984).

Pause for Thought

Twenty years ago, most psychologists believed that acquiring appropriate gender-role behaviors was an important developmental goal. Today, many people are questioning the merits of channeling children into gender stereotypes. Given that today's young parents were raised at a time when traditional gender-role behaviors were highly valued and encouraged, how might their experiences affect the way they raise their children to be girls or boys?

Gender Differences

Gender roles ascribe behaviors to each sex. But are these *true* differences in behavior, or are they merely the result of socialization? It is difficult to separate the influence of genetic biological factors from the influence of early

The most consistent research finding on gender differences indicates that males are more aggressive than females even from an early age.

learning on behavior. By examining reported gender differences in behavior in widely different cultures and environments, researchers have been able to draw some conclusion about universal gender differences in behavior. On the basis of their comprehensive review of 1400 published studies, Maccoby and Jacklin (1974) concluded that there are few behavioral differences that can be attributed to gender alone. The authors found only four characteristics that seemed to appear in almost every culture. These characteristics included aggression and three cognitive and intellectual skills.

Aggression   The most consistent research finding on gender differences indicates that males are more physically aggressive than females and from an early age (Block, 1983; Maccoby & Jacklin, 1974, 1980). This conclusion is supported by naturalistic and laboratory studies of children and adults as well as by numerous animal studies. Males engage in more rough-and-tumble play, are more likely to imitate aggression when it is modeled, and exhibit more antisocial behavior than females. Although the accumulated evidence suggests a greater aggressiveness for boys, it has been suggested that boys express their aggression overtly, whereas girls are more concerned about their aggressive tendencies, and thus, more likely to censor their expression of aggression (Brodzinsky, Messer, & Tew, 1979).

Cognitive and Intellectual Skills   Maccoby and Jacklin (1974) found support for female superiority in verbal skills. Girls learn to speak and read earlier and have fewer difficulties in reading when compared to boys. Later in childhood, girls also score better on tests of spelling, grammar, and verbal comprehension. While adolescent boys and men excel on tests of visual–spatial abilities, girls and women do not (Feingold, 1988). In a recent study in which the spatial abilities of 1800 school children were assessed, boys outperformed girls by the age of 10 and continued to do better on spatial ability tests through to age 18 (Johnson & Meade, 1987). Some studies have found, however, that this visual–spatial superiority depends on the particular test used, and does not emerge until at least the tenth grade (Tavris & Wade, 1984).

Men and adolescent boys tend to show greater mathematical ability, although there seems to be no such gender difference in the childhood years (Maccoby & Jacklin, 1974). This difference in mathematical ability is not as widely supported as the other three differences noted above (see Tobias, 1982), and has even been the subject of recent controversy. One study compared the gender differences in cognitive abilities by examining standardized aptitude test scores collected on high-school students between 1960 and 1983 (Feingold, 1988). While overall gender differences declined considerably in recent years, the one exception found was in mathematics. High-school males scored higher than females in upper-level mathematics skills.

In examining these studies, it is important to remember that the evidence supporting gender differences on certain traits and skills does not answer the question of whether these traits are innate or learned. The fact that boys as a group are more aggressive than girls as a group may be the result of differing parental expectations. A girl who is aggressive may be reprimanded or punished, while a boy may be expected and encouraged to act aggressively. In one study in which 13- to 14-month-old children were observed with adults in a play group, adults were more likely to respond to girls when they used gestures or gentle touches or talked softly, whereas the boys received adult attention when they used physical means or when they cried, whined or screamed (Fagot, Hagan, Leinbach, & Kronsberg, 1985). Eleven months later when the researchers observed the children again, they found that boys were more assertive and girls talked to their preschool teachers more.

Other Gender Differences   Aside from aggression and the three cognitive skills discussed above, what other psychological differences between males and females can be supported by research results? Maccoby and Jacklin (1974) found little consistent evidence to support some of the traditional gender-role stereotypes. There was no evidence to support the view that girls are more sociable than boys or that girls are more suggestible. In a recent updated review of studies examining gender differences, Deaux (1984) concludes that gender differences are less pervasive than previously thought. There are greater individual differences among girls and boys as a group than there are group differences between girls and boys. Eagly (1983) raises the concern that many laboratory studies that report gender differences may be biased in the direction of one gender over another. Subjects tested in a laboratory provide information on what people of different genders *can* do, not what they *actually* do in natural settings.

Gender-Role Socialization

Young children acquire a specific view of gender-appropriate behavior from the moment of birth. From the beginning of life, parents perceive their newborn boys and girls differently. In one study, parents interviewed within a day of their child's birth rated girls as smaller and softer than boys (Rubin, Provenzano, & Luria, 1974). Fathers described their sons as stronger and harder and their daughters as more delicate, even though there were no objective differences between the male and female newborns. Adults interact differently with infants depending on the perceived gender. Prompted by a children's story appearing in *Ms.* magazine about "Baby X" (Gould, 1972), an experiment was conducted in which adults were observed interacting with a three-month-old (Seavey, Katz & Zalk, 1975). Some adults were told the infant was a girl; some were told it was a boy, and others were not given any suggestion about the infant's gender. Men were more likely to offer the infant a gender neutral toy and handle the child least while women offered gender stereotypic toys more and handled the child more. These differences in behavior held true regardless of the actual gender of the infant (Sidorowicz & Lunney, 1980).

During the preschool years, children may be differentially rewarded for gender-appropriate behavior. Boys are discouraged from playing with dolls and encouraged to explore and manipulate objects. Girls are encouraged to stay close to home and mother, to be nurturant, and are discouraged from being aggressive or physical (Block, 1983). Despite the numerous studies highlighting the specific ways in which parents selectively encourage different behavior from girls and boys, more recent research by Jacklin and Maccoby (Turkington, 1984) suggests that parents have reduced their stereotyping of their children. They appear to treat little girls and boys much the same. By studying 275 children from birth to the first grade, for example, the researchers found that parents seemed to be equally warm, nurturing, and accepting or restrictive of boys and girls. The only exception was that fathers tended to offer their children more gender-role-stereotyped toys and were more likely to engage in rough play with their sons than with their daughters.

Play with gender-stereotyped toys is one of the earliest manifestations of gender typing. By age three, children show a definite preference for toys that are considered by others to be appropriate for their own gender. Recent naturalistic studies in which toddlers were observed in their homes suggest that children as young as two years old have a preference for gender-stereotyped toys (Eisenberg, Wolchik, Hernandez, & Pasternack, 1985; O'Brien & Huston, 1985). Parents contribute to the gender role socialization of their children by providing them with gender-typed toys to play with. Nancy Eisenberg and her colleagues videotaped mothers and fathers in their homes as they interacted with their one- to two-year-old children. They rated children's toys as either masculine (trucks, toy hammers and tools, balls), feminine (dolls, cleaning and kitchen tools, stuffed animals) or neutral (Play Doh, puzzles, books). Parents of boys chose neutral or masculine toys for their children to use during their interaction, while parents of girls picked more neutral toys. By selecting girl or boy toys, parents channel their children toward one gender orientation and away from another. Often the decision about what toy to buy a child is influenced not only by the gender appropriateness of the toy, but by the child's interest and enthusiasm for the toy. Thus, in the case of toy selection and availability it may be the case that children influence their own socialization.

The influence of gender-role training on the child's self-concept is substantial, particularly during this preschool period when early views of self are

Parents serve as powerful gender role models for their children. This young boy will probably be comfortable in the kitchen because of his father's example.

being formed. Jeanne Block (1983) suggests that gender-differentiated socialization also has a profound impact on the child's cognitive development. She argues that males are systematically exposed to more opportunity for independent problem solving leading to different competencies for males than females. These differential skills result in different self- and worldviews for the sexes.

Gender-role behavior is not fixed, but rather undergoes change throughout the lifespan. Thus while three-year-old Andrew may believe it is not appropriate for a boy to like to take care of babies, it is likely that he will become more nurturant and display these more feminine role behaviors when he reaches adulthood (Nash & Feldman, 1981). Furthermore, children are exposed to their parents as gender-role models at different times in their parents' gender-role development. A child who first learns about gender roles when her mother goes back to work and her father becomes more involved in child care may develop a different view of gender-role behaviors than the child whose mother remains at home and whose father is relatively uninvolved in child care.

Pause for Thought

Toys are supposed to be fun. Is it wrong for a boy to play with a Barbie doll makeup kit if it gives him pleasure? Is it wrong for a girl to play with trucks, tools, or a football? Why should it matter what a child uses in play?

The Child in the Family

Sometime during the child's second year of life, the parent's role shifts in emphasis from that of a caregiver to that of a socializing agent. Parents become more deliberate in their task of teaching young children how to control their emotions and how to adjust their behavior to meet the needs of others and themselves. The task of socializing the child is a long-term one that is accomplished over a number of years extending well beyond the preschool period. Parents use their own childhood experiences of being socialized by their parents to guide them in what to teach their children. In addition, the degree to which parents are effective in helping their children adjust to the world is influenced by the child's own reactions and by the quality of the broader social context in which the family is embedded (Belsky, 1984; Weinraub & Wolf, 1983). The earliest lessons in how to get along with others are learned in the family. In many ways the family—parents and siblings—provides a training ground for acquiring social skills that will serve the child in later years.

The Parenting Role

In most, but not all cultures, the responsibility for rearing and socializing children is assigned to their parents. This responsibility is a broad one. Parents are expected to provide for the physical and psychological care and safety of their children while at the same time serving as their first teachers.

The long-term goal of parenting is to encourage and teach skills and attitudes that will enable children to live healthy and productive lives as adults. However, in the day-to-day tasks of teaching and providing for their children's care, parents often lose sight of this ultimate goal. They become distracted by a more immediate goal of teaching their children to be compliant and pleasant in their interactions. Child-rearing practices are often focused upon ways to teach children to be obedient and responsive to the adults who would teach them. Child-rearing practices vary considerably, from culture to culture, from parent to parent, even for the same parent over time. As Richard Bell (1968; Bell & Harper, 1980) has pointed out, parents are influenced by their children just as children are influenced by their parents. New parents are likely to be anxious and somewhat rigid in their style of child-rearing. With experience, however, they are likely to become more relaxed and less demanding in their role. Also, since parents adjust their behaviors to the characteristics of the child, the socialization practices to which the easy child is exposed are likely to be different from the parental practices used with a more difficult child. Nevertheless, a few generalizations can be made regarding overall parenting styles.

Parenting Styles

Parents usually talk about their child-rearing practices in terms of discipline. **Discipline** in this sense refers to the parents' strategies for eliciting compliance to their authority. Discipline includes the selective use of rewards and punishments for obedience or disobedience to rules set by the parents. However, parents teach the child how to get along with others by their actions as well as by instruction. Often, when parents describe how they interact with their children, they describe their intentions and their disciplinary efforts, but they neglect the impact they make as models of appropriate behavior. For

Discipline The strategies used by parents to get children to comply with their rules.

The way in which parents care for their children is influenced by the culture in which they live.

this reason, it is important in the study of parental behaviors to observe the parent–child interaction as well as to collect parents' self-reports of child-rearing practices.

Early research on parental styles identified two basic dimensions on which parents differ: loving warmth vs. hostility, and permissiveness vs. authoritarian control (Schaefer & Bayley, 1963). The warm, loving parent is accepting, supportive, rewarding, gives praise and comfort, and is interested in the child. The hostile parent is described as critical, derogatory, insensitive, and generally unappreciative of the child's company. The permissive parent does not clearly state or enforce rules and frequently gives in to the child's demands, while the authoritarian parent imposes strict, arbitrary demands and applies a high degree of control in disciplining the child.

Later research by Diana Baumrind (1967, 1971, 1980) examined the way in which parental styles affected the developing social competencies of young children. By observing the behavior of preschool children enrolled in nursery schools, she was able to classify children in terms of their independence and social competence. Socially competent children were those who were rated as friendly, cooperative, and able to assert themselves in an individual and creative fashion without being irresponsible (Baumrind, 1977). Baumrind then assessed the styles of the parents of these preschool children by evaluating them on seven characteristics.

These characteristics included, (1) the degree to which parents provided children with a clear set of rules to govern behavior, (2) the degree of firmness used in enforcing the rules, (3) the degree of encouragement they gave for independence and self-assertion, (4) the degree they expected children to help out with family chores, (5) the degree to which they saw themselves as the infallible authority in the family, (6) the extent to which they used explanations and reason with children, and (7) the extent to which they encouraged social conformity.

By studying data collected from 300 families, Baumrind found three common styles of parenting, which she labeled as *Permissive, Authoritarian,* and *Authoritative*. The characteristics of the three types were summarized by Baumrind (1978) as follows:

1. The authoritarian parent values obedience as a virtue and favors punitive, forceful measures to curb self-will at points where the child's actions or beliefs conflict with what the parent thinks is right. Believing that the child should accept a parent's word for what is right, the authoritarian parent believes in keeping the child subordinate and in restricting autonomy, and does not encourage verbal give and take. Authoritarian parents may be very concerned and protective, or they may be neglecting.

2. The permissive prototype of adult control requires the parent to behave in an affirmative, acceptant, and benign manner toward the child's impulses and actions. The permissive parent sees him- or herself as a resource for the child but not as an active agent responsible for shaping and altering the child's ongoing and future behavior. The immediate aim of the ideologically aware permissive parent is to free the child from restraint as much as is consistent with survival. Some permissive parents are very protective and loving, while others are self-involved and offer freedom as a way of evading responsibility for the child's development.

3. The authoritative parent attempts to direct the child's activities in a rational, issue-oriented manner. He or she encourages verbal give and take, shares with the child the reasoning behind the parental policy, and solicits the child's objections when the child refuses to conform. Both autonomous self-will and disciplined conformity are valued by the authoritative parent. Therefore, this parent exerts firm control when the young child disobeys, but does not hem the child in with restrictions. The authoritative parent enforces the adult perspective, but recognizes the child's individual interests and special ways. Such a parent affirms the child's present qualities, but also sets standards for future conduct, using reason as well as power and shaping by regimen and reinforcement to achieve parental objectives.

In general, Baumrind found that children of authoritative parents seem to be the most self-reliant, self-controlled, explorative, and content. Children of authoritarian parents, however, showed little independence, and were more discontented, withdrawn, and distrustful. Children of permissive parents seemed to be the least self-reliant, self-controlled, or explorative of the entire group of children studied.

While Baumrind's general conclusions hold true for boys and girls, some gender differences in the effects of parenting styles were observed. Authoritarian parenting seemed to be more damaging to boys than girls. For example, sons of authoritarian parents were less likely to be independent and self-reliant and more likely to be angry and defiant. Authoritative parenting was more strongly associated with self-reliance and achievement in girls than boys.

Other researchers have identified a fourth parenting style, the *uninvolved* parent (Maccoby & Martin, 1983). This parent is not committed to being a parent and appears indifferent to the child's need for discipline or affection. The uninvolved parent is more focused on his or her own comfort than on the care of the child. The main effect on children of this indifferent style is a lowered self-esteem often accompanied by aggressive and disagreeable behavior.

It is important to keep in mind the fact that parents vary considerably in the way they respond to and direct their children. In a two-parent family, the child is likely to be influenced by parents who use different socialization practices. Even in the same family, parents differ in the way they respond to

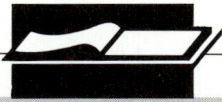

Human Development in Practice

Parent-Education Programs

Parents are the first and most influential teachers that children will ever have. Yet, until recently, few parents received any formal training in child development or parenting. In fact, by virtue of taking this course in human development, you are already better informed about child development than most parents.

The earliest years of a child's life, time that is primarily spent with parents, is a period of enormous intellectual and social growth. While numerous preschool programs have been developed for children over three years of age, there are few programs designed to help stimulate development in children under three years of age. Parent-education programs are the exception.

The goal of parent-education programs is to teach parents how to observe, stimulate, and oversee the development of their infants and children. By working directly with new parents in their early days as caregivers, specially trained teachers connected with the Missouri New Parent as Teachers Project (NPAT) were able to change the home environment of young children for the better (White, 1988). Begun in 1982, the model parent-education program was set up in four school districts in Missouri: one urban, one suburban, one small town, and one rural. One full-time and two part-time parent educators were trained to serve between 60 to 100 families in each district. The parent educators met with each family twice a month, once in the home and once with a small group at a school, until the babies were five months of age. After that, the parent educators went to each home once a month, and the parents met in groups every six weeks (Meyerhoff & White, 1986). Mostly, mothers were the ones who were involved in the parent education, but fathers, grandparents, and babysitters were all encouraged to participate.

The project began during pregnancy and lasted until the child was three years old. Parents were given basic information on effective parenting practices, on stages in infant and child development, and on stimulating activities for young children. A resource center containing books, magazines, toys, and videotapes was set up for parents to use. The social and intellectual progress of children in the project was carefully monitored as was the parents' knowledge and awareness of child development.

How effective was this model parent-education project? According to Burton White, NPAT senior consultant, the project was extraordinarily successful. Compared to a control group of children, project children were more advanced in social, intellectual, and linguistic skills. Furthermore, the parents in the NPAT project were more knowledgeable about the capabilities of young children than were the control group of parents who were not enrolled in the parent-education project.

different children. In a recent study (Dunn, Plomin, & Daniels, 1986) in which mothers were observed with their two children when the children were each two years old, little similarity was found in the mothers' disciplinary actions with the children. Even when dealing with the same child, it is unreasonable to expect that parents will use the same style all the time. As the child develops or changes behavior, the parent may adopt a different style.

Pause for Thought

Many parents today rely on their own childhood experiences of being parented to guide them in the care of their children. Since their model of parenting was observed at least 20 to 30 years ago, what problems might there be for adults who treat their children just like *their* parents treated them?

Encouraging Compliance

Controlling behavior often seems like a full-time occupation for parents of preschool children. It is during this period of time that parents develop their disciplinary strategies. As Baumrind's research suggests, the way the parent controls the child has an impact on the child's developing personality. Common sense suggests that parents use a variety of techniques to encourage compliance from their children. What particular disciplinary strategies are most effective with children? How effective is punishment in socializing children?

The most effective form of discipline for children occurs when parents are warm, nurturant, and *consistent* in their use of rationally based demands (Lamb, 1982). When parents' responses to behavior are predictable, it is easier for children to learn what is expected of them. By providing a rational explanation to children about the consequences to other people of their actions, parents are more likely to instill appropriate social skills. For example, when Andrew grabs a toy from another child, his mother is likely to frown and tell him, "It is not nice to take things without asking. If you grab things, other children won't want to play with you." In order for a reasoning strategy to be effective in teaching the child, the explanations given must match the intellectual level of the child. Also, a short explanation will be more effective than a longer one when disciplining preschool-age children.

Punishment

Parents frequently use punishment to control and socialize their young children. While punishment is effective for eliminating some behaviors and establishing new ones, it can have undesirable effects. Parents use a variety of punishments, from actually hitting or hurting the child, to verbal criticism or rebuke, withdrawal of love or attention, and withholding privileges.

In a review of studies on punishment, Martin (1975) concluded that children who were harshly punished at home were more likely to be aggressive with other children and teachers. Further, children, especially boys, who were harshly punished were more likely to become antisocial delinquents in adolescence. Although the parent's use of physical punishment temporarily inhibits the child's undesired behavior, it also provides the child with a potent model of aggression (Bandura, 1977). When a child is controlled by physical force, he or she learns not only that aggression is an effective way for parents to obtain what they want, but, at the same time, how to use it for his or her own purposes in other situations.

A second problem with physical punishment, or with too frequent a use of this form of punishment, is that children learn to avoid the punitive parent, thus reducing that parent's opportunity to correct inappropriate behavior.

Punishment is also more likely to *suppress* rather than change behavior. A young girl who is punished for biting her nails may temporarily stop the nail-biting behavior but is unlikely to give up the behavior pattern completely. In addition, punishment sometimes results in just the opposite response that parents intend. For example, punishing a child for whining, crying, or clinging—all forms of dependent behavior—may actually result in increased dependence in the child (Yarrow, Campbell, & Burton, 1968).

Results from several research studies (Parke, 1977) have provided some suggestions for more effective use of punishment. First, the sooner in time the punishment follows an undesired action, the more effective it will be. When a child is punished immediately after breaking a rule, the child is more likely to associate the punishment with the act. Second, if also provided with a reason when punished, the child is more likely to change his or her behavior. Third, inconsistent punishment is less effective than consistent punishment. Finally, the more affectionate and nurturant the parent, the more effective he or she will be in using punishment to change the child's behavior (Sears, Maccoby, & Levin, 1957).

Alternatives to Punishment

Parents have other ways of dealing with disruptive and inappropriate behavior. Sometimes when Andrew is misbehaving, his mother may gently but firmly remove him from the situation and put him in a quiet place such as his room. This common practice is called **time out** by psychologists who have studied children's behavior in social settings. Often, for example, when a little boy acts up, he receives attention for his actions from other children and sometimes adults. By removing the child from the setting the disruptive behavior is not reinforced by this attention. It is important that the time-out area be an unrewarding but not aversive place. Sending the disruptive child out to play may actually reinforce his actions if the child would rather be playing.

Sometimes parents are effective in controlling disruptive behavior in their children by anticipating the child's actions and preventing their occurrence by managing the situation (Patterson, 1980). In an observational study of mothers and their two-and-a-half-year-olds in a supermarket, Holden (1983) found that mothers used two types of control: (1) *reactive controls*, in which mothers responded to their children's disruptive behavior, and (2) *proactive controls*, in which mothers avoided potential conflict by distracting their children before the disruptive behavior began.

Preventing or eliminating undesirable behaviors in young children is only part of the parents' function. Parents also teach the child what is appropriate behavior—and the best way to do this is to catch them being good. Rewarding a child when the child behaves appropriately encourages positive behaviors that contribute to the child's socialization. An additional bonus for parents who use positive reinforcement is that they are learning what the

Time Out A strategy for changing behavior by removing a person from the setting in which the behavior to be changed is being reinforced.

child does right instead of focusing their attention on what the child does wrong, as is the case with punishment. Also, children are more likely to imitate parents who provide them with positive rewards.

Children are also more likely to cooperate with a parent who has been cooperative with them in the past. Mary Parpal and Eleanor Maccoby (1985) observed three-and-a-half-year-old children's compliance with their mothers' requests to put away toys after they had experienced one of three kinds of interactions in their laboratory. Some of the children and mothers had played freely for 15 minutes as they would at home; some of the children had played with their mothers while they acted responsively, letting the child initiate all the play with toys and cooperating with the child's intentions, and some of the children had played alone while their mothers were busy filling out a questionnaire. Children were more likely to comply after the noninteractive session and after responsive play. In both of these sessions the mothers did not attempt to control their children. Children received neither reinforcement for compliance nor punishment for noncompliance. Thus, the children who complied were allowed to take a dominant role in the play setting. Children whose parents are less controlling and more cooperative in their interactions are more likely to be compliant.

The Changing Family

Over the past 20 years, the character of American families has undergone some changes. In the traditional nuclear family, consisting of parents and children who live together, the father typically was the parent who went off to work outside of the home, while the mother remained at home to care for the children and the household. Today, however, this description of families is no longer a representative one. Mothers as well as fathers are often employed outside of the home, and fathers are now assuming more child-care responsibilities than was the case a generation or two ago. Furthermore, with more marriages ending in divorce, a greater number of children live in single-parent households. In 1979, approximately 20 percent of the households in the United States involved single-parent families (U.S. Bureau of the Census, 1980).

Maternal Employment

Today, more children than ever before have mothers who are in the work force. For example, in 1950, only 12 percent of married women with children under six years of age worked outside of the home. In 1982, however, 46 percent of women with preschool children were in the work force. In 1983, more than 40 percent of mothers of infants under a year of age were employed (Klein, 1985). (See Table 6.1.) In the last decade, over 50 percent of married mothers of school-age children were employed (Hoffman, 1979). For single mothers (divorced or never married) with children younger than six years of age, the percent who are employed full time is 56 and 45 respectively (Clarke-Stewart, 1982).

While many mothers work because they have to—that is, for economic reasons—many women are choosing to combine both motherhood and a career. The mother's decision to work is influenced by a number of factors including the quality and availability of alternate child care, the support and

Table 6.1 ▪▬▬▬

Employment Status of Women with Children under Five Years Old: 1977, 1982, and 1985

% Employed	Age in Years of Youngest Child				
	Less than 1	1	2	3	4
1977	24.0	31.0	39.7	39.2	45.7
1982	33.7	40.4	44.1	43.1	47.3
1985	— —	49.4*	54.0	55.1	— —

*This percent includes children up to one year of age.

Source: Data from O'Connell & Rogers (1983) and U.S. Bureau of Labor Statistics, *Monthly Labor Review*, February 1986.

cooperation of the spouse, the type of employment available, the degree of self-fulfillment in the job, and the age of the child. Since most out-of-home child care is costly, economic gain from a second income is often used to pay for child care.

A question that many people ask is, "How does a mother's working affect the child's development?" The general consensus 30 years ago was that it was better for children when their mothers were not employed. Today, however, new evidence collected from the growing number of children with working mothers has altered our earlier belief. (It should be noted that the term *working mother* is used to refer to a mother who is in the work force. Any mother, especially one with preschool-age children, will tell you that caring for the physical and psychological needs of children is work!)

Effects   The first thing parents arrange when the mother returns to work is child care. Most of the preschool-age children whose mothers are employed are cared for in their own homes either by a relative or a neighbor (see Table 6.2). About 48 percent are cared for in some form of day care outside the home. In Chapter 5, we examined the impact of day care on young children;

Table 6.2 ▪▬▬▬

Child-Care Arrangements for Preschool Children Whose Mothers Work Outside the House

Care Arrangements	Children Using Arrangement (%)
In own home	
father	20
other relative	20
nonrelated babysitter	12
In day-care home	
relative	15
nonrelative	20
In day-care center	13
Total:	100

Source: From A. Clarke-Stewart. *Day care.* Cambridge, MA: Harvard University Press, 1982.

the overall research results suggest that quality day care does not result in any adverse effects on young children.

The concern that employed mothers may have reduced contact and hence reduced impact on their preschool children seems not to be supported by the research data (Hayes & Kammerman, 1983). Goldberg (1977) found that there is no difference between employed mothers and mothers who are not employed in the amount of one-to-one contact with their preschool children. The *quality* rather than *quantity* of care a child receives from the mother seems to be the important factor (Hoffman, 1974, 1979).

Children of working mothers may benefit from the mother's dual career. Aside from enhancing the family's economic status, the employed mother provides a less stereotyped female model for her children. Children, especially daughters, whose mothers are employed are likely to have a broader and less stereotyped view of the female gender role. Teenage daughters whose mothers are employed are more likely than daughters of nonemployed mothers to name their mothers as the person they would most like to be like (Huston-Stein & Higgins-Trenk, 1978). Furthermore, in families in which the mother works outside the home, the father often has an increased responsibility for child care or domestic activities. This increased involvement of men in traditionally feminine activities presents a less traditional gender-role model to the children. Research by Gold and colleagues (Gold & Andres, 1978c; Gold, Andres, & Glorieux, 1979) compared four-year-old, middle-class children who since birth had employed mothers, with a comparable group of children of mothers who were not employed. The children of employed mothers showed better social adjustments and had more egalitarian views of the male and female gender roles. For school-age children, the impact of maternal employment is evidenced by a greater flexibility in gender-role definition when the mother is satisfied with her role as an employee (Gold & Andres, 1978b). School-age children of working mothers are more likely to share in household chores, have more training in independence, and learn to be more responsible (Hoffman, 1974). The families of working mothers are more structured and are characterized by more clear-cut rules. There is a division of the work among all family members, although not an equal distribution since mothers who work outside the home still do more housework than other family members. Furthermore, school-age daughters of mothers who are in the labor force display greater academic achievement and score higher in self-esteem than do daughters whose mothers are not employed.

Pause for Thought

At different times in history, women have entered the workplace in large numbers (e.g., World War II). Today's dramatic increase in the number of employed mothers has stimulated changes in the structure and activities in many American families. What are some of these changes and what impact might these changes have on future generations of families?

Divorce

According to the latest census reports, a million children each year experience the divorce of their parents. By the year 1990, it is predicted that 40 percent of all children under the age of 18 will have experienced the breakdown of their parents' marriage (Clarke-Stewart, 1982; Glick, 1979). In 90 percent of the cases, custody of the children in these families is awarded to the mothers, although there is an increase in the number of fathers who are being awarded custody. As a result, many children spend a portion of their growing years in a single-parent household. The psychological effects on children of having one parent instead of two are diverse and dependent on the reason for a parent's absence. However, most single-parent households are a result of divorce.

Divorce is an unpleasant and stressful period for all involved because the basic structure and function of the family are temporarily shaken and disorganized. Most researchers examining the impact of divorce on the people involved view divorce as a process extending over several years rather than a single event marked by the divorce decree (Furstenberg, Nord, Peterson, & Zill, 1983; Hetherington, 1979; Hetherington, Cox, & Cox, 1982; Wallerstein & Kelly, 1980). The initial period of the divorce process begins with the parents' decision to divorce and their subsequent separation. This period is usually the most stressful time for parents and children and lasts for about one year.

During this time, children react to the tension and conflict in the family in a number of ways. The most commonly reported reactions of children during this time are anger, fear, depression, and guilt (Hetherington, 1979). Children experience several changes in their lives—the loss of a parent, family upheaval and fighting, change and uncertainty in the parent–child relationships, change of residence, and the perceived threat of abandonment. Children experience concerns and stresses at a time when parents are least available emotionally to provide support or encouragement to the children because of their own personal distress. The biggest concern of children during this period is what will happen to them as a result of the divorce. Even if the family has been having a lot of problems, most children prefer the familiar home and family members to a divorce (Wallerstein & Kelly, 1980). "Who will take care of me?" "Where will I sleep?" "Will I see my father?" These are typical concerns expressed by both young children and adolescents. Children are also likely to react to divorce with anger. Young children are likely to display this anger through aggression in school, while older adolescents are likely to blame the parents rather than themselves for the family breakup.

The initial period surrounding a divorce lasts for about a year. By the end of this period, most children have learned to cope with changes brought on by the divorce. In families experiencing multiple stresses, the initial period may, in fact, last longer. The second stage in the divorce process is the transition period, which lasts approximately two to three years and is marked by a variety of social, economic, and structural changes in the family. During this time many parents re-establish a dating relationship, and many remarry. There usually is a substantial decline in the family's standard of living, which may require the custodial parent to seek new employment or to change to a less expensive residence. Despite these tangible transitions, most children appear to function at a normal developmental level.

Wallerstein and Kelly (1980), in a longitudinal study of children experiencing divorce, reported that for many children, return to normalcy occurred even when the parent–child relationships were not especially improved. However, about 25 percent of the children in the Wallerstein and

Kelly study did experience anger and depression that affected their school performance and overall social adjustment. Most of those affected were younger children. Wallerstein and Kelly also described a third stage in the divorce process that generally occurred five years after the marital breakup. During this period, many parents stabilize their families or start new ones by remarrying. For some children, these new family structures represent a return to a normal family life; but for others, the new situations are no better than the predivorce family situation.

Effects   Children's reaction to the disruptive set of transitions that occur when parents divorce is dependent on the children's age at the time of the divorce, their gender, and the quality of the parent–child relationship before and throughout the divorce process.

Preschool-age children have difficulty in comprehending the reason for the parents' breakup and are more likely to blame themselves for the divorce. The egocentric, preoperational child may think, "Daddy and Mommy are angry at each other because I have been naughty." Young children also fantasize the reconciliation of their parents (Wallerstein & Kelly, 1980). Older children are better able to understand the divorce and have greater access to peers and other adults for support during the family crisis. Despite these resources, adolescents experience pain and anger during the initial stages. Later, they are able to assign responsibility for the breakup to one or both parents and to cope with the immediate aspects of their own lives. Some, in fact, are able to gain a greater maturity and independence during their parents' divorce (Wallerstein & Kelly, 1980).

Boys generally have a more difficult adjustment to their parents' divorce than do girls, and the negative effects seem to last longer. In research conducted by Hetherington (1979), she found that boys were often aggressive, lacking in self-control, dependent, and anxious. These characteristics were reported by teachers in school as well as by the parents (Zill & Peterson, 1982). Two years after the divorce, however, these disruptive behaviors had declined. Since most of the children of divorce live with their mothers, it is not surprising to note that custodial mothers have more difficulty dealing with their sons than their daughters (Colletta, 1978; Hetherington, Cox, & Cox, 1982). In addition, boys receive less positive support and nurturance and are viewed more negatively by mothers, teachers, and peers following a divorce (Hetherington, Cox, & Cox, 1982; Santrock & Tracy, 1978). Immediately following a divorce, fathers usually have more contact with their children than they did before the divorce. However, this contact rapidly diminishes so that by the second year after a divorce children rarely see their fathers (Furstenberg et al., 1983).

The quality of the parent–child relationship before and after a divorce is a critical factor in children's adjustment. Hess and Camara (1979) report that adjustment is easier when there is less hostility between the parents and when the child is able to maintain a good relationship with both parents. Because of the increased stress associated with a divorce, parents are often not as effective in their parenting roles in comparison to parents from intact families. They are often less affectionate, less consistent in discipline, poorer at communication, and are less inclined to make maturity demands of their children (Hetherington, Cox, & Cox, 1982). Custodial mothers are likely to be more indulgent but less available to their children. Recent studies by Ahrons and Rogers (1987) of the relationship between divorced spouses suggests that not all partners remain hostile and antagonistic. Half of the couples she studied were either cooperative or friendly with each other. The consequences of divorce for children are considerably reduced when the parents maintain a cooperative and friendly relationship.

Single-Parent Families

It has been estimated that 4 out of 10 children born in the 1970s will spend some time in a one-parent family (Clarke-Stewart, 1982). Most of the single-parent families in the United States are headed by women as a result of bearing children out of wedlock, or becoming divorced, separated, or widowed. In most situations, the single-parent family is a result of divorce.

The most significant characteristic of single-parent families is that they are economically stressed (Brandwein, Brown, & Fox, 1974). There are several reasons for their economic plight. Child support payments often are not adequate to meet children's needs, and in many families, payments are never made. More than one out of two black children live in a single mother household (see Figure 6.1). Single mothers often work full time at low-paying jobs. Many single mothers work longer hours than comparable married working mothers. Compared to married mothers, single mothers were also found to receive substantially less social or community support for their parental roles (Weinraub & Wolf, 1983). Single fathers typically receive help with child care

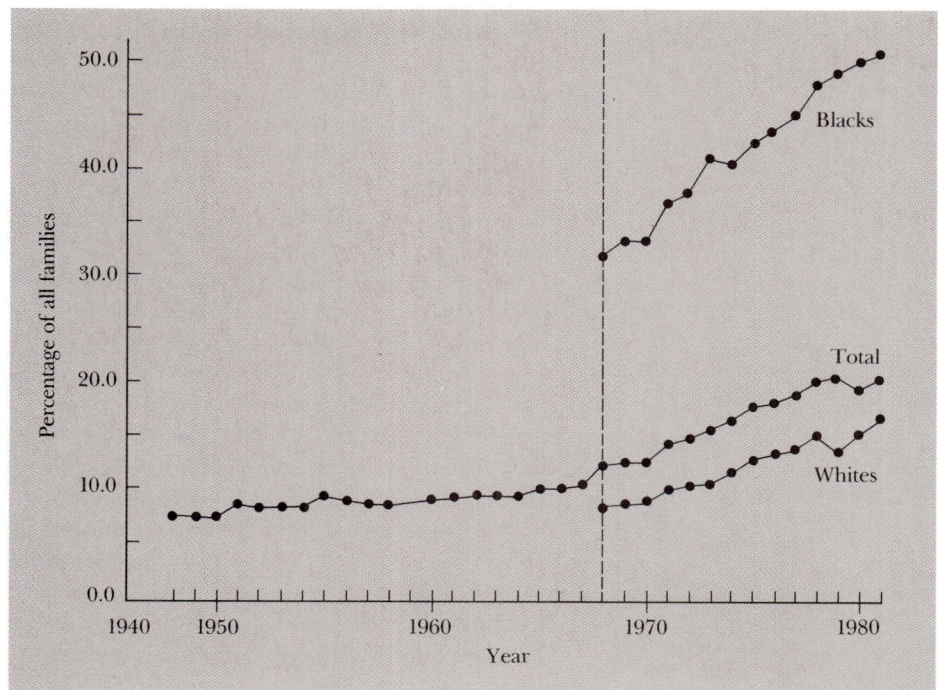

Figure 6.1 Percentage of all families with own children under 18 maintained by only one parent: 1948–1981.

or household chores from concerned friends or relatives, whereas the single mother generally assumes these duties unassisted. With no second adult to share the responsibilities, single-parent families have children who are likely to become more independent, more responsible, and more active in family decision making than children in two-parent homes (Weiss, 1979).

Despite the increased pressures and reduced social supports, many single mothers are able to function effectively in their parental roles. This is especially the case when the parents have resolved their differences enough to support the custodial parent (both financially and psychologically) in the care of the children. In families where the children are encouraged to spend time with the noncustodial parent and where children have warm relationships with other adults, the anticipated negative effects of living in a single-parent family do not occur.

Stepparent Families

Closely tied to the increase in the number of divorces and single-parent families is an increase in the number of stepparent families. It is estimated that at least one out of every three children growing up today will have a stepparent before they reach the age of 18. The remarriage of adults with children creates a **reconstituted family** that can include a stepfather or stepmother, stepsiblings, and even stepgrandparents. Little research has been done on reconstituted families. However, there are some common characteristics and difficulties that distinguish them from other families (Vishner & Vishner, 1978). Members of a reconstituted family must make more adjustments to new family members, sometimes to new households, communities, and cultures. Some, or even all members of the reconstituted family have had to deal with the disruption of a close relationship. Parent–child relations may be strained as a result of this disruption. Stepparents enter their new role as parent without the benefit of having already established a close relationship with their stepchild. Furthermore, children often resist or resent their parent's new spouse. Stepmothers have to overcome the biases against them set up by fairy tales such as *Cinderella* and *Hansel and Gretel* and sometimes by the children's biological mother who may be resentful of the stepmother (Nelson & Nelson, 1982).

Children in reconstituted families often belong to two households, their mother's and the father's households each of which may include stepparents and stepsiblings. The difficulties in coordinating the activities of one household are amplified when there are two sets of families with differing rules and activities (Hetherington, Cox, & Cox, 1982). Furthermore, the adjustments children make may differ depending on their gender. In one study, boys and girls in intact families were compared with children whose mothers were divorced and single, or divorced and remarried (Santrock, Warshak, Lindberg, & Meadows, 1982). Boys in stepfather families displayed more competent social behavior than boys in intact families, whereas girls in stepfather families were more anxious than girls in intact families. Boys in remarried families showed more warmth to their stepfathers than did girls.

The impact on children of growing up in a stepfamily depends on the relationships that develop between stepparents and stepchildren. Most of the research studies have focused on stepfather families where the biological

Reconstituted Family
A family created through the remarriage of adults with children.

mother has custody of the children. Until recently, little research had been done on stepmother families probably because it had been more common in the past for mothers than fathers to be awarded custody of children in a divorce. In a more recent study, it was found that girls who have frequent visits with their biological nonresident mothers are more likely to have a less positive relationship with their stepmothers (Clingempeel & Segal, 1986). However, the longer stepdaughters lived with their father and stepmother the more positive were the stepdaughter–stepmother relationships. When children in stepfamilies are compared with children in nuclear families, there is little difference between them on adjustment or cognitive functioning.

Child Abuse

Incidence

While many parents cope with their life stresses and provide a warm and safe environment for their children, there are an alarming number of cases being reported in which children are physically, sexually, or psychologically abused or neglected by their parents or stepparents (Parke & Lewis, 1980). *Child abuse* includes physical or emotional injury, sexual abuse, and negligent treatment or maltreatment of children under the age of 18 by adults entrusted with their care. Since many incidences of child abuse go unreported, accurate statistics are difficult to compile. One estimate suggested that one out of every 43 American children under age 14 was abused in 1982 ("Parents on the Brink," 1983).

Causes

The abusive treatment of children by people entrusted with their care is a growing social problem. Instead of viewing child abuse as an isolated action on the part of a disturbed parent, many professionals are exploring the multiple factors that determine maltreatment. Belsky (1980), for example, believes that child abuse is determined by stress-disturbed parents, certain characteristic behaviors on the part of the abused child, dysfunctional patterns of family interactions, stress-inducing social forces such as unemployment and isolation, and cultural values that promote abuse.

Many abusive parents were themselves mistreated during their childhoods, a fact suggesting that these parents may have learned a dysfunctional way of caring for children (Spinetta & Rigler, 1972). Some parents still believe that to spare the rod is to spoil the child and that the best way to train a child to obey is through harsh physical discipline that they have seen their own parents use. Abusive parents have little patience with their children. They often have unrealistic expectations and are upset when the child does not live up to them. For example, an abusive parent may interpret a two-year-old's fantasy as a deliberate lie or be angry when the two-year-old wets its pants or spills its milk. Often, abusive parents are upset when the child does not supply them with love or emotional support, something a child usually looks to the parents for.

Social–cultural stresses such as unemployment and lack of contact with church, neighborhood, or community groups also are associated with child abuse. Some studies (Burgess, 1979; Gil, 1970; Pelton 1978) report more child abuse in lower-socioeconomic families. Being poor means that parents may have greater difficulty providing for the physical needs of the family. Zigler (1980) points out that low-income families are not inherently abusive, but rather experience more stressful conditions of living.

Another factor contributing to child abuse is the social norm that condones the use of physical punishment to discipline children, particularly within the context of the family. Not too many years ago, corporal punishment was an integral part of many school systems. Our societal values may actually serve to condone or encourage parents in the use of physical actions against their children. Over half the incidences of child abuse appear to have begun as a disciplinary action that got out of control. For this reason many professionals target the broader social network as the culprit in child abuse. According to Zigler (1982), "So long as corporal punishment is accepted as a method of disciplining children, children will be abused in our country."

Effects on Children

There is no question that child abuse is bad for children. In some cases, abusive treatment is fatal. Surprisingly, until recently, there has been little research on the developmental effects of abuse on children. Most of the earlier studies described the characteristics of abused children without drawing comparisons to nonabused children (Belsky, Lerner, & Spanier, 1984). Maltreated and abused children are often described as aggressive, irritable, clingy, and difficult to manage. While you may be quick to infer that these characteristics are the *result* of being abused, you must also consider that these characteristics may be the cause of their abuse. Overburdened and stressed parents are more likely to abuse their children, particularly the most troublesome child. Low-birthweight infants and hyperactive or mentally retarded children have a higher incidence of being abused. One reason for the higher incidence may be that these children are less alert, less responsive, more difficult to care for, and less attractive, thus making greater demands on the parents (Belsky, 1980; Belsky, Lerner, & Spanier, 1984).

Results from studies using control groups of nonabused children suggest that abused children are generally more emotionally distressed, more socially inhibited and withdrawn, more difficult to manage and display more aggression in many different settings (Belsky, Lerner, & Spanier, 1984; Main & George, 1985; Oldershaw, Walters, & Hall, 1986).

Treatment

The most effective way of treating child abuse is by preventing future incidences. Parent education for abusing parents allows the parents to learn new ways to deal with their children. Many state social-welfare agencies not only provide assistance to abusive parents in managing their children but have programs to identify families at risk for child abuse. Families with many children or a disabled child, and families that are experiencing economic, psychological, or marital strains are viewed as high-risk families. By improving community resources and support systems for these families under stress, the incidence of child abuse may be reduced. Support services such as employment and educational opportunities for mothers and children, self-help groups for parents, child-care facilities, homemaker services, and hotlines help to reduce child-abuse rates (Parke & Slaby, 1983; Crittenden, 1985).

Human Development in Practice

Identifying Child Abuse

Health-care professionals are often the first to suspect and detect signs of child abuse and neglect. Because children usually do not talk about their maltreatment, and parents frequently deny the existence of abuse, the responsibility for identifying child abuse in its early stage frequently falls on the nurses and physicians who see the abused child in a hospital emergency room or physician's treatment room. State laws require that physicians report their suspicions of child abuse and take steps to insure that identified children are protected from further abuse. The earlier the diagnosis of abuse is made, the better the outcome for the child.

The nature of the physical ailment or injury often can be a sign of abuse. Unexplained eye damage is a common finding in battered children. Multiple bruises, burns, lacerations, and abrasions in various stages of healing are other signs of frequent, recurring abuse. If a child displays a painful inability to move certain parts of the body, this might suggest dislocations or fractures. Head injuries may be diagnosed through neurological tests. Many children who die as a result of battering have had human bite marks on their bodies. Nonaccidental poisoning is another common occurrence in child-abuse cases. Neglected children frequently appear malnourished, underweight, and unclean.

Another source of suspicion of child abuse is the parents' behavior. Often the parents' account of a child's injury does not explain the symptoms. For example, a parent of a two-month-old infant with multiple bruises and fractures might explain the injuries as a result of the infant rolling over in a crib. Sometimes an abused child may be brought for the medical care of a cold or flu when the child has severe beating symptoms that the parent seems to ignore. Some abusing parents will delay seeking medical help for their injured child and when they do seek help they are reluctant to provide information about the child to medical personnel. The abused child is often described by the parents as "bad" or "different" and may indeed appear different either physically or emotionally. Abusive parents often have unrealistic expectations of their children and overreact emotionally to them when they disobey or act immaturely.

When child abuse is suspected, physicians are urged to hospitalize the child to assess the degree of injury and provide protection from additional abuse. X-rays may reveal previous incidents of abuse and provide documentation of injuries. Many hospitals have established child-abuse committees to assess suspected cases of child abuse and neglect. The committees are usually composed of a pediatrician, nurse, social worker, psychiatrist and hospital administrator. The committee decides whether the child has been abused and also provides suggestions for managing the child's care.

Unexplained eye damage is a common finding in cases of child abuse.

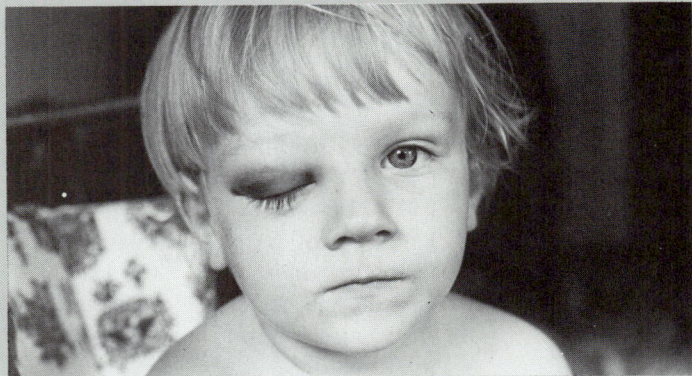

Pause for Thought ▬▬▬▬▬▬▬▬▬▬▬▬▬▬▬▬
The United States has a particularly high rate of reported physical violence in the family and specifically child abuse compared to other countries. What aspects of the American culture might contribute to the high rate of reported abuse?

Sexually Abused Children

In 1973, the U.S. Congress passed the Child Abuse Prevention and Treatment Act, and in 1978, amended the act to include as child abuse: "the obscene or pornographic photographing, filming, or depiction of children for commercial purposes, or the rape, molestation, incest, prostitution, or other such forms of sexual exploitation . . ." (*Congressional Record,* 1978). This federal legislation also mandates the reporting of suspected cases of child abuse, including sexual abuse. As a result, statistics on reported sexual abuse have risen dramatically in the 1980s, and these figures are viewed as conservative since many cases go unreported and sometimes undetected even within the families in which they occur. One estimate by David Finkelhor of the Family Violence Research Program at the University of New Hampshire is that between 1.5 and 3 million children are sexually abused each year in the United States (Krupnick, 1984). Most of the cases involve a sexual molestation of children by an adult who is known to the child; three-quarters of child molesters are friends, neighbors, or relatives.

While more than 90 percent of child molesters are men, women have been known to sexually abuse young boys and to participate in organized sexual abuse of children. However, boys are more likely to be molested by male strangers or casual acquaintances (Tierney & Corwin, 1983).

In the case of incest, the sexually active abuser is often a parent or a parental figure, and the victim is usually a female child. In two-thirds of the incest cases, the offender is not the biological parent but the stepfather. Perhaps the most devastating effect of sexual abuse is that the child is often tricked into participating in the activity and believes the act to be his or her fault. When the offender is a parent, relative, or friend, the child not only experiences the trauma and stress of the sexual molestation, but also is forced to keep a secret for fear of getting the grownup in trouble. The young victims experience a severe conflict when they are subjected to habitual sexual activity with an adult upon whom they depend. Secrecy may also be obtained when the molester threatens harm to the child for revealing the abuse. In some cases, children who have been sexually abused are also physically abused, even killed by the offenders. Many times, parents unwittingly dismiss the child's attempts to tell about the incident as lies, because sexual abuse is too horrifying for people to accept.

The terror, shame, guilt, inhibited rage, and anxiety that are typical reactions of victims of sexual abuse often stay with these victims throughout their childhood and into their adult years. The effects of incestuous activities, for example, are often reflected in poor sexual adjustment in later life. Often the victims have difficulty trusting others and establishing intimate relationships.

Psychologists and educators concerned with the growing number of cases of reported abuse urge parents to teach their youngsters to say no to adults who seek to touch them in sexual ways and that to keep secrets about grownups who touch them is wrong. Sexual abuse is a form of child abuse that occurs as a result of secrecy. To prevent them from becoming future victims, children can be protected by providing them with a way to say no.

The Child's Social World

We have seen that during the preschool period, from two to six years of age, children are learning about themselves and other people through numerous interactions with parents, relatives, and other adults. Personality and social development are not only a result of the way people treat the child but also the result of the child's growing impact on others. Children develop an ever-growing battery of social skills that puts them in greater or lesser contact with other people. One of the reasons parents send their preschoolers off to nursery school is to give them a chance to refine their social skills.

Aggression

Aggression refers to behaviors intended to hurt another person. Aggressive behaviors can be described as *instrumental*, that is, designed to accomplish an end, such as when Jonathan grabbed the puzzle piece from Andrew's hand. They can also be described as *hostile*, that is, designed to harm or hurt another person, as when a child punches someone out of anger. Many acts of aggression are the result of frustration.

Most children younger than two have outbursts of anger and may engage in instrumental aggression. Often the child is only interested in getting a toy, not in being hurtful or dominating. Gradually, however, as the child develops awareness of others and their actions, more aggressive behaviors emerge. The classic temper tantrum may be viewed as an early form of aggressive behavior. Later, the three-year-old may target aggressive behaviors at a particular person, perhaps a sibling who is stealing the parent's attention. Most of the preschooler's aggression occurs amid struggles over toys or control of space and emerges during social play. Many observant parents and preschool teachers, for example, have learned that putting more than three children together in a small room is likely to result in a fight or squabble. Interestingly, the children who are the most sociable and competent are also the ones more frequently involved in fights (Maccoby, 1980).

After the age of six or seven, children change the form of their aggressive behaviors from physical to verbal attacks on others. They also learn other more socially acceptable ways of resolving disputes, and hence the frequency of overtly aggressive behaviors declines as the child ages. Parents who respond to their children's aggression by physically punishing them actually encourage aggression by their example.

Another potent source of modeled aggression for preschoolers are the aggressive actions presented on television. When young children watch cartoons or other television programs, they are exposed to numerous examples of violence and aggression. That many of these programs are fiction and pure fantasy does not dilute their potency as models of behavior for children. Young children often do not make the distinction between fantasy and reality during the preschool period. After viewing aggressive actions on television, young children imitate these actions during their free play with peers (Friedrich & Stein, 1974). Children who are already more aggressive compared to their peers become even more aggressive when they watch violence on TV (Stein & Friedrich, 1975). TV programming thus provides examples and reinforcement for aggression in children. In Chapter 8, we will discuss the impact of TV on children's development in more detail.

Prosocial Behavior

As children mature, they acquire alternative ways to accomplish their goals— ways that are more socially acceptable than aggressive behavior. In addition to learning new social skills, young children also become aware of the hurtfulness of their actions. As they develop more positive feelings toward others and become aware of people's feelings, they begin to inhibit their aggression. The development of **prosocial behavior,** positive actions that are directed toward other people, occurs as a result of socialization and the child's growing self-awareness.

Empathy

The first step in the development of prosocial behavior begins when the child is able to empathize with another person. According to Norma Feshbach (1974), empathy includes "the shared emotional responses which the child

Prosocial Behavior
Positive actions that are directed toward other people.

The ability to empathize involves being aware of someone else's emotional distress. Researchers have found that children as young as two years of age respond to another child's distress.

experiences on perceiving another's emotional reaction." Further, she suggests that empathy involves three components: (1) The child must be aware of the emotional reaction in another; (2) the child must be able to assume the perspective and role of another person; and (3) the child must be able to experience some emotional reaction as a consequence of seeing another person's reaction. According to Piaget, young children in the preoperational period do not possess the cognitive maturity to be able to take another person's perspective. While research has generally supported his views, indications exist that preschoolers have a rudimentary awareness of different social roles as early as two to three years of age (Hoffman, 1981; Watson & Amgott-Kwan, 1983).

Several studies have demonstrated that children as young as two are able to recognize emotional states in other children and respond to them in a caring way (Denham, 1986; Iannotti, 1985; Zahn-Waxler, Iannotti, & Chapman, 1982). Carolyn Zahn-Waxler and her colleagues (Zahn-Waxler, Cummings, McKnew, & Radke-Yarrow, 1984) found that mothers who themselves were more empathic and who disciplined their children when they caused distress in others, were more likely to have children who engaged in prosocial activities such as comforting, protecting, or defending others. Other researchers (Dunn, 1983) have examined the role that early sibling interactions play in the development of empathy and later prosocial behaviors. Most children have brothers and sisters with whom they share similar interests and activities. Because of this common interest and familiarity, it is easier for siblings to understand each other's experience and practice and refine their empathic skills. Dunn reports that children who are encouraged by parents at a young age to cooperate and be kind toward their siblings are more likely to be advanced in their development of prosocial behaviors. We will discuss sibling relationships in more detail in Chapter 8.

Altruism

When people recognize the emotional reactions of other people and respond to them with acts of kindness, they are engaging in altruistic behavior. Helping, comforting, protecting, defending, or sharing are all considered to be altruistic actions. With encouragement from parents and opportunity to practice these behaviors, young children have been known to display altruism toward other children at an early age. Despite the restrictions placed on children's understanding of other people's situations by their cognitive immaturity and egocentricity, they can acquire the prosocial behaviors that foster altruism. Parents who actively talk to their children about how other people feel and at the same time discipline them for causing distress to others have children who display higher rates of altruism at an early age. When a child's attention is called to his or her actions and the effect they have on another, the child is more likely to be able to share the aggrieved person's distress at the time. When Andrew shoved Jonathan in nursery school, the teacher kindly disapproved of his actions and called his attention to how he had distressed Jonathan. Then she asked Andrew to help Jonathan pass out the cupcakes for the class party. By doing so, the teacher was teaching Andrew that hurtful actions are not acceptable or rewarding *and* that helpful ones are. The effectiveness of adult models in teaching altruistic behavior to children also depends on the nature of the children's relationship to the model. If the model has an affectionate and nurturant relationship with the child, then the child is more likely to imitate the model's altruistic behaviors.

Social Play

Early Play

The earliest form of social play may start almost as soon as the baby is born. Mothers, fathers, grandparents, and many others coo at babies, wave rattles at them, sing nursery rhymes, bounce them, and hold them up in the air. The baby responds at first by smiling and later by screaming with delight. The baby does not initiate this play, but there is no doubt that it is play and that it is social. Later the infant will play peekaboo and pat-a-cake.

A six- or seven-month-old baby, terrified of strange adults, will be completely absorbed and fascinated by other children. The older infant can always distinguish other children, including teenagers, from adults. Even by the age of 10 months, one child's play will be highly influenced by that of another child (Eckerman & Whatley, 1977).

Types of Play

The steps in the development of social play are solitary play, parallel play, associative play, and cooperative play. At first, in *solitary play* children play with their toys alone, but within earshot of their mothers. At school, they will play independently without reference to what any of the other children are doing. Later, in *parallel play,* they play within sight and earshot of another child, perhaps playing with a similar toy but in their own way. In the early phases of peer interaction, children seem to be more engrossed in objects than in each other (Mueller & Lucas, 1975). The next type is called *associative play,* in which two or three children use the same equipment and participate in the same games, but each in his or her own way. Then gradually children begin to participate in *cooperative play*—they share playthings, organize games, make friends. Cooperative play reflects children's growing capacity to accept and respond to ideas and actions that are not originally their own.

Summary

A child's self-concept gradually develops over the period from ages two through six through numerous social interactions. Part of the child's self-concept includes gender identity and the development of gender-appropriate behaviors.

Erikson believes that preschool children experience a developmental crisis of initiative vs. guilt. Overcritical reactions to a young child's initiative can lead to a sense of guilt.

Through the process of identification, children take on characteristics of their parents including gender-appropriate behaviors. Gender-role behaviors are learned by observation of models and through reinforcement. Although the differences between the sexes on psychological characteristics are smaller than the differences within each sex considered separately, males have been found consistently to be more aggressive than females.

Parents socialize children within the family by disciplining inappropriate behaviors and reinforcing socially acceptable behaviors. Four styles of parenting have been observed: authoritarian, authoritative, permissive, and uninvolved. The most effective style of parenting is one that combines firm control and warmth.

Discipline includes the use of punishment when children do not obey. Punishment is most effective, however, when consistently applied with a rationale. Alternatives to punishment include managing the situation and catching the child being good.

In families in which mothers are employed outside the home, the children benefit from a more flexible female role model. Divorce produces stresses for both children and parents that lasts for about one to two years. Single-parent families have multiple stresses that affect the parent–child relationship, including financial difficulties. Stepfamilies have the added difficulties of adjusting to different family rules and new members and styles of parenting.

Child abuse is a serious problem caused by parents' inappropriate use of physical punishment and from stresses that overburden the caregivers' ability to cope with children. Abused children are usually more aggressive and avoidant than nonabused children. Treatment of child abuse involves providing abusive families with community support and re-education. In sexual abuse, children are molested or coerced into performing sexual acts. The way to prevent sexual abuse is to teach children to say no to anyone who would touch them in sexual ways.

Children display physical aggression in their play activity. By six years of age, the frequency of aggression decreases as the child acquires self-control and alternative ways of dealing with frustration.

Prosocial behavior develops in the preschool period when the child becomes aware of other people's feelings. Empathy precedes the development of altruistic behavior. Parents can encourage sharing, helping, and other prosocial behaviors by providing examples and disapproval of actions that cause distress in others.

Social play develops in a progression: solitary play, parallel play, associative play, and cooperative play.

Further Readings

Belsky, J., Lerner, R., and Spanier, G. *The child in the family.* Reading, MA: Addison-Wesley, 1984.
Written by well-known researchers in the field of family and child development, this book describes the reciprocal relationship between changes in children's development and changes in the family. A lifespan perspective is used to highlight changes in parent–child relations. Characteristics of families in conflict, teenage pregnancies, and dual worker families are discussed.

Mussen, P., and Eisenberg-Berg, N. *Roots of caring, sharing and helping.* San Francisco: W. H. Freeman, 1977.
The development of prosocial behavior in children is explored in a conversational style. The biological, cultural, cognitive, and situational determinants of altruism, empathy, and sharing are described. Possible ways to encourage prosocial behaviors are presented for parents and educators.

Tavris, C., and Wade, C. *The longest war: Sex differences in perspective (2nd Ed.).* New York: Harcourt Brace Jovanovich, 1984.

In this revised edition, the authors present an updated account of research on differences between the sexes from a biological, social learning, sociological, and anthropological perspective. The authors address the political implications of gender differences in contemporary life.

Wallerstein, J., and Kelly, J. *Surviving the breakup: How children and parents cope with divorce.* New York: Basic Books, 1980.

The authors present the results of their longitudinal study of 60 families from the initial stages of divorce to a follow-up five years later. The psychological impact of the divorce on children and parents is detailed with summary statistics and revealing case-study material. In this compelling and well-written account, the authors provide a rich source of clinical material on divorce.

Walters, G., and Grusec, J. *Punishment.* San Francisco: W. H. Freeman, 1977.

This book represents a comprehensive synthesis of the research on learning, with particular emphasis on the effects of punishment on behavior. The effective use of punishment and alternatives to punishment with children are discussed, and relevant research studies are highlighted.

Observational Activities

6.1 *Gender Typing in Young Children's Play*

When young children play together, they often act out the gender roles they are exposed to in the family and on TV. Children practice gender-appropriate behaviors in play in many ways. The purpose of this observation is for you to observe young children playing and to identify the examples of gender-role behavior in their activities. For this observation, choose a playground or an indoor play area where children are allowed to play on their own. You will want to observe a group of girls and boys, at least two of each sex. Local nursery schools, day-care centers, or church nursery groups are good places to locate a group of two- to six-year-olds. Be sure to obtain permission to observe the children from the teacher or director. Your school may even have a drop-in day-care center that you could use for this activity.

When you have found a group of preschoolers, spend at least 30 minutes observing them. Notice the games they play. Children at this age often use a lot of imagination and fantasy in their play. Use the following questions to guide your observations:

1. Are the girls and boys playing similar games? What behaviors do they engage in? How are they different?
2. Notice the type and frequency of aggressive actions, both verbal and physical. How do the boys and girls differ in amount or type of aggression displayed?
3. Do the children play pretend games? Do they imitate adult roles such as mother, father, firefighter, or nurse?
4. How do the boys treat the girls? How do the girls treat the boys? Are there differences? Similarities?
5. Do the children seem to have an understanding of their own gender? How do you know? What do they do or say that would suggest they know how girls or boys should act?

Stay long enough to collect the information you need to draw some comparisons between the girls' and boys' behavior in play. What differences did you notice? Are these differences consistent with your view of gender-appropriate behaviors? In what ways are the two sexes alike? Summarize your observations and draw some conclusions about the way young children acquire gender-appropriate behavior. Be sure to include what personal insights you have gained in your own understanding of gender-roles.

6.2 *Parenting Styles*

By the time children reach two or three years of age, parents begin to acquire a strategy for raising them. Parents reward some behaviors and punish others. In addition, parents may become sensitive to their function as role models for their young children. In order for you to understand parenting styles more fully, and for you to appreciate the differences between parents in their approaches to child-rearing, you will be asked to interview two sets of parents of preschool-age children. You may have friends or relatives who are parents of young children and would cooperate with you in doing this. Your instructor may be able to suggest other sources of parents for this interview.

Once you have selected the parents, you will need to develop a list of questions you would like to ask them about child-rearing. Include in your list of questions the following:

1. How old and what gender are your children?
2. How do you expect your children (child) to act toward you? toward other children? (Ask for examples.)
3. How do you go about teaching your children (child) these behaviors? Do you provide an example or model for them?
4. What do you usually do when your children (child) disobey you or do not behave in the way you would like them to?
5. Do you allow your children to make decisions? If so, what kinds of decisions? (Ask for examples.)
6. What are the most difficult aspects of raising your children? The easiest?
7. Are there similarities in the way you raise your children and the way your parents raised you? If so, describe. Are there differences? If so, describe.

With your list of questions in hand, interview each parent separately. Begin by introducing yourself (if the parent is a stranger) and your purpose in asking the questions. Then ask the parent the questions you have prepared. You may want to ask to tape-record the interview so that you can listen without taking notes. Be sure to ask for permission. After you have interviewed all parents, reread the section in this chapter on parenting styles and compile a description of each parent's style of caretaking. Compare the different styles. What similarities and differences do you notice? What did you learn by conducting these interviews? Share your observations about parenting with your classmates. You might even want to ask your own parents to respond to your list of questions on parenting. Good learning!

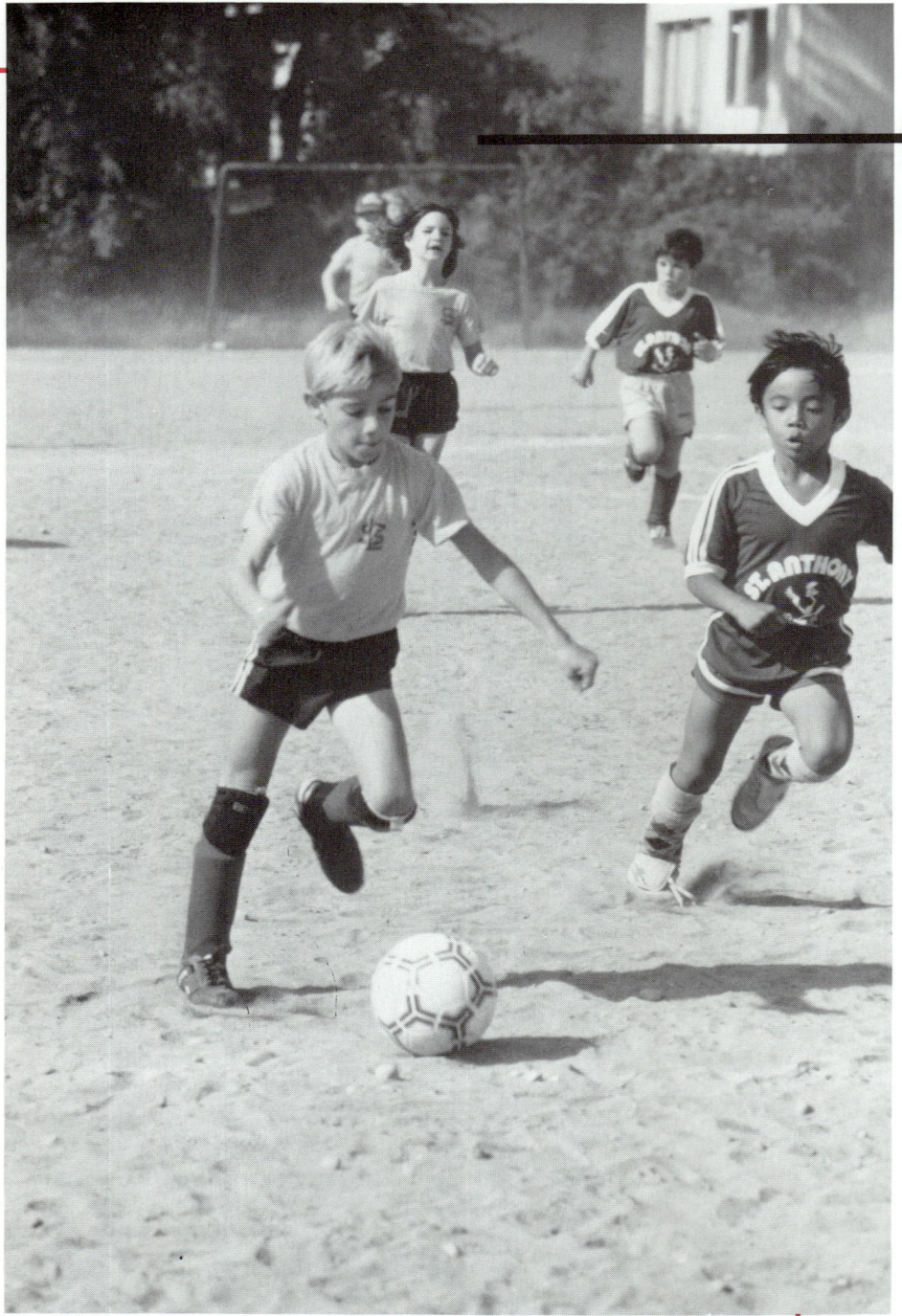

P A R T
THREE

Middle Childhood

*D*evelopmental psychologists call the time from age six through 12 the middle-childhood period. During this six-year period, children refine behaviors they acquired in early childhood such as motor skills. At the same time, new intellectual skills emerge. From a lifespan perspective, the middle-childhood period is the time when children are exposed to an increasingly greater range of social, cultural, and intellectual experiences. Children spend a good deal of their time during the middle-childhood period in school with teachers and in the company of their peers. The influence of parents continues to be important, but is balanced by children's experiences outside the home.

Middle childhood is a time when children develop the competencies that will enable them to mature into independent adolescents and young adults. They learn to do things, to work at a task, to play with their peers, and how to be a friend. It is these changes in development that people remember when they think back over their lives.

In the next two chapters, we explore the developmental changes that occur during the middle-childhood years and their impact on later development. In Chapter 7, we consider the children's physical and intellectual development; in Chapter 8, we consider the changes that occur in personality and social development.

Middle Childhood: Physical Growth, Cognition, and Learning

*I*t was a big day in seven-year-old Ian's life when he came home from school and proudly announced, "I am the best reader in my class!"

Now Ian could read the words in the comic books like his older cousin Adam did. He was also learning how to add and subtract. Now he could go into the local candy store and buy baseball cards and bubble gum on his own! In addition, his second-grade teacher, Mrs. McNulty, was helping him to learn how to write his name and how to draw dinosaurs. He looked up to her and many of the other teachers because they seemed to know how to do so many things.

Ian's parents noticed that he seemed to behave differently at home. His thinking was more like their own—he had become "reasonable." Instead of insisting that things be done his way, as he had when he was four and five years old, now he was open to suggestion and could see things from other people's point of view. His mother learned that Ian could follow her instructions. At times, he even generated his own rules—on his bedroom door he had posted the sign "no girls or babies allowed in."

In his bedroom, carefully arranged on display, was Ian's model spaceship collection, which he had painstakingly constructed from kits received on his birthday. He was eager to build the next model, which, of course, would be better and more complicated than his last one.

In the present chapter, we begin our discussion of middle childhood with a description of the physical changes that occur in this period. Changes and increases in the child's understanding of concepts will be the focus of the second section in this chapter. In the third section, we examine the strategies children use to process information. Finally, we describe the various ways in which psychologists and educators measure children's abilities, and include a discussion of learning disabilities. How these changes affect later development across the lifespan will be a running consideration throughout our discussion.

Physical Growth

Over the next several years known as middle childhood, from six to 12, Ian can be expected to steadily expand his newly found cognitive skills. As he grows in size, strength, and coordination, he will acquire greater skill and poise in his physical world. The period of middle childhood is punctuated with numerous examples of children's mastery of ideas, skills, and tools—part of the enlarged competencies that will eventually transform them into adults.

Size and Proportion

During middle childhood, children's growth is more uniform than it was previously. Instead of large spurts in height or weight, size increases gradually

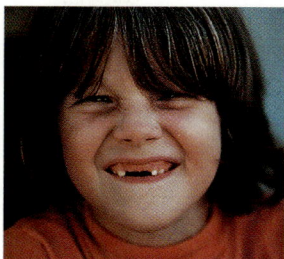

A readily obvious physical change that occurs in the school years is the loss of baby teeth. Soon this five-year-old will be sprouting permanent teeth.

from age six to about 10 or 12, at which age there is a growth spurt. Height increases from an average of 47 inches at age six to about 59 inches at age 12. Likewise, weight gain is relatively constant during middle childhood at a rate of about five to six pounds per year. The average six-year-old weighs approximately 45 pounds, while the average 12-year-old weighs 86 pounds. This weight gain is a result of growth in muscle and bone tissues, accompanied by a gradual decrease in fatty tissue as children grow taller and leaner. Body proportions change gradually over this six-year span as children develop a more adultlike body.

Between the ages of six and eight, the myelinization of neurons is approaching completion, and by eight years of age, the brain is nearly its mature size. In addition, brain waves reflecting the electrical activity increase in frequency, producing a more mature level of brain activity (Epstein, 1980).

Notable gender differences occur in growth during the school years. By age 12, girls are two years ahead of boys in height and weight, even though boys are heavier at birth than girls. Between the ages of nine to 10 years, girls experience a growth spurt. They grow taller and retain more fatty tissue than boys. As a result, girls develop softer, rounder contours, while boys' bodies are becoming more muscular and angular. Boys also have greater forearm strength than girls, even though the average girl is taller and heavier.

One readily obvious physical change that occurs in the school years is the loss of baby teeth and the eruption of permanent teeth. Beginning at ages five or six, children start to lose their teeth; girls typically lose their teeth earlier than boys. By age 12, the larger, permanent teeth are developed, giving the child's face a more grown-up look.

There is considerable variability in size among school-age children, so much so that if a seven-year-old of average height were to stop growing for two years, the child would still be within the normal range for height at age nine (Tanner, 1978). In the United States, heredity rather than diet seems to account for most of the differences among children in size. However, in other areas of the world, environment may be a contributing factor. Meredith (1982) found a consistent difference in size between schoolchildren from urban and rural settings. Urban children were, on the average, taller and heavier than rural children. He attributed this difference to a greater access to health, nutritional, and medical resources in the urban settings.

Motor Development

There is considerable variation in height among school-aged children.

Accompanying the gradual increase in size is an increase in strength and coordination. As the muscles increase in size, the child develops greater muscular control over the body. Children acquire greater precision in gross motor skills; they can run, jump, hop, and skip with grace and agility. The child of six can jump rope, ride a bicycle, and roller skate. Fine motor precision takes a little longer, as can be witnessed by the child's improvement in handwriting from the first to the sixth grade. With greater hand and finger control, school-age children can learn to play the piano and other musical instruments, learn to sew, construct models from kits, or paint by numbers. With practice, many children perform these skills nearly as well as adults do.

During this period, children practice and refine their motor skills by becoming members of sports teams such as Little League or local soccer

One of the consequences of muscle growth during middle childhood is a greater precision in gross motor skills such as skipping rope.

Physical Fitness The body's degree of optimal functioning measured by muscular strength, heart rate, and lung capacity.

leagues. They also learn to follow rules and to cooperate with their fellow team members. Many children gain a sense of self-esteem through their athletic achievements. Accumulated ribbons and trophies provide children with tangible evidence of their growing competencies. Not all children, however, distinguish themselves through motor skills and, consequently, find other arenas in which to display their skills. Physical maturity, practice, and encouragement are all important in the development of proficiency in motor skills. The child who is not particularly good at throwing a ball may not be interested in playing ball with other children, and hence not gain the precision in ball throwing that results from practice.

Physical Fitness

A nationwide survey of over 8800 children between the ages of 10 and 18 revealed that children today are fatter and less physically fit when compared to children in the 1960s (National Children and Youth Fitness Study, 1984). **Physical fitness** refers to the body's optimal level of functioning and is measured in terms of heart rate, muscle strength, and lung capacity. Despite the fact that children in the middle-childhood period are better coordinated and have the time to develop fitness skills, many do not. Instead, many children spend a large amount of their in-school and after-school time being physically inactive (e.g., watching television or staying indoors).

Many schools have reduced or eliminated physical-education and recreation programs from their curricula in an attempt to save money. However, these cuts may be shortsighted. It is during the school years that many children acquire the physical skills (e.g., swimming, tennis, running) that they will continue to use throughout their adult lives. Physical-fitness habits learned in childhood can help prevent such adult disorders as high blood pressure, obesity, and heart disease. Many of the sports that are emphasized in the schools are team sports (e.g., soccer, football, baseball). After children leave school and certainly when they reach adulthood, it is difficult for them to continue their physical activity through team sports. Far too few schools expose their children to sports that they are likely to continue in their adult years (e.g., running, golf, skiing, tennis, bowling).

There is another drawback to the lack of physical fitness in childhood. Many children are aware of how they look to others, especially to their peers. A physically unfit and overweight child is not only unhealthy, but may also be unpopular. Generally, the larger, more muscular child is also the child who is popular with peers. In part, this is because the more muscular the child, the more likely he or she will be adept in sports and physical games.

Obesity is a physical characteristic that carries a negative stereotype. It has long been known that young children have negative attitudes toward obesity—even overweight children express such attitudes (Lerner & Korn, 1972; Reaves & Roberts, 1983). In one study (Young & Avdze, 1979), the researchers wondered if the behavior of an obese child would reduce the negative image caused by obesity. The results showed, first, that the child of average weight is preferred to the obese child, and second, the obese child who was shown to be obedient was preferred to the normal-weight child who was disobedient. Thus, a child's behavior can override the negative force of obesity, but only if the behavior is "good."

Good behavior, unfortunately, will not completely solve the social stigma of a child's obesity. Another researcher (Sallade, 1973), using a self-concept scale, found that obese children in the third, fourth, and fifth grades had poorer self-concepts than average-weight children. If children express their negative attitudes toward their obese peers (and it is most certainly the case that they do), the results may have profound consequences for the social adjustment of these children (See Box, Obesity in Children).

Human Development in Practice

Obesity in Children

Many health-care professionals recognize the immediate and long-term hazards associated with obesity in childhood. Obesity is defined as weight that is 20 percent or more above the ideal weight for a person based on height, age, and gender. According to one report (Dietz in Kolata, 1986), there has been a 50 percent increase in the number of school-age children who are obese. Furthermore, 40 percent of children who are obese at age seven become obese adults.

One popular theory about obesity is that it is a hereditary condition; fat adults are likely to have fat children who will become fat adults. Results from a recent longitudinal study of adopted children and their biological and adoptive parents suggest that genetic factors play an important role in obesity (Stunkard, Thorkild, Sorenson, Hanis, Teasdale, Chakraborty, Schull, & Schulsinger, 1986). Adopted children were more similar in weight and body build to their biological parents than to their adoptive parents who raised and fed them. If one parent is obese, the risk of having an obese child is estimated at 40 to 50 percent (LeBel & Zuckerman, 1981). If both parents are obese, the risk increases to 80 percent (Mayer, 1975). However, these figures must be interpreted with caution because overweight parents are also likely to overfeed their children and to serve as models of overeating.

Diet and eating behaviors are considered to be another significant factor in obesity. People who consume more food than their bodies need accumulate excess fat. Obese people who have been overweight since childhood have as much as twice as many fat cells in their bodies as do nonobese people (Hirsch, 1975; Winick, 1975). Clearly, diets that are high in fat and carbohydrates (such as fast and snack food) add to the problem of maintaining normal weight. Further-

more, overfed infants develop more fat cells than infants who are not overfed (Winick, 1975). Once added, fat cells remain in the body throughout life. However, it is not at all clear that developing an excess number of fat cells in infancy automatically results in obesity in later childhood and adulthood. Many obese children are not obese as adults, and many obese adults were not overweight as children (Roche, 1981).

A low level of physical activity is a third contributor to obesity. Obese children do not move as often or as vigorously as nonobese children, and hence, they do not burn up excess calories and fat as quickly. One researcher (Dietz in Kolata, 1986) has suggested that second to prior obesity, television viewing is the strongest predictor of obesity. When children spend long hours in front of the television, they not only are inactive, they also eat more food. Attractively presented commercials promote a host of snack foods, many of which are shown being eaten by thin people, thus encouraging viewers to eat without concern of weight gain.

What steps can be taken to help obese children lose weight? The first step is a complete medical checkup to eliminate the possibility of metabolic disorders. Then, parents and their obese children must cooperate to change family eating behaviors. Balanced diets and a regular program of physical activity are essential ingredients of any weight-control program. Furthermore, if the obese child takes an active part in the weight-control program, it is more likely that the weight lost will not be regained. Children whose weight loss is under parental control rather than self-control may lose weight, but they are also likely to regain the weight at a later time (Cohen, Gelfand, Dodd, Jensen, & Turner, 1980).

Pause for Thought

Children during the school years compare themselves to their peers and draw conclusions about themselves as a result. Physical size and fitness is a fairly obvious characteristic for comparison. How might a child's view of self be affected by making physical comparisons? What factors might affect the degree of children's physical activity?

Cognitive Growth

Around the age of six or seven, children appear to make a remarkable shift in their ability to understand and think in a rational, logical manner. They become reasonable! Parents and teachers often recognize the transition from prelogical thought to logical thought when the child responds to rules and requests, or when the child supplies a reason for his or her behavior that is guided by logic. For example, five-year-old Lisa might explain a sunset by referring to magic or some other fantasy such as "the sun goes to bed at night," whereas seven-year-old Ian is likely to recognize that the sun is inanimate and may even be able to explain why he does not see the sun at night.

Piaget's Theory: Concrete Operational Thought

Describing the change in children's thought processes in his theory of cognitive development, Piaget stated that, by age seven, children enter the third stage of cognitive development—**concrete operations.** This stage is characterized by the acquisition of several conceptual skills that permit a logical manipulation of symbols. Many of the limitations of preoperational thinking (described in Chapter 5) disappear as the child begins to think logically. This stage is labeled "concrete" because the child's thinking is still limited by reliance on what the child observes, on tangible or concrete objects or events. For example, a six- or seven-year-old may have difficulty understanding what a democracy is since it is an abstract concept referring to a variety of actions the child cannot actually see. However, if the teacher were to lead the class in an election based on democratic principles, children may be able to understand the concept of democracy through their real-life experience of it. The challenge for many educators is to make their lessons concrete enough for students to understand. The ability to logically manipulate abstract and unobservable concepts does not emerge until about age 11 or 12, when the child enters Piaget's last stage of cognitive development, **formal operations.**

Decentration and Reversibility

Even though children reason primarily using information that is directly perceived, they become more flexible in their use of information. Unlike the preoperational thinker, the child is now able to shift attention from one perceptual attribute to another. This process, **decentration,** actually begins before the period of concrete-operational thought but becomes more generalized and applied to increasingly more complex problems during middle childhood.

A second accomplishment during the concrete operational period is seen in children's ability to reverse their thinking. **Reversibility** is the ability to mentally retrace actions in thought. For example, in the water-jar problem described in Chapter 5, the child is presented with two identical glasses filled

Concrete Operations Within Piaget's theory, the third stage of cognitive development; characterized by the development of logical thought and the ability to manipulate symbols.

Formal Operations Within Piaget's theory, the fourth, and final, stage of cognitive development that emerges during adolescence or later; characterized by abstract, logical, and hypothetical reasoning.

Decentration According to Piaget, the child's ability to shift his or her attention from one perceptual attribute to another.

Reversibility According to Piaget, the child's ability to mentally retrace his or her actions or thoughts or to think backward.

with identical amounts of juice. When the liquid of one glass is poured into a taller and thinner glass, the concrete-operational thinker recognizes that the glasses still contain identical amounts of juice because the child can mentally retrace the steps in the sequence of pouring the juice from the original to the taller glass. The child also is able to decenter—to shift perceptual focus to include the height and width of the fluid in the glasses. Hence, the child is able to judge them as equivalent.

Conservation Skills

In recognizing that the amount of juice has remained the same even though the container has changed, children demonstrate the achievement of conservation of liquid quantity. With the general understanding that some aspects of an object or substance do not change even though its shape may be transformed, children introduce some stability to their perceptions of the physical world. The acquisition of conservation skills allows children to make logical predictions about what will happen to physical objects with which they come in contact daily.

Piaget and Inhelder (1969) maintain that all children go through the same stages in mastering conservation of the different characteristics of objects. However, children do not achieve conservation of these characteristics at the same age. (See Table 7.1.) The idea that children acquire conservation of different characteristics at different ages is referred to as **horizontal decalage.** Piaget believed that children in all cultures learn to conserve different quantitative characteristics in the same invariant order, although the rate at which they acquire the concepts may vary as a function of specific experiences (i.e., whether they have attended school or not). Thus, conservation of number is achieved before quantity, and conservation of quantity occurs before weight conservation, which precedes volume conservation (Brainerd, 1978).

Horizontal Decalage According to Piaget, the idea that children acquire conservation of different physical characteristics at different ages.

Classification Skills

During the concrete-operational period, children demonstrate their understanding of true classes by coordinating the two crucial properties of *class intention* and *class extension*. Unlike the preoperational child, the concrete-operational thinker is able to define a class (class intention) and list all of the members of that class (class extension). Throughout the school years, children become more skilled at making groupings and relating these groupings to one another. One of the most frequent pastimes of children between the ages of six and 12 is collecting things and arranging them in relation to each other. Ten-year-old Sally has been collecting colorful stickers for two years and has arranged them using several dimensions: color, size, content of the sticker (e.g., rainbows, unicorns, Garfield characters), and type (scented vs. unscented). By explaining her arrangement of the stickers in her album, she also demonstrates a fairly sophisticated understanding of classification and arrangement of elements in a hierarchy.

Pause for Thought

Being able to organize "things" into logical groupings is a skill that begins in childhood and continues to be useful throughout a person's life. Think of the different ways in which you are able to function better because you can group things together.

Table 7.1

The Development of Conservation

Type	The Child Is Shown:	The Experimenter:	The Child Responds:	Age (in Years) Conservation Is Usually Achieved
Liquid	two equal short, wide glasses of water and agrees that they hold the same amount.	pours water from the short, wide glass into the tall, thin one and asks if one glass holds more water than the other.	*Preoperational child:* The tall glass has more. *Concrete operational child:* They hold the same amount.	6
Number	two rows of checkers and agrees that both rows have the same number.	spreads out the second row and asks if one row has more checkers than the other.	*Preoperational child:* The longer row has more checkers. *Concrete operational child:* The number of checkers in each row hasn't changed.	6
Length	two sticks and agrees that they are the same length.	moves the bottom stick and asks if they are still the same length.	*Preoperational child:* The bottom stick is longer. *Concrete operational child:* They're the same length.	6–7
Area	two boards with six wooden blocks and agrees that the blocks on both boards take up the same space.	scatters the blocks on one board and asks if one board has more unoccupied space.	*Preoperational child:* blocks on board B take up more space. *Concrete operational child:* They take up the same amount of space.	7–8

Table 7.1

(Cont'd.)

Matter	two equal balls of clay and agrees they are the same.	rolls one ball of clay into a sausage and asks if one has more clay.	*Preoperational child:* The long one has more clay. *Concrete operational child:* They both have the same amount.	7–8
Volume	two balls of clay put in two glasses equally full of water and says the level is the same in both.	flattens one ball of clay and asks if the water level will be the same in both glasses.	*Preoperational child:* The water in the glass with the flat piece won't be as high as the water in the other glass. *Concrete operational child:* Nothing has changed; the levels will be the same in each glass.	11–12

Children's Humor

School-age children are notorious for telling bad jokes—jokes that adults consider off-color or too obvious. The ability to tell and understand a joke develops along with the child's growing cognitive skills. A joke that is obvious to an adult may not be immediately obvious to an eight-year-old and not at all understandable to a five-year-old.

Children in the concrete operations stage of thinking are able to appreciate a joke because they can consider several ideas at once. They appreciate puns because they recognize that words can have more than one meaning, and they can simultaneously consider these double meanings.

Consider the following riddle taken from a children's riddle book:

Q: How do you stop a bull from charging?
A: Take away his credit card.

To appreciate this joke, a child must have accumulated enough experience in the world to first of all know what a "charging bull" and a "credit card" are. A four- or five-year-old may not yet have learned the meaning of these words. Secondly, the child must recognize the incongruity in the idea that bulls can use a credit card. A child of four or five is unlikely to get this joke, whereas the eight- or nine-year-old will. To an adult, this joke may be

As children develop their cognitive skills, they also appreciate the humor in jokes they tell one another.

funny the first time it is told, after which the joke presents no challenge and loses its value.

Jokes are funny to the extent that there is some incongruity, some unexpected situation or outcome. The pleasure of a joke comes from figuring it out (McGhee, 1979). A joke must be moderately complex or challenging to be considered funny, however. If the joke is too difficult or beyond the listener's level of cognitive understanding—or too obvious or easy—it is unlikely to be considered funny.

In one study, school-aged children's ability to appreciate, produce, and understand humor was measured and related to their overall competence in school (Masten, 1986). Children who were better at producing, understanding and appreciating humor were viewed by their teachers as more attentive, cooperative, and generally more competent in the classroom. Their peers viewed these children as more popular, outgoing, and happy.

As school-age children become less egocentric and can take another person's perspective, they take delight in telling a joke that fools the listener, particularly when the listener is an adult. Consider this "knock knock" joke told by 10-year-old Sally to her father:

Knock, Knock!
Who's there?
Banana.
Banana who?
Knock, Knock!
Who's there?
Banana.
Banana who?
. . . and so on for about seven or eight more times until Sally recognizes that her father is growing tired of the joke, at which point she says:

Knock, Knock!
Who's there?
Orange.
Orange who?
Orange you glad I didn't say "Banana"?!

An awareness of her father's perspective is needed for Sally to tell and appreciate this joke. Also, in telling the joke, Sally takes pleasure in being in the authority role. She, rather than her father, now is the one with the answers. Children use jokes to entertain as well as tease others. The older the child, the more aware he or she is of the entertainment value of a joke (Fowles & Glanz, 1977). Children realize that not only is it fun to tell a joke, it is also fun to hear it. Twelve-year-old Joel recognizes that a joke would be spoiled for the listener if it is heard too often, so he tells his jokes sparingly and privately to maximize their enjoyment.

Perspective Taking and Social Cognition

By about age six or seven, children begin to demonstrate that they realize that others often perceive the world differently than they do. They begin to move away from the egocentric thinking that is typical during the preschool years. At this time, children begin to differentiate between their thoughts about an object, person, or event and the way others think about the object, person, or event. In recognizing the possibility that their view of things may not necessarily reflect another person's view, children are now in a position to benefit from other people's perspectives on issues. One characteristic of seven-year-olds often noticed by parents and teachers is that they are open to adult input, and often solicit adult opinions on problems they are facing.

During the years from six to twelve children gradually become more aware of other people and learn to care about others.

The loss of egocentrism also means that children can consider other people in their actions. For example, they are able to understand what it is like to be a parent and what behaviors are expected of a mother or father (Watson & Amgott-Kwan, 1983). They can take the other person's position and imagine what it is like to be that person. When a teacher admonishes a seven-year-old child for his aggressive behavior by asking "How do you think Johnny feels when you shove him?" the child is likely to be able to answer her question and correct his behavior. With a decrease in egocentrism, co-operation with others increases as the child becomes more aware of the effect his or her actions may have on others.

Taking the viewpoint of others is closely related to the comprehension and use of social-relational terms. For a girl to understand that she is her sister's sister, for example, or her mother's daughter, she must grasp the nature of reciprocal relationships. This, in turn, implies the mastery of reversibility in thinking, which is the achievement of concrete-operational thought. Obviously, the development of this ability to decenter from oneself and to take the role of others has important consequences for the child's ability to understand the feelings of others and to function socially. Hence, cognitive growth facilitates the development of social behavior and morality.

Social Cognition The child's knowledge and understanding of social relationships and reactions.

Knowledge about social relationships and reactions is called **social cognition.** It may be generally described as awareness and understanding of how other people think, feel, and see things; what they intend; and how to describe other people. Social cognitive skills (which are developmental) are primitive in the preoperational child, but some three- and four-year olds can assume another person's visual perspective in a familiar environment (Shantz, 1983). Over the years from six to 12, children gradually obtain a fuller understanding of others and their relationship to them. For example, children as young as five or six infer disposition states in other people based on behavior, but it is not until age nine or so that children view the behavior of another as indicative of more permanent dispositions that are consistent across time and situations (Rholes & Ruble, 1984). As we shall learn in Chapter 8, children's growing awareness of other people affects their relationship with and acceptance by peers (Ladd & Oden, 1979), and their view of themselves (Damon, 1977).

Moral Reasoning

Moral Reasoning A person's ideas or judgments about whether some action is right or wrong, based on a set of rules.

Moral Behavior A person's actions based on their moral reasoning.

Ten-year-old Erin was upset when her girlfriends at school began to make fun of the way Dudley carried his books. Although she did think that Dudley carried his books in an odd way, she didn't think it was right to tease him. Yet she didn't want her friends to reject her or, worse, make fun of her. Erin truly was in a dilemma about what was right and what was wrong in this situation. In this case, Erin's behavior (not to tease Dudley) was not in conflict with her belief that it was wrong to tease. It is helpful in our discussion of moral development to distinguish between **moral reasoning**—the person's judgments about the appropriateness of an action based on some set of rules—and **moral behavior**—the actions in which a person engages. Moral reasoning is a cognitive act. As children become more capable of thinking abstractly, of coordinating more than one idea, and of seeing other perspectives besides their own, they are also able to make more sophisticated moral judgments. Even though children may understand and accept moral standards defining right and wrong, they do not always act on these standards. For example, 10-year-old Sally knows that it is wrong for her to use her brother's stereo without first obtaining his permission. When her friends were visiting and wanted to hear a new record, however, Sally played it on her brother's stereo, even though she was fully aware that she was doing something wrong. This discrepancy between moral reasoning and moral behavior is normal and to be expected from children during middle childhood.

Piaget's Views

Piaget (1965) believed that the essence of morality is found in the child's respect for rules. Rules of appropriate conduct dictate the rightness or wrongness of an action. By studying the changes in the way children use rules in playing a game of marbles, he was able to distinguish three stages in the development of moral reasoning. In the first stage, *premoral judgment*, characteristic of ages two to five years, children do not possess the cognitive structures necessary to make moral judgments. They are not even aware of rules or the need for them. When playing marbles, for example, the child at this stage focuses more on its own pleasure in shooting the marbles than on following the rules of the game.

Around five years of age, the child enters the second stage of moral development, *moral realism,* in which rules are regarded as sacred and unchangeable. Children now use rules as guidelines for proper and acceptable behavior. This is the age when the often-heard refrain "It's not fair!" has its origin. Rules are viewed as absolute extensions of higher authority, handed down by God or by parents. At this stage, children also judge the goodness or badness of an action in terms of its consequences, rather than the intentions of the actor. For example, a child at this stage would consider a child who accidentally breaks five teacups to be naughtier than the child who intention-

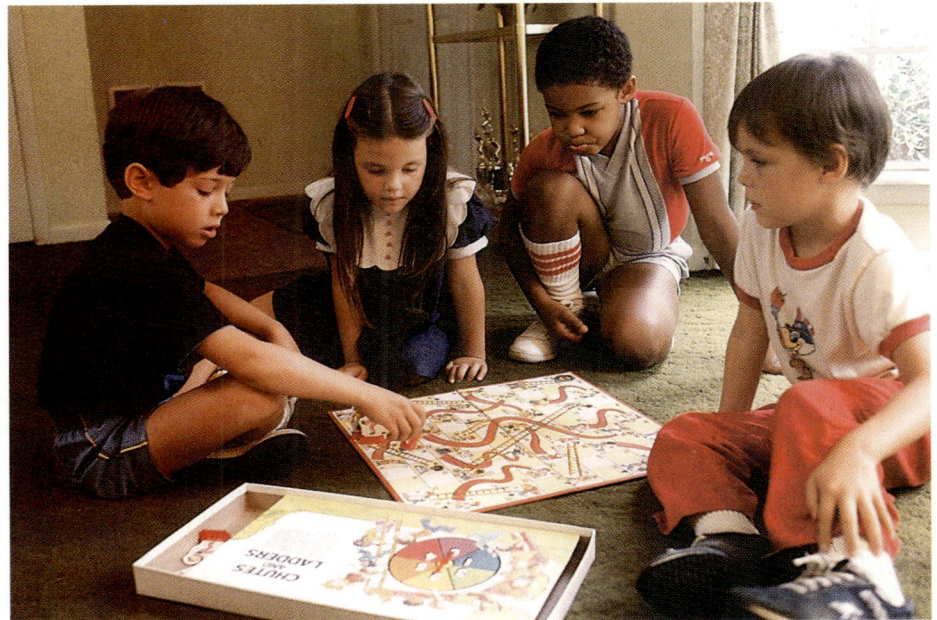

By studying the changes in the way children use rules in playing games Piaget was able to distinguish different stages in children's development of moral reasoning.

ally breaks one teacup. Children view punishment as a natural consequence of breaking rules and often suggest harsh and severe punishments for bad acts.

By about 10 years of age, children give evidence of more mature moral reasoning in the third stage known as *autonomous morality*. Shifting from a blind acceptance of rules and authority to growing awareness that rules are made by people, children realize that the purpose of rules is to help people meet their needs; to the extent that rules do not serve this purpose, they can be changed. Often children at this stage readily make up their own rules as they play games or modify existing ones. There is a shift in children's judgment of behavior. Now, actions are judged by the person's intentions and not the consequences of the behavior. The child who purposely broke the teacup would be judged as naughtier than the child who accidentally broke five teacups. Punishment is viewed as a way to teach the offender that his or her actions are inappropriate. Children at this age also believe that punishment should lead to some restitution to the victim of the inappropriate action. For example, a 10-year-old may suggest that the child who purposely broke the teacup pay for a new one and be made to wash the dishes for a week.

Kohlberg's Theory

Inspired by Piaget's work, Lawrence Kohlberg developed a theory of moral reasoning based on his studies of children of differing ages. Like Piaget, he postulated that children go through different stages of moral reasoning as their cognitive skills mature. Kohlberg (1963, 1964, 1976) based his theory on extensive analysis of interviews with boys ranging from 10 to 16 years of age in which they were presented with 10 hypothetical moral dilemmas. Each dilemma consisted of a story in which disobedience to a rule or an adult resulted in either a reward or punishment. The following is an example of one of the dilemmas Kohlberg (1976) used:

> In Europe a woman was near death from a special kind of cancer. There was one drug that the doctors thought might save her. It was a form of radium that a druggist in the same town had recently discovered. The drug was expensive to make, but the druggist was charging ten times what the drug cost him to make. He paid $200 for the radium and charged $2,000 for a small dose of the drug. The sick woman's husband, Heinz, went to everyone he knew to borrow the money, but he could only get together $1,000 which is half of what it cost. He told the druggist that his wife was dying and asked him to sell it cheaper or let him pay later. But the druggist said, "No, I discovered the drug, and I am going to make money from it." So Heinz got desperate and broke into the man's store to steal the drug for his wife. (Kohlberg and Gilligan, 1971, pp. 1072–1073)

Was Heinz correct in stealing the drug? What Kohlberg was most interested in was not the answer to this question but in the reasoning behind the answer. He proposed that moral reasoning develops in a three-level, six-stage sequence that is summarized in Table 7.2.

Children between the ages of four and 10 seem to function at the level of preconventional moral reasoning in which morality is based on anticipated rewards or punishments. A good act is one that is rewarded and a bad act is punished. At Level I, Stage 1, children focus on the physical consequences

Table 7.2 ▬▬▬▬▬▬

Kohlberg's Levels of Morality

Level I	Preconventional Morality	
	Stage 1	Obedience and Punishment Orientation: Obeys rules set by authority to avoid punishment.
	Stage 2	Instrumental Exchange Orientation: Follows rules to get rewards or return a fair exchange.
Level II	Conventional Level	
	Stage 3	Good Boy/Nice Girl Orientation: Conforms to rules to gain approval.
	Stage 4	Law-and-Order Morality: Conforms blindly to rules or laws for the good of society.
Level III	Postconventional Morality:	
	Stage 5	Social Contract Orientation: Sees rules and laws are relative to the group that makes them and agrees to uphold them.
	Stage 6	Universal Ethical Principles Orientation: Follows self-chosen universal principles that are valued above laws or social agreements.

of their actions. Thus, a child at this level may reason that Heinz should not steal the drug because he might get put in jail or he should steal the drug because it is not really worth $2000. In Stage 2, children reason that good acts serve one's own purpose. Thus, a child may reason that it is appropriate for Heinz to steal the drug because he needs it to save his wife's life or he should not steal it because the druggist is simply trying to earn a living.

At Level II, the level of conventional morality, there is a shift in reasoning. At this level, children conform to and maintain the status quo—that is, the laws and convictions that have been developed by one's family and society. A child at Stage 3 might say that Heinz should not steal the drug because it would not be his fault if his wife died; he did what he could do to help her, or he should steal the drug because saving her life is part of being a good person. At Stage 4, the reasoning for or against stealing the drug would be based on Heinz's duty either to his wife or his duty to uphold the law that prohibits theft.

During middle childhood, Level I (preconventional) morality generally predominated. However, Kohlberg (1963, 1964) did report that 40 percent of his 10-year-old subjects functioned at the conventional level of moral reasoning. (A more detailed discussion of Levels II and III will be presented in Chapter 9.)

Evaluating Kohlberg's Theory

While Kohlberg's ideas have generated a lot of interest and research projects on moral development, his views have been criticized. One criticism leveled by Carol Gilligan (1982) is that Kohlberg's ideas are based on a male perspective of morality (recall that Kohlberg's views were developed from boys' responses to his moral dilemmas). Kohlberg defined the highest standard of moral development in terms of a masculine focus on rules and justice. In contrast, women are more likely to be concerned with the social interpersonal aspects of a situation when making moral judgments. Using Kohlberg's system of assessing the level of moral reasoning, girls would be judged to be less mature than boys in their moral development if they placed concern and caring for others above the value for laws.

Kohlberg maintained that his three levels of moral development were universal, that is, they could be applied to people from all cultures. Nisan and Kohlberg (1982) studied the moral development of people in Turkey and found evidence for the stage sequence. However, there were differences within the Turkish population—city dwellers were judged to be at a higher level of morality than people who lived in rural areas. Other researchers have reported that the moral standards of other countries are not always consistent with those held in the United States (Bronfenbrenner & Garbarino, 1976).

Pause for Thought
Social learning theorists believe that morality is learned just as all behaviors are learned, that is by reinforcement, or by exposure to appropriate models. Cognitive developmentalists believe that morality is limited by the level of cognitive functioning a person has achieved. Can these two views both be correct? How would you decide which view was the "right" one? Can you think of situations in which both views would apply?

Training Moral Behavior

Social learning theorists view moral actions as learned behavior. One factor influencing the acquisition of moral behavior is children's ability to comprehend the moral significance of their actions. Thus, children who do not understand the difference between right and wrong are not likely to engage in moral behavior. Once children have acquired the ability to reason morally, they can act morally. Parents and teachers can facilitate children's acquisition of appropriate behavior by rewarding desired behavior and punishing undesired behavior. Generally, adults who provide children with clear and direct instructions about the appropriateness or inappropriateness of their actions in a loving and firm manner are more likely to encourage moral behavior. Punitive or excessively critical disciplinary actions are likely to discourage moral growth because children are usually too emotionally aroused by the punishment to focus on the moral aspect of their behavior. Reprimands that direct children's attention to the consequences of their actions on others are more likely to help children acquire moral behavior. For example, if the child has lied about something, parents should tell the child that it is wrong to lie because other people will not be able to believe or trust the child in the future.

Children who can take another person's perspective, who understand that other people have feelings and beliefs that may differ from their own are more likely to act kindly and helpfully toward others. Role-taking skills are a necessary ingredient for moral behavior. Being able to imagine how another child might feel if her toy was stolen might help a child resist the temptation to steal. Role-taking skills increase throughout the middle-childhood period, but studies suggest that children can be trained to take the role of another person (Ianotti, 1978).

Pause for Thought

Many fairy tales and fables have moral messages woven into them. Think of your favorite fairy tale from your childhood. What possible moral messages are contained in the story?

Information Processing

Paralleling the child's cognitive skills are the child's expanding capabilities in memory, attention, and problem solving. Taken together, these skills allow the child to process information, which, in turn, influences cognitive achievements. Likewise, it is difficult to separate the influence of cognition from memory, attention, and problem solving. For example, Ann Brown and her colleagues (Brown, Bransford, Ferrara, & Campione, 1983) report that children use their newly developed classification skills as an aid in memory—by grouping objects together, children can remember more.

Attention

Not only are children able to remember information better as they get older, but they also become more attentive to specific sources of information. While younger children are easily distracted by irrelevant information, older children are able to filter out the irrelevant to focus their attention on the necessary information. They develop strategies that allow them to scan material to select the desired piece of information (Miller & Bigi, 1977).

Another feature of attention is that children become more selective in the way they direct their attentional resources—they can concentrate on a task

The use of computers allows people to have command of large amounts of information. How might the use of computers change the way people process information?

at hand. More complex cognitive tasks can be attempted because the children are better able to direct their attention to appropriate elements of a task. For example, performing the arithmetic problem 3×4 is a simpler cognitive task than the problem 32×14 because the solution requires fewer steps. To successfully complete the 32×14 task, the child must selectively focus attention on the processes of multiplication, carrying, and addition. This ability to selectively focus attention advances with age (Kail & Bisanz, 1982) and is expressed in numerous areas in the elementary school.

Memory

Strategies

By age six or seven, children's capacity for memory improves significantly, primarily because they begin to use strategies that permit greater recall. The ability to recall information is the product of two activities: **encoding** or processing information into a set of cues that can be used for the second memory activity, and **retrieval**, the ability to remove information from long-term memory. Forgetting then can be a storage problem or a retrieval problem or both. In one study, it was found that older children forgot less than younger children because they were better able to retrieve information (Brainerd, Kingma, & Howe, 1985). School-age children remember things better because they recite the items they want to remember, a process that cognitive psychologists call verbal rehearsal. In one study, only 10 percent of preschoolers spontaneously used verbal rehearsal to recall items in a picture. However, 60 percent of the seven-year-olds and over 85 percent of the 10-year-olds used verbal rehearsal (Flavell, Beach, & Chinsky, 1966).

The use of **mnemonic devices**, strategies to aid recall, increases with age during the middle-childhood period. Older children generally acquire and use more strategies and are more adept at selecting a strategy to match the memory task (Miller, Haynes, DeMarie-Dreblow, & Woody-Ramsey, 1986). For example, if you were asked to remember the names of the people in your class, and you were in a large class and had lots of names to remember, you might attach a unique cue to each name and rehearse the list. If you only had a few names to remember, you might make up a little rhyme or song that included all the names. You have learned to use different strategies for different tasks. It is not until about age 10 that children become adept at using mnemonic strategies (Kail, 1979). Between the ages of six and nine, however, children refine their use of such strategies as *chunking*, a coding strategy for storing and retrieving information. For example, it may be difficult to recall a long string of numbers such as 0 3 7 2 8 9 5 1 0. However, when these numbers are grouped, as in 037-28-9510, they are easier to store and recall.

Another strategy involves *clustering*, or grouping items to be remembered into relevant classes. In an experiment on memorization strategies (Neimark, Slotnik, & Ulrich, 1971), children from first to sixth grades were shown sets of pictures related to four categories: animals, furniture, clothing, and transportation. Without telling them that all the pictures belonged to these four categories, the experimenters asked the children to arrange the pictures in any way that would help them remember the pictured objects. Children from the first to the third grades for the most part made no effort to classify

Encoding A process in memory in which information is stored using cues which later can be used to retrieve information for recall.

Retrieval A process in memory referring to the ability to remove information from long-term memory.

Mnemonic Device A strategy used to recall information from short- or long-term memory.

the pictures. However, the older children made increasingly harder efforts to categorize the pictures. Furthermore, the more proficient they were in organizing the pictures into classes, the better they were in recalling the pictures at a later time.

Making a sentence out of the first letters of an otherwise meaningless sequence is another common coding strategy that aids memory. Ian, for example, was unable to recall the names of the lines on his music staff until his teacher taught him the sentence "*Every Good Boy Does Fine.*"

Pause for Thought

In the United States and in other western countries, the number of school-age children with computer skills has increased dramatically. Computers allow people to store and process large amounts of data. In what ways might the wide availability and use of personal computers change the way people process information?

Cognitive Styles

Cognitive Style A person's particular pattern of thought and the behavior used to respond to cognitive tasks.

Children vary in their approach to learning and problem solving. Some are quick to respond with an answer to a problem, while others may be more apt to ponder a problem before generating a solution. **Cognitive style** refers to both a person's particular pattern of thought and the behavior used to respond to cognitive tasks (Kogan, 1983). A cognitive style reflects an individual's personality and preference, not his or her ability or intelligence. For example, when Ian looks at a group of buildings he thinks about how each building may be used (a functional understanding), whereas his cousin Adam notices the age and architectural styles of the buildings (a structural understanding). Both boys are equally logical and intelligent, but they differ in their style or manner of understanding the buildings. Each boy reflects a different style of learning.

Field Dependence–Field Independence

Some children are more influenced than others by perceptual information that is irrelevant to a problem's solution, but nonetheless is present. People who are *field dependent* have difficulty in separating out a relevant feature from the context or *field* in which it is embedded. The *field independent,* on the other hand, can ignore the irrelevant perceptual information to consider an object or even an experience separately from its field. One way in which this cognitive style is identified is by using the Embedded Figures Test, in which the subject is asked to locate a geometrical figure embedded in a larger one (see Figure 7.1). Compared to field-independent children, field-dependent children are less able to ignore the irrelevant background lines and shapes and thus have more difficulty with this task.

Research suggests that people become more field independent as they move through the middle childhood and adolescent years (Witken, Goodenough, & Karp, 1967). In addition, field-independent children generally are more successful in academic and problem-solving areas (Witken & Goodenough, 1981), including Piagetian-type skills such as conservation, placing objects in a series, spatial perspective taking, and formal operations (Brodzin-

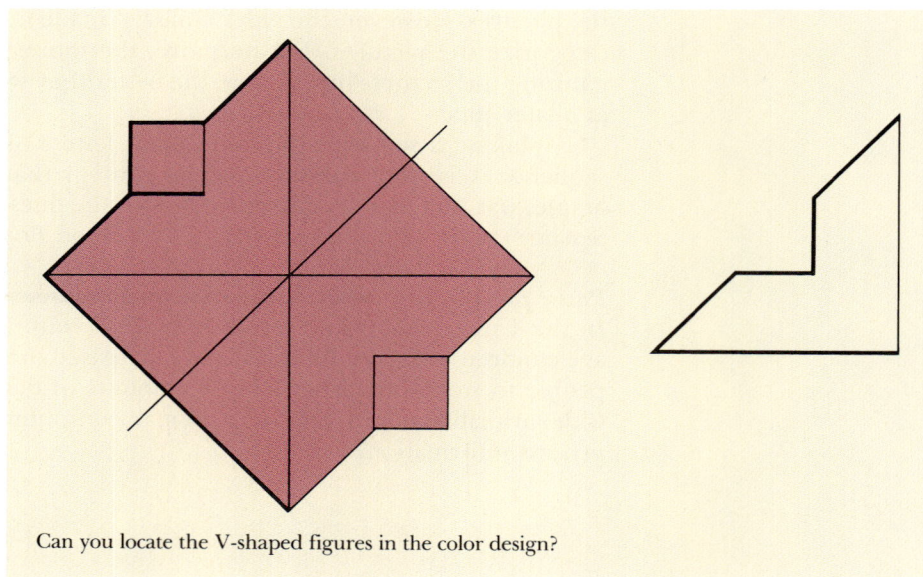

Figure 7.1 An item from the Embedded Figures Test used to measure field independence-field dependence.

Can you locate the V-shaped figures in the color design?

sky, 1985). Other research suggests that field-dependent people may be more skillful in social domains because they are adept at depending on other individuals for cues about how to act in situations in which there are no clear standards (Witken & Goodenough, 1977).

Impulsivity–Reflection

When presented with a problem, some children respond in a quick, cursory, and inaccurate manner, a style that is labeled *impulsive*. Others respond with more deliberation and withhold their answers until they have carefully evaluated their ideas. These children are said to employ a *reflective* style of thinking. Jerome Kagan (1965) developed the Matching Familiar Figures test to measure reflectivity and impulsivity (see Figure 7.2). Children are asked to find a figure from an array of items that exactly matches the standard figure. To be successful in this task, the child must make a careful and detailed examination of each figure. Impulsive children do poorly on this test because they respond too quickly, and often give the first answer that pops into their heads. Thus, they frequently make errors. Reflective children, however, take more time as they systematically scan the task items and consequently are more accurate (Messer, 1976).

Some researchers view reflectivity and impulsivity as two different cognitive styles each of which has adaptive value (Zelniker & Jeffrey, 1976, 1979). Others consider the differences between reflective and impulsive responders to be a matter of differences in abilities, with reflective responders being more adaptive. For example, Messer and Schacht (1986) reviewed a large number of studies and concluded that impulsivity is a maladaptive style of responding. One idea is that impulsive responders may be defensive about appearing incompetent and thus respond too quickly to appear competent. In one study (Wapner & Conner, 1986) involving school-age children, boys who scored

Figure 7.2 Items from the Matching Familiar Figures Test to measure the cognitive style of reflection-impulsivity.

high on a test for defensiveness also scored high on tests for impulsivity. Reflective children have been shown to be more effective problem solvers both in natural settings such as school, as well as in more contrived settings such as the psychological laboratory (Messer, 1976). Furthermore, like field-independent children, reflective children are more successful on concrete and operational tasks (Brodzinsky, 1985).

Research studies suggest that children become more reflective with age, at least through early adolescence (Salkind & Nelson, 1980). In a longitudinal study (Gjerde, Black & Black, 1985), it was found that although children's rate of response changed over time, their error rate did not. This finding suggests that the difference between impulsivity and reflectivity may not so much be a matter of style as ability.

Pause for Thought

Some tasks or activities demand concentration and thought; other tasks call for speed and a high rate of response. What particular jobs or occupations might be better done by impulsive and reflective responders? Do you think our society values one cognitive style over another?

Assessment of Mental Capabilities

Perhaps as early as the first grade, children are evaluated on the basis of their mental capabilities. The most frequent assessment made on schoolchildren is that of intelligence. Educators use measures of the child's basic mental capabilities as one guide to use to place the child in classes and curricula that will enhance the child's potential for success.

IQ Tests

Mental Age The highest age level for which a person passes most of the items on an IQ test.

Intelligence Quotient A measure of a person's intelligence or mental capabilities.

The first practical test to measure the mental capabilities of schoolchildren was published in 1905 by Alfred Binet, who was commissioned by the Paris school system to develop a test to identify those children who were unable to benefit from normal classroom instruction. The test he developed consisted of a variety of items keyed to particular skills appropriate to each age level from three to 15 years of age. Children who could pass the items appropriate for their age would also benefit from the schooling. Those who could not were given special instruction separate from the regular school curriculum.

Binet's test was brought to the United States and adapted by Lewis Terman at Stanford University; it has since been known as the Stanford-Binet Intelligence test. Items of the Stanford-Binet include naming common objects, identifying missing parts from familiar figures, sorting, remembering numbers in a series, defining words, and copying figures. Each age level has a series of items that must be answered correctly for the child to receive a score for that age. By assessing the highest age level for which the child passed most of the items, the child's **mental age** (MA) can be determined. For example, a child who passes most of the 10-year-old items would have a mental age of 10. One way to calculate the **intelligence quotient** (IQ), a measure of the child's mental capabilities, is to divide the child's mental age (MA) by his or her actual chronological age (CA) and then multiply by 100, as in the following formula: IQ = (MA/CA) × 100. In our example, if the child is 10 years of age, the IQ score would be 100:

$$IQ = \frac{10}{10} \times 100 = 100$$

If the child were only eight years of age, the score would be: IQ = 10/8 × 100 = 125. A score of 100 is considered to be average, while a score of 125 would be considered to be superior (see Table 7.3). IQ scores are also determined by referring to charts that translate mental age into IQ scores.

Later, David Wechsler developed a series of tests similar to the Stanford-Binet to measure IQ. Each test is designed to use with a particular age group. The Wechsler Adult Intelligence Scale-Revised (WAIS-R) is used to assess people 15 years or older; the Wechsler Intelligence Scale for Children–

Intelligence is often measured using standardized tests such as the Wechsler Intelligence Scale for Children–Revised Edition (WISC-R).

Table 7.3 ▬▬▬▬

Intelligence Score Distributions

IQ	Percent of Population	Classification
160–169	0.03	
150–159	0.2	very superior
140–149	1.1	
130–139	3.1	superior
120–129	8.2	
110–119	18.1	high average
100–109	23.5	normal or average
90–99	23.0	
80–89	14.5	low average
70–79	5.6	borderline defective
60–69	2.0	
50–59	0.4	mentally defective
40–49	0.2	
30–39	0.03	

Source: R. L. Thorndike, E. P. Hagen and J. M. Sattler. *Stanford-Binet intelligence scale technical manual*, 4th ed. Chicago: Riverside Publishing Company, 1986, p. 127.

Revised (WISC-R) is designed for ages six to 16, and the Wechsler Preschool Primary Scale of Intelligence (WPPSI) is designed for ages four to six-and-a-half. One difference between the Wechsler series and the Stanford-Binet is that the Wechsler IQ tests are divided not by age, but by *skills needed* to perform the various tasks on the test. Two general skills are assessed by the Wechsler tests: verbal and performance skills. Within each of these areas, subtests are used to measure specific abilities (see Table 7.4).

The Stanford-Binet and the Wechsler IQ tests are examples of standardized tests. They are administered individually according to a set standard of instructions. The score that a child receives is translated into an IQ score by comparing the child's performance with the standardized group performance.

Interpreting IQ Scores

Typically, children who score high on IQ tests also do well in school. This finding should not be too surprising since the tests were originally developed to predict school performance. However, IQ tests have been used to predict overall mental abilities and not just school performance. As a result, they have been subject to much criticism and debate. Some argue that the tests are biased in favor of white, middle-class children for whom most of the tests were originally developed. Others point to the heavy emphasis placed on what the child has already learned and not on the child's ability to learn new ideas. In fact, IQ tests measure achievement as well as ability. Some psychologists have suggested that the test be relabelled as a test of *school ability* or *academic*

Table 7.4

Functions of the Subtests of the Wechsler Intelligence Scale for Children—Revised (WISC-R)

Verbal Subtests		*Performance Subtests*	
Information	range of knowledge— statement of learned facts; alertness to the environment	Picture completion	capacity to identify and discriminate between essential and nonessential details in pictures
Comprehension	comprehension of behavioral situations, largely social in nature	Picture arrangement	social alertness and common sense; perception, visual comprehension, and planning
Arithmetic	ability to manipulate number concepts; alertness and concentration	Block design	perception, analysis, synthesis, and reproduction of abstract designs
Similarities	ability to see relationships between facts and ideas; problem-solving ability	Object assembly	visual motor coordination, concentration, and simple assembly skills; ability to see spatial relationships and assemble known objects into a meaningful whole
Vocabulary	organization of ideas into verbal meanings; provides information about quality and kind of language used; best single measure of general intelligence	Coding	ability to learn symbols and shapes and to recreate them; visual motor dexterity, speed and accuracy
Digit span	ability to attend to rather simple situations; immediate auditory recall or memory		

aptitude, instead of intelligence tests (Reschly, 1981). By doing so, the new labels may help avoid the implication that the tests are an index of overall innate ability.

Another criticism of IQ tests is that they place too much emphasis on verbal and logical cognitive skills and do not measure such talents as creativity or artistic or musical aptitude (Ellison, 1984; Gardner, 1983). Furthermore, children not proficient in English or those with language disorders are likely to be mislabeled as mentally retarded on the basis of their IQ score.

Measures of intelligence vary not only from person to person. IQ scores can and do vary for the same person when measures are taken at different times in their development. Children go through spurts in their intellectual development as they do in their physical development. Typically, there is a spurt in intellectual growth at age 6 and then again around age 10 or 11. However, by about age 10, IQ scores stabilize; you can expect to make fairly accurate predictions about intellectual ability in adolescence and adulthood using the IQ score. For example, in one study, the relationship between IQ scores taken at age 10 and IQ scores measured at age 18 was similar. (Honzik, Macfarlane, & Allen, 1948).

Although IQ scores have been overused and misinterpreted by those who have equated IQ with overall general intelligence, the tests do serve a useful purpose when used correctly—they help to predict school achievement. Using the IQ score as one type of guide, educators can discover children who can benefit from a specialized program of instruction tailored to meet their needs and abilities. They can be used to identify the slow learner, who may require more individualized programs, or the gifted child, who may be overlooked in the classroom.

Learning Disabilities

By age six, most children start school and learn basic reading, writing, and arithmetic skills, the "3 Rs." While most children acquire these basic skills, some experience considerable difficulty in the learning process. Compared to their age mates, they may be two or more grade levels behind in reading or arithmetic skills. Years ago, such children would probably have been mislabeled as lazy or mentally deficient. Today, however, most teachers are aware of the possibility that the child may have a learning disability.

Learning Disability
A problem in learning involving one or more of the basic processes that are necessary for understanding and using language and numbers.

Learning disability refers to a problem in one or more of the basic processes that are necessary for understanding and using language and numbers. As such, the term is difficult to define precisely because the specific disorders can vary from person to person and the symptoms may not be obvious early in development. Typically, these problems are not identified until children start school, where they are expected to perform specific learning tasks such as reading, drawing, and writing. Learning-disabled children have normal abilities but for various reasons are unable to express their ability in their actual performance.

Characteristics

Estimates of the incidence of learning disabilities among children vary greatly from 1 percent to over 30 percent (Hallahan & Kauffman, 1982). Four times as many boys as girls are affected by some form of learning disability (Lerner, 1976). Furthermore, some children have multiple difficulties that are obvious as soon as they enter school, while the symptoms for other children may be more subtle. The difficulties in learning may not emerge until later on in childhood, adolescence, or even adulthood, when learning tasks become more complex and demanding.

While there is no universally agreed upon definition of the specific characteristics of learning-disabled children, commonly reported behavioral characteristics do exist (Meier, 1971). The most obvious characteristic is that these children are unable to perform specific cognitive skills at grade level. (See Table 7.5.)

Dyslexia The inability to read as a result of difficulties in combining information from different sensory avenues.

One common type of learning disability is **dyslexia**, the inability to read as a result of difficulties in combining information from different sensory systems. For example, the child may not be able to distinguish the letter "b" from the letter "d" or may have difficulty associating the sound of a letter with the sight of the letter. Other children with dyslexia may not be able to

Table 7.5 ▬▬▬▬▬▬

Types of Learning Disabilities

Dyslexia	Inability to read or spell
Dysgraphia	Difficulty in writing
Dyscalcula	Inability to calculate numbers
Dyskinesia	Motor difficulties, poor coordination, and awkwardness
Hyperactivity (Attention Deficit Disorder)	Unusual energy and restlessness, short attention span, and inability to complete work
Aphasia	Inability to speak or comprehend what is said

Dysgraphia The inability to translate ideas or sounds into written words.

Dyscalcula The incapacity to mentally manipulate numbers or calculate.

organize the words they see into a sentence or be able to distinguish between the meaning of "in front of" and "in back of." **Dysgraphia** refers to difficulty in translating ideas or sounds into written letters and words. Some children, for example, display *mirror writing*, that is, from right to left and backward instead of left to right. The inability to learn basic arithmetic skills because of the incapacity to mentally manipulate numbers is called **dyscalcula.**

Causes

The difficulties in academic performance found among learning-disabled children are not the result of mental deficiency. In fact, learning-disabled children typically score normal or above on IQ tests. Nor are these deficits the result of uncorrected sensory handicaps such as poor vision or hearing loss. Children with learning disabilities may experience a loss of self-esteem as a result of their "failures" in school, and many are aware of their deficits (Cohen, 1983). Many children with undiagnosed learning disabilities often develop behavior problems as a result of frustration at school. Learning disabilities, however, are usually not considered to be a result of emotional or behavioral disturbances.

One explanation of learning disabilities is that these difficulties are a result of a developmental lag. Many of the specific difficulties observed in school-age, learning-disabled children are normally observed in less developmentally mature preschool-age children. For example, most preschoolers reverse or rotate letters of the alphabet, such as "b" for "d" and "q" for "p." While mirror writing, poor motor coordination, short attention span, and distractibility are all frequently observed in younger children, between the ages of five and seven, most of these characteristics disappear. Learning-disabled children, however, seem to be developmentally behind schedule since it is not until the age of twelve that most hyperactivity and attentional problems decrease in learning-disabled children.

Hyperactivity Unusual energy and restlessness, short attention span, and inability to complete work; also referred to as Attention Deficit Disorder (ADD).

Attention Deficit Disorder (ADD) See Hyperactivity.

Some researchers believe that these developmental and learning deficiencies are the result of some neurological dysfunction. In the past, the term minimal brain damage had been used to explain neurological developmental delay resulting in learning deficiencies and other behavioral disorders. Brain damage could occur as a result of birth trauma or accidents, or may be the result of a genetic brain dysfunction. The view that learning disabilities are produced by slight abnormalities in brain development is controversial. Many psychologists believe that the relation between brain functioning (an area still not fully understood) and learning disabilities is an indirect and complex one (Naylor, 1980). (See Box, Attention-Deficit Disorders)

Human Development in Practice

Treating Children with Attention-Deficit Disorders

Teachers may be the first to call attention to the child who does not adjust well to the classroom routine. In the latest revision of diagnostic classification (DSM III), the label **hyperactive** was changed to **attention deficit disorder** (ADD). The new term more precisely describes the symptoms of a disorder that is probably the most commonly diagnosed disorder in childhood (Minde, 1983).

The primary feature of attention deficit disorders is the child's inability to maintain attention. In school, these children have short attention spans, are easily distracted, and seem inattentive. They may daydream a lot and consequently may have difficulty in the classroom or at home, although it is not unusual for ADD children to display attentional difficulties in one setting and not in another. A second characteristic of ADD children is they have a low tolerance for frustration. They give up easily on tasks, may respond physically and aggressively when upset, and generally have difficulty delaying gratification. In short, they act immaturely compared to their age mates. A third characteristic relates to the former label of hyperactive. ADD children display an excessive level of aimless activity. They fidget, run and jump around, and appear restless.

The problem with ADD behaviors is heightened in a school setting where children are expected to pay attention and not be disruptive. Typically, their school performance suffers and they have trouble getting along with other children and sometimes with their teachers. Furthermore, hyperactive children often become poorly adjusted adults (Cantwell, 1972).

There are several hypotheses about the cause of ADD. One possibility is that the disorder is the result of genetic defects. Parents of ADD children tend to have been described as overactive in their early years and to have more psychiatric problems than parents of normal children (Morrison & Stewart, 1973). Boys are much more likely to have ADD than girls. While this gender difference may be explained by differences in socialization particularly in the classroom, others hypothesize that the differences are better explained by biological or genetic differences.

Attention deficit disorder has been treated by drugs that reduce some of the symptoms. Stimulants such as Ritalin seem to help children increase their attention spans and calm themselves down. However, the stimulants must be taken in frequent and often high doses and often have immediate negative side effects such as reduced appetite and insomnia. For some children, a long-term side effect of the stimulant may include a slow down in growth (Puig-Antich, Greenhill, Sassin, & Sachar, 1978).

A different treatment approach is based on the hypothesis that ADD may be caused by food allergies or reactions to certain food additives, flavorings, or artificial colors (Swanson & Kinsbourne, 1980). However, research studies on the effectiveness of additive-free diets on ADD have not been conclusive (Minde, 1983). A third type of treatment involves the use of behavior modification using reward and punishment. Hyperactive children have been shown to decrease their disruptive behavior while under treatment, but these changes in behavior do not seem to generalize to nontreatment settings.

No one treatment approach has been proven to be successful in curing attention deficit disorders. And there is controversy about the cause of the disorder. However, there is agreement among professionals that children with this disorder are best helped when they are diagnosed at an early age.

Pause for Thought

There is considerable variation in the incidence of dyslexia from one country to another. United States has a very high rate; Japan has a very low rate. Italy has a lower rate than the United States (Lindgren, DeRenzi, & Richman, 1985). What possible explanations can you offer for these differences?

Treatment

The best approach to helping children who are likely to experience extended difficulty in learning is to diagnose the disability early enough in their schooling to prevent the buildup of frustration and loss of self-esteem from poor performance. Once recognized, usually by alert teachers, parents, or pediatricians, learning-disabled children benefit from individualized instruction in a setting designed to reduce distraction and increase attentiveness. Most importantly, children need to learn early on in their school years that they can learn and succeed at what they do. By tailoring the lessons and instruction to the child's particular abilities, teachers and parents can help offset the difficulties presented by learning disabilities.

Summary

Physical development during middle childhood is more uniform as children grow taller and leaner. Fine and gross motor coordination improves as children practice physical activities. Physical fitness and skills contribute to the child's self-concept and help establish lifelong habits.

According to Piaget, children attain the level of concrete-operational thinking at about six to seven years of age. They are able to reverse their thinking and decenter. Conservation and classification skills develop throughout the period from six to 12.

Children's appreciation of humor is closely linked with their level of cognitive development. Being able to understand and tell a joke adds to children's sense of competence.

During the concrete-operational period, children lose their egocentric perspective and are able to consider another viewpoint in addition to their own. Social cognition refers to the child's growing awareness of other people and understanding of other people's motives.

Children shift in their understanding of morality at about age six. Piaget described three stages of moral reasoning: premoral judgment, moral realism, and autonomous reasoning. Kohlberg's three levels and six stages of morality are a refinement of Piaget's early work. Children in middle childhood reason for the most part on Level I, preconventional morality.

Kohlberg's theory has been criticized as being biased toward males, as not being universal, and as not related to moral behavior. Adults help children acquire moral behavior by reinforcing their behavior.

Children in middle childhood become more capable of processing information about the world. Attention span increases and children are less easily distracted as they grow older. Their memory skills increase throughout the period from six to 12 because they make more efficient use of strategies.

Children develop their own style of processing information and solving problems. Two cognitive styles that have been studied are field dependence–independence and impulsivity–reflection.

The IQ test was originally developed to predict school performance, and is used in many schools to guide educators in their programs for children. Two popular standardized tests are the Stanford-Binet and the Wechsler IQ series.

IQ tests have been criticized for being too narrowly constructed and biased. IQ scores stabilize at about age 10.

Some children have difficulty learning school subjects because they have a form of learning disability. While the causes of learning disabilities are not fully understood, psychologists and teachers recognize the importance of early diagnosis and treatment.

Further Readings

Cowan, P. *Piaget with feeling: Cognitive, social, and emotional dimensions.* **New York: Holt, Rinehart and Winston, 1978.**
Piaget's stages of cognitive development are described in this readable book. For each stage and substage, the author describes the child's social and emotional development as well. Particular attention is given to the transitional periods between stages. Educational complications of Piaget's approach are included.

Gardner, H. *Frames of mind: The theory of multiple intelligences.* **New York: Basic Books, 1983.**
In his book, Gardner presents his theory that the mind is not a single entity but a constellation of seven specific intelligences. He criticizes the traditional view of intelligence as being too narrowly conceived, and includes such talents as musical ability, bodily talent, spatial perception, and personal sensitivity. His theory and book are thought provoking.

Hamill, D., and Bartel, N. *Teaching children with learning and behavior problems.* **Boston: Allyn and Bacon, 1975.**
This book provides the reader with a review of common problems in learning and behavior encountered in school. Guidelines for assessing and teaching children with specific learning problems are presented along with clear behavioral examples.

Kail, R. *The development of memory in children.* **San Francisco: W. H. Freeman, 1979.**
The developmental changes in memory are described and related to cognitive functioning. This book presents comprehensive coverage of such topics as mnemonic strategies, metamemory, and individual differences in memory.

Moursund, J. *Learning and the learner.* **Monterey, CA: Brooks/Cole, 1976.**
This book is written for the would-be teacher to familiarize the reader with the different facets of learning. Coverage of basic theoretical notions of conditioning, imitation, memory, and thinking is balanced by more specific topics such as cognitive styles, motivation, creativity, and humor. Each chapter has a section in which implications for the classroom are detailed.

Observational Activities

7.1 *Memory in School-Age Children*
During the elementary-school years, children become better at memorizing and remembering things. This is because they develop strategies or plans to help them remember. You probably are aware of different techniques that you use to remember material for exams. By about age 10, children can describe their memory and the techniques they use to remember things. The purpose of this activity is for you to learn the different ways in which children have acquired metamemory. You will need to locate three or four children between the ages of 10 and 12. Perhaps you have younger siblings in this age range who would cooperate with you. Another possible source of children would be to approach the troop leader of a Girl Scout, Boy Scout, or Camp Fire Girls' pack and explain the nature of this assignment.

Once you have located the children, tell them that you are interested in learning how they remember things. It would be helpful if you tape-recorded each of the interviews so that you can talk more spontaneously with the children. In individual interviews, ask each child the questions listed below, being sure to take your time so that he or she can respond fully.

1. Can you tell me what memory is? What do we mean when we say someone has a good memory? Are there different kinds of memory?
2. Are some things easier to remember than others? Give me an example of what is easy to remember. Give me an example of what is hard to remember.
3. How good are you at remembering things? Compared to the rest of the children in your class, how good is your memory?
4. Suppose you were going to a skating party with your friends after school tomorrow and you wanted to be sure to bring your skates. How could you be really certain that you didn't forget to bring them? Can you think of anything else? How many ways can you think of?

After completing your interviews with the children, compile the information you have gathered on their awareness of memory. Reread the section on memory in this chapter and describe the children's strategies for remembering. Note any possible differences between the children's awareness of memory and compare them by age. Share your observations about children's memory with your classmates. What did you learn from doing this activity?

7.2 *Classification Skills and Collections*

Collecting things is a familiar part of childhood. Children collect all sorts of things from stamps, rocks, stickers, and dolls to baseball cards, model airplanes, and bottle caps. As children develop a greater understanding of classes and relations between classes, they apply this knowledge to organize their collections. Because children during childhood are still fairly concrete in their thinking, it is sometimes easier for them to demonstrate their classification skills than it is for them to discuss them. For this activity, you will need to find a child between the ages of seven and 12 who has at least one collection of things. You may have a younger sibling, relative, or neighbor who would be willing to show you his or her favorite collection or collections. You will need to look at the child's collection and make some observations.

1. Ask the child to explain how the objects in the collection are arranged. What dimensions are used to sort the different items of the collection?
2. Notice the way the child has grouped the objects. Ask the child to explain how he or she knows where to place a new addition to the collection.
3. Are there subgroupings in the collection? Ask the child if there are categories that could be combined within the collection (for example, baseball cards from the different teams in the American League).
4. Ask the child to explain what he or she likes about collecting things. In what ways does he or she enjoy the collection? What does the child do with his or her collection?

After you have fully absorbed the details of the child's collecting, go back over your notes and describe the child's collection as an example of classification skills. What can you say about the benefit of collection for school-aged children? What did you learn for yourself in doing this activity? Take a look at your collections and ask yourself the same questions you asked the child in this activity.

CHAPTER

8

Middle Childhood: Personality and Social Development

*I*t was a rainy Saturday afternoon and 12-year-old Lorrie and her cousins were growing bored waiting for the rain to stop. At her mother's suggestion, Lorrie set up the Monopoly game in the family room. Right away, Adam, the oldest and biggest cousin, appointed himself banker of the game. Immediately, Ian, age seven, protested "That's not fair! You were the banker the last time!" As they argued about who should be banker, Lorrie and her nine-year-old sister Amy distributed the play money. Ten-year-old Sarah meanwhile picked her favorite playing piece, the Scottie dog, and then set about to organize her piles of play money.

The bickering had stopped as Adam and Ian resolved their differences of opinion—Adam would be the banker since he was better at making change, and Ian would be in charge of passing out the deeds to the property. Fortunately, the order of the players was determined by a roll of the dice, and it was not long before the five of them were involved in moving along the board, acquiring property, and amassing their fortunes.

Lorrie had earned the reputation of being good at Monopoly because she could remember which properties paid the highest rents. Her younger sister Amy consulted her several times in the game for real-estate advice. Adam was the cousin to consult for advice on making loans to other players. Ian was the one who had mastered the actual rules of the game, while Sarah took pride in the fact that she always managed to land on the "Lucky Chance" spot. The five children were learning about the things they could do, and do well. They were also learning to fill social roles and to form friendships as they played their game. During this period of middle childhood, the focus of attention for children was shifting from their parents to their peers as they learned to establish themselves in their social world.

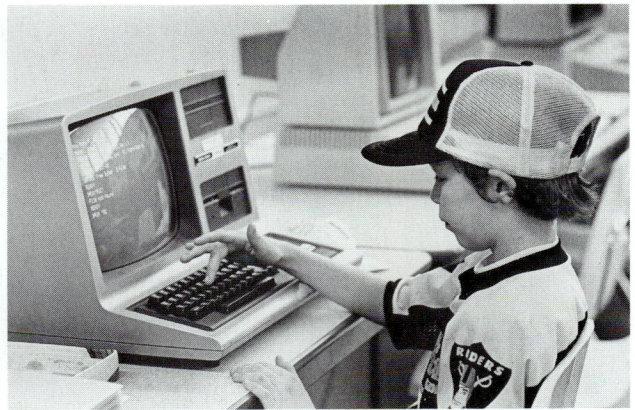

During the period from six to twelve children in all cultures receive instruction in the ways of the world. In some cultures this might be instruction on preparing foods; in other cultures, it might mean learning how to use a computer.

During the period from six to 12, children become more aware of themselves and how they compare with other children and adults. In this chapter, we begin our discussion of the child's personality and social development by examining the development of self-esteem in school-age children. In Chapter 6, we discussed the ways that the family influences a child's view of self. In the second section of this chapter, we will explore other potent sources of socialization—siblings and peers and how they have a significant influence on the child's behavior during the school years. Discussion of socialization would not be complete without mentioning the impact of television in a child's life during middle childhood. As you read this chapter, keep in mind that the changes that occur during the school years are likely to also have an impact on development in later years.

Personality

Most of us can recall many of the events of our school days. These memories helped shape our view of ourselves and our personality, that consistent and unique pattern of social and emotional behavior. The successes and failures in the classroom, playground, and backyard become part of the child's lasting self-concept. Especially significant during the school years is the impact of friends, relatives, and teachers because the child is more aware of other people and their view of him or her. The concrete-operational thinker is capable of seeing the self as others do and is able to combine information about the self from a variety of sources.

Freud's Latency Stage

Freud viewed the period from six to 12 as a quiet one with respect to psychosexual changes. Strong sexual feelings are dormant or latent and children are less emotional in their behavior. Thus, according to Freud, children's psychic energy is freed, allowing them to apply themselves to developing cognitive and social skills.

Erikson's Stage of Industry vs. Inferiority

The period from six to 12 years of age corresponds to Erikson's (1963) fourth stage of psychosocial development, the stage of *industry* vs. *inferiority*. During this period, children develop a view of themselves as workers, as people who can make things that have significance in the culture at large, and in the classroom, home, or playground in particular. Their views of self become part of their adult personality.

It is during the period of ages six to 12 that children in all cultures receive instruction in the ways of the world. In our culture, most of this is formalized in the school curriculum, whereas in other cultures, instruction occurs in less formal settings. This is the age when the young are taught how to hunt, how to cook, make clothing, and care for animals. In many rural cultures, children perform important work for the family and community in which they live. In more industrial-technological cultures, such as our own, children acquire work skills in school subjects: reading, writing, arithmetic, and computing skills. Regardless of the type of work the specific culture demands, all children acquire a sense of their ability to be useful and industrious workers. Children form a sense of industry as a result of their productivity. To the extent that they are able to apply their mastery of the tools of their culture to real problems, they develop a sense of their ability to make things. For example, seven-year-old Ian took great pride in being able to read. Having this skill puts him on the same level as older children and adults. He is now able to do "real" work, not pretend work. He can use his reading skills to help his mother at the grocery store or to play the game of Monopoly with his peers. Success and tangible accomplishments in school or in sports provide children with evidence of their ability to initiate and complete a task. When children enter the first grade, they often bring with them an eagerness and enthusiasm to do things that demonstrate their newly developed skills. Because they are focused on accomplishments, they often admire adults because of their talents. When Sarah was seven, for example, she demonstrated her awe of her mother's cooking skills by stating "My mother makes the best cookies in the world!" Then, when she was able to make cookies on her own under her mother's instruction and guidance, she was able to value her own accomplishments: "Taste the cookies *I* made!"

Not all children, however, find an area in which to demonstrate their competence. Instead, some children experience repeated failure or are made to feel like failures as a result of feedback from others. Consequently, they form a view of themselves as inadequate, incompetent, inferior. Believing that they cannot succeed, these children are easily discouraged from trying out new skills or from persevering on a task long enough to achieve success. They often give up on a project before it is begun.

A child's negative resolution of Erikson's fourth stage may be the result of several factors. The child may have accumulated failures because he or she has selected projects or tasks that are too difficult for the present level of mastery. The child may be attempting to meet the unrealistic expectations of parents who are exerting pressure to achieve before the child is ready. An-

School-aged children evaluate themselves in terms of how they are esteemed by their peers.

other negative influence on the child's psychosocial development is when the child's accomplishments are unrealistically compared to others and thereby diminished. Often the school-age child will use rigid standards to evaluate his or her own accomplishments. When Sarah's mother praised the artwork she had brought home from school, Sarah objected by saying, "Mine was not as nice as Winnie's; hers was much neater!"

Pause for Thought

Being a productive and contributing member of a group is an adult characteristic that has its roots in middle childhood. In what ways can parents, teachers, and other adults encourage children to see themselves as valuable contributors to their families or social groups?

Development of Self

Self-concept refers to the person's sense of his or her own identity, including an awareness of his or her physical characteristics and psychological traits. Throughout middle childhood, self-awareness changes as children develop the cognitive skills that allow them to make more detailed distinctions between themselves and others. Older children are not only more aware of other people's views of them but are better able to integrate these views with their own self-awareness to form a more complex and meaningful concept of self.

Changes in Self-Awareness

The developmental changes in self-concept were the focus of research by John Broughton (1978), who interviewed children about the self. He asked them such questions as "What is the self?" and "What is the mind?" From the answers the children gave, Broughton distinguished two levels of self-awareness in school-age children. In early childhood, the self is regarded in physical terms such as parts of the body. For example, seven-year-old Ian might distinguish himself as different from his cousin Amy because he has freckles and blond hair, while she has brown hair and no freckles. Self-definitions of younger children also include their possessions and toys as well as physical characteristics of their bodies. Gender, age, size, and appearance are critical defining features that young children use in defining the self (Damon, 1983). Physical activities are also included in children's views of themselves.

By about age eight, a shift occurs in the way children view themselves. According to Broughton (1978), at this age children begin to distinguish between mind and body, between what they think and feel inside and what they do or how they look. Older school-age children describe the self in psychological rather than physical terms.

Robert Selman (1980), using a different procedure to assess children's awareness of self, found a similar developmental shift in children's self-concept. He presented children with the following dilemma:

> Eight-year-old Tom is trying to decide what to buy his friend Mike for a birthday party. By chance, he meets Mike on the street and learns that Mike is extremely upset because his dog Pepper has been lost for two weeks. In fact, Mike is so upset that he tells Tom, "I miss Pepper so much that I never want to look at another dog again!" Tom goes off, only to pass a store with a sale on puppies. Only two are left and these will soon be gone (Selman, 1980, p. 94).

The children are asked to decide whether or not Tom should buy the dog for Mike. Using children's responses, Selman has identified three levels of self-awareness in children. In the first level, *physicalistic conception of self,* children view "self" only in physical terms, including their actions. So when Mike says he doesn't want to see a puppy again, young children interpret this statement to mean just that. They do not make any distinction between feelings and actions. The second level of self-awareness emerges at around age six when children begin to distinguish between subjective inner states and more material outer states. Selman called this level *awareness of distinction between actions and intentions.* They recognize the difference between a person's psychological and physical experience but believe that the two types of experiences are consistent with each other. So they interpret Mike's psychological experience of missing his dog to be consistent with his physical or behavioral reaction of saying he doesn't want another puppy. When Mike says he never wants to look at another dog, he means it. Children at this level do not believe that people can distort their outward expression of their inner feelings and psychological experience. They do not yet reflect on their own inner thoughts and feelings.

It is not until the third level, at age eight, that children recognize that a person's inner psychological experience may not be consistent with physical or outer appearance. At this level, which Selman calls *the emergence of an introspective self and the second-person perspective,* children realize that Mike may want another puppy even though outwardly he had indicated that he does not. Children now learn to manipulate their inner states and external appearance. For example, in playing Monopoly, Lorrie may want to buy Park Place but does not express this desire in her behavior because she does not want cousin Adam to recognize her plan and hence thwart it by buying it before she does. Lorrie's strategy is based on her recognition of the distinction between inner and outer aspects of the self and her awareness that others use her external reactions to judge her internal experience.

During middle childhood, children become more aware of personal characteristics in others and use them as standards to evaluate themselves and others (Rholes & Ruble, 1984). Ruble (1983) found that children's use of social comparisons of competence to define themselves dramatically increases after the age of seven. Furthermore, children develop a more differentiated view of themselves as they grow older (McCandless & Evans, 1973). Instead of simply describing themselves as "good" or "bad" as younger children do, children in the later part of middle childhood describe themselves in more specific ways: "I'm good at team sports but not so good at individual events" or "Most of the time I get along well with my friends except when I have to choose between spending time studying or playing." Children also become more self critical as they get older (Harter, 1983). Nine- and ten-year-old children are particularly sensitive to correction and embarrassment in part because they themselves are so self-critical.

Self-Esteem

Self-Esteem An affective evaluation of one's self expressed as positive or negative.

According to Damon (1983), **self-esteem** is an affective evaluation of one's self, generally assessed in terms of positive or negative traits. The self-concept is the cognitive aspect of self. Unlike self-concept, which changes as the child's ability to understand events changes, the child's evaluation of self seems to be more stable throughout middle childhood.

William James (1890) was one of the earlier psychologists who studied self-concept and the evaluation of self. He believed that a person's self-esteem was a result of three factors: (1) the extent to which our successes or achievements meet our aspirations; (2) the degree to which our achievements or successes are also valued by communal standards of success or status; and (3) the extensions of the self—the material possessions and reputation a person has accumulated. If we achieve our aims, if society views them positively, and we value our acquisitions, we will have high self-esteem.

Since James' early formulation, other researchers have studied self-esteem, particularly in children. Notable is the research of Stanley Cooper-smith (1967), who studied 85 fifth- and sixth-grade boys and their mothers to determine the antecedents of self-esteem. He interviewed the mothers and children separately, and asked each child to fill out his Self-Esteem Inventory (SEI). Children were asked to read a variety of statements and check whether each of these is "Like me" or "Unlike Me." The statements include the degree to which they felt sorry for themselves, were proud of their school achievements, felt they were popular with their peers, got along with their parents, and so on. Coopersmith found that boys' self-esteem did not change much over the three-year period studied. Children who had a positive view of themselves at 10 were the same children who viewed themselves positively at age 13.

Coopersmith found that children with high self-esteem were more independent and creative than children with low self-esteem. They did better in school and were more likely to be assertive, socially outgoing, and popular among friends. They would also express their views on a topic even when they anticipated criticism for their beliefs. Further, they were less conforming and yet had fewer difficulties in forming friendships when compared to other children. Coopersmith noted that high self-esteem boys seemed to lack a self-consciousness that would impede them from presenting themselves in a confident manner. Children with low self-esteem did not display the self-confidence that typified the high-esteem boys.

Body Esteem   A person's evaluation of his or her body.

A review of self-esteem research (Wylie, 1979) suggests that self-esteem generally becomes more positive during adolescence. However, the situation for overweight children may be somewhat different. Self-esteem refers to a person's self evaluation. **Body esteem** refers to a person's evaluation of his or her body. In normal weight children, self-esteem does not systematically change with age nor is it related to body esteem. However for overweight children between the ages of 11 and 17, the relationship between self-esteem and body esteem is closely linked (Mendelson & White, 1985). Those children who had low self-esteem also had a low body esteem. For younger overweight children (8–10-year-olds) there was no relationship between body esteem and self-esteem. Mendelson and White also found that overweight boys suffered a low self-esteem between the ages 11 and 13, while overweight girls' self-esteem suffered more in late adolescence.

Pause for Thought

Self-concept refers to how children see themselves, and self-esteem refers to how much they like what they see. These perceptions and evaluations are made against a background of family and cultural values for traits and behaviors. In what ways might self-concept and self-esteem be different in different cultures? In what ways might children's self-concept and self-esteem affect their behavior in adulthood?

Parental Influence on Self-Esteem

Coopersmith examined the characteristic behaviors of the parents of the boys in his study. He found that certain child-rearing practices were related to high self-esteem in their children. Such parents were more accepting and affectionate toward their children; they took an interest in their children's activities and friends and were generally more attentive to their children. Second, they were strict—setting clear limits on behavior. Parents of high self-esteem boys enforced rules in a firm and decisive manner. Even though they were strict, they did not use coercive kinds of discipline to enforce their rules. They were more likely to punish their children by denying privileges than by using physical punishment or withdrawal of affection to control their children. These parents were also more likely to include a rationale along with punishment. They allowed their children greater individual expression. They believed that children should have a say in making family plans and were more likely to allow their children to set their own bedtimes. Coopersmith believed that parents who set and enforced clear limits on acceptable behavior were also the parents who accepted their children's views and allowed them to exercise more self-control as opposed to parental control of behavior. Children whose parents present no limits or ambiguously defined ones are less likely to know what is expected of them and, therefore, to be less likely to evaluate their own behavior. According to Coopersmith (1967), "parents who have definite values, who have a clear idea of what they regard as appropriate behavior, and who are able and willing to present and enforce their beliefs are more likely to rear children who value themselves highly" (p. 236).

One final finding from Coopersmith's study is that the parents of high self-esteem children were themselves active, poised, and relatively self-assured people. They had high self-esteem and confidence in their abilities to cope with the responsibilities and duties of child-rearing. An interesting finding was that the mother's work history had an influence on self-esteem. The higher the child's self-esteem, the more likely it was that the mother was regularly employed and satisfied in her job.

Socialization in Middle Childhood

During the school years, there is a notable shift in children's social behavior. They now spend less time under the direct scrutiny and instruction of their parents and more time playing with siblings and peers and in school with their teachers. The impact of parents on children's behavior is augmented by what they learn as a result of play and school interactions. As is the case with parent–child relationships, child–child relationships are not static or unidirectional—the child is not only affected by others but, in turn, elicits certain reactions from siblings and peers. We begin our examination of the social influence on elementary-school-age children's development with a discussion of siblings.

During middle childhood children spend less time with their parents and more time with their peers.

The Impact of Siblings

More than 80 percent of American children have one or more brothers or sisters. Children between the ages of two and 10 spend countless hours in play and other activities with their siblings. The impact of siblings on each other's lives is further enhanced by the trend toward smaller families. With fewer children in a family, siblings have more intense and powerful relationships with each other (Bank & Kahn, 1982). Siblings serve as powerful behavioral models for each other. They are a source of support and comfort in times of distress and help teach social roles (Lamb, 1982b).

Sibling Status: Birth Order

Beulah harshly reprimanded her sister Kit for using too much butter on her bread. Kit, being three years Beulah's junior, reluctantly gave in to her older sister's authority and used less butter. This scenario may sound familiar to those of you who have experienced the pecking order among siblings. You might be interested to know that Beulah is 90 years old and Kit is 87! Even though siblings establish their status with each other in early and middle childhood, their order of birth in the family can affect their relationship throughout their lifespan.

Birth Order   A person's rank in a family relative to the number of siblings based on the order of birth.

The impact of **birth order** on behavior and development has been studied by many researchers. Firstborn children are more likely to be high achievers. They are more likely to go to college, score higher on IQ tests, and generally do better in school (Sutton-Smith, 1982). Other studies suggest that firstborn children are more conservative, more dominant, more dependent on others' approval, more affiliative, and more responsible than later-born children. However, the effects of siblings' status are influenced by the gender of the child and sibling, and age spacing between siblings (Minnett, Vandell, & Santrock, 1983; Sutton-Smith & Rosenberg, 1970). For example, second-

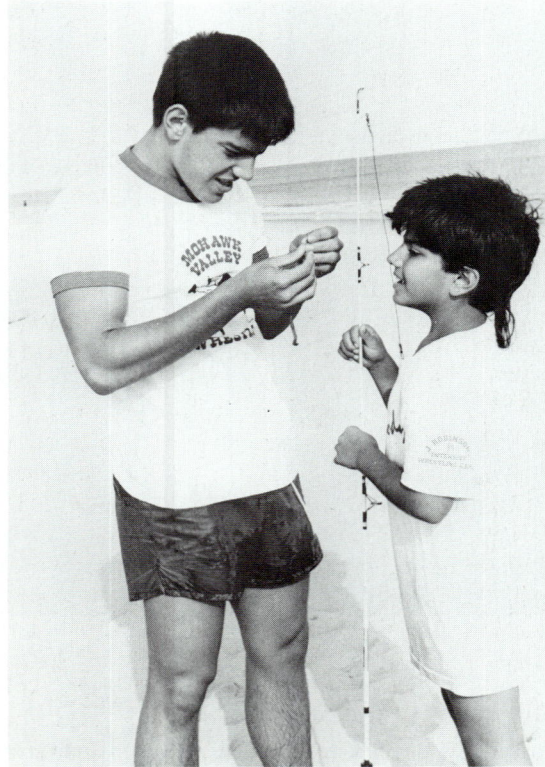

Older siblings often serve as powerful role models for younger siblings, especially when they are of the same gender.

born siblings often model their behavior after firstborn siblings, but the amount of imitation is greater if the older sibling is of the same gender. Furthermore, while the tendency for siblings to imitate an older sibling is very common for females, it is less often the case for males. Some males seem to counteract the influence of their older sisters by asserting themselves through gender-role characteristic behaviors. They may use physical aggression to reverse the dominant role the older sister has as a result of age (Sutton-Smith & Rosenberg, 1970).

Generally, older and firstborn siblings exercise more power over younger siblings, while later-born siblings acquire more social skills in negotiating with and accommodating others (Bryant, 1982). Older siblings assume the role of teacher and manager more often than younger siblings; young siblings, like Kit, are generally more compliant to their older siblings' role of teacher and guide (Brody, Stoneman, MacKinnon, & MacKinnon, 1985). Furthermore, female school-aged siblings are more likely than male siblings to assume the role of teacher.

Only children have a reputation for being more egocentric, less cooperative, less likely to get along with people than children who have siblings. However, the research studies on only children do not always support this view. Only children are more likely to be cooperative rather than competitive in games (Falbo, 1979). Other researchers have reported that only children have fewer friends and are less likely to seek out the company of their peers (Miller & Maruyama, 1976). The culture and customs of the country may have an influence on the behavior of only children. For example, in mainland

China, families are encouraged to have only one child. In comparing 180 matched pairs of only and sibling children, Jiao, Ji, and Jing (1986) found that only children were more egocentric, whereas children with siblings were more persistent, cooperative, and were held in higher prestige by their peers. The researchers concluded that only children being the sole targets of parental attention and family resources did not have to learn to cooperate with others in a communal setting as did children with siblings.

Sibling Interactions

Siblings interact with each other in ways that are different from parent–child interactions. For example, children generally behave in a more negative manner toward each other than parents do toward children (Baskett & Johnson, 1982). Even though some older siblings assume the role of babysitter and provide caretaking services for young siblings, they do not make good substitute parents (Bank & Kahn, 1982). For one thing, older siblings, even some adolescents, do not possess the cognitive maturity or experience to function effectively in the role as parent. They cannot impart values as parents do nor do they demonstrate the same degree of emotional poise characteristic of adult caregivers. Second, younger siblings are often resistant to the older sibling's efforts to provide care (Baskett & Johnson, 1982), and will often be more disruptive when under the care of siblings than when cared for by parents or other adults. Also, older siblings do not have access to the same resources as adults when caring for younger children. Their power base is considerably different than the parents', and younger siblings are likely to recognize this. For example, when Lorrie attempted to control her sister Amy's behavior of spitting, she was stopped by Amy's angry retort "You can't make me!"

Sibling rivalry or jealousy is a common occurrence in childhood. Children often see themselves in competition with each other for parents' attention, affection, or praise. Alfred Adler (1928) maintained that the "dethroning" of the firstborn child by a second child is bound to produce jealousy and hostile aggression. If parents respond to the aggressive behavior by punishing the transgressions, children often devise less obvious ways of getting back at their rivals by such actions as tattling or teasing.

Parents often find themselves in the middle of sibling conflict. By admonishing one sibling for inappropriate behavior, they may be inadvertently providing the other sibling with ammunition for a later taunt ("Ha Ha, you got caught!"). One study (Dunn and Kendrick, 1982) found that following the birth of the second baby, mothers spent less time and were less sensitive to the needs and interests of their firstborns. The researchers also found that mothers who talked to the older sibling about the care and needs of the new baby as a person and valued the older child's participation in caregiving, had firstborns who developed a more positive approach to the new sibling. Thus one way to reduce sibling rivalry among children is for parents to provide individual attention to each sibling based on the child's needs. Sometimes parents actually foster the sibling rivalry by drawing comparisons among them. For example, telling one child that his school work is not as good as his sister's may intensify the brother's rivalrous feelings. Recognizing the child's achievements independent from the sister's accomplishments provides the child with the recognition he desires without contributing to sibling rivalry.

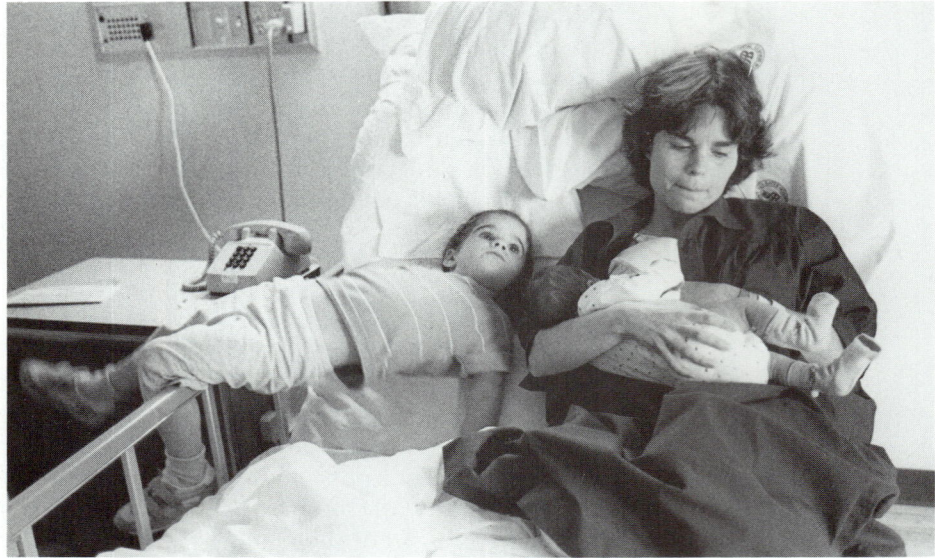

Sibling rivalry is enhanced when parents ignore the needs of one child in favor of another child.

Sibling interaction is marked not only by its negative affective tone, but by positive feelings as well (Dunn, 1983). As early as three years of age, siblings have been known to have warm, positive, and helpful reactions toward each other. Older siblings often function as teachers for young siblings. Sometimes, siblings are in a better position than parents to teach their younger siblings because they are on a more similar level of understanding and can communicate with each other more effectively (Cicirelli, 1977).

Sibling interactions are different from peer interactions. With siblings, children are able to practice social roles that they cannot practice with their peers. In two different studies (Stoneman, Brody, & MacKinnan, 1984; Brody, Stoneman, & MacKinnan, 1982) in which siblings and peers were observed playing, it was found that older siblings assumed the dominant roles of manager–teacher with their siblings; egalitarian roles of playmate in their peer interactions, and a combination of dominant and egalitarian roles when interacting with peers and siblings together. By switching from one social role to another in play with peers and siblings, children acquire more experience and sophistication in seeing themselves in various social roles.

Pause for Thought

In the United States, there is a growing tendency toward smaller families. Many adults are choosing to have only one child; some are choosing to have none. In what ways might this shift from larger to smaller families have an impact on the personality development of children growing up today?

Peer Interactions

Characteristics

During middle childhood, children interact primarily with others of their own gender and race (Sagar, Schofield, & Snyder, 1983). With the exception of sibling interactions, children are more likely to play with age-mates. In part, this is due to the greater familiarity and availability of classmates, but may also reflect the greater similarity in interests and cognitive maturity.

Peer interactions are qualitatively different from adult–child interactions. Children seek out other children for companionship, affection, and for common amusement, whereas child–adult interactions are more often based on the child's need for protection, care, or instruction (Damon, 1983). Unlike parent–child relationships, children for the most part choose their own friends and freely end these relationships when they are dissatisfied with the interactions. Children are more likely to practice and refine their social skills with each other rather than with adults because they are on a more equal footing with each other.

Functions of the Peer Group

Peers serve a variety of functions during middle childhood. Williams and Stith (1980) have identified five functions of the peer group. First, peers *provide companionship,* someone to be with, talk to, and pass time with. Through the subculture of peers, children learn jokes, riddles, and games, and enhance their collections of baseball cards and comic books. In addition, peers pass along the numerous games and superstitions that are a part of childhood. Sarah and Lorrie spend hours practicing the string game of cat's cradle, an activity their parents have long forgotten.

Second, peers *provide a testing ground for new behavior,* particularly behaviors that adults are likely to prohibit. Cursing, spitting, and performing acts of bravado are more readily practiced with peers, especially when these acts are likely to win admiration. Older children, particularly between the ages of 10 and 13, are more likely to engage in antisocial activities as a result of peer influence (Bixenstine, DeCorte, & Bixenstine, 1976). By looking to their friends for approval, children form an alliance that provides a buffer to the adult world. The peer group provides encouragement and opportunity for

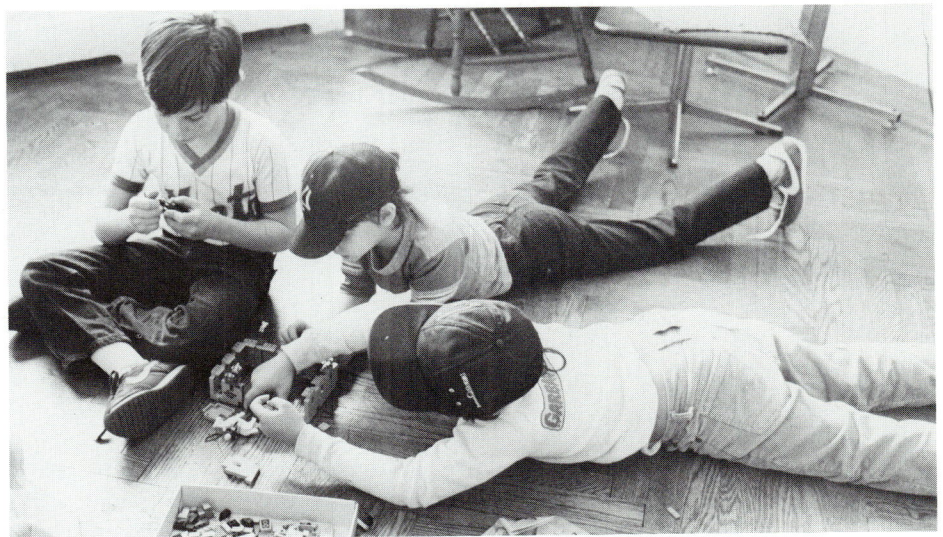

Peers provide companionship for one another; they play together, build houses, share experiences.

children to be independent from their parents' values and standards. They also provide children with an opportunity to acquire positive social skills such as cooperation and negotiation.

Third, peers *help pass on knowledge,* not only knowledge of children's games but more worldly knowledge as well. Children more readily accept information (and misinformation) from their peers. For example, Ian learned how to sail a boat from his older cousin Adam, and Amy learned about using a computer from her friend at school. Many school systems are recognizing the benefits of peer instruction for both the teacher and the learner. Not only do peers deliberately impart knowledge to each other, but also provide potent models of behavior to each other. Because children are more likely to imitate models they perceive as similar to themselves, children are more likely to acquire behaviors from their peers. Modeling effects are easily seen in later childhood when children imitate each other's manner of dress and gestures.

The peer group *teaches children rules and logical consequences,* and they learn to adhere to rules and codes of conduct generated by peers. Often peers apply harsh consequences for violating these codes of acceptable behavior, however. Peer-generated rules cover a wide range of behaviors and are usually couched in negative terms: Don't tattle, don't be a teacher's pet, don't cheat on a friend. Children often form informal clubs structured by a set of special rules. Those who abide by the rules are rewarded by peer acceptance and membership in the club. Those who violate the rules are expelled from the club.

Finally, peers also *help reinforce gender-role behaviors.* During the elementary-school years, children are acutely aware of the differences between boys and girls as a result of peer pressure. A girl who acts like a boy or plays with boys is likely to not gain acceptance into the "girl's club." Children also learn about sexuality through peer discussions, particularly during later childhood. Through peer relations, children gain experience presenting themselves to each other. Friendships in particular provide a context for the growth of a child's social self, a context within which the child can learn the appropriate self-image to project in social situations (Fine, 1981). By developing the social skills necessary for getting along with others, children acquire a varied and positive definition of themselves. Ten-year-old Sarah describes herself as a nice person because she is helpful to her friends in school. This view of herself with respect to her friends will probably generalize to other situations later in life.

Pause for Thought

When parents express concern about the company their children keep, they are in part responding to the power that peers have to affect each other's behavior. In what ways might parents have an influence on the selection of their children's friends? Do you think parents should have a say in their children's peer selection?

Peer Status

Peer Status The degree to which a child is liked and accepted by his or her peers.

One aspect of children's peer relationships that has been a popular area of research is **peer status,** the degree to which a child is liked and accepted by his or her peers. In any group of children, there are usually some children who are popular and accepted by the majority of their peers, and there are

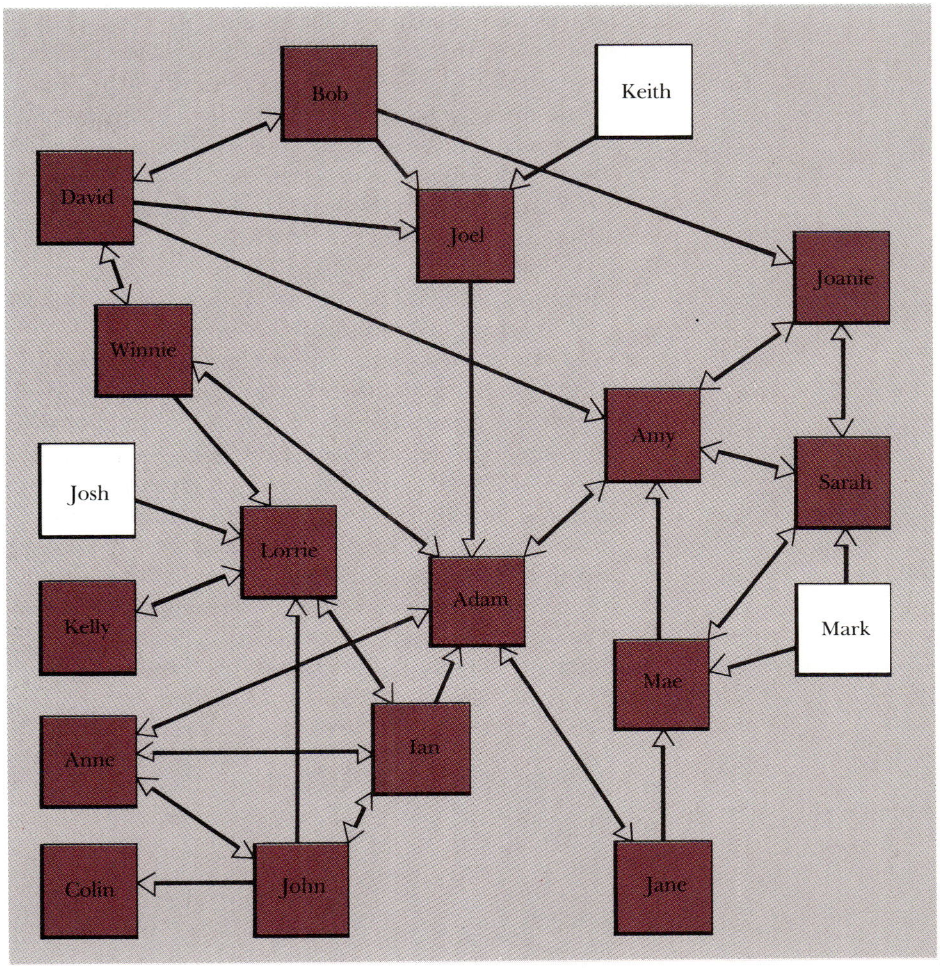

Figure 8.1 A sociogram. Popular children, such as Adam and Lorrie, have many arrows pointing to their names. Unpopular children, such as Mark, Keith, and Josh, have none.

a fair number of children who do not have many or any friends at all. Some children are openly rejected by their peers, while others are simply neglected. Furthermore, it appears that low-status or rejected children maintain their unpopular status over the years of middle childhood. The children who had a low status within their peer groups during the third and fifth grades maintained their low-status positions for five years (Coie & Dodge, 1983).

What factors account for the difference in social status among school children? One popular way of studying social relations among peers is called **sociometry.** Patterns of attraction and rejection among children in a group are determined on the basis of children's answers to questions such as: Who in the class is your best friend?, Which of your classmates do you like the least?, Who would you like to go on a picnic with? Who are the ones that aren't liked by others? The children's answers can be charted graphically in a **sociogram** by drawing a colored arrow to indicate a child's preference for a particular child and drawing a different colored arrow to indicate a child's dislike or rejection of a child (see Figure 8.1). On the basis of these sociograms, researchers can identify the *stars*, or popular children (those who receive many

Sociometry A quantitative method of studying social relations among peers.

Sociogram A diagram representing social acceptance and rejection among a group of people.

positive choices from other children), the *isolates,* or neglected children (those who are neither positively nor negatively chosen), and the *rejects* (those who are actively disliked) (Hartup, 1982). Another peer status category that is sometimes identified is *controversial* children—those who are strongly liked by some of their peers and strongly disliked by others (Dodge, 1983).

A number of characteristics and traits have been associated with popular and unpopular children. Popular children are physically more attractive (Dodge, 1983; Kleck, Richardson, & Ronald, 1974). Not surprisingly, they also appear to be friendlier, more outgoing, more cooperative, and nicer than unpopular children. Popular children are academic achievers and have higher IQs than do unpopular children.

Rejected or unpopular children have few friends, are more likely to act aggressively, and exhibit more behavior problems than do popular children (French & Waas, 1985). In a study conducted by Garry Ladd (1983), popular, average, and rejected third- and fourth-graders were observed during recess periods. The unpopular, rejected children spent less time in prosocial behavior and more time in antagonistic and unoccupied behaviors than did the other children. They spent more of their time playing with either younger-aged or other unpopular children. Unpopular children are also more likely to have an uncommon and unattractive first name (McDavid & Harari, 1966). Furthermore, negative peer status during middle childhood is associated with later problems in adjustment (Hartup, 1983).

Rejected and isolated children spend less time with their peers, unlike popular children who are friendlier and more outgoing.

In sociometry, children are asked to make judgments on peers whom they already know. These choices are made on the basis of reputation, that is, on what they believe to be true about their peers rather than on the actual observed behaviors of the children. The question remains: Are unpopular children aggressive because they are unliked by their peers or are they disliked because they are aggressive? It is likely that peer status and the style of social interaction are bidirectional, each influencing the other (Asher, 1983; Dodge, 1983; Rubin, 1983).

In order to answer the question of what causes children to have high or low status with their peers, recent studies have observed the development of peer status in groups of unfamiliar children (Coie & Kupersmidt, 1983; Dodge, 1983; Putallaz, 1983). What is emerging is a clearer picture of the differences in social competencies between popular and unpopular children.

Human Development in Practice

Type A Behavior in Children

The leading causes of death among adults are cardiovascular diseases. While the origins of cardiovascular disease are not entirely understood, two cardiologists, Friedman and Rosenman (1974), identified a pattern of behavior that characterized people at high risk for heart disease. Type A people typically are extremely competitive, hostile, aggressive, easily aroused, and are driven by an ever present sense of urgency. As a group, they are more likely to develop heart problems than are Type B people. Type B people are the opposite of Type A: They are relaxed, unhurried, and not aggressive.

Recently, researchers have been studying Type A behaviors in children (Matthews & Angulo, 1980; Vega-Lahr & Field, 1986; Whalen & Henker, 1986). The Matthews Youth Test for Health (MYTH) is a 17-item scale that has been used to identify Type A and Type B children. The scale includes such statements as "I am easygoing—I am hard driving," "I walk fast—I walk slowly," and "It does matter if I am late—It doesn't matter if I am late." Scores on the MYTH scale are related to behaviors of impatience, aggression, and assertiveness. Using this scale and versions of it that have been adapted for use with preschool children, researchers have identified several characteristics of Type A children. In a study by Nitza Vega-Lahr and Tiffany Field (1986), Type A preschool children showed more annoyance, were more aggressive in their play,

won more contests, and more frequently answered first in interviews when compared to Type B children. Type A children have also been found to have more stress in their lives (Thoresen, Eagleston, Kirmil-Gray, & Bracke, 1985). They were more hostile, angry, and had lower self-esteem than children who were low on the Type A scale.

Although Type A children do not have heart attacks (which are rare in children), their overall health does seem to be affected. In addition to being more stressed, Type A children reported higher levels of muscle tension and sleep disturbances. They were often sick, usually with sore throats and headaches, although their school attendance and number of visits to physicians were no different from low Type A children (Thoresen et al., 1985).

There are some practical applications to being able to identify people at risk for heart disease early on in their lives. There is a growing body of evidence that suggests that some heart diseases begin early in life (Berenson, Frank, Hunter, Srinivasan, Voors, & Webber, 1982). Not only is it easier to correct or stop a disease in its early stages, but it is easier to teach good health habits in childhood than to try to change bad health habits in adulthood. Thus, recognizing the behavioral clues for possible heart disease risks could be a step in the direction of reducing deaths attributed to heart disease.

Social Competencies and Peers

A growing body of evidence suggests that unpopular children are lacking in social skills. Popular children, on the other hand, seem to acquire their status as a result of social competence displayed in social interactions. Asher (1983) has described three dimensions of socially competent performance. The first dimension is *relevance*—children who gain entry into ongoing interactions seem to be able to read the social situation and adapt their behavior to the ongoing flow of interaction. A second dimension of competence is *responsiveness*—children who are effective with peers respond more positively to other children's initiations of contact. Generally, popular children are approached more frequently by other children and approach others less often. A third dimension is the *understanding of the process of relationships*—high-status children recognize that relationships are built over time, not in the moment. As a result, they are likely to go about forming a friendship slowly and in a less direct fashion. Whereas unpopular children are more likely to start right in playing with a new peer, or even asking "Will you be my friend?," popular children are more likely to start a relationship by suggesting an after-school bike ride and letting the friendship build over time.

Development of Children's Friendships

Children's understanding of friendship changes with age. It is not until the end of childhood that children can fully appreciate the meaning of friendship. In an interview study in which 130 children (ages 6–14) were asked questions like "What is a friend?" and "How do you make friends?" Youniss and Volpe (1978) found that six- and seven-year-olds defined friends as playmates with whom they shared toys and physical activities. Nine- and 10-year-olds, however, spoke of friends as persons who respond to each other's needs, someone to call on for comfort and support.

On the basis of numerous open-ended interviews with people age three to 45, Robert Selman (1981) has presented a developmental theory of friendships. Five stages in children's ability to make and sustain friendships were identified.

Stage 0. The first stage (3–7 years) is labeled Stage 0 because children do not really form friendships. Rather, a close friend is someone who lives close by and with whom the child happens to be playing at the time. In this stage, described as *momentary playmateship,* friends are valued for their toys, physical attributes, and proximity.

Stage 1. In the first stage (4–9), a close friend is someone who does what you want. This stage is labeled *one-way assistance* because a friend is seen as important because he or she performs specific activities that the child wants accomplished. If the friend does not comply, the child is likely to say "You are not my friend!"

Stage 2. The second stage (6–12) is labeled *fair-weather cooperation* because children become aware of the two-way reciprocal nature of friendships. When friends disagree or argue, the friendship dissolves.

Stage 3. The third stage (9–15) is labeled *intimate and mutually shared relationships.* Friendships are seen as a basic means to develop mutual intimacy

Childhood friendships often are formed among playmates who share physical activities.

and mutual support. Friends share personal problems and secrets and do not dissolve their relationship because of disagreement or conflict of ideas. Friendship at this stage is exclusive and possessive, hence cliques develop.

Stage 4. In the final and highest stage of development (12 to adulthood), friendships are characterized by their *autonomous interdependent quality.* Friendships can grow and change as each person accepts the other's need to establish relations with others for personal growth. Friends still rely on each other for emotional support, but they are not possessive or clinging in their relationships.

Pause for Thought

In addition to coping with disabilities, children who are physically, mentally, or emotionally handicapped may have difficulties establishing and maintaining friendships with their peers. In the United States, many handicapped children are taught in the same classroom with non-handicapped children. What are the possible merits and drawbacks to this policy with respect to children's peer interactions and friendships?

The Impact of Television

Today, more than 95 percent of American families have at least one television; some have two or more. Children spend a significant amount of their time in front of the TV. One estimate is that children under two spend, on the average, two and a half hours per day, every day, watching television. The amount of viewing time increases for eight- to 10-year-olds to an average of four hours per day (Liebert, Sprafkin, & Davidson, 1982). Based on these national averages, it is estimated that by the time of high-school graduation, the child would have spent 15,000 hours in front of the TV. According to the 1985 Nielsen report (National Audience Demographics Report, 1985), schoolchildren between the ages of six and 11 spend an average of 26 hours and 34 minutes per week watching television. Preschool children spend an average of 28 hours, 20 minutes per week. These figures for television viewing are startling. It appears that children are spending as much time in front of the TV as they do in direct classroom instruction. Clearly, television is an important socializing agent that has an impact on several aspects of a child's life.

Questionnaire and diary studies indicate that systematic viewing of television begins at two-and-a-half years, is at a high level during the preschool and early school-age years, declines during adolescence, and then reaches a relatively high level among elderly people (Anderson, Lorch, Field, Collins, & Nathan, 1986). Anderson and his colleagues videotaped families in their TV viewing rooms and found that children spent about one-third of their time with the television on while they were engaged in other activities such as playing with toys, reading, or interacting with parents. TV in this case is the background noise, much like elevator music.

Cognitive and Affective Development

Television programs are carefully produced to capture and hold the viewer's attention. The format of commercial TV programs, particularly children's shows, contains rapid-fire, action-packed sequences that are highlighted by audio and visual special effects. Children's attention is especially captured by the television format of cartoons (Wright & Huston, 1983). Children spend endless hours, particularly on Saturday morning, watching the humorous

Cartoons are designed to capture the attention of young children.

(and often violent and aggressive) adventures of animated cartoon characters. The faster the pace of the program, the more receptive children are to it. It has been suggested that the format of children's programs can be arousing to them and can lead to aggressive behavior, even when the content of the program is nonviolent (Huston, Wright, Wartella, Rice, Watkins, Campbell, & Pitts, 1981). The slow-paced, laid-back style of "Mr. Rogers' Neighborhood" is not as well received by children. However, once children are exposed to the "Mr. Rogers" show, studies indicate that they do acquire more prosocial behavior (Singer & Singer, 1983).

Research on the effects of TV viewing on development suggests that it does influence both learning and behavior. This can be beneficial. A study (Ball & Bogatz, 1972) of cognitive development of children who watch "Sesame Street" concluded that three- to five-year-old youngsters from a variety of backgrounds acquired simple and complex cognitive skills as a result of watching "Sesame Street." Those who watched the most gained the most and three-year-olds gained more than five-year-olds.

Television has a rich and as yet untapped potential for educating children and for enhancing their development (Singer & Singer, 1983). It is an excellent vehicle for presenting new ideas and information about the world beyond the child's (or adult's) immediate experience. Lorrie and Amy, for example, learned about life in the Himalayas by watching a TV special. However, the benefits to children from many "good" television programs may depend on an adult being present (Singer & Singer, 1981). Adults who watch the shows with children provide guidance, and help children understand the programs that they watch. Young children can also learn about the use of their language by listening to television; often children imitate many of the jingles and sayings they hear on television in their play (Rice, 1983).

Some of the more recent children's programs have attempted to help children deal more effectively with their fears. For example, by watching a television character overcome a fear of animals, children are able to deal more effectively with their own fears.

However, what is learned from television depends on the child's level of cognitive development. First- and second-graders, for example, are not yet able to follow a complex plot line from one scene to the next, so they may miss the moral lesson contained in many TV plots (Rubinstein, 1983). Furthermore, before age nine, children believe much of what they see on TV to be realistic. They do not distinguish fantasy from reality well (Eron, 1980, 1982). Thus, they may acquire misinformation about the world when they watch cartoons or unrealistic programs. Heavy television viewing may also interfere with other activities that contribute to children's learning. Such activities as reading, playing games, constructing things, or discussing their ideas with others are considerably reduced when children spend many hours a day watching television.

Violence and Aggression

Perhaps the most studied issue is the effect of TV violence and aggression on children's behavior. The results of research studies support the view that violence on television leads to aggressive behavior by children. By observing highly attractive models engaging in a variety of aggressive and physically violent behaviors, children are encouraged to act in a similar fashion. The extent to which children imitate aggressive acts is influenced by the age of the child. The time when children are most sensitive to learning aggressive behaviors from watching televised aggression is between eight and nine years of age (Eron, Huesman, Brice, Fischer, & Mermelstein, 1983). Also, if children are already predisposed to aggressive behaviors, they are more likely to imitate aggression seen on TV. When parents watch aggressive or violent shows with their children and discuss the events afterward, this seems to reduce the negative effects and enhance the positive effects of TV. Fortunately, many television stations provide announcements for parents concerning the impact on children of the program they are about to see.

Pause for Thought

Family television programs often feature the continuing dramas or comedies of fictional television families like the "Bill Cosby Show" or "Little House on the Prairie." Are television families realistically portrayed? What might children infer about how to get along with others from watching these and similar television programs?

Problems in Adjustment

Sources of Stress

During the elementary-school years, all children experience some difficulty in the process of growing up. While most children learn to deal with the stresses and challenges confronting them in school or with their peers, some experience problems in making these adjustments. Other children have difficulty because of physical or psychological handicaps that interfere with normal adjustment.

Research has shown that referrals to mental health facilities increase significantly during the school years and that most of the problems reported are school related (Achenbach, 1978). About 33 percent of children between the ages of six and 12 have some form of emotional problem, and boys are four times as likely as girls to have difficulty. However, most of the problems children experience while growing up are resolved without professional help; only about 10 percent of school-aged children are seen by professionals.

There are several reasons for the increase in referred emotional problems during middle childhood. Some of the children's problems have had their origins in the preschool period and are not noticed as problems until they reach school. For example, aggressive behaviors are a commonly reported problem that becomes more apparent when the child goes to school. During the preschool years when children are normally more aggressive, the problem behavior may not have been identified or may have been dismissed with the hope that the child would grow out of it. By the school years, children's problem behaviors that earlier may have only affected their parents and a few neighborhood children, may now be affecting the entire classroom. Thus, as children enter school, it is more likely that their problems will come to the attention of professionals. The child is now observed by more people and can be more readily compared to age-mates.

Another reason for an increase in adjustment problems during middle childhood is that there are more adjustments that children must make. As children mature and demonstrate their abilities to understand and cooperate with others, parents and teachers place greater social, cognitive, and emotional demands on them. The second-grader may find that it is no longer acceptable for her to throw a tantrum when things do not go her way. Now she may be expected to control her emotions and cooperate with others. In addition, because children are able to consider future events and the influence that other people have on them, they are likely to react more strongly than younger children in anticipation of an event. For example, by about age nine, children worry about the threat of a nuclear war (Escalona, 1982; Schwebel, 1982). In one study (Chivian, Mack, & Waletzsky, 1983), 98 percent of Soviet children and 58 percent of American children said they were "worried" or "very worried" about a nuclear attack. They worried about how they would be able to live without their families, friends, and teachers to love them and take care of them.

Another source of stress for schoolchildren concerns changes in their family structure. Many mothers decide to go to work when their children enter school. An increasing number of children live in families disrupted as a result of separation and divorce. Making adjustments to single-parent families and families combined through marriage may result in a stressful period for children. While some of these changes may actually be beneficial to children in the long run (such as when mothers are happily employed), children often react to the transitional and temporary upheaval with disturbing behavior and emotional problems. The loss of family members or friends through death is another stressful change (see Chapter 17).

Peer status can be another source of frustration for schoolchildren. Children commonly react to stress by acting aggressively, and are often excluded or rejected because of their aggressive behavior. Thus, stress or difficulty in one area of a child's life may lead to problems in another area.

Children living in families in which one or both parents suffer from psychiatric disorders are more vulnerable to emotional disorders and are more likely to have a diagnosed psychiatric problem themselves (Rutter, 1979; Weissman, Prusoff, Gammon, Merikangas, Leckman, & Kidd, 1984). However, when children have access to a caring adult and a supportive social network such as their schools, the stressful effects of having to cope with a disturbed parent are greatly reduced. In fact, research on young children of manic-depressive parents suggests that these children may acquire such social competencies as empathy and helpfulness as a result of having to cope with their parents (Zahn-Waxler, Cummings, McKnew, & Radke-Yarrow, 1984).

Resilient Children

Of equal interest to developmental researchers are those children who come from stressful family and social environments who rise above their misfortunes and develop normally. Children of emotionally disturbed parents who do not display emotional problems, abused children who develop close personal relationships, orphaned children who bear no emotional scars—these are but a few examples of children who seem to be *resilient* or *invulnerable* to

Human Development in Practice

Slow Down for the Hurried Child

Teachers who motivate their students to learn, who encourage achievement, are generally considered to be good, effective teachers. But is there a danger in overemphasizing achievement or pushing children to accomplish things too early? Are the pressures of competition too big a burden for children?

Some psychologists and educators think so. David Elkind (1981), a developmental psychologist, has written about the pressures on children to grow up. He argues that today we are pressuring our children to mature as never before. "Hurried children" and "children without childhood" are common euphemisms for this phenomenon.

Elkind observes this process operating in numerous ways in our society. Chief among them is the pressure for early intellectual attainment. Beginning sometimes in infancy, but more often in the preschool years, are attempts by parents and educational specialists to accelerate children's acquisition of academic skills. The general feeling among parents and teachers is that we must begin very early in children's lives if we wish to maximize their intellectual potential.

In addition to the pressures for early academic achievement, Elkind also observes the

Elkind believes that some children are encouraged to look, dress, and act like adults well before they are capable of handling it emotionally.

pressure on children to grow up in the "adultification" of their dress and behavior. According to Elkind, we encourage children to look, dress, and even act like adults well before they are ca-

the effects of stressful experiences. The personality and social factors that distinguish resilient children from vulnerable children are yet to be fully understood (Garmezy & Rutter, 1983), however, two factors do seem to be important. The availability of social support from a caring adult friend or relative frequently helps to offset the negative effects of stress. The second factor is the child's ability to understand and cope with the situation at hand. As a group, resilient children are friendly, independent, and have high levels of self-esteem; they also get along well with other children and do well in school. Together, these two factors—social support and personal strength— combine to provide children with some protection from the negative effects of difficult conditions.

Fear of AIDS in School

Of growing concern to all people, adults and children alike, is the rising number of cases of AIDS, acquired immune deficiency syndrome. AIDS is caused by a virus that attacks the immune system of the body thus rendering pable of handling it emotionally. For example, we often see preschool and early school-age children in miniature versions of adult dress. Well-known designers have even begun producing high-priced fashions for infants and toddlers. The media has also contributed to the pressure on children to grow up. Promotion of teen-age sexuality is an everyday occurrence in television, film, music, literature, and advertising. Even children's play and sports activities are not exempt from this "pressure cooker" atmosphere. The proliferation of specialized camps for such sports as baseball, basketball, football, skating, wrestling, gymnastics, and the like is a case in point. In these environments, the carefree camp atmosphere of days-gone-by has been replaced by daily rigorous routines to foster highly specialized competitive athletic skills. This emphasis on competition can also be seen in organized sports such as Pee Wee hockey, Little League baseball, and high-school athletic programs.

What effect does this pressure to grow up have on children? One common reaction is intense anxiety. Pressured by parents, teachers, and even peers to perform and achieve beyond their years and often their abilities, many children respond to the stress by becoming highly anxious—most often because they believe they cannot live up to the expectations of others. Sometimes children feel a sense of helplessness in response to a lack of control in their lives. Undue pressure to grow up may also produce a premature structuring to the child's life. In this case, the child spends so much time involved in highly specialized activities (e.g., sports, music, etc.) that he or she does not have the opportunity to develop other aspects of the self.

What can teachers do to alleviate some of the pressure from "hurried" children? The obvious intervention is to slow down the pace for these children by establishing reasonable standards of achievement and by encouraging more cooperative interactions in and outside of the classroom. By showing children that they do not have to perform or be "stars" to be accepted by them, teachers can help relieve the pressure. Many times children's advanced achievements blind teachers and parents to the fact that these children do not respond emotionally in the same way as adults.

Elkind argues that we must give our children the time to grow up—we must not deny them their childhood.

the victim vulnerable to a host of life-threatening diseases. At present, there is no known cure for the disease. Although the disease is easily spread through sexual contact and blood transfusions, it is not spread by casual contact. In 1981, approximately 500 children in the United States were known to have contracted the disease primarily through blood transfusions or as a result of being infected by their mothers during pregnancy or birth.

While the number of children with AIDS is small relative to the total population of AIDS victims, in some communities, there has been widespread panic among parents and some children about the presence of AIDS-infected children in the classroom. Some parents have boycotted schools that have AIDS-infected students. People who have been infected by the AIDS virus may not show any symptoms but may nonetheless pass on the disease through sexual contact or exchanges of blood. Since most children are not sexually active, the risk to other school children is not high. No cases of AIDS have been known or suspected to have been transmitted from one child to another in school, day-care, or foster-care settings (The Health Information Network, 1987).

The United States Public Health Service recommends that children infected with AIDS should be allowed to attend school and after-school day care. After consulting with the child's parents, teachers, physician, local school board, and public health officials to determine the best way to care for the child's medical, educational, and psychological needs, a decision can be made as to whether it would be in the child's best interest to attend school. For the afflicted child, the situation is a particularly unfortunate one.

Adjustment Reactions of Children

Aggression

One of the more common behavior problems in middle childhood is physical and verbal aggression. Boys are more likely than girls to respond to frustration by bullying their peers, by tantrums, or by destructive actions. Often, the child who is not doing well at school academically or who experiences frequent failures displaces his or her frustration by acting aggressively. Hyperactive children and children with learning disabilities often act aggressively toward their peers.

In many cases, children's aggression stems from their inept and immature attempts to make contact with others and to gain attention. Social-learning theorists believe that learning to channel aggressive actions in socially appropriate ways is a major aspect of socialization during the school years. Aggression, like many other behaviors, is maintained by the consequences it elicits. The aggressive boy, for example, not only learns that hitting or bullying someone results in his getting his way, but he also learns that adults will pay attention to him—even if the attention is negative. Children also learn to be aggressive by watching others engage in aggressive actions. Many television

Physical aggressiveness is a common behavior problem in middle childhood.

programs provide children with numerous examples of aggression. Parents who physically punish their children are also teaching them to be aggressive with others.

The best treatment approach for changing aggressive behaviors in children is to change the consequences of these actions. Withdrawing reinforcing attention from the child who is acting aggressively reduces the frequency of aggressive behavior. A procedure also used with younger children, **time out** is often effective: The disruptive child is removed from the setting and placed in a socially isolated and nonstimulating environment for a specified period of time. When the time period is up, the child is allowed to return to the original social setting. So long as the behavior is appropriate, that is, nonaggressive, the child is allowed to remain with others.

In addition to reducing negative aggressive behaviors, intervention approaches should include teaching the child more acceptable ways of dealing with frustrations. Exposing children to people who demonstrate greater maturity and control of their emotions while frustrated can also help children acquire the necessary alternatives to aggression.

Fear and Anxiety

Childhood stress is a term that is used to describe children's reactions to a variety of situational and developmental changes in their lives (Miller, 1982). Two commonly experienced stress reactions are fear and anxiety. Fear is a natural reaction to real or imagined danger. When children do not understand or cannot control events in their lives, they are likely to perceive them as dangerous. The specific events or things that are frightening to children change, however, as they develop a better understanding of their world.

In a five-year study of children ranging in age from five-and-a-half to 14-and-a-half, Maurer (1965) found that fear of animals, particularly snakes, was almost universal. As children got older, their fears diminished. For example, fear of the dark usually disappears by age seven, fear of nonexistent monsters and ghosts disappears by age 10. Older children are more likely to fear realistic events. Fear of natural hazards increases with age. As we mentioned earlier, an increasingly common fear among schoolchildren today is a fear of nuclear war and annihilation (Yudkin, 1984). Children also report fears of social situations involving possible embarrassment, such as when Sarah was worried about not remembering her lines in the school play.

It is generally understood that fears are learned. Sometimes as a result of a previous trauma or accident, a child may be conditioned to fear similar situations or events. Other times, children acquire fears through observational learning, by watching someone else express fear to particular objects or events. When Amy noticed her sister Lorrie's fearful reaction to caterpillars, she soon acquired a similar fear. When children express fears, they often elicit a more nurturant and attentive response from adults. In doing so, they may learn that being afraid has advantages.

Anxiety, like fear, is a response to a felt danger, which may or may not be real. However, anxiety is usually not directed toward a specific object or situation. Often children are unaware of what specifically is worrying them. They may experience physical reactions such as an uneasy feeling in their stomach, headache, fatigue, or difficulty in breathing, or they may simply experience a deep apprehension. Children facing hospitalization for surgery or medical tests often experience anxiety that interferes with their recuperation. In one study (Melamed & Siegel, 1981), children who were scheduled for surgery were shown a film about a seven-year-old boy as he prepared for a hernia operation. The boy in the film, while anxious, demonstrated his ability to cope with his initial fears. Watching this film helped to reduce the children's preoperative anxiety.

Childhood Depression

Ordinarily, people do not think of children as being depressed, partly because it conflicts with their belief that childhood is a happy time. However, psychologists are recognizing that some children are sad and experience a diminished sense of their self-worth.

Children do not express their depression in the same ways that adults do. The way they express their sense of despair is keyed to their age—younger children, for example, may stop growing, have a poor appetite, and be listless, while school-age children may manifest their depression by hostile and aggressive behavior toward their parents. Often discontented and dissatisfied with their lives, such school-age children derive no pleasure from their activities. Sometimes their depression is masked by vague physical symptoms such as headaches, stomachaches, and dizziness. Some children are so depressed they are suicidal.

Childhood depression seems to be a reaction to a loss, either of an object, person, or state of well-being. Loss of a parent in a child's life not only has a devastating effect on young children (Bowlby, 1973; Bradley, 1979); but may predispose the child to depression in adulthood (Seligman, 1975).

Another contributing factor to childhood depression is a hostile, overly critical, or unstable family environment. When parents are constantly fighting with each other, when the child is consistently belittled, or when there is considerable disruption in the family, as with separation or divorce, some children respond with depression. The most effective therapy for a depressed child in such situations involves restoring order and reducing the adverse quality of the home (Bakwin & Bakwin, 1972).

Summary

The child's personality is influenced by many experiences during middle childhood. The evaluations of significant others become part of the child's view of self.

According to Erikson, children during the school years must resolve the crisis of industry vs. inferiority. In doing so, they form an attitude about their ability to work and be productive.

Self-concept is composed of several aspects: The child's physical appearance (including gender and activities), the child's psychological experience (including feelings), and the child's social sense of self.

Children's self-esteem is influenced by their successes and accomplishments and by the degree of firm, affectionate direction they receive from their parents. Self-esteem is related to body esteem.

Siblings play an important role in each other's development as models of behavior, as sources of comfort, and as competitors for parental attention.

Sibling interactions provide a way for children to learn how to get along with others.

The order in which children are born can have an effect on achievement and social interactions. Only children do not have to learn to cooperate or share resources with other children.

Peer interactions are different from parent–child interactions and more frequent during the school years. Peer groups serve several functions including providing social approval, companionship, and a source of knowledge.

Peer status is influenced by the degree of acceptance by others. Factors in acceptance are friendliness, prosocial behavior, attractiveness, and social competence. Rejected and unpopular children are often aggressive and lack social skills.

Children's understanding of friendship changes during childhood. Selman's theory of friendship includes five stages in which children develop abilities to make and sustain friendships.

Television is a significant and pervasive socializing agent that has an influence on children's aggressive behavior, social attitudes and behavior, and general knowledge.

Children's reactions to stress depend upon the degree of family and social support, their ability to understand events, and on their own personal strengths. Fear of AIDS has created additional problems for children infected with the disease.

Some children have difficulty in making the many adjustments to school and family circumstances. Some common problems include aggressive behaviors, anxiety and fears, and childhood depression.

Further Readings

Asher, S., and Gottman, J. *The development of children's friendships*. New York: Cambridge University Press, 1981.
A comprehensive collection of papers focused on aspects of children's friendships. This book is divided into two sections, one dealing with various aspects of the peer group and the other with the interplay between cognitive and social development in friendships.

Axline, V. *Dibs: In search of self*. New York: Houghton Mifflin, 1964.
A moving account of the treatment of a bright five-year-old boy who was emotionally and socially disturbed as a result of his family environment. This popular book, written by the person who helped him, illustrates the use of play therapy with children.

Bank, S., and Kahn, M. *Sibling bond*. New York: Basic Books, 1982.
The material in this readable book is based on a decade of research and clinical evidence collected about siblings. Special attention is given to the ways sisters and brothers affect each other's personalities and lives.

Coopersmith, S. *Antecedents of self-esteem*. San Francisco: W. H. Freeman, 1967.
A study of the characteristics of parents of children with differing levels of self-esteem. This book is a classic in the study of self-esteem and includes a description of Coopersmith's Self-Esteem Inventory, a measure used in many self-esteem studies.

Damon, W. *Social and personality development*. New York: Norton, 1983.
This book provides a broad-based and integrative account of how the child's social relations and search for self-identity merge into his or her personality. Each chapter

presents a chronological description of relevant personality and social changes. Relevant concepts are clearly presented with the aid of examples and case histories.

Observational Activities

8.1 *School-Yard Peer Interactions*

One of the ways that researchers use to learn about friendship patterns in children is through naturalistic observation. While observing children's social interactions in a classroom or in the laboratory may provide some useful information about how peers relate to each other, children's behavior in these settings is usually structured or constrained by the presence of adults or formal activities.

In the playground, however, more spontaneous social interactions are possible. Schoolchildren often make friends and establish their status among their peers through their interactions in the school yard. The focus of this activity is to gain a better understanding of how children interact with their peers and form social groups. You will need to locate a school play yard so that you can observe children playing either before school or during recess or lunch breaks. Your local YM/YWCA may also have playgrounds where groups of school-age children play. You will need to observe the same group of children for a period of three to five days. Watch the children playing for at least 20 minutes each visit. On each visit, make note of the following behaviors among the children:

1. *Type of play:* Solitary play in which children play alone, associative play in which two or three children use the same toys or equipment but are independent of each other, or cooperative play in which children share toys or organize their activities with each other.
2. *Aggression:* Verbal aggression such as shouting, name-calling, sneering and taunting, and physical aggression such as hitting, shoving, tripping, or spitting.
3. *Prosocial behaviors:* Helping, listening, cooperating, displaying signs of affection such as touching, hugging, and winking.
4. *Social approaches:* The way in which children gain entry into an existing group of children. Does the child wait his or her turn to speak? How many entry attempts does each child make? What does the child say in attempting to gain entry into the group? What is the reaction of the children in the group?

On the basis of your observations, draw some conclusions about the kinds of behaviors used by children to gain peer acceptance. Did you notice which children were the most and least popular in the playground? What behaviors distinguish these children from each other? Share your observations about children's social interactions with your classmates. Compare your observations. What did you learn about yourself by doing this activity?

8.2 *Television: The Electronic Teacher*

Most of you probably watch television for recreation. In this assignment, you will be watching TV as a learning experience. Television provides factual information and knowledge (e.g., how gorillas mate and how to build an igloo). Television also provides the young viewer with a view of the social world, suggesting how people should and do interact with one another in various social roles (e.g., how women relate to their employers, or how housewives act). There are numerous television shows specifically produced for children. Your assignment is to watch three different types of children's shows to analyze the content in terms of what children are likely to be learning while watching these programs.

Select (1) a cartoon program offered on commercial television, (2) a family TV program in which the adventures of at least one child living in a family setting are portrayed (e.g., "Little House on the Prairie," "Family Ties," "Valerie's Family," or "The Cosby Show"), and (3) a children's program offered on educational or noncommercial television (e.g., "Sesame Street," "3–2–1 Contact," "Mr. Rogers' Neighborhood") If you are uncertain about which programs are suitable for each type, ask your instructor for suggestions.

While watching each show, keep a record of the amount of aggression or violence, the presentation of gender-sex role or ethnic stereotypes, number of prosocial actions, and the number of messages about healthy behaviors.

Compile your observations for each show and compare and contrast the three types. What differences do you notice? What similarities are there in the three types of shows? What benefits are there for children who watch these shows? What possible harmful effects exist? What did you learn from watching these shows?

PART

FOUR

Adolescence

*T*he developmental period of adolescence is easy to recognize but hard to define. Typically this period includes the years from age 12 to age 18. However, age is not always a useful marker for development since individuals vary considerably in their pace of development. From a lifespan perspective, developmental periods are signaled not by chronological age but by the emergence of a series of predictable changes in body, thoughts, feelings, and behavior. These changes occur as a result of biology, culture, and experience. The beginning of adolescence is biologically triggered by bodily changes. Since adolescence represents a transitional period between childhood and adulthood, the end of this period ends when adulthood begins. However, what constitutes being an adult varies considerably from culture to culture and from generation to generation. Adolescence is a time of dramatic changes in physical characteristics, in thought, in personal identity, and in social relationships. The adolescent period can be viewed as the dress rehearsal for adult life. The changes that occur in this period can often set the tone and direction for later adult development. In the next two chapters, we consider these changes and their impact on development across the lifespan.

CHAPTER
9

Adolescence: Physical, Cognitive, and Moral Development

David's fourteenth year was certainly one of change. He seemed to grow overnight. Just last week when he measured his height, he was taller than his mother, and he was looking forward to the time when he would surpass his father's height. As his voice grew deeper and lower, people often mistook David for his father on the telephone.

His body was changing in other ways. The light peach fuzz under his arms and in his groin was becoming coarser and thicker. His interests were beginning to turn from comic books to pin-up calendars as he fantasized his first sexual encounter.

David's mother was both surprised and delighted that he had changed his attitude and behavior about his personal appearance and hygiene. During his thirteenth year, he had abandoned showers. Now it was difficult to get him *out* of the bathroom. Constantly combing his hair and making faces in the mirror, he was now concerned that he look "cool." He was sure everyone would notice when he wasn't "cool"!

David's father bought him a set of light weights, and every night David would "pump iron" while watching himself in the mirror. He was no muscle man, but he could see that his body was getting stronger and he liked that.

Age 14 brought another dramatic change—David was becoming a more vocal contributor to the adult conversations around the house. He seemed to have an opinion on just about every topic from world politics to religion. The intensity with which he presented his ideas was characteristic of a beginner in the world of social exchange. He talked adamantly and freely about his ideas of right and wrong and eagerly generated many reasons and examples to back up his point of view.

For some of you, adolescence was just yesterday and may still be fresh in your mind. Many of you may have younger teenage siblings, and some of you may have returned to school after raising a family that includes teenagers. All of you, then, can think of adolescents you have known. From your experience, you know that all adolescents are not the same. They vary considerably in behavior and in their reactions. For some teenagers, this period is stormy and stressful; for others it is relatively smooth. David's reactions are just one example of the many styles of behavior found in adolescence. Your own experiences and reactions provide another example. In this chapter, we will examine some of the important characteristics of the adolescent experience. We begin with a discussion of the changes in physical growth and sexuality that occur among teenagers, including some of the problems that accompany such changes—for example, teenage pregnancy, AIDS, and venereal disease. Next, we highlight the emergence of newly developed adolescent thinking skills, especially the capacity for abstract reasoning. Finally, our discussion focuses on the changes in morality and values that occur at this time and on the relationship between such changes and the adolescent's emerging political awareness.

Physical and Sexual Development

Puberty The stage of development when the individual reaches sexual maturity and becomes capable of reproduction.

Some people confuse the terms *adolescence* and *puberty*. Adolescence can be roughly defined as the period from the onset of puberty to adulthood. **Puberty,** however, is the shorter period of adolescence during which an individual reaches sexual maturity (Chumlea, 1982). Puberty lasts from two to four years and is marked by great physical and psychological changes: Adolescents' bodies become capable of functioning sexually, and their attitudes and behavior become more adultlike.

The outward signs of the development of sex organs and a mature body type are not the first physical changes in adolescence. Many months before those outward signs become visible, the body is changing in unseen ways, particularly in its hormonal makeup. This prepares the way for sexual maturity and the ability to procreate.

Physical Growth

Adolescent Growth Spurt The period of acceleration of growth that occurs in early adolescence.

Human beings grow most rapidly at two times during their lives: before they are six months old and then again during adolescence. The second period of accelerated growth, often called the **adolescent growth spurt,** usually lasts from two to three years (Barnes, 1975).

The most obvious physical alterations in the adolescent are changes in height and weight, body proportions, and the development of secondary sexual characteristics. All of these changes are closely controlled and integrated by the central nervous system and the endocrine (hormonal) system (Chumlea, 1982).

In girls, the adolescent growth spurt usually begins between the ages of 9 and 11 and reaches a peak at an average of 12-and-a-half years. Then growth slows down and usually ceases completely between the ages of 15 and 18. The growth spurt in boys generally begins about two years later than it

The most obvious characteristics of adolescence are the changes in height, weight, and body proportions.

does in girls and lasts for a longer time. The male growth spurt begins between the ages of 11 and 14, reaches a peak at about age 15, and slowly declines until the age of 20 or 21 (Malina, 1978; Roche, 1979).

The teenager's body grows at differing rates, so that at times adolescents look a bit awkward. Big feet and long legs are the early signs of a changing body. But even these changes do not occur at the same time. First the hands and feet grow, then the arms and legs, and only later on do the shoulders and chest grow to fit the rest of the developing body. Other changes in body proportion occur. The trunk widens in the hips and shoulders, and the waistline drops. Boys tend to broaden mostly in the shoulders, girls in the hips. One part of the adolescent's body that does not undergo much change is the brain. By about age 10, the brain reaches adult size. However, the shape of the head and face change so that adolescents look more like adults. Foreheads become wider and higher, and the size of the head relative to the body is smaller than it was in childhood.

One of the earliest changes in both sexes is the addition of a layer of subcutaneous (under the skin) fat in the hips and legs. This fat soon diminishes in boys, but remains with girls. By 17 years of age, girls have two to two-and-a-half times as much body fat as boys. In contrast, *lean body mass* (total body weight less total body fat), or LBM, is significantly greater in boys than girls. For girls, LBM peaks around 15 years of age, whereas for boys, LBM continues to increase into late adolescence or early adulthood (Forbes, 1972). (See Figure 9.1.)

Growth in lean body mass in adolescence is due to an increase in muscle mass. In turn, increases in muscle mass produce increases in strength and motor performance. For girls, strength increases gradually throughout adolescence, eventually leveling off between 16 and 18 years. For boys, the increase in strength follows a similar growth path as in girls until about 13 years, when there is a dramatic rise in strength (Malina, 1974, 1979). The effect of this rise is that, from the adolescent period on, most males are significantly stronger than most females.

Heredity and nutrition influence the timing of the adolescent growth spurt in several ways, one of the most important being their effect on the secretion of hormones by the endocrine glands. A growth hormone released by the pituitary gland is primarily responsible for the rapid growth at the beginning of adolescence. The thyroid gland aids in this development by releasing larger amounts of the hormones that permit the conversion of food into tissues and energy. The gonads — the ovaries in the female and the testes in the male—are stimulated by hormones secreted by the adrenal glands and the pituitary. It is the gonads that bring about sexual development. They also play an important role in stimulating the physical development that occurs before the visible signs of puberty appear.

Pause for Thought

Although there is considerable variability in the rate of growth during adolescence, most teenagers resemble one or both of their parents in size and shape by the time they leave this developmental period. What effect might all the changes in size and shape have on how adolescents see themselves or how others see them? How might their parents be affected by their adolescents' growth?

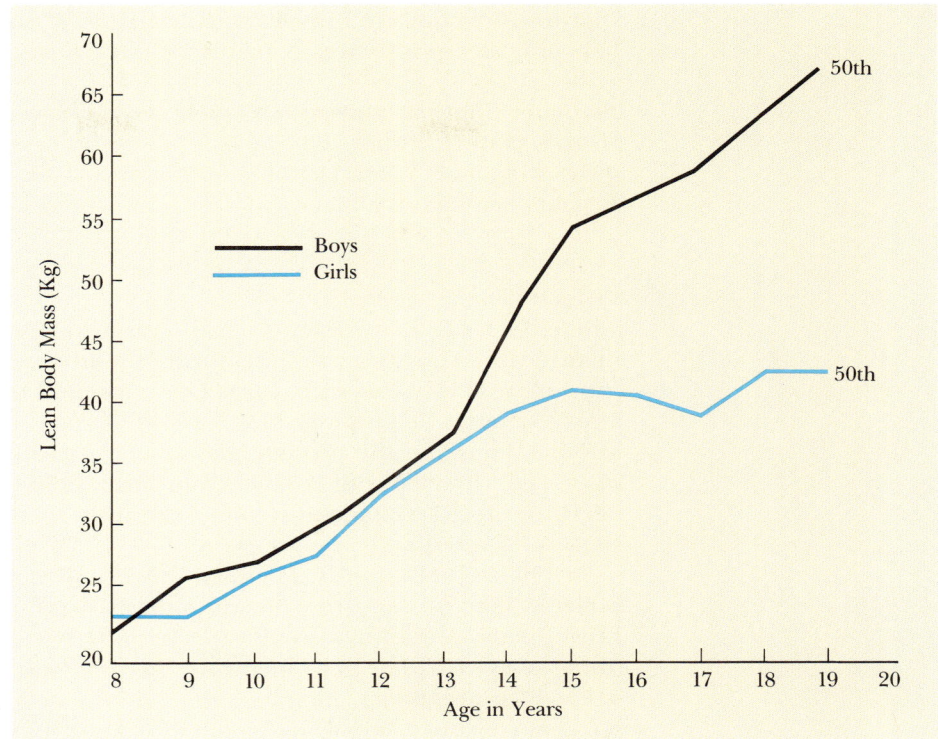

Figure 9.1 Changes in 50th percentiles of Lean Body Mass (LBM) in boys and girls.

Puberty

Perhaps the first sign you had that you were entering puberty was the eruption of pubic hairs. Most women remember the time they started their first period—another sign of pubertal growth. These obvious changes are accompanied by other changes in the body. Sex organs develop along with **secondary sex characteristics,** the nongenital physical features that distinguish the sexes. Semen, a lower voice, the growth of the penis and testes in boys and the onset of menstruation and development of breasts in girls are often taken as signs of the onset of puberty. About one to two years before the outward signs appear, the gonads begin secreting androgen in boys and estrogen in girls. These hormones initiate the striking physical and mental changes of adolescence.

Puberty can be divided into three stages. In the *prepubescent stage,* the secondary sex characteristics begin to develop, but the reproductive organs do not as yet produce ova and sperm. In the *pubescent stage,* the secondary sex characteristics continue to develop and the reproductive organs become capable of ova and sperm production. In the *postpubescent stage,* the secondary sex characteristics are well developed and the sex organs are capable of adult functioning. The great majority of American girls have their first menstruation—an event known as **menarche**—between the ages of 10 and 17; the mean age is 12.7 years (Bullough, 1981; Zacharias, Rand, & Wurtman, 1976). Puberty for boys seems to occur with greater variability than for girls. However, one study found that approximately 50 percent of boys show evidence of

Secondary Sex Characteristics   Physical features other than genitals that distinguish women and men.

Menarche   The first occurrence of menstruation.

sperm production by 14.9 years (Richardson & Short, 1978). As these numbers indicate, girls generally mature about two years earlier than boys.

Pause for Thought

If girls mature earlier than boys in adolescence, why is it that boys exceed girls in sports? What factors would affect a teenager's interests and performance in school athletics?

Primary Sex Characteristics

The male testes are present at birth, but are only about 10 percent of their mature size. They grow rapidly during the first year or two of puberty, then grow more slowly, not reaching mature size until the age of 20 or 21. Shortly after the testes begin to develop, the penis starts to grow in length, and the seminal ducts and the prostate gland enlarge. Although the penis is capable of erection by means of contact from birth, only during adolescence does it begin to erect spontaneously or in response to sexually provocative sights, sounds, or thoughts.

The female's uterus, fallopian tubes, and vagina grow rapidly through puberty. The ovaries grow during puberty, too, and although they begin to function about midway through this period, they do not reach full adult size until the age of 20 or 21. The ovaries produce ova and secrete the hormones needed for pregnancy, menstruation, and the development of the secondary sex characteristics. Following menarche, menstruation may come at irregular intervals at first. For six months to a year or more, ovulation may not always occur.

Secondary Sex Characteristics

The secondary sex characteristics—breasts, body hair, voice change—are not directly related to reproduction. In boys, the first to develop are sparse patches of light colored, straight pubic hair. This hair takes on its characteristically dark, curly appearance after a year or two. Axillary (underarm) and facial hair begin to appear when the pubic hair has almost fully grown in. Like the pubic hair, this hair at first is light colored, fine, and sparse. As for facial hair, few boys find that they need to shave before they are 16 or 17. Hair also appears on the arms, legs, and shoulders, and later on the chest. Body hair continues to develop for some time, often into adulthood, with the amount and density determined by heredity. Perhaps the most noticeable change in boys, however, is the deepening of the voice. Usually by the time a boy is 13, his voice has begun to take on a huskier tone. Caused by an enlargement of the larynx and lengthening of the vocal cords, voice change generally is complete by 17 or 18.

Girls' secondary sex characteristics generally develop in the same sequence as do boys'. The first indication of approaching sexual maturity in a girl is budding of the breasts (Chumlea, 1982). Occurring at an average age of 10 or 11, the bud stage involves a slight elevation of the nipple and increasing fullness of the surrounding areola. Before menarche, there is an increase in the amount of fat underlying the nipple and the areola, and the breast rises in a conical shape. After menarche, the breasts become larger and rounder with the development of the mammary glands. In addition to breast development, there are also noticeable changes in the size and shape of a girls' hips, which grow wider and rounder. This development is caused in part by enlargement of the pelvic bone and in part by increases in subcutaneous fat. Coinciding with these changes is the emergence of pubic hair, which has the same texture and appearance as does boys'.

For both sexes, skin becomes coarser and thicker during puberty, and the pores enlarge. The *sebaceous,* or fatty, glands in the skin become active at this time and produce an oily secretion, as persons suffering from acne know all too well. The sweat glands in the armpits also begin to function at this time, even before the axillary hair appears, and result in increases in the amount and odor of perspiration. Many teenagers are embarrassed by the large underarm sweat rings that occur when they least want to appear "uncool." Another telltale sign (or odor) of adolescence is sweaty, smelly feet and shoes, especially sneakers. Fortunately, the activity of the sweat glands decreases later on in adolescence.

Secular Growth Trends

Secular Growth Trends Variation in physical growth patterns that characterize populations over a period of time.

Secular growth trends is the term that biologists who study human beings use to describe variations in human physical growth found throughout the world (Roche, 1979). To measure secular growth trends, biologists record the height, weight, and body changes in defined groups—usually national ones—over long periods of time, usually several decades.

Children in different parts of the world seem to be reaching puberty earlier than their parents did, and growing taller and heavier as well (Roche, 1979). For example, records show that in the United States, a young man will, on the average, be one inch (2.5 cm) taller and 10 pounds (4.5 kg) heavier than his father. A young woman will probably be almost an inch (2.5 cm) taller than her mother and two pounds (.9 kg) heavier, and will reach menarche 10 months earlier than her mother did. In addition, today's adolescents reach full adult height earlier than their ancestors did. At the turn of the century, girls reached full height at the age of 18, whereas the modern girl stops growing at age 17. A century ago, boys did not reach full height until age 23 or 24, but now an adolescent boy stops growing around the age of 20.

Among European populations, the age of menarche has decreased over the past century from a range of 15 to 17 years to between 12 and 14 years (Malina, 1979; Roche, 1979). In poorly developed countries, however, menarche still occurs relatively late. Eveleth and Tanner (1976) reported that in New Guinea, first menstruation occurs between 15.5 and 18.4 years of age.

Although no one is certain what causes secular growth trends, they are generally believed to be both environmental and genetic in origin. There is, for example, some apparent relationship between crop production, urbanization, family size, and mortality. This relationship does not clearly indicate cause, however. Important factors in secular growth trends are improved health and better care during childhood. Genetic factors, altered by such events as a change in immigration and marriage patterns, may also be important, as may changes in socioeconomic status, eating patterns, and environmental stress (Malina, 1979).

Varying Rates of Development

If you have ever attended a seventh- or eighth-grade class assembly, you most likely have noticed the vast differences in size and shape of the students. Not only do the girls appear to tower over the boys, but within each of the sexes you would likely notice considerable variability in physical growth. Within any age group of adolescents, one can observe significant variations in physical maturity, as well as concomitant variations in areas of emotional and intellectual development.

Early and Late Maturation

Among the many adjustments that adolescents must make, certainly one of the most important is integrating a "new" body into an emerging picture of the self. This is a time of increased preoccupation with physical appearance (Clifford, 1971), and a time when many people report considerable dissatisfaction with the way they look (Rosenbaum, 1979; Simmons & Rosenberg, 1975). Who we are is very much related to how we look physically. For adolescents who seem to be growing and changing physically overnight, self-image is greatly affected. Furthermore, the age and rate at which an adolescent grows can have an impact on self-evaluation.

Research has shown that boys who mature early have a distinct advantage in a number of areas over those who mature late (Jones, 1957, 1958; Mussen & Jones, 1957). They tend to excel at sports, achieve greater popularity, and become leaders in student government and extracurricular activities. Early-maturing boys also tend to be more poised, relaxed, and good-natured, and they are more interested in girls. In adult life, they are likely to be more successful vocationally and to be more conventional in career and lifestyle choices. In contrast, late-maturing boys are not only smaller and less well developed than almost everyone in their age group, but they also are not very interested in dating, and when they do become interested in girls, they often lack social graces or are rebuffed by the prettiest and most popular girls. These boys also are more likely to be characterized as impulsive, restless, and lacking in self-confidence. In adulthood, however, many of these disadvantages disappear, or are compensated for by other traits. As adults, late-maturing individuals tend to be insightful, independent, curious, and less bound by rules and routines. They are also less conventionally successful (Jones, 1965; Peskin, 1973). Early maturing boys tend to be treated more as adults because they look more like adults than do late maturing boys. Pressured by adult expectations to act like adults, early-maturing boys run the risk of prematurely adopting a personal and career identity (Livson & Peskin, 1980). Late-maturing boys have more time to explore and experiment with their options before becoming fixed in their identity.

In a more recent longitudinal study (Blyth, Bulcroft, & Simmons, 1981), early maturation for girls (as defined by the onset of menstruation) was found to be a mixed blessing, whereas early maturation for boys (as measured by rate of height growth) was found to have positive effects. Blyth's five-year study tracked girls and boys from the sixth to the tenth grade. Early-maturing girls did not perform as well academically, had more reported school behavior problems, and were more dissatisfied with their bodies during the ninth and tenth grades. However, early-maturing girls were found to be more independent and socially active than their late-maturing peers.

In part, the psychological significance of puberty is a product of the times during which adolescents mature. Current opinion and values will affect the status of adolescents who are slower or faster to mature physically. In the 1960s, when the first longitudinal data on maturation rates were collected (e.g., Jones, 1965, 1958, 1957; Mussen & Jones, 1957), there was not nearly as much importance placed on teenagers looking like adults as there is today. At that time, people were not legally considered to be adults until they were 21 years of age. By that age, most of the men and all of the women would have reached physical maturity. Today, however, the legal adult age has been lowered to age 18. At this age, many men do not yet look adultlike and they may feel greater pressure to look adult at an earlier age than did their counterparts who were born a generation earlier.

The Impact of Menarche

No area of adolescent female development has been marked by as much psychological and sociocultural significance as menarche—the first menstruation. In about half the world's cultures, this event is celebrated with elaborate rituals and ceremonies (Paige & Paige, 1981). But what is the meaning of menarche for the young adolescent? And what factors influence her adjustment to this maturational event?

Psychological theories have been mixed in their characterization of the impact of menarche on the young female (Grief & Ulman, 1982). Some have suggested that the first menstruation is inevitably traumatic; others have described the event as a positive experience in the girl's development. Research by Ruble and Brooks-Gunn (1982) has yielded results that tend to support a more moderate position. That is, young adolescent girls, when asked to describe their first menstrual experience, were both negative (e.g., upset) and positive (e.g., excited) in their reactions. These researchers also noted that young adolescents who received greater preparation and had more knowledge about menarche prior to experiencing it, were more likely to have positive reactions to their first menstrual period and be less self-conscious than girls who were poorly prepared.

Girls' physical and emotional reactions to menstruation are affected by the attitudes they have about having periods. Girls who believe that menstruation is a painful experience, are more likely to have painful menstrual cramps (Gunn & Peterson, 1984). Furthermore, girls' adjustment to menstruation is influenced by whether they see themselves as fitting in with their social peers. Whether a girl is "on time" for starting her period is based more on social rather than biological considerations. If all of her friends have not yet started their periods, a girl who is a late maturer will not feel out of step. However, the early-maturing girl may feel awkward about starting her period when all her friends have not. Ballet dancers who were on time in development with respect to their general peer group but were ahead of their dancing peers had a more difficult adjustment to puberty (Brooks-Gunn & Warren, 1985).

Pause for Thought

Twenty-five years ago, boxes of sanitary napkins were sold with a brown paper covering on them to avoid any embarrassment to the purchaser. Today, television commercials and magazine ads discuss menstruation freely and provide consumers with much information. What effect has this shift in marketing had on young adolescents' attitudes toward menstruation?

Sexuality emerges in full bloom during adolescence. It is a time for exploring sexual feelings and developing sexual relationships.

Sexual Attitudes and Behavior

As adolescent's bodies become more adultlike, their interest in sexual behavior increases sharply. In early adolescence, sexual explorations are tentative and generally self-centered. The 12- or 13-year-old, for example, usually is more concerned with meeting his or her own needs than the needs of another. In late adolescence, on the other hand, sexual relationships are more often based on *mutuality*—a concern for meeting the needs of both the self and one's partner. According to surveys reported by Hass (1979), 70 percent of the boys and 45 percent of the girls said they had masturbated by age 15, and about two-thirds of the boys and one-half of the girls between the ages of 16 and 19 said they masturbated at least once a week.

Heterosexual Behavior

It is important to keep in mind that compared to previous generations, teenagers today are more willing to talk about and admit their sexual behavior. However, Dreyer (1982) notes that the growing acceptance of sexual expression among adolescents is not unconditional. Although the vast majority of adolescents approve of premarital sexual intercourse, they do so only within a relationship that is loving and affectionate. Promiscuous behavior and sexual exploitation are considered unacceptable by most adolescents.

Although research evidence has documented substantial increases in acceptance of adolescent sexual behavior, actual participation by young people in such behavior has been considerably more modest. In fact, Siegel (1982) has suggested that changes in adolescent sexual behavior are better characterized as *evolutionary* (implying a steady, gradual change) rather than *revolutionary* (implying a sudden and dramatic change). For example, one study of 15- to 19-year-old adolescents reported that whereas 95 percent of the boys and 83 percent of the girls approved of "heavy petting" (defined as genital touching), only 55 percent of the boys and 43 percent of the girls had actually engaged in such behavior (Hass, 1979).

In another more recent study (Zabin, Hirsch, Smith, & Hardy, 1984) of 3500 junior and high school students, 83 percent of the sexually active students thought that the best age for first sexual intercourse was older than the age that they experienced it themselves. Eighty-eight percent of the teenage mothers thought that the best age for first birth was older than they were when they had their babies. In other words, the adolescents' values regarding sexual behavior were not in keeping with their behavior.

The epidemic rise of the sexually transmitted disease AIDS has been a stimulus for many adults and teenagers to reconsider their values regarding sexual behavior. Some people are considering limiting their sexual activities or abstaining from sexual intercourse until they have a longstanding relationship with their partner. The greatest changes in adolescent sexual behavior over the past few generations have occurred for girls. Dreyer (1982) reports that from 1925 to 1979, the percentage of high-school girls who had experienced premarital sexual intercourse more than quadrupled, from 10 percent in 1925 to 44 percent in 1979. Boys also showed an increase in premarital coitus over this time span, from 25 percent in 1925 to 56 percent in 1979. The less dramatic rise in sexual intercourse for boys clearly reflects the fact that, until recently, boys have enjoyed substantially more freedom in the expression of their sexuality—hence their rates of sexual behavior always have been higher than for girls. In summarizing the statistics on adolescent sexual behavior, Fox (1979) observed: "More teenagers are sexually active, more are active with a greater number of partners and with increasing coital frequency, and more teenagers are initiating their sexual activity at increasingly younger ages" (p. 21).

Homosexuality

The first reliable data on homosexual behavior came from the research of Kinsey and his colleagues (Kinsey, Pomeroy, & Martin, 1948, 1953). Their studies showed that a surprisingly large number of people had had some homosexual experience during their lives—about 37 percent of males and 19 percent of females. For most of the males and about half of the females, these experiences had begun during adolescence. It was also found, however, that most of these people were not exclusively homosexual. Many of them had both homosexual and heterosexual contacts during the same general period of time, and felt comfortable in both. Also, many who engaged in homosexual activity in adolescence or early adult life gave it up later on. Most of them were never identified as homosexuals by their heterosexual friends or co-workers.

In a more recent study, 15 percent of boys and 10 percent of girls reported having had a homosexual experience (Dreyer, 1982). Studies of adolescent homosexuality indicate that such sexual experiences are usually more frequent before age 15, and more likely to occur for boys than girls (Hass, 1979; Sorensen, 1973). Most young people are tolerant of homosexuality. In a questionnaire study, nearly 70 percent of the 16- to 19-year-olds accepted sexual relations between two women, and only slightly less than that accepted such relations between two men (Hass, 1979). Since 1981, when the AIDS virus began to appear in the United States among homosexuals, there has been a cautious shift in peoples' overall acceptance of homosexuality. While homosexuality is no longer viewed as an illness as it had been viewed in the

Human Development in Practice

Sexually Transmitted Diseases

Before 1981, when the AIDS virus was relatively unknown, public health officials were concerned about the rising number of adolescents who were afflicted with a sexually transmitted disease (STD). STDs are occurring in epidemic proportions. Of all the infectious diseases, only the common cold occurs with greater frequency. In one recent study, the highest incidence of STD occurred in the group between the ages of 20 and 24. Next came the 15- to 19-year-old group, with 10 percent of all youngsters between the ages of 13 and 19 having had a sexually transmitted disease at some time. About 11 percent of females and 12 percent of males 16 to 19 years of age have had a STD, and the figures show a significant upward trend. In fact, people under age 25 make up more than three-fourths of all reported cases of STD (Green & Horton, 1982).

With the spread of the AIDS virus has come an even greater awareness among people in the health fields of the need to educate adolescents on sexual health habits. The habits and attitudes that teenagers establish concerning their sexual behavior could have a drastic and long-term effect.

Sexually active adolescents, either heterosexual or homosexual, can reduce their chance of contracting a sexually transmitted disease by taking certain precautions. The Public Health Service recommends the following steps:

1. Recognize that abstinence or a stable sexual relationship with one person (monogamy) is the best protection against sexual transmission of the AIDS virus.
2. Do not have unprotected sex with multiple partners or with people who have had multiple partners.
3. Do not have unprotected sex with anyone who has the AIDS virus. Protected sex involves using a latex condom from the start to the finish of sexual intercourse.
4. Avoid sexual activities that could cause cuts or tears in the skin.
5. Do not have sex with prostitutes or drug abusers.
6. Do not use intravenous drugs or share syringes.

Not only is it important to teach teenagers how to protect themselves from sexually transmitted diseases, health professionals need to teach people to act responsibly toward other people. If you have been exposed to someone with AIDS or some other STD, then anyone with whom you have sexual intercourse is equally exposed and needs to be informed of that risk *before* you engage in sexual behavior.

Nurses and physicians who treat adolescents can help teenagers learn more about AIDS and other sexually transmitted diseases by offering information about the diseases and by encouraging teenagers to talk about how they can protect themselves and their partners. It may be easier for adolescents to enter into a discussion about sexually transmitted diseases with a nurse or doctor, than with parents, teachers, or peers. The challenge for health professionals involves teaching adolescents how to have safe sex.

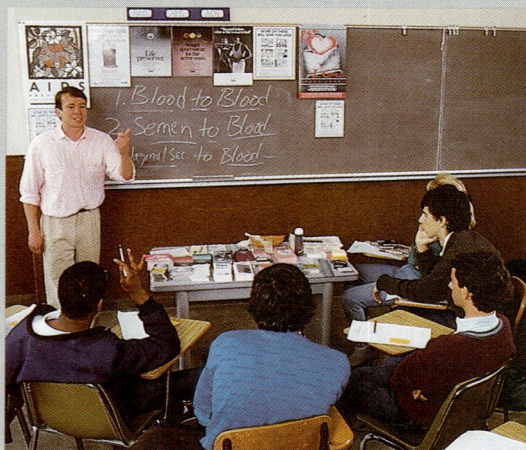

Teenagers who are informed about AIDS and ways to protect themselves and others from the virus are more likely to alter their sexual habits.

past, the dangers of contracting AIDS and other sexually transmitted diseases has resulted in less openness about their sexual orientation among gay people (see Box, Sexually Transmitted Disease).

Teenage Pregnancy

In the United States today, for every 1000 girls between 15 and 19, 96 get pregnant. The rate is almost twice as high among black teenage girls as among whites. These rates are the highest rates for teenage pregnancies among the industrialized nations of the world. In France the rate is 43, in Sweden the rate is 35 (Mall, 1985). The increase in sexual activity does not account for these differences in rate since sexual activity has increased among teenagers in other countries. Of the teenage pregnancies in the United States, nearly 40 percent are terminated by abortion (Henshaw & O'Reilly, 1983). In 1982, there were 523,531 infants born to adolescent mothers; 125,305 of these babies were known to have been fathered by men under the age of 20 (NCHS, 1982). Once a teenager gets pregnant for the first time, the odds are that she will be pregnant again within three years. In one study, half of the pregnant teenagers became pregnant again within three years (Furstenberg, 1979).

Teenage pregnancy creates risks for both mother and child. The babies of teenage mothers have twice the normal chance of being born prematurely or with low birthweight, neurological defects, or birth injuries. These babies run two to three times the normal risk of dying in infancy. The younger the mother, the greater the risk. Teenage mothers themselves are 60 percent more likely than women in their twenties to suffer complications or death during pregnancy or delivery, with hemorrhage, miscarriage, toxemia, and anemia as the most frequent causes.

Once the baby is born, the long-term care of the baby must be decided. Whereas the majority of unmarried teenagers, particularly white teenagers, once gave up their babies for adoption, only a small percentage do so today (Dreyer, 1982).

Roughly one-third of all teenage mothers are married at the time their baby is born. But the likelihood of these marriages breaking up within six years is three times greater than it is for older couples. Due to their relative lack of education and to their own immaturity, teenage couples often cannot meet the economic pressures and the parental responsibilities of raising a child. They often have difficulty completing their high-school studies, and without a diploma, their chances for job security are limited. Furthermore, teenage parents must deal with all the difficulties of working parents while they are in school. Someone must care for their child, and the parents (or single mother) must divide their time between work or school demands and the demands of a new baby.

Adolescent fathers as a group have not been studied as systematically as teenage mothers primarily because it is more difficult for researchers to identify them. The studies that have been done reveal that adolescent fathers are concerned about their newborn children; many young fathers are interested in caring for their children (Elster & Hendricks, 1986). They want to play a meaningful role in the lives of the teenage mother and child, while at the same time they want to ensure the financial stability of their young families by completing their schooling. The stresses adolescent fathers experience are similar to those of the mother. Both must deal with the transition to parenthood while also adjusting to a couple relationship, often while still living in

Teenage fathers are frequently concerned about and involved with their children.

their parents' home. All these adjustments occur in addition to the developmental adjustments associated with the adolescent period.

Sex Education

Many funny stories are told about teaching young people about the "facts of life" or "the birds and the bees." While most adolescents have some idea about how conception occurs, many are confused about specific details concerning sexual reproduction. For example, some teenage girls may not know at what point in their menstrual cycle they are most likely to get pregnant (the middle of the cycle). Often what teenagers do know about sexual reproduction and behavior they have pieced together from conversations with their peers or older siblings. Many adolescents feel embarrassed or shy about talking about or asking questions about their sexual behavior.

Many parents, though willing and interested, also shy away from talking about sex with their children (Bennett & Dickinson, 1980; Fox, 1979; Norman & Harris, 1981). When direct instruction does occur, it is usually from mother to daughter and, less frequently, mother to son. In the studies examined, "the most notable aspect about the father is his almost complete absence as a source of sex education for his children" (Fox, 1979, p. 22). The research suggests that when parent–child communication does occur, it appears to restrict the frequency and nature of adolescent sexual involvement, although the reasons behind this influence have yet to be clearly understood. Furthermore, increased mother–daughter communication appears to be associated with more effective use of contraceptives.

With the rise of teenage pregnancies and the dangers associated with sexually transmitted diseases such as AIDS, more parents are supporting formal sex-education classes in the schools. The issue of what to teach children and adolescents about sex and when has sparked controversy within many communities and households. While many states how have mandated sex

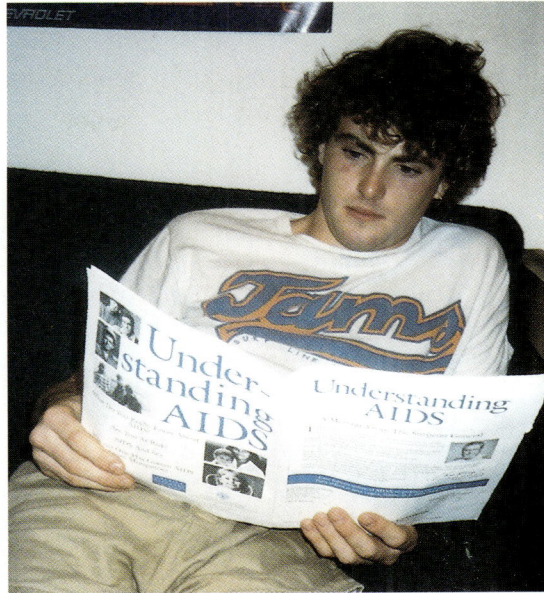

While many teenagers may be reluctant to talk with their parents about their sexual behavior, they may accept information that is offered to them. In this brochure that was distributed to all American households this young man learns about how and when to safely use a condom.

education classes, the content of these classes varies from discussion of sexual anatomy to child-care and family planning. According to Scales (1981), sex-education programs should "enable young people with the skills, knowledge and attitudes that will enable them to make intelligent choices and decisions" (p. 220). Although sex-education classes do not seem to influence an adolescent's choice to have or not have sex, there is evidence that sexually active teenage girls who have taken sex-education courses are less likely to become pregnant (Zelnik & Kim, 1982). The ideal sex-education program is one that encourages greater parental involvement in discussions on sexual behavior. A person's sexual behavior is often influenced by personal and religious values that are communicated directly and indirectly by their parents. What adolescents need is more guidance in behaving according to their values and more information about the choices they can make to prevent disease and unwanted pregnancies.

Pause for Thought
Many teenagers do not discuss their sexuality with teachers in their sex-education classes because they are afraid that teachers will talk about them to their parents or other teachers. Other teenagers are reluctant to ask questions about sex in class because they are concerned about what their peers will think of them. What precautions could be taken to encourage more discussion about sexuality in classrooms?

Cognitive Development

One of the major achievements of early adolescence is the attainment of what Piaget calls *formal operational thought* (Inhelder & Piaget, 1958). Before adolescence, children are largely concerned with the here and now, with what is apparent to their senses, and with problems that can be solved by trial and error. During adolescence, most people grow much better able to deal with problems on an abstract level, to form hypotheses, and to reason from propositions that are contrary to fact.

Formal Operations (11–15 Years)

According to Piaget, it is not until the period of formal operations—the fourth and last stage of cognitive development that is reached between the ages of 11 and 15—that a person can think flexibly enough about the world to consider abstract universals such as freedom and justice, and to grasp their intrinsic qualities. Children develop the ability to generalize before the age of 11, but they are not yet ready to understand abstract characteristics such as congruence and mass. By the age of 15 or so, most individuals can operate with these abstract concepts. They can also begin to think and operate on the level of theory, rather than being constrained by the observable facts or the apparent reality of a situation (Braine & Rumain, 1983; Moshman & Neimark, 1982; Neimark, 1982). For example, most elementary-school-age children, given the statements "Cows are larger than cats" and "Cats are larger than mice," would have little trouble concluding that "Cows are larger than mice." However, these same children would most likely reject the argument that "Mice are larger than cats, and cats are larger than cows; therefore, mice are larger than cows." The difficulty they would have in accepting the logic of this statement is that it runs counter to their everyday, observable experience—that is, they have never seen mice larger than cows. Young children cannot separate the form and content of a problem. By contrast, the adolescent, having achieved the level of formal operations, is able to make this separation, and consequently can analyze the logical implications of purely hypothetical situations or statements.

Problem-Solving Skills

Formal operational abilities are manifested in numerous areas of a person's life, particularly in the realm of scientific problem solving. In one of Piaget's experiments, subjects were shown an object hanging from a string. This pendulum could be modified by changing several factors: length of the string, weight of the object, height at which the pendulum was released, and force with which it was pushed. Subjects were asked to find out which of the above factors determines how rapidly the pendulum swings. (The experimenter knew, of course, that length of string was the key factor and that testing any one variable would necessitate controlling all others if accurate results were to be obtained.)

Children in the earlier stage of concrete-operational thought began their experiments by physically manipulating the various factors that could influence rate of swinging. They were more analytic and systematic in their approach than younger preoperational children and they made careful and objective observations of what happened. But their inferences could at best only be partially correct since they had not planned for any sort of control, nor were they capable of extrapolating beyond directly observable results. In one case, a child compared a pendulum made with a long string and a heavy weight with one that had a short string and a light weight. The child con-

Adolescents who have reached the level of formal operational thought are likely to first consider all of the possibilities in solving the problem of what would make the pendulum swing faster.

cluded that *both* weight and length were important. A truly scientific approach would have entailed using the same length of string for both pendulums, the same height, and the same force, while varying only the weight.

When working at their peak capacity, formal-operational adolescents would (and did) use just this sort of scientific approach. Moreover, they do not simply plunge into the experiment, nor is their thinking bound by immediate observable results. Adolescents first consider all of the possibilities, or hypotheses, about what makes the pendulum swing faster. They are able to imagine that one or some combination of factors is involved; and they can deduce what *might* occur if one or another possibility were tested. Thus, before even starting an experiment, they are capable of working out a detailed plan or design for systematically testing each alternative. This change in the ability to mentally think a problem through without actually performing all the intervening steps can also be seen in the adolescent's day-to-day life. Fourteen-year-old Mark, was interested in building a wooden case to hold his air rifle. In thinking about his problem, he realized that there were many possible ways he could build the case. After careful consideration, he decided on a specific design and drew up a set of plans on how he would build the case, how it might look from different perspectives (e.g., top view, side view), and what materials would be needed (including the cost of the materials). Then he presented his proposal to his father for money. Unlike a younger child, Mark was able to consider a number of possible solutions to build his rifle case. Through mental deliberations, he was able to decide on the best possible solution, on which he then proceeded to act.

The adolescent also develops a more mature notion of time—the ability to conceive the distant future concretely and to set realistic long-term goals. With this conception comes a new, sometimes poignant awareness that oneself and others are caught up in the ongoing process of growth, aging, and death.

The adolescent's increased freedom in forming hypotheses often creates problems in making decisions. Seeing not one but many alternatives can often lead to doubt and confusion about one's own judgment. It often leads to external conflict, too, especially with parents and other authority figures (Weiner, 1977). You can probably remember when you first began to challenge your parents' decisions. Adolescents often demand to know the reasoning behind the decisions and want to present the virtues of their opinions and the opinions of their peers. They are not likely to accept a decision without questions and some debate, and are likely to challenge religious and social values. You will recall 14-year-old David who, at the beginning of this chapter, was becoming critical of his family's politics and religious beliefs.

Adolescent Idealism

Interest in theoretical ideas also leads adolescents to construct ideal families, societies, and religions. As a formal operational thinker, the adolescent is freed from the bonds of personal experience and present time to explore ideas, ideals, roles, beliefs, theories, commitments, and all sorts of possibilities at the level of thought (Neimark, 1975). They see that there are alternatives to the way things are done, and they want to find ways to end human suffering and poverty, social inequity, and false belief. Utopian solutions to the world's problems—planned communities, Eastern religions, and new forms of consciousness—find many adherents in the adolescent group. As John Broughton

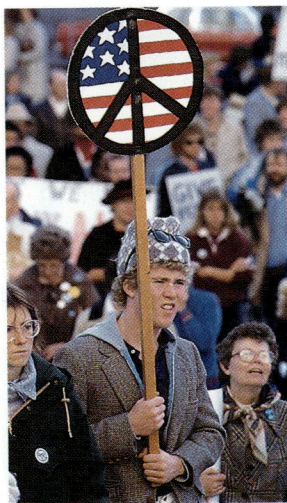

Idealism during adolescence may result in young people wanting to change aspects of their world. These teenagers are protesting the use of nuclear weapons.

(1978) has suggested, the adolescent thinker is becoming more of a philosopher in his or her approach to the world. There is increasing emphasis on the distinctions between the physical and the mental, between reality and appearance, and between subjectivity and objectivity.

Limitations of Piaget's Theory

It should be noted that several researchers regard the work of Piaget and Inhelder only as "a good first approximation" for studying the level of development beyond concrete operations. As Neimark (1975) points out, studies of older adolescents and adults in Western cultures show that formal operations may not be attained by all individuals. Also, some people apparently attain it only in certain areas of expertise. Even Piaget (1972) notes that different individuals may attain formal operations at different ages, and the manner and age at which it is displayed may depend on aptitude and experience. In reviewing cross-cultural and other research, Neimark (1975) claims that there is a need for more comprehensive studies and more objective experiments to ascertain the components of formal operational thought and to determine how variables such as class, culture, gender, IQ, education, and training affect the course of formal operational development.

Adolescent Egocentrism

As children develop, they slowly overcome various forms of egocentrism (Inhelder & Piaget, 1958; Piaget, 1969). In infancy, egocentrism is expressed by the child's incapacity to distinguish reality from his or her own point of view and immediate experiences. Infants do not even know they have a point of view. By adolescence, however, during the stage of formal operations, individuals become able to think and reason not only about their own thoughts but about those of others as well. However, it is at this point, according to David Elkind (1967), that a new form of egocentrism emerges. Adolescents,

Adolescents, searching to discover who they are, often become self-absorbed. They become preoccupied with their physical appearance.

Adolescent Egocentrism
The tendency of adolescents to believe that other people are as preoccupied with their behavior, ideas, and appearance as they themselves are.

Imaginary Audience
A term used to describe adolescents' belief that they are the focus of others' attention.

searching to know who they are, become self-absorbed. They indeed take into account the thoughts of others, but they assume these thoughts are all directed toward themselves. **Adolescent egocentrism** means that individuals believe that other people are as preoccupied with their behavior and appearance as they themselves are.

Unlike younger children, adolescents are constantly evaluating themselves and measuring themselves in terms of other people's reactions. Teenagers anticipate that others will be aware of and critical of the things they themselves find wrong about the way they look or act. Similarly, they expect others to be cognizant of and concerned with those things they themselves find attractive or appealing—even some slight gesture or personal mannerism. When parents express a negative reaction to rock music or some type of clothing, the adolescent is often surprised or confused.

Adolescents, then, are in a personal "fish bowl" and are continually creating an **imaginary audience,** as Elkind says, before whom they perform. It is imaginary because actually the adolescents are probably not the focus of attention, though their overly developed self-consciousness leads them to think they are. When young people meet, each one is playing to the audience and is at the same time an audience for the others. This testing of images takes the place of substantial interpersonal communication. Clothing, gestures, hairstyles, even the music one listens to—all become part of the image.

Elkind (1978) has distinguished between two components of the imaginary audience. One component centers on the individual's willingness to reveal to others characteristics of the self that are assumed to be relatively stable or unchanging (e.g., personality, intelligence, etc.); Elkind refers to this component as the *abiding self.* The second component of the imaginary audience is the person's willingness to reveal to others characteristics of the self that are assumed to be temporary or to vary over time (e.g., inappropriate dress or behavior, a bad haircut, etc.); this component is referred to as the *transient self.* Elkind and Bowen (1979) predicted that adolescents would be more reluctant to reveal to others aspects of the abiding self rather than the transient self. They also predicted that young adolescents would be less willing to reveal either aspect of themselves to others in comparison to younger children and older adolescents. To test these hypotheses, the researchers administered a questionnaire measuring willingness to reveal aspects of the self to 697 students in the fourth, sixth, eighth, and twelfth grades. The results of the study confirmed their hypothesis. Generally, subjects scored higher (or exposed themselves less) on items measuring the abiding self rather than the transient self. Furthermore, self-consciousness about aspects of the abiding self, but not the transient self, was associated with lower self-esteem. In addition, subjects in the eighth grade were more concerned with what others thought of them than were subjects in the fourth, sixth, or twelfth grades. Finally, girls showed an overall greater self-consciousness about revealing themselves to others than did boys. These results, backed by similar results from a study by Gray and Hudson (1984), confirm the validity of the concept of imaginary audience, and the heightened sensitivity of young adolescents to the perceived reactions of others.

In addition to the imaginary audience, many adolescents begin developing what Elkind (1967) calls the *personal fable,* an ongoing, private, and imaginary story, often full of exaggerations, in which they themselves play the leading role. As part of the personal fable, adolescents come to believe that their thoughts and feelings are unique—that they are the only ones ever to experience such euphoria or anguish. This belief in one's own specialness is often tied in with a sense of immortality.

According to Elkind, the imaginary audience provides a way of testing reality and one's self-concept. In time, adolescents begin to perceive that there is a difference between their concerns and anticipations and the real concerns of others. This usually happens when the stage of formal operations has been established (about the age of 15 or 16). At this time, adolescents can begin to develop true relationships, in which they find that others share many of the same pains and pleasures. The extreme self-interestedness associated with the personal fable is thus slowly, though probably never completely, overcome. Elkind suggests that establishing a sense of intimacy with another person serves as the replacement for the personal fable.

Pause for Thought

Teenagers are especially self-conscious during the early adolescent period because they believe that everyone is watching and evaluating them and because they hold unrealistic and exaggerated views of themselves. In what ways might adolescent egocentrism be accentuated or exploited by the mass media and by consumer marketing?

Moral Reasoning

As you read in Chapter 7, Kohlberg believes that most elementary-school-age children reason at the preconventional level of morality, which itself consists of two stages. Moral judgments at the preconventional level are based on the anticipated outcomes of a behavior—punishment and reward. As people enter early adolescence, however, there is a shift to Level II, **conventional morality.** Like the preconventional level, conventional morality is comprised of two stages. The first stage—Stage 3—involves a focus on mutual caring and affection. Here the person is concerned with maintaining good relations with others, and with winning their approval (that is, being a "good boy" or "good girl"). The second stage within this level—Stage 4—involves a focus on "law and order." Right and wrong are evaluated in terms of conformity to societal rules and regulations. If a behavior violates the law, it is wrong; if it adheres to the law, it is right. Furthermore, at this level, it is the "letter" of the law rather than the "spirit" that is most important. Thus, should a law be enacted that inadvertently benefits certain groups of individuals to the detriment of others, the person still would say that adherence to the law is essential—or morally correct—even if some people suffer.

Although the majority of adolescents (and adults) typically reason at the conventional level of morality, the ability to reason abstractly and conceptualize alternatives—both of which broaden remarkably during middle to late adolescence—increases the possible range of moral judgments for many individuals. At this time, there is increased awareness of potential conflicts among socially acceptable standards and between the rights of the individual and societal laws. Such conflicts are not readily handled by Stage 4 (law-and-order) reasoning. If adolescents (or adults) recognize the inadequacy of Stage-

Conventional Morality
According to Kohlberg, the second level of moral reasoning; morality is viewed as the desire to preserve harmonious interpersonal relationships and to obey existing formal rules, laws, and standards in a society.

Postconventional Moral-ity According to Kohl-berg, the third level of moral reasoning; morality is based on appeals to social agreements and democratic principles and to basic principles of eth-ics and human rights.

4 reasoning, they will reach for the next level of moral development, the level that Kohlberg calls **postconventional morality.**

At Level III, postconventional morality, the individual defines moral values and principles apart from the authority of the groups or persons hold-ing these principles, and apart from his or her own identity with these groups. At this level, people control their own decisions internally; that is, they base their decisions on their own evaluation and standards of what is right, rather than by conforming to social pressures and expectations. Adolescents and adults may choose to disregard rules or laws that to them are not appropriate or valid.

The postconventional level, like the previous levels, is itself divided into two distinct stages: the social-contract orientation and the universal-principle orientation. In the social-contract orientation (Stage 5), moral action is judged in terms of individual rights and in terms of policies that have been wittingly agreed to by the whole society. The person at this stage believes that if a law is unfair or unjust, it must be changed in a democratic and constitutional manner and in accordance with social rules, not by breaking a law.

The universal-ethical-principle orientation (Stage 6) recognizes right as defined by the individual's conscience in accordance with self-chosen ethical principles. These principles are abstract, and they include justice, the equality of human rights, and respect for the dignity of human beings as individual persons.

The level at which a person reasons about moral issues may vary from one situation to another. People who usually reason at the postconventional level may regress to the conventional level when their beliefs about individual rights are challenged by or in conflict with rules established by authority figures. For example, many people who were morally opposed to the war in Vietnam, nonetheless did not refuse the draft—an action that would have put them in conflict with the government and the law. Such backsliding is not uncommon during a period of time when people are forming their values and beliefs. Although people may function at different levels of moral rea-soning, their moral development is typically upward, gradual, and in a stage-like sequence (Snarey, Reimer, & Kohlberg, 1985). However, not all people may reach the highest stage of postconventional morality. As adolescents (and adults) move from conventional to postconventional levels of moral judgment, there also is an overall tendency to display increased moral behavior. In es-sence, then, adolescents tend to "practice what they preach [or believe]."

Value Systems

Setting out a philosophy of life for oneself is a task that begins in adolescence. "Who am I?" and "What is important in life?" are frequently asked questions. During earlier stages of development, children would look to their parents, families, and friends for answers to these questions. During adolescence, they look to themselves and consider various ideologies to provide them with an-swers. The ideologies that most appeal to them tend to be rigid and authori-tarian—predictable systems that impose a framework in which adolescents can work out the details of their lives. It is important to adolescents to know where they stand, and with the help of an inflexible system of values, they can be certain of their own positions. The attraction of adolescents to various

Establishing Moral Values in High School

Establishing a set of beliefs and life priorities is an important developmental task. Values and moral principles help guide people in their judgments and actions throughout their lives. Without a clear awareness of what is important and appropriate, decision making and planning is more difficult if not impossible. It is during adolescence that people consider and examine the ideals and principles that will ultimately be part of their philosophy of life.

While adolescents often take on the attitudes and values of their parents, many people believe that schools should lend a hand in the moral education of children and teenagers. In the early history of American education, moral education was the main objective in schools. Today, high schools provide an appropriate setting for students to critically explore and discover their values and moral standards. Studies have shown that moral development, the ability to reason and make moral judgments, is enhanced by formal education (Rest & Thoma, 1985; Colby, Kohlberg, Gibbs, & Lieberman, 1983). In part, this is because students who go on to college or further education are generally reinforced for thinking about issues some of which involve moral issues.

The process of moral development can be stimulated in the high-school and even junior-high classroom. In most schools, students are exposed to and governed by a body of rules and regulations that guide the behavior of all people within the school. These rules function as moral principles; students learn what is right and wrong within the school context. However, the school community can be used more effectively to help teenagers develop their values. In some schools teachers not only encourage their students to obey and respect school rules, they also encourage them to participate in establishing or changing rules. The teacher acts as a facilitator in active discussions on controversial issues or moral dilemmas. Regarding the issue, Should teachers be allowed to smoke in school? The facilitator–teacher would make sure that students expressed their views on the question and help them to identify the values underlying their views. Through the open discussion of issues, students benefit from hearing several different points of

One way to stimulate moral development is to involve students in the governance of their schools. By participating in making and changing the school rules, students are more likely to behave appropriately.

view. This process of stimulating discussion and identifying one's personal values is called values clarification. Kohlberg (1976) has advocated the use of give-and-take peer discussions of moral dilemmas as one way of increasing moral reasoning skills. The teachers' role is critical to the process. Teachers represent authority and by their involvement in the discussion group, communicate to students the importance of having values and of applying them in a responsible way in the school community. The goal in moral education is not to teach specific virtues or values, but to teach teenagers a process by which they can identify their values and increase their level of moral reasoning. By exposing them to a realistic set of dilemmas within the school community, teachers can assist students in their moral development.

religious cults such as the Hari Krishnas and the Moonies is an example of this principle. Gradually, as adolescents become more confident of their own judgment, rigid systems are usually replaced by looser, more flexible points of view.

Values change with the times. If you are in your early twenties, then you probably acquired some of your values during the mid-1980s, a time when Ronald Reagan was elected president, when rock videos became popular, and when the AIDS crisis developed epidemic proportions. However, if you are in your forties, then you entered adolescence during the early 1960s, a time when man first entered space, when the Civil Rights Act was debated and passed, when racial segregation was abolished, and when 500,000 demonstrators protested against the Vietnam War. You would have been raised by parents who believed in raising children according to strict schedules and firm disciplinary rules. Children born in the 1970s are more likely to have been raised by more liberal, less punitive, and less dogmatic parents. Clearly, one would expect to find differences between the value systems of 20-year-olds and 40-year-olds. But these differences are as much a product of history and cultural emphases as they are differences in personal experiences and development (McKinney & Moore, 1982). Studies on adolescent values conducted during the 1960s found students to be more interested in issues dealing with social and individual rights, whereas during the 1970s, students valued personal achievement more than individual and societal rights (McKinney, Hotch, & Truhon, 1977).

Political Awareness

Despite the fact that adolescents like to challenge ideologies, relatively few adolescents ever become actively involved in political movements. Even at the height of the period of civil demonstrations in the 1960s, most college students seldom worried about national welfare or the fate of humanity (Allport, 1968). What they were really concerned with was obtaining a rich, full life for themselves. This is true of today's youth as well.

The political attitudes of adolescents have been compared to their cognitive and moral development in studies (Adelson & O'Neil, 1966; Adelson, 1975, 1982) which asked subjects to respond to a hypothetical situation in which 1000 people become dissatisfied with their government and go to an island to form a new government. Thirteen-year-olds found it hard to imagine what consequences such an action might have at all, and 15-year-olds could not easily outline the community that might evolve or think of the services that the new government might provide for its citizens. Many also tended to be intolerant of civil liberties and to favor an authoritarian form of government. After the age of 15, however, the subjects of the study were able to perceive that law (not raw power) could promote the general good and produce social and moral benefits. They were able to understand the idea of an implicit "social contract" between the citizens and the state, and they recognized both the individual's right to freedom and the necessity for restraints on actions that infringe upon the rights of others or threaten social order.

Adelson (1972, 1975, 1982) also supports the idea of a developmental trend in political attitudes. Younger adolescents tended to personalize issues

Table 9.1 ■■■■■■■

Political Events and Youth Movements: 1950–1988

Period of Time	Decisive Political Events	Youth Movements

1950–1959	The Cold War—Eisenhower years
	  Growth of "military–industrial complex"
	  Dulles foreign policy
	  Recession
	  McCarthyism
	  1954 Supreme Court desegregation decision
	  House Un-American Activities Committee
		"The silent generation"

1960–1968	Kennedy–Johnson years
	  "New Frontier"
	  Civil rights demonstrations
	  Peace Corps, poverty programs
	  Vietnam escalation
	  Assassinations of Kennedy brothers and
	    Martin Luther King
	  "Great Society" programs
	  Ghetto riots and campus disruption
		New Left
		New Right
		Civil Rights and Black Power
		Protest demonstrations, strikes, violence

1969–1976	Nixon-Ford years
	  Emphasis on "law and order"
	  Voting Rights Act
	  Vietnam War ends
	  Kissinger foreign policy
	  Inflation, job squeeze
	  Growth of multinational corporations
	  Watergate
	  OPEC and Middle East oil embargo
		Women's rights
		Ecology movement
		Charismatic religious movements
		Quiet seventies

1977–1979	Early Carter administration
	  Conciliatory, practical, informal mood in
	    White House
	  Emphasis on government reorganization
	  National energy crisis
	  Inflation, job squeeze continues
	  Three Mile Island accident
		"No-Nuke" movement
		Gay liberation

1980–1988	Reagan administration
	  Nuclear disarmament talks and treaty
	  Reduction in inflation and unemployment
	  Space Shuttle disaster
	  Iran-contra scandal
	  Stock market crash
	  AIDS epidemic
		Anti-Apartheid movement
		"No-Nuke" movement

Adapted from: Richard G. Braungart, "Youth Movements," in J. Adelson (ed.). *Handbook of adolescent psychology.* New York: Wiley, 1980, p. 565.

of political philosophy. Older adolescents tended to evaluate the overall effects of events, ideas, and actions on society as a whole.

Psychologist Kenneth Keniston has suggested that political issues may serve as catalysts for moral development. Keniston believes that major events in the political life of the nation, such as the Vietnam War, Watergate, or nuclear disarmament talks, are the stimulus for moral development that otherwise might never take place. (See Table 9.1.)

If Keniston is correct, then there may be reason to worry about the amount and kind of political socialization that takes place in the school. A

Do you think that 18-year-olds are mature enough to decide on who will run the government?

number of studies have confirmed that most adolescents have little or no understanding of the way our government works; nor do they understand our fundamental liberties. In response to opinion polls, they consistently take positions against freedom of speech and freedom of religion. Moreover, as Robert Hess (1968) has pointed out, the political socialization that does take place is aimed at reinforcing the concept of obedience to authority—specifically school authority, of course, but governmental authority as well. Such socialization does not encourage efforts to arrive at one's own moral principles.

The difficulty that young, politically inexperienced adolescents have in understanding our political system is well documented by research (Sigel, 1979; Sigel & Hoskin, 1981). Using an open-ended interview procedure, Sigel sought to determine what high-school seniors comprehend about democracy—"What is it that makes any country a democracy?" She found that although most students had some notion about the meaning of democracy, it was restricted primarily to simple, sloganlike themes related to individual freedom. Only 16 percent of the 992 students interviewed displayed a sophisticated understanding of this concept—that is, they were able to delineate multiple characteristics of a democratic society and explain how these characteristics interrelated.

Many researchers have focused on the role of the family in the political development of the young, since the family influences the formation of values and attitudes toward authority figures before the child enters school. A survey of the field of political socialization (Niemi & Sobieszek, 1977) indicates that between the 1950s and 1960s, the influence of the family appears to have diminished, although studies have found that, in general, the political attitudes of children do not differ significantly from those of parents. Also noted is the fact that mothers have apparently become as important as fathers in the transmission of political values and views. An overall conclusion made in the survey is that in recent years "more amorphous factors" than school or family—for example, peers, specific political events, and the media—have emerged as important sources of political information and/or as agents of political development and activism. These factors increase the *potential* for differences between generations.

Pause for Thought

In the United States, people age 18 and over are allowed to vote for candidates and issues related to the way people are governed. Do you think that 18 is an appropriate age for the responsibility of voting? Might there be criteria other than chronological age to use as a gauge for deciding when a person is mature enough to vote?

Summary

Even before the sex organs show an outward change, hormonal changes are preparing the body for adulthood. Soon a dramatic change takes place in height, weight, and body proportions known as the adolescent growth spurt. There are always variations in physical, emotional, and intellectual development within any adolescent age group.

Puberty is the period during which an individual reaches sexual maturity, which is not necessarily synchronous with other areas of development. In the prepubescent stage, secondary sex characteristics begin to develop. In the pubescent stage, the reproductive organs begin producing ova or sperm. In the postpubescent stage, the sex organs become fully capable of adult functioning. Spontaneous erection in the male in response to sights, sounds, and thoughts first occurs during adolescence. The appearance of breasts and menstruation in girls, body hair in both sexes, and voice change in boys heralds sexual maturity.

Over the years, there have been changes in the rate of growth among children, adolescents, and adults. Today, adolescents reach puberty at an earlier age than did teenagers born several generations ago. Secular growth trends are believed to be influenced by biological and environmental factors.

The physical changes that the adolescent experiences have important consequences for psychological development, particularly for self-concept. Early-maturing boys generally excel at sports, in social activities, and in areas of leadership in comparison to late-maturing boys. The impact of timing of maturation is less clear for girls.

Girls' reactions to the onset of menstruation are influenced by their expectations and by the amount of information they have. The degree to which a girl thinks she is developmentally on time in physical maturation is dependent upon her social context.

Adolescence is a time of emerging sexuality. Today, more teenagers are sexually active and at younger ages than ever before. The greatest change in adolescent sexual behavior over the past few generations has occurred for girls. Two consequences of unprotected sexual behavior are a rising birthrate and an increasing incidence of venereal disease among teenagers.

Adolescents may experiment with homosexual behavior. Boys under the age of 15 are more likely to have homosexual experiences.

Most schools have sex-education programs for high-school students. The content in these courses varies considerably, and often does not include enough information on how to prevent pregnancy or the spread of sexually transmitted diseases. Ideally, sex-education programs would involve parents.

The ability to deal with abstractions and to reason deductively develops during what Piaget calls the stage of formal operations, which emerges between the ages of 11 and 15. The ability of individuals to consider many alternatives leads them to question their own ideas and to challenge authority figures and traditional beliefs. Adolescent egocentrism is the tendency of adolescents to become self-absorbed and have exaggerated notions of self-importance. Elkind describes the imaginary audience and personal fable, two concepts related to adolescent egocentrism.

Changes in cognitive development facilitate changes in moral reasoning. According to Kohlberg, the early period of adolescence is characterized by conventional morality—reasoning based on winning approval and maintaining the status quo. During middle to late adolescence, however, the range of moral judgments broadens for many people as they enter the period of postconventional morality. Here moral reasoning is based on self-accepted principles of ethics and justice.

The formation of a value system and political attitudes appears to follow a developmental trend. The influence of parents in these areas seems to have diminished, while the media, peers, and specific political events have emerged as important influential factors.

Further Readings

Comfort, Alex, and Comfort, Jane. *The facts of love: Living, loving and growing up.* **New York: Ballantine Books, 1979.**
This is a book for young people about their emerging sexual feelings. It deals with all aspects of human sexuality in an honest and positive way.

Elster, Arthur, and Lamb, Michael (eds.) *Adolescent fatherhood.* **Hillsdale, NJ: Lawrence Erlbaum, 1986.**
A collection of articles addressing the little-studied issue of adolescent fathers. Topics include the teenage father's education, stresses, coping strategies, use of contraceptives, and sex-role development.

Grinder, Robert E. (Ed.). *Studies in adolescence: A book of readings in adolescent development* **(3rd ed.). New York: Macmillan, 1975.**
The absent father, adolescents in the work force, and other contemporary issues are discussed in this anthology. The contributions are written from the standpoints of psychology, medicine, sociology, and other disciplines.

Hass, Aaron. *Teenage sexuality.* **New York: Macmillan, 1979.**
This study of the sexual attitudes and behavior of teenagers is based on hundreds of questionnaires and interviews. Teenagers are quoted on such topics as their romantic expectations, fantasies, ideas about various sexual behaviors, and about the double standard.

Kett, J. F. *Rites of passage.* **New York: Basic Books, 1977.**
A well-written, easy-to-read historical account of the nature of adolescence from the late eighteenth century to the present.

Rathus, Spencer A. *Human sexuality.* **New York: Holt, Rinehart and Winston, 1983.**
A comprehensive, highly readable treatment of the biological, psychological, and social aspects of human sexuality.

Observational Activities

9.1 *Adolescent Problem Solving*
During adolescence, people are better able to deal with problems on an abstract level, to form hypotheses, and to reason from propositions. One demonstration of these emerging problem-solving skills can be seen using Piaget's pendulum experiment described in this chapter.

You will need to find three teenagers between the ages of 14 and 16 who are willing to participate in a problem-solving experiment. For materials, you will need a piece of string about four feet in length and several small objects of different weights to attach to the end of the string. To construct the pendulum, attach one of the weighted objects to the string and fix the string to the ceiling or the top of a table or bookcase. Be sure to leave enough room to swing the pendulum. Proceed as follows:

1. With your subject watching, release the pendulum by pulling the string back a certain distance and pushing the weighted object. Point out to the

subject that the pendulum can be modified by changing several factors: the length of the string, the weight of the object, the height at which the object is released, and the force with which it is pushed.

2. Ask the teenager to find out which of these factors determines how rapidly the pendulum will swing. (The purpose of this experiment is not to determine if the person can figure out the correct answer [the length of the string], but rather to determine the process by which the person solves the problem.)

3. Take note of the teenager's strategy for solving the problem. Does the person systematically test one factor at a time and hold the others constant? Does the person consider the problem before manipulating the pendulum or does he or she just plunge in? Ask the teenager if he or she has any hypotheses or guesses about what influences the speed of the pendulum. Does the person have a plan for testing out these ideas?

After testing each teenager separately, compile your observations of each one's approach to the problem. Compare your observations with those reported in this chapter. What conclusions can you draw about adolescent problem-solving ability? What did you gain from doing this activity?

9.2   *Teenagers' Values*

According to Margaret Mead, children in contemporary American society cannot learn useful behavior and values from their parents because the fast pace of change has made their elders' beliefs and practices obsolete in their own time. Ask four teenagers—two males and two females—to define their values. Interview each person individually so that their replies will not influence one another. Ask them:

1. What are the three things that you feel are essential for happiness as an adult?
2. What are the three things that you think are most important to your parents for their happiness?
3. What are the three things that you think your parents would want for you as an adult?
4. What are the three things that are most important in your life right now?
5. What do you think you will be doing in the year 2010?
6. What do you think your family would like you to be doing in the year 2010?

Analyze the values reflected in the answers you get. It might be interesting for you to answer these same questions yourself and compare your answers with those of teenagers several years younger than you are. You might also want to spend some class time comparing and analyzing responses obtained by you and by others in your class.

CHAPTER

10

Adolescence: Personality and Social Development

Seventeen-year-old Erika was apprehensive as she entered Ms. Leonard's office. In her capacity as Director of Hamilton Hills Camp, Ms. Leonard was responsible for hiring summer camp counselors, and Erika very much wanted the job.

Ever since she'd been a camper herself, Erika had admired the counselors and wanted to become one. She had been gaining useful work experience for this position by babysitting, and she had even organized and run a play group for the neighborhood children. Now all she had to do was to convince Ms. Leonard that she was a good choice for the position.

On the advice of her best friend, Robin, she selected an appropriate outfit to wear for the job interview, and together they rehearsed what she would say. Erika's parents were also supportive and encouraging to her. They were pleased that Erika had taken the initiative in seeking out the job she wanted—it meant that she was moving toward independence and maturity. Erika, on the other hand, wanted the chance to demonstrate to them and to herself that she could take care of herself. She saw this as a chance to learn more about herself and to gain greater confidence in her ability to undertake and achieve important life tasks. For Erika, the counselor position was not just a temporary means of earning money, but a way of testing herself and preparing for the future.

As she shook Ms. Leonard's hand she knew she was *ready* for this job. "I understand you would like to be a camp counselor for Hamilton Hills," said Ms. Leonard. "Tell me a little about yourself."

Erika, feeling self-conscious but assertive, replied. "Well, I've always enjoyed being with children, and my friends and family agree that I am good with them. I like to dance, listen to music, and swim, and I think I would make a good camp counselor. . . ."

Erika was ready for the counselor position. She was also well on her way toward achieving her goals of independence and personal identity. Like other adolescents, she had begun to address the questions that define us as individuals: Who am I? What do I care about? What do I want to do with my life?

In adolescence, one searches more urgently than ever before for the answers to basic questions. The sense of urgency experienced by most adolescents reflects, in part, the rapid and varied transformations—in body, thought, and emotions—that each of us encounters during this time of life. It also reflects the feeling that one is searching for some ultimate and final solution to the pressing problems regarding the self. Erika, like other adolescents, will find, however, that there is no final solution, or closure, to personal identity. The answers Erika achieves at this time of her life are but a part of a dynamic and mobile construction that will change and grow as she does. This does not mean, however, that for Erika and others, personal identity is unattainable.

It simply means that one's perception of self is likely to be more fluid than fixed, and that during periods of rapid change, such as adolescence, there is likely to be greater indecision or crisis over who one "really" is.

In the present chapter, we take up the issues of adolescent identity development and the search for independence. We also discuss the role of the peer group in adolescence and the emergence of a vocational orientation. Finally, the chapter concludes with some of the major psychosocial and emotional problems experienced by adolescents today.

Adolescent Identity

Ego Identity According to Erikson, psychosocial achievement during adolescence that results in a stable and unified sense of self.

According to Erikson (1968), adolescence is the stage of development during which the crisis of identity is most acute. The major task of the individual at this time is the formation of a secure **ego identity**—one's perceptions and feelings about oneself. Ego identity includes three major components: a sense of *unity* among one's self-perceptions; a sense of *continuity* of self-definition over time; and a sense of the *mutuality* between one's self-perceptions and those held by others. Failure to achieve such an identity results in *self-diffusion*—a feeling that one lacks definition, commitment, and a sense of integration or togetherness. Ego identity is reflected in the way teenagers speak about themselves and one another, as they often use terms relating to how "together" they are and whether they have "found" themselves or not. (See Table 10.1.)

During the early stages of adolescence there is an increase in one's self-awareness (Harter, 1983), and the self becomes an object of study and interest. This change in orientation toward the self is due to a large extent to the physical changes associated with puberty, as well as to the pressures placed on adolescents by society for making role choices. For example, high schools encourage students to begin planning for the future by choosing college-oriented or noncollege-oriented courses. In doing so, students for the first time may be forced to consider their individualized skills, goals, preferences, and potential place in society. Heightened self-awareness also is related to the emerging cognitive skills associated with formal operational thinking (Elkind,

Table 10.1

Havighurst's Developmental Tasks of Adolescence

1. Acquire more mature social skills.

2. Achieve a masculine or feminine gender role.

3. Accept the changes in one's body and one's physique and use one's body effectively.

4. Achieve emotional independence from parents and other adults.

5. Prepare for sex, marriage, and parenthood.

6. Select and prepare for an occupation.

7. Develop a personal ideology and ethical standards.

8. Assume membership in the larger community.

Source: Havighurst, R. *Developmental tasks and education.* New York: David McKay, 1972.

Identity formation occurs in stages during adolescence. Often, teenagers are influenced by popular rock stars such as Madonna.

1978). The capacity for abstract, hypothetical thought, for example, allows the adolescent to speculate endlessly about the many possible identities the self may assume. This ability contrasts dramatically with the almost unquestioning self-acceptance characteristic of elementary-school-age children. Consider the musings of 14-year-old Adam: "Now that I am playing the guitar I could be a rock star . . . . I know I'd start off first with my own group and we would make our own video so that people would want to buy our records . . . . But if I didn't make it as a rock star, I could also see myself as a guitar teacher."

For most boys and girls, the transition from childhood into adolescence is marked by trading a dependency on their parents to a dependency on their peers (Steinberg & Silverberg, 1986). Conformity to the peer group may be intense. Adolescents may identify so completely with the heroes of the peer group that they seem to lose their own emerging identity. By trying out various characteristics on peers and observing their reactions, adolescents hope to get a better idea about themselves. Somewhat intimidated by the many possibilities of the future and the conflicting values offered by society, adolescents often temporarily identify with stereotyped peer-group values, thus gaining time to sort out their own values and aspirations. They may switch abruptly from utter devotion to someone or something to a complete abandonment of the same commitment. An example of this switch in loyalty can be found in pop-music trends and the tendency of young people to identify with and imitate only those star performers who currently are in favor. The individual must test the extremes, Erikson (1968) believes, before he or she can settle on a steady course.

Establishing one's identity is a process that can take up to 10 years to complete (Waterman, 1985). The adolescent latches on to one view of self, tries it on for size, wears it around the neighborhood of peers and then discards the view of self for another view. Each identification becomes part of the total view of self. All identifications must be woven together into a coherent, consistent, and unique view of self (Conger, 1978). Consider 13-year-old Melanie. Six months ago, she saw herself as similar to the funky rock star Madonna. She dressed in layers with lots of jewelry and wore a charming pout on her face. Even though she gained a reputation among her peers for being "cool," Melanie shifted her view of self by identifying with the hippielike followers of the rock–folk group *Grateful Dead*. Not only did she change the way she dressed and her preference for music, she also changed her attitudes and philosophies and even some of her friends. These shifts from funky to philosophic at will all have to be consolidated into Melanie's sense of self before her identity can be achieved.

Pause for Thought

One of the major developmental tasks of adolescents is the establishment of an identity that is separate from their parents. In fact many teenagers (and some adults) do not like to think that they are similar to their parents in any way. Yet the identity a person establishes is influenced in many ways by their parents. What are the direct and indirect influences that parents (and grandparents) can have on the adolescent's answers to the question "Who am I?"

Ethnic and Racial Identity

An important aspect of identity for adolescents is awareness of ethnic or racial origins—"roots." Adolescence is the time when people take a stand, or adopt an attitude, toward being black, Hispanic, Native American, Irish-American, Jewish, Catholic, and so on. In seeking independence from parents, adolescents are often in the position of deciding whether or not to incorporate their parents' ethnic and religious customs and tastes into their own lifestyle. Are they to accept their roots as a positive and necessary part of their emerging identity? Or are they to resist parents' customs in the interests of a new, enlightened self?

An important aspect of identity for adolescents is their awareness of their ethnic and racial origins.

In American high schools, particularly in racially mixed urban settings, adolescents may seek to define and differentiate themselves from others on the basis of their ethnic origins. One phenomenon that has helped is the recent rediscovery of ethnic pride, which has been an important factor in the shaping of today's culture. It is also becoming important in the individual's search for self-definition and identity, especially during the adolescent years. For example, a summary of cross-ethnic research (Smith, 1979) indicates that the self-concept of black students is on par with that of white students, contrary to the negative self-concept so often associated with young blacks in the past. The reason offered for this change toward a positive self-image is that black youths have been affected by the civil-rights movement and a new awareness of black culture—history, art, fashions—that allows blacks to take pride in their racial heritage and achievement. Similar racial and ethnic-pride movements among Hispanics and Native Americans may do much to give adolescents in these minority subcultures a more secure identity and to ease the transition into a well-functioning and productive adulthood.

Searching for Origins: Adopted Adolescents

Ego Continuity The sense that one's current self-perceptions are firmly connected to the self-perceptions of the past and to the anticipated self-perceptions of the future.

One problem of identity for the adolescent is establishing a sense of **ego continuity** (Erikson, 1968)—a sense that one's current self-perceptions are firmly connected to the self-definitions of the past and to the anticipated self-perceptions of the future. For most adolescents, the development of ego continuity is difficult enough, given the rapid changes associated with this period; for adopted adolescents, however, the problem is compounded by lack of knowledge about their origins.

At the time of adoption, most adoptive parents are given little information about the child's birth parents or family history; in turn, the birth parents are told little about the adoptive parents. This procedure, which is followed by most adoption agencies, is considered to be in the best interests of all involved parties.

This assumption is being challenged by a number of activist groups—in particular, the Adoptees Liberty Movement Association (ALMA), the Orphan Voyage, and Concerned United Birthmothers (CUB). These groups, and others, have argued that the sealing of records at the time of adoption not only violates the basic rights of individuals to know about themselves (and their offspring in the case of CUB members), but potentially sets the stage for serious psychological difficulties related to the adoption experience.

Genealogical Bewilderment Found among some adopted adolescents, the feelings of incompleteness and disconnectedness from one's genealogical or biological past.

Researchers have pointed out that adopted children are more at risk for psychological and academic problems than nonadopted children (Bohman, 1970; Brodzinsky, Schechter, Braff, & Singer, 1984). In adolescence and young adulthood, problems related to identity development may be particularly troublesome (Lifton, 1979; Sorosky, Baran, & Pannor, 1978). Sants (1964) has coined the term **genealogical bewilderment** to describe the feelings of incompleteness that often are experienced by adolescent adoptees when trying to connect with their past. For nonadopted adolescents, these connections are clear—there is a known family history. For most adoptees, however, there is a large void when it comes to one's ancestry. As one 18-year-old adolescent said,

> It's as if I didn't exist before my second birthday. I have no idea where I came from, and my parents either don't know or won't tell me . . . . I really don't know which . . . . I feel empty and helpless at times . . . not knowing who or what I am . . . and I don't know what I can do about it.

Thoughts and fantasies about the birth parents and the circumstances surrounding the original relinquishment are a normal part of development for the adopted child and adolescent. Nevertheless, adoptees often keep their thoughts and feelings to themselves for fear of hurting the adoptive parents, and in some cases for fear of turning the thoughts and fantasies into reality.

Adolescent Turmoil: Fact or Fiction?

If you ask people to describe the adolescent years, no doubt they will use such terms as "upsetting," "full of turmoil," "intense," "troubling," or "difficult." Ever since G. Stanley Hall's classic work on adolescence (1904), we have come to expect considerable personal upheaval during this period of life. The conception of adolescence as a time of storm and stress is built into many of our theories of development, particularly psychoanalytic theories (Blos, 1978; Erikson 1968; A. Freud, 1958). Other theorists, however, believe that psychological turmoil is not typical of most adolescents and that the course of development during this period is more often a continuation of earlier modes of adaptation rather than a dramatic emergence of new adaptive modes (Douvan & Adelson, 1966; Offer, 1969; Offer, Ostrov, & Howard, 1981).

Research on the existence of adolescent turmoil has produced inconsistent findings. One study found symptoms of anxiety in approximately 65 percent of a sample of normal adolescents, ages 12 to 18 years (Masterson, 1967). Similarly, Rutter, Tizard, and Whitmore (1970), working with a group of 14- to 15-year-olds, reported that nearly half of their sample showed evidence of emotional turmoil, such as appreciable misery or depression. Research by Offer (1969; Offer, Ostrov, & Howard, 1981), on the other hand, failed to produce results consistent with the picture of normal adolescent upheaval. He noted that for most adolescents, changes in identity, relations with parents, peer relations, and so forth, were gradual and undramatic. Similar findings were reported in a three-year longitudinal study by Dusek and Flaherty (1981), who examined the stability of self-concept in samples of adolescents from grades five through 12 using a self-report questionnaire method. These investigators found little evidence that adolescents' self-concept undergoes dramatic change. On the contrary, what changes were observed in their subject sample were of a gradual, emergent nature. Similar results were found in a longitudinal study of adolescents' self concept and self-esteem. Adolescents maintained a stable and slightly positive sense of themselves throughout this six-year study (Savin-Williams & Demo, 1984).

The overall findings suggest that adolescent emotional turmoil, while a reality for some, is certainly not a universal phenomenon. For some individuals, the passage through adolescence is accompanied by feelings of self-doubt, resentment of parents, avoidance of responsibility, and social anxiety; for others, the reaction to the physical and social-role changes associated with adolescence is much less dramatic. As in every period of development, there are individual differences in coping strategies and adjustment.

"Teenagers" are frequently stereotyped as being difficult to get along with, beset with anxiety and confusion about their identity, and being rebellious. Yet this view is not supported by research on adolescents. How can you explain this gap between research results and popular beliefs about adolescents?

Adolescents and Their Parents

During the 1960s and early 1970s, when dissent and dispute over political issues were common, the term "generation gap" was coined to refer to a generalized disenchantment that all adolescents had for their parents' way of life (Conger & Peterson, 1984; Conger 1981; Yankelovich, 1974). Not only was it the case that the majority of adolescents growing up in the 1960s and 1970s got along with their parents and were in general agreement with their views, but today there is even stronger evidence that adolescents and their parents are not natural enemies (Peterson, 1987; Hamid & Wylie, 1980; Offer, Ostrov, & Howard, 1981; Steinberg, Yankelovich, 1981).

While adolescents may differ with their parents on issues such as hairstyles, clothing, music, and curfews, they are likely to adopt their parents' views on broader social, moral, and political issues and values. During the teen years, when adolescents direct their time and attention more to their peers, parents continue to have a strong influence (Youniss & Smollar, 1985). In a study of 180 adolescents (Hunter, 1985), it was found that the frequency of discussions with parents remained unchanged between the ages of 12 and 20. However, Hunter also found that the relationship between parents and adolescents was not a mutual one. Parents tended to explain their views to their teenagers more than they tried to understand their adolescents' views. The adolescents' friends, on the other hand, were willing to explain their own views and understand someone else's views.

Often tied to the assumption of differences and conflicts between generations is the notion that ideas and ideals are passed only from the older to the new generation. A review of the research literature (Bengston & Troll, 1978; Hagestad, 1984), however, suggests that values and attitudes of youth may actually exert some influence on parental behavior and viewpoints. In some cases, the children may serve as a connection to the "larger world" and the prevailing social and cultural mood of the times. Thus, not only do adolescents learn from their parents, but parents, in turn, learn from their offspring. This finding is consistent with the bidirectional models of parent–child relationships that currently are favored by most developmental psychologists (Bell & Harper, 1980; Belsky, 1981).

Parent–Adolescent Conflict

Even though the generation gap has been greatly exaggerated, conflict between teenagers and their parents does exist and can be a source of dissatisfaction for parents and adolescents. Despite a loving relationship, most teenagers and their parents frequently find themselves in a quarrelling and antagonistic relationship (Steinberg, 1987). One study involving midteens suggests that the sources of rebellion may include a lack of sufficient freedom to make one's own decisions in areas including clothing, hairstyle, and choice of friends; a desire to provoke greater parental interest and concern ("to get my parents to pay attention to me"); and a feeling of being overcriticized. Interestingly, most of the teens questioned did not want absolute freedom in decision making but, rather, preferred their parents to be interested and actively involved in their lives (Clemens & Rust, 1979).

The degree of conflict between adolescents and parents can vary. Adolescents who have accepted many of the values of a traditional family (such as obedience, cooperation, etc.) show a greater acceptance of parental control than do other adolescents who reject these values. Authoritative parents who show a willingness to distribute family power as the child matures, appear to have more effective interactions with their children than parents who are overly permissive or authoritarian (Baumrind, 1978). Adolescent difficulties in school, social relationships, and other areas appear to occur more frequently in families in which there is "parental hostility, rejection, or neglect" (Conger, 1977). Thus, it seems that parents who allow their teenagers more of a say in what happens in the family, but who do not surrender their authority, have fewer conflicts with their adolescents.

Some adolescents may push too hard against authority. In turn, some parents may react arbitrarily or coercively to the changing needs of their child, thus fostering conflict. When 16-year-old Laura wanted to attend a party in the next town, her parents objected, saying she was too young. Laura went to the party anyway by telling her parents she was spending the night at a friend's house. When her parents learned of her disobedience and deception, they grounded her for two months, refused to allow her to talk on the telephone, and did not allow her friends to visit. They also refused to discuss the problem with her, preferring instead to allow her to "feel the effects of her deception." By cutting off communication with their daughter, Laura's parents missed the chance to teach her the importance of being honest, and to work out a mutually agreeable solution to the problem of how she can express her need to be independent and trustworthy.

Pressures from the outside world, such as school and the influence of peers and the community, may make the parent–child situation worse. The developing sexuality of the adolescent may also add to problems in the relationship with the family. Difficulties inevitably arise because the child becomes a sexually mature person while still living within the family structure. A hundred years or more ago (and today in some cultures), the onset of physical maturity was the sign that it was time for adolescents to leave home and establish their lives apart from their parents.

Lawrence Steinberg (1987) believes that one contributing factor to parent–adolescent conflict is that teenagers are physically ready to leave home before they can actually be economically independent of their parents. In highly developed industrialized countries such as the United States, teenagers reach puberty at a young age, but are not yet prepared to deal with the social and economic changes that industrialization has created. So they bicker and squabble with their parents about petty issues such as keeping a room clean, putting out the garbage, and choosing hair and dress styles. There is some evidence that the squabbling that teenagers engage in is related to the pubertal changes that are occurring. Adolescents who mature early also engage in quarrels with their parents at an earlier age than do their late-maturing friends (Steinberg, 1987). The early-adolescence period between ages 11 to

Some psychologists believe that a contributing factor in parent–adolescent conflict is that teenagers are physically ready to leave home before they can actually be independent financially of their parents.

13 is the time when parents report the most difficulty and strain with their teenagers and this is the time when pubertal changes emerge.

Establishing Independence and Autonomy

Becoming independent is a gradual process. A teenager does not wake up one morning and declare him- or herself autonomous or independent. Rather, independence is achieved in steps. Oftentimes, adolescents may not be aware of their movement toward separateness from their parents until they have already accepted responsibility for their own care and actions. Likewise, some teenagers or young adults may consider themselves to be independent but discover unknown dependencies when they move away from home. One of the difficulties college freshmen have to deal with is how much they relied on their parents for advice or for help in making decisions, or for basic support services such as laundry or housekeeping. Parents of college students also undergo changes as they accept their adolescents' maturity and independence. Parents who derive their importance solely from their role as caregivers may experience more difficulty in surrendering control of their adolescents. For example, mothers of adolescents who are employed full-time are more accepting and supportive of their teenagers' growing independence (Hoffman, 1979).

The term autonomy refers to many different characteristics and behaviors. It is not a single or simple characteristic, nor is autonomy always expressed in the same way by the same person (Steinberg & Silverberg, 1987). In one study (Moore & Hotch, 1981), college freshmen were asked how they knew when they had left home and could consider themselves to be independent from their parents. The students' responses fell into eight categories (listed in Table 10.2) including economic independence, physical separation (living in an apartment), and emotional separation (don't feel close to the family). While some of you may be able to accept your physical separation

Table 10.2

How do you know you have left home?

Category	Examples
Personal control	Less parental control Make own decisions Must do things for self now Feel mature enough
Economic independence	Financial independence Have a job
Residence	Have all my belongings with me Live in a different place Moved to an apartment
Physical separation	Distance from home Physically away from home Family is not here
School affiliation	Dorm is center of life Consider school to be home
Dissociation	Won't go back each summer Have broken the ties
Emotional separation	Have feeling of being a visitor at home Have feeling of not belonging at home Don't feel close to family
Graduation	After graduation

Adapted from "Late Adolescents' Conceptualizations of Home-Leaving" by D. Moore and D. F. Hotch, 1981, *Journal of Youth and Adolescence*, 10, pp. 1–10.

from your parents and the personal control over your decisions, you may have some difficulty accepting an emotional separation from your parents.

Pause for Thought

Parents are usually in their early to mid-forties when their children enter adolescence. By this time in their lives, most adults have established themselves in a career and a mortgage. What possible effect might their adolescents' search for identity and independence have on parents' views of themselves?

Adolescent Peer Relations

At the same time that adolescents are loosening the family ties, they are building a greater identification with others of the same age group—evolving a sense of belonging to a generation.

The Society of Adolescents

Parents and the mass media have had much to say about the "youth culture" and the "adolescent subculture." Does such an adolescent society exist? Have adults merely created a convenient stereotype as a means of explaining adolescent behavior? A classic study of midwest American high-school students by James Coleman (1961) suggests that the adolescent subculture is indeed a reality, and that it has fostered substantial differences between itself and the adult culture. These differences, according to Coleman, alienate high-school students from their parents and the academic goals of their school, and orient them toward their peers.

More recent observers of the adolescent social scene, however, have been critical of the picture portrayed in Coleman's report (McClelland, 1982). Although acknowledging the reality of an adolescent "society," contemporary sociologists and psychologists suggest that this subculture is not unified or separate from adult culture. According to McClelland, high schools serve as "the meeting place of a wide variety of subcultural strains, some of which oppose parents and the school, others of which do not, and all of which reflect one element or another of the complex adult culture" (p. 412). Thus, while adolescents organize themselves into social systems around such distinctive cultural features as clothing, hairstyle, music, recreational activities, and so forth, the attempt at separation from the world of adults is highly variable from one group of adolescents to another. Furthermore, the separation is not necessarily a revolt against institutions or norms—it is more often the way adolescents articulate their own needs and create a context in which to work out mutual problems.

Adolescents generally prefer the company of their friends to that of their family. According to one study (Czikszentmihalyi & Larson, 1984), adolescents spend more time talking to peers than in any other single activity; and they describe themselves as most happy when engaged in these interactions. The world of the adolescent is not limited to friends, however. On the contrary, their social milieu is a large one—they mix socially not only with their many acquaintances but also with relative strangers. Thus, adolescent society in our culture serves as a bridge to the mobile adult society where they will be confronted with a wide variety of colleagues and occupations. The peer interaction involved in extracurricular activities also mirrors the procedures by which

Adolescents spend much of their time talking with friends. Among teenagers, physical attractiveness is an important factor in popularity.

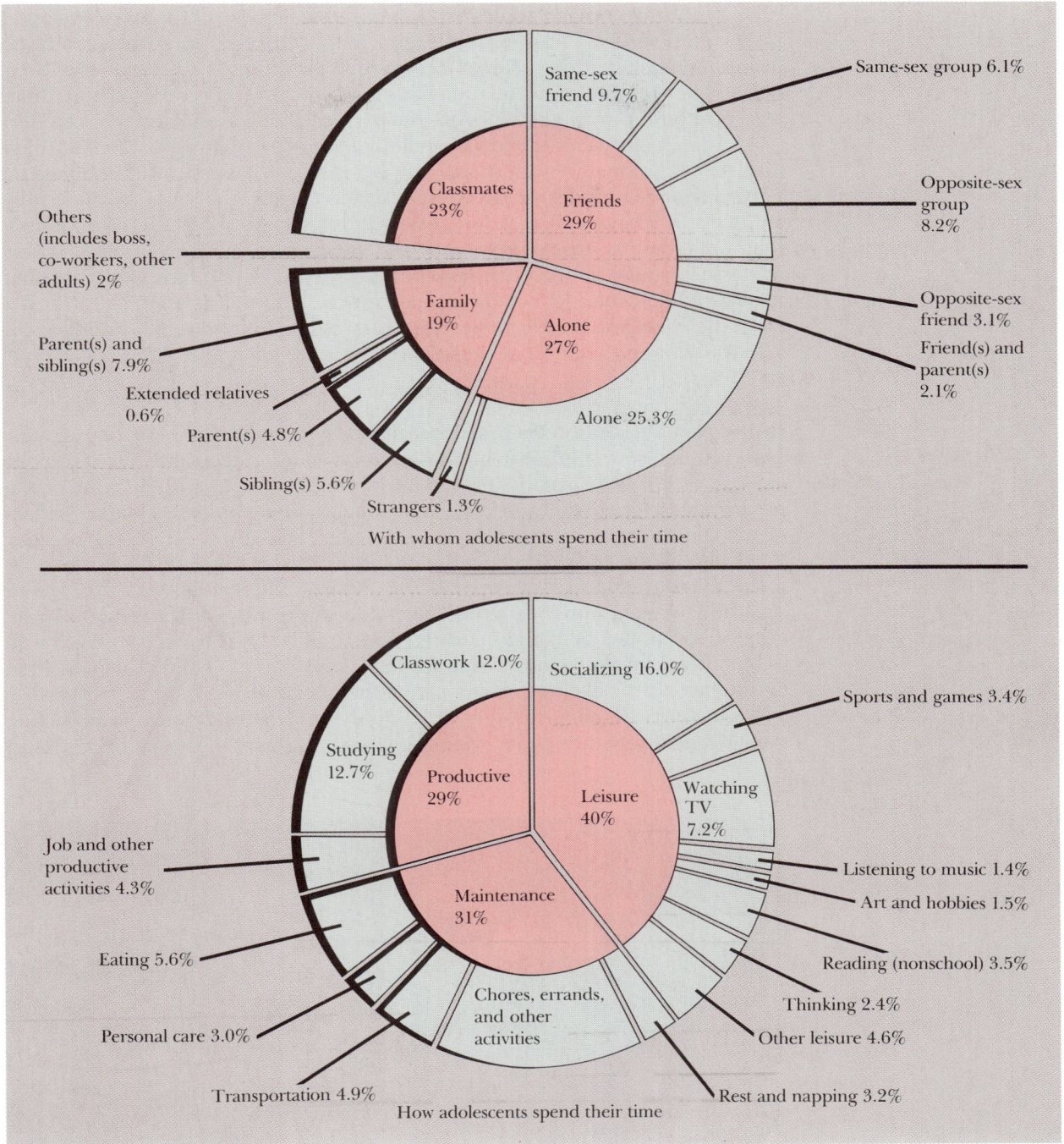

Figure 10.1 How and with whom adolescents spend their time.

organizations operate in the adult world. Student government and other activities create power hierarchies, and the adolescent learns how to deal with them. (See Figures 10.1 a and b.)

Authority in many adolescent organizations, however, tends to be lateral rather than vertical. That is, adolescents tend to spread out authority among group members and are reluctant to assume positions of authority over their peers. They see their interrelationships more as a brother- or sisterhood than a vertical power arrangement with one person having authority over another.

Adolescent society differs from adult society in other ways, too, but these differences are mainly superficial. For example, adolescent society thrives on fads, distinctive modes of dress, and slang. Feeling that they are not fully accepted as individuals in adult society, adolescents create a group identity that gives them a sense of belonging to the larger world. Despite these shows of distinctiveness, however, researchers (Newman, 1982) have observed that normal adolescents do not differ that much in moral and ethical attitudes from their parents, and in most cases, they conform to parental standards of achievement and vocational preferences.

Peer-Group Composition

In the prepubescent period, children band together in same-gender groups. In a year or so, as interest in the opposite gender increases, same-gender groups, or **cliques,** usually develop informal associations with a clique of the opposite gender (Dunphy, 1963). Individual dating is initiated by the leaders of the cliques.

The clique provides a setting for intimate personal relationships that formerly were found primarily in the family. Clique members are bound together by geographic closeness, age, education, heterosexual interest, degree of social and personal maturity, and similar social backgrounds as well as by mutual interests and similar academic orientation. There is usually little cutting across social-class lines in clique membership.

Around the clique is the larger and less rigidly defined **crowd.** The crowd is held together by its orientation to the future, the social background

Clique A small informal group of people with similar social class, education, age, and interests and who spend a lot of time together.

Crowd A large, informal group formed by two or three cliques.

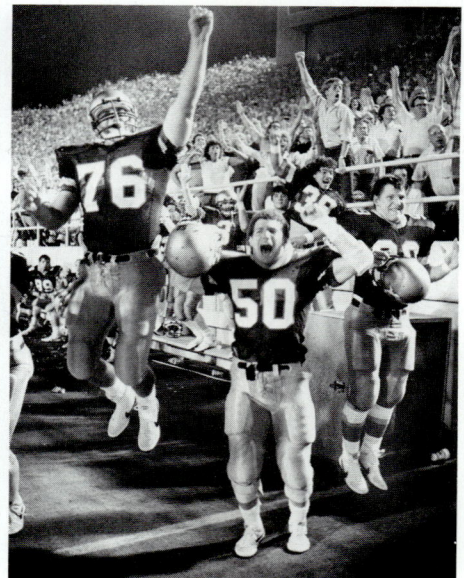

Cliques, such as "preppies" or "jocks," provide settings for informal relationships that formerly were found primarily in the family.

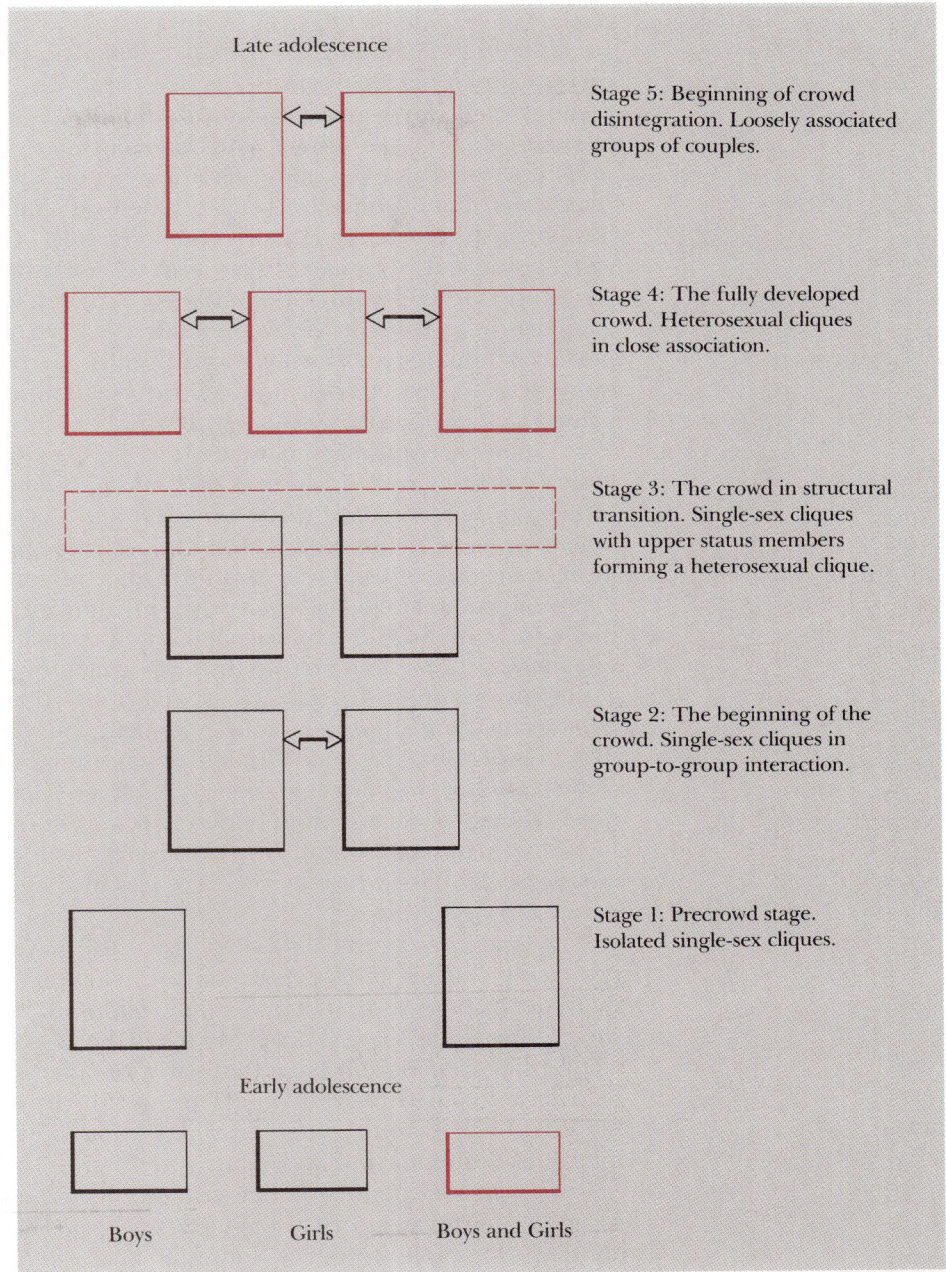

Figure 10.2 Stages of adolescent peer group development.

Late adolescence

Stage 5: Beginning of crowd disintegration. Loosely associated groups of couples.

Stage 4: The fully developed crowd. Heterosexual cliques in close association.

Stage 3: The crowd in structural transition. Single-sex cliques with upper status members forming a heterosexual clique.

Stage 2: The beginning of the crowd. Single-sex cliques in group-to-group interaction.

Stage 1: Precrowd stage. Isolated single-sex cliques.

Early adolescence

Boys   Girls   Boys and Girls

of its members, and their personality types. The loosely organized college-bound, career-oriented group of high-school students would constitute one crowd; those students choosing a vocational track in high school and oriented toward blue-collar, skilled-labor occupations would generally constitute a second crowd. In later adolescence, the crowd disappears and is replaced by cliques of couples going steady. (See Figure 10.2.)

Adolescent Friendships

In addition to belonging to crowds and cliques, adolescents usually have one or two close friends. Friendships are based on more intimate and intense feelings than clique relationships. Interaction is more open and honest and less self-conscious, and there is less role playing to gain social acceptance. The individual hesitates less about showing his or her doubts, anxieties, and resentments. Friendships are usually based on similar social backgrounds, interests, and personality characteristics (Hartup, 1983). Friendships between widely different personality types are less common.

Intimate friendships first arise in early adolescence (Berndt, 1982). In comparison to younger children, adolescents are more willing to share their personal thoughts and feelings with friends (Berndt, 1981b). They also have more actual knowledge of intimate information about close friends than do younger children (Diaz & Berndt, 1982).

Adolescent intimacy is related, in part, to the emerging ability of the individual to engage in **mutual role taking.** Only when the adolescents are capable of keeping both their own view and that of another in mind simultaneously, says Robert Selman (1981), will they be able to achieve a level of intimacy within a social relationship. Other researchers (Douvan & Adelson, 1966) have explained the emergence of intimate friendships during adolescence in terms of the psychosexual changes that accompany puberty. Such relationships serve as a vehicle through which they can express their feelings about the changes—particularly sexual ones—they are experiencing. Thus, adolescent friendships help young people cope with the impulses and drives that are pressing for expression during this period. According to Berndt (1982), adolescent intimacy also can enhance self-esteem by showing the individual that others are interested in and respect his or her ideas and feelings. In addition, intimate friendships can contribute to one's social skills and sense of security, both of which are likely to enhance intimate relationships in later periods of development.

Research suggests that boys and girls have different conceptions of friendship during adolescence and are likely to show different patterns in their development of intimate relationships (Berndt, 1982). In describing what a best friend is, girls are more likely than boys to mention someone with whom they can share intimate information (Berndt, 1981b). Girls also seem to prefer to interact with others in smaller groups than do boys (Savin-Williams, 1980), and they are less likely than boys to accept another person into their intimate circle of friends.

Contrary to popular belief, adolescents generally are not fickle in their social relationships—they usually do not jump around from one friend to another. Research evidence indicates that there is considerable stability in friendship patterns during this period of life (Berndt & Hoyle, 1985; Tuma & Hallinan, 1979)—and certainly more so than during early childhood (Berndt, 1981a). These close, stable relationships help to ease the stresses and strains experienced by adolescents in their passage from childhood to adulthood.

Mutual Role Taking
The ability to keep both one's own view and that of another in mind simultaneously; usually emerges in adolescence.

Pause for Thought

While you may still maintain your friendship with some of your high-school peers, some of your friendships may have declined. What changes have occurred to account for these changes in friendships? Is it inevitable that friendships made in adolescence will not survive into adulthood?

Conformity

Strictly speaking, conformity is simply following the norms of one's family, society, or peer group. This is not always as easy as it sounds, however, because these various norms sometimes conflict with one another. Ultimately, the individual must choose among them and adopt only the ones that are personally suitable. Children learn most of the norms of their society by the age of 11 or 12. Then in adolescence, they begin to evaluate these norms in relationship to themselves and their evolving value system.

Stereotypes about adolescents suggest that they are a highly conforming group of individuals. Pressure from peers is said to unduly influence the adolescent's choice of dress, mannerisms, values, judgments, and so forth. While it is certainly true that peers play a major role in the choices an adolescent makes, it is also true that others, particularly parents, exert considerable influence.

Are adolescents more likely to conform to peers than younger children? Apparently not, for research generally suggests either a peak in conformity in middle childhood followed by a decline in adolescence, or a continuous decline in conformity from early childhood on (Hartup, 1983). Thus, there is a tendency for individuals to increasingly think and act for themselves with increasing age.

The degree of conformity at any age, however, varies with the situation (Hartup, 1983). Under conditions of stress, for example, people are much more likely to conform to group norms than when they are not stressed. Conformity is also more prevalent in complex tasks than in simple tasks, as well as in tasks such as school exams in which an achievement orientation is fostered. In addition, the presence of a nonconformist in a group is likely to induce nonconformity in other group members, particularly if that person is admired and respected by the others. Finally, people who have high self-esteem are much less likely to conform to group pressure.

Perhaps adolescents develop solidarity with their peers as a means of coping with the threatening adult world. Under constant threat of the dire consequences of dropping out of school, getting poor grades, hanging out with the wrong crowd, and so forth, adolescents may feel that the safest thing to do is to follow the group. On the other hand, strongly conforming to peer norms may reflect the sudden absence of parental control or support that the child had relied on in the earlier years (Baumrind, 1978). Rather than seeing a coercive adult world, some adolescents may perceive an uncaring one, which allows them to flounder through feelings of insecurity and stress.

Vocational Choice

One of the most difficult and potentially frustrating tasks of adolescence is the choice of a career. In the distant past, vocational "choice" was dependent on social class. An artisan's son had few alternatives but to assume his father's trade; a peasant's son could only aspire to vocations that were appropriate to his social class; and women had no socially approved options beyond the roles of household manager, wife, and mother. In nearly all cases, personal needs and desires were subordinated to the demands of a rigidly structured economic society.

Today, both men and women have, potentially speaking, a wider margin of freedom in the choice of careers. Yet, various factors may make the job choice difficult and may impose limitations on one's actual range of choices. Those without sufficient education or training—dropouts, for example—will probably be limited to certain jobs, no matter what career they desire. Adolescents from economically or socially disadvantaged homes may not be aware of the full range of career possibilities, for they lack or have limited interactions with role models outside their primary relationships, and they may unwittingly limit their aspirations (Laska & Micklin, 1979).

Choosing a Career

The world of work is first delineated by the family. Parents provide the first models of what workers do and how one feels about work. The socioeconomic level of the family still largely determines the vocational aspirations and attitudes of the child because ideas about the kinds of work open to the child and notions about what is a "good job" are determined to a large extent by family and friends. It is usual for the children of professionals to enter the professions, for example, and for parents who are unemployed or underemployed to pass these difficulties on to their children both by example and because of the economic realities of their lives. For example, a teenager may quit school to take a job that will help support the family.

Making a vocational choice is a long and complex process, and the factors that influence it are developed through much of an individual's life. In one study of the developmental process involved in making a career choice, the researcher (Havighurst, 1964) described a pattern of decision making that parallels Erikson's psychosocial tasks. Notice that the development process envisioned here takes about 35 years and represents a major thread in the growth from early childhood into adulthood:

Age 5–10: Children identify with the worker. Their concept of working is part of their ego ideal.

Age 10–15: Adolescents develop basic working habits and learn how to use their time and energy in order to complete tasks.

Age 15–25: Older adolescents gain a worker identity by choosing a vocation and preparing for it.

Age 25–40: Adults become productive by perfecting the skills of their chosen vocation.

Career decisions and self-realization through work may be a more complicated problem for women. One study (Rosen & Aneshensel, 1978) points to the fact that there are significant gender differences in occupational attainment—women, in general, hold lower-status jobs. The researchers argue that while discrimination plays an extremely important role in this work profile, restrictions against women begin well before they enter the labor force. Their study suggests that gender differences in occupational attainment reflect the impact of traditional gender-role socialization, which places more emphasis on achievement and occupational success in the rearing of boys than girls.

Further evidence of the influence of gender stereotyping on the career development of women can be found in the literature on the effects of maternal employment. As Huston-Stein and Higgens-Trenk (1978) observe,

> The most consistent and well-documented correlate of career orientation and departure from traditional feminine roles is maternal employment during childhood and adolescence. Daughters of employed mothers (i.e., mothers who were employed during some period of the daughter's childhood or adolescence) more often aspire to a career outside the home . . . get better grades in college . . . and aspire to more advanced education. . . . College women who have chosen a traditionally masculine occupation more often had employed mothers than those preparing for feminine occupations. (pp. 279–280)

Adolescent Employment

During the 1970s, a number of commissions studying secondary education (National Commission on the Reform of Secondary Education, 1973; National Panel on High School and Adolescent Education, 1976; President's Science Advisory Committee, 1974) called attention to the failure of American education to prepare youths as workers. Their recommendations included the integration of school and work as a way of preparing students to be productive workers. Since then, youth employment has been generally viewed as a positive event (Carnegie Commission on Policy Studies in Higher Education, 1980; National Commission on Youth, 1980).

Those favoring early employment among teenagers have argued that working helps to develop such traits as initiative, autonomy, and self-reliance. Furthermore, employed youths are said to be more responsible, not only on the job, but also in their family and peer relations. Finally, working is portrayed as facilitating social competence and understanding among teenagers.

Do empirical studies support this positive picture of the effects of working on adolescents? Only in part, say Ellen Greenberger and Laurence Steinberg, who in collaboration with several other colleagues, have been investigating the impact of employment on teenagers (Greenberger, Steinberg, & Ruggiero, 1982; Greenberger, Steinberg, & Vaux, 1981; Steinberg, Greenberger, Garduque, Ruggiero, & Vaux, 1982). These researchers report that working is associated with greater *personal responsibility*—such as punctuality, dependability, self-reliance, and positive work orientation—but not greater *social responsibility*. Social cooperation, social tolerance, and social commitment among adolescents are unaffected by working. Of further interest, however, is the finding that early employment has a number of negative consequences for young people. In particular, working during the school year decreases the teenager's involvement with and commitment to activities and relationships in nonwork settings. Adolescents who work are more often absent from school, spend less time on homework and in extracurricular activities, and report that they enjoy school less. School performance, on the other hand, does not appear to be affected by part-time working. In addition, teenagers who work show less emotional closeness with peers, and in the case of employed girls, less emotional closeness with family members as well. This "distancing" from the family parallels the gains in autonomy that are especially

Some researchers believe that having a job during adolescence helps to develop such traits as initiative, autonomy, and self-reliance.

striking for employed girls. Finally, working also has been shown to lead to more materialistic attitudes among employed boys, and among teenagers in general, to more frequent use of marijuana and cigarettes, but not alcohol.

Denise Gottfredson (1985), using data collected from a large and ethnically diverse sample, found slightly different results. She found that work experiences available to students do not affect commitment to education, attachment to school or to parents. Furthermore, teenage working did not increase delinquency or have a detrimental effect on students' involvement with extracurricular activities. When work experience is carefully coordinated with the school curriculum, it can lead to a decrease in school dropout and an increase in learning and school attendance.

The discrepancy between Gottfredson's results and the results of Steinberg and his colleagues can be explained by the differences in the samples. Steinberg and his colleagues collected data from a white suburban population, while Gottfredson collected data from a primarily minority, urban, inner-city sample. The value and economic advantage accrued by having a job is relative to the adolescents' prejob level of affluence. Teenagers from poor families are more likely to value their working than teenagers who come from

Human Development in Practice

Vocational Counseling in High School

According to the Bureau of Labor Statistics (U.S. Department of Labor, 1987) more than 21 million jobs will be created in the U.S. economy between 1986 and the year 2000. Some fields such as service and managerial positions will be in big demand, while other occupations that do not require much educational preparation will decline. The complexity and increasing rate of change in today's job market makes the work of the vocational counselor both more important and more difficult than ever before. Many jobs are unappealing to youth, and many more are unknown to them. In an era of extensive specialization, not even a guidance counselor will know all the types of jobs that are available. Furthermore, new job categories open up continually, while others become obsolete. An adolescent, therefore, is faced not only with determining whether he or she will still be interested in a particular profession years after making the choice, but also whether that particular job will be available.

In an effort to help the adolescent make a career decision, some high schools offer a course in vocational planning. Students also take aptitude tests that are administered and evaluated by

trained professionals in many high schools and universities. These tests give at least some indication of a student's fundamental abilities and skills (mechanical, spatial, conceptual, and so on) and often disclose interests of which the student may not previously have been aware.

Even though high-school seniors and even college students may not be certain about the specific career they wish to enter, they can prepare themselves for the jobs of tomorrow by developing basic communication skills. Being able to read, write, solve problems, and use computers are essential skills for the future job market. Many high schools have restructured their curricula to emphasize these skills. Some high schools allow students to spend part of the school day in work settings within the community. The work experience allows students the opportunity to see whether they are suited to the job and to identify additional skills they need to develop to enhance their chances of getting into related careers.

Perhaps most helpful to adolescents are the individual counseling programs offered by many schools, church youth clubs, and government wealthier families. Furthermore, in the Gottfredson study, preworking attitudes and behaviors of the employed youths were compared with those of unemployed youths. Thus, any difference between employed and unemployed teenagers could be attributed to either their work experiences or to general differences between the groups *before* working.

Overall, the impact of employment on adolescents is determined by the type of job, the age of the teenager, the amount of support from the school and family, and the teenager's gender and socioeconomic status.

Pause for Thought

Before the Depression in 1933, the term "adolescence" was not commonly used. Up until that time, teenagers would stop going to school and get a job. Today, public education is compulsory in most states until age 16 and available at the high-school level till age 18. Some people have argued that adolescence was invented to keep teenagers out of the work force and in schools longer as a way to stabilize the effects of the Depression. Do you agree? Should education keep people out of work?

agencies. However, the need for these programs—especially among low-income adolescents who receive little or no guidance from their own families—often exceeds their availability.

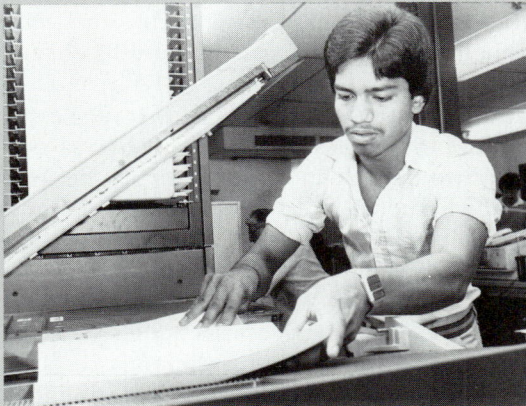

By taking a part-time job in an office, this teenager will have a clearer idea about his career options after graduation from high school.

There are not enough counselors providing the time and quality of guidance that many young people require. A partial solution to the problem of time and limited facilities is group career orientation. Lectures on vocational opportunities and planning that are offered by universities, the armed services, corporations, and independent service groups cannot possibly equal the value of individual counseling, but they can at least stimulate interest, broaden the person's understanding of the job market, and provide a realistic conception of the training and skills needed in various fields.

Teachers themselves can be potent role models for their students as they prepare for entry to a job or college. Many students see their teachers as people who teach their classes and grade their performance and do not see their teachers as workers or professionals. They may be unaware of the demands and training required of teachers. By talking openly with their students about their jobs and the steps they took to prepare for their careers, teachers can help their students in making vocational choices.

Problem Behavior

Except for dropping out of school, most of the antisocial behavior and mental-health problems exhibited by adolescents are not the exclusive domain of that age group. Certainly, adolescents have no monopoly on drug abuse and alcoholism, and such problems as depression, schizophrenia, and obesity cut across all age levels. Child psychologists and other social scientists disagree about whether these problems have specific characteristics when they originate in adolescence, but most agree that the developmental crises of adolescence—the physical and psychological upheavals that young people go through during this period—make teenagers more susceptible to some of these disorders than they might be at other times in life.

Depression

Melancholy and feelings of dejection are relatively common emotions during adolescence. In fact, there is a marked rise in prevalence of depression-like symptoms during this period (Rutter & Garmesy, 1983). Adolescent depression is characterized by a constellation of behaviors, most of which are also found in depressed adults (Carlson & Cantwell, 1982; Robbins, Alessi, Cook, Poznanski, & Yanchyshyn, 1982). Included among these behaviors are: boredom, and restlessness; irritability; disturbances in eating and sleeping; ruminations or obsessions; and hypochondrias (imaginary ill health). In addition, depressed teenagers may have a devalued self-image, which frequently leads to antisocial behavior that only produces further depression and guilt and reinforces their belief that they are bad, ugly, or inferior. Adolescent depression also has been linked to an increased likelihood of suicide threats and attempts.

Many of the symptoms of depression are frequently observed in normal nondepressed adolescents—moodiness, restlessness, boredom, and impetuousness. However, the depressed adolescent can be distinguished by three common characteristics: (1) the depressed teenager acts in such a way as to call attention to their problem—a cry for help, (2) their behavior is markedly different from their previous behavior, and (3) usually there has been a specific loss in their lives (Weiner, 1982).

Research by Seligman and Peterson (1983) suggests that depressive feelings are stable in childhood and early adolescence, at least over a period of time of up to six months. What we do not know, however, is the long-term stability of depression—that is, whether depressed children and adolescents will grow up to be depressed adults.

Psychotherapy seems to be the chief tool for treating the condition in teenagers. Antidepressant drugs, which are often administered to depressed adults with good results, seem to be less effective with adolescents. The depressed teenager is usually eager to obtain help and frequently responds well to therapy. The problem is in identifying the need for treatment. Often, teachers and parents mistake the depressed adolescents' behaviors as simply "growing pains."

Adolescent Suicide

In the United States, suicide is the second most common cause of death among 15- to 24-year-olds, after accidents (U.S. Bureau of the Census, 1982).

Suicide is the second most common cause of death among 15- to 24-year-olds. Danger signs of impending suicide include rapid mood changes, long-standing depression, changes in sleep patterns, social withdrawal, and drug use.

The rate of suicide among teenagers has doubled since the 1960s. In the United States, the number of suicides among 15- to 24-year-olds almost tripled in the years between 1955 and 1975. In 1978, suicide was the third leading cause of death in that age group. Among 10- to 14-year-olds, the rate has also risen, though the actual incidence of suicide among this age group is rather small (Hawton & Osborn, 1984). These statistics are considered by experts to be underestimates of the actual number of adolescent suicides. Because of the public embarrassment to the families involved, many adolescent suicides are listed as accidental deaths. Furthermore, attempts at suicide are also underreported. Although girls more often attempt suicide, boys are more often successful in completing the act.

Many reasons have been offered to explain these statistics. Some claim that adolescence is typically a time of special anxiety and frustration, which can trigger impulsive acts of suicide. While certain researchers (e.g., Weiner, 1977) suggest that emotional crisis and stress are not the norm in adolescence, today's competition for getting good grades, good jobs, and the "good life" may be exerting increasing pressure on young people.

Faced with strong family and cultural expectations to excel in sports, school, in the job market, some adolescents may feel cut off and detached from the mainstream (Husain & Vandiver, 1984). Overwhelmed by the competitiveness and drive to make lots of money and their sense of powerlessness, some adolescents may see suicide as the only way out of their dilemma.

Also implicated in suicide is the quality of family life. Divorce, which is disrupting families at a soaring rate, or the death of a parent, for example, makes adolescents feel insecure or abandoned. Excessive pressures from parents to succeed can contribute to a distorted self-image and loss of esteem, even if the child "fails" in minor ways. Some studies, like those involving suicidal adolescents from multiple foster-home placements indicate that continuity of care is perhaps even more important than the quality of family life (Glaser, 1978).

Danger Signs of Adolescent Suicide

Statistics on suicide are based on people who succeed in killing themselves. At the point at which a suicide is detected there is no chance of prevention. The only means of prevention is to be able to identify in advance who is likely to attempt to take his or her life. While some people who commit suicide keep their intentions to themselves, some people give off signals before they attempt suicide.

Some early warning signs of suicide among adolescents include the following:

1. A preoccupation with death in music, drawing, writing.
2. Talking of suicide, or threats such as "I wish I were dead" or "Life is not worth living."
3. Giving away prized possessions and attempting to put one's life in order.
4. Experiencing recent losses such as the death of a family member or friend, parental divorce, or the end of a love relationship.
5. Withdrawing from family and friends.
6. Disturbance in eating, sleeping, and personal-hygiene habits.
7. Having a series of accidents or physical complaints.
8. New or increased alcohol and/or drug abuse.
9. Truancy and poor school performance.
10. Sudden changes in mood and behavior.
11. A history of suicide attempts.

Having spotted some of these signs in an adolescent, what can be done to intervene? Talking directly with the person about suicide is the first step. If a person is considering killing him- or herself the question "Are you planning to kill or hurt yourself?" will bring the issue out in the open usually with lots of feelings. An attentive listener who is supportive and nonjudgmental can help the adolescent consider other alternatives to suicide. In situations in which the adolescent is under extreme emotional pressure, it is important that someone stay with the teenager until the immediate crisis is resolved or until the person is placed in a safe environment where no danger of suicide is present. After the crisis has subsided, more regular professional help by a therapist or physician may be needed.

Eating Disturbances

Being overweight or underweight may appear to be strictly physical problems, but in adolescence in particular these conditions sometimes either result from or lead to emotional disturbance. One study of adolescents categorized as "overweight," "underweight," or "average" in physique refers to the considerable body of evidence correlating appearance with self-esteem (Hendry & Gillies, 1978). Self-concept and self-perception are partly shaped by **body concept,** which, in turn, is influenced by the reactions and expectations of

Body Concept   One's perceptions and feelings about the physical aspects of oneself.

Anorexia Nervosa A psychological disorder chiefly affecting adolescent girls; characterized by voluntary restriction of food intake, resulting in chronic undernutrition and, occasionally, death.

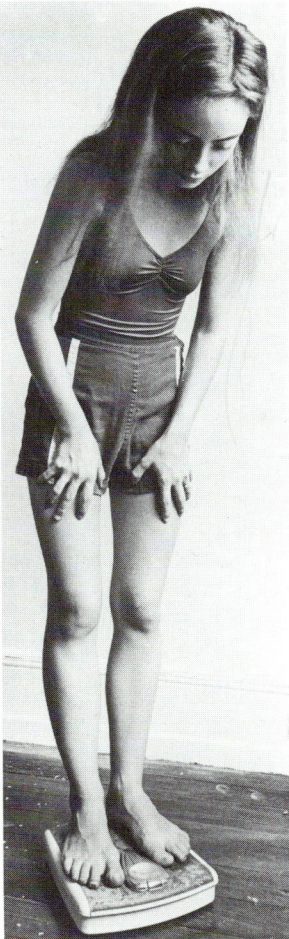

This young woman is recovering from anorexia nervosa. Treatment can help prevent long-term, serious health problems.

others to different body builds. Early on in life, children become aware of ideal body images transmitted by the culture and begin to judge their own physiques according to these standards. Both the overweight and underweight child's self-concept is thus vulnerable to injury or distortion. In adolescence the problem may be especially acute, since it is a time when each person's identity is coming into focus and adolescents are particularly self-conscious of their changing bodies.

The physiological factors that may influence overweight include (1) dietary habits and too little exercise, (2) genetic predisposition, (3) excessive number of fat cells acquired in early childhood, and (4) hormonal imbalance. Obesity may occur purely as a result of any of these conditions, but it is frequently seen in people having emotional problems as well (Stults, 1977).

The list of psychological factors that might be involved in obesity could be almost endless, but one writer on the subject (Bruch, 1961, 1973) feels that there is a basic, underlying reason for eating disturbances. She believes that the fundamental problem of serious over- or underweight people is an inability to recognize one's own bodily needs—essentially, an inability to differentiate hunger from satiety—and that this incapacity stems from a child's earliest eating experiences.

> If . . . a mother's reaction [to her child's hunger] is continuously inappropriate be it neglectful, oversolicitous, inhibiting, or indiscriminately permissive, the outcome for the child will be a perplexing confusion. When he is older he will not be able to discriminate between being hungry and being sated, or suffering from some other discomfort (Bruch, 1961).

Included in Bruch's studies of eating disorders is a condition that chiefly affects adolescent girls—**anorexia nervosa.** One of the few psychiatric disorders that can result in death, anorexia is characterized by the voluntary restriction of food intake, resulting in chronic undernutrition, weight loss, and occasionally death. Whereas most underweight adolescents may desire to have an average body and may feel self-conscious about their appearance, anorexics pursue thinness with a vengeance.

The typical anorexic may start out being slightly overweight—more commonly, she simply fears becoming "fat"—and so begins to reduce food intake drastically and to exercise frantically. Anorexics deny all feelings of hunger, yet they are always preoccupied with food. They may eat ravenously from time to time, only to remove the food through enemas, self-induced vomiting, or diuretics. Eventually, the anorexic's psychological and physiological functions become distorted. They have great difficulty sleeping and may become hypersensitive to sound, light, temperature, and pain. Hyperactivity often masks a feeling of exhaustion, although anorexics will deny such fatigue. They will also deny that their emaciated appearance is abnormal. They usually continue to perceive themselves as being overweight. These symptoms are often accompanied by increasing social isolation and a fierce preoccupation with school studies.

According to Bruch, early diagnosis of anorexia and an integrated treatment program are important. In chronic anorexia, hospitalization and the use of intravenous feeding may be necessary (see Box, Bulimia: The Binge–Purge Syndrome).

Human Development in Practice

Bulimia: The Binge—Purge Syndrome

In 1980, the American Psychiatric Association designated **bulimia** as a psychiatric disorder in the Diagnostic and Statistical Manual of Mental Disorders (DSM III). The disorder is characterized by episodic, uncontrollable binge eating. The bulimic hoards and eats large quantities of food in short periods of time. Usually the food consumed is high in calories and can be easily ingested (e.g., ice cream, candy, cakes, and cookies). One study estimated bulimics average 3415 calories in a typical binge episode; a few bulimics reported binging on 5000 calories, 10 times a day for a daily total of 50,000 calories (Mitchell, Pyle, & Eckert, 1981).

Sometimes the binge eating is followed by self-induced vomiting or by the use of laxatives or diuretics to purge the body of the binged food. Patients who resort to vomiting or laxative abuse run the risk of dehydration and other serious medical conditions and possibly death (Russell, 1979). Ninety percent of bulimics are female (Katzman, Wolchik, & Braver, 1984; Pope, Hudson, Yurgelun-Todd, & Hudson, 1984; Striegel-Moore, Silberstein, & Rodin, 1986). Most bulimics are not extremely overweight; many are of normal weight or about 10 to 30 pounds above normal weight. Furthermore, bulimics are aware of their abnormal eating behavior and are usually ashamed and depressed about their binge episodes. Bulimic women are more likely to be college educated. Boarding schools and colleges, especially those in which dating is heavily emphasized, have a higher prevalence of bulimia than other settings (Rodin, Striegel-Moore, & Silberstein, 1986; Squire, 1983).

The recent rise in reported cases of bulimia has been attributed to several factors including the overemphasis on the importance of thinness, physical fitness, and physical attractiveness within the culture (Striegel-Moore, Silberstein, & Rodin, 1986). A prolonged history of repeated dieting attempts may increase the risk of bulimia (Polivy & Herman, 1985). Excessively denying oneself particular foods may lead to later binge eating of the forbidden food. Bulimia may also be influenced by genetic factors. Women who are heavier than their peers are more likely to develop bulimia (Boskind-White & White, 1983; Fairburn & Cooper, 1983; Johnson, Stuckey, Lewis, & Schwartz, 1982). Further, many bulimics have a genetic history of depression and other mood disorders within their family suggesting that personality and genetic makeup may be a contributing factor (Johnson & Maddi, 1986).

The treatment of bulimia depends upon whether the patient is underweight or normal to overweight. Underweight bulimics must be carefully monitored, usually in a hospital, to prevent dehydration. Normal or overweight bulimics are treated by psychotherapy combined with a nutritionally sound weight-maintenance diet. Some bulimics respond well to antidepressant medication. The ultimate treatment goal is to eliminate the binging and purging behaviors and to establish normal, healthy eating habits.

Bulimia An eating disorder characterized by episodic, uncontrollable binges in eating, sometimes followed by self-induced vomiting.

Conduct Disorders A form of psychopathology in which the individual persistently violates the basic rights of others and/or the norms of society.

Conduct Disorders

In reviewing the research on adolescent **conduct disorders**—that is, those persistent behaviors that violate the basic rights of others and/or the norms of society—Herbert Quay (1982) reported that in 1979 there were 2,143,369 arrests of persons under 18 years of age—22.5 percent of all reported arrests for that year. Moreover, the arrests were not just for minor crimes such as shoplifting, vandalism, or possession of marijuana. On the contrary, many involved crimes of violence, although not nearly as many as crimes against property. Quay noted that slightly over 20 percent of all people arrested in

1979 for violent crimes (defined by the FBI as murder, forcible rape, robbery, and aggravated assault) were under 18 years of age. Data from the 1984 U.S. Census indicate that nearly half of the arrests for acts of vandalism, car thefts, burglary, and arson involved adolescents under the age of 18. Even though the overall crime rate in the United States has declined since 1960, the rate of serious crimes committed by adolescents has increased compared to the crime rate for adults (U.S. Bureau of the Census, 1984).

Researchers generally differentiate between unsocialized delinquents and socialized delinquents (Rutter & Garmesy, 1983). This distinction is based on evidence showing that the groups differ in terms of family background and outcome. For example, **unsocialized delinquents** tend to come from broken homes characterized by high levels of family hostility and parental rejection. As a result, these individuals typically fail to establish a normal degree of affection, empathy, and attachment to others. **Socialized delinquents,** in contrast, are more often products of social disadvantage and parental neglect (rather than rejection). Generally speaking, these individuals do form close relationships with others, and come to value and adhere to their reference group's standards and mores. Unfortunately, the individuals that socialized delinquents tend to identify with and emulate are themselves "social outcasts"—other delinquents, con artists, and so on.

Although most research shows little change in the prevalence of conduct disturbance during the middle-childhood and adolescent years, the actual pattern of delinquent acts does change during this period. Theft and property offenses decline in frequency during the transition from childhood and adolescence to young adulthood, whereas drunkenness and violent crimes increase in frequency (Cline, 1980; West, 1982). Furthermore, in comparison to the adolescent period, there is a substantial decline in overall delinquency and convictions during early adulthood.

What about the long-term stability of conduct disorders? Will today's young delinquents grow up to become tomorrow's hardened criminals? In summarizing data on this issue, Robins (1978) concluded that most antisocial teenagers do *not* become antisocial adults. With entrance into adulthood, the majority of teenage delinquents, particularly socialized delinquents, gradually blend into the larger culture and become productive and law-abiding citizens. Robins also reported, however, that when adults do become criminals, the origins of this lifestyle can usually, but not always, be traced to antisocial attitudes and behavior in childhood and adolescence.

Some studies view the home environment or family as a major determinant of antisocial adolescent behavior. Negative outcomes in adolescence have been related to overly permissive or overly harsh and authoritarian attitudes and behavior of parents (Baumrind, 1978). A study by Patterson and Stouthamer-Loeber (1984) found that parents of delinquent boys were not interested in or aware of their son's whereabouts and behavior, suggesting that parental indifference may be a factor contributing to delinquent behavior. However, others suggest that while the family plays some role in delinquency, the causal link is far from clear or direct.

One investigation (Johnstone, 1978) found that the strongest relationships between the family and delinquency were in the areas of drug use and status violations. (A *status violation* includes those behaviors that are legal offenses because of the adolescent's minor status in society; for example,

Unsocialized Delinquency A form of conduct disorder in which the person typically fails to develop a normal degree of affection, empathy, and attachment to others; usually associated with homes characterized by parental rejection and hard discipline.

Socialized Delinquency A form of conduct disorder in which the person typically develops the capacity for forming attachment relationships (usually to other delinquents or social outcasts); associated with social disadvantage and parental neglect (rather than rejection).

truancy, running away from home, sexual promiscuity, etc. Generally, adults are not held accountable for similar behavior.) <u>Peer influence was related most strongly to status violations</u>, drug use, and property offenses, such as vandalism and shoplifting. However, <u>violent acts,</u> such as fighting or using a weapon, and serious violations of the law, such as burglary, were most significantly related, not with peer or family influences, but ra<u>ther with community poverty and external pressures,</u> including high unemployment or a high crime rate. Johnstone's study goes on to suggest that problems in family relationships may have a stronger, more direct effect for adolescents growing up in an oppressive and hostile external environment.

Pause for Thought

Although boys commit nearly four times as many delinquent acts as girls (Federal Bureau of Investigation, 1984), the rate of female delinquency has been steadily increasing, especially for crimes that involve aggressive behavior such as theft, vandalism, and drug use. How do you account for these changes in girls' criminal behavior?

Substance Abuse

Probably no area in the teenager's life is of more concern to parents, and to a growing number of teenagers themselves, than the illegal use of drugs. Widespread concern stems from findings indicating that drug use is associated with health problems (in some cases leading to death), academic failure, delinquency, psychological maladjustment, and rejection of societal values and standards (Sutker, 1982).

The most frequently used drugs among adolescents are alcohol, nicotine (in cigarettes), and marijuana (Sutker, 1982). A study by Johnston, Bachman, and O'Malley (1985) of over 17,500 high-school students indicated that almost all seniors reported some drinking, and over half had tried marijuana. Experimentation with other drugs such as amphetamines, cocaine, and barbiturates, while not uncommon, was certainly less frequent than alcohol and marijuana use.

The use of illicit drugs by adolescents has gradually and steadily declined, since the peak in 1979. The majority of high-school seniors in the Johnston, Bachman, and O'Malley study expressed a concern about their health. This concern is reflected in a decline in daily marijuana use from 10.8 percent in 1978 to 5 percent in 1984. Nonetheless, marijuana is still the most widely used illicit drug.

The use of alcohol by adolescents has remained at a fairly stable but high level since 1975. According to Johnston, Bachman, and O'Malley (1985), nearly all of the teenagers had tried alcohol by the end of their senior year (93%). About one in 16 seniors were reported to be daily drinkers. Because marijuana and alcohol are used more than other substances, the remainder of this section will focus on these two drugs.

Alcohol

Alcohol is the most frequently used (and abused) drug among teenagers in the United States. Opinions are divided on the dangers or advantages of letting teenagers and children become acquainted with alcohol. Those in favor point out that few alcohol problems are found among Italians, Spaniards, Chinese, Lebanese, or orthodox Jews, who are traditionally exposed to wine or beer early in life as part of family meals and celebrations. For them, drinking is no proof of adulthood, and it is not regarded as either a virtue or a vice, or as the prime focus of any occasion. While abstinence is considered socially acceptable, excessive drinking or drunkenness is not.

For teenagers in this country, with its various prohibitions and its general mystique about drinking, alcohol acquires all sorts of connotations beyond being a pleasant accompaniment to meals and conversation. It often becomes a symbol of independence, adulthood, virility, or defiance. In as much as these have to be demonstrated to oneself or to others, incentive is provided for an immoderate use of alcohol. This may lead to alcoholism in the long run.

But consistent use and abuse of alcohol creates numerous problems for the young drinker, not the least of which is an addiction to alcohol. Furthermore, when adolescents become dependent on alcohol, they develop academic problems and tend to abuse other drugs (Burkett, 1980; Chase, Jessor, & Donovan, 1980).

A growing concern is the impact of alcohol on the young driver. The number of people killed while driving under the influence of alcohol has caused many states to raise both the legal drinking and legal driving age. Adolescents are encouraged to decline a ride in a car from someone who has been drinking. Many high-school students have formed volunteer groups to provide a safe ride home from a party to any teenager who does not want to accept a ride from a person who has been drinking.

An estimated 1 million teenagers drink too much, and girls are beginning to drink as much as boys, according to the National Council on Alcoholism (NYCA, 1978). For those teenagers with drinking problems who seek

A serious consequence of teenage use of alcohol is drunk driving. Many students have formed volunteer groups such as Students Against Drunk Driving (SADD) to help reduce the number of teenage auto accidents.

help, group therapy and individual counseling is available in most cities. Alcoholics Anonymous (AA) helps people of all ages, including an increasing percentage of teenagers. Many high schools include classes on drug and alcohol awareness in their curricula.

Marijuana

With any drug that is deliberately introduced into the body, one must ask what harmful side effects it can have, either immediately or in the long run. Concerning marijuana, both questions have been under continuing study.

Millions have taken marijuana as a "recreational" drug because it usually induces a sense of relaxed well-being, a subjective increase in perception, and an altered awareness of space and time. Negative psychological reactions do occur, however. In 1978, they resulted in more than 10,000 visits to hospital emergency rooms by marijuana smokers exhibiting transitory paranoia and acute anxiety, symptoms that appeared to be dose related. Also, marijuana frequently aggravates the condition of people who suffer from depression or other disturbances, and it is known to trigger latent severe disorders such as schizophrenia (Treffert, 1978).

The body's immediate, measurable responses to inhaling marijuana include a slight contraction of the pupils and reddening of the eyes, a greatly increased heart rate (which is dangerous for people with heart ailments), and decreased reaction time. While the intoxication lasts, it impairs certain functions, especially the processing of new information and its transfer from short-term to long-term memory. It also diminishes the ability to make judgments and respond to new situations. This makes drivers under the influence of marijuana a menace to themselves as well as others because they take too long to respond to unexpected events; the greater the demands of the situation, the less they can cope. Additional dangers are that the impairment may last for several hours after the "high" has passed, and that any simultaneous consumption of alcohol multiplies the impairment, rather than merely adding to it. Prolonged use of marijuana also increases the risk of lung cancer.

With regard to learning activities, it has been amply proven that materials and concepts studied in an undrugged state are significantly better understood (Clark, Hughes, & Nakashima, 1970; Klonoff, Low, & Marcus, 1973) and remembered than others studied while "high" (Tinklenberg & Darley, 1975). With regard to social and intellectual pursuits, there is some concern that their development may be impeded by frequent use of marijuana, since it gives teenagers the option of artificial relaxation as an alternative to learning how to deal with difficulties and frustrations.

What damage long-term use of marijuana may do has not as yet been established, largely because its use in Western society is of recent origin, and data from elsewhere are few and unscientific. Furthermore, deliberate and controlled experiments on long-term use can be conducted only on animals, not on humans. The reliance one can place on studies that have failed to find evidence of lasting damage is, therefore, limited, and it is further reduced by one important factor: There has been a great increase in the potency of "street" marijuana over the last decade. In 1975, the psychoactive ingredient THC (delta-9-tetrahydrocannabinol) found in confiscated samples rarely exceeded 1 percent, while it was commonly 5 percent in 1979; and so-called *hash-oil,* a marijuana extract that was not commonly available a decade and a half ago, averages 15 to 20 percent THC, and may contain as much as 29 percent. Since higher dosages create greater immediate impairment and disorientation than lower doses, they may also cause some long-term damage.

Summary

Adolescence is the period in which the individual establishes an integrated identity. An important aspect of identity for adolescents is awareness of ethnic or racial origins. Although many adolescents experience emotional upheaval over identity, parent relations, peer relations, and so on, others pass through this period with considerably less stress and strain. Adopted adolescents may have more difficulty establishing their identity if they are uncertain about their birth history.

Even though adolescents and their parents experience conflicts, the majority of teenagers get along with their parents. The conflicts that do occur concern choice in hair and dress styles, independence, and sexuality. Parents who are overly controlling are more likely to have conflicts with their adolescents.

In order to establish their own identity, people must become independent of their family. They must find other ways to meet their material and emotional needs, must make their own decisions about how to behave, and must work out their own values.

The peer group is an important agent of socialization during adolescence, one that often conflicts with the standards and values of the family. Intimate friendships begin to emerge in adolescence and become a vehicle through which the individual copes with the stresses associated with this period. The pursuit of popularity often leads adolescents to conform to group pressures. Some degree of conformity with peers is normal, and indeed unavoidable, because working out personal values takes time; meanwhile, one needs some guide to action.

Because most young people have such a wide variety of vocational choices, the decision is often difficult, although guidance counseling and publications on various vocations can be a great help. Gender stereotyping imposes vocational limitations on women and deprives them of much encouragement that men usually get.

Adolescents who work gain useful social and work skills. However, youth employment may have negative consequences for some adolescents depending on the type of job and type of support from school and family.

Adolescents are prone to many of the same social and psychological problems as adults, including suicide, depression, eating disorders, conduct disorders, and substance abuse. The two most frequently abused drugs among teenagers are alcohol and marijuana.

Further Readings

Chapin, W. *Wasted: The story of my son's drug addiction.* **New York: McGraw-Hill, 1972.** A father's account of drug abuse by a middle-class youth and the family's struggle to understand and deal with it. Mark Chapin started smoking marijuana at 14 and moved on to LSD and amphetamines. He was in a mental hospital when the book was written by his father.

Czikszentmihalyi, M., & Larson, R. *Being adolescent: Conflict and growth in the teenage years.* New York: Basic Books, 1984.
The day-to-day activities of typical middle-class American teenagers are the focus of this text. Teenagers were given electronic beepers and reported their thoughts, feelings, and activities at selected times during the day. A readable description of what it's like to be a teenager.

Erikson, E. (Ed.). *The challenge of youth.* New York: Doubleday, 1965.
Through a series of articles written by well-known social scientists, including Erikson, Keniston, and Bettelheim, the reader is exposed to many of the intrapsychic and societal factors that come into play in the adolescent's development of identity.

Frank, A. *Diary of a Young Girl.* New York: Simon & Schuster, 1982.
Anne Frank was a young Jewish girl who grew into adolescence while in hiding from the Nazis during World War II. Her poignant diary captures her experience of growing into physical maturity and falling in love. A moving book.

Krementz, J. *How it feels to be adopted.* New York: Knopf, 1982.
Nineteen children and adolescents provide firsthand accounts of how it feels to grow up in adoptive homes. Issues related to identity, family relationships, and fantasies about (and experiences with) birth parents are described in a sensitive, moving way.

Twiford, R., and Carson, P. *The adolescent passage: Transition from child to adult.* Englewood Cliffs, NJ: Prentice-Hall, 1980.
This nontechnical book gives a complete overview of adolescent psychological development.

Observational Activities

10.1   *Adolescent Friendships*

Peer relations and friendships are an important part of an adolescent's life. Teenagers prefer to spend more of their time away from family and in the company of their peers. Intimate friendships begin to emerge in early adolescence and become part of a teenager's identity. Girls and boys have different conceptions of friendship and are likely to behave differently with their friends.

The purpose of this activity is for you to gain a better understanding of adolescent friendships. You will need to locate four male and four female teenagers and interview them about their ideas of friendship. It would be best to interview the teenagers individually. Use the following questions to structure your interview.

1. How would you define a friend? What characteristics do you look for in a friend?
2. Think about three of your own friends and describe the characteristics you like in them.
3. What do you like to do with your friends? What activities do you engage in with your friends?
4. Why is it important to have friends? What role or function do friends play in your life?

5. Are you more likely to interact with your friends individually or in groups? How many friends would you usually be with at a time?
6. How does having a friend or friends influence the way you see yourself?

After completing your interviews, compare the responses of the girls and boys. Notice the differences in their conceptions of friendship. How are they similar? Summarize the teenagers' views on friendship and compare them with those reported in the text. How do the teenagers' views compare with your own views? What did you gain from doing this activity?

10.2   *Problems of Adolescence*

For the first time in their lives, adolescents begin to be aware of, and have to cope with, problems we usually associate with the adult world. Develop a questionnaire for five teenagers to complete anonymously. Select 15- to 16-year-old males and/or females; be sure to ask them to give their age and gender on the forms. You might give them a stamped, self-addressed envelope to help them protect their identity. Your questionnaire might look something like this:

Adolescents often face problems and decisions that can affect their whole lives as adults. Please number the following problem areas from most important (put a number 1 in front of the one you think is most important to you personally) to least important (number 10):

_____ having safe sex	_____ getting into college
_____ drinking alcoholic beverages	_____ keeping my weight where it should be
_____ smoking cigarettes	_____ teenage pregnancy
_____ choosing a career	_____ feeling depressed
_____ taking drugs	_____ staying out of trouble at home and at school

When you have collected the data, compare your results with those collected by your classmates. What patterns emerged in your data? How do these patterns compare with the information in the text?

PART

FIVE

Early Adulthood

*I*n the chapters that follow we change our organization of topics to reflect a shift in emphasis toward the importance of social, family, and occupational development in adulthood. In earlier chapters we divided the lifespan into developmental segments by chronological age and gave equal coverage to physical and cognitive changes in one chapter and social and personality development in another chapter. During those earlier parts of the lifespan, when rapid and numerous changes in physical and cognitive structure predominate, the organization of chapters worked well. However, during adulthood, social, family, and work issues exert a much stronger and pervasive influence on peoples' lives and thus demand a more focused presentation. Although changes in physical, cognitive, and personality characteristics are important in understanding adult development, their influence is not as dominant. Changes in social, cultural, and societal values and norms have a much greater impact on the quality of an adult's life. Therefore, in Chapter 11, we explore the physical, cognitive, and personality influences on development and then focus on family and occupational development in Chapter 12.

CHAPTER

11

Early Adulthood: Physical, Cognitive, and Personality Development

*T*o most people who knew him, 28-year-old Peter was a very eligible bachelor. He was attractive, got along well with people, and kept himself in good physical condition by running and playing racketball regularly. Although he dated several different women, he was not interested in making a commitment to any one person.

Just last spring, he and Jeannie had broken off their steady dating relationship when they realized each was interested in different goals. Jeannie was the manager of a health and fitness club and wanted to get married. She talked of the challenge of maintaining a dual career as worker and mother. However, Peter wanted to establish his career in telecommunications before he made a commitment to a wife and children. He just wasn't ready. So they parted as friends and saw each other only on an occasional basis.

For Peter, commitment to another person seemed premature. How could he take on that responsibility, he thought, when he was not even sure who he was or what he wanted out of life. The fact that Peter questioned occasionally whether he really was an adult yet—as his age implied— only reinforced the idea that he was not ready for a serious commitment to someone else. By settling into a career path and developing a career identity, Peter hoped to become more secure about himself—to feel more responsible and adultlike. Intuitively, he knew this decision was necessary before he could commit himself to marriage and a family.

Peter's reliance on his career as a means of defining himself as an adult and achieving a stable sense of self is not unusual. We all know individuals who identify strongly with the work they do. "I'm a telecommunication specialist"—as Peter might say—is a common type of response elicited by questions such as "Who are you?" or "Tell me about yourself." Taking on a particular job or career, however, is not the only way in which young people achieve an adult identity. Many people define their place in the world and achieve a stable adult sense of themselves through interpersonal relationships and family life.

Do you consider yourself an adult? If you are older than 18 years you are considered to be a legal adult. However, parents of some 18-year-olds may not consider them to be adults. In our society, adulthood is defined more in terms of social roles assumed than age or physical maturation. Thus, to be an adult means no longer being a child, teenager, or student, but rather a worker, husband or wife, or parent. In the transition to adulthood, people vary considerably in the timing of tasks accomplished and roles assumed—in other words, they attain adult status at different times. Some 20-year-olds, are students involved in exams and "relationships," whereas others are parents budgeting their income and bringing up their children. Some men and women enter the job market immediately after high-school graduation; others, such as developmental psychologists, do not undertake full-time employment until the age of 27 or 28.

Nonnormative events such as winning a cash lottery can dramatically alter a person's life.

Influences on Adult Development

When adults think about their past, for many it seems as if their childhood was separate and different from their current lives. There appears to be little continuity between their responses today and their experience as children. In part, this perception is due to the selective way in which we recall our own personal histories. But the discontinuity between childhood and adulthood is a product of the changes in influences that affect development across the lifespan. According to Baltes, Reese, and Lipsitt (1980) there are three types of influences on development: (1) *Age-normative* influences such as biological and maturational growth; (2) *History-normative* influences including major historical events such as wars, economic depressions, and epidemics; and (3) *Non-normative* influences including events that can occur at any time in life that have a serious impact on people's lives such as death of a spouse or child, illness, divorce, career changes, or even lucky wins in a sweepstake. The effect of these influences changes across the lifespan, as can be seen in Figure 11.1. In adulthood, the role of age-normative influences is sharply reduced compared to childhood, and the influence of non-normative and history-normative influences is much stronger.

Consider the social–historical information presented in Table 11.1. People who were born in 1912 experienced an economic depression in their twenties, a war in their thirties and fifties, and peace and prosperity in their forties. A complete study of changes in their development across the lifespan would have to include these critical events. People who were born in 1936, to parents who were born in 1912, experienced different social–historical events when they entered adulthood. We would expect to find differences between the 1912 cohorts and the 1936 cohorts as a result of the times and events they experienced.

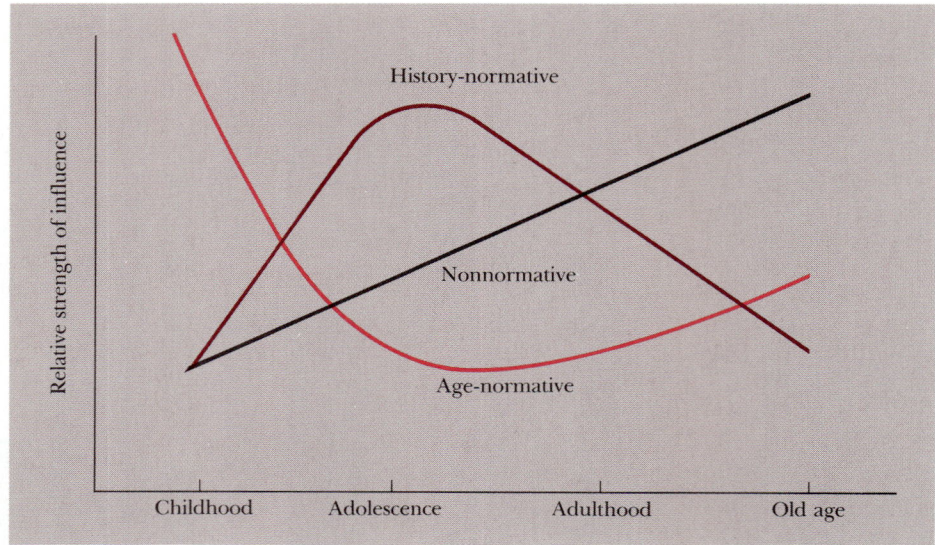

Figure 11.1 Developmental influences across the lifespan. The relative impact of various influences is believed to shift over the lifespan as shown in this hypothetical profile. Age-normative, history-normative, and nonnormative influences interact to produce age-related changes in development.

Pause for Thought

In the height of the Vietnam War, the U.S. government eliminated the draft exemption status for college students. In the 1970s, federal contributions to research and higher education were significantly decreased, and college-tuition costs rose dramatically in the 1980s. What immediate and long-term impact might these political events have had on people who were born in 1960? What other changes in the culture may have had an influence on people's lives during the time period from 1960 to 1989?

Perceived Age

Perceived Age   How old one feels.

Another way of defining adulthood is in terms of **perceived age**—how old one feels. Clearly, our perceptions of ourselves reflect many different aspects of our lives—chronological age, physical maturity, assumed roles, psychological adjustment, and so on. Some people may feel and act like adults at 16 or 17 whereas others in their middle to late twenties, such as Peter, may still be struggling with conflicts between their childlike needs and desires and their emerging adult personalities.

In early adulthood, people usually form serious personal commitments, marry, start their families, and take their place in the world of work. During this period, people define their relationship to society through love, work, and play. Adults are people who are in charge of their own lives; they earn their own keep. They make the decisions, both important and petty, about their own lives independent of other people's dictates, and accept the responsibility and consequences of these decisions. The number of years that people take to accomplish this varies—and for many people the break between

Table 11.1

Changing Times Affect Different Age Cohorts

	1932	*1944*	*1956*	*1968*	*1980*	*1989*
	Depression High unemployment No social security system	World War II Social security system established	Post-war boom Time of peace and prosperity	Vietnam War Oral contraceptives available Space age	Reagan era Unemployment high, inflation Lower birth rate	Present AIDS epidemic
Life Expectancy						
For men	58.1	60.8	65.6	67	70	71
For women	61.6	65.2	71.1	74	78	78
Divorce Rate (per 1000)	—	—	2.6	2.2	5.3	
Percent of Working Mothers with Children under 18	—	—	18.4 (1950)	27.6 (1960) 39.7 (1970)	54.1	

If you were born in						
1912	20 years old Just starting out in life	32 years old Parenting/ career	44 years old Middle age	56 years old Pre-retirement with adult children	68 years old Retired	77 years old Elderly/ deceased
1924	8 years old School child	20 years old Starting out in life/draft age	32 years old Parenting/ career in progress	44 years old Middle age	56 years old Pre-retirement with adult children	65 years old Retired or close to it
1936		8 years old School child	20 years old Starting life	32 years old Parenting/ career in progress	44 years old Middle age	53 years old Middle age
1948			8 years old School child	20 years old Starting out/ college age	32 years old Parenting/ career in progress	41 years old Middle age Parenting/ careers
1960				8 years old School child	20 years old Starting out/ college age	29 years old Settling into a career and relationship
1972					8 years old School child	17 years old About to graduate from high school
1984						5 years old Starting school

Sources: U.S. Bureau of the Census, *Statistical abstracts of the United States, 1982–1983*, Table 723. Washington, DC: Government Printing Office, 1983; U.S. Bureau of the Census, *Statistical abstract of the U.S.*, Washington, DC: Government Printing Office, 1981.

adolescence and adulthood is less a moment in time than it is a long and gradual process.

In the present chapter, we focus on several aspects of the individual's development that are important for understanding the transition to adulthood. We begin with a brief discussion of the period of youth, a new stage of life brought about by our complex, rapidly changing society. Next, we focus on the physical and cognitive changes that emerge during this time. Finally, attention is focused on personality development in young adulthood and, in particular, on the development of adult identity and its relationship to interpersonal intimacy.

Youth: An Optional Period

The concept of **youth** has been introduced to deal with the postadolescent period of life that sometimes precedes adulthood (Keniston, 1970). Those young people who take a long time to "settle down" are said to have entered an optional period of development called *youth,* which stretches from the point at which the person is legally an adult (generally at 18) to the point at which he or she actually undertakes adult work and family roles. A person may be legally an adult, old enough to vote, drive, drink, and join the armed forces, and yet may not feel "grown up" until he or she is supporting him- or herself and a family some five to 10 years later.

One of the developmental tasks of early adulthood is selecting a mate; marriage is one way to accomplish this task.

Table 11.2

Havighurst's Developmental Tasks of Youth and Early Adulthood

A. Developmental Tasks of Youth

   1. Learning to take responsibility for self

   2. Establishing an identity

   3. Developing emotional stability

   4. Getting started on a career

   5. Establishing intimacy

   6. Finding a mate

   7. Maintaining one's own residence

   8. Establishing ties to a social community

   9. Deciding on parenthood

B. Developmental Tasks of Early Adulthood

   1. Selecting a mate

   2. Learning to live with a marriage partner

   3. Starting a family

   4. Rearing children

   5. Managing a home

   6. Getting started on an occupation

   7. Taking on civic responsibility

   8. Establishing a social network of friends

Source: Havighurst, R. J., *Developmental tasks and education* New York: D. McKay, 1974.

Robert Havighurst (1974) has proposed a series of developmental tasks that are important for people to accomplish in order to feel satisfied with their lives. (See Table 11.2.) The developmental tasks he identifies for youth are more psychological in nature (e.g., establish an identity, intimacy, and emotional stability) than tasks important in early and later adulthood (e.g., select a mate, start a family, job, and home). While these tasks may reflect some of the important life events in youth and early adulthood, it is important to keep in mind that individuals vary considerably in the way in which they live. Some people may select a mate in their youth, divorce in early adulthood, and then select another mate. Others may have established ties to a community only to find they must relocate their residence to maintain or advance their careers or that of their spouse.

Youths may reject such conventional ideas as "settling down." Especially if a person enjoys a prolonged youth, he or she may demonstrate what Keniston calls a "refusal of socialization" (Keniston, 1970). A woman may realize that she has no wish to follow in her mother's footsteps as "someone's wife"; instead, she may choose to remain single and become a career person. A man may decide, after self-analysis, that the 9-to-5 work pattern he has been taught to respect is for him inappropriate—that rural life or entrepreneurial craft-work makes more sense. Often, adults become suddenly aware that they do

Youth is a period of time when people can explore their life choices; sometimes this might mean taking a long trip or just "dropping out" for a while.

not fit into the enduring "system." There is also, for most young adults, a new need to forge intimate relationships outside the family, and perhaps outside traditional forms. There is a need to make commitments to moral, political, or religious ideologies on the basis of the person's own rather than parental experiences. A youth may join a church or political party different from the one to which the rest of the family belongs.

With respect to emerging values, Yankelovich (1981) has identified a radical shift in areas of commitment among today's youth that can be traced back to societal changes during the 1960s. Young people now are more concerned with self-fulfillment—in interpersonal relationships, in sexual areas, on the job, and in family life—than self-sacrifice. This focus on fulfilling our human potential is clearly linked to the wider range of choices, and to the increasing freedom to explore alternative lifestyles, which we find in today's society as opposed to the society of past generations.

Because youth is a new and optional period of life, we have not fully integrated it into our understanding of early adulthood. It is enough to say that during the uncharted period between adolescence and middle adulthood, certain psychosocial developments occur. As we describe these developments, we shall refer to a period of early adulthood with the understanding that in some lives, it is appropriate to identify a more tentative, exploratory period of youth within this period.

Pause for Thought

In any culture or society, there are established expectations for adulthood. For example, adults buy homes, have families, carry on the values of the community. Yet societies change and often this change is spearheaded by young people who refuse to accept the status quo. What are some of the dilemmas young adults have to resolve as they establish themselves as adults within a community? How can one balance the need for change with the need for acceptance in adulthood?

The capacity for vigorous activity involving speed, strength, and endurance reaches its peak in young adulthood.

Physical Development

During early adulthood—the twenties and early thirties—the individual is at the peak of life biologically and physiologically. Not all systems of the body peak simultaneously, however; nor do all systems peak during this period of life. Each system of the body has its own unique pattern and rate of development. Early adulthood is characterized both by biological maturation and decline. Yet, when we consider the body as a whole, it is clear that this period is one of optimal biological functioning.

During early adulthood, most people reach their full height, women around 17 or 18, and men, somewhat later, around 21 (Roche, 1979; Roche & Davila, 1972). Maximum weight, in contrast, generally is not achieved until middle adulthood (Kent, 1976). Peak physical strength usually follows the attainment of mature stature, but is not achieved until the middle to late twenties. The capacity for vigorous activity requiring not only strength but speed, coordination, and endurance also is greatest during this age period. Most Olympic and professional athletes, for example, are in this age group. One study found that all of those competing in short-distance running, jumping, or hurdling—sports that demand high agility and speed—were between 18 and 30 (Tanner, 1964). The age at which athletes reach their peak in skill varies according to the sport (Fries & Crapo, 1981). Gymnasts reach their peak in adolescence, while golfers do better in later adulthood. Thereafter, physical strength declines gradually—approximately 10 percent between the ages of 30 and 60 (Troll, 1975).

A number of sensory and neural functions also are at optimal levels during young adulthood. Visual acuity and hearing are sharpest around 20, the former remaining relatively constant into the middle-adult years, while the latter showing a gradual loss over the same period of time. In addition, full brain weight and mature brain-wave patterns are achieved during early adulthood.

Most athletes reach their prime in their field during early adulthood.

Premenstrual Syndrome
Physical and psychological symptoms, including breast tenderness, abdominal swelling, water retention, irritability, anxiety, and depression.

Young adults are the healthiest individuals in our society. They are much more likely to die from violent causes—accidents, suicide, or homicide—than from diseases (Fuchs, 1974). Still, some of the health problems of later life are discernible in this age group. King and Cahill (cited in Scanlon, 1979) note that "by the time we reach young adulthood, the lesions of the diseases that will prove catastrophic later on are already present." These early manifestations of disease processes, which these researchers have labeled "silent disease," include rheumatic fever, atherosclerosis, emphysema, lung cancer, cirrhosis of the liver, kidney disease, and arthritis. King and Cahill report that young adults also are susceptible to disorders that are associated with stress. Included in this category are hypertension, drug and alcohol abuse, mental depression, ulcers, and obesity.

Perhaps because people are the fittest they have been during this period of their lives, they are less likely to practice preventive health habits such as proper nutrition, rest, and physical examinations. Yet it is during early adult-

Human Development in Practice

Premenstrual Syndrome

Every month, approximately 30 to 40 percent of the adult female population report physical and psychological symptoms just before the onset of their menses (Rose & Abplanalp, 1983). Physical symptoms include breast tenderness and swelling, abdominal bloating, retention of water, backaches, and headaches. Psychological symptoms include depression, irritability, anxiety, and hostility. In addition, changes in energy level, eating and sleeping habits, and interpersonal activity are also commonly reported. Taken together, these symptoms have come to be known as **premenstrual syndrome (PMS).**

What causes PMS? Most researchers have focused their attention on the relationship between hormone fluctuation and presenting physical and psychological symptomatology. Carroll and Steiner (1978), for example, proposed that PMS resulted either from a combination of high prolactin and low estrogen levels (producing premenstrual depression) or from high prolactin and low progesterone levels (producing premenstrual anxiety and irritability). In contrast, Dalton (1964, 1977) has been a forceful proponent of the theory that women who suffer from PMS have a deficiency of progesterone relative to estrogen during the premenstrual days. Unfortunately, as Rose and Abplanalp (1983) point out,

there is no firm, consistent evidence linking a specific hormonal abnormality to premenstrual distress. Nevertheless, the search goes on.

Recently, a number of studies have questioned the concept of a negative premenstrual syndrome caused entirely by physical factors. Diane Ruble at Princeton University conducted a study of premenstrual symptoms in which the women who were the subjects in the experiment were duped into thinking that they were either premenstrual or intermenstrual—halfway in their cycle from the onset of menstruation—when, in fact, they were all about six days from the time of their monthly period (Ruble, 1977). Ruble hypothesized that the women who thought they were premenstrual would be more likely to experience premenstrual symptoms than those who thought they were not premenstrual.

In the first phase of the experiment, the women were hooked up to a large oscilloscope (a machine that translates bodily electrical activity into a visible wave form on a screen) which, they were told, would be able to determine their place in their menstrual cycle. On a random basis they were then told they were premenstrual or intermenstrual; the control group was told nothing. They were then administered the Menstrual Distress Questionnaire developed by R. H. Moos.

hood that people can more easily change health habits that will have a long-term effect. Stopping smoking, establishing a personal exercise program, and regulating weight are habits that can contribute significantly to a person's health in middle and late adulthood. They are habits that literally last a lifetime.

Optimal biological functioning has important implications for the personal, social, and occupational adjustment of young adults. Indeed, in the occupations that rely on physical and sensory abilities, early adulthood is considered the prime of life. A construction worker or foot soldier, for example, may be said to be in his occupational prime at 20 or 25, and past it at 40. For some individuals, there is no drop in measurable performance with advancing age, however. Such musicians as Artur Rubinstein and Pablo Casals and artists such as Picasso and Georgia O'Keeffe were still at the height of their powers in their mid-eighties, with little diminution even as they approached their nineties.

The "premenstrual" group scored significantly higher than the "intermenstrual" group in three of the four predicted symptoms: water retention, pain, and change in eating habits. An unanticipated variable, sexual arousal, also reached statistical significance.

Commenting on these findings, Ruble (1977) said "that the results did *not* suggest that women never experience pain or water retention, nor that such symptoms never accompany the premenstrual phase." Rather, the findings seemed to indicate that women, because of cultural attitudes, associate such symptoms with the premenstrual phase so that they tend to look for such symptoms when they are premenstrual as well as to think they are premenstrual if they experience these symptoms.

Most women develop coping routines if they experience monthly pain or negative feelings, such as keeping busy or making time for a little extra sleep to combat fatigue. Usually these strategies are successful. Regular exercise and increasing exercise during the premenstrual period seems to help relieve some of the symptoms. Cutting down on caffeine, carbohydrates, and salt also has lessened some PMS symptoms. Only a small percentage of women—perhaps as little as 5 percent (Rose & Abplanalp, 1983)—appear to

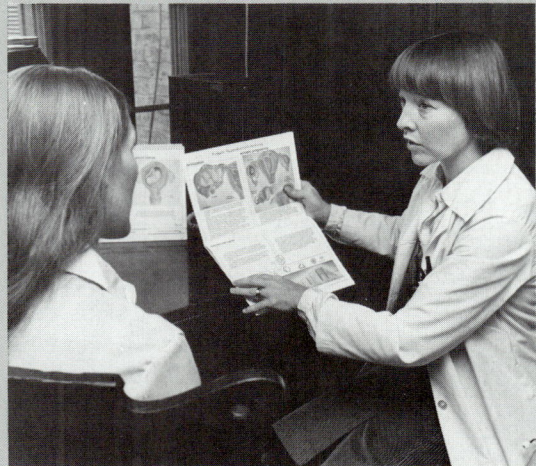

Women who suffer from premenstrual syndrome can learn to develop coping strategies to avoid some of the physical and psychological symptoms that occur just prior to the start of their period.

develop symptoms so severe that they require professional help. More research is needed to identify the causes and treatment of premenstrual syndrome.

For women, reproductive capacity is at its peak during young adulthood. Biologically speaking, the best age for a woman to become pregnant for the first time is in her twenties. This is because the organs and physiological systems involved in reproduction are better developed and coordinated during young adulthood than either earlier or later in life. During young adulthood, women are more likely to produce fertilizable eggs; their hormone cycle related to reproduction is more regular; and their uterine and pelvic environment is more conducive for sustaining a pregnancy and facilitating a safe delivery. Though many women comfortably bear children during the teenage years or into the early forties, fertility is not as high; delivery is sometimes more difficult; and there is a greater incidence of defects in the infants during these periods than in the twenties.

Except in rare cases of disease, disfigurement, or abnormal growth, physical development usually is taken for granted by young adults. It is in middle adulthood that *observable* signs of aging begin to generate concern, and physical skills begin to be measured against past performance. In other words, the optimal physical characteristics of early adulthood tend to be noticed only in retrospect, during the middle and elderly years of life.

Pause for Thought

For some people, signs of physical aging such as graying hair, loss of muscle tone, and wrinkling skin begin to show in the latter part of early adulthood. The extent to which these early signs are viewed negatively depends on the value of physical attractiveness and youth within the culture. Typically, aging women are viewed as less attractive than aging men. Why do you think this difference exists? What are the consequences of the different standard for men and women?

Cognitive Development

Like physical skills, certain intellectual abilities appear to peak during the early adult years. Research indicates that tasks requiring quick response time, short-term memory, and the ability to perceive complex relations, are performed most efficiently during the late teens and early twenties. Certain creative skills, particularly those involving the development of unique or original ideas or products, also reach their highest level during young adulthood. Most other abilities, however, continue to develop beyond this age period. Intellectual skills related to verbal ability and social knowledge, for example, show increases well into the fifties and possibly later (Horn & Donaldson, 1980). These are skills that improve with education and experience. The question of adult development and decline in intellectual areas, however, is complicated by methodological problems. As we shall see in Chapters 13 and 15, the high performance of young adults and the relatively low performance of middle-aged and elderly adults on IQ tests, may be a result or "artifact" of the cross-sectional research design.

In the broader areas of intellectual functioning, some developments in early adulthood have been tentatively identified by Piaget and others. Originally, Piaget's scheme of cognitive development ended in adolescence, with

Formal operational thought involves the use of abstract thought and problem solving. These skills increase with education.

the period of formal operations (the period characterized by hypothetical reasoning and abstract thought). Piaget stated that this stage was reached between 12 and 15, and indeed for many people, it is. However, in later writings, Piaget (1972), suggested that the period of formal operations may not develop or become consolidated until late adolescence or young adulthood (ages 15–20), and that it may be expressed more narrowly than was first supposed. A young adult may demonstrate hypothetical reasoning in her particular field of specialization, but not in other fields. A financial analyst may show highly developed reasoning as she isolates the causes of poorly performing subsidiaries, yet may be unable to apply the same logical skills to problems in an experimental or unrelated situation. Empirical research has documented that not everyone can use formal thought to generalize from one field to another. DeLisi and Staudt (1980) found that college students could express formal operational principles much more easily within their own major than in areas outside of their major. Physics students were successful on a task dealing with the isolation of variables determining the frequency of oscillation of a pendulum. In contrast, they had considerable difficulty in applying formal operations to a political-socialization task and to a literary-styles task. Political-science majors, on the other hand, were most successful on the political-socialization task and relatively unsuccessful on the other two tasks, while English majors were successful in applying formal operations only on the literary-styles task.

What are some of the factors that determine the variability in development and expression of formal-operational thought? Undoubtedly, cultural factors, such as the technology of the society, play a crucial role. Societies with advanced technologies are more in need of individuals capable of high-level abstract thought. Consequently, such societies are likely to provide avenues for the development and eventual expression of this type of thought. One such avenue is education. Research indicates a positive relationship between the number of years of schooling and an understanding of formal-operational principles (Papalia, 1972). Another factor related to formal thought is intelligence level. As one might expect, people who are more intelligent are more likely to develop and use formal operations.

It has been widely argued that not all adults, perhaps no more than half, ever reach the cognitive level of formal operations (Arlin, 1975). The adults who are said not to reach this level tend to fall into certain groups such as the aged (Papalia, 1972), especially non-Western aged (Dasen, 1972), and for some measures, women (Elkind, 1961, 1962; Leskow & Smock, 1970). Other researchers, however, have suggested that it may not be that these people are unable to reason logically according to Piaget's concept of formal operations, but that certain response tendencies, and the characteristics of the tests themselves, do not allow everyone to display their competence equally (Brodzinsky, 1985; Neimark, 1981; Overton & Newman, 1982). If a person is not interested in the task, or is highly anxious about being evaluated; or if the skills needed to solve the task are "rusty" from disuse, then performance is likely to be poorer than if the person is motivated, shows only moderate evaluation apprehension, and is well practiced in the skills necessary for task solution. In addition, both Brodzinsky and Neimark have argued that *cognitive style*—a person's habitual pattern of approaching problem solving—affects performance on Piagetian-type tasks, including those measuring formal operations. People who are reflective—that is, those who are cautious, systematic, and use planning in their problem-solving approach—do well on such tasks. So too do field-independent people—those who are more easily able to distinguish relevant from irrelevant information in problem-solving contexts. However, people who are impulsive in responding to problem situations, and those who are field-dependent—that is, who have difficulty recognizing and isolating what is relevant to a particular problem containing other information—do relatively poorly on these tasks.

Beyond Formal Operations

Although Piaget believed that the highest level of intellectual development was reached with the attainment of formal operations, other researchers have attempted to define levels of cognitive processing beyond this stage. One of the limitations of Piaget's theory is that it doesn't account for changes in thinking as a result of the specific environment or situation. Changes in thought are seen as changes in the person's cognitive structures. However, a lifespan approach sees cognitive growth as a multidirectional and multiply determined process that results from a changing person in an ever-changing environment (Labouvie-Vief & Chandler, 1978). Viewed from a lifespan-contextual perspective there is no fixed end point to cognitive growth. If the environment or context is sufficiently stimulating, change is possible (Rebok, 1987).

Problem Finding

Problem Finding According to Arlin, the ability of the person to generate new and relevant questions about the world; linked to postformal levels of reasoning.

Arlin (1975, 1977, 1984), has identified a fifth stage of cognitive development termed **problem finding,** which focuses on the ability of the individual to generate new and relevant questions about the world. In problem finding, a person poses new problems rather than just attending to old ones. Or a problem finder might discover new ways of looking at old problems in order to make new solutions possible. Arlin believes that problem finding might be the process that links Piagetian cognitive structures to creativity. Arlin's data suggest that formal operations is a necessary, but not sufficient, condition for problem finding. However, others have questioned the validity of this fifth stage both on empirical and logical grounds (Commons & Richards, 1978; Fakouri, 1976).

Dialectical Thought

Dialectical Process According to Riegel, a characteristic of mature thought in which the individual recognizes, accepts, and even seeks out intellectual conflict or challenge.

A second suggestion for an additional adult cognitive form of thought comes from the work of Klaus Riegel (1973b, 1975). According to Riegel, adult thought is characterized by a **dialectical process**—that is, a recognition and acceptance of, and even a desire for, conflict or contradiction. Riegel criticizes the notion that formal operational thought—the highest stage in Piaget's theory—is the most mature form of thinking. He is especially critical of the view that mature thought seeks equilibrium—a tensionless state where "everything fits together." According to Riegel, mature thought does not seek balance or a lack of tension, but intellectual crisis. The mature mind needs constant stimulation. It welcomes the apparent contradiction that accompanies two or more opposing viewpoints, for this is the foodstuff that fosters the growth of intellect. Dialectical thinkers seek to discover what is left out of existing ways of ordering and making sense of the world; they wish to create new orderings that include ideas and observations that did not fit in the earlier orderings (Basseches, 1984).

Riegel notes that dialectical thinking can occur in any one of Piaget's stages, although the content of the dialectical process is much less complex at lower stages. The preschooler, for example, at first attributes absolute qualities to characteristics such as "big," "small," "heavy," "light." A person is either big or small, heavy or light. Later on, however, children become aware of a conflict with respect to these qualities. An older sister is big when compared to oneself, but at the same time, she is small when compared to Mom. How can a person be both big and small? The young child resolves this apparent contradiction by recognizing that certain characteristics have a *relative* quality—that is, they can be understood only in a particular context, or in relation to something else. This resolution not only solves the immediate problem for the child—understanding how someone can be both big and small at the same time—but also provides the child with the cognitive ingredients necessary to view the world in a broader, more sophisticated sense.

Youths and young adults, like preschoolers, according to Riegel, engage the world through a dialectical process although at a much higher level. The contradictions that are confronted are more often on the level of abstract ideas. Mature adults struggle with conflict in their lives in such areas as morality, ethics, politics, religion, and the meaning of life. And yet they do not necessarily need to resolve the contradictions they confront. According to Riegel (1973b), in maturity "the individual accepts these contradictions as a basic property of thought and creativity."

Contextual Model of Adult Cognition

Consider the following story used in a study by G. Cohen (1979):

> Downstairs, there are three rooms: the kitchen, the dining-room, and the sitting room. The sitting room is in the front of the house, and the kitchen and dining room face onto the vegetable garden at the back of the house. The

> noise of the traffic is very disturbing in the front rooms. Mother is in the kitchen cooking and Grandfather is reading the paper in the sitting room. The children are at school and won't be home til tea time. (p. 416)

Who was being disturbed by the noise? If you said "Grandfather" you would be responding the way the college students in Cohen's study did. However, when Gisela Labouvie-Vief (1985) asked older adults the same question, many of them interpreted the story differently depending on the context they were using. Some thought that Grandfather was deaf and so was undisturbed by the traffic noise, otherwise he would have left the sitting room. The level of cognitive maturity present in the older adults' reasoning is more complex. Labouvie-Vief (1982) believes that adult thought that includes a consideration of the context and the practical real-life implications of an event is more sophisticated than formal-operational thought. Being an adult involves making logical choices and decisions on the basis of the responsibilities and commitments they have made to themselves and to their family. What may appear to be a logical choice for one person may not be a logical one for another person in a different context. Some of you may have found yourselves in the dilemma of responding to a multiple-choice item in which the "correct" answer would depend on the specific situation you imagine. In this case, context has become an important part of your thinking.

Characteristics of Mature Adult Thought

Although there is no consensus among developmental theorists on the existence and nature of a qualitatively distinct postformal stage of cognitive development, an increasing number of research studies have documented changes in adult thinking that are not easily handled within Piaget's theory (Commons, Richards, & Armon, 1982). In reviewing this literature, Kramer (1983) has identified three such characteristics of adult thought. First, adult thinking is *relativistic*. Unlike the adolescent, who tends to think of the world in absolutistic ways, adults are more likely to accept the existence of mutually incompatible systems of knowledge. This results, in part, from the adult's expanding social world, which includes many differing, and potentially incompatible, viewpoints and roles. A second feature of adult thought is the realization that *contradiction* is an inherent aspect of reality. No longer is there a need for necessarily resolving cognitive conflicts or contradictions. On the contrary, as Riegel (1973b) notes, the mature thinker not only accepts contradiction in reality, but actually is drawn to it. The final characteristic of adult thought, according to Kramer, is the tendency to *integrate*, or *synthesize, contradictory knowledge* into an overriding and more inclusive whole—what Commons, Richards, and Kuhn (1982) have called *metasystems*. Thus, whereas the adolescent is restricted to the development of a single abstract system of thought organized around formal-operational principles, the mature adult thinker begins to view knowledge as the integration and coordination of multiple, potentially incompatible systems of beliefs. For the mature thinker, therefore, the existence of vastly different conceptions of religion, which are often contradictive in their description and explanation of spiritual and earthly matters, is no longer so perplexing as it once was. Instead of looking for the single, correct answer to questions, whether in religion or not, the postformal adult thinker now recognizes that knowledge is always a synthesis or integration of different points of view. Each experience, looked at from a different angle or from a different perspective, yields new information and new insights. Thus, knowledge and the person's ability to know something is ever-changing.

Pause for Thought

Mature adult thought embraces much more than knowing "the correct" answer on a test. What types of questions or problems could be used to assess your knowledge of the material presented thus far in this course that would also challenge your adult thinking? Share your creative ideas with your instructor and present a rationale for them based on postformal-operational thought.

Moral Development

Young adulthood is a time when people acquire a strong sense of right and wrong based on their own experiences. Moral development, or the development of a personal value system, is closely related to cognitive development. It appears that a given logical ability is necessary before a person can reason at a given moral level. Kohlberg (1973) has argued that one must reach the formal-operational level of cognition before one can engage in principled or postconventional moral reasoning. However, the higher levels of moral development seem to require more than just the achievement of a certain level of cognitive reasoning. They require certain kinds of personal experiences as well. For example, leaving home and entering a college environment typically expose one to conflicting values, emotional choices, and new perceptions of self. Many college students react with skeptical relativism, a position that what is right is merely relative and depends on the person, his or her needs and circumstances, and so on. This position reflects the student's new awareness

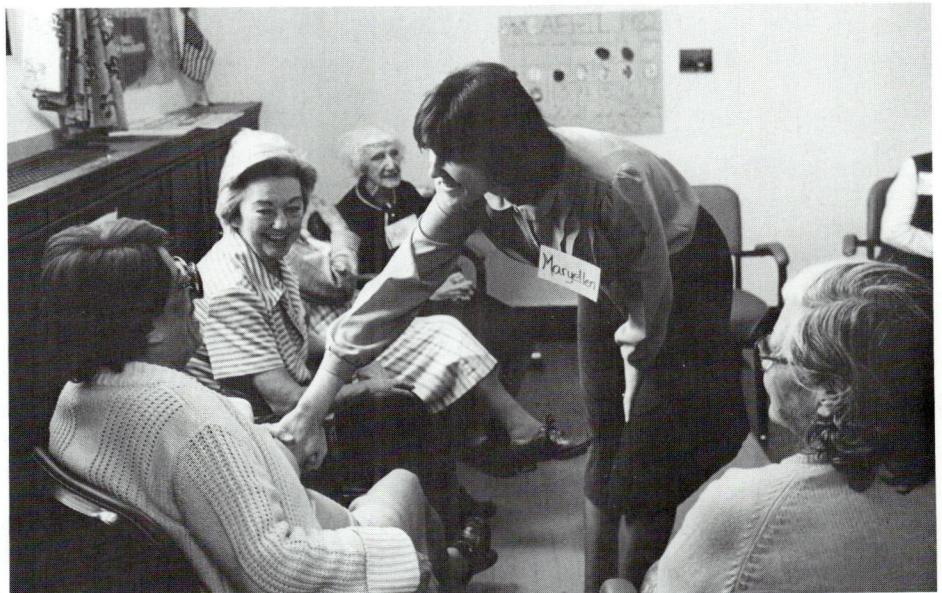

By volunteering in this adult health center, this young woman is likely to continue to be more concerned about the welfare of others. Experiences such as these can affect a person's moral development.

of the diversity in values and people. As students consolidate their identity, however, they achieve a higher level of moral judgment. They may proceed to the social-contract orientation of Kohlberg's Stage 5, and in rare cases, to the universal ethical, principled orientation of Kohlberg's Stage 6.

In our discussion of the two stages of the postconventional level in Chapter 9, it was noted that only about 28 percent of all moral judgments made by 16-year-olds were at this level. Subsequent research suggests that the college experience is critical to these stages of moral development. In one study, none of the subjects who went directly to the adult occupations, bypassing the stage we called "youth," showed evidence of Kohlberg's highest moral stage (Kohlberg & Kramer, 1969). Other studies, however, suggest that educational attainment is not the critical factor, but that adult life experiences are—they enable people who have not been to college to "catch up" to their more educated peers (Papalia & Bielby, 1974). A study by Edward Lonkey, Cheryl Kaus, and Paul Roodin (1984) found that adults who reasoned at the principled level of morality are more able than adults who reasoned at the conventional level to deal positively and constructively with significant losses in their lives such as the death of a family member or the end of a relationship. Thus, life experiences can provide a training ground for moral development and also be better understood and accepted as a result of a higher level of moral reasoning. Kohlberg believes that the experience of sustained responsibility for the welfare of others is critical to higher levels of moral reasoning.

Criticisms of Kohlberg's Theory

Kohlberg's theory, particularly the adult stages at the level of postconventional morality, has come under attack (Murphy & Gilligan, 1980). Most researchers accept the first two levels, but in research tests, according to Murphy and Gilligan, too many people show retrogression back to an earlier stage rather than development to a higher one. This lack of fit between the predictions of Kohlberg's theory and actual research results prompted Murphy and Gilligan to call for a revision of the adult aspects of the theory. In particular, whereas Kohlberg and others believe that formal operations is a sufficient cognitive foundation for the development of postconventional morality, Murphy and Gilligan (1980) argue that a more advanced, postformal level of reasoning underlies the adult postconventional moral thought. The shift from adolescence to young adulthood, according to these authors, is accompanied by a shift in the way in which formal thought is applied to moral issues. As noted earlier, adolescents use formal logic in an *absolutistic* way when dealing with moral–ethical issues, whereas adults, because of their greater experience with moral conflict and choice, are more inclined to appreciate the "gray" areas of life—that is, to recognize and accept multiple perspectives in considering moral situations. Thus, according to Murphy and Gilligan, the absolutism of adolescent logic gives way to a more *relativistic* approach to moral dilemmas during young adulthood. For example, when asked whether his moral beliefs had changed since he entered college, one person in Murphy and Gilligan's study answered that as a result of trying to get his beliefs into practice he had become

> more considerate, taking into account other people's feelings and other people's lives and how you as a person affect their lives. And seeing whether your effect is a good effect or a bad effect. And before, I didn't really care

about that too much. My first responsibility was mainly to myself, and the other just went along. (Murphy & Gilligan, 1980, p. 99)

Another criticism of Kohlberg's research that was discussed in Chapter 7 is the way in which women have been described as functioning at a lower level of moral reasoning based on research studies using Kohlberg's scoring system. The issue of gender bias in assessing moral reasoning has been raised by Carol Gilligan (1982). She argues that Kohlberg's theory is focused on concepts of justice and not on concepts of care. Men and women define morality using different perspectives. Women more often than men resolve moral dilemmas by seeking a solution that deals with the social relationships of the people involved. Men, on the other hand, are more likely to seek a "just" solution. For example, in the Heinz dilemma, high-scoring women are more likely to emphasize Heinz's responsibility for his wife's care (Stage-4 reasoning), whereas high-scoring men are likely to emphasize the value of human life over money (Stage-6 reasoning). The problem is not so much with Kohlberg's theory as with the dilemmas that are presented to assess moral reasoning. When women are presented with a dilemma that pits justice against caring, they more often focus on caring. When other dilemmas are used that are centered on justice alone, they reason on the basis of justice.

Although controversy continues to surround the nature and origin of Kohlberg's advanced moral stages, it is generally agreed that while postconventional morality may *begin* to develop during late adolescence, it is not until adulthood—when people have finally attained the freedom to make their own life choices and have begun to assume responsibility for others—that this higher form of moral thought is established. According to Kohlberg (1973), "while cognitive awareness of principles develops in adolescence, commitment to their ethical use develops only in adulthood." It is then that people make serious commitments—to themselves, to others, to ideas, and to ideologies.

Personality and Adjustment

In the past, adult personality development has been an issue that has not commanded as much research attention as personality development in childhood and adolescence. However, adults continue to grow and change throughout the lifespan. The nature of these changes varies depending on the experiences and life events that occur and on the individual's personality. For example, people who are more extroverted (that is assertive, positive, outgoing) are more likely to be satisfied with their lives regardless of the life events or age (Costa & McCrae, 1984).

As more researchers adopted a lifespan perspective and turned their attentions to adulthood, several questions about adult personality development have emerged: Are there predictable changes in adult development over the lifespan? Is there a set order for these life changes? How important are life events in the development of adult personality?

Developmental Tasks of Early Adulthood

Based on a study of 524 men and women, Roger Gould (1978) proposed seven developmental stages in adult life. The first stage occurs in adolescence and centers around teenagers' desire to escape parental control. The second

Table 11.3 ■■■■■■■■■

Gould's Developmental Stages of Adult Life

Stage	Approximate Age	Developmental Tasks
1	16–18	Desire to escape parental control
2	18–22	Leave family, establish peer-group relationships
3	22–28	Develop independence Commit self to career and family
4	28–34	Transitional questioning of life goals, reevaluation of marriage and career commitments
5	35–43	Urgent awareness of time running out; realignment of life goals
6	43–53	Settling down, acceptance of one's life
7	53–60	Acceptance of past, greater tolerance; general mellowing

Source: R. Gould. *Transformations: Growth and change in adult life.* New York: Simon & Schuster, 1978.

developmental change occurs around the ages 18–22 and involves leaving the family and establishing a peer-group orientation. Between the ages of 22 to 28, Gould's third stage, young adults are developing their independence by making commitments to careers and family. In the fourth stage (ages 29 to 34), adults question their roles in life and in their marriage and career goals. By the mid-thirties, yet another transformation occurs—the awareness that time is running out and the need to realign life goals. The sixth stage occurring between the early forties and fifties is a settling-down time when people accept their lives as they live them. Finally, the last stage that Gould proposed, though certainly not the end of one's life, occurs between 53 and 60 years of age. At this stage, Gould describes adults as having more tolerance and acceptance of things past; they mellow. Gould's stages of adulthood (or more correctly, early and middle adulthood) are based on clinical observations and questionnaire data and provide a broad description of changes that occur as people consider themselves within the contexts of their changing life circumstances. (See Table 11.3.)

Another view of adult developmental tasks is presented by Daniel Levinson (1978, 1986). In his book *Seasons of a Man's Life* (1978), Levinson reported on the results of his study of 40 men and the changes they went through. Levinson suggests that each adult at selected points in life creates a

Era of late adulthood: 60–?

Era of middle
adulthood: 40–65

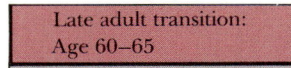

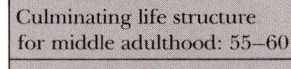

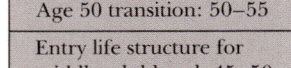

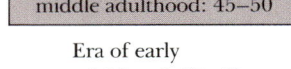

| Late adult transition:
Age 60–65 |
| Culminating life structure
for middle adulthood: 55–60 |
| Age 50 transition: 50–55 |
| Entry life structure for
middle adulthood: 45–50 |

Era of early
adulthood: 17–45

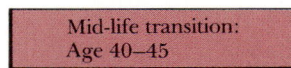

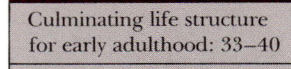

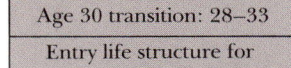

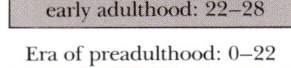

| Mid-life transition:
Age 40–45 |
| Culminating life structure
for early adulthood: 33–40 |
| Age 30 transition: 28–33 |
| Entry life structure for
early adulthood: 22–28 |

Era of preadulthood: 0–22

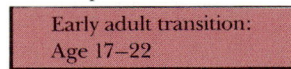

| Early adult transition:
Age 17–22 |

Figure 11.2 Developmental periods in the eras of early and middle adulthood.

Life Event   A personal experience that requires a significant change in the ongoing life pattern (e.g., divorce, death of parents, serious illness, etc.).

life structure made up of a combination of interrelated social and occupational roles that are adapted to the individual's personality and skills. The life structure is the person's pattern or life design. It is the answer to the question "What is my life like now?" Because life circumstances change, our life structure is not always stable. In different periods in people's lives their life structure is in a state of transition. (See Figure 11.2.) The period of early adulthood is embraced by a series of developmental periods leading to the mid-life transition. The first three periods of early adulthood, from roughly 17 to 33, Levinson (1986) refers to as the novice phase because they provide an opportunity to build a life structure that may not be suitable throughout life, but will move people out of adolescence. The Early Adult Transition is the bridge between preadulthood and adulthood. The Entry Life Structure for Early Adulthood is the time when people establish their initial way of living (e.g., they get married or remain single, choose a career, a geographical location to live). During the Age 30 Transition people get a chance to reappraise their earlier life and plan and modify it (e.g., switch jobs, opt to get married, have children, buy a house). The last early-adulthood period in Levinson's scheme is called the Culminating Life Structure for Early Adulthood. It is at this point that adults seek to realize the goals and dreams they established in their early twenties. The Mid-life Transition is the great divide between early adulthood and middle age. At this point, a person may be in search of a better life structure than the one used in earlier years. Levinson does not describe what is a "normal" or "appropriate" life structure; he doesn't believe that one period is more advanced than another. Instead, Levinson's periods represent the developmental tasks that everyone must work on in successive periods of their lives.

Life Events and Adjustment

Another way of looking at adult development and adjustment is to examine the way in which people confront and deal with important life events. Hultsch and Plemons (1979) have argued that particular life events and transitions underlie many of the behavioral changes and adjustment patterns that commonly are found among adults.

What is a **life event?** At the most general level, it is any experience that is deemed noteworthy or significant by the individual. More specifically, however, it is an event "whose advent is either indicative of or requires a significant change in the ongoing life pattern of the individual" (Holmes & Masuda, 1974, p. 46). Some life events are experienced by virtually all adults in our society—for example, entrance into the world of work, or illness in a family member; other events, however, are experienced only by certain people—for example, the death of one's child, imprisonment, or chronic unemployment.

Within this perspective, all life events are viewed as potentially stressful, and hence, require some adaptation on the part of the individual. Certainly, this makes sense when one is talking about such experiences as death of a spouse, divorce, loss of a job, and so on. However, life-event theory suggests that even experiences generally regarded as positive—for example, marriage, birth of a child, and job promotion—can be stress inducing, and thereby require some psychosocial adaptation. Nevertheless, the more personally cata-

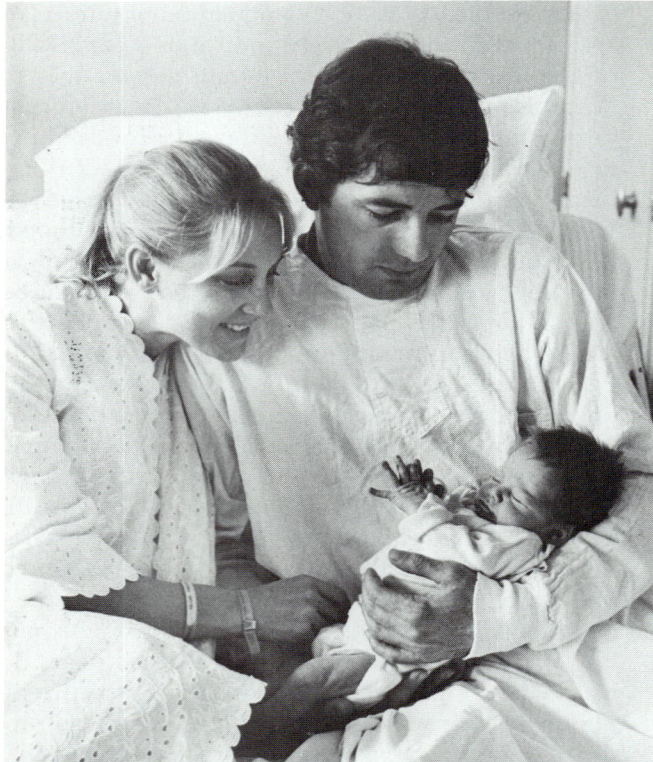

Life events such as the birth of a child require some adaptation and can be stressful to some individuals.

strophic the event, the greater the stress and the need for readjustment by the individual.

In young adulthood, the individual is confronted with a number of important life events and developmental transitions. The more common ones—some of which we will discuss in this chapter as well as in Chapter 12—include the development of intimacy relationships, leaving the nuclear family, marriage, pregnancy, birth of a child, divorce, entrance into the job market, change in financial status, change in social activities, and so on. Lowenthal, Thurnher, and Chiriboga (1975) found that although young adults generally report exposure to more life events than middle-aged and older adults, they also report more positive stresses than the other two groups, whereas the latter report more negative ones. These researchers also found that the greatest stresses in the life of youth and young adults were in the areas of education, dating and marriage, and changes in residence. Lowenthal and his colleagues point out, however, that the mere occurrence of an event is not the critical factor in determining the impact of the event on the person. What appears to be more important is the person's *perception* of the event. Two individuals can be exposed to the same high level of stress and yet experience the event differently. These investigators found that individuals who are exposed to high stress and who perceive their lives as highly stressful are likely to feel "overwhelmed." In contrast, other adults, exposed to the same high levels of stress, but who perceive their lives as unstressful, are likely to feel "chal-

Graduation from college is an important life event for many people in their early adulthood.

lenged." These findings suggest that the stress of life events does not reside within the event *per se,* or within the individual, but is a mixture of the two (Lazarus & Launier, 1978).

Timing and Sequencing of Life Events

We have noted that youth and young adulthood are the times when people begin to adopt roles—worker, spouse, parent, and so on. People do not always adopt these roles at the same time, however. Whereas some individuals leave the nuclear family at 18, others may still live at home at 28.

Generally speaking, most people have a sense of whether they are "early," "on time," or "late" with regard to the adoption of specific adult roles. Research suggests that being off time with respect to role adoption usually is upsetting for adults (Bourque & Back, 1977; Lowenthal, Thurnher, & Chiriboga, 1975). For example, failing to achieve a promotion on the job at a time when one's peers are moving up the career ladder is likely to be experienced as stressful and personally disruptive for the individual.

The order in which people choose to do things also varies during this period. In the past, fairly rigid customs prevailed. Young women were expected to marry and bear children soon after high school—if their education even reached this far. Young men were expected to finish their education and military service, and then get a job. Only after these steps were taken, were they expected to marry and have children. Over the past few decades, however, the *timing* and *order* (or sequencing) of life events have become less clear-cut for both sexes. Do these deviations from the customary order of life events in the young-adult period make a difference in people's lives?

One researcher (Hogan, 1978) examined the order of completing schooling, taking a first job, and marrying among 33,500 men born between 1921 and 1950. Most men, it was found, followed the expected order of life events described above, although there were socioeconomic and ethnic differences in this regard. White males were less likely to follow the expected pattern because they completed their education much later than other groups of men. Black men were more likely to marry, and Hispanic men were more likely to work before finishing their education. For men who deviated from the usual order of life events, there was a higher rate of marital separation and divorce. Marital disruption was 17 percent higher among those who married before finishing school.

The effects of early and delayed childbirth have been the most frequently studied aspects of deviation from the expected life events among women. Researchers have found that 10 percent of women questioned became pregnant before finishing high school, and 40 percent of the live births to these women occurred before marriage (Green & Polleigen, 1977). One consequence of the disruption in life events for these teenage women was that 80 percent of those who gave birth to a child did not finish high school. Furthermore, it appeared that women whose education is interrupted by childbirth at any age, in general, do not make up the educational deficit later in their lives (Moore & Waite, 1977). Other research has found that if a woman marries after becoming pregnant and before school is completed, she is likely to have a greater number of children—and to have them closer together in time—and her marriage is two to three times more likely to end in divorce. At the other extreme, women who postpone their first pregnancy until after their education is completed and after they have been married a year or two, are more likely to work before the birth of their first child and to expect and get more help from their husbands (Presser, 1978; Scanzoni, 1975). (See Box, Educating for Life.)

Pause for Thought

Many of the personality and adjustment characteristics associated with a mature adult are also linked to specific social roles such as worker, parent, or spouse. People who have not accepted these roles in adulthood may be labeled by some as "immature." Do you think that the acceptance of social role should be used as a standard by which to measure individual maturity? What other ways could you use to assess adult personality development?

Identity

Youth and young adults often find themselves searching for meaning in their lives. Having tackled the basic issue of identity in adolescence and, it is hoped, having achieved some, if only temporary, resolution about self-definition, young adults are often preoccupied with the expansion of self into society, by establishing new friendships, by joining volunteer groups and social clubs,

Human Development in Practice

Educating for Life

While the aim of most high schools and postsecondary schools is to help their students prepare for a successful career or life after graduation, many do not include in their curricula courses specifically designed to help students make the transition from the classroom to real life. Many young adults and some adolescents abruptly face the challenges and changes in lifestyle when they become full-time workers or parents. Even though some of the changes that young adults experience such as a new, higher-paying job, or entry into college, ultimately lead to positive changes, many people are unprepared for their new roles and are stressed as a result. Educators are becoming more aware of the beneficial role they can play in helping young adults prepare for and adjust to some predictable life events. One life event that is both abrupt and stressful is becoming a new parent. Young adults must switch their focus of concern from themselves and each other to their new and dependent baby, oftentimes without the benefit of child-care skills and experience. Many high schools offer as part of a health or family life course, training and information on child care, parenting, and managing a household. The aim is to educate students about the adjustments they may soon have to make as they enter adulthood.

Entering college is another milestone demanding a series of personal adjustments in the use of time, money, and personal freedom. Students may enter a college or university that is many times larger and more complex in structure than their high schools. New friends must be made, courses and majors selected, and new activities established—all while students are living away from home, many for the first time. To ease this transition, colleges and universities have developed freshman seminar courses, sometimes referred to as *survival courses*. In these courses, students are oriented to the physical environment of college (e.g., Where do you go to register for classes? Where is the computer center?) and informed about the support services available to help them design and accomplish their academic goals. In the process of the seminar, students also meet other freshmen and have more direct contact with faculty. As a result, students develop a sense of belonging to their college campus and are more likely to continue their studies.

Other similar life-event transition courses are needed to help young adults meet the challenge of adulthood. Some high schools combine work experiences with classroom study. However, what students need is more explicit training in entering a job market and staying there. Teachers can be excellent role models for their students by discussing with them the challenges of finding a new job and place to live. Teachers can help their students anticipate the life events ahead of them; they can point out the importance of social supports (e.g., friends, coworkers, spouse) and can lend to their students the benefit of their own experiences. By providing students with a positive way of interpreting life events and by showing them ways of coping with these new challenges, educators can help prepare their students for life outside the classroom.

and by finding new ways of defining themselves through their interests and activities.

In youth and early adulthood, individuals begin to stabilize their identity. Especially if they are attending college, young people are likely to find themselves changing the identity they forged in adolescence (Waterman, Geary, & Waterman, 1974). As a result of challenges during the freshman year, the student may reexamine many values and self-images. A new form of identity crisis will probably occur. Whereas the adolescent asks, "Who am I?" the young adult tends to ask "Where am I going—and with whom?" Youth or early adulthood is the period in which a person tackles the question of how to find a place in society. The person begins to establish a personal lifestyle, and to make commitments, more often than not in the belief that decisions are irreversible (Sheehy, 1976)—which, of course, they are not.

Identity Statuses in Early Adulthood

As we noted in Chapter 10, Erikson (1968) described the identity crisis confronting adolescents as *ego identity*—the achievement of a relatively consistent sense of self—vs. *identity diffusion,*—the feeling of a confused sense of self resulting from being overwhelmed by role possibilities. However, Marcia (1966, 1980) has suggested that the resolution of the identity crisis in youth and young adulthood is more complex than the description offered by Erikson. Marcia has identified two factors as critical to the resolution of identity in this period: (1) the existence of a personal crisis in such areas as occupation, religion, or politics, and (2) the person's degree of commitment to issues in these areas. Marcia defines a crisis as a time when a person is confronted with several meaningful alternatives in life and must choose one.

Combining these two factors, crisis and commitment, Marcia created four resolution patterns of the identity crisis that he termed **identity statuses. Identity achievers** are individuals who have experienced crises in some area of their life (e.g., occupational, religious, and political areas) and have reached a personal decision or commitment. Their choice may or may not agree with their parents' desires and viewpoints. Rather their commitment is based on a true decision-making process and not parental wishes. In contrast, individuals who are characterized by **identity foreclosure,** while also making lifestyle and value decisions, do so without experiencing a crisis and without making a personal-value commitment. These individuals give in to parental desires and points of view either out of emotional or financial pressure, fear of disapproval, or feelings of inadequacy and incompetence. For example, consider the young man who enters the family business because "it is expected of him." Marcia believes that although such individuals may appear to have strong ideological and career commitments, they actually lack a strong ego identity because they have avoided personal confrontation and crisis in these areas.

Individuals categorized as in **moratorium** or as being **identity diffuse,** unlike identity achievers and foreclosures, show no evidence of commitment. On the contrary, they are indecisive about life decisions and values. Individuals in moratorium, in contrast with identity-diffuse individuals, are, however, at the height of crisis about these issues. They are struggling to achieve a degree of consistency about who they are and where they are going. Peter, the young man in our opening example, may be described as being in moratorium since he is still struggling with the question of who he is and where he is going with his life. Identity-diffuse individuals appear less concerned or preoccupied with these issues; not only are they uncommitted to specific lifestyles or values, but they also show no evidence of personal crisis with respect to these issues. (See Table 11.4.)

Developmental Aspects of Adult Identity

One problem with categorizing people into any classification system—including Marcia's ego-identity statuses—is that it tends to foster a rigid, unchanging view of people. Of course, this is not the nature of human beings, nor

Identity Status   According to Marcia, the specific resolution pattern the person adopts in handling issues of crisis and commitment in areas of identity.

Identity Achiever   According to Marcia, the individual who has confronted various crises in life and who has made firm commitments to values, ideals, life patterns, and so on.

Identity Foreclosure According to Marcia, an identity status characterized by avoidance of personal crisis by identifying with the values and ideals of parents and other significant figures.

Moratorium   According to Marcia, an identity status characterized by heightened personal crisis but no firm commitment with regard to specific values, ideals, life pattern, etc.

Identity Diffuse   According to Marcia, a type of individual who has avoided personal crisis in areas of identity and who shows no firm commitment to specific values, ideals, etc.

Table 11.4 ▰▰▰▰▰▰

Marcia's Adult Identity Statuses

	Crisis	*No Crisis*
Commitment	Identity Achievers	Foreclosure
No Commitment	Moratorium	Identity Diffuse

is it the way in which Marcia intended the construct of ego identity to be interpreted.

Alan Waterman (1982) has presented a model that describes the *pattern* of ego-identity development (Figure 11.3). His model suggests that people begin their development of identity in a state of diffuseness and confusion. Individuals can either remain in a diffuse state, or move forward in one of two directions. One possibility is for people to latch on to an identity suggested by parents or other significant figures without really considering other courses of action—in other words, a foreclosure pattern. Bob, for example, may take over management of one of his father's used-car lots, and Sharon may enter medicine—both at the suggestion and direction of their parents and without consideration of other career choices. A second possibility is for these individuals to begin to consider a number of alternative life paths and consequently to enter a state of moratorium while they search and explore further goals.

People who adopt a foreclosure pattern either can maintain this identity status as they move into adulthood, or they can change in one of two ways. Should their earlier commitments suddenly become challenged by life events,

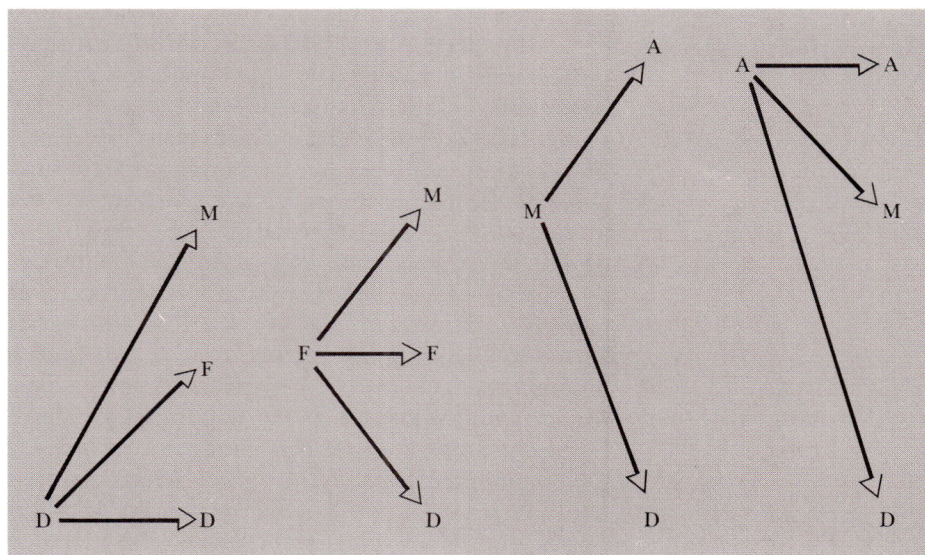

Figure 11.3 A model of the sequential patterns of ego identity development. (D = identity diffusion; F = foreclosure; M = moratorium; A = identity achievement.)

and consequently lead them to consider alternative values and lifestyles, these individuals would then move into a state of moratorium. Should Bob discover that selling cars is unrewarding or should Sharon become disenchanted with medicine, they could begin to seriously consider other life options, thereby moving toward greater personal crisis, or in other words, a state of moratorium. On the other hand, should the challenge to previous commitments by life events not lead to an active consideration of alternative life paths, the individual would then regress to a diffuse state of identity. In this state, people remain indecisive about what it is they want to do with their lives.

Having reached the level of moratorium—where one is clearly in crisis over life commitments—two patterns of identity adjustment are seen as being possible. The more beneficial one involves the transition from a state of moratorium to a state of identity achievement, where people have settled on specific identity commitments based on their personal evaluation of the many options open to them. In the example, Bob may decide, after much consideration, to return to school to prepare for a career in auto-design engineering. Similarly, Sharon may decide that greater challenges and rewards await her as a teacher of medicine rather than as a practitioner. The second, less desirable, transition from the moratorium level involves a regression to a state of diffuseness as a result of not being able to find something worthwhile to commit oneself to.

Finally, Waterman (1982) suggests that having reached the state of identity achievement, the individual still has several paths that future ego identity can take. As long as the person's commitments remain satisfying and firm, it is likely that a pattern of identity achievement will be maintained. However, should the person's values and lifestyle be challenged by life events, it is likely that he or she will regress to either a state of moratorium, where alternative courses of action are reconsidered, or, in rarer cases, to a state of diffuseness, where no life alternatives seem worthwhile.

The way in which the environment can foster development of identity in young adults is highlighted in a study in which researchers examined the influence of the psychological climate within different types of academic departments on the identity development of college-age students (Adams & Fitch, 1983). Eight different university departments including business administration, engineering, elementary education, art, psychology, family and child development, forestry, and outdoor recreation were rated by students in terms of the degree to which the department atmosphere (including its organization, curricula, and philosophy) emphasized such issues or characteristics as practicality, community or group welfare, awareness of societal concerns, propriety or conventional standards, and scholarship. Measures of ego identity and ego functioning were also collected. The researchers found, among other things, that the general atmosphere of the university department can play an important role in fostering ego identity. Departments emphasizing an awareness of societal issues were significantly more likely to facilitate development of ego identity than were departments characterized by other qualities. In commenting on this result, Adams and Fitch note that a focus on societal issues tends to broaden one's perspective and foster exploration of one's current thoughts and ideas. In other words, it creates conflict and challenges the individual's conceptions of self—exactly the type of situation Marcia suggests is the basis of identity development.

It is clear that as people enter into adulthood they show considerable variation in identity development: Some remain diffuse; others move into a foreclosure or a moratorium pattern; and still others continue forward to achieve a firm and personally created sense of self. In turn, these individual differences in identity are reflected in differences in personality and adjustment. Adult identity must be thought of as a lifelong *process*—an everchanging aspect of the human being that is responsible to, and reflects the unique experiences of one's life.

Pause for Thought

Many college freshmen believe they will never change their academic major. Yet, many do in fact change their minds about their career goals especially when they have had some exposure to new ideas. Based on Marcia's and Waterman's ideas about identity, can you offer a convincing argument for allowing college students a year or two of study *before* they select their academic major?

Intimacy

Intimacy   According to Erikson, a critical psychosocial achievement for young adults; a relationship quality characterized by warmth, mutuality of feeling, and deep commitment.

From the beginning of life, intimacy—physical and emotional—is critical to development. Infants and their mothers, the junior-high-school girl and her best girl friend, the Little Leaguer and his dad, are examples of intimate relationships that occur in the course of development. In the early adult period, however, a new kind of **intimacy** becomes possible. This is the intimacy freely chosen by two equal persons who have worked through the adolescent crises and know basically who they are.

Erikson theorized that the ability to become intimate with another—the central psychosocial task for the young adult in his theoretical model—awaits the resolution of the identity crisis during adolescence. In other words, it is only after one achieves a sense of identity that it becomes safe to risk fusing this identity with that of another person.

Researchers who have undertaken to measure ego identity and intimacy variables have largely substantiated this hypothesis, at least for males. For females, in contrast, the relationship between identity and intimacy may be more complex. As Marcia (1980) notes, identity in females is closely tied to interpersonal areas—that is, to areas promoting intimacy. Thus, whereas males may be likely to develop a sense of identity in areas of achievement and then transfer this identity to interpersonal areas, for females, the development of identity and intimacy may develop in a more concurrent fashion (Gilligan, 1982).

Intimacy and Attachment

According to some developmental psychologists, the foundation of adult intimacy can be traced to the early attachment bonds between infants and other human beings, particularly their parents (Troll & Smith, 1976). For some individuals, these early socioemotional relationships produce a sense of security, trust, and the desire to be close to others; other individuals become frustrated and insecure, providing the seed for later problems in forming mature relationships based on respect and mutuality.

Attachment is a lifelong process influencing the frequency and quality of all interpersonal relationships—both sexual and nonsexual (Bowlby, 1969). Some researchers have even suggested that when we become attached to groups, ideas, or objects, the critical factor in all of these examples is a strong emotional involvement (Kalish & Knudtson, 1976).

While attachment is a pervasive and enduring process throughout life, the nature and object of our attachments change with age. In earlier chapters, we have noted examples of attachment among family members and peers and the emergence of tentative, heterosexual attachments in adolescence. In young adulthood, new forms of attachment develop—to spouse, children, job. These attachments, some strong and others weak, are the bonds of adult life— the bonds by which people find meaning in their lives.

Sexual Intimacy

Before the resolution of the identity crisis, attempts at sexual intimacy are usually of the searching, self-serving kind in which something is given or someone is reassured. Sexual relationships are not likely to develop into deep personal commitments, especially since the individuals do not have a clear idea of themselves, let alone their sexual partners.

By contrast, the intimacy of early adulthood is characterized by *mutuality;* ideally, one cares for the other person as much as one cares for oneself. Mutuality entails the willingness to make sacrifices and compromises. It involves mature sexual functioning in genital love, which as defined by Erikson, involves choosing a partner with whom one is willing to work, play, and establish a family. In these sexually intimate relationships, individuals experience a desire to make lifelong commitments. For example, couples may decide to have children as a natural extension of their mutual care and affection for one another.

Naturally, researchers have been interested in determining when young people achieve mature sexual intimacy, and what variables affect the outcome. It does seem that the potential for mature sexuality occurs for most people in young adulthood rather than during adolescence. And yet, although most people begin to establish sexual relationships in early adulthood, not everyone experiences sexual intimacy. Sexual union can be the all-encompassing development described by Erikson, or, reduced to its most common denominator, it may become "the joining of separate almost disembodied anatomical parts" (Masters & Johnson, 1975). It appears that the outcome of the identity crisis and the resulting strength of the ego influence the quality of sexual intimacy.

In one study, college students who scored high on ego identity were found to score high on intimacy as well. These students were able to share worries, and express anger as well as affection toward their partners (Orlofsky, Marcia, & Lesser, 1973). On the other hand, students who scored low on identity measures were shown to have developed alternatives to intimacy—"stereotyped" relationships, or relationships characterized as "pseudointimate."

In *stereotyped* relationships, the partner is treated more or less as a sexual object, and the person seeks not intimacy, but sex for its own sake. In *pseudointimate* relationships the commitment is usually more permanent. The couple look and behave like partners, but the relationship is largely based on convenience. A woman may couple with a man because he provides status; the man may couple with a woman because she bolsters his ego. On the emotional level, however, the couple hardly communicates. A typical statement of the pseudointimate partner is, "My partner meets my needs and doesn't make demands on me, so why should I complain?"

The opposite of intimacy in Erikson's model is **isolation.** Some young people isolate themselves from close personal or sexual relationships with others. In some cases, this is an indication of emotional disturbance. For example, a man may have been so psychologically damaged by a parent's having abandoned him that he is unable to engage in satisfactory interpersonal relationships. In another case, a woman may be in a state of identity moratorium. Problems involved in breaking free of parents or choosing a career may leave her with little energy or desire to get involved with another person, either in a sexual or nonsexual relationship.

While people may desire sexual intimacy, not everyone is comfortable with the idea of engaging in sexual intercourse as a means of establishing intimacy. With fears of catching AIDS or other sexually transmitted diseases at an all-time high, many adults are cautious about starting a sexual relationship before they have an established relationship.

Isolation   According to Erikson, a feeling that one is disconnected from others, empty, and abandoned; this quality often develops in the absence of true, intimate relationships.

Pause for Thought

Sexual behavior, including intimacy, is influenced by cultural values and customs. In the United States, adults are exposed to many examples of sexual behavior in films, novels, and magazines. Judging from these examples, what kind of conclusion might a foreign-born adult make about the value of sexual behavior in our culture?

Nonsexual Intimacy

Intimacy in heterosexual love relationships is not the only kind of intimacy that is first achieved in early adulthood. New relationships with peers and elders become possible in response to what White (1975) calls the "freeing of relationships" from childhood expectations. Adults are no longer perceived in terms of parental stereotypes, but are appreciated as people in their own right. "For the first time," says a returning college student, "I was able to talk to my mother and my older brother as if they were real people—or friends." In large part, this is because in young adulthood people begin to have experiences that they can truly share with their parents—getting married, obtaining a job, buying a house, creating a family, and so on. These are experiences that are common to all adults and consequently they serve to bring the generations closer.

"Psychological apprenticeships" to older people may be formed during this period (Keniston, 1970). At work or in college and graduate school, *mentors*—teachers, advisers, or "parental figures" who may be eight to 15 years older than the young person—become important (Levinson, Darrow, Klein, Levinson, & McKee, 1977). Finally, the quality of friendship changes. Whereas adolescents tend to choose friends who remind them of themselves or what they want to be, young adults choose people for their own sakes; that is, they respect individual differences (Vaillant, 1977).

Summary

Adult development is influenced by age-normative events, non-normative events, and historical events. The impact of these influences varies across the lifespan.

Early adulthood is a time of greater diversity than earlier stages. Some young adults are students, some are already parents, some hold jobs, some live with their parents, some live alone. Because many positions in modern society require extended preparation, young adults may stay in school or live at home until their late twenties. *Youth* is the term used to cover the time between age 18 and that time when individuals adopt adult commitments, identities, and lifestyles.

In early adulthood, people are at their biological and physiological, peak in terms of speed, coordination, strength, endurance, and health. For women, early adulthood is the best biological time to bear children. The ability to perform cognitive tasks that require quick response time, short-term memory, and perception in complex relations is at its sharpest.

Recent work suggests that Piaget's period of formal operations (the period characterized by hypothetical reasoning and abstract thought) may not develop until late adolescence and is expressed more narrowly than was first supposed. Some investigators have speculated on the existence of a cognitive stage beyond formal operations. Although there is no consensus on the nature of this so-called *postformal stage,* three characteristics of thought have frequently been identified with it: Thinking is relativistic; contradiction is seen as an inherent aspect of reality; and contradictory knowledge is integrated into higher-order, more inclusive systems of knowledge.

Adults consider the context and practical real-life implications of an event. Based on their experiences, adults may interpret situations differently.

Moral development requires both cognitive development and personal experience to foster its growth. In youth and young adulthood, challenges to one's values and ideology, as well as resolution of identity issues, are likely to influence moral reasoning and behavior.

Criticisms of Kohlberg's theory have been directed at the way in which women's moral development is assessed and at the way postconventional morality ignores the use of multiple perspectives in resolving moral dilemmas.

Personality development in adulthood is affected by the accomplishment of specific developmental tasks. Developmental tasks or stages have been presented by Havighurst, Erikson, Gould, and Levinson.

Patterns of adjustment in young adulthood are influenced by the type of events people encounter during this time. Life-event theory suggests that both positive (e.g., marriage) and negative (e.g., divorce) life events are potentially stressful and require readjustment by the person. The timing and order of experiencing life events vary from one person to another, which, in turn, makes a difference in the subsequent life of the individual.

A major question for young adults is how they are to relate to society — where do they fit in, and what roles will they adopt? These are issues that are closely tied to the stabilization of ego identity. Marcia proposes four separate identity statuses in youth and young adulthood—identity achiever, identity foreclosure, moratorium, and identity diffuse. Identity is an ever-changing quality that is sensitive to the many experiences confronting people in their lives.

Once people have established their own identities, a new kind of intimacy becomes possible, an adult intimacy based on mutuality. In Erikson's model, the opposite of intimacy is isolation. People may isolate themselves from close friendships and contacts, either because of some emotional disturbance or because they are in a moratorium state. Intimacy in nonsexual as well as sexual relationships can be fully realized at this time of life.

Further Readings

Fries, J., and Crapo, L. *Vitality and aging.* San Francisco: Freeman, 1981.
Written by two physicians at the Stanford University School of Medicine, this highly readable book offers an optimistic view of human aging. The authors believe that disease and death can be postponed so that people can live a vital life up until the time they die.

Keniston, K. Youth: A new stage of life. *The American Scholar*, Autumn 1970, 631–654.
Keniston explores the many societal factors that have fostered the emergence of a youth culture. He describes the unique characteristics and developmental tasks associated with this stage of life.

McCrae, R., and Costa, P. *Emerging lives, enduring dispositions: Personality in adulthood.* Boston: Little Brown, 1984.
The results of numerous longitudinal studies of personality, including the Baltimore Longitudinal Study of Aging, are used to support the conclusion that adult personality is basically stable across the lifespan. Special attention is paid to the NEO model of personality traits: neuroticism, extroversion, and openness facets.

Rubin, Z. *Liking and loving.* New York: Holt, Rinehart and Winston, 1973.
A description of the process of interpersonal attraction and the many variables that influence it. Rubin, a social psychologist, examines how people are drawn together, court, and eventually make commitments to one another to create a family unit.

Scanlon, J. *Young adulthood.* New York: Academy for Education and Development, 1979.
This is a summary of the Third Annual Conference on Major Transitions in the Human Life Cycle. Scanlon provides the reader with an overview of the biological, psychological, occupational, and lifestyle changes that are common in young adulthood.

Yankelovich, D. *The new morality: A profile of American youth in the 70s.* New York: McGraw-Hill, 1974.
Yankelovich, a public-opinion expert, compares a survey of young people polled in 1967 with one in 1972. One of his findings was that although the teenagers of the 1970s still rated interesting work highly, they had become more concerned about money and security.

Observational Activities

11.1 *The Meaning of Adulthood*

People have different conceptions of adulthood. For some people, being an adult means being self-supporting. For others, perceived age or how they feel influences their definition of adulthood. Accomplishing certain life events such as getting a job or getting married is a signal of adulthood.

To gain a more detailed understanding of the way people define adulthood, interview 10 young adults between the ages of 20 and 30. Be sure to select a varied sample of people—male and female, college students and those who do not attend college, married and single people. Interview your respondents individually and ask them the following questions.

1. What does it mean to be an adult? What do you consider to be important characteristics of adults?
2. Are there certain roles or behaviors that are generally expected of adults?
3. Consider the following life events: getting a job, getting married, moving out of your parents' home, starting a family, completing your education, and buying your own house. At what age do you think a person should best accomplish these different events? In what order should one complete them?
4. Are there times when you feel like an adult and other times when you don't? Explain.

Before you interview the people you have selected, ask yourself these questions. Then, when you have completed the interviews, compile your findings and summarize them. Are there differences between men and women in their definitions and expectations of adulthood? Do college students differ from noncollege students in their responses? Are there differences in responses between the married and single people? What other differences can you identify? How do your own answers compare with your respondents' answers? What did you gain from this activity?

11.2 *The Development of Intimacy*

According to Erikson, young adulthood is the time in which people strive to develop an intimate relationship with another person. Some young adults are successful in achieving interpersonal intimacy; others are not. To better understand what characteristics exemplify an intimate relationship, interview eight to 10 young adults between 20 and 30 years of age. Be sure to interview both men and women. Interview these people individually and ask them these questions.

1. Do you believe you have achieved an intimate relationship with another person?
2. In what sense is the relationship intimate? How would you define intimacy? How do you know when an intimate relationship has been achieved?
3. What experiences have you had that facilitated or inhibited the growth of intimacy in your interpersonal relationships?

Compile the responses to these questions and compare them with the responses collected by your classmates. Do men and women differ in their level of intimacy? Do they perceive intimacy to be characterized by the same type of qualities? Describe the different kinds of experiences reported by these people that affected their development of intimacy patterns. How do the results of this survey compare with the information in the text?

Early Adulthood: Family and Occupational Development

*I*t had been five years since Kate and her first husband Tim ended their four-year marriage. High-school sweethearts, they seemed to drift apart as they grew older and developed different interests. Their divorce was not complicated by children or property. Still, the process of ending their relationship was a stressful time for Kate. Her parents and brother and sister were a source of support to Kate as she established a new life for herself as a single woman. She went back to school and completed her nurse's training. She dated, and eventually met and fell in love with Michael. Even though her parents held different values, they did not interfere or object when Michael and Kate began living together. In fact, when Kate and Michael got married, they held the informal wedding party at Kate's parents' home.

Now that Kate was 30 years old, she was eager to have a child. She was physically and emotionally ready to devote her energies to the care of their baby. She looked forward to sharing the experience of childbirth with Michael and to the challenge of parenting. Coming from a large family, she had many opportunities to watch adults care for children. Now she wanted to establish her own family.

Michael equally was looking forward to starting a family. Now that his contracting business was well established, he felt confident that he could support Kate and the baby. Both agreed that it would be best for their baby if Kate took a leave of absence during the early months after the baby's birth. Michael looked forward to sharing with Kate the responsibility and delight of caring for their child. He looked forward to teaching his son or daughter how to fish and how to build a birdhouse. He was eager to demonstrate to himself and others that he was a good father and breadwinner.

Even though Kate and Michael were confident in their decision to have a child, they did have some concerns. Having a child would mean that they would have to change the way they related to each other. They would not have as much time alone with each other. Would this change affect their love for one another? Kate had enjoyed the stimulation and challenge from her job as a nurse. Would being a full-time mother prove as satisfying to her? How would Michael react to the new demands on his time? What would happen when they did not agree on how to raise their child? These were the concerns they talked about as they made their decision. By expressing their worries to each other, Kate and Michael were able to plan more realistically for the birth of their child and a change in their lifestyle.

Early adulthood is the time when people begin to make commitments in personal relationships and on the job. By contributing to the care of others, young adults like Kate and Michael also broaden their view of themselves. In this chapter, we will discuss the different ways in which young adults develop by establishing families and by becoming active and contributing members of a community. We begin with a discussion of family life, including the nature and function of families in today's society, the processes of mate selection and courtship, and the various factors related to marital adjustment. Next, we focus on divorce and various nonmarital lifestyles found among young adults. Following this discussion, we take up the issue of parenthood and the way in which it affects marital life. Finally, the chapter ends with an examination of occupational development during young adulthood.

Family Life

From the moment we are born we encounter the most popular and enduring of all the social groupings known—the family. Although the specific nature and function of families may vary from culture to culture, from generation to generation, and from family to family, the significance and importance of belonging to a family increases throughout the lifespan. As people reach adult status, they become more aware of the role that families play in personal development.

In childhood and adolescence we were the *objects* or recipients of the care, direction, and instruction from our parents and older family members; in early adulthood, however, we become the *agents* of socialization and the caregivers to our own and other people's children. As people leave their family of origin and establish their own nuclear families, they perpetuate a process that began hundreds of years ago—the *family life cycle*. For most people the knowledge that they are participating in this cycle of life is reassuring and inspiring. One of the warmest wishes to a newly married couple is that they live to see their children's children marry and continue the family tradition they hope to set into motion by marrying.

Family Life Cycle

Just as people change and develop as they age, families undergo changes across the lifespan. The lifespan of families is a bit more difficult to delineate. An individual's lifespan begins at birth and ends at death. The family life cycle begins with marriage and ends when the surviving spouse dies. At this point, another second- or third-generation family may have been established.

In the past two decades or so, an increasing number of psychologists, sociologists, and demographers have begun to look at families from a *developmental* or *life-cycle* perspective. Basic to this perspective is the assumption that family life can be characterized as a series of stages, each with its unique developmental tasks and conflicts to be confronted and resolved (Nock, 1982). The **family life cycle** begins, of course, with marriage; it ends with the process of bereavement of the surviving spouse. Between these points are a series of stages — the exact number of which varies according to the theorist—describing different family structural patterns, role expectations, and life events that challenge family members and demand new patterns of coping from all of them.

Family Life Cycle
Beginning with marriage and ending with the death of the surviving spouse, the changes in growth and development that mark the life of the family.

Family Life Cycle Models

Evelyn Duvall (1977) was an early proponent of the family life-cycle perspective. Her eight-stage model (see Table 12.1) is based on changes in the size and composition of families as well as on changes in the social roles. The

Table 12.1 ■■■■■

Duvall's Family Life Cycle, by Length of Time in Each of Eight Stages.

Stage

I.	Married couples (without children)
II.	Childbearing families (oldest child, birth–30 months)
III.	Families with preschool children (oldest child 30 months–6 years)
IV.	Families with school children (oldest child 6–13 years)
V.	Families with teenagers (oldest child 13–20 years)
VI.	Families launching young adults (first child gone to last child leaving home)
VII.	Middle-aged parents (empty nest to retirement)
VIII.	Aging family members (retirement to death of both spouses)

Source: Based upon data from the U.S. Bureau of the Census and from the National Center for Health Statistics, Washington, DC. Adapted from E. M. Duvall, *Marriage and family development* (5th ed.) Philadelphia: J. B. Lippincott, 1977, p. 148. Copyright 1977. Reprinted by permission of the publishers, J. B. Lippincott Company.

amount of time spent in each of the stages will depend upon the age at which parents have children. Thus, if a couple have their first child when they are in their late twenties, they would be in stages II to IV during their early adulthood years. A couple who postpones having children may spend six or seven years without children and this will affect the rest of the cycle; for example, the "empty nest to retirement" stage will be shorter. Duvall's model is based on the assumption that changes in the life of the oldest child profoundly affect the entire family as members adjust to new experiences such as a child entering school or a teenager gaining new independence. In resting her model on this assumption, Duvall ignores the impact that other children have on family life.

It is worth noting, too, that although we tend to picture families as young adults with young children (the kind of group attractively portrayed in advertisements), the amount of time people spend in the first three stages of family life is relatively small—no more than a dozen out of a total of perhaps 50 years (Duvall, 1977). Almost half of the family life cycle occurs after the children are gone. Thus, adjustments, such as how a person uses leisure time, worked out in the young-adult period are not necessarily appropriate for later periods.

A more widely used family life-cycle model has been developed by Reuben Hill (1964). Hill's nine-stage model (see Table 12.2) is broader in scope than Duvall's because it incorporates into its stages the presence of children other than just the oldest one in the family. Hill also acknowledges the importance of changes in the role of the breadwinner in Stages VIII and IX; however, his focus is restricted to the father and excludes any employment by the mother.

Limitations of Family Life-Cycle Models
Although the usefulness of family life-cycle models has been demonstrated by developmental psychologists, sociologists, and historians (Vinovskis, 1988), they have been criticized by some because of their limited scope and for their

Table 12.2

Hill's Model of the Family Life Cycle

Stage	
I.	Establishment (newly married, childless)
II.	New parents (infant–3 years)
III.	Preschool family (child 3–6, and possibly younger siblings)
IV.	School-age family (oldest child 6–12, possibly younger siblings)
V.	Family with adolescent (oldest 13–19, possibly younger siblings)
VI.	Family with young adult (oldest 20 until first child leaves home)
VII.	Family as launching center (from departure of first to last child)
VIII.	Postparental family, the middle years (after children have left home until father retires)
IX.	Aging family (after retirement of father)

inability to capture the dynamic quality of family life. While the models are useful for describing changes in traditional families through the life cycle, they fail to take into account the considerable proportion of people who divorce or are widowed, who remarry, or who have a second family. Many of these people will spend some years as single parents or may bring up children not their own.

Another limitation is that the models fail to acknowledge the overlap and interaction of family life cycles across generations. For example, a family composed of a young couple with preschool children would be classified as being in Stage 3 within Duvall's model. At the same time, however, these individuals remain part of a different family as children of their own middle-aged or aging parents, and thus can be classified as being in Stage 7 or 8 (depending on whether their parents are retired or not) with respect to their family-of-origin life cycle. Thus, the impact of life-cycle events on people must be viewed within the broader perspective of **intergenerational relations**—that is, the relations between members of a family from different generations. In other words, to understand the development and adjustment of the adult at any particular life-cycle phase, one must understand the "fit" between the expectations and experiences a person has derived from the family of origin and those derived from his or her current nuclear family. We will have more to say about intergenerational relations in Chapter 14.

Intergenerational Relations The relations between members of a family from different generations.

Pause for Thought

The family life-cycle model is useful to historians who study characteristics of family life in the past; the model helps them organize and analyze the data collected from historical documents. What other fields or disciplines might benefit by using the family life-cycle perspective?

Nature and Function of the Family

Exactly what is a family, and what role does it play in the lives of parents and children? Although the answer to these questions may seem rather obvious

The structure of families can vary from a small three-member family to a large family made up of several generations.

at first, thoughtful consideration will reveal their complexity. To begin with, families can be defined either structurally or functionally. *Structural* definitions focus on the pattern of organization that characterizes this societal unit. Specifying who the family members are and how they are related to one another would constitute a structural approach to understanding families. By contrast, a *functional* definition of the family focuses more on family activities and on the role the family plays in the lives of its members (Garrett, 1982).

Although most families are formed initially in the usual way—that is, a man and woman marry and subsequently conceive and bear children—the stability of this family unit is becoming increasingly shaky. Norton and Moorman (1987) report that young people today are marrying at a later stage in early adulthood. Furthermore, they project that about 56 percent of all women will end their first marriage in divorce. Separation and divorce rates have peaked in the 1980s, and there are a large number of single-parent households. Furthermore, since the majority of people who divorce get remarried, there also has been a rise in blended or stepfamily arrangements. In addition, 10 to 15 percent of couples generally find that they have a fertility problem (Rathus, 1983), leading them to either remain childless or adopt children. There are also those adults who choose not to have children, as well as those who never marry, and those who choose to live together—with the opposite or same gender—without the societal sanction of marriage. The point is that the "traditional" family, while not actually a myth, represents fewer and fewer family arrangements in today's world. And, when one considers the radical changes that are taking place in role adoption, both within and outside of the home (for example, greater blending of family roles by husbands and wives, and the entrance of women into the work force), the notion of "traditional" family life would seem to be losing even more of its meaning.

Regardless of the structure of the family, and the specific roles played by its members, the family, as a social unit, serves a number of important functions that bind family members together and, at the same time, link them to the greater community (Garrett, 1982). First, families are the context for *legitimate procreation;* they are the legal unit responsible for the care of children born in that unit.

A second function of families is to *socialize* its members; to train both the adults and children how to get along with other people. Usually, children are the primary targets of socialization; although couples with or without children have a socializing effect on each other. Parents nurture, care for, and teach children the skills and behaviors necessary for effective coping in the world outside the home. By contrast, adults experience more indirect socialization as they interact with each other and with their offspring. For example, it is well known that the behavior and attitudes of parents are shaped by the responses they produce in their children (Belsky, 1984; Bell & Harper, 1977). We consider this an indirect socialization effect since children usually do not intentionally "try to" alter their parents' behavior in the same way that parents intentionally try to shape their children's behavior.

Finally, families also function to foster a *companionship role between marital partners.* In so doing, the family unit facilitates intimacy among its members and provides a basis for physical and emotional support. Family members share leisure activities, celebrate holidays together, and listen to each other's problems. They are not only relatives, but sometimes also good friends.

Pause for Thought

A traditional family is composed of a mother, father, and their offspring and is usually maintained in one household. Despite the increase in "nontraditional" families over the past 25 years, research studies have tended to focus their attention on traditional families. What factors might bias researchers to study one type of family rather than another?

Marriage

Marriage is a life event that about 80 percent of adults in the United States experience some time during their adult lifespan (Norton & Moorman, 1987). Over the past 10 years, the age at which people marry has increased and the marriage rate has declined (Norton & Moorman, 1987; Rodgers & Thornton, 1985).

In the past 25 years, the percentage of women who postpone marriage has doubled for women between the ages of 20 to 24 years of age and tripled for women 25 to 29 years old (Tanfer, 1987). Furthermore, women with higher levels of education (college and postgraduate) are postponing marriage in favor of establishing themselves in a career (Houseknecht, Vaughan, & Stratham, 1987; Spanier, Roos, & Shockey, 1985).

Although the age at which people marry for the first time has risen since the last generation, many young adults may experience pressures from family, friends, and even themselves to get married "on time." Bernice Neugarten (1979) believes that each society has a typical timetable for major adult life experiences and marriage is one of them. What really matters is the individual's perception of whether he or she is "late" in marrying. Most people who marry also have children and since the age of childbearing is limited by biological factors, many women over the age of 30 may experience a greater push to get married. Marriage today, or at least the traditional early marriage, appears to be but one of several possible lifestyle choices. Although most young adults still choose to get married, an increasing number of men and women are making the choice to remain single, or to postpone marriage until their late twenties or thirties.

Mate Selection

One of the most obvious problems to be faced in regard to marriage is the choice of a partner. The field seems large enough; there are millions of unattached people in the world. Realistically, however, the range of selection for each person is limited. All the while one is seeing, meeting, and going out with potential partners, a selective screening process is taking place. In the end, people seem to choose their mates from a narrow group of individuals who are much like themselves.

There are three factors that influence the mate-selection process: physical attractiveness, propinquity, and homogamy. *Physical attractiveness* has been found to be the best predictor of mutual liking between new acquaintances. In a study at the University of Minnesota, male and female freshmen were matched randomly at a dance. Four student ushers secretly evaluated the attractiveness of each student. Results showed that the higher the attractiveness rating, the greater the liking, and the more the subject expressed a desire to see the person again. The correlation between attractiveness and liking was even higher when the rating was done by the subjects themselves (Walster, Aronson, Abrahams, & Rottmann, 1966). Later, in establishing a relationship, however, personality traits and other characteristics gain more prominence — and may even weaken the effects of physical attraction (Mathes, 1975). A recent study on the continuing effects of physical attractiveness in marriage revealed that husbands but not wives were less attracted to their spouses who become less physically attractive with age (Margolin & White, 1987). In a survey in which men and women were asked to rate various physical, social and personality characteristics in terms of their importance in selecting a romantic partner, males placed greater importance on physical characteristics while females emphasized characteristics such a warmth, honesty, and faithfulness (Nevid, 1984).

Propinquity means nearness. People are more likely to choose a mate from among those who live or work nearby, if only because they are more likely to meet such people and have a greater opportunity to get to know them. In a study of married couples, Clarke (1952) found that slightly more than half of the couples he studied lived within 16 blocks of each other while dating.

Homogamy refers to the general practice of choosing a mate who is similar to oneself in social or personality characteristics. Marriage choices in the United States, for example, tend to be homogamous. Thus, people will tend to choose a partner who is of the same race and ethnic group, the same religion, the same social class, of roughly the same age, the same level of education, and whose values and worldview are similar.

Some homogamy factors are stronger than others, however. Judging by the scarcity of interracial marriages, race would seem to be the single, most powerful homogamous factor in mate selection. Religion is still important: Over 90 percent of Protestants marry other Protestants; over 90 percent of Jews marry other Jews; and over 75 percent of Catholics marry other Catholics

People usually select as marriage partners people who are similar to them in social and personality characteristics.

(Carter & Glick, 1970). Social class also exerts a strong influence. However, when people marry outside of their own class, men tend to marry women of lower social class, while women tend to marry men of higher social class.

Courtship

In the past, mate selection would usually begin with casual dating, then lead to going "steady," becoming engaged, and finally getting married. Today, however, it is obvious that not all couples who casually date move on to the other phases of courtship or in the same sequence. Becoming a "serious" couple is a process that is dependent upon many factors. Murstein (1970, 1976, 1982), has developed a three-stage theory of marital choice. The first stage is the *Stimulus (S) stage,* during which the person responds to certain stimulus values or characteristics in the other person. These characteristics include the person's physical attractiveness, reputation, adopted roles, and other information about the person. Generally, the stimulus stage involves brief contacts with the other person and is a time for forming initial impressions.

If each person evaluates the other in approximately equal ways, they may progress to the second, *Value-Comparison (V) stage* of courtship. This phase of couple development is characterized by the couple engaging in conversation aimed at gathering information about each other. Most of the information gathered focuses on the couple's interests, attitudes, beliefs, needs, values, and their past. Murstein notes, however, that the couple is unlikely to have developed sufficient intimacy by this stage to share their innermost feelings and thoughts. What is accomplished in successful relationships at this stage, however, is mutual acceptance of the other person in terms of his or her interests, values, and so forth. Generally, there then develops some consensus as to what constitute the important values of the relationship.

If a couple has survived the stimulus and value-comparison stages, they may (but do not necessarily) move on to the *Role (R) stage.* It is usually at this point that the couple begins to plan for marriage or for a long-term commitment such as to live together. In so doing, they evaluate the compatibility of their individual roles, as well as the "fit" between these roles and their perception of the way they want their relationship to develop. This also is a time when people share their intimate feelings and behaviors. It is also the time when the couple will talk about what they want in a spouse and co-parent, or if they want children at all.

Murstein notes that the stimulus, value-comparison, and role stages are not actually temporally separate from one another (see Figure 12.1). In other words, individuals within a couple relationship continue to respond to certain stimulus characteristics of their partner beyond the initial stage of courtship. However, these characteristics play a more important role during the early part of this process. Similarly, there is a constant comparison of values, interests, needs, and so on throughout the development of a relationship. However, such comparisons are more important during the middle phase of the courtship. Other researchers (Windle & Lerner, 1984) believe that the comparison process takes place very early on in relationships and does not take the months or years that Murstein suggested.

One of the more important insights gained from Murstein's **stimulus—value—role theory** of marital choice is that individuals do not necessarily have to be similar in characteristics to have a successful relationship. Murstein

Stimulus–Value–Role Theory Murstein's theory of courtship; the process begins with people responding to the overt characteristics of others; it progresses to value comparison; and eventually leads to an evaluation of role compatibility as the couple seriously considers marriage.

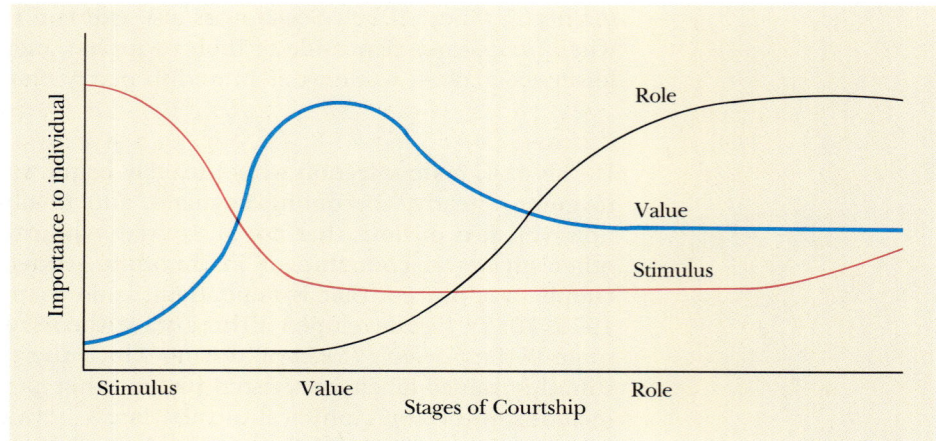

Figure 12.1 Stages of courtship in SVR theory.

(1982) points out that what is more important is that there be *equity* in the rewarding power of the partners. In other words, each individual in a relationship must have the ability, regardless of his or her characteristics, to meet the needs of the other person. In some relationships, this may result when couples share similar interests and characteristics; in other relationships, it may result when each person complements the interests and characteristics of the other, as when one person likes to cook and another likes to eat.

Pause for Thought

Many young adult college students look to their college experience as an opportunity to meet and develop a romantic relationship. Some publications describing colleges and universities include such information as the ratio of male to female students and the quality of the campus social life. In what ways might the selection of a college affect the process of mate selection for young adults?

Marital Adjustment

Sexual Adjustment

Apart from difficult decisions about the nature of engagement and marriage ceremonies, a major issue faced by the married couple is the nature of sexual adjustment and commitment. Premarital sex is, by now, common: Fully 97 percent of men and 81 percent of women between the ages of 18 and 24 are not virgins when they marry (Hunt, 1974). This represents a much more substantial increase in the incidence of premarital sex for women over the past few decades (Bell & Coughey, 1980). The increase in premarital sexual behavior for men has not been nearly as dramatic. Despite the fact that many couples enter marriage with sexual experience, many must face sexual adjustments within a marriage or committed relationship.

Sex, like other social behavior, is learned. People come to the sex act, however, weighed down with all kinds of psychological and emotional bag-

To avoid the trap of a dull and routine sex life, romantic seduction may be needed.

gage. They have ideas as to how they should feel and how they should behave. Some people believe that if they are in love, satisfying sex will just follow naturally. They may have to discard some of their strongly held notions, as they set about the task of adjusting to a sexual relationship—they have to discover in practice what causes sexual arousal for them, what acts they are comfortable with, and then be able to communicate and coordinate their preferences with those of their partners. The issue of what constitutes permissible sexual technique may arise as partners gain experience with one another. New contraceptive planning may be called for as the couple considers long-range plans for or against having children.

Even if the couple has lived together before marriage and has worked out some of these issues, new issues may arise. As Garrett (1982) observes, the trap of a dull and routine sex life needs to be avoided. Seduction must play a continuing role in the couple's sex life if this aspect of their marriage is to remain satisfactory. Unfortunately, for some couples, the "long periods of intimacy and heavy petting [experienced before marriage] are replaced with watching television, reading, or puttering around the house doing a thousand and one odd jobs" (Garrett, 1982). Another new issue that must be dealt with is marital fidelity. Are the partners expected to be faithful to one another in the traditional sense, or are casual sexual encounters or even extramarital affairs to be tolerated, in theory or practice?

Despite the change in attitude in recent years toward premarital sexual activity, there is little change in regard to extramarital sex. From 80 to 90 percent of the couples interviewed by Hunt (1974) found extramarital sex unacceptable, although young people are unwilling to say it is wrong under all circumstances (Athanasiou, Shaver, & Tavris, 1970) or should never be forgiven. There is some feeling that extramarital sex may be "OK" if both partners agree to it; or if it is part of the initial marriage contract or understanding. What is unacceptable is deception, because this compromises intimacy and usually requires lying and dishonest behavior. Nevertheless, 50 percent of all married men eventually commit adultery; so do some 25 percent of married women by the time they are 54 years of age; in only one of five marriages does the spouse know about it (Hunt, 1974).

Sexual activity is much more frequent among newly married couples. The longer couples are married, the less they engage in sexual intercourse. The average monthly frequency of sexual intercourse for newlyweds is 15, while for couples married for fifteen years, the average monthly frequency of sexual intercourse is six times.

Marital Roles and Work Roles

Especially significant for the young couple in the 1980s and 1990s are issues involving gender roles and work roles. When both partners work outside the home, as is increasingly the case today (Masnick & Bane, 1980), the traditional pattern of male dominance may be compromised. In one study, married women who were homemakers showed greater tendency toward passivity than employed wives; husbands of homemakers were also more dominant than the husbands of employed women (Burke & Weir, 1976a). When marital satisfaction is measured, employed wives appear to be more satisfied and to perform more effectively than wives who do not work outside the home. However, Burke and Weir found that husbands of employed wives tend to be more dissatisfied; they report greater job pressures, more worries, and they seem to have poorer physical and mental health (Burke & Weir, 1976b).

On the positive side, husbands of employed wives reported greater agreement with their wives over important issues (such as friends and sexual relations) and were more likely to solve disagreements in an egalitarian manner. A subsequent study by Booth (1977) refuted Burke and Weir's findings, however. Booth found that husbands whose wives were employed showed no more signs of stress and marital discord than did husbands whose wives were full-time homemakers. If anything, Booth concluded, husbands of employed women were happier and under less stress. They more often reported their wives as "loving" and "less critical." According to Booth, when stress does appear, it is likely to be the result of a transition period—for example, wives entering the labor force and employed women who became homemakers showed signs of stress.

Ideally, when both husband and wife work, they must balance the demands of their jobs with regular household chores such as cleaning, cooking, and laundry. Bahr (1973) reported that husbands of wives who work outside the home perform significantly more household tasks than husbands of non-employed wives. Women feel more justified in asking husbands to help with housework and child care when they themselves are employed. However, other research that compared the work activity of husbands and wives around the house has found that husbands spend a much *shorter* time actually engaged

When both husband and wife are employed they must balance the demands of their jobs with domestic duties.

in household tasks than wives (one-and-a-half-hours for men as compared to five hours a day for women), and that wives generally are responsible for, and perform, most of the household and child-care tasks, as well as meal preparation (Maret & Finlay, 1984; Pleck & Rustad, 1980; Walker, 1970). Husbands, in turn, spend their time on traditionally masculine-oriented tasks such as washing the car and fixing things, which occur less frequently than the tasks for which wives are responsible.

When the married couple have children, they must balance their work roles with their marital and parental roles. A crucial factor in the successfulness with which dual-earner families share their work is the gender-role attitude of the spouses, particularly the wives. In a recent study, Rosalind Barnett and Grace Baruch (1987) reported that the wife's attitude toward the male role was a major predictor of their husband's participation in child care and housework. When the wife's attitude was liberal, her husband did more; when it was traditional, he did less.

Pause for Thought

Blumstein and Schwartz (1983) in their book *American Couples*, suggest that for relationships to be satisfying and long lasting at least one member must be "relationship centered" rather than "work centered." How might relationships be affected when both couples are involved in careers?

Divorce

When a couple marries, the partners pledge to love, honor, and cherish one another until they die. Many people are unable to fulfill that pledge, however, as the stresses and strains common in marriage lead to separation and divorce. More than one out of three of all U.S. couples who marry today can be expected to divorce. Most of these divorces will occur in early adulthood and within the first seven years of marriage (Reiss, 1980). The typical divorced person is between 35 and 39 years of age (Norton & Moorman, 1987). The divorce rate is higher among the poor, the working class, the poorly educated, and those who marry outside of their social class or religion (Garrett, 1982). In the United States, divorce is more common in the West than in the East. A California demographic study yielded the following data: Every married man in that state will marry an average of one-and-two-thirds times, and every woman can expect to spend six-and-one-half years as a divorcee (Schoen & Nelson, 1974).

Nobody knows for certain what accounts for all these divorces, apart from the increased social acceptance of divorce itself. However, we do know that one of the best predictors of divorce is age at first marriage. Teenage marriages, for example, are nearly twice as likely to fail as marriages that occur when the couple are in their twenties (Norton & Moorman, 1987). The tendency for early marriages to end in divorce and for marriages generally to break down in the early years suggests some underlying developmental issue. One or both of the marital partners may not have succeeded in becoming emotionally free from parents, or in making a commitment to his or her own values or occupation. Not having done so makes it difficult to establish a relationship based on mutuality with another person.

Women who marry after a premarital birth or give birth within seven months after marriage are more likely to end their marriages in divorce. Further, first marriages of women over 30 are the most stable, although those who do divorce tend to do so sooner than women who marry at a younger age (Norton & Moorman, 1987). Whether people's marriages end in divorce may be influenced by whether their parents were divorced. Several studies have suggested that people whose parents divorced are more likely to divorce than people whose parents had stable marriages (Glenn & Kramer, 1987; Glenn & Shelton, 1983; Kobrin & Waite, 1984; Mueller & Cooper, 1986).

Research suggests that divorce is highly stressful for the adult, and second only to death of a spouse in terms of the demands placed on the person for major reorganization of his or her life (Holmes & Rahe, 1967). It is not just the divorce itself that is stressful, however. Chiriboga and Cutler (1980) note in their research that women reported equally high levels of stress during the period before the decision to divorce and the period of separation itself. By contrast, men reported least stress in the predecision period, somewhat greater stress during separation, and an even higher degree of vulnerability in the postdivorce period. Other research suggests that postseparation adjustment also is related to the preparedness of the person for divorce. Individuals who initiate the divorce proceedings, take a more active role in the decision-making process, and who generally are better prepared for the divorce show a higher level of adjustment in the postseparation phase (Wallerstein & Kelly, 1980).

The emotional reactions to separation and divorce are highly variable, and to a great extent dependent on the nature of the process that preceded it (Kelly, 1982). The happy wife who comes home to find a note taped to the refrigerator will react with shock; the wife who has been locked in self-destructive conflict with her husband for years may well react with relief. There is much evidence, though, that both will suffer a great deal of pain, and will need time to "mourn" the relationship. Some people, however, are never able to adjust to the divorce. They react to the breakup of their marriages with profound depression and anguish, in some cases, to the extent of contemplating suicide. However, not all couples that divorce end up as enemies. Some remain friends and maintain contact with each other through their mutual interests in their children (Ahrons & Rogers, 1987).

The divorced person will also encounter an identity crisis in the course of building a new lifestyle (Wiseman, 1975). The woman who married young may have tied her identity to that of her husband and to her married status. Now she has the new status of divorcee, and possibly single parent. She will need to establish a career identity, or at least find a job. And she will need to resolve issues of sexual identity. The search for sexual identity may be expressed in the often-observed "candy store" phase, in which divorced people sample a variety of sexual experiences with people to whom he or she feels little emotional commitment. The reworking of identity is also observed in the avoidance of relationships, in a refusal to socialize, and a preference for "crying into one's pillow" or one's "drink." Such a divorced person is temporarily unwilling to risk personal intimacy although this is what may ultimately be desired.

At the same time that individuals are resolving the crisis of identity and experimenting with sexual intimacy, they are also likely to be confronting a host of practical problems. For most young couples divorce brings financial distress and a lowering of the standard of living, perhaps by as much as 25 percent. If there are children, new parental relationships must be developed. This is especially true for the father, who does not usually have primary responsibility for child care.

Most divorced people eventually remarry. About one-quarter do so within the year; within three years, one-half are remarried; within nine years, three-quarters (Norton & Moorman, 1987). Men tend to remarry sooner than women. Although divorce rates are higher for second marriages, the majority of those who marry again remain married. For many, divorce is seen as a growth experience by means of which they are able to find not only a new and more suitable partner, but a greater awareness of themselves.

Nonmarital Lifestyles

A great deal has been written in recent years about such alternatives to marriage as cohabitation, remaining single, living in a commune, living an open homosexual life, having a child and bringing it up without a spouse, and adoption of children by single parents. Each of these alternatives to marriage—which are chosen by relatively few individuals—provides life satisfactions, problems, and developmental possibilities that are only beginning to be studied by psychologists and other social scientists.

Cohabitation

An increasingly common lifestyle is cohabitation, in which an unmarried couple live together and maintain a sexual relationship. Living together may come about as a result of a dating relationship. In many cases, the couple does not make a deliberate decision to live together; they gradually drift into the relationship. Other relationships constitute a "trial" marriage during which each partner works at emotional commitment, but with the security (and insecurity) of knowing that one or the other can pack up and leave. Some couples live together for unromantic reasons. They may share living quarters for financial or other reasons and subsequently develop a sexual relationship. And in still other cases a couple may live together because the partners cannot legally marry—for example, because they are of the same sex or because one or both may be married to another person.

No one knows for certain how many unmarried adults live together. Recent estimates, however, place the figure between 1.75 and 2 million people (U.S. Census, 1985)—slightly over 4 percent of all couple households in the United States. This figure is up substantially from what it was in the 1960s. A random sample of males between the ages of 20 and 30 for example, showed that the stereotype of the liberal-minded college couple may be misleading. Living together was more common among blacks than whites, and more common among high-school dropouts than high-school or college graduates (Clayton & Voss, 1977).

Among never-married women between the ages of 20 to 29, cohabitation with a man is a common occurrence (Tanfer, 1987). The cohabitation relationships that do not end up in marriage last an average of 18 months.

In a national survey of college students, 23 percent of women and 34 percent of men reported having lived with a member of the opposite gender to whom they were not married (Bower & Christopherson, 1977). Nearly all students expected that their parents would disapprove of the arrangement; nearly all (96 percent) said that they wanted to marry some day. Other research suggests that premarital cohabitation has little impact, either positively or negatively, on subsequent mate selection, gender-roles in marriages, or marital success in general (Jacques & Chason, 1979; Newcomb, 1979). Males are more willing than females to enter into a long-term cohabitation relationship, as well as most alternative forms of marital and family life. They are more reluctant, however, to take part in marriages and relationships characterized by a reversal of the traditional male–female roles (Strong, 1978).

Reiss (1980) has suggested that cohabitating couples fall into two broad categories. For one group of cohabitants, living together is simply another form of courtship, not an alternative to marriage. The primary feature of these couples is their attitude toward having children while living together—generally, they are against it. Macklin (1978) notes that in this type of relationship, should pregnancy occur, the couple would be likely to opt for an abortion or getting legally married. Thus, in the eyes of these individuals, parenthood is reserved for marital relationships. The second, and by far the smaller, group of cohabitants believe it is acceptable to bear children within their relationship. Thus, these individuals tend to view cohabitation as an alternative to marriage rather than as merely part of the courtship process. *Nonlegal marital cohabitation*—as Reiss (1980) calls this pattern—involves a desire for a life-long commitment to one's partner; and a desire to develop the same type of family environment, including children, that is found in marital relationships.

Singlehood

Although 25 may be the age by which many young people plan to be married, about 33 percent of all men and 22 percent of all women find themselves single on their twenty-fifth birthday. At 30, the percentages are approximately 15 and 7, for men and women, respectively (Quindlen, 1977). A significant number of people in our society live much of their early adulthood as singles.

Garrett (1982) has argued that two different decision-making processes can lead a person to singlehood. One involves the "push" toward singlehood as a way of avoiding marriage. The alternative is the "pull" of singlehood in response to its perceived benefits. In other words, some people remain single because of their fear of being trapped in marriage and becoming bored with one's partner; or because they equate marriage with limited sexuality, inhibited self-growth, social isolation, and limited mobility within a career. In each case, singlehood is a response to the perceived *negative* qualities of marriage. By contrast, other people choose to remain single because of the perceived *advantages* singlehood affords: freedom for individual change, greater mobility, self-sufficiency, a greater variety of experiences, sexual freedom, and increased career opportunities. In one study (Goldscheider & Waite, 1987), women who left their families' homes in early adulthood to live on their own were less likely to get married than women who continued to live at home.

Single people tend to live in, or be drawn to, urban centers, where opportunities for employment and social interaction are high. They tend to associate with other singles, and to be concerned with establishing relationships that meet the need for intimacy, companionship, and emotional support

Single people tend to live in urban centers, where there are more opportunities for employment and social activities.

(Stein, 1980). Indeed, it may be that the well-adjusted single enjoys richer friendships—friendships characterized by greater age and ethnic diversity—than do married couples in the same age range.

Homosexual Lifestyle

In recent years, more and more men and women have openly declared their homosexuality. Many of these individuals are married and have children; others are single and living alone, or with a lover. The number of homosexuals in the United States today is difficult to determine. Estimates range from 5 to 20 million people (Hume, 1984; Hunt, 1974). Of course, the definition of homosexuality affects this estimate. More conservative estimates usually reflect the number of people who are mainly or exclusively homosexual; more liberal estimates include not only these individuals, but those who have sporadic homosexual encounters and/or who are bisexual.

As homosexuals "come out of the closet," many of the myths regarding their lifestyle are being challenged. One in particular involves the notion that all homosexuals are alike—that they are promiscuous and unable to form lasting intimate relationships. Bell and Weinberg (1978), however, found considerable variability in the lifestyles of gay men and women. Specifically, five different life patterns were identified, accounting for over 70 percent of their sample. Some homosexuals (28 percent of the women and 10 percent of the men) form *close couple* relationships that resemble marriage. These relationships are characterized by a high level of intimacy and fewer social and psychological problems than other types of homosexual relationships. Approximately equal percentages of gay men (18 percent) and lesbian women (17 percent) live as *open couples*. These couples live together, but are less committed to the relationship than close couples. They also are likely to have affairs outside the relationship. Homosexuals in open relationships, although

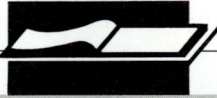

Human Development in Practice

Teaching Children from Alternate-Lifestyle Families

Since the 1960s, traditional family life has been changing in many ways. Increasingly, more young adults have sought an alternative way of living their lives and raising their children. Some have entered into cohabitating relationships; some have sought out religious or spiritual movements; and still others have chosen to remain single—often with the intention of having and bringing up a child by themselves. Furthermore, with an increase in divorce and remarriage rates, many families now consist of a single parent with children or a reconstituted family with stepparents and stepsiblings. The traditional nuclear family is in some places the exception rather than the rule.

Teachers can no longer assume that the children in their classrooms are the products of traditional families with traditional values. Some teachers may themselves come from nontraditional families. In what ways are children who grow up in nontraditional families different from children from traditional families?

This question, and others, have been the focus of a longitudinal project being conducted by Bernice Eiduson and her colleagues (Cohen & Eiduson, 1975; Eiduson, 1978; Eiduson, Cohen, & Alexander, 1973; Eiduson, Kornfein, Zimmerman, & Weisner, 1982). Eiduson has studied over 200 families and their children from the last trimester of the mother's pregnancy until, in the most recent reports, the children had reached six years of age. The families were broken down into four groups: traditional two-parent families, single-mother families, social-contract or cohabitating families, and communal-living families. (This last group was actually composed of two subgroups—those in which the members identified with an established religious or spiritual movement and/or who had a spiritual leader, and those who lived together simply because they liked one another.) All families were composed of adults between 18 and 35 years of age and all were from middle- or upper-middle-class backgrounds.

One of the first observations made by Eiduson and her colleagues was that the values of nontraditional parents were different from the values of traditional parents. Adults living in alternate lifestyle arrangements were more apt than traditional adults to reject conventional definitions of achievement, to be more egalitarian, to prefer "natural" ways of doing things, to be more oriented toward immediate gratification and less toward the future, to be less materialistic, to rely more on intuitive and mystical sources of knowledge, and to be more antiauthoritarian. By contrast, the groups did not differ in terms of basic humanistic values, in their desire for strong interpersonal relationships, and in their concern for the problems of others.

In keeping with these findings, Eiduson also found a number of differences in child-rearing attitudes and practices between the groups. Although all groups reported common modes of disciplinary behavior when the children reached toddlerhood and the preschool years, traditional married couples (and those adults in spiritually led communes) placed a much higher value on teaching their children obedience and respect for authority. These two groups also were involved in religious life more than were other groups. In addition, traditional parents tended to be more directive in their caregiving than other groups, and more often hovered around their children during activities.

One interesting question that needs to be addressed is whether children growing up in these different forms of family life show different patterns of behavior and development. Eiduson notes, they do not—at least through the first three years of life. In areas such as intelligence, attachment, persistence, fantasy, tolerance for frustration, cooperativeness, and hostility, little if any effect of lifestyle could be found in the children's behavior. This finding suggests that there is no single way of fostering healthy, normal development. As long as parents are warm, loving, concerned, consistent, stimulating, and so on, the *specific* lifestyle adopted by parents is unlikely to be a major factor in promoting a normal adjustment pattern.

not as well adjusted as those in close relationships, are nevertheless comparable in adjustment to heterosexuals. Other homosexuals live a "single" life, arranged around homosexual activities. These *functionals,* as Bell and Weinberg refer to them, account for 15 percent of gay men and 10 percent of lesbians. In general, these individuals tend to be social and political, and are well adjusted—second only to homosexuals in close-couple relationships. A fourth group of gays, which includes 12 percent of the men and 5 percent of the women, are called *dysfunctionals.* Generally, these individuals live alone and are troubled by their homosexuality. As a result, the incidence of sexual, social, and psychological problems is higher for this group than for other homosexual groups. The final group of homosexuals identified by Bell and Weinberg are the *asexuals* (16 percent of gay men and 11 percent of lesbians). These individuals tend to be older, sexually inactive, or at least less interested in sex, and have difficulty in forming intimate relationships.

Research also has found consistent gender differences in the lifestyles of homosexuals. Overall, lesbians tend to have fewer sexual partners than do gay men. They also are more concerned with romantic love and affection in their relationships. In this sense, they are comparable to their heterosexual counterparts.

Since the mid-1980s, when the deadly AIDS virus began to spread among sexually active gay men and intravenous drug users, there has been considerable concern among gays and heterosexuals about the negative impact this disease may have on people's tolerance and acceptance of gay people in general. Out of their fear of AIDS some people may shun normal contact with gay people, even though the virus is spread through sexual contact or through the blood and not by touching or sharing food or drink. Furthermore, gay people, especially gay men, who are sexually active need to take precautions to avoid the spread of the disease. Health centers have been set

Gay Rights organizations have taken on the challenge of educating homosexuals and heterosexuals about AIDS.

up to provide confidential AIDS testing for gay people and telephone hot lines have been established in many cities to provide information on how a person can protect him- or herself from getting AIDS.

Pause for Thought

Many young adults have opted to delay making decisions about marriage or starting a family until their late twenties or early thirties. For a period of about 10 to 12 years then, single people may live independently from others. Do you think that an extended period of singlehood during the young adult years helps people choose the lifestyle that is best for them? Could there be disadvantages to remaining single too long?

Parenting

One of the most powerful drives in living things is the drive to preserve the species: to establish and care for a new generation. In the course of life, most human beings become, through choice or chance, fathers or mothers. Nearly 90 percent of all couples in the United States have at least one child (Pohlman, 1970).

In Erikson's model, in which he speaks of the crises in psychosocial development, parenthood emerges in response to the crisis of *generativity vs. stagnation*. Following the resolution of the intimacy-vs.-isolation crisis, the young adult typically begins to express the crisis of **generativity** in decisions and feelings about parenthood. Erikson sees the desire to care for others as an important commitment to the past as well as to the future. Erikson recognizes, however, that some people, because of misfortune or genuine gifts in other directions, achieve generativity through means other than parenthood—through work or through meaningful interaction with parents and children.

Generativity According to Erikson, a critical psychosocial achievement for young and middle-aged adults; a concern for contributing to the maintenance of society through nurturing of others and through one's productions.

One way many people meet the mid-adulthood need of generativity is to become a parent and care for children.

On the other hand, merely wanting or having children does not amount to true generativity. Some people are unable to develop as parents due to difficulties experienced at earlier points in development. For example, couples who have not developed the capacity for mutuality and sacrifice in their relationships are often unprepared for children. Instead of caring for a new generation, they may indulge themselves as if they were their own or one another's only child (Erikson, 1963).

Fertility Motivation

"Should we have a baby?" is an important question for most young married couples. Researchers in **fertility motivation** — reasons for having or not having children—have studied the factors that influence the decision. They have found that the value of children to parents differs, and the reasons for having children differ, too.

What motivates couples to make the transition to parenthood? One factor usually cited is social pressure, particularly pressure from their own parents, the prospective grandparents. Other factors include a delight in children for their own sakes; a desire for emotional comfort that children may provide in old age; a desire for heirs to whom one can bequeath the resources, ideas, and tastes acquired over a lifetime; and a sense that one's work may not be all there is to life—that children may be needed to "make it all worthwhile." Those who decide to have children in their thirties tend to mention feelings about their own mortality and the need for something that will outlive them.

In a recent study (Gormly, Gormly, & Weiss, 1987), college students who said they wanted to have children at some point in their lives were asked to describe their reasons for wanting children. Their responses were coded into nine categories that are presented in Table 12.3. Most of the students' reasons reflected an interest in establishing an identity or social network, needs that may not have yet been fulfilled during the late teens and early twenties. For young adults who delay childbearing until their late twenties or early thirties,

Fertility Motivation People's reasons or motives for wanting children.

Table 12.3

Motivations for Parenthood among College Students

Rank	Percent Subjects Who Gave This Response	Motive
1	48.29	To expand myself, have someone to follow me
2	47.91	To achieve adult status or social identity
3	45.25	To provide a family for myself
4	32.70	For the fun and stimulation children bring
5	23.19	To be able to influence or control someone
6	19.39	Because it is the morally correct thing to do
7	8.37	To compete or compare myself with others
8	6.84	For the sense of accomplishment or creativity
9	4.56	For the economic benefit

Source: Gormly, Gormly, & Weiss, "Motivations for parenthood among young adult college students," *Sex Roles*, 1987, vol. 16, 31–39.

the reasons for wanting children may reflect different needs such as a need to nurture or care for others.

Not all motives for having children are good ones. Caseworkers placing children with a couple for adoption tend to be critical of such motives as having a child to improve their marriage, or to prevent the marriage from deteriorating. Some persons want a child as an escape from boredom ("something to do") or from an unsatisfactory job. Some see a child as a form of social status. Finally, some women, either single or unhappily married, want a child because, in the absence of adult intimacy, they need someone with whom to form a genuine attachment.

Adjustment to Parenthood

With the birth of the child, the couple becomes parents and the heads of a new nuclear family. They begin the process of socializing the infant and are, in turn, socialized by it. That is, parents teach the child eating, toilet habits, and gender-role behavior. At the same time, they learn such things as how to speak to their baby, how to keep it comfortable, how to make it smile, how to relate in new ways to its grandparents, and so on.

The transition to parenthood has been described as a crisis point in the life of the couple, requiring adjustments for which they are often not prepared (Rossi, 1968). In one study of over 2500 adults, the birth of the first child was rated as the sixth most stressful life event out of 102 possible events (Dohrenwend, Krasnoff, Askenasy, & Dohrenwend, 1978). Part of the problem is that society does little to prepare people for parenthood, either before or after the child arrives. Furthermore, the transition to parenthood is an abrupt one. One day the couple are by themselves, and the next day they have "another mouth to feed," a human being for whom they are responsible. The transition is even more abrupt when an unplanned pregnancy occurs.

Parenthood disrupts the two-person routine of the married couple and frequently interrupts the career of the wife and places time restrictions on the husband. The arrival of an infant restricts the parents' activities outside of the home, as well as their privacy within. Communication of feelings and ideas between the parents is sharply curtailed. Indeed, one researcher found that young parents talk to one another about half as much as newly married couples—and then they tend to talk about the child (Schulz, 1972).

The birth of a child to a couple who have been childless for many years of their marriage or for couples who remarry at a later age may require additional adjustments. Women and men may feel a bit "out of step" with their peers who started their families at a younger age. In the case of reconstituted families, the birth of a baby may create feelings of rivalry or even a sense of betrayal in other older children from a previous marriage.

The evidence suggests that marital satisfaction decreases with the advent of the first child (Belsky, Spanier, & Rovine, 1983; Miller & Sollie, 1980). Furthermore, the quality of marital relationships continues to decline as additional children are added to the family (Belsky, Spanier, & Rovine, 1983). In the later stages of family life, particularly after the departure of the children from the home, marital quality increases once again (Alpert & Richardson, 1980; Schram, 1979). However, the drop in marital satisfaction with the arrival of children does not occur for all couples. Hoffman and Mavis (1978) reported that if children are planned and desired, they can strengthen rather than weaken the marital relationship.

The new status of parenthood necessarily leads to new relationships between the couple and society. New mothers seek out other new mothers for companionship and advice. Many new parents show increased pleasure in the company of their own parents as well, using these individuals for their emotional and material support and for baby-sitting services. Parenthood also brings renewed contact with institutions that may have been ignored during single life and early marriage. As the child progresses through the preschool years, parents begin evaluating the parks and libraries and especially the schools of their neighborhoods. For some this leads to community activism, perhaps on behalf of better playground maintenance or in opposition to indecent advertising and violence on television. For others, dissatisfaction with the neighborhood can lead to great changes in lifestyle. A move from city to suburb, for example, will have considerable effect on a family's consumption and commuting patterns.

Pause for Thought

Typically, over 90 percent of surveyed adults say they want to have children and most married couples do have children. But some couples who want to have children cannot because of infertility problems. What impact does involuntary childlessness have on a couple's relationship? What differences in behavior or attitudes might you expect between couples who choose not to have children and couples who physically cannot have children?

Occupational Development

A large part of the person's identity—about 40 years of life — are bound up with work. For men, the question "Who are you?" has traditionally been expressed in the question "What do you do?" Today women, too, are expected to be able to answer this question. "I am an English instructor, a programmer, a hospital administrator."

Stage Theories

For most people, career choice is not a one-shot decision made in early adulthood. The life cycle imposes many different tasks at different periods of life; consequently, people develop and change in respect to their vocations. While some researchers have suggested that these changes can best be conceptualized in terms of a stage model of occupational development, others have characterized occupational development in different ways.

Super's Theory of Occupational Development

Donald Super (1957, 1963) has suggested that people go through five stages of occupational development. During adolescence (14–18 years) there is a *crystalization* of one's ideas about work. At this time the person is likely to be exposed to many different occupational areas, through media, schooling, family friends and relatives, and through firsthand experience in part-time jobs.

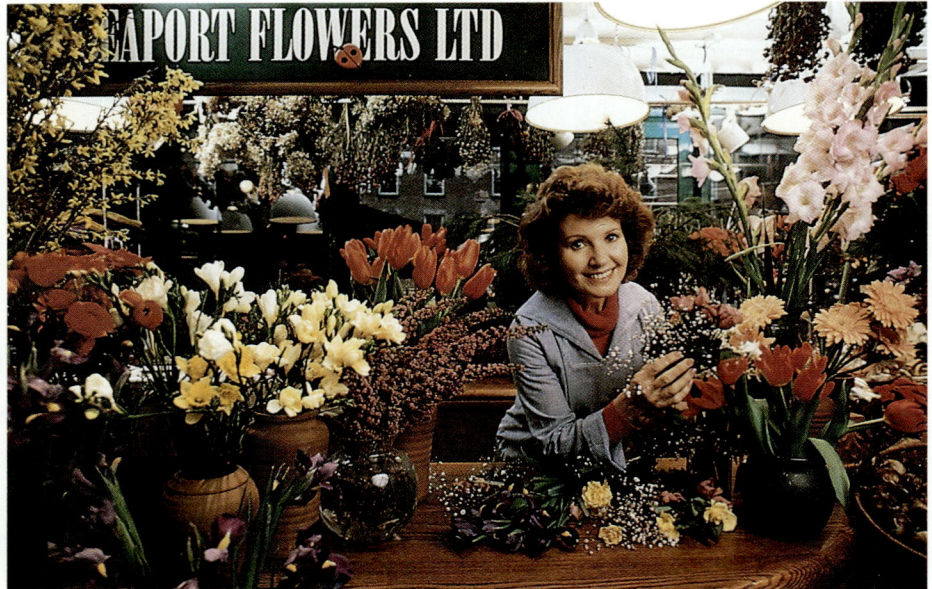

During the phase of job stabilization people become established in their jobs and take pride and pleasure from their work.

While this is going on, the adolescent is comparing possible career paths with his or her skills, interests, personality characteristics, and so on. The second stage (18–21 years) involves the *specification* of a particular occupational preference and the beginning of job training. Frequently, this involves specialized education such as that found in post-high-school vocational training centers or in career-oriented college programs. After specifying a particular career path, the next step in the process (21–24) is the *implementation* of one's training and entry into the first job. This step marks a major change in self-perception for some people, for with the adoption of the worker role many young people begin to see themselves as adults for the first time. Following the implementation phase, workers enter into the stage of job *stabilization* (24–35 years). This is the time when people become established in their fields and begin to develop job reputations—"good worker," "reliable," "a potential leader," "overly cautious," "lacks motivation." The fifth stage within Super's model (35 years and on) is the period of *consolidation and advancement* within a field or on the job. This stage represents the greatest span of time within the person's career life cycle; it is also the time when most individuals are at their peak earning power.

Super has noted that as people go through these stages of vocational development there is continual updating and implementing of self-concept. As we have already discussed, self-concept is constantly changing. A woman may undertake a new vocational identity as her household responsibilities shrink, by becoming an officer in a bank rather than a part-time, customer-service representative. The research scientist becomes the director of the research and development division of a chemical company, gradually moving from meticulous solitary work to the supervision and management of a large number of people. Such change may coincide with other developmental events, for example, a broadening of family responsibilities, and the management of a larger household.

Levinson's Theory of Occupational Development

Daniel Levinson's theory of occupational development does not project such a straight line in occupational development as suggested by Super's model. Working with a sample of men from four different occupations from unskilled worker to professional writer, Levinson proposed a stage model of adult development that includes more tentative exploration of career paths and several crisis periods of reassessment (Levinson, Darrow, Klein, Levinson, & McKee, 1977). Levinson has said that it is a cruel myth to believe that at the end of adolescence you choose your career, settle down, and continue this way more or less indefinitely.

In early adulthood, the individual enters a stage that Levinson calls *getting into the adult world.* Here, the young man tries to settle on an occupation or an occupational direction in line with his own interests and his sense of his own identity. He explores the possibilities in the work world and at the same time tries to match what he finds with his sense of his own potential. His task is to build a *life structure,* forging a link between the work world and how he sees himself. This is a period of provisional choices. From the ages of about 28 to 32, many men experience a *transitional period*—a crisis of reassessment. For every choice made, parts of the self are ignored. These aspects of the self come to the surface and must be dealt with. For example, a man who has gone into the manufacturing business with his father may not want to settle for just making money—he may want to have a try at writing plays. He may stay home for 18 months, complete a play, and then find a new career as an advertising copywriter and account executive. Some people find the right combination of career and identity and make a deeper commitment. Levinson's observations led him to hypothesize that if a significant start is not made by the age of 34, chances are small that a man will find a satisfactory life structure with an occupation consistent with his identity and interests.

Sometime in his early thirties a man *settles down.* This is a period of deeper commitment to work and to family. The individual makes and pursues long-range plans and goals. Although he feels autonomous in his work, he may be subject to many restrictions imposed by higher-ups or by the rules under which he works. This may push him into the next stage.

Becoming your own man may occur from the late thirties to early forties. At this time a man wants desperately to have society affirm him in his work role—to be made foreman or manager of his department. This period comes to an end with another crisis, the *midlife transition* around 40 to 45. Whether or not a man achieves the recognition he feels he deserves, he may go through a period of reassessment. "Is this after all what I want? Am I the kind of person who is a manager (or who failed to become a manager)?" The man must make peace with himself or drastically change his life structure. Great personal growth can result from the midlife transition.

Since the men in Levinson's sample have not yet lived through middle adulthood, the stages are not yet complete. Growth and change are seen as characteristic of occupational development, however, as well as of other aspects of a man's life.

Unfortunately, Levinson did not include women in his sample and there has not been a similar systematic long-term study of women's occupational development. In part, this is a reflection of an old bias that places greater value on male occupational development. It is also true that today more young

For parents of young children the decision to work also involves finding appropriate child care.

women are selecting career paths that include work outside the home *and* planning for a family (Archer, 1985a, 1985b). Women's occupational development is thus more complexly influenced by their combined career and family roles. Many women with children interrupt their work pattern for periods of time to have or care for children. However, continuous work patterns are an important ingredient for occupational success. In a seven-year longitudinal study of women who were between the ages of 30 and 44 at the start of the study, it was found that women who worked continuously had the highest salaries (Van Velsor & O'Rand, 1984). Furthermore, those women who worked before having children and then returned to the same type of job after their children entered school earned higher salaries than women who switched jobs or who entered the job market after they had had children. Women who work continuously are also more likely to be promoted in their jobs than women who have breaks in their work patterns (Betz, 1984). Continuous commitment to occupational choice may be difficult, if not impossible, for some women who also have family commitments.

Career Choice, Self-Concept, and Gender-Role Identity

When the individual takes a first serious full-time job, in many cases it represents an implementation of his or her self-concept. For example, the person who believes that he has the qualities of empathy, genuineness, and understanding may well become a mental-health professional because he perceives his personality characteristics to fit the requirements of this career. By contrast, this same person would be less likely to choose a career as a computer programmer since his interpersonal skills are less useful in this job. Research, using trait description checklists, has shown that there is a high correlation between people's self-concept and occupational stereotypes or images to which they aspire (Holland, 1973).

Self-concept influences more than just initial occupational choice. Havighurst (1982) notes that following entry into the first job there may be some floundering as the young person finds that his or her initial choice of a career is not as satisfying as was expected. Perhaps the job requirements were inappropriately evaluated; perhaps the person's self-evaluation was inadequate. Whatever the reason, the "fit" between the job requirements and self-concept is poor, leading the person to seek employment in another field. Levinson et al. (1977) have emphasized that the reevaluation of the match between one's career and self-concept can take place at any point in the life cycle. As people experience significant life events—marriage, parenthood, separation or divorce, death of a loved one—self-concept is likely to change. Such change increases the chance of bringing about a crisis regarding career commitment—as one begins to question the fit between the new sense of self and occupational goals.

One aspect of identity involved in career choice is *gender role*. People entering their twenties today find that entrance into many occupations is determined less by gender than it used to be. Women who had assumed that they would enter a feminine "caring" profession, such as teaching, nursing, or social work, are being encouraged by popular spokespersons, as well as the Equal Opportunity Act, to reconsider their options. For some young women this has meant taking the risk of expressing abilities and lifestyles believed by

Human Development in Practice

The Crisis in the Nursing Profession

A generation ago, the career opportunities available to women were limited. Then, a woman would typically aspire to be a teacher or a nurse. Today, however, there are many more career options and one consequence of this change is a crisis in the nursing profession.

Throughout the United States and in other countries, the number of people entering the nursing field has dropped dramatically. Furthermore, trained nurses are leaving their chosen profession in favor of other higher-paying jobs.

Ironically, the shift away from nursing has occurred at the same time that the nursing profession has made a concerted effort to change its public image. At one time nurses were seen as handmaidens to physicians. Their job was to carry out the doctor's requests and to provide comfort and care to the doctor's patients. Today, nurses define themselves as medical professionals whose primary responsibility is providing for the health and well-being of their patients. Many nurses have earned a college degree and have taken additional specialized training to keep them up on the changing medical technology. Because their focus is on providing the best patient care rather than on serving the attending physician, it is not unusual for nurses to question or even challenge the physician's judgment about the care of a patient. But the demands and job pressures in nursing make the field a less desirable choice for women who can enter other equally challenging professions. The hours and work schedules for hospital nursing are frequently limiting—evening shifts or weekend or holiday duty are often expected. Furthermore, the patients that nurses care for in the hospitals require more attentive care. In recent years, state and federal reforms in medical-insurance payments have meant that fewer people are treated in the hospital; therefore those that are hospitalized are usually sicker. Nurses are keenly aware of the role they play in safeguarding the lives of their patients. An intensive-care patient may be connected to several life-sustaining machines and monitors that a nurse must carefully watch. If the nurse does not do his or her job well, the patient

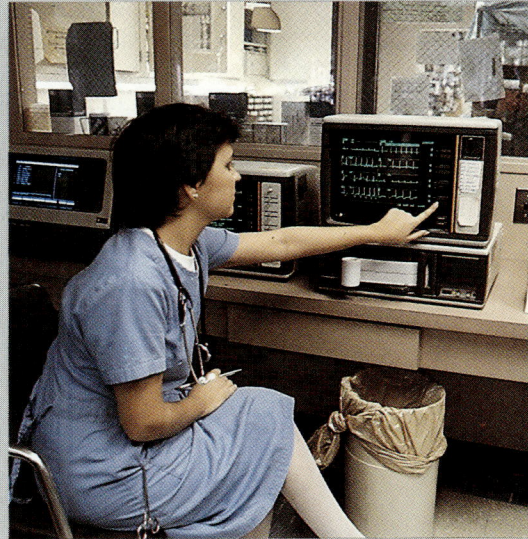

The stress of caring for critically ill patients is one reason fewer people are selecting nursing as a profession.

may not survive. The stress of caring for critically ill people is compounded when hospitals are understaffed, as many now are, and nurses must increase their patient load. Furthermore, nurses, like physicians, are burdened with the threat of a malpractice lawsuit, should their patients suffer damage or death while in their care.

The solution to the nursing crisis is not a simple one. With fewer people entering nursing programs, the shortage is likely to continue while the responsibilities and pressures on people in the health professions increase. The long-term solution is for nursing to attract more young adults to the field. But before that can happen, salaries must be increased and the public image of nurses as trained professionals must be strengthened. The status and work conditions for nurses must also improve. More flexible work hours, increased benefits and protections, and greater recognition for nurses will go a long way toward relieving the crisis.

Many more women are selecting career paths. Unfortunately, there are not as many role models for women as there are for men.

the parental generation to be masculine. Women have become mine workers, engineers, corporate managers, firefighters, and ministers—not always, however, without some social and interpersonal stresses. A mother, for example, may caution her "manager" daughter that success may stand in the way of personal fulfillment in marriage. Or, her male co-workers may harass a female steelworker on the job, making it difficult for her to do her work comfortably.

When your grandparents (or great grandparents) were young adults, they probably approached their work roles with a different view than couples today. In the past, it was expected that men would be employed until they retired and women would be involved in maintaining the home and caring for the family. Today however, things have changed somewhat. Men and women are both in the work force and many share in child care and household responsibilities. Furthermore, it is much more difficult for one employed spouse to change jobs without there being a significant impact on the other employed spouse and other family members. Today, couples with children are less likely to place job or career interests above family concerns. A survey of managers in large corporations found that even in this high-achieving group, there was a growing reluctance among younger subjects to uproot their families for the sake of a promotion. There was also more openness with respect to the possibility of second careers, suggesting that identity was less rigidly tied to the job or the company than in earlier samples (Williams, 1977). A related phenomenon is the tendency of men and women to prefer jobs that offer maternity or paternity leave to be able to care for newborn family members.

Pause for Thought

One of the inspiring characteristics of human beings is their capacity to change. In just one generation, gender roles have changed to include a wider range of career options for women and men. However, institutions such as professional schools, corporations, and certain industries do not change as quickly as the individual. What kinds of problems might a person have to confront when entering a career that has traditionally been associated with a specific gender (e.g., a male nurse or a female chief executive officer)?

Two-Provider Families

One of the more important social trends in the past few decades is the increase of women in the labor force, and consequently, the emergence of increasing numbers of two-provider, or dual-earner, families. In 1979, over 52 percent of married women with children under 18 were employed, including 43 percent of those with children under six years (U.S. Department of Labor, 1980).

There are a number of reasons for the rise of two-provider families in our society. The first, and most important, is the financial need of the family. Moen (1982) notes that the majority of dual-earner couples see their situation as an economic necessity, rather than an option. This is especially true in inflationary times. In addition, a declining birthrate has freed more women from the responsibility of child care at an earlier stage in their lives. Also, changes in societal attitudes concerning female and male roles have helped women make the transition into the work world. Once there, these more flexible attitudes have opened up a greater range of career opportunities for women.

Much has been written about the relationship between work and the family, and the special costs and benefits found in two-provider households (Moen, 1982; Rapaport & Rapaport, 1976). The trend today is for more and more young women to look to both careers and family relationships as a source of personal satisfaction (Regan & Roland, 1985). One of the more difficult problems faced by dual-earner couples is how to manage their time. There is only so much time in the day and if both spouses work, less time can be allocated to other activities—child care, social activities, hobbies, and just being together as a couple, or alone. Managing work and family life also takes a great toll on the person's energy level. As Moen (1982) observes, the stresses and strains of work can be great, particularly for those individuals who are moving up the career ladder. The physical and emotional drain that results can interfere with satisfactory adjustment in the nonworking areas of one's life.

Role Overload   A condition in which a person takes on, or is expected to take on, the responsibilities associated with many roles; produces increased stress in the individual.

The meshing of work and nonwork roles also produces **role overload** for many people, particularly women. Although husbands of employed wives are more likely to contribute in household tasks and help with child care than husbands of nonemployed wives (Pleck, 1979), the bulk of the domestic chores in two-provider families still falls on the shoulders of the wife (Maret & Finlay, 1984; Pleck, 1977; Slocum & Nye, 1976). The additional strain on women produced by role overload can be a contributing factor in the development of marital dissatisfaction among dual-career couples. It should be noted, however, that two-provider families are not necessarily doomed to greater conflict than single-earner families. In one study (Benin & Nienstedt, 1985) that looked at the causes of happiness and unhappiness among housewives, working wives, and their husbands it was found that in dual-earner families, marital satisfaction and job satisfaction were equally important in determining a person's happiness. For both single and dual-earner families, marital happiness was the most important determinant of overall happiness. Job satisfaction (or lack of it) was the most important determinant of unhappiness. Employed wives' level of happiness (but not their husband's) varied depending on where they were in their life cycle. During the stage when their children are young women are likely to experience more strain as they balance family and work demands. Benin and Nienstedt's findings are similar to the earlier findings of Hoffman and Nye (1974) that when employed wives in middle-class families enjoy their work, the dual-earner couple actually experiences greater marital satisfaction than single-earner couples.

A woman's decision to work when her children are young is often a difficult one to make. Research suggests that one of the factors associated with the decision is the woman's perception of the effects of separation from the infant. Hock (1978) found that women who planned to return to work were less anxious about the separation, and were more trusting of others to care for their infants than were nonworking women. In contrast, women who had not planned to return to work following childbirth, but who subsequently changed their minds, were more anxious about separation from their infants than nonworking mothers (Hock, Christman, & Hock, 1980).

The motivation for working following childbirth plays a major role in the subsequent adjustment of the mother and, in turn, the rest of the family.

A person's career choices may be influenced by his or her definition of the gender role.

When work is viewed as an avenue of self-expression and development, women are much more likely to be successful in integrating occupational and family roles than in situations when women work primarily for financial reasons. When adequate substitute child care and other support systems are available to the woman, there is better integration of work and parental roles. Some women who work to help support their families cannot afford, or do not have available, the kind of support they need to meet the day-to-day household responsibilities—child care, cleaning, shopping, cooking, and so on. For these women, the period of early adulthood is often marked by task overload, and accompanying feelings of frustration and despair, especially if they did not chose to work or have children.

Although it is difficult for families when both spouses work, there also are some important benefits that must not be overlooked. One of these is the financial security provided by two incomes instead of one. With more money coming in, dual-earner families are better able to meet their material needs, as well as have enough for some of the "extras" that make life more enjoyable—vacations, a second car, a new stereo system, additional toys for the children, and so on. Working also broadens the person's social network. In fact, one of the major complaints of nonemployed women is their sense of social isolation (Ferree, 1976). Finally, work serves as a basis for consolidation of identity and evaluation of the self. It has long been known that identity in men is tied closely to their occupational positions. In recent years, however, we have come to recognize that this is also true for women—although possibly not to the same extent. Research indicates that employed women, if they enjoy their jobs, report more positive self-esteem, higher levels of competence, and greater life satisfaction than unemployed women (Hoffman, 1974).

Summary

Family life has many different periods during which new developmental tasks or issues arise. The family life cycle begins at marriage and ends with the death of the remaining spouse. Duvall and Hill have proposed several stages of the family life-cycle. Early adulthood is the time during which the family is first formed through the time when children reach the preschool years. The family life-cycle models are useful for describing changes in traditional families. Their limitations are that they do not explain changes in nontraditional families and they don't acknowledge intergenerational relations.

Social scientists define families structurally, in terms of who the family members are and how they are related to one another, and functionally, in terms of the family activities and the role the family plays in the lives of its members.

The age at which people marry and the way they marry are influenced by social norms. Some of the factors affecting the courtship process are physical attractiveness, propinquity, similarity in background and values, achievement of rapport, mutual self-disclosure, role-taking ability, and the fitting together of roles and needs.

The newly married couple must learn to deal with conflict in a mature way and to make adjustments in areas dealing with money, sex, relatives, and the possibility of children. Adjusting to their new roles as husband and wife usually requires some personal change. Most young people today prefer a marital relationship of shared responsibilities. When both partners work, there seems to be more satisfaction in the marriage.

Among couples who marry today, nearly one in three can be expected to divorce. Most divorces occur within the first seven years of marriage. After a divorce, people seem to need to rework their lives and identities. Whereas most divorced people make adjustments to their new status, and eventually remarry, many have a difficult time adjusting to divorce. Most Americans marry at least once, yet cohabitation is an increasingly common arrangement. Other people remain single throughout much or all of their young adulthood. Women who remain single exhibit better mental health and fewer neurotic tendencies than married women or single men. Today, a growing number of men and women are openly declaring and living homosexual lifestyles.

In Erikson's model of development, parenthood emerges in response to the crisis of generativity. However, some people choose to express this generativity through their work. In either case, it represents a commitment to the past and to the future.

The reasons for having (or not having) children vary from one couple to another. Yet, each couple experiences similar kinds of adjustment problems associated with parenthood. The arrival of the infant restricts parental activities and privacy, imposes a financial burden on the family, and often disrupts the career of the wife. Research indicates that marital satisfaction decreases with the advent of the first child, although it often increases again in later stages of family life. However, if the children are wanted and planned for, they can strengthen the marriage.

People first enter the work world during young adulthood and begin the process of moving up the occupational ladder. According to both Super and Levinson, the changes in occupational development can be conceptualized as a series of stages, each with its unique tasks or issues.

Initial job choice is influenced by many factors including one's self-concept and gender-role identity. People entering the work force today find that entrance into many occupations is less gender determined than it once was. This is having a significant impact on career development in women. Families with two providers are finding that there are many costs as well as benefits to this lifestyle. Personal motivation for working and job satisfaction are two important factors in the adjustment of these families.

Further Readings

Beyer, Eugenia H. *Parents as partners in education.* St. Louis: Mosby, 1981.
A text designed to help parents and school personnel work together effectively.

Cohen, Judith B. *Parenthood after 30? A guide to personal choice.* Lexington, MA: Lexington, Books, 1985.
Many women are delaying pregnancy until their careers have been established. This helpful book details the pros and cons of parenthood and the medical, personal, and social dilemmas of delayed parenthood. An annotated list of resources is included at the end of the book.

Gilbert, L.A. *Men in dual-career families.* Hillsdale, NJ: Lawrence Erlbaum, 1985
This book is about men whose wives have careers. The author conducted extensive interviews with 51 men and relates their experiences along with a review of theory and research on dual-career families.

Green, Maureen. *Fathering.* New York: McGraw-Hill, 1976.
A discussion of the changes that the traditional role of the father has undergone. Green deals with the father's role in other cultures, the relationship between fathers and children, divorced fathers, and the future of the father's role.

Hall, Francine S. and Hall, Douglas T. *The two-career couple.* Reading, MA: Addison-Wesley, 1979.
New research, common sense advice, interviews, and questionnaires on such topics as competition, transfers, managing the home and family, sex, and splitting up.

Murdock, Carol V. *Single parents are people, too!* New York: Butterick, 1980.
A timely account of the single-parent lifestyle. The book emphasizes the need for social support.

Observational Activities

12.1   *The Value of Children to Young Adults*
In the past two decades, with the rise of the women's movement and the increase in dual-career families, the decision of whether or not to have children has become an important issue. More and more young adults are consciously weighing both the costs and benefits of raising children before committing themselves to a decision concerning parenthood or even marriage.

Interview five married couples and five men and five women who are not married about the value of having children. Ask your respondents the following questions:

1. What do you think are the benefits of having children?
2. What are the drawbacks?
3. Should people be married before having children?
4. If you do want to have children, when in your life would you like to have them? What factors would influence your decision to have a child?
5. What influence would your career plans have on your interests or decision to have or not have children?
6. What changes in your life would you expect following the birth of a child?

After interviewing the people, compare the responses you received with those of your classmates. What are the major benefits and costs of parenthood for today's young adults? How many people plan to remain childless? What factors appear to be important in this decision? How do you interpret the data on the costs and benefits of parenthood in light of the changes that have taken place in society over the past few decades?

12.2   *Shared Roles in Marriage*

In the past, when a man and woman married, each had a reasonably clear idea of the responsibilities and roles each would assume. The husband "provided" for the family and assumed those roles requiring leadership, strength, and technical knowledge. In turn, the wife's primary responsibilities centered on domestic activities and raising the children.

The expectations that young adults bring to marriage today may be different. Traditional marital roles no longer seem so clear-cut.

Interview several couples who have been living with each other for at least a year about the roles and responsibilities that each partner assumes. Try to get a sample of married and unmarried couples. Ask each partner in the couple:

1. To what extent do you have your own specific roles and responsibilities? What are they?
2. Do these roles correspond to traditional gender-role expectations?
3. To what extent are your roles shared?
4. In what areas of your relationship, if any, have traditional, gender-related roles prevailed?
5. Do you like the way the roles and responsibilities in your relationship are divided? Explain.

From the information you have gathered, does it appear that traditional gender roles are breaking down in relationships? Are there differences between married and unmarried couples? Do you have any suggestions for the ideal relationship?

SIX

Middle Adulthood

*P*erhaps *when you were a child you thought that anyone who was 40 years old or older was very old indeed. By the time you reached early adulthood, you might have softened your perspective a bit to recognize that the period of life known as middle adulthood represents a time of reassessment and change. For some people the time between the early forties and early sixties is their prime time; for others, it may be the beginning of their journey to old age and the end of their lives. With life expectancy in the mid-seventies, the early forties marks the second half of the lifespan. With half a time behind them, many people look upon their middle-adulthood years as a time to reconsider the choices they made in earlier stages of life. Family commitments may change as their children grow into adults and their parents grow elderly. Greater confidence and wisdom gained from a wealth of life experiences may stimulate people to break tradition and start new lifestyles or careers.*

The impact of the physical changes characteristic of middle adulthood varies from person to person. But the recognition that life is not forever has a profound effect on everyone. Health concerns become more prominent as past health habits show their effect and as parents or friends become ill.

The middle-adulthood period is a period of challenge and change. Although the changes are less obvious to observers, to the individual, their personal changes can dramatically alter the quality of life. In the next two chapters, we will consider the impact on people of the physical, cognitive, and personality changes during middle adulthood and then examine the changes that occur in their family and work lives.

CHAPTER

13

Middle Adulthood: Physical, Cognitive, and Personality Development

As she looked into the mirror, 45-year-old Karen noticed how gray her hair was becoming. Other signs of aging were also visible—the slight wrinkles around her eyes and mouth, the age spots on her hands, and the thickening of her waistline were all signs that she had reached middle age. "No doubt about it," she thought to herself, "You are definitely not getting any younger!"

Even though Karen did not particularly like the idea, she acknowledged that she was now a middle-aged woman. Not too long ago, she mused, this label had applied to her own mother. Still, with two children ready to enter college and her own parents now official, card-carrying Senior Citizens, Karen recognized that she could not deny the obvious—she had made the transition from the "young generation" to middle adulthood.

Actually, Karen was not that distressed about entering the middle years of life. For one thing, she *felt* young, and despite the physical changes she had begun to notice, she still felt attractive. Certainly, she and her husband continued to have frequent and satisfying sexual relations. If anything concerned Karen about getting older, it was the uncertainty about how she would spend the rest of her life. Karen needed to commit herself to something meaningful, to be creative, and to push herself into new areas.

For the past 20 years, Karen had directed most of her time and energies to the care of her children, family, and home. She took pride in the everyday cooking and sewing projects and in the way she had decorated her house. When the children were younger, she had spent much of her time supervising and assisting them in their activities. As she catalogued her activities and skills, she continued to look for other ways to use her many talents.

Maybe it was the result of what her friends called the "midlife crisis," but she found herself seeking new challenges and goals. She had considered going back to work as a librarian, but decided to try her hand at writing children's books. When her children were young she would make up bedtime stories to tell them. Karen's stories were popular, and her husband had encouraged her to write them down in the hope that she would be able to share them with others someday.

As she sat rereading one of her many bedtime stories, Karen was convinced she had found a way to use her talents. "Imagine, a middle-aged homemaker and mother turned author. Now *that's* a good way to spend your life," she mused.

When considered from a lifespan perspective, development during the middle-adulthood years is a challenge to describe and explain. The changes in physical characteristics, in cognition, and in one's outlook on self and life are affected by the culmination of 40 or more years' life experiences. Events occurring as far back as early childhood can have an impact on the quality and meaning of life in middle adulthood. Significant social, cultural, and historical changes can alter the individual's life experiences. Middle-aged women today, for example, have far greater career opportunities available to them than their mothers did during their middle-adult years. The impact of the broad cultural changes will depend on the individual's life course.

Genetic and biological influences contribute to the changes that occur during middle adulthood. The timing of the transition from young adulthood to middle adulthood is also variable from one person to another. Some people perceive themselves to be middle-aged in their thirties; others, like those in a study reported by Busse, Jeffers, and Christ (1970), continue to view themselves as young or middle-aged well into their sixties. Regardless of when it is perceived, though, this period of life brings with it new tasks and challenges.

In the present chapter, we consider the various changes that are associated with middle age. We begin with a discussion of some of the more important issues in physical development and health confronting the middle-aged person. Next, we take up midlife changes in intelligence, reasoning, and creativity. We conclude the chapter with an examination of the psychosocial tasks of middle age and a discussion of the stability of personality across the adult years.

Physical Development

The most obvious signs of physical aging are those evident to others—manifested on the exterior of the body. In middle age, the skin loses some of its elasticity, laugh lines become facial wrinkles, and the waistline becomes flabbier (a condition affectionately referred to as "love handles"). Hair begins to thin out and often turns gray or white, especially in the armpits and pubic areas. The percentage of body weight that is fat also increases significantly in middle adulthood, both for men and women, although the problem of obesity is more often found in women (Weg, 1977).

Muscular strength declines slowly, but steadily, from young adulthood onward. Troll (1982) notes that between 30 and 80 years of age, maximum muscular strength in men declines 42 percent. This does not mean, however, that middle-aged, or even old people are incapable of activities that require muscular effort. People accustomed to physical work will continue to be productive even into the late fifties and early sixties, particularly if they have engaged in regular physical activity in earlier stages of their lives.

With increasing age, there is a noticeable reduction in breathing efficiency; the person is more easily winded when running or climbing. The heart, too, must work harder to achieve less. This is especially true of people who are overweight or have *atherosclerosis*, a degenerative condition involving thickening and hardening of the artery walls. Both conditions are more common in the late fifties.

Changes in the sensory systems are also marked. Visual acuity peaks in early adulthood and remains relatively stable until the fourth decade, after which there is a slow but steady decline (Timiras, 1972). In almost all cases, however, visual acuity problems can be corrected with glasses. The size of the pupil becomes smaller around age 50, resulting in less light entering the eyes. This means that the person may need brighter lighting to see adequately. At this time, problems with depth perception, recovery from glare, and adap-

Presbycusis A progressive loss of hearing, especially for tones of high frequency, caused by degenerative changes in the auditory system; the most common auditory problem associated with aging.

tation to darkness also are observable (Troll, 1982). The most common auditory problem associated with increasing age is **presbycusis,** a progressive loss of hearing, especially for tones of high frequency, caused by degenerative changes in the auditory system. This condition more often affects men than women (Corso, 1977). Under ordinary circumstances, however, hearing loss has little impact on the day-to-day life of the middle-aged or older adult. Some loss of taste, smell, and sensitivity to touch also occurs in the late forties and fifties but is not generally noticed by the individual until later in life.

The nervous system undergoes changes, which, under ordinary circumstances, have a minimal effect on behavior, perception, and intelligence during middle age. Brain weight decreases after age 20, gradually at first, and more rapidly in later life. However, studies involving electroencephalograms (EEGs), which record the electrical activity of the brain, show little difference between healthy young and old people in many instances (Bromley, 1974). Simple reflex time (e.g., the hammer-on-the-knee) remains about the same from 20 to 80 years (Hugin, Norris, & Shock, 1960). Reactions to complex stimuli involving more complex transmission of impulses, however, become slower. There also seems to be a slowing of conductivity in the peripheral nerves and across synapses, which may result in a generalized slowing down of bodily functions and processes (Timiras, 1972).

Although the middle years bring a gradual decline in physical functioning from the peak reached in the twenties, the human organism does not experience a sudden reversal from growth to deterioration. Even in early life, both processes are taking place. For example, since nerve cells do not multiply after the first year of life, their number declines. Because of the overabundance of such cells, the loss is insignificant, at least until the late sixties and, more often, the seventies. The heart (cardiovascular) diseases of middle age are also the result of cumulative rather than sudden conditions. For the average person, cardiac output (as measured in a state of rest) begins to decline not in middle age but around 19 or 20, at about the rate of 1 percent a year (DeVries, 1975); perhaps at age 50 a problem will be noticed. Similarly, some medical authorities claim that the first lesions of atherosclerosis are laid down in the first years of life (Timiras, 1972). Midlife, then, is not a sharp turning point; it simply marks the point at which the balance begins to shift, gradually and inevitably, from growth to decline.

Pause for Thought

The impact on people of the physical changes associated with aging depends on the value that cultures place on age. In the Chinese culture where elderly adults are held in high esteem, growing old is viewed more positively than in a culture where being young is valued. How does the American culture value growing old? How is this value communicated to people?

Factors Related to Health and Aging

It has been long recognized, and more recently documented, that an individual's rate of physical decline is partly determined by *heredity*. There are families whose members seem to be particularly long-lived. Insurance companies and other actuarial accounts show that a person whose same-gender parent suffered a condition such as cardiovascular disease or breast cancer is at risk by virtue of heredity. Striking similarities have also been found in the aging patterns of identical twins. Even family photographs reveal the similarity of smile and facial wrinkles from one generation to the next. How well the organism wears, and which diseases it is vulnerable to, thus, are partly influenced by the original genetic endowment established at conception.

Aging is not merely a biological process, however. Many *environmental* factors are involved. For example, a recent study has shown that a series of life changes—death of a spouse, divorce, change of job or residence—may be so stressful as to result in rapid aging or increased vulnerability to a variety of disease processes (Rahe, Mahan, & Arthur, 1970). (See Table 13.1.) Moreover, statistics show that married people, especially men, tend to live longer than their unmarried cohorts; that white, middle-class people live longer than poor whites or minority-group members in our culture; and that certain Russian peasants who live in cohesive social structures live longer and have more vigorous lives than certain urban, American populations (Benet, 1976).

Health and Nutrition

The way in which people conduct their lives plays a major role in the extent to which they can offset the physical changes that accompany aging. Belloc and Breslow (1972) reported that seven personal habits are related to the health status and longevity of middle-aged and older adults. These habits include: smoking cigarettes, drinking immoderately, sleeping less than seven hours a night (and to a lesser degree, more than nine), failing to eat breakfast, weighing too much (and to a lesser degree, too little), failing to exercise on a regular basis, and eating between meals.

Smoking dramatically raises mortality and disease rates of middle-aged adults.

The risk of cancer and other diseases is reduced by eating a nutritious diet, especially one which includes fibers found in whole grains and cereals.

The mortality rate of men who practiced four or more of these habits was four times higher than those who had none of them; among women the death rate was doubled. Moderate alcohol consumption, one or two drinks per sitting, was positively associated with good health; teetotalers had slightly higher death rates. A complete lack of exercise doubled the death rate for both men and women, but there was no difference shown between moderately active and very active people. Even a little exercise kept people healthier than no exercise at all. For this reason, many corporations are including as part of their job benefits access to exercise programs and facilities on the work site.

More important than all the other health habits mentioned above, however, may be a proper diet. Not only is it best to eat only at meal times, but the calories eaten should be chosen carefully. According to a recent surgeon general's report on diet and disease, the typical American diet is too high in fats, sugar, cholesterol, and salt, and too low in fiber.

Scientists have estimated that as many as half of human cancers are diet related. A high intake of fats is associated with cancers of the breast and colon and may promote the growth of other cancers as well, according to Dr. Arthur Upton, director of the National Cancer Institute (Brody, 1979). The risk of colon cancer is reduced by eating fiber, which is found in whole grains (bran) and cereals, and fresh fruit and vegetables.

Health and Middle-Adulthood Stress

Another health-related factor for middle-aged adults that has received increased attention is general life stress. Theorell and Rahe (1974), for example, have noted a positive relationship between the incidence of heart attacks and the number and type of such major changes in the person's life as death of a spouse, divorce, loss of a job, or retirement. Throughout life, people must adjust to numerous stressful events and transitions. Not all of these events are necessarily negative ones. For example, in a scale of stressful life events developed by Holmes and Rahe (1967) (see Table 13.1), marriage and the

Table 13.1

Social Readjustment Rating Scale

Rank	Life Event	Stress Value
1	Death of a spouse	100
2	Divorce	73
3	Marital separation	65
4	Jail term	63
5	Death of a close family member	63
6	Personal injury or illness	53
7	Marriage	50
8	Fired at work	47
9	Marital reconciliation	45
10	Retirement	45
11	Change in health of family member	44
12	Pregnancy	40
13	Sex difficulties	39
14	Gain of new family member	39
15	Business readjustment	39
16	Change in financial status	38
17	Death of a close friend	37
18	Change to different line of work	36
19	Change in number of arguments with spouse	35
20	Mortgage over $10,000	31
21	Foreclosure of mortgage or loan	30
22	Change in responsibilities at work	29
23	Son or daughter leaving home	29
24	Trouble with in-laws	29
25	Outstanding personal achievement	28
26	Wife beginning or stopping work	26
27	Beginning or ending school	26
28	Change in living conditions	25
29	Revision of personal habits	24
30	Trouble with boss	23
31	Change in work hours or conditions	20
32	Change in residence	20
33	Change in schools	20
34	Change in reaction	19
35	Change in church activities	19
36	Change in social activities	18
37	Mortgage or loan less than $10,000	17
38	Change in sleeping habits	16

Table 13.1 (con't.) ▬▬▬▬

39	Change in number of family get-togethers	15
40	Change in eating habits	15
41	Vacation	13
42	Christmas	12
43	Minor violations of the law	11

Source: From "The Social Readjustment Rating Scale" by T. H. Holmes and R. H. Rahe, *Journal of Psychosomatic Research*, 1967, *11*, 213–218.

birth of a child are ranked among the top stressors. Both of these events, while generally cause for celebration, require people to make changes in the way they lead their lives and define themselves. They often result in other related changes such as a change in family income and place of residence.

Holmes and Rahe's Social Readjustment Scale is widely used to assess the level of stress in people's lives. People are asked to check off the events that have occurred during the past six or 12 months. A total stress index is then derived by summing up all the stress values associated with the checked life events; the more events in people's lives, and the more changes they had to make, the greater the level of stress. According to Holmes and Rahe, the higher the score, the more the person is at risk for a major health problem. A score over 300 is likely to be associated with a major life crisis and a significant decline in health (Holmes & Masuda, 1974).

What is not included in Holmes and Rahe's listing of stressful events are the daily and chronic hassles that seem to erode the quality of life and contribute to a person's level of stress (Lazarus & DeLongis, 1983; Lazarus & Folkman, 1984). Getting stuck in traffic jams, misplacing one's keys, arguing with sales clerks or adolescent children—although relatively trivial compared to the death of a spouse or close friend—when experienced on a daily basis,

This man has several bad health habits which contribute to a shorter lifespan. Can you identify at least one of them in this picture?

Getting a parking ticket is just one of many daily hassles which can add stress to a person's life.

can combine to affect one's emotional well-being. The 10 most frequently reported hassles among middle-aged adults are listed in Table 13.2 Depending on where a person lives and on their socioeconomic status, some events may be more or less troublesome. For example, a person who lives in a noisy and crowded apartment complex may be bothered more by the physical environment than someone who lives in a more spacious or tranquil setting.

Other common sources of stress during middle adulthood can include role conflicts for employed parents or dual-earner families, changes in the

Table 13.2

Ten Most Frequent Hassles among Middle-Aged Adults

1 Concern about weight
2 Health of a family member
3 Rising price of common goods
4 Home maintenance
5 Too many things to do
6 Misplacing or losing things
7 Yard work or outside home maintenance
8 Property, investments, or taxes
9 Crime
10 Physical appearance

Source: From "Little hassles can be hazardous to your health" by R. Lazarus, *Psychology Today*, 1981, July, p. 61.

size and composition of the household through divorce, remarriage, or the exit of adult children, or the physical and mental decline of one's parents. Events such as parents' aging, children leaving home, and divorce and remarriage are more likely to occur during the early part of middle adulthood. They may even occur simultaneously.

Furthermore, a life event may be the source of stress for one person and not for another. There is wide variation in the meaning and reaction to life events. Thus, it is not so much that specific life events are stressful as it is that a person's stress level is influenced by the way in which he or she copes with the combined stresses of living.

Pause for Thought

Many life events are transitions in which people must solve the problem of how they will readjust their lives to meet the new demands. Furthermore, the way in which people construe the meaning and consequence of a life event can affect their level of stress. Clearly, there must be a connection between people's emotional well-being and their cognitive development. What might this connection be? Can people be trained to experience less stress in their lives?

Type-A Behavior: A Factor in Heart Disease

Whereas the leading causes of death for young adults are accidents and suicide, during middle adulthood, the major causes are cardiovascular diseases and cancer. Nearly 40 percent of deaths in this age group are due to heart disease, of which 80 percent of the victims are men (U. S. Department of Health, Education & Welfare, 1978). Cardiovascular diseases have been associated with heredity, diet (particularly foods high in cholesterol and fat), smoking, overweight, and lack of exercise. However, 50 percent of all heart-disease victims could not be linked to any known causal factor. Recently, scientists have identified a pattern called *Type-A behavior* as one possible missing link and a major contributor to coronary heart disease (Cooper, Detre, & Weiss, 1981).

Type-A Behavior A behavioral and emotional pattern associated with coronary heart disease; includes explosive and accelerated speech, impatience with delay, excessive competitiveness and achievement striving, restlessness, undue irritability, and a chronic sense of time urgency.

According to Matthews (1982), the **Type-A Behavior** pattern, which was first identified by Friedman and Rosenman (1974; Rosenman & Friedman, 1983) in their work with middle-aged cardiac patients, is not a personality trait, but a continuum of behaviors associated with varying degrees of risk for heart disease. At one end of the continuum are the Type-A related behaviors, which include explosive, accelerated speech, impatience with delay, excessive competitiveness and achievement striving, restlessness, and undue irritability. The Type-A pattern also is characterized by a chronic sense of time urgency — the person feels that there is just too much to do and not enough time to do it. In response to the time pressure and the tendency toward achievement striving, Type-A people find themselves in a constant struggle to control and master their environment. In addition, this pattern is associated with a heightened pace of living—Type-A individuals move, walk, and even eat rapidly and often attempt to accomplish two tasks simultaneously. Compulsive in their acquisition and quest for "numbers," Type-A people measure their self-worth by how fast they achieve high-status goals. They also possess an aggressive drive that may become free-floating hostility. A simple conversation or sporting event, for example, can become a hostile, angry struggle. At the other end of the continuum are Type-B related behaviors, which are directly opposite to the Type-A behaviors—a relaxed, unhurried approach to the world, low aggressiveness, low-to-moderate achievement striving, and so on.

The causative link between Type-A behavior and heart disease is based on four findings: (1) the presence of Type-A behavior patterns in those individuals already afflicted with coronary heart disease; (2) the extreme vulnerability of Type-A persons to the disease—Type-A behavior is associated with at least twice the occurrence of heart disease as Type-B behavior (Jenkins, Rosenman, & Zyzanski, 1974); (3) the presence of certain coronary biochemical abnormalities in Type-A persons; and, most important, (4) successful experiments in which Type-A behavior was induced, following which coronary biochemical changes were found. Other research suggests that Type-A people are so busy and preoccupied that they may ignore important physical symptoms. This may actually contribute to the risk of heart disease by preventing them from seeking medical attention or altering their behavior to reduce tension (Matthews & Brunson, 1979; Weidner & Matthews, 1978). Although the stereotype of the Type-A person is the hard-driven, compulsive male executive, research evidence suggests that women who exhibit this behavior pattern are also at greater risk for heart disease (Eisdorfer & Wilkie, 1977).

Furthermore, recent research (Steinberg, 1988) suggests that the Type-A behavior pattern is likely to have had its origins in early childhood, when the characteristic behaviors are likely to be interpreted as temperament. Such dimensions of temperaments as low activity, negative mood, low sensory threshold and high adaptability are associated with adult Type-A behavior pattern for males. For Type-A females, early temperamental characteristics are high activity, high adaptability for achievement and low adaptability for impatience and negative mood. That early temperamental characteristics are associated with the adult Type-A behavior pattern does not mean that all children who display these characteristics will grow up to be Type-A adults. Throughout the course of development from childhood to middle adulthood, socialization and life experience can significantly interact with temperament to affect behavior patterns.

Menopause and the Climacteric

During middle adulthood, people undergo a number of changes in their reproductive and sexual organs, a process that generally is referred to as the **climacteric.** These changes are linked to a decrease in the production of gonadal, or sex, hormones—specifically, estrogens and testosterones produced, respectively, by the ovaries and testes. Although the pituitary gland continues to send strong messages to the gonads, and although the adrenals, thyroid, and pancreas continue to function as before, the gonads simply become less productive in the middle-adult years.

For women, the mid-forties mark the beginning of a decline in estrogen and progesterone levels. The decrease in estrogen levels eventually leads to **menopause,** the cessation of the menses, when women stop menstruating and can no longer bear children. The cessation of menstruation takes place over

Climacteric Changes in the reproductive and sexual organs that usually accompany middle age.

Menopause The cessation of ovulation and menstruation signaling the loss of fertility in women, usually occurring between ages 45 and 55.

a period of from two to five years. The decline in estrogen levels results in thinning of the vaginal walls, a slowing down of the vaginal lubrication response, cessation of ovulation and menstruation, and a shrinking of the ovaries and uterus.

The way in which these changes are experienced somewhat parallels adolescent development. Women experience a clear beginning to "womanhood" in the first menstruation (menarche) but for the first year or so, the menstrual cycle may be *anovulatory,* which means that the young girl may be infertile or only irregularly fertile. During the climacteric, women again experience relatively clear signs of change in the menopause. Twelve consecutive months without menstruating is experienced on the average at 50 years of age (Weideger, 1976), although there is wide individual variation. Again, like the adolescent girl, the older woman is irregularly fertile; she may be anovulatory one cycle, and surprised to find herself pregnant the next. These changes, however, are not experienced primarily in terms of sexual activity; that is, a woman can participate in and enjoy sexual intercourse no matter what her fertility status. In fact, Hyde (1979) reports that for many women, menopause is sexually liberating since the fear of pregnancy no longer exists. (See Box, Midlife Pregnancy).

Researchers have also noted that a number of unpleasant symptoms have been correlated with menopause, including profuse sweating, "hot flashes," dizziness, headaches, irritability, depression, insomnia, and weight gain. Approximately 30 percent of all menopausal women seek medical attention for one of these symptoms (Weideger, 1976). One long-term effect of a decreased level of estrogen is **osteoporosis**, a condition in which bones become thinner and hence more fragile and breakable. Although the effects of osteoporosis are more visible in late adulthood, the condition begins much earlier in the lifespan. Likewise, the disease is more readily prevented by steps taken in early and middle adulthood. Adding calcium to the diet and starting an exercise program such as walking, running, bicycling or dancing are two measures that are recommended for preventing osteoporosis. Some people are at higher risk for the disorder, namely women who begin menopause at an early age because their ovaries have been surgically removed. In high-risk cases, doctors recommend the administration of estrogen (National Institutes of Health, 1984). Estrogen therapy has also been used to reduce other menopausal symptoms.

Recently, however, medical studies have shown a strong relation between prolonged use of estrogens, as part of a program of estrogen replacement therapy, and the incidence of cancer of the breast and endometrium (the lining of the uterus) (Antunes, Stolley, Rosenshein, Davies, Tonascia, Brown, Burnett, Rutledge, Pokempner, & Garcia, 1979; Hoover, Gray, & Cole, 1976; Nathanson & Lorenz, 1982). Thus the use of estrogen replacement in menopausal women is a controversial treatment.

Some women have strongly objected to the medical-model approach to menopause, which stereotypes this biological state as a disease. Goodman (1980) reminds us that menopause refers to the cessation of menstruation, which sometimes, but certainly not always, is accompanied by unpleasant physical symptoms. She found that these same symptoms are often present in premenopausal women. In fact, the only difference Goodman found in her research between menopausal and premenopausal women, after adjusting

Osteoporosis A condition that results in the thinning of the bones in old age.

Human Development in Practice

Midlife Pregnancy

Although most women start and complete their families during their early adulthood years, more women are delaying both marriage and their childbearing until they have settled into a career. The result of these shifting trends is that more women are choosing to have a child during their middle-adulthood years. This trend is in contrast to the past when most midlife pregnancies were the result of "change-of-life" unplanned conceptions.

According to Ian Morrison (1975), "the label 'high risk' in a modern obstetrical context applies to the fetus." With careful prenatal care and a nutritious diet, there is no longer a greater risk to the life of an elderly (defined by doctors as over 35) pregnant woman than to a younger woman. The risks involve the infant. There is a greater likelihood of stillbirth or a neonatal (within the first month of life) death; there is a greater likelihood that the fetus will be smaller over the nine-month period, resulting in a greater chance of miscarriage, stillbirth, or premature birth; and there is a greater chance of neonatal morbidity, that is, that the infant will have central nervous-system problems or respiratory problems related to the birth itself. Despite these alarming statistics, the mortality rates are low. The mortality rate for infants of elderly mothers, is still only 47 per 1000 births—more than twice the national infant mortality rate but an unlikely event for any individual mother. Furthermore, infant mortality rates for high-risk pregnancies combine the birthing experience of two different groups of women. First is the elderly mother who has had more than one child (referred to as *multiparous*). If she is poor, not in good health, and perhaps malnourished during her pregnancy, this woman has a poor chance of having a healthy baby in midlife. The older woman having her first child (referred to as *primagravida*) but who is middle class and in excellent health usually seeks out the best care for herself and should have no problems. It is important to note that general health is a better predictor of the outcome of pregnancy than age.

As mentioned in Chapter 2, the incidence of Down syndrome (mongolism) is related to age.

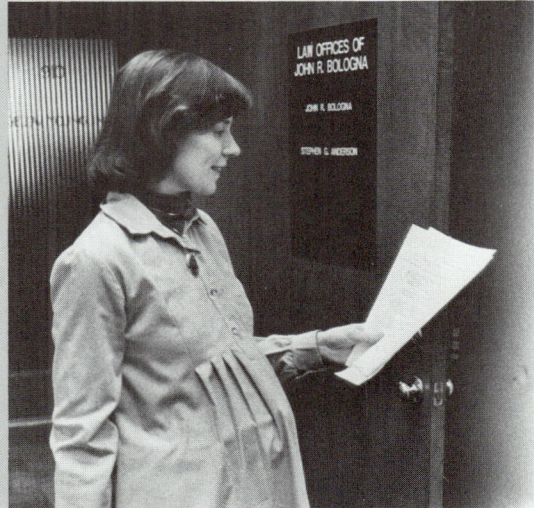

Today, more women are delaying having children until they have established themselves in their career. With good medical care this woman will probably have a healthy baby even though she is over 35.

The chances—about one in 1000 at age 30—rise to less than one in 100 by about age 45. One other statistic that climbs for elderly mothers is the rate of delivery by cesarean section, a surgical procedure. One explanation is the greater readiness of obstetricians to perform cesareans on older mothers. It is generally accepted by obstetricians that a cesarean will prevent many of the complications that might arise during the delivery of a child by an older woman. Rather than judge each case on its own merits, some obstetricians prefer to be safe and remove the infant surgically.

Clearly, the advantage of a midlife pregnancy is the maturity a woman and her husband can bring to the experience. An older woman knows herself better, has had a greater depth of experience in the world, and can handle any problems that arise more wisely and with greater strength. She should not be threatened by the idea that at 35 or 40 she is too old to bear and rear children of her own.

for age differences between the groups, was that the former more often had surgery related to female disorders. No difference was found for the incidence of sweating, headaches, nervous tension, and other "common menopausal symptoms."

Only a small percentage of women have symptoms so severe that they are prohibited from going about their daily routine (Neugarten, Wood, Kraines, & Loomis, 1963). Yet the stereotype remains, often contributing, and unnecessarily so, to problems in midlife adjustment.

Male Climacteric

What about men? Do they also undergo a menopause? Strictly speaking, they do not, for they have never menstruated. Yet there are clear changes in male reproductive and sexual organs during the middle-adult years. At about the age of 50, men experience a decline in testosterone, which is more gradual than the estrogen decline experienced by women. This decline results in a slight decrease in the number of healthy, active sperm and in the size of the testicles; a reduction in the force of ejaculation and the volume of fluid ejaculated also is experienced, as is an enlargement of the prostate gland (Weg, 1975). Middle-aged males also find that they require more time and stimulation to achieve an erection, and a longer period between erections than they did in adolescence and young adulthood. On the other hand, erections can usually be maintained for longer periods of time by the middle-aged male. Unlike women, the climacteric has little effect on male fertility status; most men remain fertile throughout life. In fact, one consequence of remarriage is that more men are becoming fathers during middle adulthood because they marry younger women, who are still in their childbearing years.

Although some men report a sudden increase in insomnia, irritability, headaches, and other "menopausal" symptoms in middle age, the majority seem unaware of the physical changes that are taking place. The climacteric, if experienced at all, usually is felt as a falling off of desire (less frequent and spontaneous erections) or decline in performance (usually caused by impotence anxiety). Seldom does a man consult a doctor about the climacteric. Unlike women, men do not usually have an ongoing relationship with a physician who is especially concerned with reproductive functions.

Midlife Sexuality

In the past, it was more or less assumed that middle-aged people did not approach sex with anything like the vigorous interest of the young. Whether due to fatigue, impotence (or the fear of it), or declining physical attractiveness, the middle-aged person was thought to experience a falling off of desire. Today, however, it is understood that this stereotype is an oversimplification of the facts. With good health, good spirits, and an available and interested partner, sexual activity can be a vital part of the life of the middle-aged and older adult.

To some extent, sexual expression in midlife (as in adolescence) is influenced by cultural expectations. There is increased willingness of middle-aged people to respond honestly to researchers' questions about sex, and there are more relaxed attitudes toward sexual matters since the 1960s and 1970s.

Table 13.3

**Frequency per Week of Martial Coitus:
Male and Female Estimates Combined**

Kinsey, Pomeroy, & Martin: 1948, 1953		Hunt: 1974	
Age	Median	Age	Median
16–25	2.45	18–24	3.25
26–35	1.95	25–34	2.55
36–45	1.40	35–44	2.00
46–55	.85	45–54	1.00
56–60	.50	55+	1.00

There also seems to be greater and more varied sexual expression among today's middle-aged than the middle-aged that Kinsey reported on in his ground-breaking research over 35 years ago. The average frequency of marital intercourse for couples in all age groups has increased from the time of Kinsey's sampling (Kinsey, Pomeroy, & Martin, 1948, 1953) to Hunt's sampling (1974); the increase was proportionately greatest for people over age 55. Moreover, the 35-to-44-age group in the 1974 sampling was more active than the 26-to-35 age group a generation ago (Hunt & Hunt, 1975).

Nevertheless, there are differences between the sexuality of youth and middle age. Sometime between the ages of 46 and 55, the majority of men and women become aware of a decline in sexual interest and activity (Pfeiffer, Verwoerdt, & Davis, 1972) (see Table 13.3). Although middle-aged men and women experience complete and satisfying sexual relationships, sexual response is usually slower, characterized by more leisurely and imaginative foreplay. While the older male may require prolonged physical stimulation before he achieves erection (Kaplan, 1977), such activity may actually enhance the intimacy between partners.

There are a number of reasons that middle age brings new sexual satisfaction to some couples. For women, there is reduced fear of pregnancy and, after 50 to 55, little fear at all. Birth control can be safely ignored. With the launching of the children from the home, privacy increases, promoting sexual expression and other forms of communication that enhance intimacy and sexual response. Finally, there is cultural support, as never before, for pleasurable and guiltless sexuality among people of all ages.

Pause for Thought

By the time many parents reach middle adulthood, their children have become sexually active teenagers or young adults at their physical peak. Most parents do not discuss their own sexual behavior with their children. The net result is that many teenagers and young adults find it hard to imagine their middle-aged parents as sexually active. What impact might the presence of sexually active children living in the home have on the sexual behavior of middle-aged parents?

Cognitive Development

Until fairly recently, it was assumed that intelligence, like muscular strength or height, was fully developed by late adolescence or the early twenties. This assumption recognizes the physical basis of intelligence—that is, the brain and related neurological foundations. More recent work has suggested that although some aspects of intelligence may develop only until young adulthood, intellectual development continues into later adulthood. Some cognitive skills such as wisdom and expertise in living may not even appear until mid- or late adulthood (Baltes, 1987). Furthermore, depending upon how intelligence and cognitive ability are defined and measured, different conclusions can be drawn about whether there is an overall decline in cognitive development with age (Salthouse, 1982). Many of the earlier theories of intellectual and cognitive development grew out of either an interest in test development (psychometric movement) or an interest in the formation of cognitive capabilities in childhood and young adulthood (e.g., Piagetian theory). Today, lifespan-development researchers are taking a new look at cognitive and intellectual development. A lifespan perspective views intellectual development as a multifaceted process that can proceed in different directions across the lifespan (Baltes, 1987). Knowledge and understanding are also influenced by the culture and times of a person's life course.

Intelligence

The intelligence quotient (IQ) has long been the measure of intelligence in school-age children. Standardized intelligence tests measuring IQ have also been given to large adult populations, as for example, to army recruits. When different age groups are tested in a cross-sectional design, that is, testing all ages at one time, age-related patterns emerge. These patterns are naturally of interest to psychologists studying intelligence over the lifespan.

In an early large-scale administration of a standardized intelligence test, Jones and Conrad (1933) discovered that individuals about 20 years of age scored higher than middle-aged and older adults; this was interpreted to mean that intelligence began a long decline at age 20. In more recent cross-sectional studies of adult intelligence, however, the average peak of performance seems to occur between 25 and 35 (Schaie, 1979, 1983). Middle-aged and older people do less well on these tests than younger adults.

A problem with the cross-sectional design is that we cannot assume that the differences between age groups are solely the result of aging. Younger subjects may score higher than middle-aged subjects not because they are more intelligent, but because of such variables as more formal education, better nutrition, and greater childhood exposure to television. Just as important is the greater experience that most younger people have with taking standardized tests. The higher scores, then, may represent *generation* or *cohort* effects as opposed to (or in addition to) effects of aging.

The possibility of large cohort effects for intelligence is impressively illustrated in a study by Flynn (1984). This investigator showed that every Stanford-Binet and Wechsler intelligence test standardization sample from 1932 to 1978 established norms of a higher standard than its predecessor. As Flynn notes, the obvious interpretation of this pattern is that representative samples of Americans did better and better on IQ tests over a period of 46 years, the total gain amounting to a rise in mean IQ of 13.8 points. What is unclear is whether the finding means that people today are more intelligent than people tested 40 to 50 years ago, or whether people today are simply better test takers. (A further discussion of cohort effects will be found in the later section of this chapter on personality development.)

In order to minimize generation effects and gain a clearer picture of changes in intelligence over time, longitudinal studies have been conducted. In these studies, the same individuals are tested and retested at different points in their lifespan. Based on this approach, little or no decline in intelligence has been found in middle age. In fact four major studies showed that middle-aged adults performed better than they had as young adults (Bayley & Oden, 1955; Eichorn, Hunt, & Honzik, 1981; Nisbet, 1957; Schaie, 1979, 1983)—although this increase may have been a reflection of the highly select, intellectually superior sample of subjects.

The longitudinal studies have their own biases, however. For one thing, it is the highly motivated and healthier individual who remains in the study (which may continue for 20, 30, or even 40 years). The results, then, may reflect intelligence as it operates in the more vital and thoughtful individual. A second point is that longitudinal studies may be affected by changes in environment. For example, if testing were to become much more frequent during a given decade, all respondents tested after that time might do better— on the basis of their experience in the testing situation—than they had done 20 years earlier. Similarly, being given the same or similar tests repeatedly over a period of time sensitizes people to the test-taking situation — that is, they learn how to take tests, and consequently, may do better on later tests. In each case, an increase in test scores would reflect more than aging.

A study by Schaie and Hertzog (1983) supports the belief that little, if any, significant decline in intellectual functioning takes place during middle adulthood. Using a sophisticated methodological design that allowed them to separate age effects from cohort effects, these investigators noted that marked decreases in most areas of intellectual performance do not occur until after 60 years of age. When declines were observed prior to 60, they did not appear to be, in the words of the authors, "of sufficient magnitude to be practically important." Perhaps the best conclusion regarding intelligence in middle-aged adults is that decreases in performance, if they exist at all, are certainly not universal.

Fluid and Crystallized Abilities

In order to test intelligence, researchers must define what it is they are testing. Over the years, the concept of intelligence has included a large number of factors such as verbal abilities, long- and short-term memory, reasoning ability, general information, and quickness of response. Because of the need to distinguish between intelligence acquired as a result of education and absorption of one's culture, and intelligence acquired as a result of more "casual learning influences" (Horn & Donaldson, 1980), some researchers have proposed a model in which intelligence is divided into two patterns they call fluid and crystallized intelligence (Cattell, 1963; Horn, 1972; Horn & Cattell, 1966).

Crystallized intelligence is culturally derived, that is, it is a result of accumulated knowledge and of problem-solving techniques learned initially

Crystallized Intelligence Abilities that depend on the individual's acquisition of information and skills important to his or her culture.

in school and more generally through direct instruction and socialization; it involves a knowledge of one's language and of the skills and technology of one's culture. Examples of crystallized intelligence include such abilities as vocabulary, general information, social judgment, reasoning ability related to formal logic, and mechanical knowledge such as the use of tools and the understanding of mechanical principles. Crystallized intelligence is associated with the use of principles common to the culture in which one lives.

Fluid Intelligence
Abilities that enable a person to perceive relationships, draw inferences, conceptualize, abstract information, and comprehend implications.

Fluid intelligence relates to abilities such as seeing relationships among stimulus patterns (such as in putting puzzles together), drawing inferences about relationships, and comprehending their implications. As Horn (1982) notes, this component of intelligence represents the fundamental features of reasoning, abstraction, and problem solving that are not dependent on direct training and socialization within a culture. Research suggests that fluid intelligence is directly linked to neurophysiological intactness in the individual. This finding explains why fluid intelligence is more affected than crystallized intelligence by hereditary factors as well as injury to the central nervous system.

What is the relevance of fluid and crystallized intelligence to aging? Fluid intelligence peaks between the ages of 20 and 30 and thereafter declines. Crystallized intelligence, on the other hand, increases as one gets older (Horn, 1982; Horn & Donaldson, 1980). (See Figure 13.1.) Horn and Donaldson try

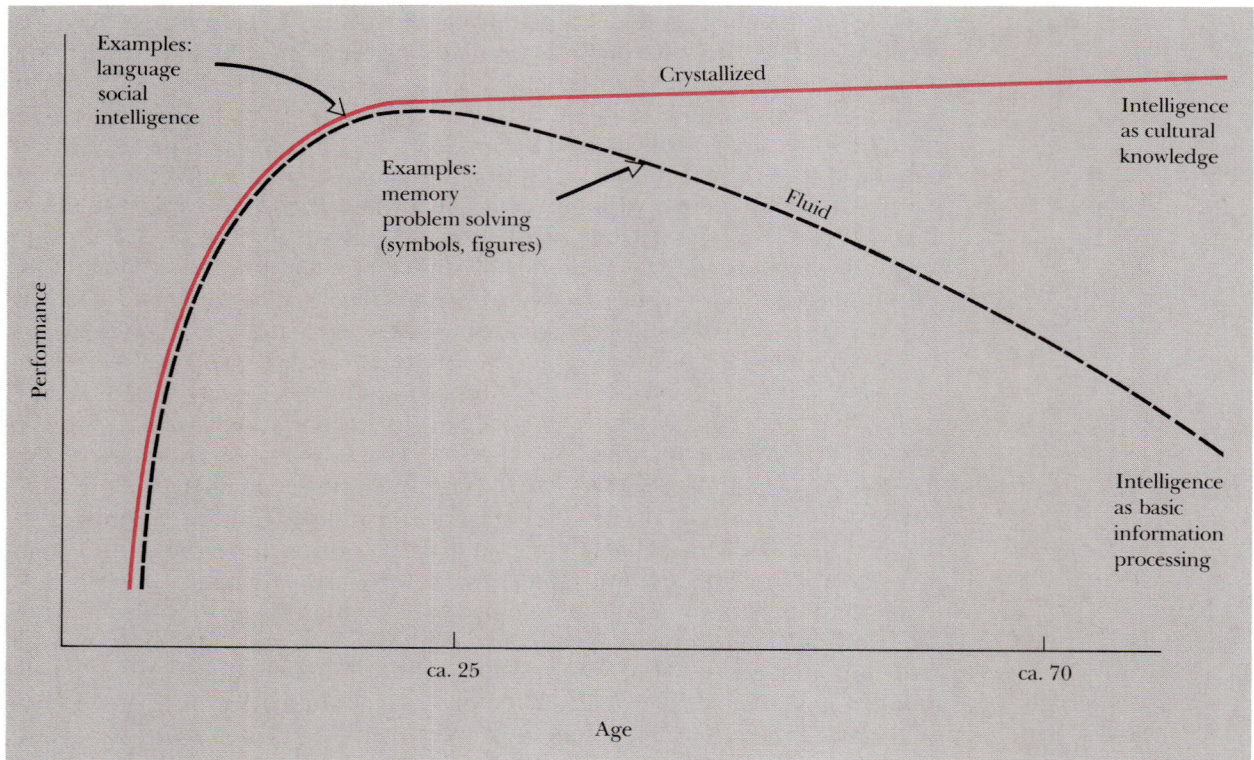

Figure 13.1 Changes in fluid and crystallized intelligence over the adult years.

to explain these differences by pointing to the learning process. If one is concentrating one's energies on a learning task, the quality of learning is enhanced. These researchers point to the years from 20 to 30 as a period of great intensity in learning one's occupation as well as making sexual and marital adjustments. Thus, one's fluid abilities are strained to the utmost in finding personal solutions to life's problems. At the same time, one builds one's crystallized intelligence on the retention of what was learned during these years. For example, it is a lot easier to learn how to operate a computer terminal if you have already learned how to type.

Pause for Thought

Cognitive and intellectual skills are obviously related to the health and functioning of the brain and nervous system. In what ways might the differences in measured abilities between young and middle-adulthood people be affected by their health status? (e.g., cardiovascular diseases, cancer)?

Creativity

While most researchers interested in intellectual functioning across the life-span have focused on the skills and knowledge represented in standardized intelligence tests, or Piagetian-type measures, others have sought to examine the more creative aspects of human functioning. One researcher (Lehman, 1953) studied the quality of the creative work of recognized artists and scientists and found that his subjects made fewer high-quality creative contributions as they became older. Creative breakthroughs were more often the work of young adults; there was a falling off in the quality of creative productions in middle age. Another researcher (Dennis, 1966) studied productivity, that is, the number of contributions, regardless of quality, in males who had lived to 80 years of age. Artists, such as musicians and poets, reach their peak productivity earlier than scientists and scholars. However, scientists and scholars whose creative work involved extensive collection and evaluation of data as, for example, historians and geologists, were especially productive in middle and late adulthood.

Some researchers have found that the creative abilities of middle-aged adults increased with their level of self-esteem.

What factors might be related to the decline in creativity of artists from young adulthood through old age, and to the later productivity of scientists and scholars? Bromley (1967) measured creativity in three groups of adults with a mean group age of 27, 47, and 67 years. Creativity was measured by asking the subjects to produce unique or novel arrangements and sortings of different colored and shaped blocks. Bromley found that the number of unique responses declined with increased age such that people in the 67 year-old mean age group produced only 50 to 60 percent as many responses as the people in the 27-year-old mean age group. Since all of the subjects were of similar and superior intelligence (IQ scores for the groups range from 121–123) the researcher excluded the possibility that declines in creativity were due to declines in intelligence. Rather, the age differences were interpreted as a reflection of the combined decline in three cognitive skills: persistence, flexibility of thought, and abstraction. Alpaugh and Birren (1977) identified two variables that are related to a decline in the creative contribu-

Human Development in Practice

Middle-Aged Student Teachers

You could always spot the student teachers in the classroom. They were younger and quieter than the other teachers and usually had a worried or unsure look about them. Today, however, if you were to peek into an elementary school you might not be able to tell the new teachers from the more seasoned ones. That's because a growing number of middle-aged people are entering college and some of them are entering the teaching profession.

In 1978, 13 percent of all adults between the ages of 35 and 54 were enrolled in some kind of formal education. Both men and women are returning to school; however, women make up the majority of returning students. From 1975 to 1979, the number of women over 35 attending college increased by 66.8 percent (U.S. Bureau of the Census, 1979). Many of these women are single parents who are seeking to improve their career opportunities and financial earnings.

For some, middle adulthood corresponds with the time when their children are well on their way to independence and when they are seeking new intellectual and personal challenges. For these who select education as their major focus of study, it is an opportunity to meet their need for generativity by using their knowledge and skills to educate children.

Middle-aged new teachers are likely to have an advantage in the classroom because they do not look like novices and because their life experiences can often be put to good use in teaching children.

tions of older people: *divergent thinking* and a *preference for complexity*. Divergent thinking includes the ability to think of many different ideas appropriate to a situation; originality; and the ability to change and transform ideas from one state to another. A preference for complexity of ideas has been equated with creativity itself (Barron, 1963; Helson, 1967). Alpaugh and Birren, working with a cross-sectional sample of subjects from 20 to 83 years of age, carefully controlled for education, found systematic declines in both variables with increasing age, whereas their measures for intelligence remained constant. They concluded, therefore, that in addition to declines in such factors as energy and vigor, declines in creative production across the lifespan—as related to cognitive processes—can be explained in terms of a decrease in divergent thinking and preference for complexity rather than any decline in intelligence per se.

Other researchers, however, have not confirmed a linear decline in divergent thinking from young adulthood through the elderly years. Jaquish and Ripple (1981) observed that middle-aged adults performed better than

For women who enter college after years of being out of the classroom and in the home, the initial prospect of being a student may be stressful. Most of their classmates and some of their faculty may be younger than they are. The role of student is one more role that they must balance in addition to wife, mother, neighbor, and daughter. They may experience feelings of self-doubt and uncertainty about their ability to do well "at their age." The peak of fluid intelligence occurs in adolescence and slowly declines throughout adulthood. Would this put the older student at a disadvantage in a classroom full of 18- to 20-year-olds?

Apparently not. Research studies show that the typical older student, after an initial period of adjustment, does better in college than the typical 18-year-old. One reason for their superior performance may be that older students usually have clearer personal goals and greater motivation. Furthermore, older students have higher levels of crystallized intelligence; in their years of experience they have accumulated a wide array of general information and problem-solving skills that can readily be applied to their studies.

Adult students are usually conscientious about their education. They attend all their classes, read and prepare their assignments, and seek ways to apply their classroom knowledge in the real world. In many cases, the older education major has the advantage of having experienced years of teachers and school curricula from the other side as a parent of students. They are more likely to bring their vivid experiences into their education classes or to challenge lecture material when it seems to contradict their understanding. Adult students actively involve themselves in their education.

Once in the classroom, the adult student teacher has the advantage of not looking like a novice. Working with and around children may not be a new experience for adults who have raised children for 15 or 20 years. They can more readily bring into their teaching the many ideas, observations, and objects they have collected over their adult years. For example, quilting may have once been a hobby for a young mother. Once in the classroom as a teacher, she can use her knowledge in a lesson plan on American folk traditions. Perhaps the most compelling aspect of older "new" teachers is the example they set for their students and colleagues: You are never too old to learn.

younger and older adults on a variety of divergent thinking tasks. Furthermore, these researchers reported that the creative abilities of their middle-aged and elderly subjects were positively correlated with self-esteem. That is, people who had high self-esteem were more likely to be creative. It would appear, therefore, that a positive view of the self is a motivating force underlying a person's desire and willingness to seek creative solutions to problems.

There are some problems in studying creativity across the lifespan. Measures of creativity in adulthood and early adulthood may not be equivalent to measures used for an older and more experienced adult population (Romaniuk & Romaniuk, 1981). For example, on a task that asks subjects to think of unusual uses for common objects such as a plastic cup, people from different ages or cohort levels may have different levels of experience with the objects. Furthermore, the meaningfulness of the task may vary considerably from one age group to another. What may be a fun and challenging task to a child or teenager may be perceived as trivial and boring to an adult.

Personality Development

To some people, personality development in midlife seems improbable. Middle-aged people are said to be "set in their ways." Put more positively, they have achieved a welcome stability of personality. Middle-aged people are not the last to subscribe to this image. In one study (Gould, 1972), subjects in their early forties showed a striking increase in agreement with the position, "My personality is pretty well set." The same group tended to agree with statements such as "It is too late to make any major changes in my career," or "Life doesn't change much from year to year."

On the other hand, observation, as well as the psychological literature, suggest that middle age can be a period of extraordinary growth and change. The old saying, "life begins at forty," supports this position, as do many popular and scholarly descriptions of the midlife crisis. Indeed, many writers go so far as to compare the onset of middle adulthood with adolescence, coining the term *middlescence* to account for a troubled midlife passage, as well as its new social role (Fried, 1967). Middlescence is seen as an opportunity to carry forth and resolve the identity crisis of adolescence. It is a second chance to "do your own thing, sing your own song, to be deeply and truly yourself," in one middle-aged writer's popular statement (LeShan, 1973). "Instinctual reawakening," "rebirth experience," "fresh vigor of human midlife," are a psychiatrist's words for the same phenomenon (Vaillant, 1977).

Personality Stability and Change

Having raised the issue of personality change in adult development, let us examine it more closely. The focus of the issue has to do with the effect of aging on personality. Do individuals show systematic changes in such aspects of personality as character structure, values, and beliefs as they move from young adulthood to midlife, and finally to old age? Or is personality stable across the adult lifespan?

Measuring Personality Change

At first glance, it would appear that these questions would be easy to answer—simply measure some trait or cluster of traits at one age, say 20, and then again at a later age, say 40. To the extent that personality is stable, one would expect people to remain the same over the 20-year period—that is, the hostile–aggressive 20-year-old should also be hostile–aggressive at 40; the warm, nurturant young adult should develop into a warm, nurturant middle-ager. If personality changes with increasing age, however, these patterns would not be expected—hostile–aggressive or warm, nurturant young adults would not necessarily be the same type of people at midlife as they were during early adulthood.

Unfortunately, the answer to the question of personality stability vs. change is not so easily discerned. Personality is a complex aspect of the individual and difficult to measure over time. Many theorists differentiate between genotypic and phenotypic continuity with respect to personality (Livson, 1973; Neugarten, 1977). **Genotypic continuity** refers to the stability of an underlying personality structure or pattern of traits—a structure that may be expressed, however, in different behaviors at different times. Thus, a hos-

Genotypic Continuity
The degree of continuity or similarity of a person's underlying personality structure over time.

Phenotypic Continuity
The degree of continuity or similarity in a person's overt behavior or characteristics over time.

tile–aggressive person may be physically assertive and verbally caustic during young adulthood—directly confronting people, arguing constantly, and even occasionally getting into fights. That same person during middle age, however, may express hostility in more indirect, passive–aggressive ways, by repeatedly "forgetting" to invite a colleague to join the group at lunchtime, for example, or by "misplacing" an important report that the boss needs for a conference presentation. In this example, it is assumed that the basic structure or trait pattern of personality, that is, hostility, is stable over time—it is only the behaviors representative of hostility that have changed. **Phenotypic continuity,** in contrast, refers to the degree of similarity in overt behavior at two different times. In the above example, phenotypic continuity would be low since the overt behaviors representing hostility have changed dramatically from early to middle adulthood. Thus, it should be clear that the lack of similarity in overt behavior from one time to another is not necessarily evidence of instability or change. Likewise, similarity in behavior does not necessarily imply continuity or stability. Two identical behaviors can be based on different underlying motives. Workers who offer help to colleagues may do so because of a genuine desire to assist others, or because they need to inflate their own self-image by letting others know of their incompetence and inferiority in specific areas—a passive–aggressive "put down" of others.

Another important distinction that needs to be made is between *relative stability* and *absolute stability* of personality dimensions. Relative stability refers to the ordered distribution of scores of a sample of subjects across a period of time. A personality trait or behavior would be relatively stable if the ordered ranking among individuals remained reasonably constant from one measurement period to another. Thus, subjects who scored higher on a personality trait than other subjects would still score higher at some future time regardless of whether the overall group of subjects increased, decreased, or remained the same with respect to the trait. Absolute stability, in contrast, refers to whether people maintain the same score, or level of functioning, from one evaluation to another. For example, since people increase in level of self-awareness from childhood to middle age, the absolute stability of this component of personality is low. Note that any behavior or trait that changes with development has low absolute stability.

As in measuring intelligence, there is the problem of distinguishing between differences in personality that are due to *development* and those that are due to *cohort,* or *generational,* effects. Changes due to development would be true for most people as they progressed through the lifespan. Generational effects would be observed only for a particular cohort of people who lived through a specific historical period — for example, people who were young during World War II, or those who were members of the "now" generation in the 1960s. Woodruff and Birren (1972) examined personality changes in adolescents tested in 1944 and then retested 25 years later when they were in middle age. To examine cohort differences, the personality scores of the subjects also were compared to a set of scores of adolescents and youth tested in 1969. The researchers found that personality changes from adolescence to middle adulthood were small in comparison to the differences due to cohort experiences. The major difference between the adolescents tested in 1944 and those tested in 1969 were that the 1944 adolescents scored higher in self- and social adjustment than the 1969 adolescents.

Personality Stability

Aside from these theoretical and methodological problems, much of the research evidence supports the assumption of personality stability in adulthood. This is particularly true of those studies that have utilized longitudinal designs (Costa & McCrae, 1977, 1980b, 1984; Costa, McCrae, & Arenburg, 1980; Haan & Day, 1974; Leon, Gillum, Gillum, & Gouze, 1979; Schaie & Parham, 1976; Woodruff & Birren, 1972). Some of the most stable characteristics include values (aesthetic, religious, economic, social, and political) and vocational interests. When cross-sectional designs are used, as Neugarten (1977) notes, the findings are more complicated, with some but not other studies reporting age differences in such personality characteristics as rigidity, cautiousness, conservatism, self-concept, and life satisfaction.

Some researchers such as Paul Costa and Robert McCrae (1980b, 1984) argue that adult personality remains remarkably stable. Costa and McCrae conducted a longitudinal study of men between the ages of 20 and 90 years and tested their subjects every six years. On the basis of the data the researchers categorized personality traits into three major dimensions: *neuroticism,* including such characteristics as anxiety, depression, hostility, and impulsiveness; *extroversion,* including such traits as attachment, outgoing personality, assertiveness and excitement seeking; and *openness,* including such traits as openness to ideas, fantasies, feelings, and values. When measured over time on these clusters of traits, the men were found to be remarkably consistent in their personality. Men who were highly extroverted in young adulthood described themselves as extroverted in later adulthood.

Another longitudinal study of adult personality development was reported by Haan (1981). The investigator was among a group of researchers (Eichorn, Clausen, Haan, Honzik, & Mussen, 1981) who examined physical, mental health, and personality data on several cohort groups of men and women studied longitudinally from early adolescence (and in some cases, from childhood) through middle age. Haan's contribution to this massive research effort was an investigation of the relative stability and developmental changes in six common personality dimensions. The first dimension studied, *cognitive investment,* indicated ease and skill in dealing with intellectual matters, deliberate reflectiveness, and interest in personal achievement. The second dimension, *emotional under- overcontrol* was a bipolar dimension. One extreme represented a pressured, dramatic, and aggressive approach to interpersonal exchanges; the other extreme, an emotionally bland, constricted, and submissive approach. The third dimension, *open–closed self,* represented the degree of openness to one's thoughts, feelings, and experiences, as well as ease of self-expression. The fourth dimension, *nurturant–hostile,* was defined, on the one hand, by warmth, consideration, and responsiveness to other people and, on the other hand, by hostility, suspiciousness, and wariness of others. The fifth dimension, *under- overcontrolled heterosexuality,* referred to variations in one's expression of sexuality. At one extreme are individuals who are impulsive and self-indulgent in their sexual relations, and who tend to eroticize most situations; at the other extreme are individuals who are overcontrolled, aloof, fearful, intellectualized, and asexual in character. Finally, the last dimension studied was termed *self-confidence* and dealt with the degree of poise, assertiveness, productivity, self-satisfaction, and confidence one displayed in interpersonal relations.

Haan correlated personality ratings for her subjects across the adolescent, young-adult, and middle-adult years. Her results indicated that for the most part the personality dimensions were reasonably stable; that is, subjects rated high on particular dimensions at one time tended to be rated high on those dimensions at later times. Not surprising, the length of time between ratings affected the degree of stability found. Haan observed greater stability from adolescence to young adulthood, and from young adulthood to middle adulthood, than from adolescence to middle adulthood. She also found that dimensions most directly concerned with the self—cognitive investment, open-closed self, and self-confidence—tended to be the most stable. Furthermore, women's personalities were generally more stable than men's—the latter shifted in personality most radically between adolescence and adulthood when they took on responsibilities such as career and financial independence.

Haan also found some interesting developmental patterns for these personality dimensions. For example, she observed that people increased in cognitive investment, openness to self, nurturance, and self-confidence from adolescence to middle age. No developmental change was observed, however, for emotional under- overcontrol. Finally, a rather complex developmental pattern was noted for under- overcontrolled heterosexuality. Following a peak in undercontrolled sexuality in adolescence, people became more controlled in young adulthood, only to show a resurgence in self- and sexual expression at midlife, perhaps coinciding with people's concerns about pregnancy.

In summarizing her findings, Haan emphasized that from adolescence to middle adulthood, people change slowly, while maintaining a reasonable degree of continuity with their past. In other words, personality development is characterized by a low degree of *absolute stability* (since people often increase or decrease in their level of functioning with age) and a moderate degree of *relative stability*. Adult personality development is not, generally speaking, characterized by large and pervasive changes in beliefs, attitudes, and values.

Research suggests that people increase in cognitive investment, openness to self, nurturance, and self-confidence as they go from adolescence to middle age.

In particular, the midlife crisis, if it is experienced at all, involves more of a reshaping and reorganization of existing personality characteristics than a complete transformation of the person into a "new human being."

Pause for Thought

The fact that personality remains relatively stable throughout adulthood may be reassuring to anyone considering marriage or any other lifetime commitment to another person. Imagine the confusion that could result in relationships if people changed their personalities dramatically. Can you think of situations in which abrupt personality changes may occur?

Developmental Tasks of Middle Adulthood

Although the evidence suggests that basic personality structure does not change much during adulthood, certainly the developmental tasks confronting adults do. Moreover, some theorists have speculated that the way in which people cope with life crises may well undergo some transformation as they are confronted with the new tasks of middle adulthood.

Erikson's Theory

In Erikson's psychosocial scheme, the central crisis for middle-aged adults is the resolution of **generativity vs. stagnation.**

Generativity vs. Stagnation According to Erikson, the primary psychosocial crisis of middle age. Generativity refers to a concern for establishing and guiding the next generation; in the absence of generativity, a feeling of personal impoverishment, boredom, or stagnation occurs.

Erikson notes that "evolution has made man a teaching as well as a learning animal, for dependency and maturity are reciprocal" (Erikson, 1968). Generativity, then, is primarily the concern for establishing and guiding the next generation. For some individuals, generativity is expressed in the context of the family, through loving and nurturing relationships with spouse and children. For others, it is found in job productivity or in mentorship to younger workers—guiding and helping them in their career development. Generativity is a person's link with the future—the means by which one can transcend one's own mortality. The opposite of generativity in Erikson's the-

Generativity, the concern for guiding the next generation, can be expressed in many ways. For this man, his need for generativity is met by helping these children learn how to play soccer.

ory is stagnation, a feeling of personal impoverishment, boredom, and an excessive concern or preoccupation with the self. Erikson points out that the experience of generativity is more difficult for adults who have not become parents. However, it is not essential that adults foster the development of their own biological offspring. In a longitudinal study of infertile men (Snarey, Son, Kuehne, Hauser, & Vaillant, 1987), it was found that infertile men who became fathers, either by adoption or birth, were more likely to be generative in middle adulthood than were infertile men who remained childless. The infertile men who had become adoptive fathers had a higher rate of experiencing generativity than did fertile men. Perhaps because of their intense interest and persistence in overcoming their reproductive disabilities, infertile men were more invested in the significance of taking care of others.

Peck's Theory

The work of Robert Peck (1968) echoes some of the themes found in Erikson's theory. Peck outlines four major challenges or tasks for middle-aged adults who are attempting to cope with the changes taking place both within and outside themselves. (1) People must come to value wisdom over physical strength and attractiveness; they must acknowledge and accept the inevitable decline in physical areas, and rely more on experience, knowledge, and mental processes for life satisfaction. (2) They must redefine relationships with others; people, including spouses, should increasingly be viewed as individuals and companions—relationships, on the whole, become broader, more social, and less sexualized at this time. (3) Middle-aged adults must also be able to demonstrate what Peck calls *cathected flexibility*, that is, the capacity to shift one's emotional investment to new people or activities. This capacity becomes especially important in middle age because of the increased exposure to "breaks" in relationships during this time—parents die, children grow up and leave home, certain activities (such as vigorous athletics) may have to be put aside. To adjust to these changes, middle-aged people must be able to "let go" of relationships—with parents, children, a job—and then reinvest themselves in something new. (4) Peck suggests that successful adjustment to middle age also requires remaining mentally flexible and open to new experiences or ways of doing things. If people continue to rely on well-worn ideas or answers, they may become slaves to the past. Instead of controlling their lives, their lives may control them.

Havighurst's Theory

Another perspective on midlife challenges is offered by Robert Havighurst (1974). He notes that developmental tasks arise from changes within the person, from societal pressures, and especially from pressures laid down upon the person by his or her own values, standards, and aspirations. Middle age is a unique time of life. At no other point in the lifespan does the person have as much influence upon society. And yet it is also the time when society makes its greatest demands on the person. Middle-aged adults must cope with important tasks at home; for example, assisting teenaged children to become responsible, happy adults and maintaining a harmonious relationship with a spouse. They face pressures at work and must reach and maintain a satisfactory level of occupational performance. And at the same time, they are asked by society to accept and fulfill their social and civic obligations and responsibilities. The middle-aged person, according to Havighurst, must also find

Table 13.4

Havighurst's Developmental Tasks of Middle Age

1. Achieve adult civic and social responsibility

2. Establish and maintain an economic standard of living

3. Develop adult leisure-time activities

4. Assist teenager children to become responsible and happy adults

5. Relate oneself to one's spouse as a person

6. Accept and adjust to the physiological changes of middle age

7. Adjust to one's aging parents

Source: R. J. Havighurst. *Developmental tasks and education (3rd ed.).* New York: McKay, 1974.

new outlets for leisure time; outlets that reflect changes in body, interests, values, financial status, and family structure. (See Table 13.4.)

Levinson's Theory

We introduced Daniel Levinson's (1986) theory of life-course development in Chapter 11 and then discussed his work on occupational development in Chapter 12.

In his theory, Levinson addresses the major transitions from one era of people's lives to the next. During the era of middle adulthood, which roughly corresponds with the years from 40 to 65, adults become "senior members" of their community and take on the responsibility for their work and for the development of the next generation of adults. From Levinson's perspective, the middle-adult years are the time for consolidation of interests, goals, and commitments. The transition to middle adulthood actually begins in the early to mid forties (see Figure 11.1 in Chapter 11). This period represents a bridge between the early and middle years of adulthood—or, as Levinson notes, between the past and future. It is a time when people take stock of themselves. Questions reminiscent of the adolescent period such as "Who am I?" "Where am I going?" and so on, become important again. The person begins to evaluate personal achievements in light of previous goals, and to reorganize those goals in light of both current and anticipated achievements. According to Levinson, successful resolution of this midlife transition necessitates working through discrepancies between what is and what might be. For those individuals who are able to come to grips with and accept the realities of their life structure, a new level of stability emerges as they enter middle adulthood, usually between 45 and 50 years. Levinson notes that during this period qualities such as wisdom, judiciousness, compassion, and breadth of perspective often emerge. He also notes that men who reported good relationships with mentors in their early years are likely to become effective mentors themselves at this time—guiding and nurturing the development of younger, less experienced co-workers.

Overview of Theories

Although each of these theorists portrays the tasks of middle age in somewhat different ways, a common thread runs through their writings. Each sees middle age as a time of continued challenge for the individual—challenge that may require considerable adjustment in areas such as self, family relations, social interactions, career development, and leisure activity. Yet successful adjustment to the tasks of midlife, as to all periods of development, is dependent upon many factors and takes many forms. Middle-aged adults are not a homogeneous group. Each person is a unique individual with unique experiences, and each will adjust to the challenges of midlife in his or her unique way. As one 50-year-old schoolteacher recently said: "As I watched my father go through middle age, I saw a person I loved begin to fall apart. He lost interest in everything, became preoccupied with his health and what he saw as a 'looming death.' He was no fun to be around. Now I'm at the point in my life that he once was and I still can't understand his reaction. Sure, it's no fun to get old. But I'm finding new interests all the time—new things to do. My job has become somewhat less important as I discover these interests. Many I can share with my husband; others are just for me. I don't feel that old and I just don't worry about getting older . . . life is just too short to be preoccupied with those kinds of thoughts. I'm middle-aged, I guess, but I feel good about where I'm at."

Summary

Middle age is accompanied by a gradual physical decline from the peak reached in the twenties. The individual does not experience a simple reverse from growth to deterioration; both processes have been taking place since early in life. As for the changes themselves, they do not represent disabilities in our society. Judgment, experience, and management ability have come to be valued more than physical strength.

As people enter the middle years of life, concerns regarding physical health become more common. Cardiovascular diseases and cancer are the two leading causes of death during this time. Stressful life events such as death of a spouse, divorce, or change of jobs can contribute to health problems. Daily hassles and multiple stresses occur often and can erode people's sense of well-being. Individuals react to stress in different ways; the most adaptive approach is to actively evaluate one's priorities and make appropriate changes. Research indicates that emotional and personality factors—particularly Type-A behavior—are major contributors to the health problems of middle-aged adults. Type-A behavior patterns may have their origins in childhood and are linked to heart disease in adulthood.

One effect of aging is the climacteric, the changes in the reproductive and sexual organs that result from a decrease in the production of gonadal hormones. For women, the decline in estrogen and progesterone levels brings a clear signal of biological change: menopause. Menstruation gradually ceases over a period of a year or two. For men, the results of a decline in testosterone levels are less clear-cut.

Cognitive development continues in middle age in abilities that are influenced by experience, such as verbal ability, social knowledge, and moral judgment. A decline in intellectual function through the middle years is found only in studies based on a cross-sectional design. Longitudinal research, however, in which the same people are measured more than one time in their lifespan, does not show decline in intelligence during middle age.

Some theorists propose two components of intelligence. Peaking in early adulthood, fluid abilities are closely related to neurophysiological intactness. Crystallized abilities, which are the result of acculturation, remain unchanged or even increase during middle age.

Creativity, as measured by products, declines with age. Divergent thinking and preference for complexity also decline with age and may contribute to the decline in creativity. Different kinds of creativity may emerge at different ages.

It is difficult to determine whether adult personality is basically stable, or whether people undergo major personality changes across the lifespan. Some theorists have suggested that although the basic personality structure or trait pattern of the individual remains essentially the same across the adult years, the behaviors representative of the underlying structure may well change. Most research, particularly those studies using longitudinal designs, supports the assumption of personality stability in adulthood. Some of the most stable characteristics include values and vocational interests.

Different views exist of personality development in midlife. Most theorists do agree, however, that middle age is a time of challenge for the individual—challenge that may require considerable adjustment in such areas as the self, family relations, social interactions, career development, and leisure activity. Erikson sees the midlife crisis as one of generativity — a concern for the next generation— vs. stagnation—a sense of boredom and preoccupation with the self. Other views of middle-adulthood development have been proposed by Peck, Havighurst, and Levinson.

Further Readings

Block, M. R., Davidson, J. L., and Grambs, J. D. *Women over forty.* New York: Springer, 1981.
A very readable account of the physical changes that women experience in middle age and late adulthood.

Chew, Peter. *The inner world of the middle-aged man.* New York: Macmillan, 1976.
A compassionate and fascinating exploration of the changes occurring in the middle-aged man. Chew examines such aspects of the middle-aged crisis as impotence, employment difficulties, and the drive to recover lost youth.

Eichorn, D. H., Clausen, J. A., Haan, N., Honzik, M. P., and Mussen, P. H. (Eds.). *Present and past in middle life.* New York: Academic Press, 1981.
An edited volume containing comprehensive analyses and discussion of longitudinal changes across the adolescent to middle-adult period in physical development, mental health, personality, and career development. The chapters are technical and well written.

Levinson, Daniel J. *The seasons of a man's life.* New York: Knopf, 1979.
Levinson outlines the developmental stages of a man's life. His theory is based on a 10-year study, and the book includes many case histories. Levinson's writing is poetic and readable.

Sheehy, G. *Passages: Predictable crises of adult life.* New York: Dutton, 1976.
Sheehy offers a highly readable account of the turmoils, struggles, and triumphs of every age stage past adolescence. Her writing is journalistic and engaging.

Observational Activities

13.1 *Physical Changes in Middle Adulthood*
Between 40 and 60 years of age, people begin to notice signs of their physical aging. Wrinkles appear on the face and hands, age spots erupt, and the skin

loses its elasticity. Hair begins to thin out and turn gray. The timing and specific course of physical aging are influenced by many factors and differ from person to person during middle adulthood. To appreciate these physical changes, locate and interview at least 10 people in their middle-adult years about the physical changes they have noticed about themselves. Use the following questions to structure your interview:

1. Describe the changes you have noticed in:
   a. Your skin: for example, age spots, wrinkles, dry spots, sagging, elasticity.
   b. Your hair: for example, thinning or graying
   c. Your vision: for example, do you need reading glasses?
   d. Your physical strength
   e. Your hearing
   At what age did you first notice these physical changes?
2. Describe what types of physical activity, if any, you engage in regularly.
3. Have you altered your diet over the past five years? Explain.
4. What changes are you most bothered by, if any?

While you are interviewing each respondent, take note of the different physical characteristics of the people and ask their ages. Once you have completed your interviews, compile your results. What changes seem to be the most commonly reported ones? Which physical characteristics did you notice most frequently in your respondents? How similar were the respondents in the ages at which they noticed these physical changes? What conclusions can you draw about physical aging in middle adulthood?

13.2   *How Old Is Old?*

How old will you be when you start to "get old"? Perceptions of age, especially relative age such as young, middle-aged, and elderly, are based on many social and personal experiences. Some of these experiences are objective in nature, such as the satisfaction with life goals one has achieved, or the perception of time left to pursue those goals. Because people differ in their social and personal experiences, perceptions of the aging process vary considerably among people.

Develop a short questionnaire with the purpose of ascertaining the perceptions people have about age.

1. Ask, for example, at what age does a person stop being young? When is a person middle-aged? When is a person old?
2. Keep track of such data as age and gender, and perhaps a rough estimate of social class (as shown by such indicators as employment and education), and direct your questions to about 40 people.
3. Tabulate your results.
4. What differences in perception of aging did you find for different age groups, males vs. females, or social classes?
5. Do single adults view aging differently than married adults?
6. What factors seem to be most influential in a person's perception of aging?

Summarize your data and draw some conclusions. Finally, answer this question: "Is it really true (based on your findings) that you are as young or as old as you feel, or as you perceive yourself to be?"

C H A P T E R
14

Middle Adulthood: Family and Occupational Development

At 55 years old, John was at a good point in his life. The difficulties he had experienced in his first marriage were long since resolved and he had been happily remarried for many years. He enjoyed his work as a high-school English teacher, especially since he had taken on the task of improving the writing skills of his students.

For years he had taught the literature course, but he really wanted to teach the creative-writing course. It was a bit ironic that he should be so keen on effective writing since as a student he did not do particularly well in his composition classes. However, his father had been insistent that he acquire good writing skills. "You cannot call yourself educated if you cannot put your thoughts on paper," was the refrain. He chuckled whenever he heard himself giving the same message to his tenth-grade students. Even his son Danny from his first marriage, who was a senior at the local university, had learned to value his own writing skills.

John had earned the reputation at the high school of being a conscientious, concerned, and particularly effective teacher. Often, younger faculty members would ask to sit in on his classes to learn to be better teachers themselves. John was more than pleased to be able to share with others what he had learned over his 30 years of teaching. His own personal definition of success was found in the way his students were able to broaden their views of the world and pass on new information to others. A large part of his success he attributed to his second wife Helen.

Over the 15 years they had been together, John and Helen had remained good companions and friends to each other. Often when John was frustrated with the lack of progress in his students, he would come to Helen and talk about the problems he was having. By listening and encouraging him to find a way to reach the students, she was invaluable to him. She often read the students' compositions and offered her opinions on them. Together, they planned their summer vacations to different parts of the country every year. Each summer was a new adventure as they set off in their camper van. From each new city or region they visited, they sent postcards to John's students describing in fluent, but concise detail their many experiences.

John's interest and dedication to his work and his involvement with his family represent his own way of addressing the psychosocial tasks of middle adulthood. As we saw in Chapter 13, middle age brings with it a new sense of challenge—in Erikson's (1968) scheme, a challenge of *generativity vs. stagnation*. Nowhere is this challenge better expressed than in the context of family and work life.

In middle age there is a broadening of interests and a turning outward toward others. Having found their own place in society, mature adults, like John, reorient their energies toward the future—to the next generation. The issue of generativity involves the need to teach and otherwise become responsible

Mentor Relationship
Exists when an older, more experienced worker guides the training and development of a younger worker.

for the development of the next generation. Within the family, middle-aged parents give encouragement and support as their offspring prepare to set out from home and make their own way. The middle-aged worker expresses generativity not only in managing people and policies, but in training and guiding one or several younger employees in **mentor relationships.** Thus, the fruits of middle age, according to Erikson, are found primarily in relationships based upon generativity. Midlife identity may also be linked to adults' desire to have an effect, to leave their mark. As they watch the next generation emerge, middle-aged adults cannot escape the realization that their years remaining are limited. As they witness the decline of their own parents' generation, adults seek meaning for their lives. Are they part of a continuous cycle of families that produce new families? What contributions will they leave behind them for those who follow?

Not all adults are successful in achieving generativity, however. For some, family life is a constant source of frustration and irritation. Previous or ongoing emotional problems may prevent the person from engaging in supportive, friendly relationships with spouse, children, and friends. At work, too, some people are unable to interact effectively with others. A woman may become disillusioned because she believes her work or ideas are unappreciated by her superiors. A man may feel defeated because he has failed to achieve some earlier established career goal. For such people, the midlife "harvest" may be sparse. If they are unable to reach out to others in personal areas, their lives may take on the hollow feeling of stagnation.

In this chapter, we describe the different facets of family and occupational development during middle age. We begin with a discussion of family life, with particular emphasis on intergenerational relations and quality of midlife marital adjustment. The second part of the chapter deals with the world of work, and specifically with the way in which middle-aged adults advance within their careers and develop feelings of satisfaction or dissatisfaction with this aspect of their life.

Family Life

The nature of family life changes dramatically during middle age. Because most middle-aged adults married in their twenties and had their children soon thereafter, by the time they are in their early forties, their oldest children may be out of high school. For some families, the exit of young adult children from the household creates a very different day-to-day family atmosphere. Without the parade of teenagers and young adults using the phone, watching TV, or listening to music, the house is likely to be quieter. In a few more years, the youngest and last child may be launched into society as an independent adult, leaving the middle-aged couple by themselves. In other families, adult children may continue living in their parents' home or return home after a few years on their own at college or in a nonmarital relationship. Nonetheless, most couples will spend fully one half of the family life cycle living together alone after the children have grown and finally left their household.

Most middle-aged couples are in the launching stage of the family life cycle. Their family size is no longer expanding, but instead gets smaller as adolescent and young adult children mature. The point in people's lifespans when their family composition and functions change depends on several factors—the age at which they married and began childbearing, the number and spacing of children, whether they experience divorce and remarriage, the presence of stepchildren, and even the decision to remain child free.

While the stereotypical middle-aged couple is one which is getting ready to launch their first child into the adult world, this image does not fit for couples who delayed having their first child until their mid-thirties or for the remarried couple who have a child after children from previous marriages may be adults or teenagers. Couples who marry and have children at a young age may have already launched their adult children from the family home only later to experience their children's reentry to the home in times of financial need or marital breakdown. Single-parent families and families that have extended family members (e.g., grandparents, aunts, uncles, cousins) living in the household may have a different sequencing and timing of events in the family life cycle.

Pause for Thought

The launching stage of the family life cycle corresponds with the peak load of family expenses as children need financial help for college or career training and as they seek to leave home and set up a residence independent from parents. Many middle-aged earners have already reached the peak of their salary scale and must take on extra work to meet the high costs of launching young adults. What kinds of personal dilemmas might be created for middle-aged adults who finance the launching of adult children from the home?

Intergenerational Relations

As Hagestad (1982) has observed, the phrase "parents and children" is likely to evoke a picture of young to middle-aged adults in interaction with children between the ages of one and 16. Less often do we think of these same young and middle-aged adults as children to their own aging parents.

As life expectancy has increased and families have become smaller and more closely spaced, a sizable percentage of families have become multi-generational in nature. It is quite common, for example, for three or four, and in rarer cases, even five generations to coexist within a family line. Family life-course theorists speak of the various tiers of parent–child relationships as **generational stations** (Hagestad, 1982).

Generational Stations
The various tiers of parent–child relationships that exist within a family.

Until recently, little interest was shown by social scientists in the issue of intergenerational relations. In part, this neglect stemmed from a narrow view of primary familial relationships. Rather than conceiving of parent–child relations as a lifelong process, most researchers focused almost exclusively on the early period of the family life cycle—that is, the period when the couple reproduced and reared its young children, up to the point when these children were launched into the world. Furthermore, popular stereotypes suggested that once young adults were out on their own, they neither needed nor wanted a high level of contact with their parents. We now know, however, that adult children and their parents maintain a reasonably high level of contact throughout their adults lives and that the relationship is usually beneficial to both parents and adult children.

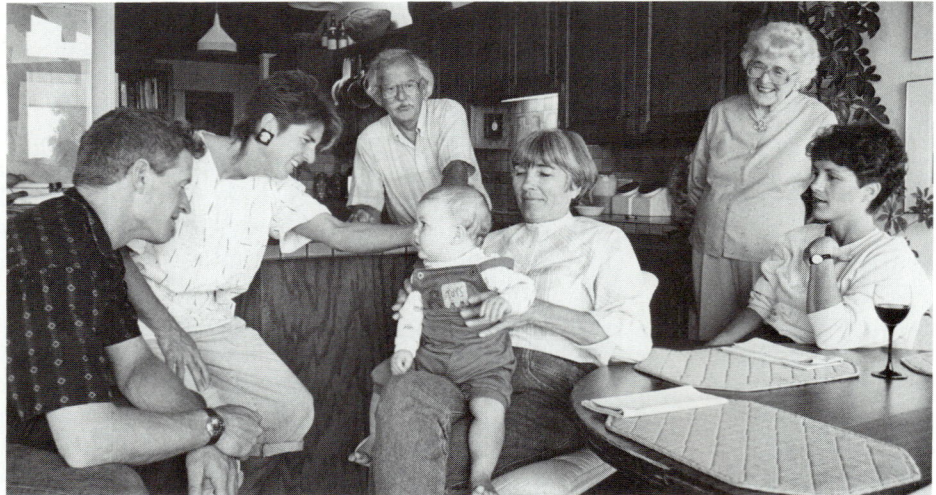

Because life expectancy has increased, families have become multigenerational. This family gathering has four generations represented.

In studying intergenerational relations, two frequently asked questions are the degree to which one generation influences the development of the other and whether the intergenerational influences observed are primarily *unidirectional* (i.e., parents guiding and shaping the behavior and adjustment of their children) or *reciprocal* (i.e., parents and children mutually affecting each other's development). Bengston and Troll (1978), in discussing the relationship between young adults and their parents, emphasize that family socialization in adulthood is a complex, interrelated process characterized by continuous feedback and a system of mutual influences. Moreover, they also note that intergenerational transmission of values, standards, patterns of behavior, and so on are affected not only by the specific characteristics of the individuals involved, but by factors outside of the family—for example, the specific historical period in which the people live and their ethnic and cultural background. A person who grew up during the Depression, a time when material goods and money were hard to come by and being resourceful was essential, is more likely to continue to value hard work and resourcefulness in later adult life and to pass these views on to his own offspring either by example or by socialization. (See Elder, Downey, & Cross, 1980.)

The bidirectional nature of intergenerational influences is supported by the research of Gunhild Hagestad (1984). Family relationships across three generations of adults in 150 families were studied—aged parents, middle-age parents/children, and young-adult children. In areas as varied as diet and health practices, political attitudes, and childrearing views, Hagestad found evidence of socialization influences both up and down the generational lines. Not only did parents influence their children's views, but children had an impact on their parents' views.

Advice up the generational chain from middle-aged children to older parents dealt mostly with health or practical matters such as managing households and use of time. Older parents gave their middle-aged children advice on health, work, and money matters. The youngest generation tried to influence their middle-aged parents on health matters, social attitudes and how to keep up with the changing times. Children (of all ages) were more likely to get their parents to change than parents were to get children to change.

In the study of intergenerational relations, the middle-age period is a significant one. Middle-aged adults are influenced both from the top-down and from the bottom-up.

In reviewing the literature on intergenerational transmission, Troll and Bengston (1982) report that most researchers have focused on attitudes, values, and orientations in five areas: politics, religion, sex, work, and lifestyles. For example, similarity in political-party preference has been found to be consistently high across generations. Thus, Democratic parents usually have Democratic adult children, Republican parents have Republican adult children, and so on. General political orientation and values—for example, liberalism, egalitarianism, dedication to causes, and so forth—also show cross-generational continuity, although usually not as high as political-party affiliation. Research on religious affiliation and religious values also has found consistently high similarity between parents and their adult children. In contrast, less intergenerational similarity has been reported for gender-roles, lifestyle, and work orientation.

In studying intergenerational relations, the middle-adult period takes on special significance. Middle-aged adults are the link between the younger and older generations. Being in the middle of the family line also means that one is likely to be influenced both from top-down (elderly parent to middle-aged child) and bottom-up (adolescent or young-adult child to middle-aged parent) family processes. Consequently, the individual during middle age finds it necessary to integrate seemingly discrepant family roles into his or her sense of self—that is, the assertive, power-based roles associated with being a parent to one's children, and the more submissive, dependent roles associated with being a child to one's aging parents. Needless to say, this psychosocial task poses considerable challenge for the middle-aged person.

Families with Adolescents

In Chapter 10, we discussed the nature of the adolescent–parent relationship primarily from the perspective of the developing teenager. As adolescents seek to establish their independence and autonomy within the family, their parents more often than not are also facing the personal challenge of defining themselves within a much broader context. Middle-aged parents who can see the end of their active role as parents may be asking themselves the same question their adolescent children are asking: Who am I and what do I want to be doing with my life?

Middle-aged parents of adolescents not only have to resolve whatever conflicts exist between them and their growing children, they must also come to terms with their own inner conflicts (Steinberg & Silverberg, 1987). One conflict, which we discussed in Chapter 13 is that adults may not want to accept the decline in their physical capabilities made ever more apparent when they compare themselves to their physically mature (and strong and youthful) adolescents. Teenagers are not only younger looking and stronger, they also have more energy than middle-aged adults. Recognizing that their adolescent children are functioning at a different physiological and developmental level helps parents "let go" of their children.

In many ways, the emergence of adolescents as independent and autonomous is like the final examination or report card for parenting. Parents' overall long-term goal may have been to be able to assist their children in becoming self-sufficient. Adolescence and youth are the first developmental periods when that goal could be achieved. Perhaps with "success as parents" in their sights, many parents focus their energy on supporting and assisting their adolescents in their search to establish identities, identify career choices

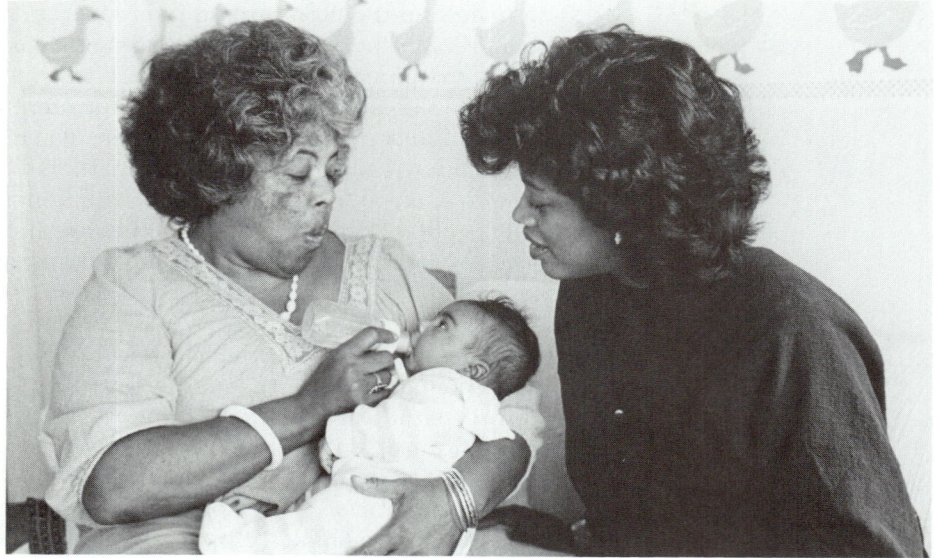

This grandmother is modeling appropriate parenting behaviors for her teenage granddaughter, the mother of the young infant.

and prepare themselves for the adult world. Parental assistance in career exploration can be critical for adolescents seeking to identify their adult career paths (Grotevant & Cooper, 1988). Parents not only serve as role models of career orientations, they serve as a source of encouragement, information, and financial support. In a recent survey of youth (Hedin, Erickson, Simon, & Walker, 1985) adolescents named their parents as the most important influence on their thinking about careers, more so than their high-school guidance counselors. Mothers more than fathers play an influential role in career exploration. Sons and daughters of mothers who had established careers are much more likely to enter less traditional careers and to have high career aspirations (Hoffman, 1979; Rollins & White, 1982; Shapiro & Crowley, 1982). Although fathers serve as a source of information and expectations about careers, daughters are less likely to enter into candid discussions with their fathers about their career concerns or hopes (Youniss & Smollar, 1985).

As adolescents take on adult roles such as worker or parent, their parents may have greater influence. Parental concern about adolescent sexuality may shift dramatically if their children should become parents themselves. In a study that looked at the role that middle-aged black grandmothers played in the lives of their teenage daughters who became mothers, Stevens (1984) found that the presence of the grandchild provided the context for the grandmothers to teach their daughters about infant development. The grandmothers not only modeled appropriate parenting behavior, they served as child-rearing consultants for the teenage mothers. In adolescent families without the presence of grandchildren, the socialization of parenting skills is less likely to occur.

Thus, while parenting of adolescents may be a period of conflicts, it is not necessarily a time of continual stress and strain. If middle-aged parents see their role as influential rather than as intrusive in their adolescents' lives, this period can be one in which both parent and child accomplish some of their developmental tasks.

Families with Adult Children

At some point in the family life cycle, parents and children begin to "let go" of one another. Parents begin to accept that their children—now legally adults—have become independent, self-reliant individuals. This stage of parenting, which almost always occurs in middle age, is a poorly researched phase of family life (Hagestad, 1982). It is often referred to as the "postparental" period, as if the launching of children into the world relinquishes adults of all parental needs, responsibilities, and obligations. In reality, people do not cease to be parents simply because their children no longer live with them—just as adults, regardless of age, are still their parents' children even though they may be married, have children of their own, and lead relatively autonomous lives.

The relationship between middle-aged parents and their adult children is different from parent–child relationships of earlier periods of the family life cycle (Hess & Waring, 1978; Thompson & Walker, 1984). Since both parents and children are adults, they are in some ways social equals, at least insofar as privileges and responsibilities are afforded them by their adult status. Independent living, increasing financial autonomy, establishment of one's own nuclear family, recognition by peers and co-workers, all bolster the status of the young-adult child and, in turn, help to realign the power imbalance that characterized the earlier parent–child relationship. Another difference between parent–child relationships at this time as compared to earlier ones is that primary emotional investments and obligations are redirected toward new individuals. For young adults, concerns for spouse and children take precedence over concerns for parents. Likewise, middle-aged parents begin to focus more attention on each other and less on their independent and relatively self-reliant, adult children. For many middle-aged adults, their level of satisfaction and contentment in life is not dependent on having regular contact with their adult children, even when they enjoy the company of their children and grandchildren (Cicirelli, 1982; Lee & Ellithorpe, 1982; Lee & Ihinger-Tallman, 1980).

The introduction of in-laws also complicates parent–child relations at this time. Middle-aged parents often find that they must share their children's time, energy, and emotional investments with the parents of their daughter- or son-in-law. For some, this realization brings with it a sense of resentment and jealousy. Finally, parent–child relationships are more voluntary than they once were. Independent living means that a greater effort must be made for parents and adult children to maintain their relationship. Some adult children may live in a different town or state than their parents, making contact more difficult. Increasingly, parent–child interaction is part of leisure-time activity rather than part of the daily routine.

Despite these changes, research suggests that parent–child relationships remain important for people during this stage of the family life cycle. Troll, Miller, and Atchley (1979) point out that generally the ties between adult children and their parents are close. Young-adult children frequently rely on their parents for financial help, for child care, and for emotional support. In turn, middle-aged parents receive emotional satisfaction from their relationship with their adult children, as well as companionship and a sense of achievement of generativity. They have produced independent, responsible, and loving offspring who will carry on after they are gone. Middle-aged parents also share vicariously in the accomplishments of their adult children—at work, at home, and at play. They take pride in their daughter's graduation from medical school, and their son's promotion within the company; they share the joy of their children's marriages, and the birth of grandchildren. For some middle-aged adults, the success of their children becomes the avenue for fulfilling some of their own unmet needs and goals.

Yet the "empty nest" of family life—as this period has been called—is not without its problems. Some parents experience considerable stress when their children finally leave home for good. Bart (1970), who studied midlife depression in women, identified the **empty-nest syndrome** as a factor in her sample of depressed middle-aged women. These women had devoted themselves (and their identities) to being the ever caring and helpful mother. When their children grew up and no longer needed or wanted their mother's care, these women experienced the loss of no longer having a meaningful role to play in their family. Mothers are not the only ones who may be upset by the departure of the children from the home. Lewis, Frenau, and Roberts (1979) found that 22 percent of their sample of fathers reported considerable unhappiness over the departure of the last child from home. Furthermore, it was the older father, who had few children, who was more involved in nurturing relationships, and whose marriage showed evidence of problems, who was the most affected by the absence of children.

Recent studies have shown that the empty-nest syndrome is not as common as it had been in the early 1970s. Many middle-aged parents are happy to see their children leave the nest. Women who have juggled parental and work roles may find it a lot easier to deal with the transition of having fewer roles to fulfill than it was to balance the roles of mother, wife, and worker (Bee, 1987). Furthermore, most studies on marital satisfaction find the empty-nest period to be the time when couples report the most satisfaction. Many parents greet the departure of their children with a sense of relief and psychological well-being (Harkins, 1978). As one 52-year-old female executive commented: "I love my children, but God, how glad I am that they are out on their own. Suddenly I feel free . . . . It's just me and my husband now . . . . The funny thing is that the kids and I get along better now . . . I guess the strain of a career *and* managing a house full of kids can kind of get to you."

Relationships with Aged Parents

As middle-aged adults become free from the responsibilities and obligations of raising children, it is natural that more of their time, energy, and concern will be transferred to their own parents, who are now into the later years of life. Historically, this redirection of emotional investment toward one's aging parents is a recent phenomenon, for just two generations ago, middle-aged adults usually were the oldest surviving members of the extended family— that is, their own parents were no longer alive. Furthermore, the nature of involvement with one's aging parents is different today than it was for middle-aged adults even a few decades ago. Hess and Markson (1980) note that today's middle-aged adults are the first cohort of offspring who are relatively free from the responsibilities and obligations of providing at least minimum income maintenance and health care to their aging parents. Federally subsidized income (Social Security) and health care (Medicare and Medicaid), better retirement plans, planned retirement communities, and so on have softened (but certainly not eliminated) the impact of retirement and aging on the older person, and, in turn, this has lessened the middle-aged child's burden

Empty-Nest Syndrome An emotional pattern, including depression and loss of self-worth, that some middle-aged adults experience after their children leave home.

for caring for his or her aging, and possibly, ailing parent. Many elderly people today not only enjoy relatively good health, but are also financially better off than they were in the past (Aldous, 1987). This is not to say that middle-aged adults are entirely free of responsibilities toward the older generation. Indeed, many middle-aged adults provide emotional and physical support, and often assume financial responsibility for many aspects of their parents' lives. In fact, there is sometimes a reversal of parent–child roles during this time, as middle-aged people become the providers and nurturers for their aging parents. This is usually true, though, only where the parents are well into the aging years. Most research indicates that older parents do not want to be dependent upon their middle-aged children; on the contrary, they show a strong preference for remaining independent as long as possible (Yankelovich, Skelly, & White Inc., 1977). Regardless of this attitude, however, research indicates that contact between adult children and their aged parents is important and beneficial for old people's psychological well-being (Alpert & Richardson, 1980; Aldous, 1987).

There are difficult decisions to be made by the children of aged parents. How long can you let old people live alone who are not in good mental or physical condition? Can you put your own mother or father in a nursing home, no matter how well-managed? The line is a delicate one to draw between taking over and destroying old people's sense of their own independence, and protecting them from physical harm.

Grandparenthood

Although the stereotype of grandparents is that of gray-haired, wrinkled, and bespectacled old people whose favorite pastimes are sitting in a rocking chair or baking cookies or cakes for the family, today this image is not appropriate (Troll, 1980). With the changes in fertility and mortality patterns, and the shift in population characteristics over the past century, becoming a grandparent is more a middle-age than old-age event. Troll (1983) notes that in our culture, the typical age of becoming a grandparent is around 49 to 51 years for women and 51 to 53 years for men. Furthermore, teenage pregnancies often produce grandparents who are in their early to mid-thirties. Thus, first-time grandparents are likely to be healthy, working at full-time jobs, and living independent and active lives. In fact, a few middle-aged people find it difficult at first to accept the grandparent role—they may feel it casts a shadow of age on the youthful self-image they are maintaining.

Research suggests that grandparents play an important role in family systems. They provide the younger generations with emotional support and with advice concerning basic values, lifestyle, occupation, education, parenting, and so on (Troll, 1980). Grandparents, especially maternal grandmothers, have been shown to be extremely important for promoting well-being in single-parent, child-rearing units, particularly those involving teenage mothers (Stevens, 1984; Tinsley & Parke, 1983). Often grandmothers fill the important function of child care while the single parent is working. Similarly, Hetherington, Cox, and Cox (1982) found that the adjustment of mother-headed households following divorce was greatly affected by the contributions of grandparents.

Just as individuals differ in their personalities and styles of parenting, so, too, do they differ in their styles of grandparenting. In what has become a classic study, Neugarten and Weinstein (1964) identified five styles of interactions with grandchildren among middle-class grandparents in their fifties and sixties:

1. *Formal:* shows interest in the grandchild and occasionally provides special gifts or services, such as baby-sitting, but does not interfere in the raising of the child; leaves the parenting to the parents.
2. *Fun-seeker:* an informal, leisurely orientation toward grandparenting; assumes the role of playmate and expects mutually gratifying experiences with the grandchild.
3. *Surrogate Parent:* grandparent (almost always the grandmother) assumes the child-care responsibilities while the parents are working.
4. *Reservoir of Family Wisdom:* grandparent (usually the grandfather) adopts an authoritarian role in the family; all family members, including parents, are subordinate to him; he dispenses resources, knowledge, and advice to others.
5. *Distant Figure:* has little consistent relationship with the grandchild; visits on holidays or special occasions; adopts a benevolent but emotionally distant role.

Neugarten and Weinstein also noted that many grandparents experience a sense of biological renewal—a feeling of carrying on the family line—as well as a sense of emotional self-fulfillment in their new family role. The older mother may relive her pregnancy, delivery, and early mothering through her daughter's or daughter-in-law's early parenting experiences. The new grandfather, in turn, may realize that he has the time and interest for his grandchildren that he never had for his own children. Robertson (1977) reports that many people find grandparenting easier and preferable to parenting. It is not uncommon, in fact, to hear grandparents assure themselves that they are better grandparents than they were parents.

Pause for Thought

When adults divorce and remarry, there often is family conflict and confusion about how to stay in contact with ex-relations. What are the common assumptions or stereotypes present in our culture that contribute to the strained relationships among families in which divorce and remarriage have occurred?

Marriage

With the advent of the empty-nest stage of the family life cycle, the husband and wife enter a new phase of married life. The absence of children from the home allows the couple to refocus their attention on each other and their marriage. This is a time in which couples rediscover one another—and sometimes recognize the gulf that lies between them. And it is a time in which marital patterns are reexamined.

Midlife Marital Adjustment

Probably the most frequently studied aspect of midlife marriage is marital adjustment. One early and important study suggested that most couples become progressively disenchanted over the course of a marriage (Pineo, 1961). More recent studies, however, show an upturn in marital satisfaction in the

Human Development in Practice

Parents and Teachers as Partners in the Classroom

Helping the next generation deal more effectively with their lives is a major goal for middle-aged adults seeking to meet their generativity needs. Parenting is one way to achieve generativity, teaching is another. Traditionally, parents and teachers have operated in separate domains even though their targets (the children) were the same. Parents and teachers might meet at back-to-school, open-house events or parent–teacher conferences, but their contact and involvement would primarily consist of reporting on planned classroom activities and discussing the overall performance of the student.

Today, a new type of parent–teacher relationship is actively being encouraged. Fueled by research reports that underscore the importance of the home environment in increasing student achievement (Walberg, 1984), many school systems are seeking new ways to involve parents more directly in the education of their children. Parents are a largely untapped resource for schools. Parents have skills that can be applied in the home to encouraging their children to do well in school. Most children, young children and adolescents alike, look to their parents as models of behavior, attitudes, and values. Furthermore, parents are their children's first and most influential teachers. Through daily conversations with their children about school activities, about news events, and shared hobbies and travels, parents can stimulate numerous opportunities for learning. When parents are made more aware of their important function as co-teacher and when teachers invite greater parental involvement in day-to-day instruction, everyone benefits—students, teachers, and parents.

Most parents and many teachers need to learn more specific ways in which to join forces in education. Becker and Epstein (1982) surveyed 3700 Maryland teachers and found that although teachers were receptive to the idea of having parents cooperate with implementing the school curriculum, many were skeptical about whether parents would know what to do. The teachers who had already involved parents in such projects as home reading, at-home tutoring, and school-performance contracts were already

Parents are a largely untapped resource of skills, expertise, and creativity for teachers. This parent has volunteered to teach schoolchildren about the guitar.

convinced of the productive contributions parents could make.

Parental-involvement programs work regardless of the socioeconomic or educational status of the parents. One ingredient for success is that teachers actively promote parent involvement through specific activities. Teachers who are more successful in promoting parent participation in the elementary grades use such strategies as asking parents to read aloud to their children, to sign homework papers, and to set up areas in the home for study. Encouraging parents to discuss school activities with their children or to drill students on math and spelling, inviting parents into the classroom to talk with students about their careers, special interests, or hobbies are other ways teachers can reinforce their partnership. Some middle-aged adults are also new parents as a result of either remarriage or delayed parenthood. Other middle-aged parents have children in secondary schools. Parent participation in education not only encourages their children to do better in school, it helps stimulate greater community involvement in raising the quality of education for generations to come.

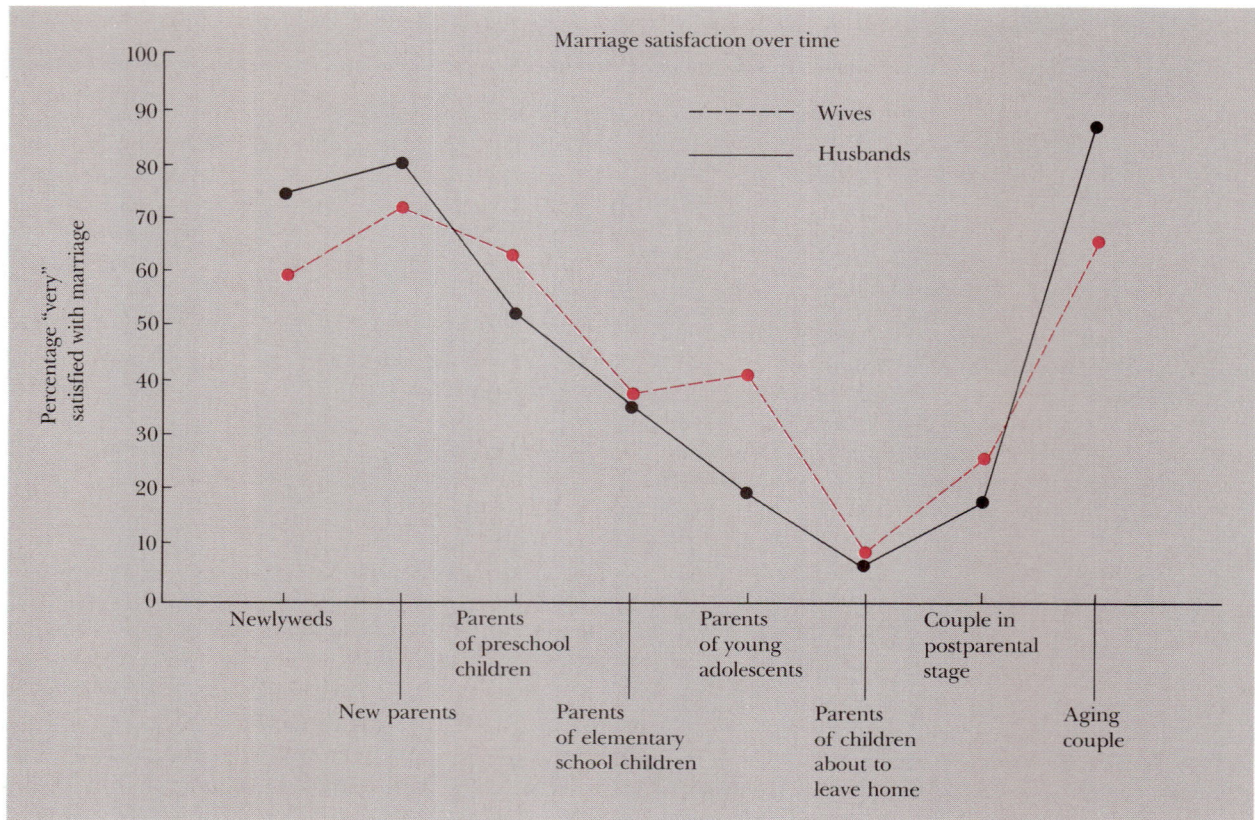

Figure 14.1 Marriage satisfaction over time.

later stages of married life. For both husbands and wives the stage when children are school aged represents a low point, whereas the postchild and retirement stages are positively viewed (Huyck, 1982; Schram, 1979). Although the period when children have left home is often a time of stress, the dissatisfaction seems to be with children and/or parenting, rather than with marriage or each other.

What accounts for the rise in marital satisfaction during this period of life? To begin with, research suggests that the role strain experienced during the earlier years of marriage is lessened during the postchild and retirement stages of family life (Spanier & Lewis, 1980). Women, in particular, are freed from the burden and pressures of coordinating work and parenting roles. The renewed interest in sexual matters for many middle-aged adults, as discussed in Chapter 13, also is likely to enhance the intimacy between marital partners. Another factor that may explain the more positive marital evaluations by middle-aged and elderly adults is that couples who are the least satisfied with their marriage have already separated or divorced by this period of family life. Hence, the "marital survivors" represent a select group of individuals who are more satisfied and better adjusted. If this interpretation is true or even partly true, the research findings regarding lifespan marital satisfaction are less a reflection of true developmental changes in the quality of marital life than they are a methodological artifact related to selective dropout of subjects. Finally, Spanier, Lewis, and Cole (1975) suggest that couples who have invested considerable time and energy in one another—as is true for middle-aged and elderly adults—are the most likely to place a high value on their relationship. Furthermore, they are likely to be motivated to see things in a similar, or at least in a compatible, way. This striving for cognitive consistency would then be reflected in similar and more positive marital evaluations.

Marital Styles

We have discussed the stages in the family life cycle that are related to marital satisfaction, and yet we have not defined what we mean by this term. What constitutes a happy marriage? Is there some optimal form of marriage toward which all of us should be striving?

It is obvious that people differ in their personalities, interests, needs, fantasies, and life goals. In turn, marital adjustment is, in part, determined by the kind of characteristics the husband and wife bring to the marriage relationship. Does marital happiness, however, necessarily imply that the husband and wife share the *same* interests and needs? Some researchers believe so. In reviewing the research on this issue, Clore and Byrne (1977) concluded: "Marriage, and stable marriages in particular, are composed of people with similar personalities, attitudes, and other characteristics" (p. 548).

In contrast, other researchers have argued that marital adjustment is determined by *complementarity* in the relationship—the two individuals possess different and yet compatible traits. Winch (1974) was interested in the complementarity of role playing. He chose two sets of complementary roles (dominance–submission and nurturance—receptiveness) to arrive at four types or styles of complementary relationships in marriage: (1) the Ibsenian relation-

Some researchers suggest that stable marriages result when people share similar interests.

ship (named after the author of *A Doll's House*), characterized by a dominant, nurturant male and a submissive, receptive female; (2) the Thurberian relationship (named after James Thurber's view of male–female relationships), involving a nurturant, submissive male and a dominant, receptive female; (3) the master–servant girl relationship, in which a dominant, receptive male marries a submissive, nurturant female; and (4) the mother-son relationship, involving a submissive, receptive male and a dominant, nurturant female.

Most of the marriage and family research to date suggests that the complementarity theory is inadequate for explaining mate selection and adjustment in the early stages of marriage. Other researchers have speculated that the longer the couple remain together, the more likely the marriage relationship will be characterized by complementarity of roles. Furthermore, as we noted in Chapter 12, Murstein (1982) has suggested that the most satisfying interpersonal relationships do not necessarily occur between the most similar individuals, but between those who are equally capable of meeting the other's needs. Research also suggests that marital satisfaction is highest in egalitarian couples, where power is distributed relatively equally between the partners, and lowest in couples headed by dominant wives (Gray-Little & Burk, 1983).

Types of Marriages

Just as there are individual differences among people, there are differences among the types of marriage that people establish. As people mature and change with time, they also change the way they interact with each other in relationships. Family changes such as the birth of a child or when a young-adult child leaves home can also affect the way in which married people relate to each other. Thus, marriages can develop in many ways depending on the life events and personalities involved. Cuber and Harroff (1965) studied over 400 marriages that had lasted at least 10 years. None of the husbands and wives had seriously considered separation or divorce, so these marriages would be considered to be "good" ones. There was considerable variation in the type of relationships established in the marriages. Nonetheless, Cuber and Harroff identified five basic types of marriages.

1. *Conflict–habituated:* The marriage is characterized by considerable conflict and tension, which becomes a habitual but acceptable pattern. In fact, the consistency of arguing and bickering may even provide a sense of stability to the marriage.
2. *Devitalized:* The couple believe that they love one another, and yet there is little zest or vitality to the marriage. At one time their marriage may have been a vital one, but now it has little passion or intimacy. Although they may appear disenchanted, the couple still view their marriage as a good one even though they may be painfully aware of their lost passion.
3. *Passive–congenial:* The couple are content and comfortable with what they have. There is little effort, however, at improving or changing the marriage. Conflict is avoided if possible. In fact, partners have little to do with each other.
4. *Vital:* The marriage is characterized as vibrant and exciting. The couple are highly involved with one another, particularly in areas related to family life—finances, child care, recreational, and social activities.
5. *Total:* Like the vital marriage, this one is characterized by a high degree of involvement between husband and wife, only to a greater and more complete extent. This relationship is rare.

Marital Companionship
An aspect of marital life characterized by caring, emotional attachment, trust, commitment, and a sharing of interests.

Companionship and Marriage

If asked to name a key factor for determining a couple's marital satisfaction, many people would respond: sexual compatibility. Although this aspect of marriage certainly is important for the couple's happiness, research suggests that **marital companionship** is an even more important factor (Garrett, 1982).

Companionship implies more than simply spending a great deal of time with one's spouse. It involves caring, emotional attachment, trust, commitment, and a sharing of interests. In terms of the marital styles described by Cuber and Harroff (1965), one is more likely to find companionship in vital and total marriages.

One reason why companionship relations are linked to marital satisfaction is that they provide marital partners with a haven for venting the pressures, tensions, and frustrations that build daily in life. Garrett (1982) observes that in the security of such a relationship, spouses can "blow off steam" without fear of criticism, reprisal, or rejection. Having someone who is a willing and interested listener and who offers encouragement and occasional advice also brings a balance to the marital relationship and promotes a sense of mutuality within the couple.

Although companionship relations can be found in all socioeconomic groups, Garrett (1982) notes that they are more frequent in middle- and upper-class marriages than lower-class (or working-class) marriages. This finding is related to the more rigid division of labor in working-class families, in which the husband typically is the "breadwinner" and the wife, the "mother and housewife." Role rigidity such as this tends to break down communication between marital partners and, along with financial concerns, contributes to the lower marital satisfaction found among working-class as opposed to middle-class couples.

Family Violence

Law-enforcement officials estimate that there are 28 million victims of wife beating—women who are physically assaulted by their husbands. Research indicates that at least one-sixth of all married couples experience one "violent episode" every year. Studies show that up to 60 percent of all married women are subjected to physical violence by their husbands at some time during the marriage (*FBI Law Enforcement Bulletin*, 1978). One study showed that 20 percent of all husbands beat their wives "regularly" according to their own report, from daily to six times a year (Gelles & Straus, 1979). Furthermore, physical violence cuts across socioeconomic and racial lines (Tavris & Offir, 1977).

Wife beating can be explained psychologically in the context of social learning and role theory. People learn the approved roles of their own and the opposite gender. In Western society men play the dominant role. The laws are created and enforced by men. Furthermore, although ours is a violent culture, only one-half of the population is encouraged in violence, while the other half is encouraged to avoid and fear it. So in the case of domestic violence, women are likely to be socially conditioned to the victim role and men to the aggressor role (Pagelow, 1979).

What about the victim? What kind of women find themselves victims of their husband's beatings? Any woman may find herself in a battering situation and find it difficult to extricate herself from it. Despite the danger to herself and to her children, she may stay with her husband because of lack of financial

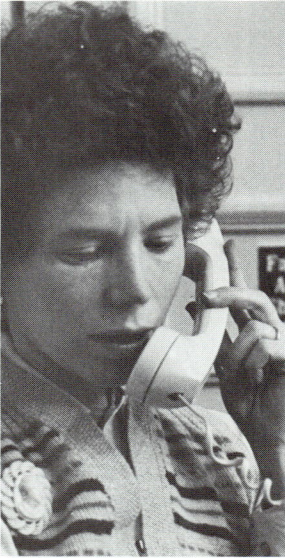

Shelters for battered women provide temporary support and counseling for abused women and their children.

resources, dependence, terror, for the sake of the children, and often because she has nowhere else to go.

It is fairly commonplace to blame the victim, the beaten wife. It is thought, even by some professionals, that many of these women provoke their husbands; or that they enjoy being beaten. Such ideas could not be further from the truth. As one battered woman stated, "No one has to provoke a wife beater. He will strike out when he is ready, and for whatever reason" (quoted in Fleming, 1979).

In most communities, shelters for battered wives provide women with an alternative to staying in the home and violent marriage. Victims find psychological and legal counseling in these shelters as well as help in setting up a new life for themselves and their children.

Pause for Thought

Battered women are often mothers as well as wives. Financially dependent on their husbands, they often stay in a destructive marriage for the sake of their children. But their children are also victims as they witness family violence. What short-term and long-term effects might there be for children who watch their mothers being beaten by their fathers?

Midlife Divorce

Over one-third of all marriages end in divorce; approximately 15 percent of these divorces occur after 15 years of marriage, and therefore involve middle-aged partners (Norton & Moorman, 1987). The divorce of couples who have been married for 20 or 25 years was formerly uncommon; today nearly everyone knows at least one couple who has divorced after many years of marriage.

Divorce in midlife occurs for many reasons. For some couples it is a response to the stresses of midlife career crises or extramarital affairs. For many others, however, it reflects differential growth of the marital partners. Troll (1982) has presented a model of couple adjustment that is based on the "fit" between individual growth patterns of each partner (see Table 14.1). According to this model, the marriage has the best chance of remaining intact if both individuals either remain stable in personality, or grow (or even deteriorate) in synchronous and compatible ways over time. Marital discord, in contrast, is likely to result from any pattern reflecting a deteriorating fit between the couple. This can occur (1) when one spouse remains stable and the other grows (or deteriorates) in personality; (2) when there is personality change in the same direction for both spouses, but the rate of change is radically different for one individual as opposed to the other; or (3) when there is personality change in the opposite direction for the partners. Take, for example, the case of a couple in which the wife has established a new career for herself after having completed her job as child-rearer and is now ambitiously achieving success. The husband, meanwhile has spent the past 20 to 30 years driving himself on the job, and is now more interested in traveling or spending leisure time with his wife. In this case, the spouses are changing in different and possibly incompatible directions.

Historical trends and expectations may also be linked to the rising divorce rate during midlife. Many of today's middle-aged divorced people claim to have married at the socially prescribed time without much thought. They

Table 14.1 ▬▬▬▬▬▬▬

Troll's Model of Couple Development

Development of Husband	Development of Wife		
	None (stable)	**Becomes more complex**	**Becomes less complex**
None (stable)	Match should remain good. Perhaps dormant while children intervene, but, when they leave, may get a "second honeymoon."	Match deteriorates. Wife's needs no longer met.	Match deteriorates. Husband's needs no longer met.
Becomes more complex	Match deteriorates. Husband's needs no longer met.	Relationship has chance to develop if individuals' changes are on same path. But they could each develop in different directions and would no longer match.	Match deteriorates. Husband's needs no longer met.
Becomes less complex	Match deteriorates. Wife's needs no longer met.	Match deteriorates. Wife's needs no longer met.	Relationship has chance of staying matched if negative developments of both are synchronous; could be like "cooling off." But if not, synchronization will disappear.

did what was expected. Now social attitudes have changed and these couples have an opportunity to make corrections. In a recent analysis of the U.S. Census Current Population Survey (Norton & Moorman, 1987), it was found that women who marry after age 30 are less likely to divorce than women who marry in their early twenties. By delaying marriage until personal and career goals are established, women may be less likely to have second thoughts about their marriages in midlife.

For many middle-aged couples, divorce is seen as a growth experience. They may not experience some of the problems of the young divorced person. Young children, economic sacrifice, and disapproval of parents may not present problems for the divorcing middle-aged couple. On the other hand, the couple has built up a more extensive household, and has made investments and purchases together. There are joint checking and savings accounts;

Midlife divorce is often followed by remarriage, usually within three years after being divorced.

joint car ownership; and the deed for the house may be in both names. The couple has also developed a larger network of mutual friends, and these relationships may be strained upon separation.

Divorce at midlife, as in earlier points in development, is painful. It is typically followed by loneliness, self-doubt, mood swings, and many practical adjustments in living (Kelly, 1982). For example, the divorced woman may be starting to date at the time she begins to experience doubts about her attractiveness; she also is expected to consider sexual relations after a number of years of intimacy (or the painful lack of it) with one partner. Fear of sexual inadequacy may also inhibit the divorced middle-aged male from pursuing new relationships with female companions.

If midlife divorce is almost always followed by uncertainty and stress, it is also usually followed by marriage, on average, within three years after being divorced. Middle-aged men are more likely to remarry than women (Reiss, 1980) and very often to a younger never-married woman.

Of those adults who remarry, about half will divorce a second time (Glick, 1984; Norton & Moorman, 1987). However, for those couples who remarry at midlife, married life is more successful (Hunt & Hunt, 1975; Norton & Moorman, 1987). Although the risk of divorce among remarried couples is higher than for first marriages, the majority of remarried people—particularly men—report that they are happier than they were in their first marriage. This generalization may hold especially well for midlife marriages that are made between potentially more mature people and that are not plagued by custody and stepparent arrangements.

Widowhood

Widowhood is usually associated with old age, but, according to Troll (1982), in the United States, there are over 90,000 men and women under 60 years of age who are widowed, and half of them are under 45. Women are outliving men in an ever-widening margin (Berardo, 1968), with the result that widowhood is beginning to be seen as an inevitable and almost universal phase of life—and one frequently associated with middle age.

Many of the problems of widowhood are related to the problems of later adulthood. (Indeed, a woman may define herself as "old"—as having entered the final stretches of life—after she loses her husband.) Among the problems unique to the middle-aged widow, however, is the fact that she may be the first, or one of the first, to lose her husband. Her friends are still married, and she may consequently come to think of herself as the fifth wheel at any social occasion. Friends may be insensitive—alternately exhorting her to socialize and then forgetting to invite her. She also tends to be less willing than the older woman to resign herself to life without masculine companionship and sexuality; yet she may be unable to meet single men (especially widowed men) who can understand her experience. Consequently, for many women widowhood can be an extremely lonely and alienated period of life (Troll, 1982).

Pause for Thought

Compared to middle-aged men, women in their midlife have a higher incidence of depression, more so than at any other period of the lifespan. Separation, divorce, and death of their spouse are a few life events that may contribute to depression. Why should women be more susceptible to depression at this age than men?

Singlehood

Approximately 5 percent of all middle-aged adults in the United States are single people who have never been married. There is relatively little research on this group, and almost none on the positive aspects of its adjustment. Ordinary observation, however, produces many examples of single people who, in the absence of immediate family obligations, have achieved an especially intense career commitment: Obvious examples include the dedicated priest, schoolteacher, or charity worker.

Naturally, single, middle-aged people encounter special problems. They must accept the social identity of a single—spinster or bachelor—which even today carries some stigma. They must plan for a late adulthood that does not include support from, or involvement with, children, although, of course, they may be involved with other people's children. And they are less protected against illness or misfortune. For example, if they become mentally disturbed they are more likely to be hospitalized than are married people, who may be cared for by their families.

The single, middle-aged person, however, is not usually a loner. Most single people develop close relationships with friends—single as well as married. Singles, particularly women, also often maintain close contact with their nuclear and extended family.

The motives for remaining single typically are somewhat different for males and females, with a major exception noted for male and female homosexuals, many of whom choose never to marry. Never-married women are better educated, come from higher socioeconomic groups, and are more achievement oriented than single men. Moreover, it appears that the older single woman has chosen not to marry rather than having never been asked (Havens, 1973). In contrast, Spreitzer and Riley (1974) report that successful, achievement-oriented men are the least likely to remain single. In traditional and even nontraditional marriages, women take primary responsibility for household and child care. Under these circumstances, it is hardly surprising that achievement-oriented women differ from achievement-oriented men in their marital statuses. Single women can more realistically focus their time and energy on their careers when they do not have a family to care for.

Occupational Development

In middle adulthood, people have a new opportunity to become generative in their work. Generative midlife people produce goods, ideas, plans, and policies at a higher rate than they did earlier. They may also become generative in the sense of teaching what they know to others—usually younger people. In midcareer, for example, a person may train new workers; represent a union chapter; head a department; lead a state government or a multinational corporation or the board of a community organization. The worker, like the parent, feels able and wants to contribute something to the world to be inherited by younger generations. On the other hand, when people have no opportunity, or take no opportunity, to impart their skill, experience, or care to others, they may suffer from a sense of stagnation. They will feel alienated both from what they produce and from what they leave behind. In short, one of the key components of identity and self-esteem, especially for men, is occupational status (Tamir, 1982).

Occupational Advancement

In midlife, people are concerned with reaching and maintaining a satisfactory level in their occupational career (Havighurst, 1982; Super, 1963). Advancement at this stage frequently means moving from in-depth involvement in a specialty to a managerial or supervisory function. For example, the assembly-line worker becomes a foreman; the clerical worker becomes the office manager; the research chemist becomes director of a unit. Havighurst (1982) suggests that one important career task at this time is achieving a flexible work role that is perceived as interesting, productive, and financially satisfactory. Similar observations have been offered by Daniel Levinson and his co-workers, who have also noted that the middle-adult period is a time for self-evaluation regarding career development (Levinson, Darrow, Klein, Levinson, & McKee, 1977). Past goals are now revived in light of current achievements. Individuals who have achieved, or believe they will achieve, previously established career goals are likely to feel satisfied with themselves and to display a positive self-image. Conversely, the recognition that one is unlikely to achieve a desired occupational level—for example, corporate vice-president, department chairperson, division manager, company foreman, and so on—typically leads to a reevaluation of life goals and often to a reevaluation of the self. Individuals who have difficulty readjusting their career goals and aspirations to the realities of their particular life situations may feel frustrated, stagnant, and personally impoverished. They are also more likely to change jobs.

During middle adulthood, most men and women attain the highest status and income of their careers. Yet, men and women show striking differences in advancement in status and income with increasing age, with women lagging far behind, especially in income. For the older woman, discrimination at the workplace becomes particularly evident as she fails to be promoted and given salary increases, as well as responsibility commensurate with that of her male counterpart. Between the ages of 35 and 65, men's average yearly earnings are nearly double those of women. Furthermore, this gender difference in income is not completely accounted for by differences in occupation. N. S. Barrett (1979) notes that within all major occupational groups, women's earnings are far below those of men. Part of the reason for discrepancy in salary levels between men and women is that women more often drop out of the work force to establish their families and in so doing delay their career advancement and hence salary level. Studies of successful women (Betz, 1984; Van Velsor & O'Rand, 1984) suggest that women who work continuously are more likely to achieve a higher occupational status than women who step out of their jobs or who switch jobs. However, even when women are compared with men of the same level of work experience, they are paid less than men.

Personality and Occupational Advancement

In addition to gender, what differentiates the individuals who advance within their respective companies from those who do not? Having a college degree makes a big difference; college-educated people advance earlier and go further in their careers. In one 20-year longitudinal study of AT&T executives, Bray and Howard (1983) found that men who rose higher in the corporation were more committed to the job, more interested in success, showed higher achievement motives, and were more forceful and dominant than their less successful colleagues. There was no difference between these groups in life satisfaction. Regardless of their position within the corporate ladder, the executives were basically satisfied with their lives. Although Bray and Howard studied men, similar results have been found with women who work in companies similar to AT&T (Ritchie & Moses, 1983). In a different study, Clausen (1981) found that occupational success for men during middle age was associated with a host of personality factors, not only during midlife, but during the adolescent years as well. Personality variables in adolescence that predicted midlife career success included intellectual capacities and interests and factors indexing what is called the "Protestant ethic"—ambition, productivity, dependability, low self-indulgence, and objectivity. Midlife personality variables associated with career success included intellectual capacities and interests, dependability, objectivity, tolerance for uncertainty, low hostility and self-defeating attitudes, ambition, incisiveness, and flexibility in roles. Thus, it would appear that occupational achievement is to a great extent tied to motivational and personality variables—and presumably to competence. Yet, we must remember that the harsh realities of the world—sexism, racial and ethnic discrimination, and even favoritism—are factors in determining who gets the job opening or the higher salary.

Pause for Thought

According to Erikson's theory of psychosocial development, a person's attitude toward work and view of self as a worker originates during the middle-childhood period. Depending upon the individual's successes and failures primarily in the school and home, a positive or negative view is established. What kind of "successes" in middle childhood might be related to adult occupational advancement?

Job Satisfaction

The midlife phase of the occupation cycle is often a time of "truth" for many people. As in many other contexts of life, both men and women become acutely aware of the time remaining to accomplish their goals. For those individuals who are within reach of achieving their goals, this period of occupational life is experienced as exciting, challenging, and rewarding. For others, however, the large gulf between aspirations and achievements may become a major factor in triggering a midlife crisis (Levinson et al., 1977).

In middle age, most people are seeking some assurance of job stability—seniority, for example. They are less likely than younger workers to leave their company (Byrne, 1975). This may reflect the fact that older people generally take fewer risks than younger ones. But it also represents positive satisfaction with the work itself. The highest percentage of satisfied workers can be found in the over-40 category (Rhodes, 1983). These workers are significantly more satisfied than young adults, not only with their jobs but with the monetary rewards and challenges they provide (Quinn, Staines, & McCullough, 1974; Tamir, 1982). In fact, the bases of job satisfaction differ between younger and older workers—at least for white-collar workers. For the younger group, dissatisfaction with the job is likely to be tied to salary; for the older group, it is more likely to be related to the lack of challenge and the resources to get the job done. In contrast, for blue-collar workers, income level is an important factor in job satisfaction for both younger and older workers.

Middle-aged women may find greater satisfaction in their lives as a result of their careers. Coleman and Antonucci (1983) found that working women

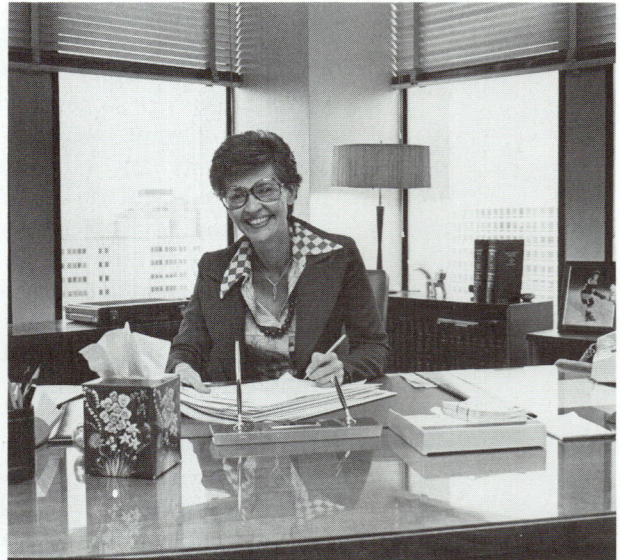

Middle-aged women find greater satisfaction in their lives as a result of their careers than do men. For some women, a career may involve working in a corporation; for other women, it might mean working on an adult education program in their community.

Human Development in Practice

Wellness in the Workplace: A New Role for Health-Care Providers

While it is not news that many large corporations and businesses have medical services available on the job for employees, what is news is that many work sites are shifting their focus to "wellness."

Back in the late 1970s, several large corporations such as Johnson & Johnson, Control Data Corporation, and AT&T began pilot health-promotion programs for their workers. These programs, which were offered to employees as part of their job-benefit package, included physical-fitness facilities (gyms, weights, saunas) and dining services that served only healthful foods. The initial focus of these early wellness programs was stress. Under pressure from escalating job demands and responsibilities, many high-level and mid-level executives were "burning out" from stress. The wellness programs were seen as cost efficient since they helped keep highly trained and experienced executives on the job. Relaxation training was provided to teach employees how to reduce stress.

Today, wellness programs are found in almost two-thirds of companies with 50 or more employees. The scope of these programs has expanded to include major health projects such as smoking, drug, and alcohol control; exercise and physical fitness; back-pain treatment and prevention; weight control; screening for high blood pressure and other health problems; education to prevent off-the-job accidents; and overall health-risk appraisals. Since many states have introduced legislation that prevents or limits smoking in the workplace, it is of advantage to companies to provide their employees with help in quitting smoking.

The results from studies on these wellness programs is encouraging. Many companies report that those who participate in the wellness programs are more likely to have lower health-care costs (*Trenton Times,* Nov. 8, 1987). This, of course, means savings to both employer and employee; absenteeism is reduced and high-cost medical care is reduced or eliminated. Most of the studies report that employees with unhealthy lifestyles cost employers more money than those with healthy lifestyles (e.g., not smoking, exercising, using car seatbelts). Furthermore, people who are enjoying good health are more likely to develop positive attitudes about their jobs and their lives in general.

The wellness-in-the-workplace projects are aimed at preventing illnesses and identifying health problems at an early and treatable stage. Many health-care workers and nurses who work with severely ill patients in understaffed hospitals may find it a refreshing alternative to work to improve the health of people on the job.

scored significantly higher on most measures of psychological well-being. Working women had higher self-esteem, less psychological anxiety, better physical health, and greater marital satisfaction than women who were homemakers. In addition, a strong trend was noted in the direction of greater happiness and life satisfaction for working women. On the other hand, no differences were noted between working and nonworking women for depression, degree of satisfaction with their role as parents, tendency to get things done, and interest in life.

These findings generally are in agreement with the few other studies that have focused on the impact of work on women (Kessler & McRae, 1982; Northcott, 1981). They also are compatible with the results of research on the impact of work on men (Tamir, 1982). However, Coleman and Antonucci (1983) note that work may not have exactly the same meaning for men and women. It is known that women's psychological adjustment, unlike men's, is less affected by salary and occupational prestige. Furthermore, the positive benefits of employment are reduced for working mothers whose spouses do not share household and child-care responsibilities for young children (Kessler & McRae, 1982).

Retraining and Second Careers

In our rapidly changing society, many middle-aged workers find that the skills learned in the earlier period of their career do not serve them as well as they once did. Technological advances have radically changed the world of work, both for the white-collar and blue-collar worker. Gone is the manual type-writer, for example. In its place, temporarily, are the electric and electronic typewriters, which, in turn, are rapidly giving way to the computerized word processor. Comparable changes are taking place in virtually every area of occupational life. In the face of such change, workers, particularly middle-aged workers, are becoming increasingly aware of the need for retraining. Corporations are spending millions and millions of dollars each year for up-grading employee skills. Community colleges across the country are booming in response to the demand from older students for job-related courses. Middle-aged workers are being challenged as never before.

In some cases, however, simply upgrading one's skills is not enough. Among the serious problems encountered by middle-aged workers are job obsolescence, unemployment, and age discrimination in hiring and job advancement. Not infrequently in our fast-paced society, the middle-aged person becomes obsolete as businesses strive to incorporate innovative and cost-efficient technological changes into their production line. Computerized robots, for example, now do the assembly-line work in automotive plants that used to be done by many workers. Should middle-aged workers lose their jobs, they may find it difficult to obtain another. Sweetland (1978) has re-viewed some of the factors working against the rehiring of middle-aged and older workers. They include: (1) unfavorable employer attitudes—"He's too old. We're a 'young' company"; (2) high salary and benefit demands in com-parison to younger workers; (3) the reluctance of older workers to relocate themselves; (4) the employer's belief that hiring older workers represents an unwise investment in the absence of long-term career potential; and (5) less education and technological skill in comparison to younger workers. Regard-less of the reasons, prolonged unemployment in midlife may cause serious loss of identity, status, and health, as well as loss of income.

A small, but growing, percentage of middle-aged people, in response to the pressures of job obsolescence or job dissatisfaction, are making career changes. As one middle-ager said, "I had the feeling I was getting nowhere. I struggled all my life to make money and be a successful business executive. But when I got there I realized it wasn't at all what I wanted. It became boring and meaningless, and that's when I decided to get out. I sold my business and got a master's degree in social work. Now I'm working in a counseling center for college kids and have never been happier." This type of career change is typical of many people going through midlife crisis. There seems to be an overwhelming fear that time is running out—a now-or-never feeling for "doing something important or meaningful." Sometimes the change is made to pursue a dream that was put aside for a secure livelihood.

These midlife feelings seem to be largely responsible for the phenomenon of second careers. More and more people in their thirties and forties are changing their lives and attempting to find more satisfaction in their work lives. Of course, not everyone is equally receptive to retraining and career change. Research indicates that the people who are most interested in such change are those who are concerned with the social–psychological aspect of jobs and who are strongly motivated to achieve but who see little chance of movement in their current job and consequently are less satisfied with what they are doing (Sheppard & Belitsky, 1966). In other words, they want to get ahead and/or do a good job, but they do not see much chance of accomplishing their goals in their current position.

Integrating Work and Leisure

Even before people look ahead to retirement, the question of "What will I do with my time?" becomes particularly relevant (Gould, 1978). During middle age, people often have more time for leisure activities, especially after the children are launched from the home. Integrating work, family, and leisure becomes an important goal for the midlife adult. Yet, in our society, leisure is not given a high priority in everyone's value hierarchy. Many people are skeptical of those who seem to have too much time for hobbies, sports, or community work. According to Gordon, Gaitz, and Scott (1977), however, leisure activities often help to bridge role conflicts at different stages of the life cycle. Thus, people may use leisure activities to achieve goals or to satisfy needs not met in other aspects of their life—particularly on the job. The owner of a neighborhood gas station, for example, might find an outlet for his sense of drama as a thirty-second degree Mason; a middle-aged medical social worker might spend her winter weekends on the ski patrol and her summer weekends marking new trails for the forest service.

People seek leisurely activities for several reasons (Gordon, Gaitz, & Scott, 1977). *Relaxation* is the least intense form of leisure and may include napping, taking a sauna, daydreaming. Leisure can also be a form of *diversion* from our daily chores or activities; watching television, playing board or card games or talking on the telephone to friends are examples. As in work, some leisure activities take on a more intense quality when people use them to improve themselves. *Developmental pleasures* include leisure activities that require practice and skill to enjoy such as weight training, bicycle racing, playing a musical instrument, or developing a special expertise in Elizabethan plays. In *creative pleasures,* people might devote a fair amount of their free time to creative artistic endeavors. Some of the creative activities may spill over into work as when a worker is asked to organize the office holiday party because his hobby is gourmet cooking. Finally, people may seek out *sensual pleasures* in their leisure activities. Sensual pleasures can include massage, rhythmic dancing, contact sports, aerobic exercise, or even high risk and excitement activities such as motorcycle racing or soaring.

The nature of leisure activity changes as one enters midlife. Between 30 and 44, leisure time is most often spent with the family. With the launching of children, however, more time is spent in personal, expressive activities, in which the family is not included (Gordon, Gaitz, & Scott, 1977). Watching television, gardening, visiting friends, walking, reading, and camping are examples of popular midlife activities.

Finally, the question of leisure time also becomes important as plans begin for retirement. Individuals who are deeply involved with avocational pursuits may be eager to retire; those who "live for their work" may find retirement traumatic. Once again, leisure activities may help the person to deal with role changes—in this case, from worker to nonworker.

Summary

Intergenerational relations become increasingly significant during middle adulthood. Being in the middle of the family line means that the middle-aged adult is influenced both by top-down (elderly parent to middle-aged child) and bottom-up (adolescent or young-adult child to middle-aged parent) family processes. Research indicates greater intergenerational transmission of political and religious values and orientations than gender-roles, lifestyles, and work orientations.

The composition of the family changes dramatically during middle age. After years of sharing their lives with their children, middle-aged partners find themselves alone together. Before the children leave, the parents must deal with the conflicts encountered in raising adolescents. They must support adolescents in their search for identity, help them with their career exploration, and prepare them to take their places in the adult world. Guiding their children is a part of the resolution of Erikson's crisis of generativity vs. stagnation.

For most parents, the "empty-nest" phase of the family life cycle signifies freedom and is experienced as a relief. For some, however, whether mothers or fathers, the absence of their children is difficult to bear—part of their self-definition and reason for living is gone.

Relations between middle-aged parents and their adult children are closer than is generally assumed. Each relies on the other for support and psychological well-being.

In middle age, a parent–child role reversal sometimes occurs, with the middle-aged child caring for and supporting aging, dependent parents. Most older people, however, neither want nor need to be dependent upon their adult children.

Becoming a grandparent for the first time is more of a middle-age than old-age event. Grandparents play an important role in the family system, offering emotional support, child care, and advice on basic values, lifestyle, occupation, and parenting. Research indicates that grandparents play a particularly beneficial role in the adjustment of single-parent families, especially those involving teenage mothers. Just as there are styles of parenting, so too are there styles of grandparenting that people begin to adopt during this period.

Most research suggests that marital adjustment is high during middle adulthood, particularly in the postchild phase of the family life cycle. When problems do arise, they are often related to differential growth of partners, finances, sexual boredom, and work pressures.

Successful marriages take many forms, from couples who are totally involved and committed to one another, to couples whose bickering and fighting form the basis for marital continuity. Although some investigators suggest that the longer a couple remains together, the more likely it is that their relationship will be characterized by complementarity of roles, most research indicates that marital adjustment is linked to couple similarity in interests, attitudes, and personality. One factor that is particularly important for successful marital adjustment is the development of a companion relationship with one's spouse, which involves mutual caring, trust, commitment, and open communication.

Each year, millions and millions of women are physically battered by their husbands. Socialization practices that foster a dominant, assertive role in men and a submissive, passive role in women also feed into family violence.

Midlife divorce is becoming a more common phenomenon, particularly as cultural attitudes toward marriage and divorce become more flexible. Divorce during middle age, as at any other time, is painful and is usually followed by loneliness, self-doubt, mood swings, and many practical adjustments in living. Most people who divorce in midlife do remarry.

Many women lose their husbands before the age of 60—thus, widowhood is often a middle-age event. Middle-aged widows must deal with such problems as meeting new male companions, starting new sexual relationships, maintaining old friendships, and adjusting to reduced finances.

For many adults, generativity is achieved not only through family relations, but also on the job by the development of ideas, products, plans, and by guiding others in their job development. In middle age, most people are concerned with consolidating their work position and advancing. They also are concerned with evaluating their level of achievement in light of past, current, and future goals and aspirations. Because of gender discrimination on the job, women lag far behind men in occupational status and income.

Research suggests that personality and motivational factors play an important role in the person's success in occupational areas. The traits most frequently associated with career success are intellectual competence, high achievement orientation, forcefulness, dominance, commitment, ambition, dependability, low hostility and self-defeating attitudes, and objectivity.

Middle-aged people generally are the most satisfied workers; moreover, among white-collar workers, satisfaction less often is tied to income than is true for younger or blue-collar workers. Technological advances have radically changed the work world, both for white-collar and blue-collar workers, and have resulted in the need for retraining for many middle-aged adults. Should the middle-aged worker lose his or her job, that person is often faced with serious problems in getting rehired by another company. Many prejudices exist in the business world that work against the rehiring of middle-aged and older workers.

In midlife, leisure activities are often pursued alone in contrast to the family-oriented activity of younger families. Such activities often help people to adapt to role changes and to find satisfaction and interest that may be absent in other areas of their lives—especially on the job. Leisure activities are usually pursued for relaxation, diversion, personal development, creativity, and for sensual pleasure.

Further Readings

Bernard, Jesse. *The future of marriage.* New York: Bantam Books, 1972.
Discusses the differences between the "his" marriage and the "her" marriage, and compares them to other lifestyles, such as being single, divorced, or widowed. The mental health of each group is discussed and compared with that of others.

Boston Women's Health Collective. *Ourselves and our children.* New York: Random House, 1978.
This practical, informative book discusses decisions and conflicts in the role of parenting; examines parenting throughout the lifespan.

Fuchs, Estelle. *The second season: Life, love, and sex—women in the middle years.* Garden City, NY: Doubleday, 1977.
Deals primarily with the complex physiological, social, and psychological concerns of the middle-aged woman: sex, pregnancy, hysterectomy, menopause, divorce, widowhood.

MacPherson, Michael C. *The family years: A guide to positive parenting.* Minneapolis, MN: Winston Press, 1981.
A practical book that addresses family issues such as limits and rules, conflicts and their resolution, and family conferences.

Schowalter, John E., and Anyan, Walter R. *The family handbook of adolescence.* New York: Knopf, 1981.
A straightforward reference book for adolescents and their parents; written from a medical point of view.

Troll, Lillian E., Israel, Joan, and Israel, Kenneth. *Looking ahead: A woman's guide to the problems and joys of growing older.* Englewood Cliffs, NJ: Prentice-Hall, 1977.
An edited volume containing many interesting papers on the middle-aged and elderly woman. Included are such topics as physical appearance, sexuality, marital relations and friendships, work and education, minority issues, mental health, and political power.

Troll, Lillian, E., Miller, Sheila, J., and Atchley, Robert C. *Families in later life.* Belmont, CA: Wadsworth, 1979.
An overview of the many forms of family life in the adult years. The authors incorporate research and theory from psychology, sociology, and family studies to achieve a truly multidisciplinary approach to the topic.

Observational Activities

14.1 *Grandparenthood*

Today, becoming a grandparent is more likely to occur during middle adulthood than in late adulthood. The stereotypic view of grandparents as being aged, wrinkled, and gray-haired, sitting in a rocking chair, has been replaced by a more youthful and active grandparent. People in middle adulthood who become grandparents differ in their styles of grandparenting. The role of grandparent is variously interpreted by adults depending on their age and family circumstances. The type and degree of involvement grandparents have with their grandchildren also differs from one family to the next. In this chapter, we discussed the five styles of grandparenting identified by Neugarten and Weinstein: Formal, Fun-seeker, Surrogate Parent, Reservoir of Family Wisdom, and Distant Figure.

For this activity, interview 10 grandparents between the ages of 50 and 65 about their experiences of grandparenthood. Ask them the following questions.

1. Describe your involvement with your grandchildren. (Use the five styles of grandparenting as a guide for asking questions.)
2. Describe your satisfaction with your role of grandparent. (Ask people to elaborate on their views as much as possible.)
3. Compare your role as grandparent with your role as parent.

Once you have completed your interviews, compile and summarize your findings. Do you notice any differences in the styles of grandparenting among your respondents? How did your respondents compare with those of your classmates? What roles do a person's age, work status, and gender play in the emergence of grandparent roles?

14.2 *Vocational Development*

Vocational development takes many forms. Some people choose a job or career early in adulthood and stick with it through their entire working lives. Others try a variety of jobs before settling into the particular one they believe is right for them. Still other people find that after many years of commitment to a job, a sense of dissatisfaction or boredom has developed, thereby leading to a midlife vocational change.

Interview five to 10 middle-aged working men and women about the nature of their vocational development. Ask each of them the following questions.

1. Describe your job history starting with your first full-time job.
2. How satisfied have you been with your job development?
3. Have you thought seriously about switching jobs recently?
4. What factors might influence your decision to change your job during this time of your life?

On the basis of the data collected, speculate on the societal, situational, and personality factors that influence the course of one's working life. Are there differences in vocational development for men and women; for blue-collar vs. white-collar workers? What factors may contribute to these differences?

SEVEN

Late Adulthood

*C*hange is a constant ingredient in life. In earlier periods of the lifespan, physical, cognitive, personality, and social changes brought new skills, new identities, and new opportunities for learning to individuals. In late adulthood, there are also numerous changes that occur in the body, in social relations, and in the way people think about themselves. Most of these changes represent a loss or decline of some sort for which people must make adjustments.

Late adulthood is the last period in the lifespan. It is the time when the effects of earlier physical and psychological changes of life events and accomplishments culminate to provide meaning to people's lives or to produce a sense of despair. People show considerable variability in the way in which they adapt to the process of growing older. There is as much if not more variation among people in late adulthood as compared to earlier periods of development. Although not everyone lives a long or healthy late adulthood, more people today are living to be in their seventies and eighties. The benefits of late adulthood are balanced by the restrictions placed upon older people as a result of physical, social, financial, and cultural changes.

In Chapter 15, you will learn about the various factors that influence the physical and cognitive adaptation in late adulthood. Issues of identity and personality adjustment will also be discussed. In Chapter 16, we will turn our attention to changes in family life and social relations and changes in work roles that occur as people retire.

Late Adulthood: Physical, Cognitive, and Personality Development

The word "elderly" had always seemed to apply to others, thought Minnie—for example, the gray-haired, frail-looking owner of the corner grocery store; the old man down the block who walked his dog past her house every day; Aunt Catherine, nearly crippled from her battle with arthritis; the residents of a nearby nursing home who often visited the park across the street; and, of course, Mother and Father, who passed away just a few years ago. By contrast, Minnie had never considered herself to be elderly. So what if she was 65 years old. She was active, healthy, and generally in better physical shape than most women 10 to 15 years younger. Her mind was clear and quick, and she was still inquisitive, still eager to learn. Furthermore, she and her husband were still active socially, as well as sexually. Overall, Minnie felt good about herself.

Things were beginning to change for Minnie, however. She noticed that people were beginning to act differently toward her. Even though the mandatory retirement age of 70 had been removed as discriminatory, some of her colleagues at work persisted in asking her what she planned to do during retirement. Most of her adult life she had prided herself for being an important employee to the large department store; now she was beginning to feel as if she was no longer an integral part of the company. Then there was the real-estate salesman who stopped by last weekend. What had he said—"Wouldn't it make more sense for you and your husband, now that you are getting on in years, to move to a smaller, more manageable house?" And finally, there was Beth, her lifelong best friend, who had died several months ago of cancer. These events, and others, had forced Minnie to recognize that she was getting older—even if she did not feel old.

Yet, Minnie was not going to enter the last phase of her lifespan meekly. She decided to enroll her husband and herself in an adult-education course on starting a postretirement business. The course would give them the extra help they needed to plan a different lifestyle for themselves that would see them through the next 10 to 15 years they saw before them.

In this chapter, we examine three aspects of the aging process. First, we discuss the many changes that take place in physical areas in late adulthood, with particular emphasis on sensory and organ functioning and their relationship to health and adjustment. Next, we turn our attention to the area of cognitive development and describe the changes in information processing, reasoning, and problem solving that occur in old age. Finally, the chapter ends with a discussion of the major psychosocial tasks confronting the older person and the role of social image, self-concept, and social interaction in life adjustment.

But before we describe the changes that occur in late adulthood, let's consider the overall impact of growing older. Although most of you may not be in the over-65 age category (we hope some of our readers are!), all of you will have contact with people from this period of the lifespan and all of you will eventually become part of the elderly population.

The Impact of Growing Older

As people get older, they are inevitably surrounded by reminders of their advancing age and mortality. For some individuals, such as Minnie, these reminders are at odds with their *perceived age*—that is, the general age with which one identifies. It can come as a shock to people to realize that society has defined them as old simply because of the number of years they have lived. For other adults, however, self-perceptions of aging come relatively early. The graying of hair and wrinkling of skin experienced in middle age, for example, are sufficient for some individuals to redefine themselves as old—or, at least, as "getting on in years."

Ageism   Any situation in which people are prejudicial on the basis of age.

Like Minnie, some people experience the unpleasant effects of discrimination and prejudice because of their age. **Ageism** (Butler & Lewis, 1982) refers to any situation in which people are negatively judged not by their behavior or personality but by their age. Negative stereotypes of the elderly persist in our culture. Mandatory retirement ages underscore the image of older employees as not as efficient as younger ones. Older people are inaccurately described as feeble or rigid. In Ronald Reagan's second campaign for the presidency, one of the issues raised was whether he was capable of using sound judgement and making decisions because he was in his seventies. The elderly are sometimes perceived as children who require instruction and supervision. Although some older adults may be physically or mentally disabled and require more care, many elderly people do not fit the stereotype of helpless, mindless, or passionless people.

The esteem or status attached to being old varies from culture to culture. In the United States today, while people wish to live a long and healthy life, they do not want to be elderly. In Japan and China, however, the elderly are given a much higher status in the family and in the cultures. The elderly are respected and honored.

The effects of ageism are subtle but nonetheless self-defeating. To view older adults negatively is to increase our own fears about growing older. For elderly people who incorporate the negative stereotypes, the effects of ageism can be lowered self-esteem, greater unhappiness, and depression. Like other forms of prejudice such as racism and sexism, ageism is reduced by education and by increased contact with vital and healthy elderly adults. With an increasingly older population of adults in the United States, it is even more important that negative stereotypes attached to being old be eliminated.

An Aging Population

In the past two decades, the behavior and adjustment of the older adult have been the focus of increased attention by numerous sectors of our society. To the physician, the psychologist, the urban planner, the economist, the politician, and even to themselves, older people have become a "hot topic." For example, advanced medical technology has not only increased the average

People over the age of 65 comprise the fastest growing segment of the American population, thus making them a political and economic power.

life expectancy, but it has raised serious medical, legal, and ethical questions regarding the definition of death in terminal patients—most of whom are older adults. In addition, the age at which people ought to retire has become an important economic issue in our society.

Due in part to increases in medical technology and to the postwar baby boom, people over the age of 65 compose the fastest growing segment of the United States population, with an eightfold increase from 1900 to 1980. The trend toward an older population will continue into the next century. The over-65 population is estimated to more than double from 26 million in 1980 to 67 million by the middle of the twenty-first century. By the year 2030, one in five people will be over 65 (Heckler, 1985). Furthermore, due to overall increases in income and improved medical care, the elderly will not only live longer, they will be healthier and financially better off. Many of these elderly will be women. Currently, more than 60 percent of people aged 65 or older in the United States are women.

Many community and four-year colleges are recognizing the importance of providing educational programs for the elderly. Many offer tuition waivers for people over age 65. It is not unusual now to see a retired person working at a fast-food restaurant or collecting tickets at the local cinema. Health-and-fitness facilities now offer special aerobic exercise programs for "senior citizens." Thus, the shifting age of the population has focused more attention on the needs and characteristics of older adults. Let's now examine some of the physical changes that appear in later adulthood.

Pause for Thought

Many adults spend a lot of time and money trying not to look their age. For younger adults, this might mean buying the right clothes for success in business or changing hairstyles. For older adults it might mean using cosmetics, hair dyes, and wigs or even cosmetic surgery to look younger. Ageism seems to have spawned a booming business market or could the reverse be true? Could ageism be a by-product of marketing and media campaigns?

Physical Development

As people age, they experience numerous structural and functional changes in the body—changes which, while not usually beginning in late adulthood, do have their most significant impact during this time of life.

Senescence: Primary Aging

Senescence The normal degenerative processes accompanying aging; also known as primary aging.

Primary Aging Another name for senescence or the degenerative processes accompanying aging.

A frequently misunderstood aspect of aging is **senescence,** which refers to the period of the lifespan when the body weakens and declines rather than grows (Rockstein & Sussman, 1979). It is a time when physical, social, and cognitive processes deteriorate. Huyck and Hoyer (1982) note that senescence, or **primary aging** as it is also called, is a normal part of growing older. Unlike disease, senescence occurs in all people across all cultures, although, of course, the timing and patterning of the decline varies from person to person. The gradual loss of neural tissue and the slowing down of central-nervous-system activity with increasing age are two examples of senescence. So, too, is the breakdown of the body's immune system as people get older. Thus, as people age, they are more likely to catch diseases and have more difficulty in recuperation.

Senescence is a gradual process. The changes in structure and functioning that it leads to are slow to emerge, unlike the sudden changes associated with accidents, stress, or disease. Senescence also takes place at many levels within the same individual. Thus, researchers have identified anatomical, biochemical, physiological, and behavioral changes with advancing age. Finally, although senescence is distinct from disease, it is important to note that disease, and other extrinsic factors such as trauma and stress, can accelerate senescence, and ultimately lead to death. Sometimes the death of a lifelong spouse or friend, or a move to a smaller apartment, may be so stressful that older people begin to deteriorate physically. The acceleration of senescence by these extrinsic factors is referred to as **secondary aging.**

Secondary Aging The acceleration of senescence, or primary aging, by factors such as disease, trauma, or stress.

Physical Appearance

The most obvious changes occurring in old age are in physical appearance. The wrinkles and gray hair that began in middle age become more pronounced now. Decreases in fat and muscle tissue result in inelastic skin that tends to hang in folds. The craggy, lined, and weathered features of the aged person's face is a popular subject for photographers. Loss of hair—including scalp, axillary, and body hair—also is common with aging for both sexes. So,

Postural stoop is caused by years of poor posture, shrinking muscles and tendons, and thinning of the bones.

too, is an increase in "age spots," irregular skin pigmentations, and loss of teeth (Rossman, 1980).

One of the most pronounced changes in physical appearance during the aging years is postural stoop. As Stevens-Long (1979) points out, this characteristic slump, with head projected forward and lower limbs and hips flexed, is probably caused by years of poor posture that is now made worse by the shrinkage of muscles and tendons, increased calcification of ligaments, compression of spinal discs, and thinning of bone. Older people also show a decrease in height that is related to spinal disc compression and probably postural stoop as well. Rossman (1980), however, cautions that much of the reported average decline in height in older people may be due to a cohort effect, since this decrease in stature with age is less evident in longitudinal studies (where cohort or generational effects are reduced) than in cross-sectional studies.

Osteoporosis, a condition that results in the thinning of the bones that affects some postmenopausal women and even fewer men, may result in a "dowager's hump" or hunchback as well as decreased height. Because their bones are thinner, older women afflicted with osteoporosis are more likely to fracture or break their bones during a fall. Fortunately, the disease can be prevented by increased consumption of calcium and exercise programs beginning early in young adulthood and continuing into late adulthood (National Institute of Health, 1984).

Sensory-System Changes

Nearly all the sensory systems show loss of efficiency in old age. In many cases, the loss is simply a continuation of the problems that arose in middle age, but at a more accelerated pace. For some people, however, new problems arise while old problems stabilize. In the area of vision, for example, changes in the lens that produced farsightedness in middle age now stabilize for the older person. On the other hand, new changes affecting the retina and nervous system result in decreased visual acuity and color vision for the aging adult (Fozard, Wolf, Bell, MacFarland, & Podolsky, 1977). Many older people also have considerable difficulty seeing in the dark, a situation that makes night driving particularly hazardous. In the aged, these changes also are exacerbated by the formation of *cataracts*—the most common disability of the aged eye—and *glaucoma*. Nearly 60 percent of the elderly suffer from cataracts and 1 to 3 percent from glaucoma (Crandall, 1980).

Probably the most usual sensory loss associated with aging is hearing. According to Corso (1977), 17 percent of people who are 65 or over show signs of advanced presbycusis—hearing loss due to degenerative changes in the auditory system. This loss is primarily restricted to high-frequency sounds, including many speech sounds. Many speakers try to compensate for the older person's auditory handicap by talking loudly, but increasing the volume of one's voice, or shouting, only serves to obscure the intelligible sounds for the older listener. To promote effective communication with the hard-of-hearing, one should actually lower one's voice, since this reduces voice pitch—the vocal quality that poses the most trouble for the aged. The potential importance of hearing loss for the elderly is documented by research showing that aged persons with reduced hearing are significantly more likely to do more poorly in areas of intellectual functioning than are persons with normal hearing (Granick, Kleban, & Weiss, 1976).

There is some evidence that sense of taste and smell also decline with age. The number of taste buds on the tongue decline sharply from young adulthood to old age (Bee, 1987) thus making it more difficult for elderly people to discriminate between tastes. In one study, for example, Grzegorczyk, Jones, and Mistretta (1979) found that among a sample of adults between 23 and 92 years, the ability to detect the taste of salt declined significantly with increasing age. The sense of smell is closely related to taste. In a study of over 2000 people from ages 5 to 99, the sense of smell was found to be the best between the ages of 30 and 60, to be less acute between the ages of 60 and 80, and then to decline sharply thereafter (Doty, Shaman, & Dann, 1984). Engen (1977) has cautioned, however, that sensory loss for taste and smell may be due primarily to some pathological condition, or to such chronic habits as smoking. In any event, the older person who has trouble tasting and smelling things is likely to be less interested in food, thereby leading to nutritional problems—a serious issue for many individuals in later life.

If many of these sensory changes suggest a pessimistic picture of late adulthood, it should be pointed out that except at advanced states—which usually occur only in very old age—these physical changes typically do not prevent a person from living a normal life. Such modern technological improvements as better medical facilities, amplified telephones, hearing aids, and eyeglasses have helped the elderly to live quite comfortably despite the reduced efficiency of their bodies. Indeed, it is primarily under conditions of stress that the age-related losses appear to make a significant difference in the adjustment of older people (DeVries, 1975). At her brother's funeral, for example, 70-year-old Jenny was disturbed because she had so much trouble hearing what other people were saying as they expressed their condolences. She felt awkward and was reluctant to respond to them because she could not understand their comments. Instead, she withdrew into herself and tried to shut out the confusing and frightening world around her.

Pause for Thought

Changes in one aspect of people's lives often affect other aspects. What aspects of a person's daily life would be affected by a significant decline in hearing, vision, and ability to taste and smell? How might regular physical checkups help to lessen the psychological impact of these changes?

Organ Functioning

Not only do older people worry about how aging has affected the way they look and their ability to see, hear, and taste things, many also worry about how the heart, lungs, and brain are working. Certainly with a slowing down of the body's ability to heal itself comes a greater possibility for problems within the body's organs. Nancy's grandfather, for example, was often heard to say "my ticker just isn't what it used to be" and "these bones can't take it anymore." With aging come marked reductions in the efficiency and ease with which the body's organs function. The cardiovascular (heart and blood vessels) system, in particular, manifests significant changes. The heart, like other muscles in the body, requires a longer time to contract, thereby increasing blood circulation time. Fatty concentrations (cholesterol) accumulated in the heart and arteries also reduce blood flow throughout the body; degeneration of the blood vessels leads to increased blood pressure (Kohn, 1977). Yet these changes, while most evident in later life, do not originate during this period. Losses in cardiac output (the amount of blood the heart can pump through the body) are evident from early adulthood.

Other organ systems also show reduced efficiency in late adulthood. Vital lung capacity decreases with age. Older people frequently report shortness of breath, particularly after mild exercise such as climbing stairs or raking the yard (Klocke, 1977). Changes in the gastrointestinal system, such as deterioration of the mucous lining in the intestinal tract, and reduction of gastric juices, contribute to the frequent intestinal and digestive complaints of the elderly. Normal immune functions also decline with age, and in the elderly may be related to an increased incidence of cancer or other diseases (La Rue & Jarvik, 1982; Makinsdan, 1977; Teller, 1972). As we mentioned earlier, the bone tissue deteriorates in older people.

Chemical changes in bone results in a thinning and weakening of bony material, particularly in the long bones. These changes increase the older person's susceptibility to fracture; and they prolong the healing process when breaks do occur.

It is estimated that there are about 10 billion neurons, or nerve cells, in the brain at the point of maximum growth. As we age, a vast number of these cells die—anywhere from 20,000 to 100,000 cells per day after the age of 30 (Huyck & Hoyer, 1982). Undoubtedly, this neural loss accounts, in part, for the decrease in brain size that is observed with increasing age. Rockstein and Sussman (1979) report that by the time a person reaches 90 years of age, there may be as much as a 20 percent reduction from maximum brain weight. Other brain changes occur on a microscopic level. Some of the more important have to do with the gradual accumulation of residue or waste products in the brain—specifically, *lipofuscan* and *argyrophilic plaque*. Researchers have speculated that the buildup of these waste products may be linked to the development of dementia, a progressive disease characterized by decline in memory, attention span, intelligence, personality, and physical self-help-care skills (Rockstein & Sussman, 1979). (See the section, "Dementias," later in this chapter.)

Central Nervous System and Behavior

The effects of aging on the central nervous system have been well studied, especially by James Birren and his colleagues. On the average, older people are found to be slower to respond to stimuli than young people; this reflects a basic change in the speed with which the central nervous system processes information (Birren, 1974; Birren, Woods, & Williams, 1980; Marsh & Thompson, 1977). Whereas young people appear to be quick or slow depending upon the demands of the situation, older people characteristically require more time to process information. When rapid decisions or movements are called for—avoiding an oncoming bicycle, for example—the older person may be unable to make the appropriate response. Older people are prone to falls and other accidents that might be avoided by quick movements and readjustments. Using an electrical analogy, Birren refers to a generalized "brownout" in the nervous system.

As the nervous system ages, reaction time slows down. Should these cyclists need to stop suddenly it might take them a little longer to react than it did when they were younger.

Vladimir Horowitz is well into his eighties yet is able to perform complicated piano pieces with ease.

The slowing down of the central nervous system appears to be significant in several areas. For instance, it may account for some of the difficulties older people experience in memory retrieval and learning. It may also explain some age-related differences in intelligence-testing situations in which speed is a factor. The slowing down of responses may even affect personality and adjustment, undercutting the self-confidence with which older people manage themselves in a fast-paced urban environment—or in a fast-paced clinical interview. This slowing down may contribute to rigidity in behavior, or to the reduced risk taking that seems to be characteristic of older people.

Although the slowing down of the nervous system normally affects many kinds of behavior, this fact is not related to the stereotype of the slow-paced, shuffling elder. The older person may take a split second too long to grab hold of the banister (and therefore fall) but will not necessarily take longer than a younger person to walk up the stairs and down the hallway. It is primarily when old people have to change the direction of their movement in response to new information that impairment occurs (Welford, 1959). If an older person is accustomed to rapid and finely coordinated movement (if such movements do not represent new kinds of decisions), responses may be so quick as to astonish the unpracticed young. Artur Rubinstein, Vladimir Horowitz, Claudio Arrau, and Rudolf Serkin are examples of well-known pianists who continue (or continued) into their late seventies, eighties, and even nineties to interpret difficult compositions even at prestissimo tempos. With regular practice, the older person loses little, and what is lost in response time is often compensated for in experience.

Health Factors in Late Adulthood

One of the most serious problems confronting the older person is increased susceptibility to disease. This is particularly true of chronic or long-term conditions. In contrast, the incidence of acute or temporary illness actually decreases with age.

Most people over 65 suffer from one or more chronic conditions. Yet, relatively few of these individuals are seriously restricted in their mobility. When all things are taken into consideration, most older people are in reasonably good health. Only 4 to 5 percent of the elderly are in chronic-care facilities, hospitals, mental institutions, or nursing homes. The remaining 95 to 96 percent of the aged live in the community and are able to "get around" despite their chronic conditions (Harris, 1978).

The prospect of illness is nevertheless a real threat to the aging adult. Older individuals are less likely to "bounce back" from an illness; once admitted to the hospital, they are likely to stay longer than the younger person. They are also more likely to die from the illness (Harris, 1978). Even acute conditions, which are contracted less frequently by the elderly, generally are more serious at this time. Influenza, for example, can progress to pneumonia, and possibly death, for the aging adult.

The most common chronic conditions restricting activity in individuals 65 and over are heart disease, arthritis, hypertension, visual impairments, and orthopedic problems (Harris, 1978). Although all of these conditions take a significant toll on the aged, some people find that the secondary effects, beyond the purely physical ones, are even more difficult to live with. The dependence on others that often accompanies these chronic conditions can be extremely frustrating, particularly for people who are used to "doing for themselves." As one 78-year-old woman said, "The pain I can bear. You can get used to that part. What really bothers me is not being able to care for myself. . . . I don't like being waited on. . . . The loss of dignity is something you can't imagine."

Hypokinetic Disease A condition in which physical functioning declines due to inactivity.

Exercise and Health

In 1981, John Kelley ran his fiftieth Boston Marathon. He was 73 years old. One minute after the race his heart beat was 64. Although a 26-mile race is not prescribed for people in their seventies, walking, jogging, running, and swimming are recommended not only for people in late adulthood, but for all men and women who live sedentary lives. Regular exercise improves mental abilities (Powell, 1974) as well as helps to combat the degeneration of the cardiovascular (heart and blood vessels) and pulmonary (lung and breathing) systems. Even after years of neglecting their bodies, people can make remarkable comebacks. One man who did not start jogging until he was 67 holds 14 field-and-track world records for his age category (Crandall, 1980).

To a large degree it has been found (Wessell & Van Huss, 1969) that the losses in physiological functioning of older people may be related as much to human inactivity—the modern sedentary life—as to age itself. Wessell and Van Huss coined the term **hypokinetic disease** (*hypo* = under, *kinetic* = motion) for the loss of function due to inactivity.

DeVries, an exercise physiologist, points out that there are three causes for physiological losses in older people: the processes of aging itself, undetected incipient diseases, and hypokinetic disease. Of the three, hypokinetic disease is reversible. DeVries (1970) set up a vigorous exercise training regimen in a retirement community. One hundred and twelve volunteers, men aged 52 to 87 (mean age 69½), exercised at calisthenics, jogging, and stretch-

John Kelly was 73 years old when he ran in his fiftieth marathon race (26 miles). Exercise in old age is a key ingredient to health.

ing or swimming for one hour three times a week. The most significant findings were related to oxygen-transport capacity. Oxygen pulse and minute ventilation improved by 30 and 35 percent, respectively. There was a 20 percent gain in vital capacity. Significant improvement was found in the ratio of fat to protein, physical work capacity, and both systolic and diastolic blood pressure. A group of men with heart trouble were placed on a modified program of milder exercise, and their improvement showed similar gains. In a subsequent study (Adams & DeVries, 1973), older women aged 52 to 79 participated in a vigorous exercise program for three months and also showed significant improvement in physiological functioning.

For elderly people who want to engage in more than vigorous walking in a regular exercise regimen, it is recommended that they consult a physician or a physical education expert. Furthermore, since it is the large muscles that influence heart and lung capacity as well as the other factors mentioned above, it is recommended that a personal exercise program consist of natural activities such as walking, jogging, running (or a combinations of these three), or swimming. For example, a 30-to-60-minute daily walk can bring about marked improvement in elderly men and women.

The best way to keep physically fit in late adulthood is to begin a program of exercise in early or middle adulthood and stick to it on a regular basis. The later in the lifespan a person begins an exercise program, the less effect it will have on increasing maximum skill or physical function (Denney, 1982). While exercise will not cure all that ails elderly people, a physically active life can enhance the prospects that people can reach their true biogenetic potential for longevity (Bortz, 1982).

Pause for Thought
"Use it or lose it" seems to be a fitting piece of advice with regard to physical activity. Think back over the lifespan and consider the other areas of change. For what other aspects of development might this advice also apply? How is it that activity promotes growth or slows decline?

Mental Health and Aging

Two categories of mental disorders have a significant impact on the aging adult—**functional disorders** and **organic brain syndromes.** The common feature of these two conditions is that they produce substantial cognitive and personality changes. Functional disorders are those for which there is no apparent physiological or biological basis. Organic brain syndromes, in contrast, are organically, or biologically, caused.

Depression
The most common functional disorders in the elderly include depression, paranoid reactions, hypochondriasis, and chronic anxiety (Butler & Lewis, 1982; Pfeiffer, 1977). Of these, depressive reactions are the most frequent and are characterized by extreme sadness, social withdrawal, inhibition, lowered self-esteem, pessimism, indecision, and occasionally, a slowing down of mental processes as well as physical movement. The suicide rate for the elderly, which is linked to depression, is higher than for any other age group—

Functional Disorders Mental disorders for which there is no apparent physiological or biological basis.

Organic Brain Syndromes Mental disorders caused by organic or biological factors.

Loss of a loved one or friend is a common factor in depression among the elderly.

especially for white males. Moreover, when the older adult attempts suicide, there is roughly one chance in two that he or she will succeed, whereas the ratio is one in seven for young adults (Pfeiffer, 1977).

Loss is a common factor in depression among the elderly. For some people the loss of physical vigor and stamina, especially with the diagnosis of a chronic, immobilizing illness can trigger a depressive reaction. Loss of sensory function (sight, hearing, taste, or smell) can contribute to paranoid feelings and social isolation, two conditions that increase depression (Charatan, 1981). Depression can be a reaction to the death of friends and relatives, to the loss of a peer group or status after retirement, or to having to relocate to a smaller more affordable residence.

Depression can be treated by individual or group psychotherapy sometimes in combination with antidepressant drugs. Exercise programs and increased social activity also contribute to reducing depressive symptoms in old people.

Although many forms of psychopathology increase with advancing age (Butler & Lewis, 1982), it would be a mistake to assume that most older adults suffer from emotional problems. Romaniuk, McAuley, and Arling (1983), for example, found that only 18 percent of community-living elderly adults reported definite or extensive symptoms of functional psychological disorders. In addition, only 10 percent reported feeling lonely often, and only 6 percent rated their life satisfaction as poor. Separate ratings by interviewers generally confirmed the overall positive adjustment reported by the elderly themselves. Ninety-seven percent of these older adults were rated as being pleasant and cooperative, 94 percent as showing good common sense in making judgments, 89 percent as having the ability to cope with everyday problems, 89 percent as being mentally alert, and 76 percent as showing enjoyment of life. The investigators also noted that mental health among the elderly was significantly related to perceived physical health, education, income, and marital status. Individuals who viewed themselves as physically healthy also rated themselves, and were rated by others, as emotionally healthy. Moreover, older adults with greater education and higher income also showed less evidence of psychological problems. Finally, married elderly adults fared much better psychologically than either their widowed or nonmarried counterparts.

Dementias

Dementia A type of organic brain syndrome characterized by a variety of behaviors including decreased mental functioning, changes in mood and social skills, and a deterioration in personal habits.

Dementia is the most common organic brain syndrome found in old age. This condition refers to a broad constellation of behavioral and psychological symptoms associated with diffuse or general brain loss of unknown origin. Over the course of the disease, brain weight can reduce as much as 15 to 30 percent. Typical symptoms include errors in intellectual and social judgment, mood changes, memory impairment, disorientation with respect to time and space, general confusion, loosening of inhibitions, and deterioration of personal habits. The behavior of 80-year-old Elsie is an example. Her adult children became concerned when they noticed that she was not dressing as neatly as she had in the past. Her usually well-kept hair now always seemed in need of a shampooing. Just last week, Elsie lost her Social Security check and left the stove on when she went to bed. When her son asked her about these problems, she seemed confused as to which day it was and when the problems had occurred. It was clear to those who knew and loved Elsie that she was declining mentally.

Alzheimer's Disease A form of dementia characterized by the slow deterioration of the brain.

The most common form of dementia is called **Alzheimer's disease** (AD), named after the German physician who first described the condition in 1907. Until recently, the term Alzheimer's disease was reserved for people under the age of 60 who showed signs of dementia, while the term *senile* was applied to people over the age of 60 with the same symptoms. Today, however, the term senile is no longer used since it is not only imprecise and blurred with negative stereotypes of the elderly, it also appears that the onset of the syndrome may begin in middle adulthood but not be clearly diagnosed until the person is older (Emr & Schneider, 1985). In Alzheimer's disease, a progressive and irreversible deterioration of the brain tissue, primarily in the cerebral cortex, results in increasing deterioration in mental, social, and personality behaviors. The risks of developing Alzheimer's disease increase dramatically with age. The prevalence of the disease among people 65 years or older is 6 percent, for people aged 75 the incidence is 20 percent and for people 85 years and older the incidence is 20 percent. People with Alzheimer's may live for 15 years or more with the disease that has been classed as one of the leading causes of death for elderly Americans (Heckler, 1985). With the growing ranks of the elderly projected for the next century, Alzheimer's disease has been targeted as a major health issue among the elderly (Rickards, Zuckerman, & West, 1985).

The symptoms of Alzheimer's disease are several and appear in a stage-like sequence. In the early stages, some of the symptoms such as forgetfulness and confusion may be overlooked or accepted as normal signs of aging—another negative consequence of ageism. Patients may show several signs of memory or cognitive deficits. Like Elsie, they may be confused and even forget the names of close family members. Then, as the condition progresses, people may show signs of personality changes, insomnia, loss of appetite, and depression. They may be unable to control their bodily functions, which adds to the difficulties in caring for them. Frequently, patients with Alzheimer's disease will show signs of depression as a result of their deteriorating condition and the stresses that result (See Box, Caring for Alzheimer's Disease Patients).

At present, there is no sure-fire test to diagnose the disorder short of brain autopsy. Work is in progress on several behavioral tests that can be used to detect early signs and symptoms (Hostetler, 1987). These tests include assessment of memory, language function, a measure of people's ability to use and understand language and their ability to control voluntary movements.

The cause and cure of Alzheimer's disease is not yet known, although there are several possibilities under investigation (Khachaturian, 1985). Heredity, toxic-waste accumulations, auto-immune responses, trauma, and slow growing viruses have been suggested as possible causes. There is a link between Alzheimer's disease and Down syndrome. Families with Alzheimer's disease have three times the likelihood of having a Down syndrome child. Furthermore, people with Down syndrome almost always develop Alzheimer's disease in their twenties or thirties, if they live that long (Bazell, 1986).

Multi-Infarct Dementia (MID) A form of dementia characterized by sporadic decline in cognitive functions caused by a series of strokes or ministrokes.

The second most common form of dementia is called **multi-infarct** dementia (MID). It was formerly referred to as *cerebral arteriosclerosis* because it was thought the dementia symptoms were caused by the hardening of the arteries that pump blood to the brain. With reduced blood flow, specific damage and deterioration in brain tissue would result, producing cognitive and emotional deterioration. However, it is now believed that the symptoms, which include increased irritability, fatigue, headaches, and memory losses, are caused by stroke or mini-strokes brought on by arteriosclerosis. The onset of this disease, which often affects more men than women, may occur as early as the mid-fifties. Because a person erratically suffers multiple strokes over the years, there is a corresponding pattern of decline and recovery of cognitive skill; ultimately, the brain can no longer compensate for the stroke damage and death occurs (Reisberg, 1981).

Pause for Thought

Alzheimer's disease presents an interesting challenge to researchers because it is a medical (organic) condition that is diagnosed by behavioral and psychological signs. Psychologists, neurologists, biochemists, and physicians have joined efforts to identify its causes, diagnostic tests, and cure. Since the distinction between the mind and body as separate systems fails with Alzheimer's disease, can you offer a convincing argument for urging physicians and psychologists to join forces in the care of the elderly?

Theories of Aging

Although there is an increased vulnerability to cancer and such cardiovascular diseases as heart failure, arteriosclerosis (clogging of the arteries), and hypertension, it is not clear exactly what part age plays in these processes. Practically everyone who has studied the aging person has remarked upon the difficulty of isolating the effects of aging per se from the effects of disease, or the gradual degenerative changes that develop with the passage of time. For ex-

Human Development in Practice

Caring for Alzheimer's Disease Patients

It is a fear that many people have—that their mind will stop working before their bodies do. When Alzheimer's disease begins, the victim looks well. Yet, someone who is physically active and capable of running five miles or hauling groceries into the house may not be able to do a simple task such as making a telephone call or preparing a cup of tea. The person can talk and recall past events, but may be unable to remember what you said 10 minutes earlier. The early symptoms of the disease are mistaken for deliberate forgetfulness and may produce frustration and irritation among family members who are affected by the victim's lapses of memory. Later, as the disease becomes progressively worse, disturbing changes in personality emerge.

From the point of view of the health-care provider, the victim's family needs attention as well as the Alzheimer victim. In the earlier stages, which may linger for many years, the primary-care providers are the families. Often the emotional needs of the family members have been ignored as they care for the increasing physical and psychological needs of the victim. Among patients who are more severely impaired, the burden of care on the family is frequently overwhelming. Alzheimer victims eventually become incapable of taking adequate care of their bodies—they must be washed, bathed, and cared for as one would a young child who had not yet learned self-help behaviors. Victims often become so confused they wander off, sometimes in the middle of the night. Thus, they must be fed, clothed, and watched carefully. All the while, the spouse or adult children are dealing with the difficulties of a loved one who is changing before their eyes.

At some point, the patients (the victim and family members) require outside assistance and support to continue their care of the Alzheimer's victim. One source of help is in the form of a *Respite* worker. As the name implies, respite care is any service that gives the primary-care providers a temporary break or rest from the continuing care of a chronically ill family member. Adult day-care programs are another alternative to full-time care in the home. Staffed by specially trained workers with medical backup, the day-care programs help reduce the need for hospitalization and reduce the stress on family members (Burdz, Eaton, & Bond, 1988).

Another source of support is available through the Alzheimer's Disease and Related Disorders Association (ADRD). Founded by relatives who have had to cope with Alzheimer's disease, this national group has local chapters that provide afflicted families with a forum in which to discuss their concerns and frustration and from which they derive help, hope, and information.

Ultimately, when the victim is severely impaired and the family can no longer provide care, hospitalization occurs. Often, this comes as a relief to family members who may also feel guilty about feeling good about being relieved of the victim's care. Any nurse or physician involved in the care and treatment of the Alzheimer's patient needs to be sensitive to the consequences this disease has on all those family members who care for the victim.

ample, is arteriosclerosis a disease or a degenerative process that only becomes evident in older people? Is heart failure the result of a disease process or the effect of age alone (Fries & Crapo, 1981; Timiras, 1972)?

There are a number of theories linking the loss of physiological function with the aging process (Shock, 1977). One is the theory of *cellular error,* in which aging and eventual death are explained as resulting from the accumulated effects of errors that occur in the sequence of the transfer of information at the cellular level. Information originally stored in the genetic code

Excessive doses of radiation during earlier stages of life can result in errors in cellular function later on in life.

must be transformed into biochemical processes. With increased age, errors occur; either the wrong biochemical message is sent or none is sent at all. As biochemical errors increase over time, cellular functioning deteriorates. The basic genetic code, carried in molecules of DNA, may also be damaged or altered over the years by radiation or other chemicals or drugs. Furthermore, there is some evidence to suggest that the cellular mechanisms that normally repair damaged DNA may deteriorate with age resulting in an accumulation of genetic errors (Mclearn & Foch, 1985). Species or organisms within species that have a more efficient cell-repair capacity are likely to live longer (Sacher, 1978). Another, more general, theory, the *wear-and-tear-theory,* compares the human organism to a machine and human cells to machine parts. Human cells wear out with prolonged use just as machine parts do. Hayflick (1970, 1977, 1980) has shown that after 50 or so divisions, human cells normally die. The inability of cells to replace themselves indefinitely means that over time the basic building block of life (i.e., DNA) will be used up, thus resulting in physiological decline and, ultimately, death (Rockstein & Sussman, 1979). A variation of the wear-and-tear theory is the *stress theory* of aging, which suggests that stressful life events reduce the energy capacities of the organism. The accumulation over time of the minor impairments caused by stress leads to a deterioration of the ability of the body to adapt (Shock, 1977). Still another theory of aging is the *deprivation theory,* which holds that aging is due to the inadequate delivery of essential nutrients and oxygen to cells; this kind of deprivation may be related to certain disease states such as arteriosclerosis. The cells begin to deteriorate under these deprived conditions and eventually die. In the *metabolic waste theory,* aging is attributed to the slow poisoning of the body by itself. According to this theory, there is a gradual buildup of the waste products of metabolism that interferes with normal cell functioning. In the *immunological theory,* the immune system of the individual gradually deteriorates with age and so cannot provide protection from foreign substances and mutant cells. This increases the chance of disease and cellular dysfunction. A variation of this theory is called the *autoimmune theory* of aging: As the immune system deteriorates, the body cannot tell the difference between normal and abnormal cells and, therefore, destroys both.

Biological theories of aging

Theory	Description
Cell division	Cells are capable of dividing a limited number of times
Genetic	Life is unnecessary after reproductive system is inactive
Mutation	Cell mutations disable DNA code
Immunity	Immunity defenses wear out
Metabolic wastes	Cells become poisoned with wastes
Wear and tear	Body parts wear out

Figure 15.1 Biological theories of aging.

Longevity has a strong genetic component; these sisters are all in their eighties.

These are but a few of the various theories of aging that exist; there are others. However, it is still unclear whether many of the processes described are causes of aging or the outcome of aging. For example, does the increased accumulation of metabolic waste in the cell cause a person to age, or is the accumulation the *result* of the aging process (Shock, 1977)?

Another issue that remains unanswered is the role of genetics in the aging process. Research has shown that longevity has a strong inherited component. Long-lived parents, for example, tend to have long-lived children (Kallman & Jarvik, 1959). Yet, the specific mechanism by which genetics controls the aging process has yet to be identified.

Pause for Thought
The search for the "fountain of youth" or the cure for aging has been a preoccupation of many people over centuries and across cultures. Suppose that a discovery was made that would slow down the aging process (or better yet, halt it), what changes would such a discovery make in people's lives? In cultural values and priorities?

Cognitive Development

One stereotype about aging is that people lose much of their mental alertness and ability as they grow older. It is commonly assumed that older people will not catch on to things so quickly or remember them so accurately. The elderly also are not expected to be "brainstormers" or initiators of ideas; nor are they expected to be creative. To examine these stereotypes, psychologists have conducted a great deal of research on intelligence and cognitive functions in later life. The results of the research, while often controversial, have provided us with one clear conclusion—namely, that the large kind of losses we sometimes imagine are by no means inevitable in the healthy older person.

Intellectual Functioning

By far the most frequently studied component of intellectual functioning in the aged is their performance on standard IQ tests. As we noted in Chapter 13, considerable controversy exists about the apparent decline in intelligence during middle and late adulthood. Cross-sectional studies often report decreases in test performance beginning as early as the third decade of life, whereas longitudinal studies indicate relative stability in most intellectual functions through the fifth decade, after which a slow but progressive decline is noticeable. In addition, even when decreased test performance is observed, it is usually only in areas measuring perceptual-integration ability, memory, and inductive reasoning—what is known as fluid intelligence—as well as in areas emphasizing psychomotor skills and quickness of response. Social knowledge, verbal–conceptual ability, and arithmetic reasoning—that is, *crystallized intelligence*—are little affected by the aging process per se (Botwinick, 1977; Horn, 1970; Horn & Donaldson, 1980).

If intellectual performance does decrease during late adulthood—even if only in select areas—it also appears to be true that the decrease is not experienced equally by all people. One interesting theory is that "age is kinder to the initially more able"—that is, subjects with high ability show less decline

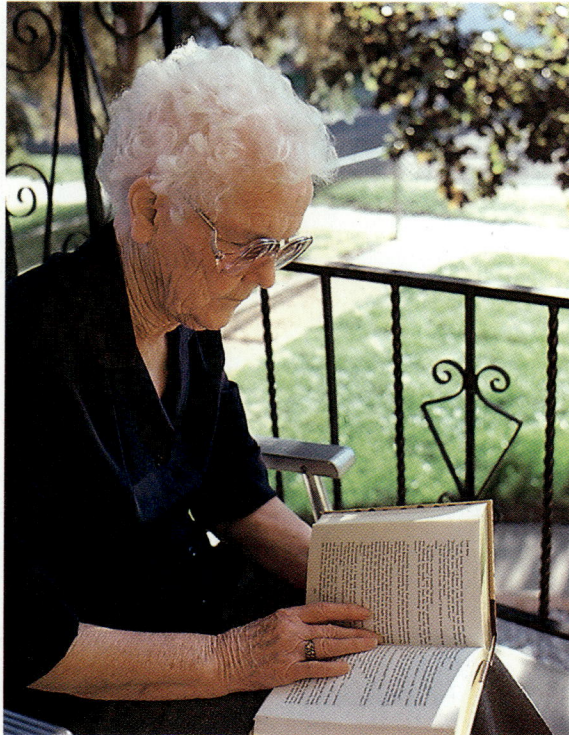

If intellectual skills are practiced they are less likely to decline.

in old age than do subjects with low ability. Since higher abilities tend to be related to higher education levels (and higher income levels), it has also been suggested that well-educated individuals experience less, if any, decline. One 20-year followup of 80-year-old subjects supports both these hypotheses—at least for a sample that included a wide range of abilities (Blum & Jarvik, 1975). The researchers suggest that keeping oneself mentally active throughout life, including the latter part of life, provides protection against intellectual decline. (Use it or lose it!) This view is supported by the work of Schultz, Kaye, and Hoyer (1980) and Nancy Denney (1982), who found that individuals who continued to use their cognitive abilities on a regular basis into their older years, were much less likely to show a decline in intelligence. The work of Baltes and Willis (1980) is also relevant to this issue. They have been concerned with the older adult's degree of *intellectual plasticity,* which they defined as the range of intellectual performance a person displays under different environmental conditions. Using extensive training procedures to enrich the intellectual functioning of their subjects, Baltes and Willis have shown that older people have a relatively high level of intellectual plasticity— that is, their performance of unexercised abilities can be improved considerably through intervention and training. These results have obvious practical implications for the education and retraining of the elderly. It is not unusual to discover elderly students enrolled in adult-education courses that are offered in many communities or in painting or poetry classes presented in retirement complexes. (See Box, Never Too Old to Learn.)

Information Processing

Although it is often said that "you can't teach an old dog new tricks," this age-old adage certainly cannot be applied to people in late adulthood. Older people continue to take in new information and make appropriate life adjustments until the ends of their lives.

On the other hand, this does not imply that the learning performance of older adults is equal to that of younger adults. The accumulation of several decades of research on the elderly suggests that there are age-related decrements in the ability to acquire and remember information. The critical issue for psychologists, then, is not whether the elderly can learn, but how they process information in the context of learning and under what conditions information processing is impaired.

Perception and Attention

Research has shown that older adults have greater difficulty processing perceptual information than younger and middle-aged adults. For one thing, the ability to process visual information becomes slower with age (Hoyer & Plude, 1980). In addition to a slowing of visual-information processing, the elderly also have more difficulty than young adults in detecting isolated parts that are embedded within a complex stimulus background (Comalli, 1970). For example, if a familiar geometric pattern such as a triangle is hidden within a complex design, the older adult will take longer to identify its location than will a younger person.

Researchers have suggested that perceptual-processing deficits in the elderly may be linked to problems in attention (Stankov, 1988). Two com-

Human Development in Practice

Never Too Old to Learn: Education for the Elderly

There once was a time when the oldest person in the classroom was the teacher. Today, it is likely that the oldest person might be a student. There is a growing trend in the United States today for elderly people to continue (or in some cases, begin) their education. At least one out of every 20 adults over the age of 60 is enrolled in classes of some sort (U.S. Bureau of the Census, 1981). Some of these older adults begin their education in their workplace, the largest single provider of adult-education classes. Others enroll in local colleges or high-school adult-education programs. State and federal support is given to stimulate the development of formal education programs for the elderly.

One such specialized program for the elderly is the Elderhostel, a network of colleges and universities that provide short-term inexpensive courses for retired people. Founded in New Hampshire in 1975, there are now over 30,000 students enrolled in courses in all 50 states (Romaniuk & Romaniuk, 1982). In the Elderhostel program, students live in the dormitories while attending classes taught by regular college faculty. Other institutions attract elderly students to their classrooms by offering tuition reductions or waivers and offering courses that cater to the interests of older adults. A higher proportion of older adults who enroll in classes have graduated

At least one out of every 20 adults over the age of 60 is enrolled in classes of some sort. This woman received her degree at age 104!

Divided Attention The ability of the person to process more than one source of information simultaneously.

Selective Attention The person's ability to attend to relevant information while ignoring irrelevant information.

ponents of attention are worth mentioning: divided attention and selective attention. **Divided attention** refers to the ability of the individual to process more than one source of information simultaneously—for example, being able to attend to multiple conversations at a social gathering. **Selective attention,** by contrast, refers to the person's ability to attend to relevant information while ignoring irrelevant information—for example, focusing on a conversation with one particular individual while ignoring all the irrelevant conversations and background noises that are going on in the immediate environment. Research has shown that the elderly are at a particular disadvantage in comparison to younger adults in situations where they must divide their attention between two or more information sources (Craik, 1977). Selective attention deficits among the elderly also have been found, but only when it is difficult to differentiate between relevant and irrelevant information—that is, when the two forms of information are highly similar (Farkas & Hoyer, 1980). Thus, an elderly person may have trouble listening to a television news from high school. With the growing trend of more and more older adults having earned at least a high-school diploma, the number of elderly who take courses is likely to increase dramatically in years to come.

Older students are extremely motivated, a critical ingredient in the learning process. Many of these adult "returning" students seek an intellectual challenge, a more stimulating environment, and an opportunity to learn new ideas. The active mind, like the active body, takes longer to decline in old age. People who seek out new learning environments are helping to forestall the cognitive deficits associated with aging. Other reasons that older people become students include wanting to achieve some personal goals, to meet new people, to have regular social activities, to keep abreast of the technological and sociocultural changes that occur, and to seek training in a postretirement activity or career.

Teachers of older adults may find that although they may have to readjust some of their classroom activities to accommodate a slower learner, they benefit from having more knowledgeable and experienced students. Older adults need to have clear and organized presentations and be given opportunities to acquire information at their own pace. Programmed instruction that provides the students with success early in the learning process works especially well with older adults who may be uncertain about their standing in the classroom. The older-adult learner is also more likely to learn when the material presented has practical, real-life value. Many older adults may be interested in taking courses that deal with the changes that occur in human development, especially during the late-adulthood period of the lifespan.

This Elderhostel group enjoys a field trip during one of their classes.

report while other people in the room are talking. Another reason that older people do not do as well as younger people on selective attention tasks is that they take longer to process the information (Madden, 1985).

Learning and Memory

It is clear that adults continue to learn as they age. However, it is also clear that learning in the aged is highly influenced by a number of factors. One of the most important variables that has been studied in learning research is *pacing*—the amount of time the person is allowed to examine the stimulus and/or to make a response. It has often been thought that fast-paced conditions place the aging adult at a significant disadvantage; and that increasing inspection and response time would decrease the performance difference between younger and older adults, and possibly eliminate it altogether. Research does indicate that learning in the elderly is adversely affected by fast-paced conditions. However, when learning occurs at a slow pace and when elderly adults are allowed to pace themselves, their performance improves. On the other hand, increased performance under self-paced conditions still does not equal the level of performance for younger adults (Arenberg & Robertson-Tchabo, 1977; Perlmutter & List, 1982).

Other factors—besides pacing—may also contribute to the performance decrement of older adults in learning tasks. Carl Eisdorfer and his associates have suggested that the reason older people perform more poorly than younger people is because they are *physiologically overaroused,* that is, overly anxious and nervous—a condition that is known to interfere with the learning process. When elderly subjects have been administered drugs to lower autonomic nervous system arousal and thereby reduce their level of anxiety, performance has improved substantially—although still not to the level of younger subjects (Eisdorfer, 1968; Eisdorfer, Nowlin, & Wilkie, 1970). The meaningfulness of the material to be learned also influences the performance of older individuals. Hulicka (1967) found that many older subjects resent having to learn material they cannot understand or find uninteresting. In her experiment, the vast majority of older adults refused to participate because the material was viewed as "nonsense." When one considers that many learning experiments employ nonsense syllables and other patently uninteresting and meaningless stimuli, one must begin to question just what the performance decrements of the elderly on these tasks represent: decreased ability or simply lack of interest and motivation?

Once information has been acquired, it must somehow be stored, so that under appropriate conditions it can be retrieved and acted upon. Whether we are talking about a laboratory experiment involving nonsense words or a more realistic and meaningful problem situation such as trying to remember which grandchild's birthday falls on January 15th, it is obvious that the process of memory is involved. Researchers often differentiate between **primary memory** and **secondary memory** (Craik, 1977; Waugh & Norman, 1965). Primary memory refers to recall of information that is still being attended to "in one's mind"—*short-term memory.* Secondary memory, by contrast, refers to information that has been encoded but is no longer the focus of active or selective attention—*long-term memory.*

Most research suggests that primary memory capacity—the number of words, letters, numbers, or bits of information a person can remember in correct order—does not usually decline with age (Craik, 1977; Hartley, Harker, & Walsh, 1980). Both older and younger adults are capable of remembering the same *number* of items, but only under ideal or undemanding conditions. To the extent that the person is required to reorganize the stimulus material (e.g., repeating the list backward), or divide attention between the "to-be-remembered list" and some other component of the task (Talland, 1965), the older adult, more than the younger, is likely to show performance decrements in primary memory.

With respect to secondary memory, the research shows that older people have significantly more problems in remembering material that is no longer actively attended to or focused upon. Furthermore, this deficit has been linked to three distinct components of memory: registration of information, storage of information, and retrieval of information. In each of these areas, evidence is accumulating to indicate that the elderly perform less well in comparison to younger adults (Craik, 1977; Hartley, Harker, & Walsh, 1980). Still, lower-level performance does not necessarily imply a lack of ability. Researchers

Primary Memory
Memory for information that is still being actively attended to. Also called short-term memory.

Secondary Memory
Memory for information that has been encoded but is no longer the focus of active attention. Also called long-term memory.

such as Paul Baltes (Baltes & Baltes, 1977; Baltes & Willis, 1980) and Gisela Labouvie-Vief (Labouvie-Vief, 1980a, 1980b, 1985; Labouvie-Vief & Schell, 1982) have argued cogently for continued mental flexibility and plasticity in the older adult despite these performance and memory deficits.

Logical Reasoning

In addition to research on information-processing capabilities, numerous studies have been conducted on logical reasoning in the elderly. One group of studies in particular is worth noting—those that have attempted to extend Piagetian theory and research to the thought processes of the aged. Papalia (1972), presented subjects, six to 65 years and over, with a battery of conservation tasks (number, mass, weight, and volume). In the older adults, Papalia found a lower level of performance primarily for the more advanced concepts—particularly conservation of volume, for which only 6 percent of the 65-and-older age group produced correct responses. Similarly, in the area of classification ability, Denney and Cornelius (1975) reported that middle-aged adults significantly outperformed two groups of elderly adults: those who lived in the community and those who were institutionalized. A comparison of the two older groups indicated that the elderly who lived in an institutionalized setting demonstrated lower-level logical reasoning when compared to the elderly who lived in the community. This difference makes sense when one considers the fact that life in an institution is not as stimulating or challenging as life in the community. Furthermore, there may be a bias in the sampling because one reason elderly people may be institutionalized is that they have demonstrated an inability to reason logically and hence care for themselves unassisted.

The strongest and most consistent decrements in performance for the elderly, however, have been found in the area of formal operational abilities—the most advanced form of reasoning within Piaget's system (Clayton & Overton, 1976). This has given rise to an interesting hypothesis that the most recent abilities to emerge in development—for example, formal operations—are the first to disappear during aging.

Cognitive Styles

In Chapter 7, we noted that cognitive style refers to the *manner* or *mode* used by a person to solve a problem, whereas cognitive ability refers to a person's *capacity* to perform. Although the distinction between cognitive style and cognitive ability has a long history (see Kagan & Kogan, 1970; Kogan, 1983), it is only recently that researchers have examined the development and expression of cognitive styles in old age (Kogan, 1982). Three cognitive styles have been the focus of attention among adult development researchers: impulsivity–reflection, field-dependence–field-independence, and categorization styles.

Although Kogan (1973) has speculated that adults are likely to become increasingly reflective with age—that is, slower, more systematic in analysis, and, hence, more accurate in problem solving—research by Coyne, Whitborne, and Glenwick (1978) and Denney and List (1979) failed to confirm this prediction. Coyne, Whitborne, and Glenwick (1978) found that elderly subjects were disproportionately represented in the impulsive category—they

Elderly people who live in institutional settings typically perform less well on tests of cognitive skills.

were fast to respond and relatively inaccurate in solving problems. By contrast, Denney and List (1979) found that older adults were slow and inaccurate, or, in other words, inefficient. Thus, no clear pattern has emerged on the effect of aging on impulsivity–reflection.

Research on field-dependence–field-independence has produced a more consistent picture. Generally speaking, researchers have found that as people age they become increasingly field-dependent—that is, they rely more on contextual cues in problem-solving situations than on their own internal judgments (Lee & Pollack, 1978; Panek, Barrett, Sterns, & Alexander, 1978). Finally, research (Cicirelli, 1976; Kogan, 1974; Pearce & Denney, 1984) has consistently shown that older adults, when given a series of objects or pictures to sort, are more likely than younger adults to group stimuli according to *relational* or *thematic* criteria (e.g., a match, pipe, and tobacco go together because of their functional relationship) as opposed to *perceptual similarity* (e.g., a wheel, ball, and donut go together because they are round) and *categorical* criteria (e.g., a cat, monkey, and giraffe go together because they are animals). The fact that these differences in categorization reflect stylistic preferences and not ability is seen in the work of Smiley and Brown (1979). These investigators not only had subjects group stimuli according to their preferred criteria, but they also requested that subjects justify both their preferred and nonpreferred categorization responses. Their results confirmed that older adults are more likely than younger adults to classify thematically, whereas younger adults are more likely to classify using categorical criteria. More important, though, was their finding that the elderly were as capable as younger adults in explaining or justifying the basis of categorical classifications. Thus, the fact that older adults display more thematic and fewer categorical classifications than younger adults is clearly a function of *stylistic preference* rather than ability.

Interpreting Age-Related Cognitive Decline

The pattern of cognitive and intellectual decline during the aging years, which has been documented repeatedly by research studies, has been variously interpreted. Schaie (1974) speaks of the "myth of intellectual decline." When cross-sectional studies are done, he says, marked differences in the skills of successive generations are found. On nonspeeded tests, at least, the elderly function nearly as well as they did when young. Still, they do not function as well as their well-educated grandchildren. Schaie suggests that in intellectual abilities, old people, if they are reasonably healthy, do not decline—they become obsolete. (There is no way of telling whether this will be true of successive generations.) Similar points have been made with respect to Piagetian performance. For example, Papalia and Bielby note that one must be cautious about interpreting the apparent decline in formal operational abilities, since many adults never attain this level. Lower performance among the elderly may reflect an initially less competent sample (Papalia & Bielby, 1974). It may also reflect changing expectations. Speaking more generally, Riegel (1973b) has said, "Generation and social change outpace the individual, and while the old person might produce the impression that he has deteriorated in his performance, it might be that he has remained stable but society has changed its conditions and standards."

Other researchers believe that health-related factors, and neurological intactness, are associated with performance decrements in the elderly. In what has now become a classic study, Birren and his colleagues (Birren, Butler, Greenhouse, Sokoloff, & Yarrow, 1963) examined physiological, intellectual, and personality functioning in young and elderly men, the latter of which were grouped into two separate categories: those who were in optimal health in every regard, and those who were without obvious clinical symptoms of disease but were found to have mild or subclinical disease through extensive examinations. In the majority of areas measured, the subclinical, older group were functioning not only below younger subjects, but also below optimally healthy, older subjects. In the area of intelligence, the subclinical group obtained poorer scores than the healthy older group on 21 of 23 tests. Of interest, however, was the fact that for verbal intelligence, both older groups outperformed the younger group, whereas in areas measuring psychomotor speed (e.g., reaction time), the reverse was found. This pattern supports the hypothesis that verbal conceptual ability does not ordinarily decline with age and, in fact, may continue to increase, whereas skills dependent upon speed of central nervous system transmission do show age-related decline. The study by Birren and his associates is important because it points to the adverse impact of disease, even a mild degree of disease, on the adaptive functioning of older people. When the elderly are free of disease, which admittedly is not that common when subclinical problems are included in one's definition of disease, there is relatively little difference between the old and the young with the major exception of a slowing down of central nervous system activity.

Another factor that has been linked to cognitive deficits in the elderly is their level of social interaction. Individuals who are isolated socially, as many older people are, have less opportunity to practice their intellectual skills than individuals who are more active. Limited contact and conversation with other people prevent the elderly from receiving information and feedback from others, which is important for correcting misperceptions, reducing egocen-

George Burns and Maggie Kuhn are elderly people who maintain their vitality by continuing to do what they do best.

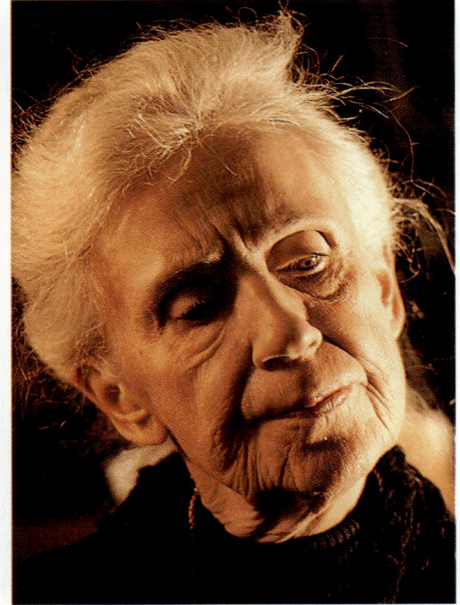

Competence As opposed to performance, what an individual knows or is capable of doing under ideal conditions.

Performance As opposed to competence, the person's actual level of functioning in a situation or on a task.

trism, and in general, stimulating cognitive growth. The impact of social interaction on cognitive functioning in the elderly is well documented in the work of Dolen and Bearison (1982). These researchers found that level of social interaction among a group of subjects aged 65 to 89 years was a more sensitive predictor of social–cognitive reasoning than was subjects' age per se. Dolen and Bearison suggested that their findings support social policies aimed at programs of intervention whose goals are the facilitation of mental functioning in the elderly through enhanced social activity. Minnie remains vital and alert, in part because of the many social activities she is involved in. She finds that joining discussion groups and social organizations provides her with a sense of challenge and help her to feel young.

One other interpretation of the relatively low test scores achieved by the elderly rests on the distinction between **competence** and **performance** (Flavell & Wohlwill, 1969). Technically, competence is defined as "what the individual knows or could do in a timeless ideal environment," whereas performance represents what the individual actually does in the task at hand. Utilizing this distinction, some psychologists suggest that the decreased performance of the elderly does not necessarily indicate decreased competence. For example, older people may perform poorly because they are not motivated. They may be put off by the toylike materials used in Piagetian tasks. They may be unable to relate to younger researchers, or even to hear the instructions. In some areas, their competence may be high, but their skills may be rusty. Older subjects may be in a position similar to that of the person who remembers having mastered Latin or the violin: They are still capable of functioning at a high level, but probably cannot do so at the present moment. The more years that go by, the greater is the possibility that skills will fall into disuse. The decline in cognitive functions in the elderly may thus represent an increasingly wider gap between competence and performance, rather than regression (Bearison, 1974). If this is so, then the performance of older people might be improved relatively easily. For example, more appropriate rewards might be introduced to counter poor motivation; short-term retraining might be expected to result in higher functioning for skills that have fallen into disuse.

Personality Development

Old age brings new challenges and new tasks to be faced and mastered. Most older individuals are just as successful or unsuccessful in confronting and handling the developmental tasks of late adulthood as younger individuals are in dealing with the tasks of their respective life periods. Furthermore, the styles of adjusting are, if anything, more variable during the later years than earlier in life. This is not to deny, however, the seriousness of the problems confronting the aged. Declining health, loss of functions, widowhood, financial problems, loss of social status, social isolation, susceptibility to crime, and impending death are but some of the real problems older people face today. Yet face them they do. In fact, the success most older people have in meeting the challenges of old age speaks to a resiliency not usually associated with this life period in the minds of most individuals. Late adulthood is a time of continued psychological growth—even in the face of physiological decline.

Developmental Tasks in Late Adulthood

Erikson's Theory

During old age, according to Erikson, the individual experiences the crisis of **ego integrity vs. despair** (Erikson, 1963). Integrity is experienced as emotional integration, as a transcendence of the limitations of the self, through full acceptance of the one and only life one is granted (Erikson, 1976). Despair expresses itself as a feeling that time is now too short, that there is no further chance of finding an alternate path to an acceptable life. As in earlier stages, there is inner struggle. Even the person who enters old age with a high degree of integrity experiences despair at the momentary thought of death—and disgust at the futility and pettiness of human life. As in the earlier psychosocial stages of Erikson's theory, it is the favorable ratio that is important. The person who achieves a favorable ratio of integrity over despair in the last years attains wisdom: "the detached and yet active concern with life itself, in the face of death itself." It is this outcome that "maintains the integrity in spite of the decline of bodily and mental functions" (Erikson, 1976).

Associated with the task of developing ego integrity is a process called the **life review.** As people reach the end of their lives, they organize their memories and reinterpret the actions and decisions that have shaped the course of their lives. Ideally, the life review is a positive experience resulting in integration of the personality. For some, the life review leads to less ego involvement with one's own situation and to more concern with the world in general. For others, it produces nostalgia and perhaps a touch of regret. In still others, it engenders anxiety, guilt, depression, and despair: Instead of reflecting on a full life, the person feels cheated and enraged (Butler, 1971). Often, elderly people share their thoughts about their lives with relatives and friends as they go through the life-review process. While fishing with his adolescent grandson, 70-year-old Carl recalled the disappointments he ex-

Ego Integrity vs. Despair According to Erikson, the primary psychosocial task of late adulthood; ego integrity represents an emotional integration and acceptance of one's life; despair expresses itself as a feeling that one's life has been without real meaning.

Life Review In old age, the process of organizing memories and reinterpreting actions and decisions that have shaped a person's life.

As this woman spends time with her grandchild, she reflects on her own life as mother and later grandmother. A life review helps people develop a sense of integrity in their life.

perienced in his career as a salesman. At the same time, however, he recalled with considerable satisfaction the pleasure he had received from his children and grandchildren throughout his life.

Peck's Theory

According to Peck (1968), continued psychological growth in the aging years centers on the outcome of three major developmental tasks. In late adulthood, most people must come to grips with *occupational retirement.* They must be able to find personal satisfaction and self-worth beyond the work activities that have been important for self-definition in earlier periods. Peck summarizes this issue in the question that he believes each person must ask him- or herself during late adulthood: "Am I a worthwhile person only insofar as I can do a full-time job; or can I be worthwhile in other, different ways—as a performer of several other roles, and also because of the kind of person I am?" (Peck, 1968). To the extent that older people can redefine themselves meaningfully in areas other than work, they are more likely to face the future with greater interest, vitality, and a sense of integrity. Having a hobby or interests outside of work often helps people in making this transition.

A second theme of old age, within Peck's theory of personality development, concerns the inevitable *physical decline* that accompanies old age. People who define happiness and well-being primarily along physical dimensions are often seriously disturbed by the bodily changes they experience during aging—even more so than by the changes in middle age. They become preoccupied with these changes, so much so that they may experience a profound sense of despair and disgust with themselves and with life itself. Older people, according to Peck, must shift their values away from the physical domain, if they have not already, and into the domain of interpersonal relations and

Table 15.1 ■■■■■■■

Havighurst's Developmental Tasks for Late Adulthood

1. Adjusting to decreasing physical strength and health

2. Adjusting to retirement and reduced income

3. Adjusting to death of spouse

4. Establishing an explicit affiliation with one's age group

5. Adopting and adapting social roles in a flexible way

6. Establishing satisfactory physical living arrangements

Adapted from: R. J. Havighurst, *Developmental tasks and education (3rd ed.).* New York: D. McKay, 1974.

mental activities. It is through these areas of human functioning, Peck says, that the elderly are most likely to experience feelings of life satisfaction and fulfillment.

The final theme emphasized by Peck is directly linked to *human mortality.* Each person in old age must face the realization of impending death; must try to accept not only the inevitability of fate, but also find meaning in it. This may well be the most significant and challenging task confronting the aging adult. Like Erikson, Peck believes that the answer is to be found in the feelings of generativity developed by the person over the years.

Overview of Theories

It is obvious that there are many common threads in the characterization of old age as portrayed by Erikson and Peck, as well as by other theorists (Havighurst, 1974; Neugarten, 1973). (See Table 15.1.) Each views the central developmental tasks of this period in terms of challenges of declining health, reduced generativity, acknowledgment and acceptance of one's mortality, and, above all, the integration of feelings about the self and life in general. Not so obvious, however, is the assumption made by these researchers that success in meeting these challenges depends, to a great extent, on the success experienced with earlier developmental tasks. The crisis of old age is a culmination of the many psychosocial crises through which the individual has passed in life.

We have already noted that both Erikson and Peck place a great deal of importance on generativity in giving meaning to the final years of life. The integrity of old age is also an outcome of the love that has emerged in intimacy, as well as the fidelity to self and to others that has issued from the identity crises. All the earlier conflicts can be seen to reach into, and to be renewed by, the level of this last developmental challenge as they have been on each level in between. It is the primary trust of infancy, writes Erikson, that provides the foundation for some faith necessary both for terminal peace, and for the renewal of life from generation to generation.

Social Image and Self-Concept

The image of old age in modern Western societies has not been a positive one, a situation that contributes to the fears that spawn ageism. Take a quick glance at birthday greeting cards and you will notice how many funny (but not so funny) references there are to the negative qualities associated with growing older. These negative images not only affect older people, they influence the way younger people view older adults. Several classic attitudinal studies have shown that young people perceive the old as lonely, resistant to change, and failing in physical and mental powers (Tuckman & Lorge, 1953). The attitudes of high school and college youth toward the elderly and their social role are mostly negative (Kastenbaum & Durkee, 1964; Lane, 1964). The older the adult, the more unpleasant he or she appears to the younger subject (Hickey & Kalish, 1968).

As for the old themselves, probably one of the most difficult things about aging is learning to define oneself as old. One study found that nearly half of the subjects 65 years and older identified themselves as middle-aged (Turner 1979). Unfortunately, the elderly cannot help but agree with some of the cultural stereotypes of old age. After all, they themselves have held these stereotypes most of their lives. A man who is biased against women, or a white man who dislikes blacks, is never himself in the position of being turned into the object of his prejudice. The young person *does* eventually become an old person, however. Activist groups that represent the elderly say that they must combat stereotypes held by the elderly about themselves as well as stereotypes held by younger generations. Still, the fact that some studies have found a decrease in self-concept and self-esteem in old age must be interpreted with caution. Kaplan and Pokorny (1970) argue that it is not aging per se that influences self-concept, but rather events that the elderly experience during this life phase—for example, a lower income level than one expected, living alone rather than as a couple, and declining health. In support of this position, Flanagan (1981) found that the two most important factors influencing quality-of-life ratings among the elderly were lack of money and health problems. Older adults who are in poor health and lack adequate financial resources are more likely to be rated as showing problems in adjustment and to display a less positive view of themselves and of aging.

Regardless of long-held prejudices, older people must at some point face up to thinking of themselves as "old" and adjust their self-concepts accordingly. Many factors enter into the definition. One is awareness of social norms. According to the classic study by Neugarten and her associates, an "old" man is between 65 and 75 years of age; an "old" woman between 60 and 75 (Neugarten, Moore, & Lowe, 1965). These age-norm definitions are reinforced and perpetuated by social policy. For example, under most circumstances people become eligible for Social Security at age 65. In some cities, they may receive a special senior citizen pass to the movies or on intercity transportation upon reaching their sixtieth or sixty-fifth birthday. All these "rites of passage" may be expected to enter into a person's awareness of advancing age. Joining an activist group for senior citizens may be the final step in accepting and exploiting the social definition.

Personality, Social Interaction, and Adjustment

With respect to personality adjustment, it is clear that age is a poor index of differences between people (Neugarten, 1977). Work and family roles, financial resources, and physical health appear to be more important to adult adjustment than the exact number of birthdays that the individual has survived. In an attempt to understand the way in which older people handle the many changes they experience—in themselves, at work, with their family, and so on—psychologists have studied age-related tendencies in selected areas of personality. They have investigated older people's perceptions of, and interactions with, their particular environments (Moos & Lemke, 1985)—environments that have become increasingly risky, dangerous, and complex.

Research suggests that there is a decrease in gender-typed qualities with increasing age. David Gutmann, one of the leading theorists and researchers in this area, suggests that during the aging process, men gradually shift from an *active–mastery approach* to the world to a more *passive–accommodative* approach. Older women, by contrast, show the opposite trend—that is, movement from a passive–accommodative to an active–mastery style (Gutmann, 1977). Given that the active–mastery style is associated with traditional "masculine"-typed qualities such as strivings for autonomy, competence, and control, and the passive–accommodative style is associated with traditional "feminine"-typed qualities such as dependence, gentleness, avoidance of conflict, and inhibition of aggressive impulses, it is clear that Gutmann is suggesting that old age brings with it a femininization of men and a masculinization of women—or in other words, increasing androgyny. For example, as they grew older together, Bob and Helen began to notice changes in each other and in their relationship. Helen was more likely to speak up for herself and make decisions for the two of them, such as where they would go on their vacation. In turn, Bob was more likely to defer to Helen's suggestions, and he even became more involved in meal preparation and cleanup.

People gradually reduce or simplify their interactions with others as they age. Older adults, for example, exhibit less role activity (Neugarten, 1973, 1977; Palmore, 1981); they engage less often in family and community activities. The drop-off in social interaction, however, is not a sharp one, but rather a gradual decline in each successive age group from the mid-fifties on (Havighurst, Neugarten, & Tobin, 1968). This is not, of course, a function of personality alone. Older people may have fewer opportunities to interact with others (just as they have greater reason to avoid the risks of their environment). Furthermore, the fact that older people show a decline in social interaction should not be taken to mean that friends and social relationships, in general, are unimportant to them. Hess (1972), for example, suggests that friends often help the older adult adjust to, and compensate for, the many losses experienced during aging. Thus, friendship and social interaction can be an important factor in the adjustment of the elderly (Tesch, 1983).

A number of researchers have suggested that older people choose, perhaps wisely, to risk less personal investment in their relationships. "There seems to be reduction in drive level, a decrease in ego involvement" (Kuhlen, 1964). Less "ego energy" is available to deal with conflict situations, especially as they involve emotions (Havighurst, Neugarten, & Tobin, 1968). Perhaps for this reason, older people seem less worried than younger people. If something does not go right, the tendency is to "let it go," to take it in stride.

Preoccupation with one's inner life seems to become more intense, leading some theorists to describe increased **interiority** as a developmental change of this period (Neugarten, 1973). Older people tend to move toward more self-centered positions. They are concerned more with their own individual

Interiority A tendency of an older person to become increasingly preoccupied with his or her inner life.

Disengagement Theory
An explanation of the changes in elderly people that lead to reflection, self-exploration, and a reduction in social and psychological investments; gradual disengagement of the person from society is said to lead to a sense of well-being and satisfaction; the opposite of activity theory.

problems and less with the problems of the outside world (Leon, Gillum, Gillum, & Gouze, 1979). Some researchers have proposed a **disengagement theory** to account for this change. Disengagement theory predicts a decrease in role activity and gradual physical and psychological detachment from others with increasing age. The process seems to be a reciprocal one between the elderly person and society. As individuals gradually disengage themselves from society, there is less and less of a place for them in the society. If the two processes occur at about the same time, then a good adjustment to aging is likely. However, if a person is cut off from society prematurely by forced retirement and a loss of social contacts, there are likely to be problems in adjustment (Cumming & Henry, 1961). Gradual disengagement of the person from society is said to lead to a sense of psychological well-being and satisfaction (Cumming & Henry, 1961). That is, disengagement is desired for its own sake.

Disengagement theory has been criticized on several points. The predictions that high activity would be associated with low morale and that disengagement is inevitable has not been supported by research studies (Maddox, 1968; Palmore, 1982; Reichard, Livson, & Peterson, 1962). The tendency for older adults to withdraw from social interaction is influenced not only by age but by their health or well being of their spouse, by their financial status, and by their work environment. People who maintain social contacts are more likely to do so because the social environment is supportive. Other researchers have found that disengagement occurs about two years before people die (Lieberman & Coplan, 1970).

Activity Theory The belief of some researchers that maintaining an earlier level of activity results in successful aging; the opposite of disengagement theory.

Other researchers have proposed an **activity theory** that suggests the opposite: Maintaining the earlier level of activity results in successful aging. Research findings suggest that much depends on the individual's style of aging. "Certain personality types, as they age, slough off various role responsibilities with relative comfort and remain highly content with life," writes Neugarten (1973). Other types are depressed by any reduction in social opportunities. Still others who have long had low levels of interaction accompanied by high satisfaction show relatively little change as they grow older. Personality type and long-standing lifestyles seem to predict the way in which individuals adapt to society as they age.

Summary

In old age, people undergo numerous physical, cognitive, and socioemotional changes. The variation among the elderly in the extent and patterning of change is considerable.

The negative consequences of ageism can affect the overall experience of growing older. In the United States, the number of people living beyond 65 is increasing.

Senescence refers to primary aging—the normal age-related changes that occur in response to biological decline. Changes in physical appearance include wrinkles, graying of hair, hair loss, age spots, loss of teeth, and postural stoop. The major changes of the body—cardiovascular, pulmonary, digestive, and neural—continue to decline in efficiency. There is an acceleration in sensory decline, particularly in hearing. A slowing down of the central nervous system accounts for many of the problems manifested by the elderly in movement and mental functioning. A regular and moderate level of physical activity and exercise can help slow down the aging process and help older people feel better.

Old people are more susceptible to disease and less likely to recover quickly. In old age, people are more likely to suffer from such mental disorders as depression, chronic anxiety, and hypochondriasis. Older white males have the highest suicide rate of any group of individuals. Loss is a common factor in depression in old age.

Dementia is a common condition in old age in which people experience declines in physical, cognitive, and personality behaviors as a result of brain deterioration or damage. Alzheimer's disease, the most common dementia, is a chronic and progressive disorder that can last for 10 to 15 years or more before the victim dies. Multi-infarct dementia refers to brain damage as a result of a series of strokes or mini-strokes brought on by reduced blood flow to the brain.

The aging process cannot be satisfactorily explained by a single theory. Some think that aging is a result of an accumulation of errors that occur in the transformation at the cellular level. Some attribute aging to the wear and tear on the body over the years. Aging is also explained by the deprivation theory as due to an inadequate delivery of essential nutrients to the cells, which then deteriorate and die. Aging has been explained in such terms as: a breakdown in the immune system, an accumulation of stresses over the years, and an accumulation of metabolic wastes. For many of these theories, it is unclear whether the explanatory factor is a cause of aging or one of the symptoms of aging. Research has shown a definite link between heredity and longevity.

Certain aspects of intelligence seem to decline with age, particularly psychomotor skills, attention, memory, and inductive reasoning. Social knowledge, verbal–conceptual ability, and arithmetic reasoning, among other skills and knowledge, are not affected by age. Declines are not experienced equally by all people. Better-educated and brighter individuals tend to experience little if any decline in intelligence.

Many factors affect the ability of older people to perform well on intelligence tests, including the pacing of the problems, an overarousal of the autonomic nervous system, and a lack of motivation. Some researchers do not believe that there is a decline in intelligence in older people if they are healthy and socially active. Other researchers believe that the cognitive changes that do take place are adaptive for the development and expression of wisdom.

According to Erikson, the crisis of old age is that of ego-integrity vs. despair. Most old people continue to grow psychologically as they face the challenges of old age. Old people must adjust to retirement, physical aging, and the inevitability of their own death. Compounding these problems is the negative image of age held by most members of society, including the aged themselves.

There are two opposing theories concerning the best means of adapting to old age. The disengagement theory suggests that old people can adjust to aging best by reducing their involvement with other people and situations and becoming more interested in themselves. Other researchers, however, do not agree. They feel that activity and involvement keep a person healthy and youthful. The way they have lived their lives seems to predict the adaptation to aging of individual old people.

Further Readings

Baltes, P. B., and Schaie, K. W. (Eds.). *Life-span developmental psychology: Personality and socialization.* New York: Academic Press, 1978.
A book of readings focusing on research about the changes in personality that occur as one ages.

Blythe, R. *The view in winter: Reflections on old age.* New York: Penguin Books, 1979.
A moving collection of interviews with people from various walks of life on the joys and problems of growing older.

Butler, R. N. *Why survive? Being old in America.* New York: Harper & Row, 1975.
A grimly realistic book on the tragic conditions of the aged in America. Butler forces us to face the fact that in this country the aged daily confront prejudice, poverty, and discrimination.

Butler, R. N., and Lewis, M. I. *Aging and mental health* (3rd ed.). St. Louis: C.V. Mosby, 1982.
An exceptionally well-written and thorough treatment of the major mental-health problems faced by the elderly. The authors also discuss the various intervention and prevention approaches that are being used to handle the problems of our older people.

Cowley, M. *The view from 80.* New York: Penguin Books, 1982.
A personal and witty account of old age from a well-known author and literary critic.

Montagu, A. *Immortality, religion, and morals.* New York: Hawthorn, 1971.
A witty and literate collection of essays dealing with our search for immortality, through children, creative works, or the survival of the soul. Montagu supports his text with evidence from the fields of anthropology, religion, and philosophy.

Skinner, B. F., and Vaughan, M. E. *Enjoy old age: A program of self-management.* New York: Norton, 1983.
With advance planning and a positive approach, old age can be a productive and satisfying period of life. That's the message that B. F. Skinner and his colleague convey in this book filled with helpful tips and suggestions on how to remember things, how to get along with younger people, how to think clearly and feel better.

Observational Activities

15.1 *Media Stereotyping of the Aged*

The image of old age in our society is anything but positive. Among other things, older people are said to be lonely, fearful, sexless, rigid, self-centered, and "out of date." Research, however, suggests that most of these stereotypes do not accurately represent the majority of older adults. Why then do the stereotypes persist? Some people believe that the media play a major role in fostering the continuation of such stereotyping.

Observe a random selection of television shows during prime time over a two-week period. Focus on the roles and behaviors of older adults in these shows, as well as other people's behavior toward the elderly.

1. To what extent are the elderly portrayed as figures of authority? As wise people?

2. Are most older adults on television active and vigorous or are they portrayed as passive and unenergetic?
3. What role does sexuality play in the lives of older television characters?
4. Are the stereotypes attributed to the aged different for men and women? Different for individuals according to racial group or social class?
5. What are the attitudes of most younger adults toward the elderly in the majority of television shows? Do they perceive the elderly as competent and adaptable or as "senile" and unchangeable?

From your observations draw some conclusions concerning the role of television in perpetuating negative stereotypes about the elderly. Are any subgroups of older adults more likely to be stereotyped than others?

15.2 *Life Review*

As people enter the later years of life, they usually engage in a process called *life review*. This involves organizing one's memories and reflecting on the significant actions and developmental milestones that have shaped one's life. It is through the life review that people attempt to gain a final understanding of themselves and the world around them.

Choose an older adult for an in-depth, life-review interview. Ask the person the following questions.

1. Who were the most important people that contributed to your development, both as a child and as an adult? In what ways were they important to you?
2. What events or developmental milestones were particularly significant in your life? Why?
3. How has aging affected you—physically, psychologically, socially?
4. How do you feel about your life? Has it been satisfactory? In what areas have you been most satisfied? Least satisfied?
5. How often do you think about your eventual death? What thoughts go through you mind when you think about death?

From your interview, summarize this person's perception about his or her life. Are the significant events and developmental milestones that shaped the person's life the same as those described in the text? How would you evaluate the person's attitude toward life?

Late Adulthood: Family Life, Social Relations, and Retirement

Although they have remained friends for over 45 years, Eric and Bill actually are very different from one another, and the paths their lives have taken also have been different. Eric, a modestly successful lawyer, is a "family man." He and his wife Jenny have developed a deep love for each other after 40 years of marriage. Together, they raised two bright, healthy, and loving children—now in their thirties—and maintain close contact with them even though they live in another state. Professionally, Eric has never been "driven" by the need for success. He has put in long hours as a lawyer, especially in the early years of his career, but he has always made time for his family, friends, and hobbies. Now that he is well into his sixties, he is giving serious consideration to retiring. Jenny, who retired from her position as a teacher two years ago, supports this decision. Eric and Jenny always planned to retire when they were still young and healthy enough to enjoy themselves—to travel, work in the garden, read, and explore new areas of life together. Fortunately, they are in a financial position to carry out their plans. For Eric and Jenny, the aging years seem bright—something to look forward to, something to share.

By contrast, Bill, who heads his own accounting firm, is anxious about getting old. His life has not been as smooth as his friend Eric's. Bill's first marriage lasted only a few years. When his wife asked for a divorce he was shocked and dismayed; he did not understand her dissatisfaction with him or their marriage. His second marriage lasted longer—15 years—and produced three children, but eventually it too dissolved. Once again, Bill was unable to fully comprehend the basis for his wife's decision to leave the marriage. She had complained that he was never around, that he was remote and unfeeling, that he did not share himself with her or the children. She resented the fact that his career always came first. Although Bill is defensive about his two divorces, he can acknowledge that he placed his desire for success ahead of his family. Ever since he was a young man in his late teens, he wanted more than anything to be successful in his career. In fact, he more than wanted it, he seemed to "need" it. Over the years, he buried himself in his career—moving from a junior- to senior-level accountant in a nationally known company, and eventually starting his own firm. After 15 years, Bill has achieved his goal—he is successful, at least financially. But now that Bill is into the later years of his life, feelings of dissatisfaction and incompleteness are beginning to emerge. Bill has no one with whom to share his life and success. He never remarried after the second divorce, and his relationship with his children is distant. In essence, he is alone, with the exception of one or two friends, especially Eric. As he experiences his own aging and becomes increasingly aware of his own mortality, he senses his isolation more and more. Bill is anxious and depressed. The thought of death frightens him. In fact, he cannot even consider the possibility of it. He wants more from life—he *needs* more. And yet he does not really understand what it is he wants, or how to go about achieving it. For Bill, the aging years are a time of despair and yearning; a time of sadness and regret.

Eric and Bill are, of course, stereotypes who represent extremes. In Chapter 15, we noted that for some people, like Eric, the later years of life are filled with joy, excitement, and a sense of continued involvement—with family, friends, and society as a whole. For other people, like Bill, old age brings with it unhappiness, loneliness, boredom, and regrets. In between these two extremes are the majority of people, those whose lives continue to be characterized by "ups and downs"; by success and happiness in some areas, and frustration and possibly failure in others.

For most people who live to late adulthood, the quality of their lives is heavily affected by the context of their family life and social relations. Certainly the changes in their physical and cognitive capabilities that result from aging influence the type of lifestyle they adopt during the last period of the lifespan. But their successful adjustment will more often center on how they spend and enjoy their time after retirement. The adjustments older adults make in their late sixties, seventies, and even eighties are a reflection of their unique personal developmental histories and the social context in which they developed over the years. In this chapter, we examine the changes and characteristics of family life and social relations for older adults. We also discuss the impact of retirement on people's lives.

Family Life

The last stage in the family life cycle is described as the time from retirement to the death of both husband and wife. For adults who married and remained married this period usually is about 10 to 15 years long (Duvall, 1977). However, for people who never married, or for those who have divorced or remarried, the last stage in the family life cycle may differ. An older man who remarried a woman 10 or 15 years or more his junior, may still have adolescent children living in the household when he is ready to retire. In general, since women live longer than men, they will have a much longer time from their retirement (or their spouse's retirement) to their death.

Historically, this period of the family life cycle is relatively new. Improved medical care, better nutrition, and greater number and quality of social services have helped to ease the burdens of aging for older adults, thereby facilitating longer lifespans. In the past, it was rare for an individual to live into the late seventies, eighties, or nineties. Now it is relatively common. Furthermore, couples are reaching these advanced years together and are experiencing the joys and problems of older married life and widowhood, of which earlier generations never even dreamed. What are the characteristics of this final phase of family life? What unique developmental tasks are confronted within the context of the family at this time, and how do the elderly cope with them?

Marriage in Late Adulthood

Imagine being married to the same person for 40, 50, or even 60 years. Perhaps you've seen newspaper photos of smiling elderly couples celebrating their "golden" wedding anniversary. Often when younger people think of aging married couples they imagine the husband and wife as unhappy, lonely,

After nearly fifty years of marriage, this couple continues to enjoy their lives together.

and isolated from each other and from their families (Streib, 1977). However, this view is an ageist stereotype that is not supported by reality. Most research, in fact, suggests that the quality of married life in old age is generally good. Like the smiling golden-anniversary couple, most couples who enter late adulthood together feel especially fortunate. In one important study, the majority of older couples described this time as the happiest period of their marriage (Stinnett, Carter, & Montgomery, 1972).

What factors determine love and marital satisfaction in old age? Are the factors the same as those found for younger couples? Researchers asked a sample of young, middle-aged, and older adults to rate a variety of statements in terms of how well the statements described their current love relationship (Reedy, Birren, & Schaie, 1981). The results of the study indicated that older couples rated emotional security and loyalty as more characteristic of their love relationship, and sexual intimacy and communication as less characteristic, than younger couples (see Figure 16.1). The authors suggested that "over time satisfying love relationships are less likely to be based on intense companionship and communication and more likely to be based on the history of the relationship, traditions, commitment, and loyalty" (p. 61). Beyond these age differences, the study also found a remarkable similarity between the three generations in what couples find satisfying within their love relationship. All age groups rated emotional security as most important, followed by respect, communication, help and play behaviors, sexual intimacy, and loyalty. Reedy, Birren, and Schaie (1981) concluded that "there is considerably more to love than sex and that at any age, emotional security—feelings of concern, caring, trust, comfort, and being able to depend on one another—is the most important dimension in the bond of love" (p. 62).

The adjustment of the older couple represents, of course, many years of being with and learning about themselves and each other. After 40 years or more together, each partner has learned to ignore small irritations and accept what cannot be changed. Eric learned for example that Jenny liked to drag out a story while telling it. Earlier in their life together, Eric had become impatient with Jenny's style, but, over the years, he pretty much came to accept her style and was able to ignore the minor irritation. In addition, as people get older, they often are less emotionally involved with situations and events, and this may contribute to a more easygoing relationship in late marriage. So too does the tendency to "block out" conflict and other stressful situations. While the elderly frequently are confronted with stressful life events, they generally are successful in coping with them—usually by "distancing" themselves, psychologically, from the events (Chiriboga & Cutler, 1980). In so doing, the elderly experience less disruption in their lives, including their marriage.

The two factors that give the older marriage its unique character are the gradual shift in focus away from the children and the retirement of the husband (and more recently the wife) from occupational life (Adams, 1975). Both events provide the couple with increased freedom from outside responsibilities and obligations; now, they are not expected to do much more than support and sustain each other. Death has usually relieved them of responsibilities toward their own parents; and their children usually ask only that they remain self-sufficient, which, of course, they mean to do. Consequently, husbands and wives often find that they have more time for each other during

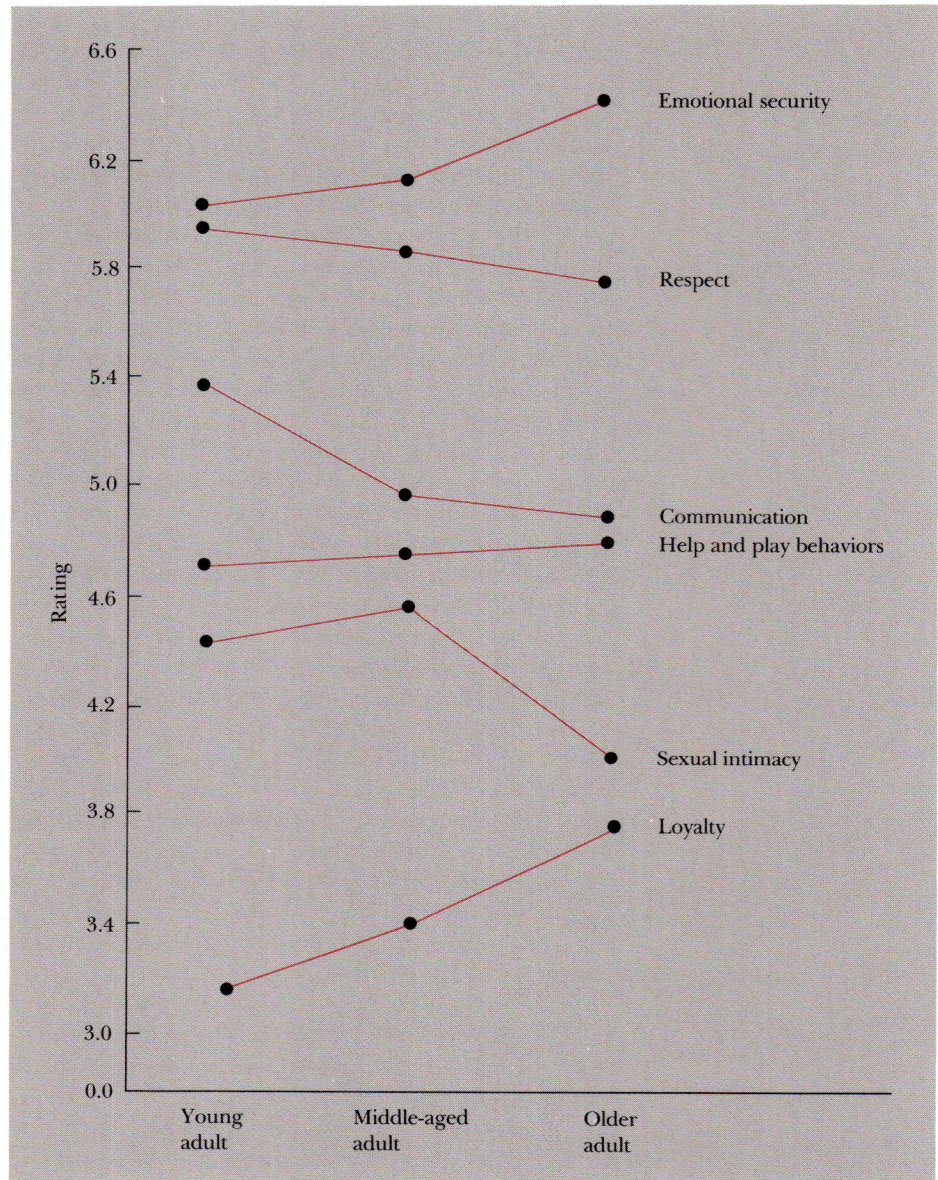

Figure 16-1 Age differences for components of love relationships.

this period than at any other time in their marriage—a factor that seems to facilitate marital happiness.

Although older couples have more time to spend with each other, the amount of love actually expressed in a marriage declines with years (Swensen, Eskew, & Kohlhepp, 1981). For couples who have had a history of sharing their time and interests, who do not have a highly gender-typed division of labor within the family, and who have learned to cope with interpersonal conflicts by discussion and negotiation, the later years of marriage prove to be loving and positive ones (Ade-Ridder & Brubaker, 1983; Atchley, 1980; Atchley & Miller, 1983; Swensen, Eskew, & Kohlhepp, 1981).

However, not all married couples enjoy a satisfactory relationship in later life. This is especially true for couples who have not shared domestic duties throughout their marriage or who have not spent much time with each other before retirement. Wives who have been primarily responsible for the running of the household may experience the retired husband as an inconvenience at first. New daily routines and household responsibilities must be established now that both spouses are at home. For women who have maintained a career and are now retired along with their husbands, there is an additional adjustment to be made: how to spend their time and how to divide the domestic chores with their spouse. Early in retirement, both husband and wife may find new tensions in their relationship as they tackle meal preparation and housecleaning with the same interest that characterized their work roles. Husbands may be unwilling to take on household activities that had been assumed by their wives. Even though husbands spend more of their time in domestic labor after retirement than at any other period of their lifespan, wives continue to spend more time involved in housework than do their husbands (Rexroat & Shehan, 1987).

Illness also tends to strain the marital relationship, reduce sexual interaction, and perhaps introduce a new dependency relationship as the spouse takes on the role of nurse or caregiver. Poverty is another source of marital discontent, especially when encountered for the first time in the later years. Retirement brings with it a substantial reduction in financial income. Consequently, the older couple must make drastic adjustments in their standard of living—adjustments that may strain the marriage if adequate decision-making processes for managing scarce resources have not been developed over the years. Generally, most couples who have been relatively well adjusted improve their relationship with old age. On many indices of marital satisfaction, the aging couple come to resemble the young childless couple. Rollins and Feldman (1970) conclude that "perhaps the outstanding characteristic of this relationship is the general feeling of peacefulness, lack of stress, and satisfaction with marriage, in which they approach the level of the newly married."

One factor that may help to explain the success of some late marriages is the interesting gender-role reversal, mentioned in Chapter 15, that characterizes some older couples. It frequently has been noted that parenthood and occupational life sharpen gender-role distinctions in many couples. As couples enter into later life, however, the demands of parenthood and work lessen, often leading to a marked reduction of gender-role differences. Some men begin to recognize and express their more affiliative, nurturant, and emotional needs, while women become more assertive (Gutmann, 1977; McGee & Wells, 1982; Neugarten, 1968). These changes are likely to reduce tension between the couple, allowing for greater ease of communication and increased sharing of feelings—both of which are likely to facilitate marital satisfaction. Jenny and Eric, for example, take comfort from each other as they talk about their past regrets and fears of their impending deaths and loss of each other.

Finally, marriage is not only quite satisfying during this age period, it is psychologically and biologically beneficial. Research indicates that older individuals who are married are less likely to experience loneliness and depression than are the unmarried elderly (Tibbitts, 1977). They also show less evidence of mental illness (Gove, 1973), and they are likely to live longer (Civia, 1967). Marital adjustment increases an individual's physical, psychological, and social well-being and can help to counteract the negative influence that family strains and other stressful life events bring to later life (Lavee, McCubbin, & Olson, 1987).

Pause for Thought

People stay married for many reasons, one of which is to be married rather than single. Others continue in a marriage to preserve family harmony for the benefit of their children. Still others stay married because they have a commitment to their spouse as a person, a friend, and companion. What differences might you find in the late-adulthood period between marriages that are based on a personal commitment and marriages for the sake of being married?

Sexuality in Late Adulthood

Contrary to the stereotyped view of the elderly as sexless people, there is sex after 60. In his eighties, actor George Burns takes pride in talking about his

Most people who are healthy and have an available and willing partner continue to show an interest in sexual relations during later adulthood.

interest in women. At one time, any older man who acknowledged or displayed his interest in women would be described as a "dirty old man" or perverted. The strongly held belief that older adults do not enjoy (or should not enjoy) sexual relations is contradicted by more current and representative research (Kay & Neelley, 1982) that supports the view that many people can and do experience their sexuality well into old age. Throughout the lifespan, sexuality is expressed in different ways and is affected by various cultural and life events. For example, the birth of a child usually reduces the frequency of sexual intercourse. Likewise, the illness of a spouse may limit the type of sexual activity. When sexuality is viewed more generally than sexual intercourse to include pleasurable intimate physical contact between couples, the stereotype of sexless elderly becomes even more absurd (Laws, 1980). Even though the frequency of sexual intercourse declines with age and as people enter late adulthood, older adults are interested in sexual pleasures and indulge with warmth and dignity (Comfort, 1980).

Why then the persistent stereotype of sexless older adults? One reason is that until recently, there was little research done using older people, especially for people over the age of 75. Sex research on the elderly has been somewhat of a taboo topic (Laws, 1980). Gerontologists had been reluctant to survey older people about their sexual behavior because they themselves found it difficult to imagine that people as old or older than their parents would be interested in sexual relations. (Can you imagine your own parents or grandparents as sexually active people?) With little research to build on, the topic of sexuality was ignored until fairly recently. The research of Masters and Johnson (1966, 1981) included a study of the sexual behaviors of men and women over age 60. They found that people who maintained an active sexual life during early stages of their life were more likely to continue to be sexually active in later life. In a large questionnaire study by Consumers Union, 81 percent of married women and 50 percent of unmarried women over age 70 reported at least some sexual activity during the past month. For men over the age of 50, the figures were 81 percent for married men and 75 percent for unmarried. Since the respondents in this study were all subscribers and readers of a consumer's magazine, they were, as a group, better educated and middle class. Nonetheless, other studies have reported similar results (Butler & Lewis, 1976; Palmore, 1981) to support the existence of sexuality after age 60.

The form of sexual activity in old age changes as a result of biological and physiological changes that take place with aging. Hormone reduction, testosterone for men and estrogen for women, that began in middle adulthood continues to alter the structure and functioning of reproductive organs in old age. For women, the walls of the vagina become thinner, shorter, and less expansive. Vaginal lubrication also decreases, thereby leading to occasional pain during intercourse. Orgasm is generally shorter and less intense as well (Weg, 1978). For men, more direct stimulation is necessary to achieve erection; and the time required for full erection is longer, sometimes as long as 30 to 40 minutes (Runciman, 1975). Older men also experience longer times between erections, and less intense orgasms. However, they are better able to control ejaculation; that is, they are able to maintain erections longer. In many cases, this increases the man's ability to satisfy his partner, and to enhance his own pleasurable sensations (Masters & Johnson, 1966).

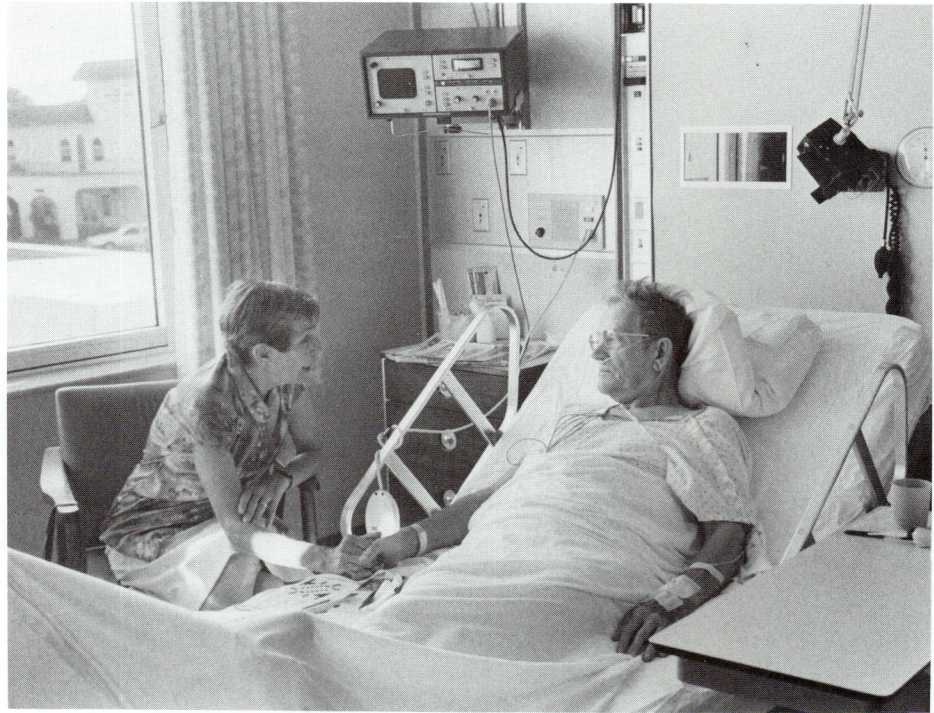

One reason that sexuality may decline in late adulthood is the lack of an available partner due to illness.

Impotence A man's inability to produce an erection.

Sexuality in old age is complicated by medical problems, however. Cardiovascular problems, diabetes, hypothyroidism, arthritis, alcoholism, drug dependence, and obesity, to name a few health-related factors, frequently contribute to a decreased sexual desire and, at times, even to **impotence.** Some prescription drugs used in the treatment of hypertension result in impotence. Certain surgical procedures also are linked to sexual problems in the elderly. Radical surgery for cancer of the colon or the rectum frequently leads to impotence in older men—sometimes because of surgical damage to the nerves that cause an erection, but more often because of the negative impact of surgery on sexual self-image. Similarly, older women sometimes lose interest in sexual activity following a hysterectomy, or mastectomy, not because of some medical complication, but because of the myths surrounding the surgery (Jacobson, 1974). They falsely believe that removal of the uterus or a breast causes loss of sexual desire or automatic sexual unattractiveness.

Although the myth that the elderly are not interested in sex has been discredited, older people continue to be adversely affected by it. For example, friends and relatives may react with consternation if an older widow or widower conducts an obviously sexual affair. As a result, many older couples court in an atmosphere of secrecy and near shame (McKain, 1972). When interviewed about their marriages, they pointedly avoid mentioning sex, referring instead to "companionship."

Pause for Thought

One of the vicious cycles perpetuated by ageism is the declining sexuality of the elderly. Believing sexuality to be inappropriate for their age, many elderly hide or inhibit their sexual feelings, thus contributing to the erroneous belief that they are sexless. How can this self-fulfilling prophecy be stopped? What social agents could help dispel the view of the elderly as passionless?

Relations with Adult Children

According to popular images, there is no room in the nuclear family for the older generation, and so they are doomed to a rejected, lonely old age. In actuality, the old are neither isolated nor abandoned. The majority of elderly people prefer to live independently, while actively participating in their family's life (Cicirelli, 1983; Troll, Miller, & Atchley, 1979; Yankelovich, Skelly, & White 1977). With changes in family size and increased longevity, more older people are living within an extended family network that can span several generations. About one-half of all persons aged 65 years and over with surviving children belong to families spanning four generations (Shanas, 1979). Most of these family members live within driving distance, thus making it easier for an elderly person to live alone but not without available assistance from family members (Shanas, 1980). Whereas at the turn of the century over 60 percent of the population over the age of 65 lived with their children, today's figures suggest that the figure is below 15 percent (Smith, 1981; Shanas, 1980). Partly, these shifts are due to increased longevity. Today, most people over the age of 65 live with their spouses. Further, the changes in living conditions among the elderly are due to an improved standard of living for older couples. Elderly couples are not as financially destitute as their predecessors because, as a group, they are better educated and often have the benefit of two salaries and pensions (Aldous, 1987).

Older people rely primarily upon their children in times of illness, and they receive an almost instantaneous response (Shanas & Sussman, 1981; Sussman, 1960, 1965). Most adults are eager to help their aging parents by assisting them in shopping, providing rides and support for doctors' visits, or by acting as their spokesperson when dealing with local or state agencies. Older parents usually are not emotionally or financially dependent upon their children. The relationship is one in which they give as well as receive. Among the types of aid that older parents give their children are emotional support, money, services such as baby-sitting or legal advice, and household services such as shopping, cleaning, and house repairing. A study of near elderly couples (people who were close to retirement or recently retired) found that older parents provided their adult children with child-care and house-and-yard care services, financial assistance in the form of loans or gifts, and transportation (Aldous, 1987). It was also found that near elderly parents were selective with their help among their children. They were more likely to maintain contact with and provide support and services to adult children who were in most need of their attention—namely their divorced or single adult children. Although some elderly may not be physically or financially able to do so, the number of older people who help their children tends to exceed those who receive help from their children (Riley, Riley, & Johnson, 1968). Troll, Miller, and Atchley (1979) suggest that this pattern is likely to continue until there is deterioration in the financial or health condition of the parents.

As independent and self-sufficient as older people wish to be, there does come a time in their lives when they need to accept help from their children, and others, and when the help received far outweighs the help given. At such times, a role reversal takes place—with adult children becoming caregivers to their own aging—and usually ailing—parents. Approximately 8 percent of the elderly in the United States are housebound, with much of the caregiving being provided by their adult children (Huyck & Hoyer, 1982). Daughters, in particular, are likely to take on this responsibility, regardless of whether it is for their own parents, or their in-laws (Troll & Turner, 1980).

Relations with Grandchildren

In old age, one's grandchildren are no longer toddlers or schoolchildren. They are adolescents, or older. The fact that life expectancy has increased, and people now reach advanced age in better health and with greater vitality than ever before, suggests that the probability of grandparental influence upon younger family members is likely to be considerable (Hagestad, 1982). Grandmothers, in particular, are likely to have an influential relationship with their grandchildren (Hagestad, 1978, 1982; Troll, 1983)—if for no other reason than that they live longer than grandfathers. This is not to deny, however, the influence of grandfathers, who are often seen as the reservoirs of family wisdom and who are especially likely to have an impact on grandsons (Hagestad, 1978).

    Grandparents vary widely in the degree of involvement with their grandchildren—some are intensely involved, whereas others appear totally unin-

Grandparents vary widely in degree of involvement with their grandchildren. Some, such as this woman, enjoy influencing and being influenced by their grandchildren; other grandparents are remote and uninterested in their grandchildren.

terested in their grandchildren. In Chapter 14, we noted that grandparents often play a significant role in the well-being and adjustment of the child–grandchild family unit, particularly in situations following such life stresses as divorce, unplanned and unwanted pregnancy, and the like (Troll, 1983). Of interest, however, is the common finding that the well-being and morale of grandparents is unrelated to the amount of contact they have with their grandchildren. Life satisfaction among the elderly has more to do with friendship patterns—and presumably marital patterns—than it does with grandparenting patterns (Troll, Miller, & Atchley, 1979).

Grandparents and adolescent and adult grandchildren often acknowledge the ways they try to influence one another. Moreover, they admit that their attempts are often successful—but only in certain areas (Troll, 1980). Interestingly, both groups realize that there are some areas in which influence should be avoided. Hagestad (1978) uses the term *demilitarized zone* in reference to these sensitive areas, sexuality and religion, for example. She suggests that family members, including those from different generations, go to great lengths to avoid interpersonal conflict. By not attempting to influence one another within these sensitive areas, which obviously will vary from one family to another, grandparents and their grandchildren avoid disrupting the stability of familial relationships. Jenny and Eric's grandchildren, for example, talk to them about their school and sports activities, their summer plans, and even their career plans, but they never mention their sexuality or enter into a debate on the pros and cons of abortion or school prayer. Likewise, Eric and Jenny know to hold their own opinions on these issues in check.

Pause for Thought

Divorce disrupts family bonds, sometimes resulting in limited contact for grandparents with their grandchildren. However, since many divorced people often remarry and reconstitute their families, divorce can also result in a much larger network of relatives. How might the role of grandparent change with the divorce and remarriage of their adult children?

Singlehood

About 5 percent of the population of adults over the age of 65 have never married (U.S. Bureau of the Census, 1983). Older people who have never married are in the special situation of having neither their own children nor grandchildren toward whom to extend themselves. Their adjustment to old age has been of interest not only to developmental researchers but to every happy single who has heard the threatening question "But what will you have when you are old and sick?" At least one study suggests that elderly single people, as lifelong isolates, do not find old age especially lonely (Gubrium, 1975). Single older people appear to feel less lonely than those who are unhappily married or widowed. Whether that is because they are lifelong isolates, or simply because they have learned to make use of other emotional resources, probably depends upon the individual. The single older person does tend to maintain closer relationships with siblings than do those who marry and have families (Shanas et al., 1968). Sister–sister ties are usually strongest. Furthermore, many single people have many friends with whom

Single people rely on friends and siblings for companionship and support.

they spend considerable time (Cargan & Melko, 1982) and can turn to when they want companionship. One study (Essex & Nam, 1987) found that loneliness in never-married women is not affected by their relationships with family and friends, but by the quality of their health; when their health is poor, never-married older women are more likely to report feeling lonely.

Widowhood

Widowhood represents the greatest emotional and social loss suffered by individuals in the normal course of the lifespan. (Other major losses, such as the death of a parent in childhood, or the death of a child, represent what we, in a more fortunate time, have come to see as unnatural, or at least uncommon, events.) One-half of the women in the United States over the age of 65 and nearly 70 percent of women over the age of 75 are widowed. The corresponding percentages for men are approximately 12 and 20 percent, respectively (U.S. Bureau of the Census, 1983).

The gender difference in widowhood represents a higher mortality rate for men than women, and the fact that older men are much more likely to remarry following the death of their spouse than are older women. Treas and Van Hilst (1976) report that among whites, there are six times more men than women over 65 who remarry after the death of the spouse.

Widowhood is, first, an experience to be lived through and, second, a social status to be lived with. The death of the spouse is an emotional emer-

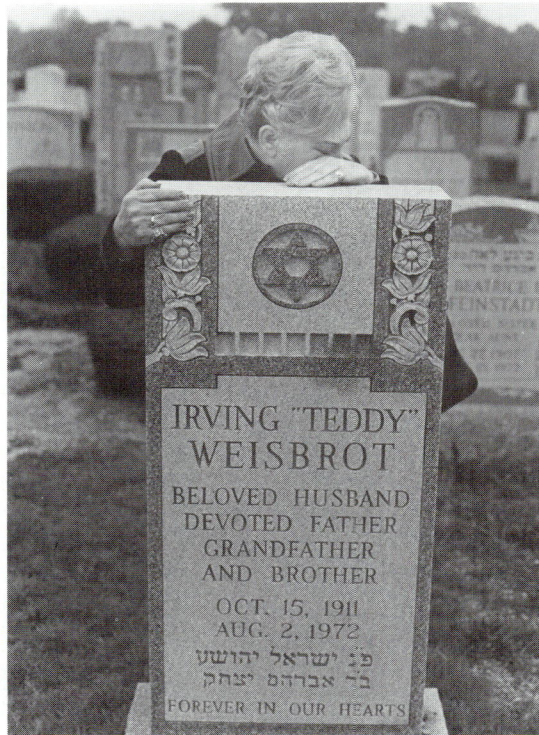

Widowhood represents the greatest emotional and social loss experienced by the elderly.

gency; only later is the bereaved person in a position to adjust, so far as is possible, to a new status and lifestyle.

Still, many widows outlive their husbands for what amounts to one or more generations. In the second stage of adjustment, the widow must establish a new relationship with society. According to Lopata (1973, 1979), who has studied this stage of the family cycle in depth, the widow has several options. One option is to return to the medium or high levels of activity she enjoyed before being widowed. This may be difficult if her activities depended on the presence of a spouse, as is often the case for middle-class, educated women. It can also be difficult for financial reasons. Lopata (1979) reported that 40 percent of the widows in her study lived at or below the poverty level. A second possibility is that the woman can choose to enter a new role and develop new friends (including widows like herself). Or, she can retreat into isolation. Lopata suggests that the first two solutions, or some combination, are ideal from the widow's standpoint.

A more immediate and practical problem for the widow is where she will live (most often expressed in the question "What will you do now?"). The widow can live alone, adopt some form of communal living, live with one of her married children, or remarry (Lopata, 1971). About one-half of Lopata's sample of 301 Chicago women lived alone, primarily because they wanted to be free and independent. Those who lived with relatives or took in roomers were more often than not the head of the household. Only 10 percent lived with married children, an alternative that is usually the least preferred one.

From 1969 to 1974, a demonstration project called the Widow-to-Widow program was conducted through Harvard University (Silverman, 1985). The purpose of the program was to reduce the risks of mental and physical decline for widows who were in the process of transition following the death of their spouse. The program was designed as an outreach program in which widows who had already made a successful adjustment in their transition from spouse to widow to single person made contact with a recently widowed person. One-to-one contact would typically be made about three to six weeks after the death of the spouse, the time when most relatives and friends would have gone home on the expectation that the widow could manage alone.

The goals of the program centered around helping the widow make changes in her life by providing practical information about bereavement; financial, legal, and housing matters; and community and social services available to her. The widow also received emotional support from and discussed coping strategies with the widow aide who could readily share some of her own experiences. Usually the widow aide would be a neighbor or someone from the widow's immediate community. Today, there are numerous programs available in the United States and Canada that have been based on the Widow-to-Widow program (Osterweis, Solomon, & Green, 1984).

One controversial question that has generated considerable research is whether widowhood differentially affects men and women. We already have noted that women are less likely to remarry following the death of their spouse than men. Widows are also undoubtedly less well off financially than widowers. On the other hand, the literature on psychological and physical adjustment following loss of a spouse suggests that men generally suffer more than women. In reviewing the research in this area, Stroebe and Stroebe (1983) conclude that "although women have typically higher rates of reactive depression, mental illness in general, and physical illness than men, when widower to married men's ratios are compared to widows to married women's ratios to assess the deterioration associated with the partner loss, the men are worse off" (p. 294). These researchers suggest that the gender difference is most easily explained in terms of greater role strain and lesser social support for older men than older women. The widower must find comfort for his loss while at the same time learn to care for a household and himself.

Pause for Thought

The death of a spouse may change the degree and quality of family interaction. Depending on the family role that the deceased person played, there may be more or less contact between adult children and grandchildren and the widowed parent. What factors might influence the frequency and type of contact an older widowed parent might have with adult children and grandchildren?

Institutionalization

Some older people who are unable to live in family or home environments are placed (or place themselves) in institutions variously referred to as nursing homes, geriatric hospitals, hospitals for the chronically ill, and old-age homes. The issue of the institutionalized care of older persons receives a great deal of media attention, with the result that many people believe that institution-alization is widespread. As we have seen, the majority of older people live independently, an hour or less away from one of their children. Only about 5 percent live in nursing homes (Townsend, 1971). If we include other forms of institutions, however, such as psychiatric or extended-care medical facilities, perhaps as many as 20 percent of the elderly are at some point institution-alized (Kastenbaum & Candy, 1973).

The average nursing-home resident is approximately 80 years old, white, and female (Butler & Lewis, 1982). Between 85 and 90 percent of those who enter nursing homes do not leave them alive. The average length of stay in the nursing home is 1.6 years, with one-third of the residents dying within the first 12 months. Most nursing-home residents suffer from chronic physical illness—a typical problem being some form of cardiovascular disease. Psychi-atric disorders are also common, either as primary conditions, or secondary conditions to physical illness. Unfortunately, little psychiatric care is provided for most nursing-home residents (Butler & Lewis, 1982).

The reasons for entering nursing homes and other long-care facilities are varied. Some older people enter voluntarily. A debilitating condition may make it impossible for some people to maintain themselves at home. They may be unwilling to become dependent on children, seeking, instead, the impersonal comfort of institutionalized care. Some older people assert their independence by deciding to enter an institution before they become unable to care for themselves (and even to select the institution). Married couples

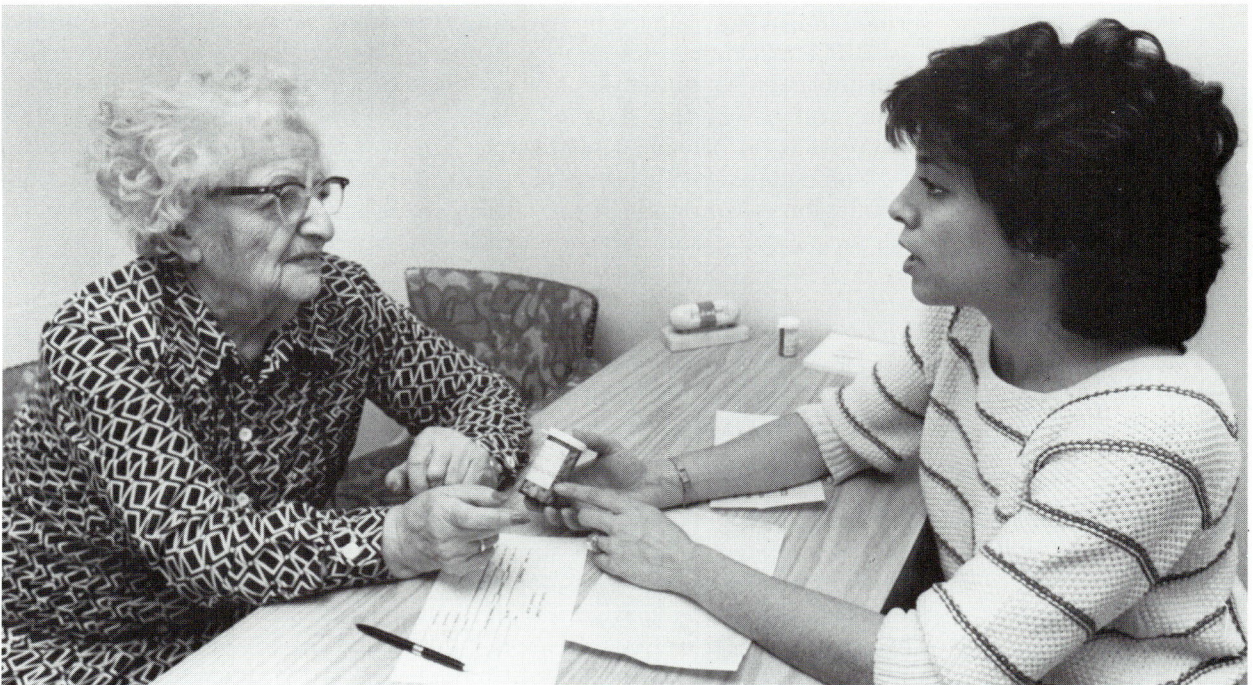

This nursing home health care worker is instructing an elderly client about the use of her medication.

occasionally close up their own home and admit themselves to the facility together—if they can afford it.

In many other cases, institutionalization seems not to be a decision, but an involuntary action on everyone's part. The middle-aged offspring say they have no choice. They may be unable, financially or physically, to care for the chronically ill parent within their homes. Even if resources exist, they may feel unable to accommodate the parent without destroying their own family relationships (including, perhaps, the relationship with the ailing parent). Whatever the justification, the son or daughter often feels guilty.

The assumption underlying these feelings is that all institutions for the elderly are unpleasant and dehumanizing places. They are often described as places where one goes to die (a seeming judgment as well as fact), and yet the institutions are so varied that it is difficult to make generalizations. They range from small convalescent homes run by religious orders to large proprietary nursing homes run by operators with "tender loving greed" (Mendelson, 1974). Some nursing homes provide basic nursing care while others offer a range of physical and recreational activities in addition to basic care. (See Box, Nursing-Home Care.)

Because most older people do not reside in nursing homes or other institutions, it frequently has been asked whether those individuals who do become institutionalized differ physically, socially, or psychologically from those who do not. In one of the most comprehensive studies on this question, Tobin and Lieberman (1976) found that, surprisingly, there was little difference between the two groups. Nursing-home residents were neither more dependent in personality nor more lacking in a confidante or close friend than were same-age residents of the community. Furthermore, both groups seemed to be characterized by the same kind of physical, social, and economic losses. The researchers found that institutionalization was most likely to occur when the person's physical condition showed evidence of increased deterioration, and there was a lack of adequate care facilities (or the inability or unwillingness to provide it) within the family or the community.

Some older people adapt well to institutionalization and communal life. If admission is voluntary; if the older person has had a part in planning it; if, in fact, it offers solutions to loneliness or other life problems, adjustment may be relatively smooth (Schulz & Brenner, 1977).

Alternatives to Nursing Homes

Most elderly people do not want to live in a nursing home and would prefer to live independently. Likewise, most families dread the thought that they might have to place their parents in an institution. Fortunately, several alternatives to institutionalized nursing-home care exist. Many cities now offer some type of residential setting for the elderly (Moos & Lemke, 1985). Some of these settings are apartment complexes that are rented only to the elderly and that provide specialized leisure and social programs and medical services to the residents. Typically, residents in these specialized settings report that they like being able to socialize and participate in the activities (Lawton, 1981). The costs of living in housing specially designed for the elderly are usually lower since many receive state and federal funds. Residents are offered independence and security in these communities, ingredients that help contribute to higher morale and a more active lifestyle for the elderly.

Human Development in Practice

Nursing-Home Care

Health-care professionals who work in nursing homes are well aware of the negative effects of institutionalization on the elderly. Rapid decline in health is often observed upon admission; mortality increases among first-year residents. As we have seen, the aged person is especially vulnerable in periods of stress. Lieberman (1961) suggests that it is entering the institution (rather than living in one) that dramatically upsets the equilibrium.

Entering a nursing home often means surrendering personal control over many aspects of a person's life. Even when the elderly person is in fairly good health, perceived loss of control over life outcomes can lead to poorer health and low morale and depression (Abramson, Seligman, & Teasdale, 1978; Fawcett, Stonner, & Zeppelin, 1980; Wolk & Kurtz, 1975). For example, patients in nursing homes often do not select their own rooms; they are assigned. Meals are usually served at preselected times, and visitors are allowed at defined times. Although the rules and operation of nursing homes are designed to meet the combined needs of the elderly patients, many of whom require medical attention, the loss of independence and sense of control over one's life can often lead to increased debilitation of the elderly patient.

The importance of perceived control for the elderly is highlighted by the research of Ellen Langer and Judith Rodin (1976). These researchers were interested in the influence of personal decision making and responsibility on the well-being of nursing-home residents. One group of residents was encouraged by staff to make decisions for themselves and was given the responsibility to care for plants. The other group of residents was assured by the staff that they were there to make the decisions and to take respon-

sibility for them. Those individuals who were encouraged to take control of their lives in the nursing home by making decisions and assuming responsibility showed significant improvement in mental alertness. They also were rated as more active and happier. Of the group that was not encouraged to assume personal responsibility for themselves, 71 percent showed evidence of debilitation. Furthermore, in an 18-month follow-up of this research, Rodin and Langer (1977) found that the "responsibility" group continued to be psychologically and physically healthier than the "no responsibility" group. The "responsibility" group even had a lower mortality rate. This research suggests that increased choice and responsibility and a sense of personal control can have a profound impact on the elderly and may even slow down some of the negative effects of aging and institutionalization.

Rather than refer to the people who enter nursing homes as "patients," many health-care workers use the term "client." Some nursing homes encourage their clients' independence and individuality by allowing them to decorate their rooms with their own furniture and plants. Some allow the residents to have a private phone in their rooms and to have unlimited visitors.

The layout and design of the nursing-care facility can also contribute to a greater sense of independence and self-control. Since many elderly people have difficulty seeing, large signs and other visual aids strategically placed around the halls and buildings can make it easier for clients to move about unassisted. Flexible and frequent scheduling of activities, especially stimulating and active ones, further adds to the quality of life by giving people more choices in how and when they will spend their time each day.

Some elderly people live in specially built additions to the homes of their adult children. Commonly referred to as "mother-in-law apartments" or "granny flats," these living arrangements allow older people privacy and independence without being cut off from their families. Some elderly are able to continue living in their own homes with the help of daily visits from visiting nurses who provide home care and social-welfare workers who provide home-maker services. Sometimes a worker is hired to live with an aging person to provide care and security when needed.

With an increasingly larger number of people living past retirement and with smaller families, the need for more flexible housing and living arrangements for the elderly is likely to become an even more important issue. The population of never-married people or child-free married couples will increase in the future, thus increasing the number of older adults who cannot rely on adult children to provide for their care (Lawton, 1981). Institution-alization does not have to be the only alternative.

Pause for Thought

Planning and designing a residential community for the elderly requires a knowledge of the physical, social, emotional, and cognitive needs and capabilities of older adults. Economic and political issues are also a consideration. If you were to design the ideal residential community for the elderly, what are some of the things you would stress?

Social Relations

"Grow old along with me. The best is yet to be"—a familiar refrain reminding us that people age within a social context. The way in which the person adjusts to that context and the degree of support that the context offers the older person determines, in part, the way in which he or she adjusts to the aging process. We have already seen that family life, as one component of the social environment, plays an important role in the adaptation of the older adult. But there are other social relations besides marriage and relationships with children and grandchildren that impact on the aging adult.

Social Integration vs. Social Isolation

Social Integration vs. Isolation The degree of interpersonal activity and organizational participation in which a person engages, and the degree of social—emotional support the person receives from others in these activities.

Social integration vs. isolation generally refers to the degree of interpersonal activity and organizational participation that a person engages in. It also refers to the extent of the person's social network and the degree of social support derived from that network (Kahana, 1982). Does the aged person belong to a social club or religious group, participate in programs for the elderly in the community, or keep abreast of what is happening in the local and national news? To what extent does the elderly person make use of the help that is available? As we noted in Chapter 15, one theory of aging—*disengagement theory*—suggests that people gradually withdraw from social interaction and social roles as they get older; and that the reduction of social obligations and responsibilities actually is conducive to heightened feelings of life satisfaction. An alternative theory, *activity theory,* suggests that satisfactory aging necessitates continued involvement in social roles and social relationships. In reviewing the research on this issue, Kahana (1982) observed that neither social disengagement nor social participation per se is consistently linked to high morale and life satisfaction among the elderly. A number of factors apparently mediate the relationship between social behavior and adjustment.

One important distinction is between *voluntary* and *involuntary* social withdrawal. People who choose to withdraw or, conversely, who choose to remain active, are much more likely to feel satisfied with their life situation than are people who are forced by personal or external circumstances to adopt a particular lifestyle against their will (Lowenthal & Boler, 1975). In essence, voluntary decision making allows individuals to feel more in control of their life. Another important factor mediating adjustment to aging is the *subjective meaning* of social integration to the elderly (Liang, Dvorkin, Kahana, & Mazian, 1980). For some individuals, being involved with other people and organizations is extremely important. In fact, it is through these activities that some individuals develop and maintain their sense of identity during the adult years. For example, even though Jenny has retired from teaching, she still attends school-board meetings and is active in professional teaching organizations. For Jenny, continued identification with the profession in which she spent her working life is important. For other individuals, however, continued social integration is much less significant—at least insofar as it impacts on identity and self-esteem. Thus, to understand the importance of social relations for successful adaptation in late adulthood, one must understand the personal meaning that social interaction and social roles have for the elderly, both at the present stage of life, as well as in earlier times.

Research also indicates that the frequency of social participation per se is a poor predictor of life satisfaction and morale among older adults (Lemon, Bengston, & Peterson, 1972). More important than the number of social contacts a person has or the number of organizations he or she belongs to, is the quality of the individual's social relations. The importance of close companions or confidantes has been linked often to successful adjustment in the elderly (Lowenthal & Haven, 1968). The most important companions for the elderly, besides one's spouse, are siblings and friends.

Siblings

Between 75 and 80 percent of people in late adulthood have living brothers and sisters. Even very old people are likely to have a surviving sibling. In a sample of midwestern older adults, those over 80 years of age still had, on the average, one living sibling (Cicirelli, 1979, 1982). Furthermore, contact with brothers and sisters is relatively frequent among the aged, although it obviously depends on the distance between residences.

Relationships with siblings plays an important role in the life of the aging adult, particularly for those individuals who have lost a spouse, are divorced, or who never married (Shanas, 1979). Siblings often provide the support and help that normally would come from a spouse. They act as confidantes; share family occasions, holidays, and recreational activities; aid in decision making, homemaking, and home repairs; boost morale; lend money in times of financial need; and provide nursing care and emotional support in times of illness. It is understandable, therefore, that the majority of older people feel "close" or "extremely close" to at least one of their siblings (Cicirelli, 1979, 1980, 1982; Scott, 1983).

Research suggests that the influence of siblings on older adults differs depending upon the gender of the sibling and the gender of the individual (Cicirelli, 1977b, 1979). Generally, female siblings exert a greater influence

Heredity is an important factor governing the aging process, as is seen in these identical twins.

on both aged men and women. They are more effective in preserving family relationships and providing emotional support. Furthermore, the presence of sisters tends to reduce the threat of aging for the older man; that is, older men seem happier and less affected by economic and social insecurities when they have living sisters. For aged women, the presence of sisters results in greater concern about social skills, social relationships outside of the family, and community activity. In other words, sisters stimulate each other and tend to facilitate a more challenging environment for the older woman.

Friends

Although much has been written about the meaning and role of friendship in childhood and adolescence, we actually have little information on the importance of friends for adults, especially older adults (Tesch, 1983). Nevertheless, common sense tells us that for most people friends are important. McCormick (1982) suggests that friends serve a number of functions. For example, Eric and Bill provide each other with approval, affection, and emotional support during difficult times. Friends also encourage self-disclosure, as well as mutual trust, respect, and obligation. In addition, friends provide us with aid, advice, and services; and they stimulate us by providing new information and experiences.

In old age, friendships help to compensate for many of the personal and social losses experienced by the individual (Hess, 1972). In times of grief and sorrow the elderly often seek to share their experiences with others, particularly those who also have gone, or are going, through similar situations. This may explain why older people, more than middle-aged adults, tend to choose friends who are close to their own age (Lopata, 1977; Norris & Rubin, 1984; Stueve & Fischer, 1978). The importance of friendships to the elderly is further highlighted by research showing that life satisfaction is more closely linked to friendship interaction than to interaction with relatives (Philblad & Adams, 1972; Wood & Robertson, 1978).

Friendship patterns differ in old age for men and women. Older men generally report more friends than older women, although they tend to spend less time with their friends and reveal less about themselves to their friends than women do (Dickens & Perlman, 1981; Powers & Bultena, 1976; Reisman, 1981). Older men also report more cross-gender friendships than women (Booth & Hess, 1974). As Troll (1982) has noted, this may imply that it is easier to be friends with women than men. That is, women may be more receptive to self-disclosure and sharing of confidences than men—characteristics that promote close, intimate friendships. Or, it may just mean that with fewer men surviving into old age, women have less opportunity than men to develop cross-gender friendships.

Pause for Thought

In a longitudinal study that looked at the social motives that affect people's lives, Veroff, Reuman and Feld (1984) found that as women got older their desire for affiliation declined. This decline was not found for older men, however. Their subjects were 21 years or older when they were first studied in 1957 and then were studied again in 1976. What explanations can you offer for the differences between men and women in their interest in being with people?

Retirement

The occupational life cycle ends with retirement. According to Atchley (1977), a person is retired if he or she is employed less than full-time year round and if at least part of his or her income is derived from a retirement pension, private or government, earned through prior years of employment. Thus, to

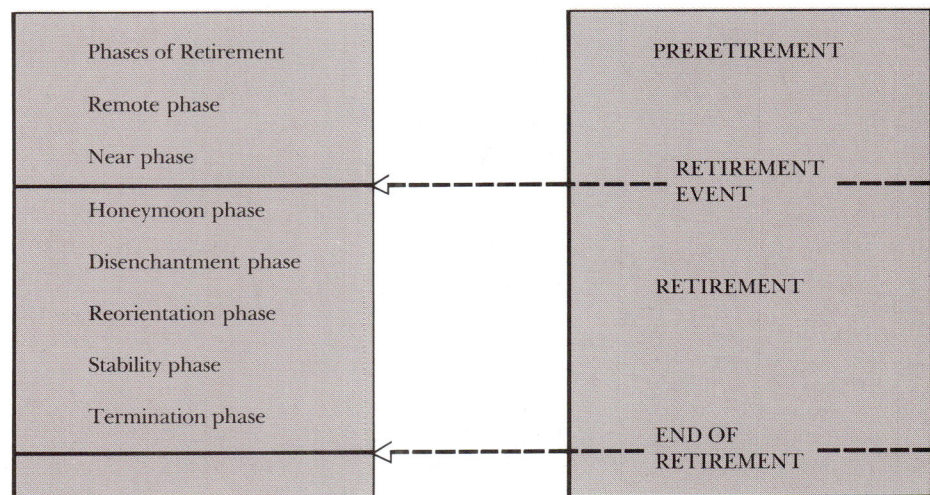

Phases of Retirement	
Remote phase	PRERETIREMENT
Near phase	
Honeymoon phase	RETIREMENT EVENT
Disenchantment phase	
Reorientation phase	RETIREMENT
Stability phase	
Termination phase	END OF RETIREMENT

Figure 16-2 Phases of retirement.

be retired does *not* mean that the person is totally unemployed. Many older people, after retiring from their primary job, take on part-time work—sometimes for financial reasons, but in many cases, because they feel more satisfied "doing something." Why do people retire? What significance and impact does the retirement role have for the older person? In this section, we address these, and other, questions.

The Decision to Retire

Retirement age is often described as an "artifact" of the Social Security system. As many psychologists, physicians, and social planners note, chronological age is a poor indication of one's ability or desire to work. Adopting 70 as a normal retirement age is a device to allow employers to dispense with higher-paid older workers, and to allow younger workers to enter and advance in the job hierarchies. Most supervisors, when questioned, say that they would prefer a variable retirement age, to account for individual differences in ability and health.

Reasons for retiring vary from individual to individual. Contrary to what most people think, retirement is less often forced on people than it is a voluntary decision. Somewhere between 40 to 50 percent of retirement is by choice (Palmore, Burchett, Fillenbaum, George, & Wallman, 1985). People from lower socioeconomic groups, however, are less likely to retire voluntarily

Some jobs are arduous and dangerous, making early retirement an attractive option.

than are people from middle- and high-income groups, primarily because the former are less financially secure. In line with this finding, Louis Harris and Associates (1975) found that black workers are less likely to retire by choice than are white workers—43 vs. 63 percent, respectively.

Those who choose to retire usually do so because of adequate financial resources, good pension plans, desire to spend more time with family, or dislike for the job. Age norms also influence a person's decision to retire. People may realize that they have reached the age when people expect them to retire. The desire to be part of the "retirement crowd," to join the activities of friends and relatives who already have retired may be an additional inducement to finally quit working.

Involuntary retirement, on the other hand, usually results from the mandatory retirement policy of the company. Another important factor is poor health. With the passage of time, chronic physical problems such as cardiovascular disease, arthritis, pulmonary disease, and so on, often begin to take their toll, and prevent, or at least inhibit, older workers from effectively doing their job. In fact, the primary reason given for "early retirement"—that is, prior to mandatory retirement age—is declining health. The combination of poor health and forced retirement is often difficult for the older person to adjust to (Atchley, 1977).

Not all workers retire, or retire completely. Self-employed people—artists, professional scholars, private practitioners in medicine and psychology, independent artisans and contractors, among others—are not affected by mandatory retirement. Furthermore, as we have noted, some adults retire from one job, only to take up a second—usually part-time—job. A study by Flanagan (1981) indicated that as many as 16 percent of men and 12 percent of women in their late sixties to early seventies work either full-time or part-time. When asked what were the most important characteristics of a job for them, these older adults reported the following: The job should be something they are competent at or do well; the job should be meaningful, challenging, and interesting; co-workers and the work environment should be pleasant; and supervisors should be friendly and interested in their welfare.

Early Retirement

Even though federal legislation has raised mandatory retirement age from 65 to 70 and some employers have eliminated any age requirement, many people are electing to retire early, that is before they have to and even before they reach their sixties. Actual retirement age in major industries averages about 58 years of age (Stagner, 1982). The major factors in deciding on early retirement are financial status and health. People in poor health or with an ailing spouse are more likely to take an early retirement if they have private pension and retirement benefits to supplement their Social Security benefits that alone are not adequate to support a family in retirement. Many people take an early retirement so that they can direct their time and energy to developing a postretirement second career. A study of college professors who had taken early retirement found that more than half of them had planned specific projects such as writing a book or doing research (Kell & Patton, 1978). (See Box, Retired Teachers Back in the Classroom.)

Other workers leave their jobs early because they do not like their work. These are people who cannot wait to leave jobs that for them may be boring

Human Development in Practice

Retired Teachers Back in the Classroom

Learning is a life-long process and teaching is a never-ending occupation. Even though teachers retire, many never lose their passion for helping people learn. Years of experience in solving problems, creating new learning opportunities, and dealing with people in a classroom are not easily set aside in retirement. It is not an uncommon reaction to hear a retired educator talk about how much he or she misses the challenge of teaching.

Changes in the Age Discrimination section of the National Employment Act now make it illegal for employees to set a mandatory age for retirement. (Four occupations were excluded from the legislation: police and fire fighters, prison guards, and tenured members of college and university faculties.) The legislation makes it possible for older teachers (nonuniversity) who do not want to retire to stay in the classroom.

For those who wish to retire, however, there are other ways they can use their teaching experience. Some retired teachers take part-time jobs as substitute teachers. Others teach English as a second language to children and adults from foreign countries. Some retired guidance teachers have set themselves up as consultants for high-school students and their parents to guide them in the selection of and admission to college or other career paths. Tutoring and remedial

work on a one-to-one basis is another way older teachers maintain contact with their profession. Students with learning disabilities require more personal instruction that can be delivered by part-time retired educators.

People who have taught for many years have acquired a wealth of information and insights in the process of teaching that can be beneficial to new teachers. By inviting retired teachers into the classroom as guest speakers or co-teachers, both the new teacher and the students benefit. By having contact with an older teacher who is respected by the school and is challenging in the classroom, students are more likely to develop more positive attitudes about the elderly. Classroom teachers who invite retired educators back to their schools benefit from the different perspective the retired person may bring to the lesson. Administrators are also beneficiaries of any efforts to engage the service of retired teachers. With the prospect of more meaningful ways of using their training and experience as educators after retiring, more teachers may consider retirement a more attractive option. A reduced work load, more time for reflection and study and the continued contact with fellow teachers and administrators may make the postretirement phase a more satisfying time for life-long educators.

This gentleman is a retired schoolteacher who has come back to the classroom to talk about the aging process with schoolchildren.

and require hard work under difficult or hazardous conditions. Some workers are offered inducements to retire earlier such as a year's salary in bonus. Usually, employers who offer such inducements are hoping to make room for more advancement for younger workers or to make substantial changes in the organization. With the added financial incentive, many older workers already close to retiring may decide to leave early. In some cases, the early retirement is not an option but the result of being laid off or fired. People who do not choose to leave work but are forced to usually have a more difficult time making the adjustment from work to retirement.

The Process of Retirement

Retirement is often thought of as an event. It is usually associated with one's sixty-fifth or seventieth birthday—with going to work for the last time, getting the gold watch or some other symbol of a "job well done," having co-workers throw a farewell party for you, and so on. In reality, though, retirement is less an event than a process—something that takes place gradually over time. Eric, for example, has been preparing for his retirement for several years. (See Figure 16.2, p. 547.) For some time now, he and Jenny have been setting money aside for the day when they would no longer be working. In addition, Eric has been purposely less involved in critical, long-term legal cases and has spent more and more of his time on leisure activities and developing hobbies.

Atchley (1977) has suggested that the retirement process involves seven phases. He noted, however, that not everyone necessarily goes through all seven phases; nor do they necessarily go through the phases in the particular sequence described. Variability in the retirement age and in the reasons for retiring means that the process of retirement will be somewhat different from one person to another. Still, Atchley's model is useful for understanding the developmental tasks confronting the older person who is undergoing the transition from worker to nonworker.

The first, or *remote phase*, occurs in the preretirement period, usually in the early part of middle adulthood. For most adults, this is a time of intense activity at work, and a time for enjoying the fruits of one's labor—job status, financial security, feelings of competence, and so forth. Thoughts about retirement, if they exist at all, are vague; little is done to prepare for retirement at this time.

As people move closer to retirement, they enter the *near preretirement phase*. This is a time for more active thinking and planning for retirement. Some workers—though a minority of those eligible—attend preretirement programs, where they are counseled about retirement and learn how to plan for this phase of life. According to Atchley, this is a time of mutual disengagement at work. Duties and obligations are gradually given up—shifted to younger workers. This period ends with the actual retirement. Eric would be described as being in this phase.

The transition from worker to nonworker is often accompanied by initial enthusiasm, by feelings of excitement and even euphoria. This is the *honeymoon phase*—the first of the postretirement phases. During this time, people often begin to implement the many activities they had long planned for—for example, a trip across the country, visiting relatives or children, beginning the many house repairs that were put off in the past, developing a garden, reading and writing, or just plain relaxing. Not all people who retire, however, experience the excitement and enthusiasm of this early retirement period. Older adults who have been forced to retire, either because of company policy or poor health, and those who find that their financial situation prevents them from engaging in the activities they had planned, usually feel a sense of dissatisfaction, frustration, and even anger.

Even those older adults who initially go through a honeymoon phase, with its accompanying feelings of excitement, will usually find that some of their plans are beyond their means, or that the plans are not as satisfying as they had expected. When this happens, a transition to the *disenchantment phase* occurs, and the retiree feels "let down," and often depressed.

For most adults, disenchantment does not last forever. Atchley suggested that as people move through the postretirement years they enter a *reorientation phase* during which they come to grips with the reality of retirement and its meaning for them. This is a time for reorienting oneself to the future and for reevaluating one's goals and the means of achieving them.

The next phase of retirement is termed the *stability phase*. Although Atchley indicated that it typically follows a period of disenchantment and then reorientation, he noted that some older people enter this phase immediately after the honeymoon period. The crux of this phase is that it is a time for deciding on long-term choices or goals and for implementing them.

The final phase of retirement is the *terminal phase*. This is a time when retirement loses much of its significance or meaning for the person. Other factors take on more importance—serious illness or impending death, for example. In this case, the older adult puts aside the role of retiree and becomes preoccupied with the role of sick, disabled, or dying person. For other adults, however, the terminal phase takes on a much different perspective. Dissatisfaction with retirement goals and activities—including those associated with extended leisure—sometimes leads the older individual to seek out employment once again, usually a part-time job and often one that is totally unrelated to past employment activities. Thus, the individual has come full circle, from worker to nonworker to worker once again.

Pause for Thought

The term "retirement" suggests a shut down or rest and perhaps contributes to some of the difficulties people have with deciding on and accepting the change from being a worker to being a nonworker. Furthermore, many women do not actually leave a job from which they can officially retire. Can you think of another term for retirement that has a more positive connotation and that applies equally well to people who shift their focus of attention from work to nonwork activities?

Attitudes Toward Retirement

A number of factors influence people's attitudes toward retirement. First is the amount of choice they can exercise in the matter, which varies with the occupation. People who are self-employed, such as the novelist, carpenter, or physician, have the option of working well beyond normal retirement age. A schoolteacher can choose to retire after 20 or 25 years—with different benefit schedules. Members of trade unions may be able to take advantage of a "flexible retirement" clause that allows them to work past normal retirement; or provides an early retirement option that allows full benefits after only 30 years. Other workers have no choice but to accept the gold watch at the specified moment. Interacting with this, of course, is job satisfaction. Unskilled workers (who show less job satisfaction) are likely to opt for early retirement within a corporation that provides this option. People who are bored with their work or who are unhappy with the control exercised over them by supervisors or co-workers also may look favorably on retirement (Troll, 1982). Other workers, particularly those in white-collar and professional jobs are more likely to choose retirement at 65 or later. Who, then, is discontented? As common sense and popular literature would have it, the people for whom adjustment is most difficult are the ones who enjoy their work but find their careers, after 40 years of competence, "brought to an end by unpleasant compulsions." Such people are thwarted in their lifelong desire "to go out with . . . job boots on" (Olmstead, 1975).

Adjustment is also difficult for those who do not have adequate savings or retirement income (Atchley, 1975; Harris and Associates, 1975). Many retired people find, in an inflationary period, that their "nest eggs" and fixed retirement incomes amount to much less than they had foreseen. Postretirement poverty is experienced differently by different retirees. For the person who has always been poor, it is just "one more economic insult." For the majority of retirees, it represents a relative deprivation and a discontinuity with the working years (Maddox, 1968). Especially for the latter group, reduced resources represent a difficult adjustment, perhaps a scrapping of retirement plans for travel and other recreations. For retired people generally, a high level of morale may be possible only if their economic status compares favorably with that of working adults (Bromley, 1974).

Leisure Activities in Retirement

Perhaps most important to retired people in terms of their attitude and adjustment to retirement is the issue of what they are going to do with their time. Their options seem to include leisure, hobbies or recreation, part-time employment, voluntary service, socializing, or doing nothing (which might mean anything from watching television to contemplating the meaning of life). Though doing nothing might be a reasonable choice after a lifetime of labor—there are societies that recognize the older person's privilege to sit and think—this is not thought to be an admirable choice in our culture.

Many people begin a leisure activity or hobby in their middle adulthood years, some do so in anticipation of their retirement years. Leisure refers to nonwork or nonobligatory time during which people engage in activities that they enjoy. An activity such as cooking a meal may be work for one person and a leisure activity for another. It all depends on whether the person feels obliged to do the activity. Thus, retired people may take pleasure in volunteering their time to counsel unwed teenage mothers or teach English to immigrants because they have made the choice to do so freely and not because they needed to work for money or because their services were required in some way.

Rather than continuing a work-related role, some older people develop new roles in voluntary services. There is ample opportunity. Among the many governmental agencies known to value the work of older people are Veteran's

Administration Volunteers Service, Foster Grandparents, Small Business Administration, Vista, and Peace Corps (Arthur, 1969). Opportunity for general community service differs, of course, with the community. Some cities have agencies that place older people in other city agencies, matching skills and interests to requirements. Even small towns and rural areas have self-help programs that depend upon the volunteer efforts of retired residents.

Most people who volunteer their time do so within a 10-year period before and just after retirement (McPherson, 1983). Furthermore, they are likely to have higher levels of education, be in better health, and come from higher social classes than do people who do not volunteer their time.

Many people are limited in the leisure activities they can pursue by lack of transportation, limited funds, and declining health (Burrus-Bammel, & Bammel, 1985). People who live in an age-segregated residential community have greater opportunity to become involved with more leisure activities because they do not have to travel and often have companions with similar interests as their neighbors.

The leisure activities that are most frequently reported by people over the age of 65 are socializing with friends and relatives, watching television, gardening, reading, and thinking—with the possible exception of gardening, all sedentary activities (McPherson, 1983). Most of the activities are home-based, indoor, and can be done alone.

Whatever the specific activities, most studies have found that people who are involved in leisure activities are more satisfied with their lives and adjust better to retired life. Leisure activities often bring people in contact with one another and create more variety and stimulation in their lives.

While it may be the case that people who have made a more satisfactory adjustment to old age are also more likely to involve themselves with other people and engage in leisure activities, keeping oneself active in the post-retirement years is nonetheless an important factor in aging.

Psychological Impact of Retirement

Due to the pivotal impact of work in our culture, retirement represents a loss of significant magnitude for most people. There is loss of a social role, loss of identity, social contacts, financial security, and power and prestige. Thus, retirement can be seen as an important life-stress process requiring numerous life readjustments (Holmes & Rahe, 1967). Like other life stressors, retirement has often been associated—at least among the general population—with declines in health and psychological well-being. But is there any validity to this stereotype?

Contrary to popular opinion, health does not deteriorate after retirement. In fact, many people improve in health in the immediate postretirement years (Troll, 1982). Furthermore, except for those who are involuntarily retired, retirement does not seem to be associated with low morale in most cases (Streib & Schneider, 1971). Nor does it lead to psychological impairment or mental illness (Lowenthal & Haven, 1968). Moreover, following retirement, family members across generations usually interact more and become closer (Friedmann & Orbach, 1974). In general, Atchley (1977) concludes that "most people continue to do in retirement the same kinds of things they did when they were working."

Summary

Many of the adjustments to aging lie within the contexts of family, social relations, and work, such as the death of a spouse, retirement, and accommodating to a reduced income. Most research seems to indicate that the quality of married life in old age is good. The two factors that characterize older married couples are the focus away from the children and retirement from work, leaving the husband and wife with more time for each other.

Poverty and illness place a strain on older married life. However, people benefit in old age from being married. They live longer, and experience less mental illness and loneliness where there is a spouse to buffer them from the stresses of old age.

Sexual activity is still important to old people. They enjoy sex but are often frustrated by the lack of an available and willing partner. Older adults focus less on sexual performance and more on sexual pleasure.

Most older people are neither abandoned nor isolated. They live independently of their children, and often, nearby. Old people rely on their children in times of illness, but give advice, emotional support, and services as well as receive them. Relationships with grandchildren vary considerably from one older adult to another—some are intensely involved and others are remote. Research suggests that older adults and their adolescent and young-adult grandchildren mutually influence one another, but only in certain areas.

Widowhood represents the single greatest loss suffered by the aging individual. Of women over 75 years of age, 70 percent are widowed. Most prefer to maintain their independence despite the problem of loneliness. Other problems are decreased income and decrease in social status.

Only about 5 percent of older people live in nursing homes. About 20 percent, however, will be institutionalized at one time or another in some form of extended-care facility. Generally, people enter an institution when their physical condition is increasingly deteriorating and there is no other care available. Mortality rates following institutionalization are high.

Alternatives to institutionalization for elderly include retirement or age-segregated residential communities, in-home care, and living in apartments attached or close to the home of adult children. Most elderly people value their independence but want to live in a secure setting.

Aging takes place in a social context. The impact of declining social roles and social relations on the elderly is determined by whether the withdrawal is voluntary or not. Besides marital relations, and relations with children and grandchildren, the older adult is influenced by interactions with friends and siblings—both of which offer emotional support in times of crisis.

People retire for various reasons. Those who choose to retire usually do so because of adequate financial resources, good pension plans, desire to spend more time with family, or dislike of the job. Involuntary retirement is associated with mandatory retirement policies and poor health.

Retirement is a process involving a number of phases. As individuals go through the phases, they develop, implement, reevaluate, and enact their plans for the retirement years. Some adults find retirement exciting and satisfying; others are disenchanted and depressed.

Leisure activities in old age are mostly confined to inside-the-home sedentary activities. Some people volunteer their time to community groups.

People who are actively involved in leisure pursuits are usually more satisfied with their postretirement life.

Attitudes toward retirement depend on the person's control over retirement, financial situation, job satisfaction, personality, degree of preretirement planning, and satisfaction with the activities he or she is engaging in during retirement. Contrary to popular belief, retirement, though often stressful, is unrelated to declining health and psychological problems.

Further Readings

Atchley, R. C. *The social forces in later life* (3rd ed.). Belmont, CA: Wadsworth, 1980.
This introductory work examines social factors that influence the elderly, and presents social stereotypes and the effects they have on older adults.

Atchley, R. C. *The sociology of retirement.* Cambridge, MA: Schenkman, 1976.
This brief book covers the various stages of retirement that one normally experiences in old age. The author focuses on the different reaction patterns of individuals at each of the stages.

Butler, R. N., and Lewis, M. I. *Sex after sixty.* New York: Harper & Row, 1976.
In this wise and compelling book, Butler and Lewis discuss the value of sex, romance, and love among the elderly. Impotence, emotional problems with sex, patterns of lovemaking, and remarriage are treated openly and honestly.

Hess, B. B., and Markson, E. W. *Aging and old age.* New York: Macmillan, 1980.
This introductory text provides a highly readable account of aging from a sociological perspective. Some of the topics relevant to our discussion include family life, politics, economics, and institutionalization in old age.

Jones, R. *The other generation: The new power of older people.* Englewood Cliffs, NJ: Prentice-Hall, 1977.
A popular account of the impact on U.S. society of the rising number of elderly. The social problems encountered by the elderly such as ageism, retirement, and economic decline are discussed.

Tisdale, S. *Harvest Moon: Portrait of a nursing home.* New York: Henry Holt, 1987.
This gentle guide to life in a nursing home was written by a staff nurse about a nonprofit West Coast institution. The author describes the difficulties and details of daily routine, financial complexities, and medical dilemmas in a nursing home.

Observational Activities

16.1 *Adjustments to Retirement*

Between the ages of 60 and 70, most people retire from the jobs they have held for many years. Retirement is a major life event for men and some women in their late-adult years. The ease and impact of leaving their jobs and adjusting to a new life at home vary from person to person. The degree of personal satisfaction during retirement also is influenced by many factors, including the extent of preretirement planning, financial resources, hobbies and meaningful activities available, and the degree of involvement with people.

In order to fully understand the impact of retirement on people, choose several retired individuals who are willing to be interviewed. Ask them the following questions:

1. How old are you and how long have you been retired? What kind of work did you do before retirement? Do you work part-time now?
2. At what point in your life did you make plans for your retirement? What sort of plans did you make? Were these preretirement plans helpful to you?
3. What do you like about your life now that you are retired? Are there things you do now that you couldn't do before retirement? Give examples.
4. What changes have you had to make in your life as a result of retirement? What has been the most difficult part of retirement for you?
5. If you are married, how has being at home affected your relationship with your spouse? Are you more involved in household tasks? Give examples.

After you have interviewed these people, summarize your findings and compare them to the findings of your classmates. What factors seem to be most important in the degree of satisfaction associated with retirement? How does retirement affect family relations? On the basis of your interview, what suggestions do you have on how a person might better prepare for retirement?

16.2   Community Services for the Aged

In response to the increase in the number of people who live until late adulthood, many communities have developed programs and services to meet the special needs of the elderly. These services are provided through private and public agencies on the local, county, state, and federal level. Through these programs, the elderly can get assistance with medical, legal, and financial problems. They can locate more appropriate housing, find a special exercise program for senior citizens and even arrange to have meals delivered to their homes if they have difficulty preparing them.

The purpose of this activity is for you to become more familiar with the community resources available to the elderly in your local area. A good place to begin to locate these resources is the front pages of your local telephone directory. Often, there is a listing of local and state agencies that provide services to the aged. Another place to contact for information about local services available to the elderly is the Social Security Administration office in your area. Your local priest, minister, or rabbi may also be able to direct you to a variety of private agencies that offer services to the aged.

1. Make a list of the various services and programs you have located to assist senior citizens; include the phone number and address if available.
2. Describe the specific services provided by each agency or group.
3. If possible, make a visit to one of these agencies to learn more about the special needs of the elderly.

What did you gain for yourself in doing this activity? Share your findings with your classmates.

EIGHT

The Final Stage of Life

Death is a natural consequence of living. Birth marks the beginning of a lifespan and death marks the end. Although everyone dies at some point, there is considerable variation among people about when and how they die. Death also affects the living. As older family members and friends die, we are reminded that life is not eternal, that we have a limited lifespan. When someone dies prematurely in childhood or early adulthood, we are more acutely aware of the ways in which our death may be affected by our behavior, our biology, or the sociocultural environment in which we live. We want to know "why did this person die so soon in life?" perhaps hoping to learn something that may help us forestall our own death. In this last chapter, we examine from a lifespan perspective some of the issues concerning death and the process of dying. We also consider the meaning of death and the effects of the loss of a loved one.

17

The Final Stage of Life: Death, Dying, and Bereavement

At 40 years of age, Bob was not prepared to accept his doctor's diagnosis that he had a rare and fatal form of bone cancer. His first reaction was one of disbelief, followed by anger and rage that such a fate should befall him in the prime of his life. There were so many things he still wanted to do.

As a bachelor professor teaching college courses in Humanistic and Eastern Psychology, he wanted to travel to China and the Near East to further his understanding of the Eastern way of life and thought. He mourned the fact that he had not married and had no children of his own. An important part of his life had been his friends and his students. Now, all that had changed with the diagnosis of cancer. He often experienced a sense of isolation when he was among people who were uncomfortable when he talked about his disease or the negative prognosis it carried.

As he came to accept his fate, he also decided to make the most of his time remaining by doing what he most enjoyed: teaching and traveling. By carefully scheduling his classes, he was able to teach, while at the same time undergoing chemotherapy to slow down the effects of his cancer. Two-and-a-half years after the initial diagnosis, Bob took a six-month sabbatical to travel to China, Nepal, and Bali. His medical tests indicated that his physical condition was deteriorating, but his spirit and enthusiasm for life sustained him.

Returning to his beloved classroom, Bob was full of enthusiasm and new ideas and insights to pass on to his students. Over the next nine months, his blood tests continued to indicate the progressive deteriorating effects of the cancer. Within a week after commencement ceremonies, Bob was hospitalized.

He was well aware of what would lie ahead. As each new treatment effort failed, he moved closer to accepting the reality of his imminent death. He took several steps to ensure that he would die as he lived, among friends and with grace and dignity.

He asked one friend to be with him and to hold him as he died; another friend was asked to be with his body when it was cremated. He asked another friend to look after his aging aunt to whom he was particularly close. Over the last three months of his life, despite the pain and discomfort of his disease, he set his life in order so that he was ready to die. He contacted old friends with whom he had lost touch; he buried old grudges and made amends with his brother. He wrote out explicit instructions for the settling of his estate, which consisted of treasured mementos from his travels. As he thought about his many friends and selected something special to leave each of them, he was filled with a deep sense of gratitude for the friendships he had made in his life. Among the four pages of instructions he left in his will was the following request: "Throw a party for all the folks . . . a happy party—very happy. If I'm ready—as I am—then you can all celebrate that fact."

By early October, he had set his life in order, said his goodbyes, and made plans for his funeral. He was ready to die. On October 7, surrounded by a few close friends and in the arms of the person he had asked to hold him, Bob died peacefully. He died as he had lived, with full involvement and dignity. The next summer, as he had requested, a joyful party celebrating his life was thrown by and for his many friends. Bob's legacy was a vivid and memorable example of how a person could live his life fully until death.

Until fairly recently, a discussion of death would be considered by many people to be in poor taste or disrespectful. Psychologists, sociologists, and physicians were equally quiet on the subject. Little research had been done on dying people and not much was known about the effects on the individual or the consequences to the friends and relatives who survived someone's death. Today we know more about this last period in the lifespan, although much more remains to be learned about the significance and consequences of this last stage of development. In this chapter, we will examine the significance of death in the lifespan of a person. We begin with a discussion of the concept of death and then examine what is known about the process of dying. Finally, we will consider the process of bereavement and discuss the ways in which people adjust to loss in their lives.

Death: The Final Stage of Life

Significance of Death

The distinction between life and death is sometimes not so easily drawn. The legal and medical definitions of death were at one time based on the moment at which the heart stopped beating and breathing stopped. Today, as a result of modern medical advances, the issue of determining death is more complex. Pacemakers and cardiac resuscitation can restore and regulate heartbeat; respirators can maintain cardiovascular and respiratory functions. These processes may even be continued long after the brain has been irreversibly damaged and is no longer functional. Many physicians have advocated a new medical and legal definition of death based on the death of the brain. Even this does not present a completely clear-cut alternative, however, since the principal measure of brain activity, the electroencephalogram (EEG), is not in itself sufficiently accurate. People whose EEGs have remained flat for several hours have been known to recover. In conjunction with other factors, however, such as a lack of spontaneous respiration and muscle movement, and the passage of time, a flat EEG could become the guideline in determining death.

Causes of Death across the Lifespan

While most of us associate death with old age, death can occur at any point of life. Death can occur at the moment of birth or even before birth in the case of stillborn births or miscarriages. Most infants who die do so within a few days of life. Most die as a result of birth defects or because their bodies have not developed sufficiently to sustain life outside the uterus. One of the

In the earlier stages of the lifespan, death is more likely to occur as a result of accident.

reasons that the average life expectancy has increased in recent years is that medical technology has improved to the point where newborns who might have died at birth now survive longer. Sudden infant death syndrome (SIDS) is a rather tragic killer of young infants. Death of an infant from SIDS is especially difficult for parents because the infant who appears to be healthy dies so suddenly.

During childhood, death is more likely to occur from accidents or illness. The leading causes of accidental death for children include automobile accidents, poisoning, drowning, death by fire, and falls from heights. Major illnesses that cause childhood death are cancer, heart disease, and birth defects. During adolescence, death is more likely to occur violently through homicide, suicide, or motor-vehicle accidents, which are often alcohol related. While not the leading cause of death, the AIDS virus is more likely to affect younger people, especially those who are sexually active.

In early and middle adulthood, people die from motor-vehicle accidents, combat, homicide, and disease, primarily heart disease and cancer. By late adulthood, most people die of disease or, in some cases, suicide.

Whenever death occurs before the person has reached middle adulthood it is considered to be premature. Often, as in the case of accidents, suicides, and homicides, the death is sudden and unexpected.

The significance of death to a person is influenced by his or her level of development, and death will be responded to in different ways at various times in the lifespan.

Pause for Thought

Part of the distress associated with death is a sense of lost time. People who die prematurely do not have as much time to live as those who live to old age. But no one really knows for sure how long they will live. How do people determine ahead of time how long they think they will live? What impact might their estimates have on the way they live their lives?

Developmental Conceptions of Death

The impact of death varies with the person's age and ability to understand the meaning of this final process. Chronological age influences the person's expectations of death as well as experience with death and bereavement. A mature, adultlike understanding of the concept of death includes a recognition of three aspects: (1) death is irreversible and final; (2) death represents the end of life, and (3) all living things die (Speece & Brent, 1984). As children develop, they gradually acquire a mature understanding of the meaning of death.

Infancy

Most of the research on children's understanding of death suggests that children under the age of two years do not comprehend death. Death represents a loss of a person in one's life. To the infant functioning at Piaget's sensorimotor level of cognitive development, an object or person that is gone is also forgotten. Until the development of object permanence at about 18 months, the infant has no idea of permanent loss or death. The young infant cannot conceive of the thing "not being," because it does not conceive of the "being" in the first place.

The child, however, soon begins to develop the necessary concepts. The early game of peek-a-boo is one in which the infant experiments with being and not being: "He replays in safe circumstances the alternate terror and delight, confirming his sense of self in risking and regaining complete consciousness" (Maurer, 1961). Psychologists see in this nearly universal activity the first steps toward appreciation of life-and-death states. It is the infant's aliveness that is joyfully restored by the contact with the eyes of his partner.

As the infant achieves object permanence, it begins to react to the disappearance of objects. However, the infant's perceptions continue to differ from those of adults in important ways, for example, by being less able to differentiate itself from the object (or person). Thus, when Mother leaves the room, the infant in a sense disappears too.

By the time children are 10 months or so, they have formed an attachment, usually to their parents. Now they can experience loss and separation, and consequently suffer separation anxiety. It is important to note that the child does not for many years attain an understanding of time as it is measured objectively by adults. A short separation will be experienced as a total loss, especially since the child wavers in its ability to understand that Mother is "somewhere else." Separation, then, remains a powerful analogy to death for the infant. What seems to counteract it, at this stage and throughout early childhood, is the reassurance of continuity (Pattison, 1977). The child experiences separations and reunions, waking and sleeping. Such death as the young child understands is identified with separation and sleep; it is temporary.

With respect to the infant's actual experiences with bereavement, we know little. Of course, some infants do lose a parent or primary caretaker during the first year of life. From the infant's perspective, it makes little difference whether this loss is permanent separation, temporary separation (as in foster placement), or death.

The loss or prolonged separation from the primary caretaker during infancy may affect the child's vitality and health. Studies of institutionalized children deprived of warm, loving, social contact report a higher mortality rate for such infants (Spitz, 1945).

Early Childhood

During the period from two to six years of age, children are able to form concepts; they are functioning at Piaget's level of preoperational thought. The preschool-age child discovers that some things are called "alive" and he begins to form concepts of life and death. At first, preschoolers ascribe the quality of life to a great many things that are not, by adult criteria, alive. A ball, the moon, clouds, and so on are alive because they are moving or changing. By the same logic, these objects can die. For example, in one study, four- and five-year-olds made statements such as "A ball is living when it goes up in the air and when the ball goes down it dies dead." . . . "The moon dies when it's blown up, but it comes back to life the next day" (Safier, 1964). At this stage of development, life and death are temporary, reversible states.

Death of people continues to be viewed as a state similar to sleep. Death may also be equated with disappearance. Because of feeling so small relative

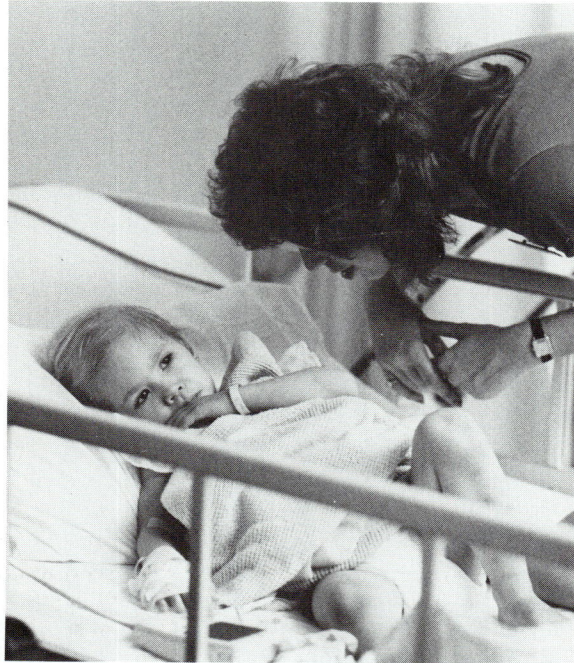

Even though this child is less than five years old, she may be aware of the seriousness of her illness. Some young children may even comprehend that they are going to die.

to other objects in the environment, the child will occasionally express fears of being sucked away or absorbed by some larger process. Children at this stage are often afraid of disappearing down the bathtub drain, or being sucked up in the vacuum cleaner.

Although not understanding the significance of death, the young child may react with seriousness to dead objects and death-related phenomena. He or she is likely to be interested in burial, and "what happens to the body." Even when quite young, the child may draw back from a dead animal with awe, saying "No more," or "All gone" (Kastenbaum, 1977). This action is like that of some higher birds and mammals who react dramatically to the death or dying of a member of their own species (Lorenz, 1966), even though (we assume) they have no real understanding of death.

In a classic study, Marie Nagy (1948) asked 378 children between the ages of three and 10 years to tell whatever came to their minds on the subject of death. She also asked them the following questions:

1. What is death?
2. Why do people die?
3. How do you recognize when someone is dead?

On the basis of the children's responses, she identified three stages of development of death-related concepts for children between three and 10 years of age. (See Table 17.1.) The preschooler sees death as reversible, a state in which dead people are simply living differently. For example, death was seen as a long sleep or a journey. Children believe that when people die they still possess the same life processes and consciousness as the living. Thus, a toddler may wonder whether a deceased relative thinks about her. Young

Table 17.1 ▪▪▪▪▪▪

Nagy's Stages of Development in Children's Conception of Death

Stage 1: Children under five years of age did not see death as irreversible but rather as a living on under changed circumstances. Eighty-six percent of the three-year-olds, 50% of the four-year-olds, and 33% of the five-year-olds were at this level of conceptual development.

Stage 2: Children between the ages of five and nine years personified death. Fourteen percent of the three-year-olds, 50% of the four-year-olds, and 67% of the five-year-olds were found to be at this level of conceptual development.

Stage 3: Children beyond nine years of age saw death as final and lawful. No child five years of age or younger was classified at this conceptual level.

children view death as a separation and ask where the dead person went. If a person goes away from the child, as when a relatives moves, the child may consider the relative to be dead. Furthermore, children at this age believe that dead people can come back to life or be reborn in another place.

Unfortunately, some children are forced to confront their own death in early childhood. It was once assumed that young children did not understand their predicament (and that this was probably a blessing). Research suggests, however, that the seriously ill child of four or five years may be aware of impending death. Anxiety takes the form of separation anxiety, loneliness, and fears of abandonment (Spinetta, 1974). They will be greatly comforted by assurances that their mother will stay with them and "never leave." Though young children normally do not realize that death is irreversible, many terminally ill children do. One researcher found that the majority of children came to understand not only that they were dying, but that this was a final and irreversible process (Bluebond-Langner, 1977).

Middle Childhood

By age six or so, the child has formed a more realistic concept about what it means to be alive and what it means to be dead. Somewhere between six and nine years of age, the child perceives that it is not movement itself that defines life, but rather spontaneous, or internally generated movement (Safier, 1964). Thus, for example, a car is no longer seen as alive (or dead) simply because it moves; it is not alive because it does not move itself. A worm, however, is alive (or dead) because it moves on its own accord.

At this stage, death, too, is perceived more nearly in adult terms. Death is no longer reversible. However, it is not yet seen as inevitable (Safier, 1964). Death is still something that one can outwit. In particular, death is a person one can outwit—something akin to a bogeyman or a black angel (Nagy, 1948).

Personification of death characterizes children's conception of death during Nagy's second stage. By making death humanlike, children are better able to understand it because death is now tangible, visible, and concrete. They are able to reduce their concerns about their own death by eluding or tricking death. Children at this age recognize that old or sick people are more likely to die because they cannot run or move fast enough to avoid the "death man." Young children do not die because they are more active and because they are small enough to hide from death (Kastenbaum, 1967).

By the time children are nine years of age they understand that death is final and irreversible.

At about age six, children also believe in their own personal mortality (Reilly, Hasazi, & Bond, 1983). Even though they recognize that they will die, most view their own death as a long way off. This awareness is related to the child's ability to use concrete operational thinking, particularly conservation. Children who have not achieved conservation typically do not believe in their own mortality. Death-related experiences (e.g., death of a parent, sibling, or close relation) also facilitate children's comprehension of their own mortality.

Children who must face terminal illness in middle childhood appear to understand their predicament (Simeonsson, Buckley, & Monson, 1979). They are aware of hospital procedures and are able to acquire information on drugs and their side-effects. Whereas the young child is concerned mostly with separation, the school-aged child fears physical injury and mutilation (Natterson & Knudson, 1960). Older children, like adults, tend to fear loss of normal bodily functions. Terminally ill children do not always verbalize their death fears (one reason why they were believed not to understand their condition). However, it is now recognized that school-aged children with a serious illness understand that they may die and need to be able to express their concerns and deal with their fears and anxiety (Furman, 1974).

At about nine or 10 years of age, children enter the third stage in Nagy's theory, in which they achieve a firm, adult concept of death (although it may not operate at all times). Death and life are seen as internal processes that belong to people, animals, and plants. The child becomes concerned about the goodness and badness of people who died, about how they felt about dying, and so forth. These concerns are related to the child's growing capacity for self-knowledge. It is also during this age period that children often experience the death of a grandparent or distant relative, thus making death more apparent to them. Discussing these deaths enables children to cope with the loss of closer relatives in later years.

Pause for Thought
Children who are concrete operational thinkers understand ideas and events better when they have a tangible, concrete way of conceptualizing them. Death can be viewed abstractly by adults but not readily by children. Why, then, are children often not included in the funeral and burial rituals of relatives who have died?

Adolescence and Youth

The adolescent, in most cases, can operate at the formal operational level and has attained a mature notion of time and physical changes, such as his or her own maturity and parents' aging. Perhaps for the first time faced with the question of a personal future and of setting long-range academic and vocational goals, the adolescent reacts to the many factors combining to produce an awareness, and even an interest, in death.

Adolescents understand death more or less the way adults do. However, their age makes their actual relationship to death different from that of older people. Adolescents and young adults are in an expansive period of life when death is uncommon. Although mortality risk increases appreciably between 15 and 25, in the United States it remains relatively low (Kastenbaum, 1977). Not surprisingly, death for young people remains a distant and abstract event—something that happens to the elderly. When young people think of death in relation to themselves or their peers, it tends to be closely bound up with ideas of fate or circumstances of violence. Death is not seen as a natural debilitating process: it is a cruel blow. (In fact, violent death, through accident or suicide, is the most common form of death in this period.)

Ordinarily, adolescents do not have a sense of longevity; the length of life is not so important as the quality. The attitude is "Who cares how long one lives so long as one lives and dies the real me?" (Pattison, 1977). The young person typically values a bright flame over a slow fire, and may be attracted to the idea of "burning himself out" through passion or creativity, in the manner of the stereotypic Romantic. Adolescents may be idealistic, willing to risk their lives for a cause. At this stage in life, there is a need to have the maximum possible number of sense experiences (Keniston, 1970), and many have observed the young person's need to flirt with death—to "speed," literally with drugs or motor engines, toward that possibility. Risk-taking behavior among the young (particularly men) appears to be common in many cultures. Not all young people are dominated by these attitudes toward life and death, but these attitudes are so often expressed by young people as to be characteristic of this age group.

Reckless behavior and risk taking reflect adolescents' belief in their own immortality.

Early Adulthood

It does not appear that any special orientation toward death is formed in early adulthood. According to most writers, the onset of significant death anxiety in adulthood occurs when the individual becomes aware of his or her own aging, usually in middle age. However, early adulthood does present the individual with events and decisions that affect the relationship to death. If it is accurate to summarize the life cycle by saying that we are born, marry, reproduce, and die, we might note that two intermediate steps are usually taken in early adulthood. Marriage, for example, asks young adults to pledge themselves until "death do us part"; to consider sharing the rest of their lifespan with (or alternately without) one person. Young adults must also consider the prospects for immortality through children. The question of whether or not to have children usually arises during this period. For some people—perhaps for all people at some level—this is experienced as a question of whether or not to extend oneself into the future (that includes our own death). Actually, becoming a parent affects our relationship to death. During pregnancy, many prospective parents worry about the possibility that the baby or mother might die during childbirth. Upon birth, various rituals, such as naming for the dead, remind the new parents of their place in the chain of generations. Indeed, thoughts of death and birth give rise to each other in many contexts, at many points in the lifespan (Kastenbaum, 1975).

A symbolic death at this stage of life is childlessness due to infertility or misfortune. Spontaneous abortion ("miscarriage"), particularly in the later stages of pregnancy, may also be experienced as a form of personal death for which the body "mourns." Sometimes similar reactions follow induced abortions—even women and men who have no antiabortion convictions may suffer feelings of bereavement.

Human Development in Practice

Death Education

While there is no easy way to eliminate the discomfort a person experiences with the death of a friend or relative or in anticipation of one's own death, information about and awareness of death within a healthy context can help reduce the stress associated with death.

Since Elizabeth Kübler-Ross began her seminars on death and dying in the late 1960s, there has been a growing interest in educating people young and old about death and the dying process. *Death education*, as this field of interest is called, does not morbidly dwell on death, but rather focuses on it as a natural consequence of life, a part of the life–death cycle found throughout nature. Being able to talk openly about death and sharing their feelings help people put their fears and anxieties about death into perspective. Death education can offer the learner practical information about how to comfort and help dying and bereaved people as well as decrease the stress associated with a personal loss. Another goal of death education is to help children and adults confront and deal with their feelings about death.

Throughout the United States—on college campuses, in medical schools, in elementary and secondary schools, and through adult-education programs—an estimated 20,000 death-education courses have been initiated since the late 1960s (Durlak, 1978–1979). The specific content of the death-education programs varies according to age and life experiences of the audience. For elementary and middle-school children, the topics generally included are life cycles of plants and animals, death and separation, grief and its expression, and funeral and burial customs (Gibson, Roberts, & Buttery, 1982). Discussion of these topics may be stimulated by a current death experience of a child, as, for example, when a national figure or a pet dies. Children's books that include the theme of death or loss may also be useful in stimulating discussion.

In high-school or college-level death-education programs, similar topics are discussed but in more detail and with greater depth. The student is capable of considering the more abstract and philosophical aspects of death such as the right

The death of a pet or other animal may be the first encounter with death for many school-age children.

to die, suicide, human destiny, and accepting one's own death.

Death education occurs not only in the schools but in the home as well. Death educators advocate that parents first examine their own feelings and ideas about death. With a clearer understanding of their own reactions, parents are in a better position to give assurance to their children when the subject of death arises. The best time to talk about death to children is when it is part of their experience. By answering a child's questions about death directly and honestly, the parent can help the child form a realistic concept of death. Telling a child that Grandma is sleeping when she is actually dead *adds* to the child's misconceptions about what happens when someone dies. As with sex, the child's interest and curiosity about death is a useful springboard for educating the child about the topic. By not hiding the fact of death from children, and by openly discussing various aspects of death, parents and educators can help children learn how to cope with death in their lives.

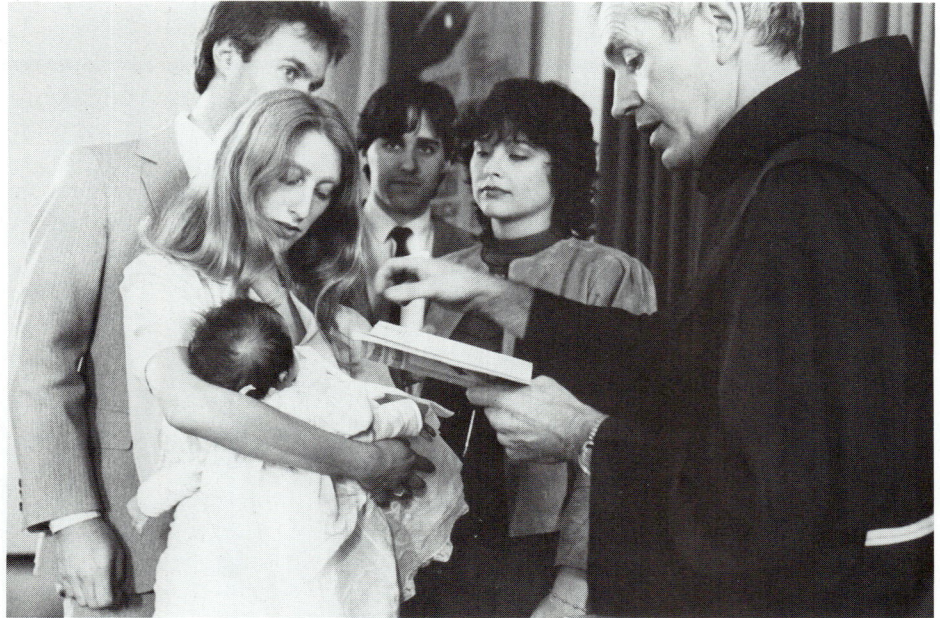

Naming a baby after a recently deceased relative calls attention to the life/death cycle.

Middle Adulthood

In middle adulthood, a person typically becomes sensitive to the aging of the body and the limits of his or her lifetime. Time perspective changes. The person begins to think in terms of time left to live, instead of time from birth (Neugarten, 1967). Concern with death appears to peak. In one study, the greatest fear of death was expressed by those in the 45-to-54 age group (Bengston, Cuellar, & Ragan, 1977). It may even be that the painful creative crisis of midlife is largely a result of the individual's confrontation with death (Jaques, 1964).

Exactly *when* a person becomes more conscious of life's finitude probably depends on personal experience. Among the precipitating events described by Sheehy (1976) are the death or serious illness of a contemporary; the death of a parent; or an unanticipated brush with death for those in their thirties or early forties. In some cases the awareness grows slowly. In others it comes like a blow, inducing panic, crying spells, or temporary breakdown. In later middle age, death fears seem to be resolved—perhaps more openly acknowledged, perhaps more fully integrated into the person's understanding of life.

The person who becomes terminally ill in middle age tends to experience death as a disruption of relationships and responsibilities toward others. Whereas the young person may rage against the loss of experiences or ambitions, the middle-aged person is acutely concerned about the emotional survival of his or her family and important others. Unlike the elderly, the person has had little time to make appropriate practical or emotional adjustments.

Late Adulthood

The older person stands in a special relationship to death. Even when physically and mentally vigorous, older people realize in old age that health is precarious and the amount of time left to them relatively short. Death becomes a realistic concern. A variety of activities may be undertaken in preparation. These range from such practical matters as deciding upon distribution of property, to internal processes, such as life review.

It is often assumed that the elderly, as a group, live in special fear of death. However, research suggests that this is not so. A classic study by Munnichs (1966) found that the most common orientations in individuals 70 and older were acceptance or acquiescence. Another study suggests that elderly subjects were less preoccupied with death fears than middle-aged subjects (Bengston et al., 1977). It appears that excessive fear or denial of death in older people represents a general failure to come to terms with their own limitations, which, in turn, may be an indication of psychological immaturity (Munnichs, 1966). Fear of death is also associated with lack of ego integrity (Erikson, 1963). On the other hand, a low level of death fear is associated with people's having experienced "purpose in life" (Durlak, 1973), and having achieved integrity.

Several reasons why older adults are less fearful of death (Kalish, 1981) include the fact that elderly people are more frequently reminded of death as same-age peers and even younger persons die. They are much more likely to have lost a spouse, sibling, or parents through death. They attend more funerals, visit more gravesites, and read the obituaries more frequently. In addition, elderly people experience the decline in their own bodies, thus compelling them to think and talk more about their own death. By confronting the realities of death, people are better able to cope with their fears of death.

The Terminal Stage

Older people also share an expectancy about their own death. Although the expected lifespan varies from individual to individual and is dependent on numerous life experiences and situations, older people generally have an idea about how long they will live. By accepting the reality of a life expectancy of 75 years or so, older people who live longer than that consider themselves to be fortunate. As people approach their seventies, they do so with the realization that their lives are coming to a completion. The diagnosis of a terminal illness or the sudden loss of mental or physical capabilities may trigger the person's awareness of the **terminal stage of life,** the time when people are aware of their impending death.

Terminal Stage of Life The time when a person becomes aware of his or her impending death.

Entering the terminal period also influences intellectual performance. Riegel and Riegel (1972) conducted a 10-year study of old people in Germany. The subjects were 190 males and 190 females who ranged in age from 55 to 75. The investigators administered a battery of tests to the subjects, including an intelligence test, a word-association test, verbal achievement tests, and a number of attitude and interest tests.

Terminal Drop A decline in intellectual performance that frequently occurs within five years before death.

Findings showed that subjects whose performance on intelligence tests was below average were closer to death than their more successful peers—indicating **terminal drop.** Riegel and Riegel analyzed the subjects' scores by going backward in age, starting with the time of death. They concluded that the decline in performance on intelligence tests was due to a sudden drop in ability that occurred within five years before the death of the subjects. Similar results have been found in longitudinal studies (Palmore & Cleveland, 1976; Siegler, McCarty, & Logue, 1982; Suedfeld & Piedrahita, 1984).

Elderly people are frequently reminded of death as they attend the funerals of spouses and friends.

For many older people, the terminal stage is characterized by loneliness. Spouses and same-age peers die, one by one, leaving the survivor feeling bereft and depressed. Often an older person does not have time to get over the passing of a loved one before another dies. This is particularly true for women, who tend to outlive men. When death takes one's spouse, the survivor is left to manage as well as possible and, often, to think about his or her own impending death. As Kastenbaum (1977) notes, "Somewhat apart from the prospect of one's own death, then, the falling away of significant others is a powerful influence upon the thoughts, feelings, and actions of old people."

Pause for Thought

Although medical and behavioral science is a long way off from developing a way to determine the onset of death in old age, what changes might occur within a family and culture, if people were to know five years in advance when they were to die? What ethical issues might arise should such a means of fixing one's lifespan be developed?

The Dying Process

In some belief systems and personal ideologies, death is not a process, but a moment of extinction. In others it is likened to a journey, with the scenery specified; or a long, restful wait before a final judgment. Some cultures have seen death as the end of all experience, and others as the beginning of salvation.

We do not know today, any more than we knew yesterday, what death is, or what developmental significance it has for the individual. However, we do have the advantages of recent research in the medical, biological, and psychological sciences. These sciences, in studying life, have necessarily granted insights into the dying that is part of life.

One seemingly new viewpoint is that dying is not a distinct moment (or even an indistinct moment) in which the person changes from alive to dead. In part because of technological advances, we have come to see that death is usually a slower process.

The *psychological* process of dying begins when a person learns that he or she has a fatal physical condition. The *physiological* process of dying, the failure of the body to function, may have begun earlier. People who die suddenly as a result of accidents or heart attacks may never know that they are dying. Most people, however, are aware of it (Kalish, 1981) and adjust lives as a result. For some people, the physician's diagnosis and prognosis of a terminal disease signals the onset of dying. In the past, physicians and family members withheld the truth about a fatal condition from the dying person on the assumption that it was kinder not to tell the person. Today, however, most physicians recognize that patients need to be told the truth about their condition so that they can make the necessary financial, psychological, and emotional adjustments (Schulz, 1978).

Kübler-Ross's Stages of Dying

The most well-known research and writings on people's psychological reactions to dying are the result of work done by Elizabeth Kübler-Ross (1969). Kübler-Ross interviewed and observed over 200 terminally ill patients. On the basis of her observations, she outlined a five-stage process of dying:

1. Denial and isolation
2. Anger
3. Bargaining
4. Depression
5. Acceptance

Stage 1: Denial and Isolation

The first reaction people usually have upon learning that they have a terminal condition is shock and numbness, followed by denial. They react to their serious illness (or loss) by saying, "No, it cannot be me." They may assert that the doctors are incompetent, the diagnosis mistaken. In extreme cases, the person may refuse treatment and persist in going about business as usual. Most patients who use *denial* extensively throughout their illness are people who have become accustomed to coping with difficult life situations in this way. Indeed, the denial habit may contribute to the seriousness of the condition, as, for example, when a person refuses to seek medical attention at the onset of the illness. Ordinarily, the person relies on denial at the beginning of the illness and, perhaps at other moments, when facing reality becomes temporarily impossible. For most patients, denial soon becomes difficult and other reactions begin to intrude.

Stage 2: Anger

The cry of the dying person at this stage is "Why me?" The person facing the great loss feels *anger*, at fate, at God, at the powers that be, at every person who, unknowing, enters the person's world. There is resentment of the healthy, particularly those who must be the person's caretakers. Angry at others for perceiving them as dying or as good as dead, they are likely to alienate others, for no one can give an answer to the anger at their shortened lifespans and lost chances.

Stage 3: Bargaining

At this stage, the person changes his or her attitude and attempts to *bargain* with fate. For example, the individual who is dying may ask God for a certain amount of time in return for good behavior, stoicism, or cooperation in treatment. A man may promise a change of ways, even a dedication of his life to the church. A woman may announce herself ready to settle for a less threatening form of the same illness and begin to bargain with the doctor over her diagnosis. For example, if she submits gracefully to some procedure, might she be rewarded by not progressing to the next stage? This stage is relatively short in duration.

Stage 4: Depression

"When the terminally ill patient can no longer deny his illness, when he is forced to undergo more surgery or hospitalization, when he begins to have more symptoms or becomes weaker and thinner, he cannot smile it off anymore. His numbness or stoicism, his anger and rage will soon be replaced with a sense of great loss" (Kübler-Ross, 1969, p. 85). At this stage, the person enters a deep *depression* over the losses he or she is incurring, for example, loss of body tissue, job, or life savings. The dying person also is depressed about the loss that is to come. In the process of losing everything and everybody he or she loves, the person must be allowed to express his or her sorrow.

Stage 5: Acceptance

Finally, the dying person *accepts* death. The struggle is over and the person experiences "a final rest before the long journey." At this point, the person is tired and weak. He sleeps often, and, in some cases, the approach of death feels appropriate or peaceful. People may limit the number of people they will see, and recall their interest from matters of the world. Silence and constancy are appreciated, and they seem to detach themselves so as to make death easier. (See Box, When a Child Dies.)

Evaluating Kübler-Ross's Theory

There is no doubt that Elizabeth Kübler-Ross has made an important contribution to people's awareness and understanding of the process of dying. Her theory and writing have provided a forum for professionals and dying people and their families to talk about death and understand their reactions.

People who care for the dying are more sensitized to the emotional needs of their patients and can more easily help friends and relatives through the difficult time as a result of being more knowledgeable about reactions to death.

However, her stages of dying have been criticized on several points. For one, the stages are not universal. Not all terminal patients progress through the stages Kübler-Ross describes. For example, a woman may die in the denial stage because she refuses to consider any other alternative or because the course of her illness is too quick to grant her the necessary time to move beyond denial. Pattison (1977) found that anger and denial are prominent throughout the dying process not just at the earlier stages. For some people, depression is the dominant mood (Schultz, 1978). Some people never accept their own death. Thus, people do not always experience the stages of dying in the order Kübler-Ross suggested, and some people never experience a sequence at all.

Another criticism of the theory is that often people experience anger at recurring times in the process of dying. Kübler-Ross herself acknowledged that patients do not limit their responses to any one stage; a depressed patient may have recurring bursts of anger. She notes, too, that all patients in all stages persist in feeling *hope.* Even the most accepting, most realistic patients leave the possibility open for some cure.

The nature of a person's reactions to dying depends on many factors such as the nature and suddenness of their dying, the age at which dying occurs, their personality, and cultural expectations surrounding death. The degree of loss associated with death often will affect the intensity and duration of depression people experience. A person who is still relatively young at the time of death may experience a greater sense of loss than an older person who has lived a full life and has already lost a spouse. People who have strong religious beliefs about life after death or heaven may find it easier to accept death than those who do not have these beliefs. Some diseases such as cancer that are associated with remissions may foster more denial than diseases such as AIDS that have no cure or remission.

One final concern about Kübler-Ross's stages is that they may be over-interpreted by health-care professionals or relatives and applied in a lock step fashion to the dying person. Angry reactions from dying people may reflect a justified objection to their care or situation and should not be dismissed as simply their reaction to the process of dying.

Dying Trajectories: An Alternative View of Dying

An approach to understanding the process of dying that differs from Kübler-Ross's stage theory has been suggested by several researchers (Glaser & Strauss, 1965; Pattison, 1977). Glaser and Strauss (1965) maintain that as people approach death, their physical condition deteriorates until the moment of actual death. By plotting the person's nearness to death on a vertical axis, and time along the horizontal axis, a *dying trajectory* can be determined (Glaser & Strauss, 1968). Not only are medical workers aware of dying trajectories, but so, too, are the people who are dying. Family and friends may also anticipate the death and make plans according to a predicted time frame for dying.

People who have accepted the reality of their own death may decide on a particular time after which they will die. For example, terminally ill patients have been known to stay alive in anticipation of a particular event (e.g., birth of a grandchild, arrival of a friend), only to die shortly after the event. Sometimes people live longer than they have anticipated, an occurrence resulting in frustration and weariness.

Some physicians express concern that the patient's acceptance of a physician's stated dying trajectory or the patient's own fantasized trajectory will

Norman Cousins believes that laughter helped him overcome a fatal disease. As part of his "treatment" he watched hours of the Marx Brothers' films.

be a self-fulfilling prophecy. Telling a woman, for example, who is not yet experiencing the disabling symptoms of cancer that she has four to eight months to live may actually trigger her psychological and physical decline. Yet despite this concern, most physicians recognize the importance of communicating directly and honestly with terminally ill patients, even young patients (Carey & Posavac, 1978–1979; Townes & Wold, 1979).

Pause for Thought

Some people faced with a prognosis of imminent death display a "will to live" that seems to contradict their medical condition. Norman Cousins (1976) fought off a fatal degenerative nerve disease by making himself laugh for long periods. Explain these events in light of dying trajectories.

Issues in the Care of the Dying

Hospice Care

One significant outcome of Kübler-Ross's work with dying people is the awareness among physicians and health professionals of the need of the dying person to be in contact with caring people who will listen as they share their concerns about and prepare for their own death. Unfortunately, many people are often frightened or repelled by contact with dying people. Today, some terminally ill patients are often isolated in sterile hospital wards and left to face the end alone, without the loving companionship of friends and family. Even adequate protection against pain is sometimes denied (Smyser, 1982). Modern hospitals, geared to aggressive life-prolonging therapies, are simply not good places to die. A quiet revolution is occurring, however, toward more humane treatment of the dying—the **hospice** movement.

Hospice A homelike setting specializing in the care of the dying.

The modern hospice concept is the work of Britain's Dr. Cicely Saunders. The idea was born out of her friendship with a Polish refugee who was dying of cancer in the noisy confusion of a busy London hospital. In 1967, Saunders founded St. Christopher's Hospice in southeast London for those afflicted with terminal cancer. St. Christopher's provides a pain-free, emotionally secure environment for the dying. The atmosphere is warm and friendly, with plenty of sunlight and fresh flowers. Patients may bring in cherished possessions; one woman brought her antique collection. Visiting hours extend from 8 A.M. to 8 P.M., and family and friends help with patients' care—holding hands, giving sponge baths, bringing special foods from home. Sophisticated use of analgesics keeps patients relatively pain free. Saunders pioneered the use of the "Brompton mix," containing such ingredients as heroin, cocaine, and gin, for the alleviation of terminal cancer pain. If feasible, patients may go home to die.

Currently, in the United States, there are more than 1200 operational hospice programs (Osterweis, Solomon, & Green, 1984). Unfortunately, the availability of these programs is limited. Most medical insurance plans do not provide coverage for hospice care, thus limiting access to these programs to the more affluent. However, recent changes in the Social Security program now permit limited federal reimbursement for hospice care under Medicare.

Since most of the hospice programs depend on the help of a family member or friend to provide for the daily care of the dying person, not everyone may be able to participate.

Hospice care is just one way in which the needs of the dying person are met. The right to die with dignity or in the presence of loved ones can be accomplished in other ways. With help and direction from trained medical and health practitioners, some people are able to die at home. Not only is home care for the dying psychologically more acceptable to people because they are not isolated from their families, it is also considerably less costly than hospital or nursing-home care.

Euthanasia

On the night of April 14, 1975, Karen Ann Quinlan lapsed into a coma. Blood tests showed that she had been drinking as well as taking the tranquilizers Librium and Valium. Fourteen months later 21-year-old Karen was still in a coma, kept alive by means of a respirator. Doctors held little or no hope for her recovery; her EEG readings indicated massive brain damage. Karen's parents, with the support of doctors and their parish priest, asked a New Jersey court for permission to have the doctors discontinue the use of the respirator to allow their daughter to die. A United States Circuit Court upheld their decision, and the life-supportive measures were stopped (Greeley, 1977).

Euthanasia The act of inducing an easy and painless death for merciful reasons.

Drawing a great deal of attention from television and newspapers, the case of Karen Ann Quinlan once again put the question of **euthanasia** before the public. Derived from the Greek (*eu*—good; *thanatos*—death), the word *euthanasia* can be used to mean "an easy and painless death," as well as "the inducing of an easy and painless death for reasons assumed to be merciful." It is the second definition of euthanasia that has generated controversy.

Because euthanasia is affected by so many factors—legal, moral, and historical—it is necessary to clarify the different meanings of the term. Many people differentiate between euthanasia by omission and euthanasia by commission, that is, ceasing the use of "extraordinary measures" in keeping a patient alive—as in the Quinlan case—vs. actively ending someone's life. For instance, the Catholic church, which is against euthanasia in general, makes an exception in cases where extraordinary measures are used to prolong life. As early as 1957, Pope Pius XII told a group of anesthesiologists that neither they nor their patients were morally obligated to use such modern devices as respirators to maintain life when there was no hope for recovery (Russell, 1977).

Living Will A document by means of which people can express their wishes for the disposition of their own lives should they lose mental competence while dying.

People wishing to ensure their right to decide how and when they will die may guarantee that no extraordinary medical attempts be made to prolong their lives by making out a living will. **Living wills** are documents by means of which people can express their wishes for the disposition of their own lives, should they later lose mental competence. The Euthanasia Education Council provides a form that people may use to formalize their wishes (see Figure 17.1). Even though a living will does not have a legal force in most states, the spirit of the document is usually honored. The difficulty is in deciding when there is "no reasonable expectation of recovery"; this decision usually is made by the attending physician.

The Living Will

To My Family, My Physician, My Lawyer and All Others Whom It May Concern

Death is as much a reality as birth, growth, maturity and old age—it is the one certainty of life. If the time comes when I can no longer take part in decisions for my own future, let this statement stand as an expression of my wishes and directions, while I am still of sound mind.

If at such a time the situation should arise in which there is no reasonable expectation of my recovery from extreme physical or mental disability, I direct that I be allowed to die and not be kept alive by medications, artificial means or "heroic measures." I do, however, ask that medication be mercifully administered to me to alleviate suffering even though this may shorten my remaining life.

This statement is made after careful consideration and is in accordance with my strong convictions and beliefs. I want the wishes and directions here expressed carried out to the extent permitted by law. Insofar as they are not legally enforceable, I hope that those to whom this Will is addressed will regard themselves as morally bound by these provisions.

Signed _____

Date _____

Witness _____

Witness _____

Copies of this request have been given to _____

_____

_____

Source: Reprinted with the permission of Concern for Dying, 250 West 57th Street, New York, New York 10017.

Figure 17-1 The Living Will.

Opponents feel that once voluntary euthanasia is approved, it could easily open the door to involuntary euthanasia. Furthermore, someone has to decide if people who request euthanasia are competent to choose their fate, or are only temporarily depressed or affected by medication. Who would make this decision? Also, since our knowledge of medicine is far from perfect, it is difficult to decide when a given situation is hopeless. Many patients whose cases were deemed "hopeless" by physicians have recovered—often enough to lead perfectly normal lives. Lastly, some opponents hold that all life is a gift from God and only God can make the decision. The question remains: If individuals without hope for recovery wish their suffering and pain to end, don't they have that right? Or is all life precious at any cost?

Pause for Thought

For some people, donating their vital and usable organs after death is one way to ease their sense of loss over their dying. Aging people donate their corneas, younger people their hearts, kidneys, or lungs. While there is controversy surrounding the issue of people's right to choose when they wish to die, there is little about people's decisions to donate parts of their bodies. What seems to be the underlying issue separating the right to end one's life and the right to decide the fate of one's body?

Bereavement

Bereavement the state or condition of loss of a loved one, usually through death.

When someone close to us dies, we experience the loss of that person in our lives. **Bereavement** refers to the state or condition of loss; the most significant loss occurs through death. However, bereavement may involve other losses such as the loss of a love relationship through divorce or desertion; the loss of a child to adoption, abortion, or miscarriage; or the loss of a home through fire, financial upset, or relocation.

Funeral and bereavement practices vary from culture to culture. While the emotional experience of grief is the same, the way in which feelings are expressed depends upon the culture.

Grief A person's emotional response to bereavement or the loss of a significant person.

Mourning The culturally prescribed, overt expression of grief and bereavement.

Grief is the emotional response to bereavement or the loss of a significant person. While it is true that the grieving process involves the experiencing of painful emotions and psychological suffering, it is also the case that bereaved people who do not grieve generally do not recover from their loss. A study on bereavement reports that during the process of bereavement, the survivors are at increased risk of dying prematurely themselves or suffering physical and mental illness (Osterweis, Solomon, & Green, 1984).

Mourning refers to the culturally prescribed, overt expression of grief and bereavement. While it is generally believed that the core experience of grief is much the same throughout the world, the way in which these feelings are *expressed* is specific to the particular culture or subculture (Averill, 1968; Kastenbaum, 1977). Funeral practices, the length of bereavement, the person's manner of dress and behavior are all dictated by the person's ethnic, cultural, or religious heritage.

The Experience of Grief

Although people's reactions to the death or loss of a significant person vary depending on their age and personal circumstances, studies of bereaved people suggest certain commonalities in their grief reactions. In 1944, Erich Lindemann described the grief reactions of over 100 bereaved people who had lost family members in the tragic Coconut Grove restaurant fire in Boston. According to Lindemann (1944), the common symptoms experienced by these bereaved included the following:

1. Sensations of somatic distress occurring in waves lasting from 20 minutes to an hour at a time;
2. A feeling of tightness in the throat;
3. Choking, with a shortness of breath;
4. A need for sighing;
5. An empty feeling in the abdomen;
6. Lack of muscular power;
7. An intensive subjective distress described as pain or tension.

Insomnia, loss of appetite, absentmindedness, difficulty in concentration or memory, and obsessive rituals were also commonly observed characteristics. Research also indicates that bereavement can produce changes in respiratory, nervous, and hormonal systems and even alter the heart and immune systems (Osterweis, Solomon, & Green, 1984).

Lindemann also noted a phenomenon he labeled *anticipatory grief,* in which people grieve in expectation of a person's death. When a relative or friend is very old or is afflicted with a terminal illness, people may begin the process of experiencing their loss of that person before the actual death. In most cases, anticipatory grief helps people cope more effectively with death and results in a better emotional adjustment during the bereavement period. Rando (1983) studied the experiences and adaptations of 54 parents for a period of three years following the death of a child from cancer. She found that parents who had experienced anticipatory grief were better prepared for the child's death and showed less abnormal grief following the death. By grieving in advance of the child's death, these parents were able to participate more in the care of the sick child; this action helped them resolve their emotional reactions of guilt after the child died. (See Box, When a Child Dies.)

Human Development in Practice

When a Child Dies

Perhaps the most sorrowful and anguishing event is the death of a child. The loss is especially felt by those who have taken care of the dying child, namely, the parents and sometimes the hospital nurses and staff. For parents, the time before and after a child's death is a difficult period. They must not only provide for the normal needs of their child—the need to feel safe, to be loved, and the basic needs for comfort, they must also prepare themselves and their child for medical treatments and the eventual death. The experiences of parents who have had their children die in hospitals has shown that the way in which nurses and staff members respond to the parents and the dying child can affect the length and severity of the grieving process. Sensitive, honest, and direct care in dealing with the parents before a child dies can help them to resume a normal life after the death (Compassionate Friends, 1986).

The traumas associated with the death of a child have been compiled by Compassionate Friends, a nationwide support group for bereaved parents. When a child is dying, parents still want to care for their child. Hospital personnel can help by letting parents participate as much as possible in the daily care of their child. Because dying children often are also patients receiving treatment or being monitored by machines, nurses may need to explain equipment and procedures to parents beforehand so that parents (and perhaps siblings) are not frightened by the medical aspects. Parents usually need and want to be with the child and can be a comfort to a frightened child.

Sometimes nurses may be reluctant to tell parents what they know about the child's condition. Rather than try to protect them from the unpleasant news, nurses should tell parents the truth, including acknowledging what they don't know. If parents ask for the information, they are usually ready to hear it. Sometimes, parents may not be ready to accept bad news and cope with it by denying it. In this case, nurses and physicians need to patiently reaffirm the unpleasant reality, remembering that ultimately the parents will come to accept the situation.

Parents need to know it is okay and healthy to express their feelings. Sometimes nurses are able to help by showing their own feelings of sadness at the anticipated loss of a child. Using the child's name, being available for reassurance and information, and making it possible for parents to be with their child at the moment of death can help ease the parents' bereavement.

Nurses can further help bereaved parents by making them aware of the grieving process, telling them what normal emotional reactions they can expect. For example, the birth or death anniversaries of the child are likely to be stressful times for parents and they need to allow themselves time to take care of their emotional needs. It is important for nurses to also recognize their own grieving process, especially if they had become attached to the dying child. By allowing time to express feelings of sadness and frustration and finding a safe outlet for these feelings, nurses become more sensitive to the needs of others in bereavement. Parents and family members may want to turn to a support group for help in absorbing the loss of a child. The telephone number for the national support group, Compassionate Friends is (312) 990–0010.

Stages of Grief

Several researchers have pointed out that people's reactions to death change over time (Averill, 1968; Bowlby, 1980; Parkes, 1972). Grief is not a fixed state, but rather a process involving a succession of emotional reactions, each one affecting the next. By investigating the course of bereavement in widows, Colin Parkes has identified four stages of grief. In the first stage, the bereaved experience *numbness* and little feeling, usually directly after learning of the

The sudden and unexpected death of John F. Kennedy was difficult for many Americans to accept. As his father's casket passes, young John F. Kennedy, Jr., salutes in tribute.

death. The bereaved person may be in a state of shock or disbelief, may experience confusion, and may be dazed throughout the funeral and burial services. This stage usually is short in duration and is followed by the second stage, which is characterized by *yearning* and *protest*. The bereaved may pine for the lost relative with crying and weeping, or they may be angry and irritable as they protest the fact that a loved one has been taken from them. Accompanying these reactions may be a sense of anxiety and fear of making it on their own, a need to relive old memories of the deceased and a general restlessness and tension.

After a period of time, which varies from one person to the next, but usually occurs within the first year after the death, people enter the third stage of grief, characterized by *disorganization* and *depression*. People may become apathetic, have no interest in their future. Their appetite may diminish, they may report physical symptoms, or they may be overwrought with guilt. Higher mortality rates for the elderly are commonly reported during this period of bereavement (Rowland, 1979). During this stage, bereaved people need the sympathetic support of friends and relatives, or they may need to talk with a professional in order to resolve their emotional reactions to their loss and get on with their lives.

The most important barrier to *recovery*, the final stage of grief, which involves a healthy resolution to one's loss, is the ability to express such emotions as anger, anxiety, or guilt. The length of time people spend in the disorganization and depression stage of grief is dependent in part on whether the bereaved are able to talk about and emotionally express their feelings about the death to a concerned listener. Spinetta and his colleagues (Spinetta, Swarner, & Sheposh, 1981) reported that the patients who effectively coped with the death of a child from cancer had a support person to whom they could turn for help during their child's illness. Recovery from the loss of a loved one usually begins within two years of the death and is highlighted by the bereaved person's decision to get on with his or her life and to renew social contacts or initiate new activities. The person is able to establish new relationships and goals instead of hanging on to painful memories of the dead. Memories of the deceased loved one are more likely to be pleasant ones, and the person experiences a sense of commitment to his or her own life and a deeper appreciation of human relationships.

Pause for Thought

People who have a terminal illness experience numerous losses in their lives before their death. They lose contact with loved ones and friends, their jobs, and their normal activities; they lose control over their lives when they enter hospitals or nursing homes. How might the grief associated with these and other losses interact with and influence their reactions to dying?

Death in the Family

According to a study by Osterweis, Solomon, and Green (1984), over 8 million Americans experience the death of a close family member each year. With the loss of a spouse, parent, sibling, or child comes a period of stress and bereavement for all members of the family. When a family member dies, the survivors must cope with their emotional reactions to the loss of a companion or loved one, and also take over new roles and duties left vacant by the deceased person. For the new widow, the death of her husband may mean assuming the job of maintaining the family car or dealing with lawyers. For the widower, the daily tasks of meal preparation or laundry may prove to be initially unsettling. Adult children may step in to fill the roles of the deceased. For example, when Bill died, Mary relied on her son to make decisions about the care of the family car. For some people, losing a parent may also signal a transition to adulthood when they realize that they can no longer rely on their parents for guidance or advice.

As we shall learn in the next section, young children and adolescents have special needs during the bereavement period. They may be struggling with concerns about who will take care of them. Often, the surviving parents may not be able to deal effectively with the immediate emotional needs of their children because they are overwhelmed by their own needs. This is a time when other less emotionally stressed family members can be of assistance. The impact of the death of a loved one on the family depends on two factors: the emotional and social resources of the family and the degree of preparation for the death.

During bereavement, people suffer distress and need the support, reassurance, and assistance of others to help them face the permanent loss of a loved one. The most important sources of support come when people are encouraged to express their feelings about their loss to understanding and accepting people.

The family that encourages open communication among its members, that allows members to share their feelings, and that has regard for each other is a rich resource to draw upon during a time of crisis or death. During the few days immediately following a death, family members help each other by talking about the life and death of the loved one, by sharing the responsibility for the funeral and burial arrangements, and by combining their personal resources in the form of friends and in-laws. When John's father died, he was touched and reassured by the offers of help and encouragement his family received from his wife's family. Later on, in the weeks and months following the death, family members can help each other deal with the sense of loneliness and depression by maintaining contact with each other.

Some families, however, are less fortunate. They may be cut off from their relatives as a result of living in different parts of the country or state and are, therefore, limited in the amount of mutual support they can provide to each other. Other families may not have close or friendly relationships among family members. Families that characteristically don't listen to each other, that deny the expression of emotions, or that do not talk openly to each other suffer from the impoverishment of emotional resources during bereavement. Often, family members are angry with one another without realizing why. Unable to communicate freely about their feelings at having lost a loved one, some people may experience their distress in the form of mental or physical symptoms that require professional treatment (Osterweis, Solomon, & Green, 1984). As a result of diminished emotional resources, many families turn to trained professionals for help, support, and information. Physicians, psychologists, clinical nurse specialists, social workers, and the clergy can provide help to families in their time of need.

The amount of preparation family members have had to ready themselves emotionally, socially, and economically for a loved one's death is a critical factor in the bereavement process. The most difficult death for most people to cope with is the untimely or unexpected death. The death of a child is an untimely and premature one that often is traumatic. Tragic or calamitous deaths by accident, suicide, or murder result in an intensification of the grief experience. Very often families experiencing unexpected deaths may require the help of extended family members, friends, or even professionals during the bereavement period.

In the case of an expected death, family members are aware of the impending death of a loved one either as a result of old age or terminal illness. As a result, the family often anticipates the changes in their lives as a result of the loss of the particular family member. Family roles are often reorganized to accommodate the care of the dying family member, and, as a result, the survivors are better prepared to deal with the changes in daily and household routines following the death. Even with an expected death, however, family members still require the loving support from each other to ease the distress of their loss and to reestablish meaningful lives.

Bereavement in Children and Adolescents

The effect of bereavement upon young children has been studied mostly in retrospect—that is, through adult case studies. Numerous researchers have found that the loss of a parent during early childhood is associated with a greater-than-average tendency to suffer depression or commit suicide in adulthood (Bowlby, 1980). Early loss may even be associated with physical conditions, such as cardiac disease (Lynch, 1977). Even before the age of two, bereavement appears to be experienced, and in some sense remembered. Physicians, psychiatrists, and psychologists occasionally encounter depressed patients who in midlife appear not to have completed the grieving process of early childhood.

When a parent or close relative dies, children frequently ask themselves three questions: Did I cause this to happen? Will it happen to me? Who will take care of me now (or if something happens to my parents)? (Osterweis, Solomon, & Green, 1984). These questions may or may not be directly expressed, but children do need to have the answers to them provided by a caring and trusted relative or friend. As irrational as these concerns may seem to adults, to children these concerns are a reflection of their need for safety and care due to their immaturity.

> The five-year-old who loses his mother is both blaming himself for her disappearance and being angry at her for having deserted him and for no longer gratifying his needs. The dead person turns into something the child loves and wants very much, but also hates with equal intensity for this severe deprivation. (Kübler-Ross, 1969, p. 4)

Unlike the adult, who may also experience ambivalent feelings, children lack the cognitive ability and life experiences that would enable them to reject their anger on rational grounds. Adults can help children during bereavement by providing information and support to them as they mourn their loss. The death of a pet can sometimes be a useful learning experience in which children learn to accept their emotional reactions to death and loss. Rather than quickly replacing the dead animal, parents need to respect the child's need to understand and feel the significance of the pet's death.

Bereavement in adolescence and youth usually means the death of a parent. Young people grieve and understand death as adults. Still, bereavement at this point in the lifespan has its special significance. The person who is at the brink of establishing an adult identity may feel cheated out of knowing the parent as one adult to another. Deprived of the opportunity to share first achievements with the parent, the adolescent cannot enjoy the parent's recognition of new adult status. If the young person loses a parent before he or she has truly established identity, development may be more directly affected. For example, a daughter's normal process of differentiating herself from her mother may become a source of guilt when separation is imposed by death. Concern for the remaining parent may cause the young adult to rework her relationship with her family of origin—taking more adult responsibilities or slipping unhappily into childlike dependency. As we noted in Chapter 10, adopted adolescents and youth experience a special case of identity loss. Having come to understand the implications of being relinquished, many adopted teenagers and young adults experience a sense of incompleteness and bewilderment about who they really are. Searching for their origins, as an increasing number of adoptees are doing, represents an attempt to resolve their loss and to establish a firmer sense of self.

Young people who lose a close friend, sibling, spouse, or lover are under "a heavy burden that comes out of season" (Shneidman, 1977). Even for the 20-year-old widower, physically in the prime of life, bereavement amounts to a life-threatening condition. Temporarily at least, the loss of a spouse or lover may be so traumatic as to make any idea of future intimacy painful and impossible.

Most people who die in adolescence or youth are victims of accidents or suicide attempts (Fuchs, 1974). The relatively few who suffer through serious diseases are necessarily aware of the great unfairness and untimeliness of death. The result is rage at lost opportunities and a fundamental uncertainty about what to do with the time remaining. Unlike the mature adult, the young person has not had to confront the hints of mortality that come with aging. A dying young man, for example, may be overwhelmed with disbelief at the seriousness of his condition. His situation is made more difficult by the inability of others to communicate with him and to accept the illness.

Summary

The determination of death—the final stage of the life cycle—has become more complex as a result of advances in medical technology. Death can occur at any point in the lifespan, although the nature of death varies with age. Accidents and birth defects are more common in early childhood; in adolescence and young adulthood death occurs more frequently by violent means. During middle adulthood, people die from disease and accidents. The impact of death varies with a person's age and cognitive ability. By the age of 10 months, infants have formed an attachment and are capable of experiencing loss and separation. Separation and sleep are both identified with deathlike experiences during infancy. In cases where separation is not temporary, such as the death of a parent, the child may preserve a feeling of anxiety into later life.

Preschoolers define all things that move as "alive." Death is seen as reversible and similar to sleep. By age six, death is no longer seen as reversible, but it is not yet seen as inevitable. Death is personified and children believe they can outwit or escape it. At nine or 10 years, the child has an adult concept of death. Life and death are seen as internal processes that belong to all living things. Terminally ill children appear to understand their predicament.

Although adolescents appear to have an adult understanding of death, they view it as distant or remote from their experience. In young adulthood, marriage and deciding on parenthood help to define a person's relationship with death.

Concern with death peaks during middle adulthood as people become aware of their own physical limitations and experience the death of their parents. In late adulthood, death becomes a realistic concern as the elderly accept death as a natural part of living.

As people approach the limits of life expectancy, they enter the terminal stage of life and begin to anticipate dying. Some people experience a terminal drop in cognitive and intellectual skills just before the onset of dying. Others experience isolation and loneliness as peers and spouses die.

Death is viewed as a process. Most people are aware that they are dying and make social and psychological adjustments as a result. Dying people need to be informed of their physical condition so that they can deal with their own death. Kübler-Ross describes five stages of adjustment that dying people experience: denial, anger, bargaining, depression, and acceptance. Other researchers suggest that people have their own dying trajectory that influences the speed with which they die. Criticisms have been expressed concerning the universality of Kübler-Ross's stages.

Hospice care has been developed to help people through the dying process with dignity and with the presence of a concerned person. Some people make out living wills to ensure that no extraordinary medical efforts are used to prolong their lives.

Bereavement is a condition of loss during which people grieve and mourn the death of a loved one. Different cultural traditions influence mourning practices, while the experience of grief is believed to be universal.

Grief is an emotional reaction to loss and can be experienced in advance of an actual loss or death. People go through stages in their grief experience: numbness, yearning and protest, disorganization and depression, and recovery.

Children who experience the loss of a parent or close relative may experience emotional reactions similar to those of adults, but they do not possess the cognitive ability or life experiences to help them understand their emotional reactions.

Further Readings

Grollman, E. (Ed.). *Explaining death to children*. Boston: Bacon, 1967.
This collection of readings concerning the many facets of death and dying as they relate to children is a useful reference for parents and educators. It includes a comprehensive bibliography of books about death to use with children.

Gunther, J. *Death be not proud: A memoir.* New York: Harper & Row, 1949.
John Gunther's son, Johnny, died at age 17 of a brain tumor. This book is a chronicle of the years and months before his death, showing in a personal way the effect that a brain tumor and the knowledge of death had on a vital, intelligent boy and his family.

Lonetto, R. *Children's conceptions of death.* New York: Springer, 1980.
This book presents a detailed discussion of the changes in a child's conception of death from ages three to five, six to eight, and nine to 12. The author includes examples of children's drawings and discusses children's fears associated with death.

Kübler-Ross, E. *On death and dying.* New York: Macmillan, 1969.
In this book, a classic in the field of death education, Kübler-Ross describes her early work with dying patients and the emotional experiences dying people have. Her five stages of dying are described with supporting case studies.

Kübler-Ross, E., and Warshaw, M. *To live until we say goodbye.* Englewood Cliffs, NJ: Prentice-Hall, 1978.
In this moving book, the various stages of dying are depicted through numerous photographs and narrative descriptions of four people. Excellent and sensitively photographed scenes capture the people's struggle and final acceptance of death. Hospice care and dying at home are also illustrated with personal glimpses.

Stoddard, S. *The hospice movement: A better way of caring for the dying.* Briarcliff Manor, NY: Stein and Day, 1978.
Hospices are places that have been set up to help terminally ill patients face death without pain or fear. The techniques used involve medication and an environment of support for the dying person. Stoddard provides a favorable overview of the hospice movement through case studies and the author's personal experience in St. Christopher's Hospice in London.

Observational Activities

17.1 *Death Awareness and Children's Literature*

One of the goals of death education is to provide children a greater and more realistic awareness of death. Since most children are fortunate and young enough to have not yet experienced the death of a close relative or friend, knowledge about death often occurs through stories told in children's books. In order for you to gain a better understanding of the ways children learn about death through literature, visit the children's section of your local or college library and examine the available books that deal with the topic of death. You may want to discuss this activity with the head or children's librarian, who can direct you to a more specific selection of books for children. Or, you may locate some of the books listed below.

1. Select at least three books, read them, and then summarize the specific information that a child would gain about death or dying by reading each book.
2. Compare and contrast the three books. How well did the authors address the emotional aspects of death? At what age level was each of the books directed?
3. What did *you* learn about death, dying, or bereavement from reading these books? What did you gain for yourself in doing this activity?

Some suggestions for children's books dealing with death include:

Abbott, S. *Old dog.* New York: Coward, McCann & Geoghegan, 1972.

Bleau, R. *Grandma didn't wave back.* New York: Franklin Watts, 1970.

Brown, M. W. *The dead bird.* Glenview, IL: Scott, Foresman, 1965.

Cleaver, V. *Grover.* Philadelphia: Lippincott, 1970.

Cleaver, V., and Cleaver, B. *Where the lilies bloom.* Philadelphia: Lippincott, 1969.

Cohen, B. *Thank you, Jackie Robinson.* New York: Lothrop, 1974.

dePaola, T. *Nana upstairs and Nana downstairs.* New York: Putnam, 1973.

Fassler, J. *My grandpa died today.* New York: Behavioral Publications, 1971.

Koch, R. *Goodbye, Grandpa.* Minneapolis: Augsburg, 1975.

Miles, M. *Annie and the Old One.* Boston: Little, Brown, 1971.

Smith, D.B. *A taste of blackberries.* New York: Crowell, 1973.

Viorst, J. *The tenth good thing about Barney.* New York: Atheneum, 1971.

Wagner, J. *J. T.* New York: Dell, 1969.

White, E. B. *Charlotte's web.* New York: Harper & Row, 1952.

Whitehead, R. *The mother tree.* New York: Seabury, 1971.

Zolotow, C. *My grandson Lew.* New York: Harper & Row, 1974.

17.2 *Bereavement in Families*

Different cultures and religions have different rituals associated with death and bereavement. Funeral customs and memorial services are ritualized and prescribed to help ease the suffering of losing a loved one. The purpose of this exercise is for you to become more familiar with the customs and traditions associated with dying. To complete this activity, you will need to talk with priests, ministers, rabbis, and other religious or spiritual representatives in your community. You may have representatives of religious groups available to you on the college campus who would be able to provide you with information about funeral services and customs in different cultural groups. Often, hospitals have personnel on site to offer bereaved families help in making funeral arrangements. When you have located a sample of different ethnic and religious people, structure your discussions with them around the following questions.

1. What happens when a member of your community (congregation, synagogue, etc.) dies?
2. What rituals or traditions exist concerning death?
3. How long do people mourn the death of a loved one?
4. Are there specific social gatherings that typically occur when a person dies?
5. Are there specific times or days when funerals can or cannot occur?

You will probably generate more questions as you discuss these issues. When you have completed your interviews, summarize the responses and draw comparisons among the different religious and ethnic groups. Compare the bereavement practices with those from your own family or culture. Share what you have learned with other classmates.

Glossary

AB̄ Error The infant's inability to locate an object that has been visibly put in a different hiding place.

Accommodation The process of changing existing schemes as a result of new experiences.

Activity Theory The belief of some researchers that maintaining an earlier level of activity results in successful aging; the opposite of disengagement theory.

Adolescent Egocentrism The tendency of adolescents to believe that other people are as preoccupied with their behavior, ideas, and appearance as they themselves are.

Adolescent Growth Spurt The period of acceleration of growth that occurs in early adolescence.

Ageism Any situation in which people are prejudicial on the basis of age.

Allele A single gene in a pair of genes, or alleles.

Alzheimer's Disease A form of dementia characterized by the slow deterioration of the brain.

Amniocentesis A prenatal test of the amniotic fluid to determine the presence of defects in the unborn child.

Amniotic Sac A membrane filled with a salty fluid that surrounds the embryo.

Animism The tendency of young children to attribute animate characteristics to inanimate objects.

Anorexia Nervosa A psychological disorder chiefly affecting adolescent girls; characterized by voluntary restriction of food intake, resulting in chronic undernutrition and, occasionally, death.

Anoxia Lack of oxygen to the baby at birth.

Apnea A condition in which regular breathing suddenly stops.

Artificial Insemination A procedure for conception in which a specimen of sperm is injected into the woman's uterus.

Assimilation The process by which a person, using existing knowledge, takes in new information about the environment.

Attachment An affectionate emotional bond between parent (or caregiver) and child.

Attention Deficit Disorder (ADD) See Hyperactivity.

Autosomes The 22 pairs of chromosomes—other than the sex chromosomes—within a cell, that are responsible for the various physical changes throughout development.

Behaviorism A school of thought that maintains that what we call development is only what we learn.

Bereavement The state or condition of loss of a loved one, usually through death.

Bidirectional View The view of development in which parents and child are seen as having an active influence on each other.

Binocular Fixation The ability to simultaneously use both eyes to focus on an object.

Birth Order A person's rank in a family relative to the number of siblings based on the order of birth.

Birthing Rooms Homelike settings in hospitals designed for both labor and delivery.

Blastocyst The hollow sphere of cells that forms within a week after fertilization.

Body Concept One's perceptions and feelings about the physical aspects of oneself.

Body Esteem A person's evaluation of his or her body.

Breech Birth   A delivery in which the baby appears in a bottom-first position.

Bulimia   An eating disorder characterized by episodic, uncontrollable binges in eating, sometimes followed by self-induced vomiting.

Centration   Piaget's term for the process of focusing attention on one detail or aspect of an object or event.

Cephalocaudal   Pertaining to the pattern of growth that proceeds in a head-to-toe direction.

Cervix   The opening to the uterus.

Cesarean Section   A surgical procedure used to deliver a baby by making an opening in the uterus.

Chorionic Villus Test   A prenatal diagnostic test in which fetal cell samples are obtained from the villi protruding from the chorion surrounding the fetus.

Chromosomes   Rodlike structures containing long segments of genes.

Classical Conditioning   A form of learning in which a person learns to make a response (CR) to a conditioned stimulus (CS) that he or she has come to associate with an unconditioned stimulus (UCS) that *automatically* evokes the response (UCR).

Classification   The ability to sort objects into categories.

Climacteric   Changes in the reproductive and sexual organs that usually accompany middle age.

Clique   A small informal group of people with similar social class, education, age, and interests and who spend a lot of time together.

Cognition   The process by which a person acquires and organizes information and knowledge.

Cognitive Development   The changes in a variety of intellectual operations such as representational thought, logical reasoning, problem solving, planning, memory, and abstract thought.

Cognitive Style   A person's particular pattern of thought and the behavior used to respond to cognitive tasks.

Cohort   A group of individuals born during the same time period who presumably were exposed to similar experiences during the socialization process.

Colostrum   A thin, watery, yellowish substance secreted from a new mother's breasts.

Competence   As opposed to performance, what an individual knows or is capable of doing under ideal conditions.

Concrete Operations   Within Piaget's theory, the third stage of cognitive development; characterized by the development of logical thought and the ability to manipulate symbols.

Conduct Disorders   A form of psychopathology in which the individual persistently violates the basic rights of others and/or the norms of society.

Conservation   The recognition that characteristics of objects remain the same so long as nothing is added or subtracted.

Constructivism   A philosophical position that suggests that our knowledge of the world at any given time results from an active process of transforming specific stimuli (and information) in accordance with our current cognitive rules and principles.

Contextual View   The view that development and behavior must be understood in terms of the total setting or context against which it occurs.

Conventional Morality   According to Kohlberg, the second level of moral reasoning; morality is viewed as the desire to preserve harmonious interpersonal relationships and to obey existing formal rules, laws, and standards in a society.

Critical Period   A time of growth and development during which the organism is changing and is most vulnerable to outside influence.

Cross-Sectional Research   A type of research design in which groups of individuals are compared at different ages on some measure at the same point in time.

Crowd   A large, informal group formed by two or three cliques.

Crowning   During the birth process, the moment at which the baby's head first appears at the opening of the vagina.

Crystallized Intelligence   Abilities that depend on the individual's acquisition of information and skills important to his or her culture.

Decentration   According to Piaget, the child's ability to shift his or her attention from one perceptual attribute to another.

Dementia   A type of organic brain syndrome characterized by a variety of behaviors including decreased mental functioning, changes in mood and social skills, and a deterioration in personal habits.

Deoxyribonucleic Acid (DNA)   Found within genes, a protein molecule made up of sugar, phosphate, and bases.

Deprivation Dwarfism   See Psychosocial Dwarfism

Developmental Psychology   The study of the physical, cognitive, personality, social, and emotional changes that occur over the lifespan.

Developmental Task   Prescriptions, obligations, and/or responsibilities that must be accomplished in order for people to feel satisfied with their lives.

Dialectical Process   According to Riegel, a characteristic of mature thought in which the individual recognizes, accepts, and even seeks out intellectual conflict or challenge.

Differentiation   (1) Changes in growth and development from simple, general forms to more complex, specific forms. (2) Within two weeks after fertilization, the process in which growth of the cell becomes more specialized.

Discipline   The strategies used by parents to get children to comply with their rules.

Disengagement Theory   An explanation of the changes in elderly people that lead to reflection, self-exploration, and a reduction in social and psychological investments; gradual disengagement of the person from society is said to lead to a sense of well-being and satisfaction; the opposite of activity theory.

Divided Attention   The ability of the person to process more than one source of information simultaneously.

Dominant Gene   A gene that is expressed when paired with the same or a different gene.

Dyscalcula   The incapacity to mentally manipulate numbers or calculate.

Dysgraphia   The inability to translate ideas or sounds into written words.

Dyslexia   The inability to read as a result of difficulties in combining information from different sensory avenues.

Dyzygotic Twins   Fraternal twins formed when two eggs are fertilized at the same time by two different sperm.

Ectoderm   The outer layer of the embryo from which the skin, sense organs, and nervous system develop.

Ego   In Freud's theory, the part of the personality system that is responsible for realistic adaptation to the world.

Ego Continuity   The sense that one's current self-perceptions are firmly connected to the self-perceptions of the past and to the anticipated self-perceptions of the future.

Ego Identity   According to Erikson, psychosocial achievement during adolescence that results in a stable and unified sense of self.

Ego Integrity vs. Despair   According to Erikson, the primary psychosocial task of late adulthood; ego integrity represents an emotional integration and acceptance of one's life; despair expresses itself as a feeling that one's life has been without real meaning.

Egocentric Speech   Speech that is uttered when the child is alone or not making an attempt to communicate.

Egocentrism   The inability to distinguish easily between one's own perspective and any other perspective.

Embryo Stage   The six weeks following the implantation of the ovum into the uterine wall.

Empty-Nest Syndrome   An emotional pattern, including depression and loss of self-worth, that some middle-aged adults experience after their children leave home.

Encoding   A process in memory in which information is stored using cues which later can be used to retrieve information for recall.

Endoderm   The inner layer of the embryo from which the digestive, respiratory, and glandular systems develop.

Episiotomy   A surgical slit made in the skin around the vaginal opening to ease delivery of the baby.

Euthanasia   The act of inducing an easy and painless death for merciful reasons.

Experimental Techniques   A data-collection strategy in which one set of variables (independent variables) are manipulated and their influence observed on a second set of variables (dependent variables).

Family Life Cycle   Beginning with marriage and ending with the death of the surviving spouse, the changes in growth and development that mark the life of the family.

Fertility Motivation   People's reasons or motives for wanting children.

Fertilization   During conception, the process in which the egg and sperm cell fuse their nuclei to become the first cell of life.

Fetal Alcohol Syndrome (FAS)   A pattern of abnormal growth and development in children of chronic alcoholic mothers.

Fetal Stage   The last stage of prenatal development when all major bodily systems are completed.

Fluid Intelligence   Abilities that enable a person to perceive relationships, draw inferences, conceptualize, abstract information, and comprehend implications.

Fontanelles   Open spaces in a neonate's skull.

Formal Operations   Within Piaget's theory, the fourth, and final, stage of cognitive development that emerges during adolescence or later; characterized by abstract, logical, and hypothetical reasoning.

Functional Disorders   Mental disorders for which there is no apparent physiological or biological basis.

Gender Constancy   The recognition that one's gender does not change.

Gender Identity   The recognition and acceptance of one's own gender.

Gender Role   The pattern of behaviors considered to be appropriate for the male and female within the culture.

Gender Typing   The process by which children acquire the culturally expected behaviors for their gender.

Genealogical Bewilderment   Found among some adopted adolescents, the feelings of incompleteness and disconnectedness from one's genealogical or biological past.

Generational Stations   The various tiers of parent–child relationships that exist within a family.

Generativity   According to Erikson, a critical psychosocial achievement for young and middle-aged adults; a concern for contributing to the maintenance of society through nurturing of others and through one's productions.

Generativity vs. Stagnation   According to Erikson, the primary psychosocial crisis of middle age. Generativity refers to a concern for establishing and guiding the next generation; in the absence of generativity, a feeling of personal impoverishment, boredom, or stagnation occurs.

Genes   Segments of specifically arranged molecules of deoxyribonucleic acid (DNA), which govern cell activity.

Genetic Counseling   A field that provides and interprets medical information about genetics to prospective parents.

Genotype   The actual genetic arrangement contained in the cell; one's genetic makeup.

Genotypic Continuity   The degree of continuity or similarity of a person's underlying personality structure over time.

Germ Cell   The egg or sperm cell.

Gerontology   The study of the aged and the aging process.

Grief   A person's emotional response to bereavement or the loss of a significant person.

Habituation   The process by which a person becomes familiar with a stimulus and decreasingly reacts to it.

Handedness   A person's basic preference for the use of one hand over the other.

Heredity–Environment Issue   The controversy in psychology concerning the relative contribution of heredity or genetics (nature) versus experience or environment (nurture) in the development of the person.

Hierarchic Integration   The process by which the differentiated parts and functions of the person become increasingly organized and coordinated into a complex system during development.

Horizontal Decalage   According to Piaget, the idea that children acquire conservation of different physical characteristics at different ages.

Hospice   A homelike setting specializing in the care of the dying.

Hyperactivity   Unusual energy and restlessness, short attention span, and inability to complete work; also referred to as Attention Deficit Disorder (ADD).

Hypokinetic Disease   A condition in which physical functioning declines due to inactivity.

Id   Within Freud's theory, an innate part of the personality system governing the expression of our most basic biological and emotional urges.

Identification   The process by which a child takes on the beliefs, behaviors, desires, or values of another person as his or her own.

Identity Achiever   According to Marcia, the individual who has confronted various crises in life and who has made firm commitments to values, ideals, life patterns, and so on.

Identity Diffuse   According to Marcia, a type of individual who has avoided personal crisis in areas of identity and who shows no firm commitment to specific values, ideals, etc.

Identity Foreclosure   According to Marcia, an identity status characterized by avoidance of personal crisis by identifying with the values and ideals of parents and other significant figures.

Identity Status   According to Marcia, the specific resolution pattern the person adopts in handling issues of crisis and commitment in areas of identity.

Imaginary Audience   A term used to describe adolescents' belief that they are the focus of others' attention.

Impotence   A man's inability to produce an erection.

Infertility   The inability to conceive or difficulty in conceiving a child.

Information-Processing Theory   A theory of thinking and cognitive development based on the workings of a computer, dealing with how people process information.

Intelligence Quotient   A measure of a person's intelligence or mental capabilities.

Intergenerational Relations   The relations between members of a family from different generations.

Interiority   A tendency of an older person to become increasingly preoccupied with his or her inner life.

Interview Techniques   A data-collection strategy involving a one-to-one interchange, usually verbal, between subject and investigator.

Intimacy   According to Erikson, a critical psychosocial achievement for young adults; a relationship quality characterized by warmth, mutuality of feeling, and deep commitment.

Irreversibility   The child's inability to mentally reverse his or her thinking.

Isolation   According to Erikson, a feeling that one is disconnected from others, empty, and abandoned; this quality often develops in the absence of true, intimate relationships.

Labor   The process of expelling the baby from the uterus.

Lamaze Method   A type of prepared childbirth involving lectures and specific exercises and routines.

Lanugo   Fine hair covering a newborn's body.

Learning Disability   A problem in learning involving one or more of the basic processes that are necessary for understanding and using language and numbers.

Life Event   A personal experience that requires a significant change in the ongoing life pattern (e.g., divorce, death of parents, serious illness, etc.).

Life Review   In old age, the process of organizing memories and reinterpreting actions and decisions that have shaped a person's life.

Lifespan Perspective   The view that development occurs throughout the course of life as a result of a changing interaction of physical, biological, social, historical, cultural, and psychological influences.

Living Will   A document by means of which people can express their wishes for the disposition of their own lives should they lose mental competence while dying.

Longitudinal Research   A research design in which the same group of individuals is repeatedly tested over a period of time.

Marital Companionship   An aspect of marital life characterized by caring, emotional attachment, trust, commitment, and a sharing of interests.

Meiosis   The process of cell division by which germ cells are formed.

Menarche   The first occurrence of menstruation.

Menopause   The cessation of ovulation and menstruation signaling the loss of fertility in women, usually occurring between ages 45 and 55.

Mental Age   The highest age level for which a person passes most of the items on an IQ test.

Mentor Relationship   Exists when an older, more experienced worker guides the training and development of a younger worker.

Mesoderm   The middle layer of the embryo from which the circulatory, excretory, and musculatory systems develop.

Metamemory   The child's conscious or intuitive knowledge and understanding of memory.

Mitosis   Process of cell reproduction in which the nucleic material is duplicated and the cell divides into two separate, identical cells.

Mnemonic Device   A strategy used to recall information from short- or long-term memory.

Molding   The coming together of the bones of the newborn's skull during the birth process.

Monozygotic Twins   Identical twins formed from one egg that divides to form two separate beings.

Moral Behavior   A person's actions based on their moral reasoning.

Moral Reasoning   A person's ideas or judgments about whether some action is right or wrong, based on a set of rules.

Moratorium   According to Marcia, an identity status characterized by heightened personal crisis but no firm commitment with regard to specific values, ideals, life pattern, etc.

Morpheme   The smallest unit of meaningful sound in a given language.

Mourning   The culturally prescribed, overt expression of grief and bereavement.

Multi-Infarct Dementia (MID)   A form of dementia characterized by sporadic decline in cognitive functions caused by a series of strokes or ministrokes.

Mutual Role Taking   The ability to keep both one's own view and that of another in mind simultaneously; usually emerges in adolescence.

Myelin   The protective sheath covering the neurons.

Nature–Nurture Issue   See heredity–environment issue.

Negative Reinforcement   A process whereby the removal of an aversive stimulus results in an increase in behavior.

Neonatal Reflexes   Automatic responses that are present in the early weeks and months of life.

Neonate   The infant during the first few weeks of life.

Object Permanence   The knowledge that objects still exist even when they are not in sight.

Observational Learning   A form of learning in which behavior change occurs as a result of watching others engage in specific behaviors.

Observational Techniques   A data-collection strategy in which the ongoing behavior of individuals is recorded with as little interaction between observer and subjects as possible.

Operant Conditioning   A form of learning in which the learner acquires a behavior as a result of the consequences of the behavior.

Organic Brain Syndromes   Mental disorders caused by organic or biological factors.

Osteoporosis   A condition that results in the thinning of the bones in old age.

Overregulation   The child's tendency to overuse the rules of a language to produce new and nongrammatical combinations of words.

Ovum Stage   The first stage of prenatal development lasting from conception to 10 to 14 days.

Peer Status   The degree to which a child is liked and accepted by his or her peers.

Perceived Age   How old one feels.

Performance   As opposed to competence, the person's actual level of functioning in a situation or on a task.

Phenotype   The expressed and observable characteristics of a person that are the result of genotype.

Phenotypic Continuity   The degree of continuity or similarity in a person's overt behavior or characteristics over time.

Phoneme   The basic unit of sound in a given language.

Physical Fitness The body's degree of optimal functioning measured by muscular strength, heart rate, and lung capacity.

Physiological Neonatal Jaundice A condition frequently found in neonates in which the baby's skin appears yellow.

Placenta A blood-filled structure that supplies the unborn child with nutrients.

Postconventional Morality According to Kohlberg, the third level of moral reasoning; morality is based on appeals to social agreements and democratic principles and to basic principles of ethics and human rights.

Pragmatics The rules for using the language in a social context.

Premenstrual Syndrome Physical and psychological symptoms, including breast tenderness, abdominal swelling, water retention, irritability, anxiety, and depression.

Prenatal Diagnosis The use of medical techniques to provide information about the unborn child.

Preoperational Stage Within Piaget's theory, the second stage of cognitive development that begins around two years of age and ends around six or seven years; characterized by the emergence of representational thinking but the absence of logical reasoning.

Prepared Childbirth Method of childbirth in which both parents are prepared to deal with the various aspects of labor and delivery.

Presbycusis A progressive loss of hearing, especially for tones of high frequency, caused by degenerative changes in the auditory system; the most common auditory problem associated with aging.

Primary Aging Another name for senescence or the degenerative processes accompanying aging.

Primary Memory Memory for information that is still being actively attended to. Also called short-term memory.

Problem Finding According to Arlin, the ability of the person to generate new and relevant questions about the world; linked to postformal levels of reasoning.

Prosocial Behavior Positive actions that are directed toward other people.

Proximodistal Pertaining to the pattern of growth that proceeds from the center to the outer or peripheral parts of the body.

Psychological Androgyny A state of being in which the individual possesses both masculine and feminine personality traits; a gender-role pattern that has been linked to more flexible patterns of adjustment.

Psychosocial Dwarfism Failure to grow as a result of an impoverished social environment; also referred to as Deprivation Dwarfism.

Puberty The stage of development when the individual reaches sexual maturity and becomes capable of reproduction.

Punishment A process whereby the application of an aversive stimulus after a response has been made decreases the frequency of the response.

Pupillary Reflex The automatic opening or closing of the iris in response to light.

Quickening The experience of feeling the fetus's movement in the uterus.

Random Selection A research technique by which subjects are drawn from a population in such a way that every member of the population has an equal chance of being selected.

Rapid Eye Movement (REM) A phase of sleep characterized by rapid eye movements.

Realism The tendency to attribute real physical properties to mental entities.

Recessive Gene A gene that is expressed only when paired with a similar recessive gene or in the absence of a dominant gene.

Reconstituted Family A family created through the remarriage of adults with children.

Reflexes Automatic and unlearned responses to particular stimuli in the environment.

Reinforcement The term that describes any stimulus that follows a behavior and results in that behavior being repeated.

Reliability The extent to which measurement of the same phenomenon by the same researchers at different times, or by different researchers at the same time, will produce the same results.

Retrieval A process in memory referring to the ability to remove information from long-term memory.

Reversibility According to Piaget, the child's ability to mentally retrace his or her actions or thoughts or to think backward.

Role Overload A condition in which a person takes on, or is expected to take on, the responsibilities associated with many roles; produces increased stress in the individual.

Scheme According to Piaget, an action sequence.

Schizophrenia A form of psychosis characterized by regression, bizarre behavior, apathy, delusions, hallucinations, destructive rages, and/or other symptoms of detachment from reality.

Secondary Aging The acceleration of senescence, or primary aging, by factors such as disease, trauma, or stress.

Secondary Memory Memory for information that has been encoded but is no longer the focus of active attention. Also called long-term memory.

Secondary Sex Characteristics Physical features other than genitals that distinguish women and men.

Secular Growth Trends Variation in physical growth patterns that characterize populations over a period of time.

Selective Attention The person's ability to attend to relevant information while ignoring irrelevant information.

Self-Concept A person's sense of his or her identity, including physical and psychological traits; the way a person views self.

Self-Esteem An affective evaluation of one's self expressed as positive or negative.

Semantics The study of meanings of words and sentences within a language.

Senescence The normal degenerative processes accompanying aging; also known as primary aging.

Senile Dementia A mental condition found in old age that is associated with general brain loss of unknown origin; symptoms include problems in intellectual and social judgment, general confusion, mood changes, and deterioration of personal habits.

Sensorimotor Stage Within Piaget's theory, the first stage of cognitive development; intelligence at this time is defined primarily in terms of the infant's motor and sensory actions.

Separation Distress The infant's protest or crying when caregiver and infant are separated.

Sex Chromosome The chromosome that determines the gender of the person.

Short-Gestation-Period Babies Infants born before the full 38 weeks of development; also referred to as preterm babies.

Sign A type of mental representation that is socially defined and accepted by other people.

Small-for-Date Babies Infants born after the full period of gestation but who are under 2500 grams or 5 lbs. 8 oz. in weight; also referred to as growth-retarded babies.

Social Cognition The child's knowledge and understanding of social relationships and reactions.

Social Integration vs. Isolation The degree of interpersonal activity and organizational participation in which a person engages, and the degree of social–emotional support the person receives from others in these activities.

Social Learning Theory Based on behavioral principles, a school of thought that also recognizes that people learn by observing and imitating others; gives greater weight to cognitive processes in learning than traditional behavioral approaches.

Socialization The process by which a child learns the expected behaviors of a culture or group.

Socialized Delinquency A form of conduct disorder in which the person typically develops the capacity for forming attachment relationships (usually to other delinquents or social outcasts); associated with social disadvantage and parental neglect (rather than rejection).

Sociogram A diagram representing social acceptance and rejection among a group of people.

Sociometry A quantitative method of studying social relations among peers.

Standardized Test A test whose material, administration, scoring, and evaluation have been so designed that it can be given reliably at different times and places by different examiners.

Stimulus–Value–Role Theory Murstein's theory of courtship; the process begins with people responding to the overt characteristics of others; it progresses to value comparison; and eventually leads to an evaluation of role compatibility as the couple seriously considers marriage.

Stranger Anxiety An infant's general wariness of unfamiliar people.

Superego In Freud's theory, the part of the personality system encompassing our conscience and set of moral values.

Symbol A gesture, drawing, or word that represents something else; according to Piaget, a type of mental representation that is unique to the child's experience.

Symbolic Play Play involving the use of symbols to represent reality such as make-believe or pretend games.

Symbolic Representation or Symbolic Function The ability to create and use symbols or images to represent something that is not present.

Syntax The rules of a language by which words and morphemes are combined to form larger clauses and sentences.

Telegraphic Speech Abbreviated speech containing only the most informative words (similar to the sentence structure used in sending a telegram).

Temperament A person's inborn, characteristic way of responding to stimuli.

Teratogens Specific environmental agents that cause abnormalities in the developing fetus.

Terminal Drop A decline in intellectual performance that frequently occurs within five years before death.

Terminal Stage of Life The time when a person becomes aware of his or her impending death.

Theory A set of interconnected statements that integrate information within a field of inquiry and suggest new relationships among the phenomena under study.

Time Out A strategy for changing behavior by removing a person from the setting in which the behavior to be changed is being reinforced.

Transductive Reasoning Reasoning from the particular to the particular.

Transformational Rules   Rules that allow the child to translate the basic meaning of a sentence into a grammatically correct sentence.

Type–A Behavior   A behavioral and emotional pattern associated with coronary heart disease; includes explosive and accelerated speech, impatience with delay, excessive competitiveness and achievement striving, restlessness, undue irritability, and a chronic sense of time urgency.

Umbilical Cord   The structure that links the embryo to the placenta.

Unidirectional View   The view of development in which the child is seen as a passive recipient of the parents' actions.

Unsocialized Delinquency   A form of conduct disorder in which the person typically fails to develop a normal degree of affection, empathy, and attachment to others; usually associated with homes characterized by parental rejection and hard discipline.

Validity   Degree to which a measure assesses what it is supposed to measure.

Vernix Caseosa   A cheeselike substance covering the newborn's skin.

Visual Accommodation   The eye's ability to change the shape of the lens to obtain a clear focus.

Wisdom   A cognitive characteristic associated with aging; related to such traits as intuitiveness, introspection, experience, intellectual integration, empathy, understanding, patience, and gentleness.

Youth   An "optional" period of development in which an individual is legally an adult but has not yet undertaken adult work and roles.

Zygote   The fertilized egg.

References

Abplanalp, J. M. Premenstrual syndrome: A selective review. *Women and Health*, 1983, *8*, 107–123.

Abramson, L., Seligman, M. E. P., & Teasdale, J. Learned helplessness in humans: Critique and reformulation. *Journal of Abnormal Psychology*, 1978, *87*, 49–74.

Abravanel, E., & Gingold, H. Learning via observation during the second year of life. *Developmental psychology*, 1985, *21*, 614–623.

Achenbach, T. Developmental aspects of psychopathology in children and adolescents. In M. Lamb (Ed.), *Social and personality development*. New York: Holt, Rinehart and Winston, 1978.

Acredolo, L., & Feldman, P. The effect of active versus passive exploration on memory for spatial location in children. *Child Development*, 1979, *50*, 698–704.

Adams, G. M., & DeVries, H. A. Physiological effects of an exercise regimen upon women aged 52–79. *Journal of Gerontology*, 1973, *28*, 50–55.

Adams, B. N. *The family: A sociological interpretation*. Chicago: Rand McNally, 1975.

Adams, G. R., & Fitch, S. A. Psychological environments of university departments: Effects of college students' identity status and ego stage development. *Journal of Personality and Social Psychology*, 1983, *44*, 1266–1275.

Adelson, J. The development of ideology in adolescence. In S. Dra-

gastin & G. Elder (Eds.), *Adolescence in the life cycle*. New York: Wiley, 1975

Adelson, J. The political socialization of the young adolescent. In J. Kagan & R. Coles (Eds.), *Twelve to sixteen: Early adolescence*. New York: Norton, 1972.

Adelson, J. Rites of passage: How children learn the principles of community. *American Educator*, 1982, *18*, 60–67.

Adelson, J., & O'Neil, R. P. Growth of political ideas in adolescence: The sense of community. *Journal of Personality and Social Psychology*, 1966, *4*, 295–306.

Ade-Ridder, L., & Brubaker, T. The quality of long-term marriages. In T. H. Brubaker (Ed.), *Family relations in later life*. Beverly Hills, CA: Sage Publications, 1983.

Adler, A. Characteristics of first, second, and third children. *Children*, 1928, *3* (14), Issue 5.

Ahrons, C., & Rogers, R. *Divorced families*. New York: Norton Press, 1987.

Ainsworth, M. *Infancy in Uganda: Infant care and the growth of love*. Baltimore, MD: Johns Hopkins University Press, 1967.

Ainsworth, M., Bell, S., & Stayton, D. Individual differences in strange situation behavior of one-year-olds. In H. R. Schaffer (Ed.), *The origins of human social relations*. New York: Academic Press, 1971.

Ainsworth, M., Blehar, M., Waters,

E., & Wall, S. *Patterns of attachment*. Hillsdale, NJ: Erlbaum, 1978.

Aldous, J. New views on the family life of the elderly and the near elderly. *Journal of Marriage and the Family*, 1987, *49*, 227–234

Alley, T. Growth-produced changes in body shape and size as determinants of perceived age and adult caregiving. *Child Development*, 1983, *54*, 241–248. (a)

Alley, T. Infantile head shape as an elicitor of adult protection. *Merrill-Palmer Quarterly*, 1983, *29* (4), 411–427. (b)

Allport, G. W. *Pattern and growth in personality*. New York: Holt, Rinehart and Winston, 1961.

Allport, G. W. *The person in psychology*. Boston: Beacon, 1968.

Alpaugh, P. K., & Birren, J. E. Variables affecting creative contributions across the adult life span. *Human Development*, 1977, *20*, 240–248.

Alpert, J. L., & Richardson, M. S. Parenting. In L. Poon (Ed.), *Aging in the 1980s: Psychological issues*. Washington, DC: American Psychological Association, 1980.

Amazing births. *Time Magazine*, January 23, 1984, p. 30.

Ambron, S., & Salkind, N. J. *Child development* (4th ed.). New York: Holt, Rinehart and Winston, 1984.

Anastasi, A. Heredity, environment, and the question "how?" *Psychological Review*, 1958, *65*, 197–208.

Anderson, D., Lorch E., Field, D., Collins, P., & Nathan, J. Television viewing at home: Age trends in visual attention and time with TV. *Child Development*, 1986, *57*, 1024–1033.

Annis, L. F. *The child before birth*. Ithaca, NY, Cornell University Press, 1978.

Antunes, C., Stolley, P., Rosenshein, N., Davies, J., Tonascia, J., Brown, C., Burnett, L., Rutledge, A., Pokempner, M., & Garcia, R. Endometrial cancer and estrogen use. *New England Journal of Medicine*, 1979, *300*, 9–13.

Archer, S. Career and/or family: The identity process for adolescent girls. *Youth and society*, 1985, *16*, 289–314. (a)

Archer, S. Identity and the choice of social roles. In A. S. Waterman (Ed.), *Identity in adolescence: Processes and content*. San Francisco: Jossey-Bass, 1985(b)

Arenberg, D., & Robertson-Tchabo, E. A. Learning and aging. In J. E. Birren & K. W. Schaie (Eds.), *Handbook of the psychology of aging*. New York: Van Nostrand Reinhold, 1977.

Arlin, P. A. Cognitive development in adulthood: A fifth stage? *Developmental Psychology*, 1975, *11*, 602–606.

Arlin, P. A. Piagetian operations in problem finding. *Developmental Psychology*, 1977, *13*, 297–298.

Arlin, P. A. Adolescent and adult thought: A structural interpretation. In M. L. Commons, F. A. Richards, & C. Armon (Eds.), *Beyond formal operations: Late adolescent and adult cognitive development*. New York: Praeger, 1984.

Arthur, J. K. *Retire to action: A guide to voluntary service*. Nashville, TN: Abingdon, 1969.

Asher, S. Social competence and peer status: Recent advances and future directions. *Child Development*, 1983, *54*, 1427–1434.

Aslin, R., Pisoni, D., & Jusczyk, P. Auditory development and speech perception in infancy. In P. H. Mussen (Ed.), *Handbook of child psychology, Vol. 2: Infancy and developmental psychobiology* (4th ed.). New York: Wiley, 1983.

Atchley, R. C. Dimensions of wid-

owhood in later life. *The Gerontologist*, 1975, *15*, 176–178.

Atchley, R. C. *The social forces in later life* (2nd ed.). Belmont, CA: Wadsworth, 1977.

Atchley, R. C. *The social forces in later life* (3rd ed.). Belmont, CA: Wadsworth, 1980.

Atchley, R. C., & Miller, S. Types of elderly couples. In T. H. Brubaker (Ed.) *Family relations in later life*. Beverly Hills, CA: Sage Publications, 1983.

Athanasiou, R., Shaver, P., & Tavris, C. Sex: *Psychology Today* reports back to readers on what they told when they filled out the sex questionnaire. *Psychology Today*, July 1970, *4*, 39–52.

Averill, J. R. Grief: Its nature and significance. *Psychological Bulletin*, 1968, *70*, 721–748.

Axline, V. *Dibs: In Search of Self*. New York: Houghton Mifflin, 1964.

Bahr, S. Effects of power and division of labor in the family. In L. Hoffman & G. Nye (Eds.), *Working mothers*. San Francisco: Jossey-Bass, 1973.

Bakwin, H., & Bakwin, R. *Behavior disorders in children*. Philadelphia: Saunders, 1972.

Ball, S., & Bogatz, G. A. Summative research on Sesame Street: Implications for the study of preschool children. In A.D. Pick (Ed.), *Minnesota Symposium on Child Psychology* (Vol 6) Minneapolis: University of Minnesota Press, 1972.

Baltes, M. M., & Baltes, P. B. The ecopsychological relativity and plasticity of psychological aging: Convergent perspectives of cohort effects and operant psychology. *Zeitschrift füer experimentelle und angewandte Psychologie*, 1977, *24*, 179–197.

Baltes, P. Theoretical propositions of lifespan developmental psychology: On the dynamics between growth and decline. *Developmental Psychology*. 1987, *23*, 611–626.

Baltes, P. B., Reese, H. W., & Lipsitt, L. Lifespan developmental psychology. In M. Rosenzweig & L. Portor (Eds.), *Annual Review of Psychology 31*. Palo Alto, CA: Annual Reviews, 1980.

Baltes, P. B., Reese, H. W., & Nesselroade, J. R. *Life-span developmental psychology: Introduction to research methods*. Monterey, CA: Brooks/Cole, 1977.

Baltes, P. B., & Willis, S. L. Enhancement of intellectual functioning in old age: Penn State adult development and enrichment project (ADEPT). In F. I. M. Craik & S. Treub (Eds.), *Aging and cognitive processes*. New York: Plenum, 1980.

Bandura, A. *Social learning theory*. Englewood Cliffs, NJ: Prentice-Hall, 1977.

Bandura, A. The self system in reciprocal determinism. *American Psychologist*, 1978, *33*, 344–358.

Bank, S., & Kahn, M. *The sibling bond*. New York: Basic Books, 1982.

Banks, M. S., & Salapatek, P. Infant visual perception. In P. H. Mussen (Ed.), *Handbook of child psychology, 2*, New York: Wiley, 1983.

Barnes, H. V. Physical growth and development during puberty. *Medical Clinics of North America*, 1975, *59*, 1305–1317.

Barnett, R., & Baruch, G. Determinants of father's participation in family work. *Journal of Marriage and the Family*, 1987, *49*, 29–40.

Barrera, M. E., Rosenbaum, P. L., & Cunningham, C. E. Early home intervention with low-birth-weight infants and their parents. *Child Development*, 1986, *57*, 20–33.

Barrett, N. S. Women in the job market: Occupations, earnings, and career opportunities. In R. E. Smith (Ed.), *The subtle revolution: Women at work*. Washington, DC: The Urban Institute, 1979.

Barron, E. *Creativity and psychological health: Origins of personal vitality and creative freedom*. New York: Van Nostrand, 1963.

Bart, P. Mother Portnoy's complaints. *Trans-action*, 1970, *8*, 69–74.

Baskett, L., & Johnson, S. The young child's interactions with parents versus siblings: A behavioral analysis. *Child Development*, 1982, *53*, 643–650.

Basow, S. A., & Howe, K. G. Role-model influence: Effects of sex and sex-role attributes on college students. *Psychology of Women Quarterly,* 1980, *4,* 558–572.

Basseches, M. Dialectical schemata: A framework for the empirical study of the development of dialectical thinking. *Human Development,* 1980, *23,* 400–421.

Basseches, M. *Dialectical thinking and adult development.* Norwood, NJ: Ablex Publishers, 1984.

Baumrind, D. Child care practices anteceding three patterns of preschool behavior. *Genetic Psychology Monographs,* 1967, *75,* 43–88.

Baumrind, D. Current patterns in parental authority. *Developmental Psychology Monographs,* 1971, *1,* Pt. 2.

Baumrind, D. Some thoughts about childrearing. In S. Cohen and T. J. Cominsky (Eds.), *Child development: Contemporary perspectives.* Itasca, IL: Peacock, 1977.

Baumrind, D. Parental disciplinary patterns and social competence in children. *Youth and Society,* 1978, *9,* 239–276.

Baumrind, D. New directions in socialization research. *American Psychologist,* 1980, *35,* 639–652.

Bayley, N., & Oden, M. H. The maintenancy of intellectual ability in gifted adults. *Journal of Gerontology,* 1955, *10,* 91–107.

Bearison, D. J. The construct of regression: A Piagetian approach. *Merrill-Palmer Quarterly,* 1974, *20,* 21–30.

Becker, H., & Epstein, J. Parent involvement: A survey of teacher practices. *The Elementary School Journal,* 1982, *83,* 85–102.

Beckwith, L., & Parmelee, A. EEG patterns of preterm infants, home environment, and later I.Q. *Child Development,* 1986, *57,* 777–789.

Bee, H. *The journey of adulthood.* New York: Macmillan, 1987.

Bell, A., & Weinberg, M. *Homosexualities: A study of diversity among men and women.* New York: Simon & Schuster, 1978.

Bell, R. Q. A reinterpretation of the direction of effects in studies of socialization. *Psychological Review,* 1968, *75,* 81–85.

Bell, R. Q., & Harper, L. V. (Eds.), *Child effects on adults* Lincoln, NE:

The University of Nebraska Press, 1980.

Bell, R. R., & Coughey, K. Premarital sexual experience among college females, 1958, 1968, 1978. *Family Relations,* 1980, *29,* 353–357.

Bell, S. M., & Ainsworth, M. D. Infant crying and maternal responsiveness. *Child Development,* 1972, *43,* 1171–1190.

Belloc, N. B., & Breslow, L. Relationship of physical health status and health practices. *Preventive Medicine,* 1972, *1,* 409–421.

Bellugi, U. Learning the language. *Psychology Today,* 1970, 32–38.

Belsky, J. Child maltreatment: An ecological integration. *American Psychologist,* 1980, *35,* 320–335.

Belsky, J. Early human experience: A family perspective. *Developmental Psychology,* 1981, *17,* 3–23.

Belsky, J. The determinants of parenting. A process model. *Child Development,* 1984, *55,* 83–96.

Belsky, J. Two waves of day care research: Developmental effects and conditions of quality. In R. C. Ainslie (Ed.), *The child and the day care setting.* New York: Praeger, 1984.

Belsky, J., Lerner, R., & Spanier, G. *The child in the family.* Reading, MA: Addison-Wesley, 1984.

Belsky, J., & Rovine, M. Temperament and attachment security in the strange situation: An empirical rapprochement. *Child Development,* 1987, *58,* 787–795.

Belsky, J., & Rovine, M. Nonmaternal care in the first year of life and the security of infant-parent attachment. *Child Development,* 1988, *59,* 157–167.

Belsky, J., Spanier, G. B., & Rovine, M. Stability and change in marriage across the transition to parenthood. *Journal of Marriage and the Family,* 1983, *45,* 553–566.

Belsky, J., & Steinberg, L. The effects of day care: A critical review. *Child Development,* 1978, *49,* 929–949.

Belsky, J., & Steinberg, L. What does research teach us about day care: A follow-up report. *Children Today,* July–August 1979, 21–26.

Benawra, R., Mangurten, H. H., &

Duffell, D. R. Cyclopia and other anomalies following maternal ingestion of salicylates. *Journal of Pediatrics,* 1980, *96,* 1069–1071.

Bender, A. E. Nutrition of the elderly. *Royal Society Health Journal,* 1971, *91,* 115–121.

Benedek, T. Parenthood as a developmental phase. *American Psychoanalytic Association Journal,* 1959, *7,* 389–417.

Benet, S. *How to live to be 100.* New York: Dial Press, 1976.

Bengston, V., Cuellar, J., & Ragan, P. Stratum contrasts and similarities in attitudes toward death. *Journal of Gerontology,* 1977, *32,* 76–88.

Bengston, V. L., & Troll, L. Youth and their parents: Feedback and intergenerational influence on socialization. In R. Lerner & G. Spanier (Eds.), *Child influence on marital and family interaction: A life-span perspective.* New York: Academic Press, 1978.

Benin, M., & Nienstedt, B. Happiness in single-and-dual-earner families: The effects of marital happiness, job satisfaction, and life cycle. *Journal of Marriage and the Family,* 1985, *47,* 975–984.

Bennett, S., & Dickinson, W. Student-parent rapport and parent involvement in sex, birth control, and venereal disease education. *Journal of Sex Research,* 1980, *16,* 97–113.

Berardo, F. M. Widowhood status in the United States: Perspectives on a neglected aspect of family lifecycle. *The Family Coordinator,* 1968, *17,* 191–203.

Berenson, G., Frank, G., Hunter, S., Srinivasan, S., Voors, A., & Webber, L. Cardiovascular risk factors in children. Should they concern the pediatrician? *American Journal of Diseases of Children,* 1982, *136,* 855–862.

Berko, J. The child's learning of English morphology, *Word,* 1958, *14,* 150–177.

Bernard, J. *The future of marriage.* New York: World, 1972.

Berndt, T. J. Age changes and changes over time in prosocial intentions and between friends. *Developmental Psychology,* 1981, *17,* 408–416. (a)

Berndt, T. J. Relations between social cognition, nonsocial cognition, and social behavior: The case of friendship. In J. H. Flavell & L. D. Ross (Eds.), *Social cognitive development: Frontiers and possible futures.* Cambridge: Cambridge University Press, 1981. (b).

Berndt, T. J. The features and effects of friendships in early adolescence. *Child Development,* 1982, *53,* 1447–1460.

Berndt, T., & Hoyle, S. Stability and change in childhood and adolescent friendships. *Developmental Psychology,* 1985, *21,* 1007–1015.

Bernstein, A., & Cowan, P. Children's concept of how people get babies. *Child Development,* 1975, *46,* 77-91.

Bertenthal, B., & Fischer, K. Development of self-recognition in the infant. *Developmental Psychology,* 1978, *14,* 44–50.

Betz, E. A study of career patterns of women college graduates. *Journal of Vocational Behavior.* 1984, *24,* 249–263.

Bielby, D. D., & Papalia, D. E. Moral development and perceptual role-taking egocentrism: Their development and interrelationship across the life span. *International Journal of Aging and Human Development,* 1975, *6,* 293–308.

Biller, A. Father absence and the personality development of the male child. *Developmental Psychology,* 1970, *2,* 181–201.

Birnbaum, J. Life patterns, personality, style, and self-esteem in gifted family-oriented and career-oriented women. (Doctoral dissertation, University of Michigan). Dissertation Abstracts International, 1971, *32,* 1834 b.

Birns, B. Individual differences in human neonates' responses to stimulation. In J. Stone, H. Smith, & L. Murphy (Eds.), *The competent infant.* New York: Basic Books, 1973.

Birren, J. E. Transitions in gerontology—from lab to life: Psychophysiology and speed of response. *American Psychologist,* 1974, *29,* 808–815.

Birren, J. E., Butler, R. N., Greenhouse, S. W., Sokoloff, L., & Yarrow, M. R. (Eds.). *Human aging: A biological and behavioral study.* HSM Publication No. 71–9051. Washington, DC: U.S. Government Printing Office, 1963.

Birren, J., Woods, A., & Williams, M. Behavioral slowing with age: Causes, organization, and consequences. In L. W. Poon (Ed.), *Aging in the 1980s.* Washington, DC: American Psychological Association, 1980.

Bixenstine, V., DeCorte, M., & Bixenstine, B. Conformity to peer-sponsored misconduct at four age levels. *Developmental Psychology,* 1976, *12,* 226–236.

Bjork, E., & Cummings, E. Infant search errors: Stage of concept development or stage of memory development. *Memory & Cognition,* 1984, *12,* 1–19.

Blasi, A. Bridging moral cognition and moral action: A critical review of the literature. *Psychological Bulletin,* 1980, *88,* 1–45.

Block, J. Differential premises arising from differential socialization of the sexes: Some conjectures. *Child Development,* 1983, *54,* 1335–1354.

Bloom, L. *Language development: Form and function in emerging grammars.* Cambridge, MA: MIT Press, 1970.

Blos, P. *The adolescent passage.* New York: International Universities Press, 1979.

Bluebond-Langner, M. Meanings of death to children. In H. Feifel (Ed.), *New meanings of death.* New York: McGraw-Hill, 1977.

Blum, J. E., & Jarvik, L. F. Intellectual performance of octogenarians as a function of education and initial ability. *Human Development,* 1975, *18,* 364–375.

Blum, M. *The day care dilemma,* Lexington, MA: Heath, 1983.

Blumstein, P., & Schwartz, P. *American couples.* New York: William Morrow, 1983.

Blyth, D., Bulcroft, R., & Simmons, R. *The impact of puberty on adolescents: A longitudinal study.* Paper presented at the annual meeting of the American Psychological Association, Los Angeles, August, 1981.

Bohman, M. *Adopted children and their families: A follow-up study of adopted children, their background environment, and adjustment.* Stockholm: Proprius, 1970.

Booth, A. Wife's employment and husband stress: A replication and refutation. *Journal of Marriage and the Family,* 1977, *39,* 645–650.

Booth, H., & Hess, E. Cross-sex friendship. *Journal of Marriage and the Family,* 1974, *36,* 38–47.

Bornstein, M. H. Human infant color vision and color perception. *Infant Behavior and Development,* 1985, *8,* 109–113.

Bortz, W. Disuse and aging. *Journal of the American Medical Association,* 1982, *248,* 1203–1208.

Boskind-White, M., & White, W. *Bulimarexia: The binge/purge cycle.* New York: Norton, 1983.

Botwinick, J. Cautiousness in advanced age. *Journal of Gerontology,* 1966, *21,* 347–353.

Botwinick, J. Intellectual abilities. In J. E. Birren & K. W. Schaie (Eds.), *Handbook of the psychology of aging.* New York: Van Nostrand Reinhold, 1977.

Bourque, L. B., & Back, K. W. Life graphs and life events. *Journal of Gerontology,* 1977, *32,* 669–674.

Bower, D., & Christopherson, V. University student cohabitation: A regional comparison of selected attitudes and behavior. *Journal of Marriage and the Family,* 1977, *39,* 447–453.

Bower, T. G. R. *A primer of infant development.* San Francisco: W. H. Freeman, 1977.

Bower, T. G. R. *Development in infancy* (2nd ed.). San Francisco: Freeman, 1982.

Bowlby, J. *Attachment and loss: Attachment* (Vol. 1). New York: Basic Books, 1969.

Bowlby, J. *Attachment and loss: Separation* (Vol. 2). New York: Basic Books, 1973.

Bowlby, J. *Attachment and loss: Loss, sadness, and depression* (Vol. 3). New York: Basic Books, 1980.

Brachfeld, S., Goldberg, S., & Sloman, J. Parent–infant interaction in free play at 8 and 12 months: Effects of prematurity and immaturity. *Infant Behavior and Development,* 1980, *3,* 289–305.

Bradley, S. The relationship of early maternal separation to borderline personality in children and adolescents: A pilot study. *American Journal of Psychiatry*, 1979, *136*, 424–426.

Braga, L., & Braga, J. *Learning and growing: A guide to child development*. Englewood Cliffs, NJ: Prentice-Hall, 1975.

Braine, M. D. S., Heimer, C. B., Wortis, H., & Freedman, A. M. Factors associated with impairment of the early development of prematures. *Monographs of the Society for Research in Child Development*, 1966, *31*, no. 4, serial no. 106.

Braine, M. S., & Rumain, B. Logical reasoning. In J. H. Flavell & E. M. Markman (Eds.), *Handbook of child psychology. Vol. III: Cognitive development*. New York: Wiley, 1983.

Brainerd, C., *Piaget's theory of intelligence*. Englewood Cliffs, NJ: Prentice-Hall, 1978.

Brainerd, C. Kingma, J., & Howe, M. On the development of forgetting. *Child Development*, 1985, *56*, 1103–1119.

Brandwein, R. A., Brown, C. A., & Fox, E. M. Women and children last: The social situation of divorced mothers and their families. *Journal of Marriage and the Family*, 1974, *36*, 498–514.

Braungart, R. Youth movements. In J. Adelson (Ed.), *Handbook of adolescent psychology*. New York: Wiley, 1980.

Bray, D., & Howard, A. The AT&T longtitudinal studies of managers. In K. W. Schaie (Ed.), *Longitudinal studies of adult psychological development*. New York: Guilford Press, 1983.

Brazelton, T. B. *Neonatal assessment scale*. Philadelphia: Lippincott, 1973.

Brazelton, T. B. *On becoming a family*. New York: Delacorte Press/Seymour Lawrence, 1981.

Brecher, E. *Love, sex, and aging*. Boston, MA: Little, Brown, 1984.

Bretherton, I. Attachment theory: Retrospect and prospect. In Bretherton, I., & Waters, E. (Eds.), Growing points of attachment theory and research. *Monographs of the Society for Research in Child Development*, 1985, serial no. 209, *50*, Nos. 1–2.

Brewer, G. S. (Ed.). *The pregnancy after 30 workbook*. Emmaus, PA: Rodale Press, 1978.

Brim, O., & Kagan, J. *Constancy and change in human development*. Cambridge, MA: Harvard University Press, 1980.

Brody, G., Stoneman, Z., & MacKinnon, C. Role asymmetries among school-aged children, their younger siblings, and their friends. *Child Development*, 1982, *53*, 1364–1370.

Brody, G., Stoneman, Z., MacKinnon, C., & MacKinnon, R. Role relationships and behavior between preschool-aged and school age sibling pairs. *Developmental Psychology*, 1985, *21*, 124–129.

Brody, J. E. Cancer agency head advises diet changes. *New York Times*, October 4, 1979.

Brody, L., Zelago, P. R., & Chaika, H. Habituation–dishabituation to speech in the neonate. *Developmental Psychology*, 1984, *20*, 114–119.

Brodzinsky, D. M. On the relationship between cognitive styles and cognitive structures. In E. Neimark & R. DeLisi (Eds.), *Moderators of competence*. Hillsdale, NJ: Erlbaum, 1985.

Brodzinsky, D. M., Messer, S., & Tew, J. Sex differences in children's expression and control of fantasy and overt aggression. *Child Development*, 1979, *50*, 372–379.

Brodzinsky, D. M., Schechter, D. E., Braff, A. M., & Singer, L. M. Psychological and academic adjustment in adopted children. *Journal of Consulting and Clinical Psychology*, 1984, *52*, 582–590.

Bromley, D. B. *The psychology of human aging* (2nd ed.). Middlesex, England: Penguin, 1974.

Bromley, D. Age and sex differences in the serial production of creative conceptual responses. *Journal of Gerontology*, 1967, *22*, 32–42.

Bronfenbrenner, U. Freudian theories of identification and their derivatives. *Child Development*, 1960, *31*, 15–40.

Bronfenbrenner, U. Toward an experimental ecology of human development. *American Psychologist*, 1977, *32*, 513–531.

Bronfenbrenner, U., and Garbarino, J. The socialization of moral judgment and behavior in cross-cultural perspective. In T. Lickona (Ed.), *Moral development and behavior*. New York: Holt, Rinehart and Winston, 1976.

Bronfenbrenner, U. *The ecology of human development*. Cambridge, MA: Harvard University Press, 1979.

Brooks-Gunn, Jr., & Matthews, W. *He and she: How children develop their sex-role identity*. Englewood Cliffs, NJ: Prentice-Hall, 1979.

Brooks-Gunn, J., & Warren, M. The effects of delayed menarche in different contexts: Dance and nondance students. *Journal of Youth and Adolescence*, 1985, *14*, 285–300.

Broughton, J. Development of concepts of self, mind, reality, and knowledge. In W. Damon (Ed.), *Social cognition: New directions for child development*. San Francisco: Jossey-Bass, 1978.

Brown, A. L. The development of memory: Knowing, knowing about knowing, and knowing how to know. In H. W. Reese (Ed.), *Advances in child development and behavior* (Vol. 10). New York: Academic Press, 1975.

Brown, A. L. Theories of memory and the problem of development: Activity, growth, and knowledge. In L. S. Cermak & F. I. M. Craik (Eds.), *Levels of processing in human memory*. Hillsdale, NJ: Erlbaum, 1979.

Brown, A. L., Bransford, J., Ferrara, R., & Campione, J. Learning remembering and understanding. In J. H. Flavell & E. Markman (Ed.), *Handbook of child psychology, Vol. 3: Cognitive Development* (4th ed.). New York: Wiley, 1983.

Brown, P. Teenage pregnancy: A national challenge, what are the facts? *Vital Issues*, 1983, *32* (6).

Brown, R. The first sentences of child and chimpanzee. In *Psycholinguistics: Selected papers*. Glencoe, IL: The Free Press, 1970.

Brown, R. Development of the first language in the human species.

American Psychologist, 1973, *28*, 97–106.

Bruch, H. Transformation of oral impulses in eating disorders. *Psychiatric Quarterly*, 1961, *35*, 458.

Bruch, H. *Eating disorders.* New York: Basic Books, 1973.

Bruch, H. Anorexia nervosa and its treatment. *Journal of Pediatric Psychology*, 1977, *2*, 110–112.

Bruck, K. Temperature regulation in the newborn infant. *Biologia Neonatorum*, 1961, *3*, 65–119.

Bruner, J. From communication to language: A psychological perspective. In I. Markova (Ed.), *The social context of language.* New York: Wiley, 1978.

Bruner, J. Interaction, communication and self. *Journal of the American Academy of Child Psychiatry*, 1984, *23*, 1–7.

Bryant, B. Sibling relationships in middle childhood. In M. E. Lamb & B. Sutton Smith (Eds.), *Sibling relationships.* Hillsdale, NJ: Erlbaum, 1982.

Bullough, V. L. Age at menarche. *Science*, 1981, *213*, 365–366.

Burdz, M., Eaton, W., & Bond, J. Effects of respite care on dementia and nondementia patients and their caregivers. *Psychology and Aging*, 1988, *3*, 38–42.

Burgess, R. Child abuse: A social interactional analysis. In B. B. Lakey & A. E. Kazden (Eds.), *Advances in clinical child psychology.* New York: Plenum, 1979.

Burke, R. I., & Weir, T. Personality differences between members of one-career and two-career families. *Journal of Marriage and the Family*, 1976, *38*, 453–459. (a)

Burke, R. I., & Weir, T. Relationship of wives' employment status to husband, wife, and pair satisfaction and performance. *Journal of Marriage and the Family*, 1976, *38*, 279–282. (b)

Burkett, S. Religiosity, beliefs and normative standards and adolescent drinking. *Journal of Studies on Alcohol*, 1980, *41*, 662–671.

Burlin, F. The relationship of parental education and maternal work and occupational status to occupational aspiration in adolescent females. *Journal of Vocational Education*, 1976, *9*, 99–104.

Burrus-Bammel, L., & Bammel, G. Leisure and recreation. In J. Birren & K. W. Schaie (Eds.), *Handbook of the Psychology of Aging* 2nd ed. New York: Van Nostrand Reinhold, 1985.

Bushnell, E., Shaw, L., & Strauss, D. Relationship between visual and tactical exploration by 6-month-olds. *Developmental Psychology*, 1985, *21*, 591–600.

Busse, E. W., Jeffers, I. C., & Christ, W. D. Factors in age awareness. In E. Palmore (Ed.), *Normal aging: Reports from the Duke longitudinal study, 1955–1969.* Durham, NC: Duke University Press, 1970.

Butler, R. N. Old age: The life review. *Psychology Today*, December 1971, *5*, 49.

Butler, R. N., & Lewis, M. I. *Love and sex after sixty: A guide for men and women for their later years.* New York: Harper & Row, 1976.

Butler, R. N., & Lewis, M. I. *Aging and mental health* (3rd ed.). St. Louis: Mosby, 1982.

Butterfield-Picard, H., & Magno, J. Hospice, the adjective, not the noun: The future of a national priority. *American Psychologist*, 1982, *37*, 1254–1259.

Byrne, J. D. Mobility rate of employed persons into new occupations. Bureau of Labor Statistics, Manpower and Employment, Special Labor Force Reports. *Monthly Labor Review*, February 1975, pp. 53–59.

Campos, J. J., Bertenthal, B. I., & Caplovitz, K. The interrelationship of affect and cognition in the visual cliff situation. In C. Izard, J. Kagan, & R. Zajonc (Eds.), *Emotion and cognition.* New York: Plenum, 1982.

Cantwell, D. Psychiatric illness in the families of hyperactive children. *Archives of General Psychiatry*, 1972, *27*, 414–417.

Caplan, T., & Caplan, F. *The early childhood years: The 2 to 6 year old.* New York: Putnam, 1983.

Carey, R., & Posavac, E. Attitudes of physicians on disclosing information to and maintaining life for terminal patients. *Omega*, 1978–1979, *9*, 67–77.

Carey, S. The child is a word learner.

In M. Halle, J. Bresman, & G. A. Miller (Eds.), *Linguistic theory and psychological reality.* Cambridge, MA: MIT Press, 1977.

Cargan, L., & Melko, M. *Singles: Myths and realities.* Beverly Hills, CA: Sage Publications, 1982.

Carlson, G. A., & Cantwell, D. P. Diagnosis of childhood depression: A comparison of the Weinberg and DSM III criteria. *Journal of the American Academy of Child Psychiatry*, 1982, *21*, 247–250.

Carnegie Commission on Policy Studies in Higher Education. *Giving youth a better chance.* San Francisco: Jossey-Bass, 1980.

Caron, A. J., Caron, R. F., Caldwell, R. C., & Weiss, S. J. Infant perception of the structural properties of the face. *Developmental Psychology*, 1973, *9*, 385–399.

Carpenter, G. Mother's face and the newborn. In R. Lewin (Ed.), *Child alive.* London: Temple Smith, 1975.

Carpenter, R. B., & Emery, J. L. Identification and follow-up of infants at risk for sudden death in infancy. *Nature*, 1974, *250*, 729.

Carroll, B. J., & Steiner, M. The psychobiology of premenstrual dysphoria: The role of prolactin. *Psychoneuroendocrinol*, 1978, *3*, 171–180.

Carter, H., & Glick, P. C. *Marriage and divorce: A social and economic study.* Cambridge, MA: Harvard University Press, 1970.

Caster, W. O. *The nutritional problems of the aged.* Athens, GA: University of Georgia Press, 1971.

Cattell, R. B. Theory of fluid and a crystalized intelligence: A critical experiment. *Journal of Educational Psychology*, 1963, *36*, 1–22.

Cavanaugh, J., & Borkowski, J. Searching for metamemory–memory connections: A developmental study. *Developmental Psychology*, 1980, *16*, 441–453.

Cavior, N., & Dokecki, P. R. Physical attractiveness, perceived attitude similarity, and academic achievement as contributors to interpersonal attraction among adolescents. *Developmental Psychology*, 1973, *9*, 44–54.

Cavior, N., & Lombardi, D. A. Developmental aspects of physical attractiveness in children. *Developmental Psychology*, 1973, *8*, 67–71.

Center for Disease Control. Basic statistics on the sexually transmitted disease problem in the United States. *Sexually transmitted disease sheet, 34th edition.* Atlanta: Center for Disease Control, U.S. Department of Health, Education, and Welfare (HEW Publication NO. CDC 79–8195), 1979, 1–37.

Charatan, F. Assessing, identifying and treating depressive illness in the elderly–I. *Carrier Foundation Letter*, 1981, *68*, 1–5.

Chase, J., Jessor, R., & Donovan, J. Psychosocial correlates of marijuana use and drinking in a national sample of adolescents. *American Journal of Public Health*, 1980, *70*, 604–612.

Chiriboga, D. A., & Cutler, L. Stress and adaptation: Life span perspectives. In L. Poon (Ed.), *Aging in the 1980s: Psychological issues.* Washington, DC: American Psychological Association, 1980.

Chivian, E., Mack, J., & Waletzsky, J. *What Soviet children are saying about nuclear war: Project summary.* Mimeograph. The Nuclear Psychology Program. Harvard Medical School, 1983.

Chomsky, N. *Language and mind.* New York: Harcourt, 1968.

Chumlea, W. C. Physical growth in adolescence. In B. Wolman (Ed.), *Handbook of developmental psychology.* Englewood Cliffs, NJ: Prentice-Hall, 1982.

Cicirelli, V. G. Categorization behavior in aging subjects. *Journal of Gerontology*, 1976, *31*, 676–680.

Cicirelli, V. G. Family structure and interaction: Sibling effects on socialization. In M. McMillan & M. Sergio (Eds.), *Child psychiatry: Treatment and research.* New York: Brunner/Mazel, 1977. (a)

Cicirelli, V. G. Relationship of siblings to the elderly person's feelings and concerns. *Journal of Gerontology*, 1977, *31*, 309–317. (b)

Cicirelli, V. G. *Social services for the elderly in relation to the kin network.* Report to the NRTA–AARA Andrus Foundation. Washington, DC, 1979.

Cicirelli, V. G. Sibling friendship in adulthood: A lifespan perspective. In L. Poon (Ed.), *Aging in the 1980s: Psychological issues.* Washington, DC: American Psychological Association, 1980.

Cicirelli, V. G. Sibling influence throughout the life span. In M. E. Lamb & B. Sutton-Smith (Eds.), *Sibling relationships.* Hillsdale, NJ: Erlbaum, 1982.

Civia, A. Longevity and environmental factors. *The Gerontologist*, 1967, *7*, 196–205.

Clark, L. D., Hughes, R., & Nakashima, E. N. Behavioral effects of marijuana: Experimental studies. *Archives of General Psychiatry*, 1970, *23*, 193–198.

Clarke, A. An examination of the operation of residential propinquity as a factor in mate selection. *American Sociological Review*, 1952, *17*, 17–22.

Clarke-Stewart, K. A. *Day care*, Cambridge, MA: Harvard University Press, 1982.

Clarke-Stewart, K. A. Interactions between mothers and their young children: Characteristics and consequences. *Monographs of the Society for Research in Child Development*, 1973, *38*, serial no. 153.

Clarke-Stewart, K. A., & Gruber, C. Day care forms and features. In R. C. Ainslie (Ed.), *The child and the day care setting.* New York: Praeger, 1984.

Clarkson, M., & Berg, W. K. Cardiac orienting and vowel discrimination in newborns, crucial stimulus parameters. *Child Development*, 1983, *54*, 162–171.

Clarren, S. K., & Smith, D. W. The fetal alcohol syndrome. *New England Journal of Medicine*, 1978, *298*, 1063–1067.

Clausen, J. A. Men's occupational careers in the middle years. In D. Eichorn, J. Clausen, N. Haan, M. Honzik, & P. Mussen (Eds.), *Present and past in middle life.* New York: Academic Press, 1981.

Clayton, R., & Voss, H. Shacking up: Cohabitation in the 1970s. *Journal of Marriage and the Family*, 1977, *39*, 273–283.

Clayton, V., & Birren, J. E. Age and wisdom across the life-span: Theoretical perspectives. In P. B. Baltes & O. G. Brim, Jr. (Eds.), *Life-span development and behavior* (Vol. 1). New York: Academic Press, 1980.

Clayton, V., & Overton, W. F. Concrete and formal operational thought processes in young adulthood and old age. *International Journal of Aging and Human Development*, 1976, *7*, 237–245.

Clemens, P. W., & Rust, J. O. Factors in adolescent rebellious feelings. *Adolescence*, 1979, *14*, 159–173.

Clifford, E. Body ratification in adolescence. *Perceptual and Motor Skills*, 1971, *33*, 119–125.

Cline, H. F. Criminal behavior over the life span. In O. Brim & J. Kagan (Eds.), *Constancy and change in human development.* Cambridge, MA: Harvard University Press, 1980.

Clingempeel, W. G., & Segal, S. Stepparent–stepchild relationships and the psychological adjustment of children in stepmother and stepfather families. *Child Development*, 1986, *57*, 474–484.

Clore, G. L., & Byrne, D. The process of personality interaction. In R. B. Cattell & R. M. Dreger (Eds.), *Handbook of modern personality theory.* New York: Wiley, 1977.

Cogswell, B., Cohen, J., Mikow, V., Kanoy, K., & Margolin, R. *Adolescents' perspectives on the health care system.* Chapel Hill: University of North Carolina, 1982.

Cohen, E., Gelfand, D., Dodd, D., Jensen, J., & Turner, C. Self-control practices associated with weight loss maintenance in children and adolescents. *Behavior Therapy*, 1980, *11*, 26–37.

Cohen, G. Language comprehension in old age. *Cognitive Psychology*, 1979, *11*, 412–429.

Cohen, J., & Eiduson, B. T. Changing patterns of child rearing in alternative life styles: Implications for development. In A. Davids (Ed.), *Child personality and psychopathology: Current topics.* New York: Wiley, 1975.

Cohen, R. Reading disabled children are aware of their cognitive deficits. *Journal of Learning Disabilities*, 1983, *16*, 286–289.

Cohn, J., & Tronick, E. Three-month-old infants' reaction to stimulated maternal depression. *Child Development*, 1983, *54*, 185–193.

Coie, J., & Dodge, K. Continuities and changes in children's social status: A five-year longitudinal study. *Merrill-Palmer Quarterly*, 1983, *29*, 261–282.

Coie, J., & Kupersmidt, J. A behavioral analysis of emerging social status in boys' groups. *Child Development*, 1983, *54*, 1400–1416.

Colby, A., Kohlberg, L., Gibbs, J., & Lieberman, M. A longitudinal study of moral judgment. *Monographs of the society for research in child development*, 1983, *48*, 1–2. serial no. 200.

Coleman, J. S., with the assistance of Johnston, J. W. C., & Jonassohn, K. *The adolescent society: The social life of the teenager and its impact on education.* New York: Free Press, 1961.

Coleman, L. M., & Antonucci, T. C. Impact of work on women at mid-life. *Developmental Psychology*, 1983, *19*, 290–294.

Coles, R. *Erik H. Erikson: The growth of his work.* Boston: Little, Brown, 1970.

Colletta, N. D. Divorced mothers at two income levels: Stress, support, and child-rearing practices. Unpublished thesis, Cornell University, 1978.

Colman, N., Helliarachy, N., & Herbert, V. Detection of a milk factor that facilitiates folate uptake by intestinal cells. *Science*, 1981, *211*, 1427–1429.

Comalli, P. E., Jr. Life-span changes in visual perception. In L. R. Goulet & P. B. Baltes (Eds.), *Life-span developmental psychology: Research and theory.* New York: Academic Press, 1970.

Cometa, N. S., & Eson, M. E. Logical operations and metaphor interpretation: A Piagetian model. *Developmental Psychology*, 1978, *49*, 649–659.

Comfort, A. Sexuality in later life. In J. E. Birren & R. B. Sloane (Eds.), *Handbook of mental health and aging.* Englewood Cliffs, NJ: Prentice-Hall, 1980.

Comfort, A., & Comfort, J. *The facts of love: Living, loving and growing up.* New York: Ballantine Books, 1979.

Commons, M. L., & Richards, F. A. The structural analytic stage of development: A Piagetian post-formal operational stage. Paper presented at the meeting of the Western Psychological Association, San Francisco, April 1978.

Commons, M. L., Richards, F. A., & Armon, C. *Beyond formal operations: Late adolescent and adult cognitive development.* New York: Praeger, 1982.

Commons, M. L., Richards, F. A., & Kuhn, D. Metasystematic reasoning: A case for a level of systematic reasoning beyond Piaget's stage of formal operations. *Child Development*, 1982, *53*, 1058–1069.

Compassionate Friends, Inc. *Suggestions for medical personnel.* Oak Brook, IL: The Compassionate Friends, Inc., 1986.

Condon, W. S., & Sander, L. W. Neonate movement is synchronized with adult speech. *Science*, 1974, *183*, 99–101.

Conel, J. L. *The postnatal development of the human cortex.* Cambridge, MA: Harvard University Press. Vol. 1, 1939, Vol. 2, 1947, Vol. 3, 1959.

Conger, J. J. Parent–child relationships, social change, and adolescent vulnerability. *Journal of Pediatric Psychology*, 1977, *2*, 93–97.

Conger, J. J. Adolescence: A time for becoming. In M. Lamb (Ed.), *Social and personality development.* New York: Holt, Rinehart and Winston, 1978.

Conger, J. Freedom and commitment: Families, youth and social change. *American Psychologist*, 1981, *36*, 1475–1484.

Conger, J., & Peterson, A. Adolescence and youth. In J. Adelson (Ed.), *Handbook of adolescent psychology*, 4th ed. New York: Harper & Row, 1984.

Congressional Record, U.S. House of Representatives, p. H2647, April 10, 1978.

Cooper, C. D., Detre, T., & Weiss, S. M. Coronary prone behavior and coronary heart disease. *Circulation*, 1981, *63*, 1199–1215.

Coopersmith, S. *The antecedents of self-esteem.* San Francisco: Freeman, 1967.

Corah, N. L., Anthony, E. J., Painter, P., Stern, J. A., & Thurston, D. L. Effects of perinatal anoxia after seven years. *Psychological Monographs*, 1965, *79*, whole no. 596, 3.

Cordes, C. Researchers make room for father. *APA Monitor*, 1983, *14*, 1, 9–10.

Corso, J. F. Auditory perception and communication. In J. E. Birren & K. W. Schaie (Eds.), *Handbook of the psychology of aging.* New York: Van Nostrand Reinhold, 1977.

Costa, P. T., & McCrae, R. R. Age differences in personality structure revisited: Studies in validity, stability, and change. *International Journal of Aging and Human Development*, 1977, *8*, 261–275.

Costa, P. T., & McCrae, R. R. Objective personality assessment. In M. Storandt, I. C. Siegler, & M. F. Elias (Eds.), *The clinical psychology of aging.* New York: Plenum Press, 1980. (a)

Costa, P. T., & McCrae, R. R. Still stable after all these years: Personality as a key to some issues in adulthood and old age. In P. Balte & O. Brim (Eds.), *Life-span development and behavior 3.* New York: Academic Press, 1980. (b)

Costa, P. T., & McCrae, R. R. Personality as a lifelong determinant of wellbeing. In C. Z. Malatesta & C. E. Izard (Eds.), *Emotion in adult development.* Beverly Hils, CA: Sage Publications, 1984.

Costa, P. T., McCrae, R. R., & Arenberg, D. Enduring dispositions in adult males. *Journal of Personality and Social Psychology*, 1980, *38*, 793–800.

Cousins, N. *Anatomy of an illness.* New York: Norton, 1976.

Cowan, P. *Piaget with feeling: Cognitive, social and emotional dimensions.* New York: Holt, Rinehart and Winston, 1978.

Coyne, A. C., Whitborne, S. K., & Glenwick, D. S. Adult age differences in reflection–impulsivity. *Journal of Gerontology*, 1978, *33*, 402–407.

Craik, F. I. M. Age differences in human memory. In J. E. Birren &

K. W. Schaie (Eds.), *Handbook of the psychology of aging.* New York: Van Nostrand Reinhold, 1977.

Crandall, R. C. *Gerontology: A behavioral science approach.* Reading, MA: Addison-Wesley, 1980.

Cravioto, J., DeLicardie, E. R., & Birch, H. G. Nutrition growth and neurointegrative development: An experimental and ecological study. *Pediatrics,* 1966, *38,* Pt. 2, 319–372.

Crittenden, A. New insights into infancy. *New York Times,* November 13, 1983, 84–96.

Crittenden, P. Social networks, quality of child rearing, and child development. *Child Development,* 1985, *56,* 1299–1313.

Crnic, K., Greenberg, M., Ragozin, A., Robinson, N., & Basham, R. Effects of stress and social support on mothers and premature and full-term infants. *Child Development,* 1983, *54,* 209–217.

Crockenberg, S. Early mother and infant antecedents of Bayley Scale Performance at 21 months. *Developmental Psychology,* 1983, *19,* 727–730.

Crockenberg, S., & McCluskey, K. Change in maternal behavior during the baby's first year of life. *Child Development,* 1986, *57,* 746–753.

Cronbach, L. J. *Essentials of psychological testing* (3rd ed.). New York: Harper & Row, 1970.

Cross, J. F., & Cross, J. Age, sex, race, and the perception of facial beauty. *Developmental Psychology,* 1971, *5,* 431–439.

Crosson, C. W., & Robertson-Tchabo, C. A. Age and preference for complexity among manifestly creative women. *Human Development,* 1983, *26,* 149–155.

Csikszentmihalyi, M., & Larson, R. *Being adolescent: Conflict and growth in the teenage years.* New York: Basic Books, 1984.

Csikszentmihalyi, M., Larson, R., & Prescott, S. The ecology of adolescent activity and experience. *Journal of Youth and Adolescence,* 1977, *6,* 281–294.

Cuber, J. F., & Harroff, P. B. *The significant Americans.* New York: Appleton-Century-Crofts, 1965.

Cumming, E., & Henry, W. *Growing old: A process of disengagement.* New York: Basic Books, 1961.

Cummings, E. M., Iannotti, R., & Zahn-Waxler, C. Influence of conflict between adults on the emotions and aggression of young children. *Developmental Psychology,* 1985, *21,* 495–507.

Cummings, E., & Bjork, E. Perseveration and search on a five choice invisible displacement task. *Journal of Genetic Psychology,* 1983, *142,* 283–291.

Dalton, K. *The premenstrual syndrome.* London: Heinemann, 1964.

Dalton, K. *The premenstrual syndrome and progesterone therapy.* London: Heinemann, 1977.

Dalton, K. Cyclical criminal acts in premenstrual syndrome. *Lancet,* 1980, *2,* 1070–1071.

Damon, W. *The social world of the child.* San Francisco: Jossey-Bass, 1977.

Damon, W. *Social and personality development.* New York: Norton, 1983.

Dasen, P. R. Cross-cultural Piagetian research: A summary. *Journal of Cross-Cultural Psychology,* 1972, *3,* 23–39.

Deaux, K. From individual differences to social categories: Analysis of a decade's research growth. *American Psychologist,* 1984, *39,* 105–116.

DeCasper, A. J., & Fifer, W. P. Of human bonding: Newborns prefer their mothers' voices. *Science,* 1980, *208,* 1174–1176.

DeFries, J. C., & Plomin, R. Behavioral genetics. *Annual Review of Psychology,* 1978, *29,* 473–515.

DeFries, J. C., Plomin, R., Vandenberg, S. G., & Kuse, A. R. Parent–offspring resemblance for cognitive abilities in the Colorado Adoption Project: Biological, adoptive and control parents and one-year-old children. *Intelligence,* 1981, *5,* 245–277.

DeLisi, R., & Staudt, J. Individual differences in college students' performance on formal operations tasks. *Journal of Applied Developmental Psychology,* 1980, *1,* 201–208.

Denham, S. Social cognition, prosocial behavior, and emotion in preschoolers: Contextual validation. *Child Development,* 1986, *57,* 194–201.

Denney, N. W. Aging and cognitive changes. In B. Wolman (Ed.), *Handbook of developmental psychology.* Englewood Cliffs, NJ: Prentice-Hall, 1982.

Denney, N. W., & Cornelius, S. W. Class inclusion and multiple classification in middle and old age. *Developmental Psychology,* 1975, *11,* 521–522.

Denney, N. W., & List, J. A. Adult age differences in performance on the Matching Familiar Figures test. *Human Development,* 1979, *22,* 137–144.

Dennis, W. The effect of cradling practices upon the onset of walking in Hopi children. *Journal of Genetic Psychology,* 1940, *56,* 77–86.

Dennis, W. Creative productivity between the ages of 20 and 80 years. *Journal of Gerontology,* 1966, *21,* 1–18.

Dennis, W. *Children of the creche.* New York: Meredith, 1973.

de Villiers, P., & de Villiers, J. *Early language.* Cambridge, MA: Harvard University Press, 1979.

DeVries, H. A. Physiological effects of an exercise training regimen upon men aged 52–88. *Journal of Gerontology,* 1970, *25,* 325–336.

DeVries, H. A. Physiology of exercise and aging. In D. S. Woodruff & J. E. Birren (Eds.), *Aging: Scientific perspectives and social issues.* New York: Van Nostrand Reinhold, 1975.

DeVries, H. A., & Adams, G. M. Electromyographic comparison of single doses of exercise and meprobamate as to effects on muscular relaxation. *American Journal of Physical Medicine,* 1972, *51,* 130–141.

Diaz, R. Bilingual cognitive development: Addressing three gaps in current research. *Child Development,* 1985, *56,* 1376–1388.

Diaz, R. M., & Berndt, T. J. Children's knowledge of a best friend: Fact or fantasy? *Developmental Psychology,* 1982, *18,* 787–794.

Dickens, W., & Perlman, D. Friendship over the life-cycle. In S. Duck & R. Gilmour (Eds.), *Personal relationships Vol. 2. Developing personal relationships*. New York: Academic Press, 1981.

Dinnerstein, D. *The mermaid and the minotaur: Sexual arrangements and human malaise*. New York: Harper & Row, 1976.

DiVitto, B., & Goldberg, S. The effects of newborn medical status on early parent–infant interactions. In T. M. Field, A. M. Sostek, S. Goldberg, & H. H. Shuman (Eds.), *Infants born at risk*. New York: Spectrum, 1979.

Dodge, K. Behavioral antecedents of peer social status. *Child Development*, 1983, *54*, 1386–1399.

Dohrenwend, B., Krasnoff, L., Askenasy, A., & Dohrenwend, B. Exemplication of a method for scaling life events. *Journal of Health and Social Behavior*, 1978, *19*, 205–229.

Dolen, L. S., & Bearison, D. J. Social interaction and social cognition in aging: A contextual analysis. *Human Development*, 1982, *25*, 430–442.

Donaldson, M. *Children's minds*. New York: Norton, 1978.

Doty, R., Shaman, P., & Dann, M. Development of the University of Pennsylvania Smell Identification Test: A standardized microencapsulated test of olfactory function. *Physiology and Behavior*. 1984, *32*, 489–502.

Douvan, E., & Adelson, J. *The adolescent experience*. New York: Wiley, 1966.

Doyle, A-B., Champagne, M., & Segalowitz, N. Some issues in the assessment of linguistic consequences of early bilingualism. In M. Paradis (Ed.), *Aspects of bilingualism*. Columbia, SC: Hornbeam Press, 1978.

Dreyer, P. H. Sexuality during adolescence. In B. Wolman (Ed.), *Handbook of developmental psychology*. Englewood Cliffs, NJ: Prentice-Hall, 1982.

Drillien, C. M., & Ellis, R. W. B. *The growth and development of the prematurely born infant*. Baltimore: Williams & Wilkins, 1964.

Dunn, J. Sibling relationships in early childhood. *Developmental Psychology*, 1983, *54*, 787–811.

Dunn, J., & Kendrick, C. *Siblings: Love, envy, and understanding*. Cambridge, MA: Harvard University Press, 1982.

Dunn, J., Plomin, R., & Daniels, D. Consistency and change in mother's behavior toward young siblings. *Child Development*, 1986, *57*, 348–356.

Dunphy, D. C. The social structure of urban adolescent peer groups. *Sociometry*, 1963, *26*, 230–246.

Durlak, J. A relationship between attitudes toward life and death among elderly women. *Developmental Psychology*, 1973, *8*, 146.

Durlak, J. Comparison between experimental and didactic methods of death education. *Omega*, 1978–1979, *9*, 57–66.

Dusek, J. B., & Flaherty, J. F. The development of the self-concept during the adolescent years. *Monographs of the Society for Research in Child Development*, 1981, *46*, serial no. 191.

Duvall, E. *Marriage and family development* (5th ed.). Philadelphia: Lippincott, 1977.

Eagly, A. Gender and social influence. *American Psychologist*, 1983, *38*, 971–981.

Eccles, J. Sex differences in math achievement and course enrollment. Paper presented at the annual meeting of the American Educational Research Association, New York, March 1982.

Eckerman, C. O., & Whatley, J. L. Toys and social interaction between infant peers. *Child Development*, 1977, *48*, 1645–1656.

Egeland, B., & Farber, E. Infant-mother attachment: Factors related to its development and changes over time. *Child Development*, 1984, *55*, 753–771.

Eichorn, D. H., Clausen, J. A., Haan, N., Honzik, M., & Mussen, P. H. (Eds.). *Present and past in middle life*. New York: Academic Press, 1981.

Eichorn, D. H., Hunt, J. V., & Honzik, M. P. Experience, personality, and IQ: Adolescence to middle age. In D. Eichorn, J. Clausen, N.

Haan, M. Honzik, & P. Mussen (Eds.), *Present and past in middle age*. New York: Academic Press, 1981.

Eiduson, B. T. Emergent families in the 1970's: Values, practices and impact on children. In D. Reiss & H. Hoffman (Eds.), *The family: Dying or developing*. New York: Plenum Press, 1978.

Eiduson, B. T., Cohen, J., & Alexander, J. Alternatives in child rearing in the 1970's. *American Journal of Orthopsychiatry*, 1973, *43*, 721–731.

Eiduson, B. T., Kornfein, M., Zimmerman, I. L., & Weisner, T. S. Comparative socialization practices in traditional and alternative families. In M. Lamb (Ed.), *Nontraditional families: Parenting and child development*. Hillsdale, NJ: Erlbaum, 1982.

Eisdorfer, C. Arousal and performance: Experiments in verbal learning and a tentative theory. In G. Talland (Ed.), *Human aging and behavior*. New York: Academic Press, 1968.

Eisdorfer, C., Nowlin, J., & Wilkie, F. Improvement of learning in the aged by modification of autonomic nervous system activity. *Science*, 1970, *170*, 1327–1329.

Eisdorfer, C., & Wilkie, F. Stress, disease, aging, and behavior. In J. E. Birren & K. W. Schaie (Eds.), *Handbook of the psychology of aging*. New York: Van Nostrand Reinhold, 1977.

Eisenberg, N., Wolchik, S., Hernandez, R., & Pasternack, J. Parental socialization of young children's play: A short term longitudinal study. *Child Development*, 1985, *56*, 1506–1573.

Elder, G., Downey, G., & Cross, C. Family ties and life chances: Hard times and hard choices in women's lives since the 1930s. In R. Turner and H. Reese (Eds.), *Lifespan developmental psychology*. New York: Academic Press, 1980.

Elkind, D. Quantity conceptions in junior and senior high school students. *Child Development*, 1961, *32*, 551–560.

Elkind, D. Quantity conceptions in college students. *Journal of Social Psychology*, 1962, *57*, 459–465.

Elkind, D. Egocentrism in adolescence. *Child Development,* 1967, *38,* 1025–1035.

Elkind, D. Understanding the young adolescent. *Adolescence,* 1978, *13,* 127–134.

Elkind, D. *The hurried child: Growing up too fast too soon.* Reading, MA: Addison-Wesley, 1981.

Elkind, D., & Bowen, R. Imaginary audience behavior in children and adolescents. *Developmental Psychology,* 1979, *15,* 38–44.

Ellison, J. The seven frames of mind. *Psychology Today,* June 1984, 20–26.

Elster, A., & Lamb, M. (Eds.) *Adolescent fatherhood.* Hillsdale, NJ: Lawrence Erlbaum, 1986.

Elster, A., & Hendricks, L. Stresses and coping strategies of adolescent fathers. In A. Elster & M. Lamb (Eds.), *Adolescent fatherhood.* Hillsdale, NJ: Erlbaum, 1986.

Emler, N. P. Morality and politics: The ideological dimension in the theory of moral development. In H. Weinreich-Haste & D. Locke (Eds.), *Morality in the making: Thought, action, and social context.* New York: Wiley, 1983.

Emler, N. P., Renwick, S., & Malone, M. The relationship between moral reasoning and political orientation. *Journal of Personality and Social Psychology,* 1983, *45,* 1073–1080.

Emr, M., & Schneider, E. Alzheimer's Disease: Research highlights. *Geriatric Nursing,* 1985, *16,* 135–138.

Engen, T. Taste and smell. In J. E. Birren & K. W. Schaie (Eds.), *Handbook of the psychology of aging.* New York: Van Nostrand Reinhold, 1977.

Epstein, H. T. EEG developmental stages. *Developmental Psychology,* 1980, *13,* 629–631.

Epstein, L. Comments at a workshop on childhood obesity, National Institute of Health, Washington, DC, March 10–11, 1986.

Epstein, M. H., Cullinan, D., Lessen, E., & Lloyd, J. Understanding children with learning disabilities. *Child Welfare,* 1980, *59,* 2–14.

Erikson, E. H. *Identity and the life-cycle: Selected papers by Erik H. Erikson.* New York: International Universities Press, 1959.

Erikson, E. H. *Childhood and society* (2nd ed.). New York: Norton, 1963.

Erikson, E. H. *Identity: Youth and crisis.* New York: Norton, 1968.

Erikson, E. H. Reflections on Dr. Borg's life cycle. *Daedalus,* Spring 1976, *105,* 1–28.

Eron, L. D. Parent–child interaction, television violence and aggression of children, *American Psychologist,* 1982, *37,* 197–211.

Eron, L. D. Prescription for the reduction of aggression. *American Psychologist,* 1980, *35,* 244–252.

Eron, L., Huesmann, L. R., Brice, P., Fischer, P., & Mermelstein, R. Age trends in the development of aggression, sex typing, and related television habits. *Developmental Psychology,* 1983, *19,* 71–77.

Ervin, S. Imitation and structural change in children's language. In E. H. Lenneberg (Ed.), *New directions in the study of language.* Cambridge, MA: MIT Press, 1964.

Escalona, S. Growing up with the threat of nuclear war: Some indirect effects on personality development. *American Journal of Orthopsychiatry,* 1982, *52,* 600–607.

Essex, M., & Nam, S. Marital status and loneliness among older women: The differential importance of close family and friends. *Journal of Marriage and the Family,* 1987, *49,* 93–106.

Etaugh, C. Effects of nonmaternal care on children. *American Psychologist,* 1980, *35,* 309–319.

Euthanasia Educational Council. *A living will.* New York: Euthanasia Educational Council, 1974.

Eveleth, P., & Tanner, J. *Worldwide variation in human growth.* Cambridge, England: Cambridge University Press, 1976.

The facts of adolescent life. *Parents Magazine,* February 1979, *54,* 69.

Fagan, J. Infant memory. In T. J. Field, A. Huston, H. C. Quay, L. Troll, & G. E. Finley (Eds.), *Review of human development.* New York: Wiley, 1982.

Fagot, B., Hagan, R., Leinbach, M., & Kronsberg, S. Differential reactions to assertive and communicative acts of toddler boys and girls. *Child Development,* 1985, *56,* 1499–1505.

Fairburn, C., & Cooper, P. The epidemiology of bulimia nervosa. *International Journal of Eating Disorders,* 1983, *2,* 61–67.

Fakouri, M. E. Cognitive development in adulthood: A fifth stage? A critique. *Developmental Psychology,* 1976, *12,* 472.

Falbo, T. Only children, stereotypes, and research. In M. Lewis & L. A. Rosenblum (Eds.), *The child and its family.* New York: Plenum, 1979.

Fantz, R. Pattern vision in young infants. *Psychological Record,* 1958, *8,* 43–49.

Fantz, R. L. The origins of form perception. *Scientific American,* 1961, *204,* 66–72.

Fantz, R. L. Visual perception from birth as shown by pattern selectivity. *Annals of the New York Academy of Science,* 1965, *118,* 793–814.

Farkas, M. S., & Hoyer, W. J. Processing consequences of perceptual grouping in selective attention. *Journal of Gerontology,* 1980, *35,* 207–216.

Fawcett, G., Stonner, D., & Zeppelin, H. Locus of control, perceived constraint, and morale among institutionalized aged. *Aging and Human Development,* 1980, *11,* 13–24.

FBI Law Enforcement Bulletin, May 1978, pp. 4–5.

Featherman, D. Life-span perspectives in social science research. In P. Baltes & O. Brim (Eds.), *Life-span development and behavior,* Vol. 5. New York: Academic Press, 1983.

Federal Bureau of Investigation. *Crime in the United States,* Washington, DC: Federal Bureau of Investigation, 1984.

Fein, G. C., Jacobson, J., Jacobson, S., Schwartz, P., & Dowler, J. Prenatal exposure to polychlorinated biphenyls: Effects on birth size and gestational age. *Journal of Pediatrics,* 1984, *105,* 315–320.

Feingold, A. Cognitive gender differences are disappearing. *American Psychologist,* 1988, *43,* 95–103.

Ferree, M. M. Working-class jobs: Housework and paid work as sources of satisfaction. *Social Problems,* 1976, *23,* 431–441.

Feshbach, N. The relationship of child rearing factors to children's aggression, empathy and related positive and negative behaviors. In J. deWit & W. W. Hartup (Eds.), *Determinants and origins of aggressive behavior.* The Hague: Mouton, 1974.

Field, T. Interaction behaviors of primary versus secondary caretaker fathers. *Developmental Psychology,* 1978, *14,* 183–184.

Field, T., Woodson, R., Greenberg, R., & Cohen, D., Discrimination and imitation of facial expressions by neonates. *Science,* 1982, *218,* 179–181.

Fine, G. Friends, impression management, and preadolescent behavior. In S. Asher & J. Gottman (Eds.), *The development of children's friendships.* New York: Cambridge University Press, 1981.

Fischer, D. *Growing old in America.* New York: Oxford University Press, 1987.

Fischer, K., Relations between brain and cognitive development, *Child Development,* 1987, *58,* 623–632.

Fishkin, J, Keniston, K., & Mac-Kinnon, C. Moral reasoning and political ideology. *Journal of Personality and Social Psychology,* 1973, *27,* 109–119.

Flanagan, J. Some characteristics of 70-year-old workers. Paper presented at the Annual Meeting of the American Psychological Association, Los Angeles, August 1981.

Flavell, J. H. *Cognitive Development.* Englewood Cliffs, NJ: Prentice-Hall, 1977.

Flavell, J., Beach, R., & Chinsky, J. Spontaneous verbal rehearsal in a memory task as a function of age. *Child Development,* 1966, *37,* 283–299.

Flavell, J., Green, F., & Flavell, E. Development of knowledge about the appearance-reality distinction. *Monographs of the Society for Research in Child Development,* 1986, *51,* no. 1., serial no. 212.

Flavell, J. H., & Wellman, H. Metamemory. In R. Kail & J. Hagen (Eds.), *Perspectives on the develop-ment of memory and cognition.* Hillsdale, NJ: Erlbaum, 1977.

Flavell, J. H., & Wohlwill, J. F. Formal and functional aspects of cognitive development. In D. Elkind & J. H. Flavell (Eds.), *Studies in cognitive development: Essays in honor of Jean Piaget.* New York: Oxford University Press, 1969.

Fleming, J. B. *Stopping wife abuse.* Garden City, NY: Anchor Press, 1979.

Flynn, J. R. The mean IQ of Americans: Massive gains 1932 to 1978. *Psychological Bulletin,* 1984, *95,* 29–51.

Foley, M., Johnson, M., & Raye, C. Age related changes in confusion between memories for thoughts and memories for speech. *Child Development,* 1983, *54,* 51–60.

Forbes, G. B. Growth of the lean body mass in man. *Growth,* 1972, *36,* 325–338.

Fowles, B., & Glanz, M. Competence and talent in verbal riddle comprehension. *Journal of Child Language,* 1977, *4,* 433–452.

Fox, G. L. The family's influence on adolescent sexual behavior. *Children Today,* 1979 (May–June), 21–25.

Fox, J. H. Effects of retirement and former work life on women's adaptation to old age. *Journal of Gerontology,* 1977, *32,* 196–202.

Fozard, J. L., Wolf, E., Bell, B., MacFarland, R., & Podolsky, S. Visual perception and communication. In J. E. Birren & K. W. Schaie (Eds.), *Handbook of the psychology of aging.* New York: Van Nostrand Reinhold, 1977.

Fraiberg, S. *Every child's birthright: In defense of mothering.* New York: Basic Books, 1977.

Frazier, T., Davis, G., Goldstein, H., & Goldberg, I. Cigarette smoking: A prospective study. *American Journal of Obstetrics and Gynecology,* 1961, *81,* 988–996.

Freeman, N., & Janikoun, R. Intellectual realism in children's drawings of a familiar object with distinctive features. *Child development,* 1972, *43,* 1116–1121.

Freidrich, L., & Stein, A. Aggressive and prosocial television programs and the natural behavor of preschool children. *Monographs of the Society for Research in Child Development,* 1974, *38,* no. 4, serial no. 151.

French, D., & Waas, G. Behavior problems of peer-neglected and peer-rejected elementary-age children: Parent and teacher perspectives. *Child Development,* 1985, *56,* 246–252.

Freud, A. Adolescence. *The Psychoanalytic Study of the Child,* 1958, *13,* 255–278.

Freud, S. *A general introduction to psychoanalysis.* London: Boni and Liveright, 1924.

Fried, B. *The middle-age crisis.* New York: Harper & Row, 1967.

Friedenberg, E. Z. *Vanishing adolescence.* Boston: Beacon, 1959.

Friedman, M., & Rosenman, R. H. *Type A behavior and your heart.* New York: Knopf, 1974.

Friedman, S., Jacobs, B., & Werthmann, M. Sensory processing in pre- and full-term infants in the neonatal period. In S. Friedman & M. Sigman (Eds.), *Preterm birth and psychological development.* New York: Academic Press, 1981.

Friedmann, E. A., & Orbach, H. L. Adjustment to retirement. In *American handbook of psychiatry,* Vol. 1. New York: Basic Books, 1974.

Fries, J., & Crapo, L. *Vitality and aging: Implications of the rectangular curve.* San Francisco: W. H. Freeman, 1981.

Frodi, A., Lamb, M., Leavitt, L., Donovan, W. L., Neff, C., & Sherry, D. Fathers' and mothers' responses to the faces and cries of normal and premature infants. *Developmental Psychology,* 1978, *14,* 490–498.

Fuchs, V. R. *Who shall live? Health, economics and social choice.* New York: Basic Books, 1974.

Furman, E. *A child's parent dies.* New Haven: Yale University Press, 1974.

Furrow, D., Nelson, K., & Benedict, H. Mothers' speech to children and syntactic development: Some simple relationships. *Journal of Child Language,* 1979, *6,* 423–442.

Furstenberg, F. Premarital pregnancy and marital instability. In G. Levinger & O. Moles (Eds.), *Divorce and separation: Context, causes and consequences.* New York: Basic Books, 1979.

Furstenberg, F., Nord C., Peterson, J., & Zill, N. The life course of children of divorce: Marital disruption and parental contact. *American Sociological Review*, 1983, *48*, 656–668.

Fuson, K., Secada, W., & Hall, J. Matching, counting and conservation of numerical equivalence. *Child Development*, 1983, *54*, 91–97.

Gallahue, D. L. *Motor development and movement experiences for young children.* New York: Wiley, 1976.

Gallup, G. Self-recognition in primates. A comparative approach to the bidirectional properties of consciousness. *American Psychologist*, 1977, *32*, 329–338.

Galton, Francis. *Hereditary genius: An inquiry into its laws and consequences.* London: Macmillan, 1869.

Gardner, H. Metaphors and modalities: How children project polar adjectives onto diverse domains. *Child Development*, 1974, *45*, 84–91.

Gardner, H. *Frames of mind: The theory of multiple intelligence.* New York: Basic Books, 1983.

Gardner, L. Deprivation dwarfism. *Scientific American*, 1972, *227*, 17–25.

Garmezy, N., & Rutter, M. (Eds.) *Stress, coping and development in children.* New York: McGraw-Hill, 1983.

Garrett, W. R. *Seasons of marriage and family life.* New York: Holt, Rinehart and Winston, 1982.

Gelles, R. J., & Straus, M. A. Violence in the American family. *Journal of Social Issues*, 1979, *35*, 14–38.

Gelman, R. Preschool thought. *American Psychologist*, 1979, *34*, 900–905.

Gelman, R., & Gallistel, C. *The child's understanding of number.* Cambridge, MA: Harvard University Press, 1978.

Gelman, R., Spelke, E. S., & Meck, E. What preschoolers know about animate and inanimate objects. In D. Rogers & J. A. Sloboda (Eds.),

The acquisition of symbolic skills. New York: Plenum, 1983.

Gelman, S., Collman, P., & Maccoby, E. Inferring properties from categories versus inferring categories from properties: The case of gender. *Child Development*, 1986, *57*, 396–404.

Gergen, K. The emerging crisis in life-span developmental theory. In P. Baltes and O. Brim (Eds.), *Life-span Development and Behavior* (Vol. 3). New York: Academic Press, 1980.

Gesell, A. The ontogenesis of infant behavior. In L. Carmichael (Ed.), *Manual of child psychology* (2nd ed.). New York: Wiley, 1954.

Gesell, A., & Thompson, M. Learning and growth in identical infant twins: An experimental study by method of co-twin control. *Genetic Psychology Monographs*, 1929, *6*, 1–124.

Gibson, B., Roberts, P., & Buttery, T. *Death education: A concern for the living.* Bloomington, IN: Phi Beta Kappa Educational Foundation, 1982.

Gibson, E. J., & Walk, R. D. The visual cliff. *Scientific American*, 1960, *202*, 64–71.

Gil, D. *Violence against children: Physical child abuse in the United States.* Cambridge, MA: Harvard University Press, 1970.

Gilder, G. *Naked nomads.* New York: Quadrangle, 1974.

Gilligan, C. *In a different voice: Psychological theory and women's development.* Cambridge, MA: Harvard University Press, 1982.

Ginzberg, E., Ginzberg, S., Axelrod, W., & Herna, J. *Occupational choice.* New York: Columbia University Press, 1951.

Gjerde, P., Black, J., & Black, J. The longitudinal consistency of matching familiar figures test performance from early childhood to preadolescence. *Developmental Psychology*, 1985, *21*, 262–271.

Glaser, B., & Strauss, A. *Awareness of dying.* Chicago: Aldine, 1965.

Glaser, B., & Strauss, A. *Time for dying.* Chicago: Aldine, 1968.

Glaser, K. The treatment of depressed and suicidal adolescents. *American Journal of Psychotherapy*, 1978, *32*, 252–269.

Gleitman, L., Newport, E., & Gleitman, H. The current status of the motherese hypothesis. *Journal of Child Language*, 1984, *11*, 43–79.

Glenn, N., & Kramer, K. The marriages and divorces of the children of divorce. *Journal of Marriage and the Family*, 1987, *49*, 811–825.

Glenn, N., & Shelton, B. Pre-adult background variables and divorce: A note of caution about over-reliance on explained variance. *Journal of Marriage and the Family*, 1983, *45*, 405–510.

Glenn, N., & Shelton, B. Regional differences in divorce in the United States. *Journal of Marriage and the Family*, 1985, *44*, 641–652.

Glick, P. C. Children of divorced parents in demographic perspective. *Journal of Social Issues*, 1979, *35*, 170–182.

Gold, D., & Andres, D. Developmental comparison between adolescent children with employed and nonemployed mothers. *Merrill-Palmer Quarterly*, 1978, *24*, 243–254. (a)

Gold, D., & Andres, D. Developmental comparisons between 10-year-old children with employed and nonemployed mothers. *Child Development*, 1978, *49*, 75–84. (b)

Gold, D., & Andres, D. Relations between maternal employment and development of nursery-school children. *Canadian Journal of Behavioral Science*, 1978, *10*, 116–129. (c)

Gold, D., & Andres, D., & Glorieux, J. The development of Francophone nursery children with employed and nonemployed mothers. *Canadian Journal of Behavioral Sciences*, 1979, *11*, 169–173.

Goldberg, S. Premature birth: Consequences for the parent–infant relationship. *Science*, 1979, *67*, 214–220.

Goldberg, S. Social competence in infancy: A model of parent–infant interaction. *Merrill-Palmer Quarterly*, 1977, *23*, 163–177.

Goldberg, S., Brachfield, S., & DiVitto, B. Feeding, fussing and play: Parent–infant interaction in the first year as a function of prematurity and perinatal medical problems. In T. Field, S. Goldberg, D. Stern, & A. Sostek (Eds.),

High-risk infants and children: Adult and peer interactions. New York: Academic Press, 1980.

Goldberg, S., & DiVitto, B. *Born too soon.* San Francisco: Freeman, 1983.

Goldberg S., Perrotta, M., Minde, K., & Corter, C. Maternal behavior and attachment in low-birthweight twins and singletons. *Child Development*, 1986, *57*, 34–46.

Golden, M., Rosenbluth, L., Grossi, M., Policare, M., Freeman, H., & Brownlee, E. *The New York City infant day care study.* New York: Medical and Health Association of New York City, 1978.

Goldman, R., & Goldman, J. How children perceive the origin of babies and the role of mothers and fathers in procreation: A cross-national study. *Child Development*, 1982, *53*, 491–504.

Goldscheider, F., & Waite, L. Nest-leaving patterns and the transition to marriage for young men and women. *Journal of Marriage and the Family*, 1987, *49*, 507–516.

Goldsmith, H. H., & Campos, J. J. Toward a theory of infant temperament. In R. Emde & R. Harmon (Eds.), *The development of attachment and affiliative systems.* New York: Plenum Press, 1982.

Goldstein, E. Effects of same-sex and cross-sex role models on the subsequent academic productivity of scholars. *American Psychologist*, 1979, *34*, 407–410.

Goodall, M. Left-handedness as an educational handicap. In R. S. Laura (Ed.), *Problems of Handicap.* Melbourne: Macmillan, 1980.

Goodman, M. Toward a biology of menopause. *Signs: Journal of Women in Culture and Society*, 1980, *5*, 739–753.

Goodnow, J. J. A test of milieu differences with some of Piaget's tasks. *Psychological Monographs*, 1962, 76 (36), whole no. 555.

Gordon, C., Gaitz, C. M., & Scott, J. Leisure and lives: Personal expressivity across the life span. In R. Binstock & E. Shanas (Eds.), *Handbook of aging and the social sciences.* New York: Van Nostrand Reinhold, 1977.

Gormly, A., Gormly, J., & Weiss, H. Motivations for parenthood among young adult college students. *Sex Roles*, 1987, *16*, 31–39.

Gottfredson, D. Youth employment, crime, and schooling: A longitudinal study of a national sample. *Developmental Psychology*, 1985, *21*, 419–432.

Gottfried, A., & Bathurst, L. Hand preference across time is related to intelligence in young girls, not boys, *Science*, 1983, *221*, 1074–1076.

Gould, L. X: A fabulous child's story. *Ms.*, December 1972, 74–76; 105–106.

Gould, R. L. The phases of adult life: A study of developmental psychology. *American Journal of Psychiatry*, 1972, *129*, 33–43.

Gould, R. *Transformations: Growth and change in adult life.* New York: Simon & Schuster, 1978.

Gouze, K., & Nadelman, L. Constancy of gender identity for self and others in children between the ages of three and seven. *Child Development*, 1980, *51*, 275–278.

Gove, W. R. Sex, marital status, and mortality. *American Journal of Sociology*, 1973, *79*, 45–67.

Graham, F. K., Ernhart, C. B., Thurston, D. L., & Craft, M. Development three years after perinatal anoxia and other potentially damaging newborn experiences. *Psychological Monographs*, 1962, *76*, whole no. 522, 3.

Granick, S., Kleban, M. H., Weiss, A. D. Relationship between hearing loss and cognition in normally hearing aged persons. *Journal of Gerontology*, 1976, *31*, 434–440.

Gray, W., & Hudson, L. Formal operations and the imaginary audience. *Developmental Psychology*, 1984, *20*, 619–627.

Gray-Little, B., & Burk, N. Power and satisfaction in marriage: A review and critique. *Psychological Bulletin*, 1983, *93*, 513–538.

Greeley, J. *Euthanasia: The debate.* Cincinnati: Pamphlet Publications, 1977.

Green, C. P., & Polleigen, K. *Teenage pregnancy: A major problem for minors.* Washington, DC: Zero Population Growth, August 1977.

Green, L., & Horton, D. Adolescent health: Issues and challenges. In T. J. Coates, A. C. Peterson, & C. Perry (Eds.), *Promoting adolescent health: A dialogue on research and practice.* New York: Academic Press, 1982.

Green, W., Campbell, M., & David, R. Psychosocial dwarfism: A critical review of the evidence. *Journal of the American Academy of Child Psychiatry*, 1984, *23*, 39–48.

Greenberger, E., Steinberg, L., & Ruggiero, M. A job is a job is a job . . . or is it? *Work and Occupations*, 1982, *9*, 79–96.

Greenberger, E., Steinberg, L., & Vaux, A. Adolescents who work: Health and behavioral consequences of job stress. *Developmental Psychology*, 1981, *17*, 691–703.

Greene, J., Fox, N., & Lewis, M. The relationship between neonatal characteristics and three-month mother–infant interaction in high-risk infants. *Child Development*, 1983, *54*, 1286–1296.

Greenspan, S. *First feelings.* New York: Viking Press, 1984.

Grief, E. B., & Ulman, K. J. The psychological impact of menarche on early adolescent females: A review of the literature. *Child Development*, 1982, *53*, 1413–1430.

Grollman, E. (Ed.). *Explaining death to children.* Boston: Beacon Press, 1967.

Grotevant, H., & Cooper, C. The role of family experience in career exploration: A life-span perspective. In P. Baltes, D. Featherman, & R. Lerner (Eds.), *Lifespan development and behavior*, Vol. 8. Hillsdale, NJ: Erlbaum, 1988.

Grzegorczyk, P. B., Jones, S. W., & Mistretta, C. M. Age-related differences in salt-taste acuity. *Journal of Gerontology*, 1979, *34*, 834–840.

Gubrium, J. F. Being single in old age. *International Journal of Aging and Human Development*, 1975, *6*, 29–41.

Gunn, J., & Peterson, A. (Eds.) *Girls at puberty: Biological psychological, and social perspectives.* New York: Plenum, 1984.

Gunther, J. *Death be not proud.* New York: Harper & Row, 1949.

Gurin, G., Veroff, J., & Feld, S. *Americans view their mental health.* New York: Basic Books, 1960.

Gutmann, D. The cross-cultural perspective: Notes toward a comprehensive psychology of aging. In J. E. Birren & K. W. Schaie (Eds.), *Handbook of the psychology of aging.* New York: Van Nostrand Reinhold, 1977.

Haan, N. Common dimensions of personality development: Early adolescence to middle life. In D. Eichorn, J. Clausen, N. Haan, M. Honzik, & P. Mussen (Eds.), *Present and past in middle life.* New York: Academic Press, 1981.

Haan, N., & Day, D. A longitudinal study of change and sameness in personality development: Adolescence to later adulthood. *International Journal of Aging and Human Development,* 1974, *5,* 11–39.

Haan, N., Smith, M. B., & Block, J. H. Moral reasoning of young adults: Political–social behavior, family background, and personality correlates. *Journal of Personality and Social Psychology,* 1968, *10,* 183–201.

Hagestad, G. O. Patterns of communication and influence between grandparents and grandchildren in a changing society. Paper presented at the World Congress of Sociology, Uppsala, Sweden, August 1978.

Hagestad, G. O. Issues in the study of intergenerational continuity. Paper presented at the National Council on Family Relations Theory and Methods Workshop. Washington, DC, October 1982.

Hagestad, G. O. The continuous bond: A dynamic, multigenerational perspective on parent–child relations between adults. In M. Perlmutter (Ed.), *Minnesota symposia on child psychology,* Vol. 17. Hillsdale, NJ: Erlbaum, 1984.

Haith, M. *Rules newborns look by.* Hillsdale, NJ: Erlbaum, 1980.

Hakuto, K. Degree of bilingualism and cognitive ability in mainland Puerto Rican children. *Child Development,* 1987, *58,* 1372–1388.

Hall, G. S. *Adolescence: Its psychology and its relations to physiology, anthropology, sociology, sex, crime, religion, and education* (2 volumes). New York: Appleton, 1904.

Hallahan, D., & Kauffman, J. *Excep-tional children: Introduction to special education* (2nd ed.). Englewood Cliffs, NJ: Prentice-Hall, 1982.

Halling, H. Suspected link between exposure to hexachlorophene and malformed infants. *Annals of the New York Academy of Sciences,* 1979, *320,* 426–435.

Halverson, H. M. An experimental study of prehension in infants by means of systematic cinema records. *Genetic Psychology Monographs,* 1931, *10,* 107–286.

Hamid, P., & Wyllie, A. What generation gap? *Adolescence,* 1980, *15,* 385–391.

Hammill, D., & Bartel, N. *Teaching children with learning and behavior problems.* Boston: Allyn and Bacon, 1975.

Hammond, D., & Middleton, R. Penile prosthesis. *Medical Aspects of Human Sexuality,* 1984, *18,* 204–208.

Hardy-Brown, K. Formal operations and the issue of generality: The analysis of poetry by college students. *Human Development,* 1979, *22,* 127–136.

Hardyck, C., & Petrenovick, L. Left-handedness. *Psychological Bulletin,* 1977, *84,* 385–404.

Harkins, E. B. Effects of empty-nest transition on self-report of psychological and physical well-being. *Journal of Marriage and the Family,* 1978, *40,* 549–558.

Harlow, H. F. The heterosexual affectional system in monkeys. *American Psychologist,* 1962, *17,* 1–9.

Harlow, H. F., & Harlow, M. K. Learning to love. *American Scientist,* 1966, *54,* 244–272.

Harris, C. S. *Fact book on aging: A profile on America's older population.* Washington, DC: The National Council on the Aging, 1978.

Harris, L., and Associates, Inc. *The myth and reality of aging in America.* Washington, DC: The National Council on the Aging, 1975.

Harris, S. L., & Ersner-Hershfield, R. Behavioral suppression of seriously disruptive behavior in psychotic and retarded patients: A review of punishment and its alternatives. *Psychological Bulletin,* 1978, *85,* 1352–1375.

Harter, S. The perceived competence scale for children. *Child Development,* 1982, *53,* 87–89.

Harter, S. Developmental perspectives on the self-system. In E. M. Hetherington (Ed.), *Handbook of child psychology. Vol. IV: Socialization, personality, and social development.* New York: Wiley, 1983.

Hartley, J. T., Harker, J., & Walsh, D. A. Contemporary issues and new directions in adult development of learning and memory. In L. Poon (Ed.), *Aging in the 1980s: Psychological issues.* Washington, DC: American Psychological Association, 1980.

Hartshorne, H., & May, M. S. *Studies in the nature of character. Vol. 1: Studies in deceit, Vol. 2: Studies in self-control, Vol. 3: Studies in organization of character.* New York: Macmillan, 1928–1930.

Hartup, W. Peer interaction and social organization. In P. Mussen (Ed.), *Carmichaels' manual of child psychology* (Vol. 2). New York: Wiley, 1970.

Hartup, W. Peer relations. In C. Kopp & J. Krakow (Eds.), *The child: Development in a social context.* Reading, MA: Addison-Wesley, 1982.

Hartup, W. W. Peer relations. In E. M. Hetherington (Ed.), *Handbook of child psychology. Vol. IV: Socialization, personality, and social development.* New York: Wiley, 1983.

Haskins, R. Public school aggression among children with varying day-care experience. *Child Development,* 1985, *56,* 689–703.

Hass, A. *Teenage sexuality.* New York: Macmillan, 1979.

Havens, E. M. Women, work, and wedlock: A note on female marital patterns in the United States. *American Journal of Sociology,* 1973, *78,* 975–981.

Havighurst, R. J. Youth in exploration and man emergent. In H. Borrow (Ed.), *Man in a world of work.* Boston: Houghton Mifflin, 1964.

Havighurst, R. J. *Developmental tasks and education* (3rd ed.). New York: McKay, 1974.

Havighurst, R. J. The world of work. In B. Wolman (Ed.), *Handbook of developmental psychology.* Englewood Cliffs, NJ: Prentice-Hall, 1982.

Havighurst, R. J., Neugarten, B. L., & Tobin, S. S. Disengagement and patterns of aging. In B. L. Neugarten (Ed.), *Middle age and aging.* Chicago: University of Chicago Press, 1968.

Hawkins, J., Pea, R., Glick, J., & Scribner, S. "Merds that laugh don't like mushrooms": Evidence for deductive reasoning by preschoolers. *Developmental Psychology,* 1984, *20,* 584–594.

Hawton, K., & Osborn, M. Suicide and attempted suicide in children and adolescents. In B. Lahey & A. Kazdin (Eds.), *Advances in clinical child psychology* (Vol. 7). New York: Plenum Press, 1984.

Hayes, C., & Kammerman, S. *Children of working parents: Experiences and outcomes.* Washington, DC: National Academy Press, 1983.

Hayflick, L. Aging under glass. *Experimental Gerontology,* 1970, *5,* 291–303.

Hayflick, L. The cellular basis for biological aging. In C. E. Finch & L. Hayflick (Eds.), *Handbook of the biology of aging.* New York: Van Nostrand Reinhold, 1977.

Hayflick, L. The cell biology of human aging. *Scientific American,* 1980, *242,* 58–66.

Haynes, H., White, B. W., & Held, R. Visual accommodation in human infants. *Science,* 1965, *148,* 528–530.

Health Information Network. *The facts about AIDS: a special guide for NEA members.* Washington, DC: 1987.

Heckler, M. The fight against Alzheimer's disease. *American Psychologist,* 1985, *40,* 1240–1244.

Hedin, D., Erickson, J., Simon, P., & Walker, J. *Minnesota youth poll: Aspirations, future plans, and expectations of young people in Minnesota.* St. Paul: University of Minnesota, Report AD-MR-2512, Center for Youth Development and Research, 1985.

Helson, R. Personality characteristics and developmental history of creative college women. *Genetic Psychology Monographs,* 1967, *76,* 205–256.

Hendry, L. B., & Gillies, P. Body type, body esteem, school, and leisure: A study of overweight, average, and underweight adolescents. *Journal of Youth and Adolescence,* 1978, *7,* 181–195.

Henig, R. The child savers. *New York Times,* March 22, 1981.

Henshaw, S., & O'Reilly, K. Characteristics of abortion patients in the United States, 1979 and 1980. *Family Planning Perspectives,* 1983, *15,* 5–16.

Herman, J., & Roth, S. Children's incidental memory for spatial locations in a large-scale environment: Taking a tour down memory lane. *Merrill-Palmer Quarterly,* 1984, *30,* 87–102.

Hernandez, A. Cardiac orienting response and habituation/dishabituation in term and preterm infants due to pure tone auditory stimuli. Paper presented at the meetings of the Society for Research in Child Development, Boston, 1981.

Hess, B. Friendship. In M. Riley, M. Johnson, & A. Foner (Eds.), *Aging and society, Vol. 3: A sociology of age stratification.* New York: Russell Sage Foundation, 1972.

Hess, B., & Markson, E. W. *Aging and old age.* New York: Macmillan, 1980.

Hess, B., & Waring, J. M. Parent and child in later life: Rethinking the relationship. In R. Lerner & G. Spanier (Eds.), *Child influences on marital and family interaction: A lifespan perspective.* New York: Academic Press, 1978.

Hess, R., & Camara, K. Post-divorce family relationships as mediating factors in the consequences of divorce for children. In T. E. Levitin (Ed.), *Children of divorce. Journal of Social Issues,* 1979, *35,* 79–96.

Hess, R. D. Political socialization in the schools. *Harvard Educational Review,* 1968, *38,* 528–536.

Hetherington, E. M. Divorce: A child's perspective. *American Psychologist,* 1979, *34,* 851–858.

Hetherington, E. M., Cox, M., & Cox, R. Effects of divorce on parents and children. In M. Lamb (Ed.), *Nontraditional families: Parenting and child development.* Hillside, NJ: Erlbaum, 1982.

Hickey, T., & Kalish, R. A. Young people's perceptions of adults. *Journal of Gerontology,* 1968, *23,* 215–219.

Hill, R. Methodological issues in family development research. *Family Process,* 1964, *3,* 186–206.

Hirsch, J. All number and size as a determinant of subsequent obesity. In M. Winick (Ed.), *Childhood obesity.* New York: Wiley, 1975.

Hock, E. Working and nonworking mothers with infants: Perceptions of their careers, the infants' needs, and satisfaction with mothering. *Developmental Psychology,* 1978, *14,* 37–43.

Hock, E., Christman, K., & Hock, M. Factors associated with decisions about return to work in mothers of infants. *Developmental Psychology,* 1980, *16,* 535–536.

Hoffman, L. W. Effects of maternal employment on the child—a review of the research. *Developmental Psychology,* 1974, *10,* 204–228.

Hoffman, L. W. Maternal employment: 1979. *American Psychologist,* 1979, *34,* 859–865.

Hoffman, L. W., & Mavis, J. D. Influences of children on marital interaction and parental satisfactions and dissatisfactions. In R. Lerner & G. Spanier (Eds.), *Child influences on marriage and family interaction: A lifespan perspective.* New York: Academic Press, 1978.

Hoffman, L. W., & Nye, F. I. *Working mothers.* San Francisco: Jossey-Bass, 1974.

Hoffman, M. Development of moral thought, feeling and behavior. In E. M. Hetherington & R. Parke (Eds.), *Contemporary readings in child psychology* (2nd ed.). New York: McGraw-Hill, 1981.

Hogan, D. The variable order of events in the life course. *American Sociological Review,* 1978, *43,* 573–586.

Holden, C. Identical twins reared apart. *Science,* 1980, *207,* 1323–1328.

Holden, G. Avoiding conflicts: Mothers as tacticians in the supermarket. *Child Development,* 1983, *54,* 233–240.

Holland, J. L. *Making vocational choices: A theory of careers.* Englewood Cliffs, NJ: Prentice-Hall, 1973.

Holmes, L. How fathers can cause the Down's syndrome. *Human Nature,* 1978, *1,* 70–72.

Holmes, T. H., & Masuda, M. Life change and illness susceptibility. In B. S. Dohrenwend & B. P. Dohrenwend (Eds.), *Stressful life events: Their nature and effects.* New York: Wiley, 1974.

Holmes, T. H., & Rahe, R. H. The social readjustment rating scale. *Journal of Psychosomatic Research,* 1967, *11,* 213–218.

Honzik, M., Macfarlane, J., & Allen, L. The stability of mental test performance between 2 and 18 years. *Journal of Experimental Education,* 1948, *4,* 309–324.

Hooper, F. H., & Sheehan, N. W. Logical concept attainment during the aging years: Issues in the neo-Piagetian research literature. In W. Overton & J. Gallagher (Eds.), *Knowledge and development* (Vol. 1). New York: Plenum Press, 1977.

Hoover, R., Gray, L., & Cole, P. Menopausal estrogens and breast cancer. *New England Journal of Medicine,* 1976, *295,* 401–405.

Horn, J. L. Organization of data on lifespan development of human abilities. In L. R. Goulet & P. B. Baltes (Eds.), *Lifespan developmental psychology: Research and theory.* New York: Academic Press, 1970.

Horn, J. L. Intelligence: Why it grows, why it declines. In J. Hunt (Ed.), *Human intelligence.* New Brunswick, NJ: Transaction Books, 1972.

Horn, J. L. The aging of human abilities. In B. Wolman (Ed.), *Handbook of developmental psychology.* Englewood Cliffs, NJ: Prentice-Hall, 1982.

Horn, J. L., & Cattell, R. B. Refinement and test of the theory of fluid and crystallized intelligence. *Journal of Educational Psychology,* 1966, *57,* 253–270.

Horn, J. L., & Donaldson, G. Cognitive development in adulthood. In O. G. Brim, Jr., & J. Kagan (Eds.), *Constancy and change in human development.* Cambridge, MA: Harvard University Press, 1980.

Hostetler, A. Alzheimer's trials hinge on early diagnoses. *APA Monitor,* 1987, *18,* 14–15.

Houseknecht, S., Vaughan, S., & Statham, A. The impact of singlehood on the career patterns of professional women. *Journal of Marriage and the Family,* 1987, *149,* 353–366.

Howes, C. Sharing fantasy: Social pretend play in toddlers. *Child Development,* 1985, *56,* 1253–1258.

Howes, C., & Olenick, M. Family and child care influences on toddler's compliance. *Child Development,* 1986, *57,* 202–216.

Howes, C., & Rubenstein, J. Determinants of toddler experiences in day care: Age of entry and quality of setting. *Child Care Quarterly,* 1985, *14,* 140–151.

Hoyer, W. J., & Plude, D. J. Attentional and perceptual processes in the study of cognitive aging. In L. Poon (Ed.), *Aging in the 1980s: Psychological issues.* Washington, DC: American Psychological Association, 1980.

Hudson, T. Correspondence and numerical differences between disjoint sets. *Child Development,* 1983, *54,* 84–90.

Hugin, F., Norris, A., & Shock, N. W. Skin reflex and voluntary reaction time in young and old males. *Journal of Gerontology,* 1960, *14,* 338–391.

Hulicka, I. M. Age differences in retention as a function of interference. *Journal of Gerontology,* 1967, *22,* 274–280.

Hultsch, D. F., & Plemons, J. K. Life events and life span development. In P. B. Baltes & O. G. Brim, Jr. (Eds.), *Life-span development and behavior* (Vol. 2). New York: Academic Press, 1979.

Hume, E. Gays see election as chance for gain: May be main political force this year. *Wall Street Journal.* January 11, 1984, p. 60.

Hunt, B., & Hunt, M. *Prime time: A guide to the pleasures and opportunities of the new middle age.* New York: Stein & Day, 1975.

Hunt, J. V., & Rhodes, L. Mental development of preterm infants during the first year. *Child Development,* 1977, *48,* 204–210.

Hunt, M. *Sexual behavior in the 1970s.* Chicago: Playboy Press, 1974.

Hunt, M., & Hunt, B. *The divorce experience.* New York: McGraw-Hill, 1977.

Hunter, F. T. Adolescents' perception of discussions with parents and friends. *Developmental Psychology,* 1985, *121,* 433–440.

Husain, S., & Vandiver, T. *Suicide in children and adolescents.* New York: SP Medical and Scientific Books, 1984.

Huston, A., Wright, J., Wartella, E., Rice, M., Watkins, B., Campbell, T., & Pitts, C. Communicating more than content: Formal features of children's television programs. *Journal of Communication,* 1981, *31,* 32–48.

Huston-Stein, A., & Higgens-Trenk, A. Development of females from childhood through adulthood: Career and feminine orientations. In P. B. Baltes (Ed.), *Life-span development and behavior* (Vol. 1). New York: Academic Press, 1978.

Huyck, M. H. From gregariousness to intimacy: Marriage and friendship over the adult years. In T. Field, A. Huston, H. Quay, L. Troll, & G. Finley (Eds.), *Review of human development.* New York: Wiley, 1982.

Huyck, M. H., & Hoyer, W. J. *Adult development and aging.* Belmont, CA: Wadsworth, 1982.

Hyde, J. S. *Understanding human sexuality.* New York: McGraw-Hill, 1979.

Iannotti, R. Effect of role-taking experiences on role taking, empathy, altruism, and aggression. *Developmental Psychology,* 1978, *14,* 119–124.

Iannotti, R. Naturalistic and structured assessments of prosocial behavior in preschool children: The influence of empathy and perspective taking. *Developmental Psychology,* 1985, *21,* 46–55.

Inhelder, B., & Piaget, J. *The growth of logical thinking from childhood to adolescence.* New York: Basic Books, 1958.

Inhelder, B., & Piaget, J. *The growth of logic in the child: Classification and seriation.* New York: Humanities Press, 1970.

Istomina, Z. The development of voluntary memory in preschool-age children. *Soviet Psychology,* 1975, *13,* 5–64.

Izard, C. E. The maximally discriminative facial movement coding system (MAX). Newark: University of Delaware, Instructional Resources Center, 1979.

Jacobson, J., Jacobson, S., Fein, G., Schwartz, P., & Dowler, J. Prenatal exposure to an environmental toxin: A test of the multiple effects models. *Developmental Psychology,* 1984, *20,* 523–532.

Jacobson, L. Illness and human sexuality. *Nursing Outlook,* 1974, *22,* 50–53.

Jacobson, S., Fein, G., Jacobson, J., Schwartz, P., & Dowler, J. The effects of intrauterine PCB exposure on visual recognition memory. *Child Development,* 1985, *56,* 853–860.

James, W. *Principles of psychology* (2 vols.). New York: Holt, 1890.

Jaques, E. Death and the midlife crisis. *International Journal of Psychoanalysis,* 1964, *46,* 502–514.

Jacques, J. M., & Chason, K. J. Cohabitation: Its impact on marital success. *Family Coordinator,* 1979, *28,* 35–45.

Jaquish, G. A., & Ripple, R. E. Cognitive creative abilities and self-esteem across the adult life-span. *Human Development,* 1981, *24,* 110–119.

Jenkins, C. D., Rosenman, R. H., & Zyzanski, S. J. Prediction of clinical coronary heart disease by a test for the coronary-prone behavior pattern. *New England Journal of Medicine,* 1974, *290,* 1271–1275.

Jiao, S., Ji, G., & Jing, Q. Comparative study of behavioral qualities of only children and sibling children. *Child Development,* 1986, *57,* 357–361.

Johnson, C., & Maddi, K. The etiology of bulimia. *Adolescent psychiatry,* 1986, *13,* 253–273.

Johnson, C., Stuckey, M., Lewis, L., & Schwartz, D. Bulimia: A descriptive survey of 316 cases. *International Journal of Eating Disorders,* 1982, *2,* 3–16.

Johnson, E., & Meade, A. Developmental patterns of spatial ability: An early sex difference. *Child Development,* 1987, *58,* 725–740.

Johnson, J., & McGillicuddy-Delisi, A. Family environment factors and children's knowledge of rules and conventions. *Child Development,* 1983, *54,* 218–226.

Johnston, L. D., Bachman, J. G., & O'Malley, P.M. *1979 highlights: Drugs and the nation's high school students: Five year national trends.* Rockville, MD: National Institute on Drug Abuse, 1979.

Johnston, L. D., Bachman, J. G., & O'Malley, P. M. Student drug use, attitudes, and beliefs: National trends 1975–1982. In M. Bloom (Ed.) *Life span development* (2nd ed.). New York: Macmillan, 1985.

Johnstone, J. W. C. Juvenile delinquency and the family: A contextual interpretation. *Youth and Society,* 1978, *9,* 299–313.

Jones, H. E., & Conrad, H. S. The growth and decline of intelligence: A study of a homogeneous group between the ages of ten and sixty. *Genetic Psychology Monographs,* 1933, *13,* 223–294.

Jones, K. L., & Smith, D. W. Recognition of the fetal alcohol syndrome in early infancy. *Lancet,* 1973, *2,* 999–1001.

Jones, K. L., Smith, D. W., Streissguth, A. P., & Myrianthopoulos, N. C. Outcome in offspring of chronic alcoholic women. *Lancet,* 1974, *1,* 1076–1078.

Jones, M. C. A laboratory study of fear: The case of Peter. *Pedagogical Seminar,* 1924, *31,* 308–315.

Jones, M. C. The later careers of boys who were early- or late-maturing. *Child Development,* 1957, *28,* 115–128.

Jones, M. C. A study of socialization patterns at the high school level. *Journal of Genetic Psychology,* 1958, *93,* 87–111.

Jones. M. C. Psychological correlates of somatic development. *Child Development,* 1965, *36,* 899–911.

Jones, R. *The other generation: The new power of older people.* Englewood Cliffs, NJ: Prentice Hall, 1977.

Kagan, J. Impulsive and reflective children: Significance of conceptual tempo. In J. D. Krumholz (Ed.), *Learning and the educational process.* Chicago: Rand McNally, 1965.

Kagan, J. *Personality development.* New York: Harcourt Brace Jovanovich, 1971.

Kagan, J. *The second year: The emergence of self-awareness.* Cambridge, MA: Harvard University Press, 1981.

Kagan, J. *Psychological research on the human infant: An evaluative summary.* New York: W. T. Grant Foundation, 1982.

Kagan, J. *The nature of the child.* New York: Basic Books, 1984.

Kagan, J., Kearsley, R., & Zelazo, P. *Infancy: Its place in human development.* Cambridge, MA: Harvard University Press, 1978.

Kagan, J., & Kogan, N. Individual variation in cognitive processes. In P. Mussen (Ed.), *Carmichael's manual of child psychology* (Vol. 1). New York: Wiley, 1970.

Kahana, B. Social behavior and aging. In B. Wolman (Ed.), *Handbook of developmental psychology.* Englewood Cliffs, NJ: Prentice-Hall, 1982.

Kahn, R., & Antonucci, T. Convoys over the life course: Attachment, roles and social support. In P. Baltes and O. Brim (Eds.) *Lifespan development and behavior* (Vol. 3). New York: Academic Press, 1980.

Kail, R. *The development of memory in children.* San Francisco: Freeman, 1979.

Kail, R., & Bisanz, J. Information processing and cognitive development. In H. Reese (Ed.), *Advances in child development and behavior* (Vol. 17). New York: Academic Press, 1982.

Kail, R., & Hagen, J. Memory in childhood. In B. Wolman (Ed.), *Handbook of developmental psychology.* Englewood Cliffs, NJ: Prentice-Hall, 1982.

Kalish, R. A. *Death, grief, and caring relationships.* Monterey, CA: Brooks/Cole, 1981.

Kalish, R. A., & Knudtson, F. W. Attachment versus disengagement: A lifespan conceptualization. *Human Development*, 1976, *19*, 171–181.

Kallman, F. J., & Jarvik, L. Individual differences in constitution and genetic background. In J. Birren (Ed.), *Handbook of aging and the individual.* Chicago: University of Chicago Press, 1959.

Kantner, J., & Zelnick, M. Sexual experiences of young unmarried women in the U. S. *Family Planning Perspectives*, 1972, *4*, 9–17.

Kaplan, H. S. Sex at menopause. In L. Rose (Ed.), *The menopause book.* New York: Hawthorn, 1977.

Kaplan, H. S., & Pokorny, A. P. Aging and self-attitude: A conditional relationship. *International Journal of Aging and Human Development*, 1970, *1*, 241–250.

Kastenbaum, R. The child's understanding of death: How does it develop? In E. Grollman (Ed.), *Explaining death to children.* Boston: Beacon Press, 1967.

Kastenbaum, R. The foreshortened life perspective. *Geriatrics*, 1969, *24*, 126–133.

Kastenbaum, R. Is death a life crisis? On the confrontation with death in theory and practice. In N. Datan & L. Ginsberg (Eds.), *Life-span developmental psychology: Normative life crises.* New York: Academic Press, 1975.

Kastenbaum, R. Death and development through the lifespan. In H. Feifel (Ed.), *New meanings of death.* New York: McGraw-Hill, 1977.

Kastenbaum, R., & Candy, S. E. The 4% fallacy: A methodological and empirical critique of extended-care facility population statistics. *International Journal of Aging and Human Development*, 1973, *4*, 15–21.

Kastenbaum, R., & Durkee, N. Young people view old age. In R. Kastenbaum (Ed.), *New thoughts on old age.* New York: Springer, 1964.

Katzman, M., Wolchik, S., & Braver, S. The prevalence of frequent binge eating and bulimia in a nonclinical sample. *International Journal of Eating Disorders*, 1984, *3*, 53–62.

Kay, B., & Neeley, J. N. Sexuality in the aging: A review of current literature. *Sexuality and Disability*, 1982, *5*, 38–46.

Kaye, H., & Marcus, J. Imitation over a series of trials without feedback: Age six months. *Infant Behavior and Development*, 1978, *1*, 141–155.

Kell, D., & Patton, C. Reactions to induced retirement. *The Gerontologist*, 1978, *18*, 173–179.

Keller, A., Ford, L., & Meachem, J. Dimensions of self-concept in preschool children. *Developmental Psychology*, 1978, *14*, 483–489.

Kelly, J. B. Divorce: The adult perspective. In B. Wolman (Ed.), *Handbook of developmental psychology.* Englewood Cliffs, NJ: Prentice-Hall, 1982.

Keniston, K. Youth: A "new" stage of life. *The American Scholar*, Autumn 1970, 631–654.

Keniston, K. *Youth and dissent: The rise of a new generation.* New York: Harcourt Brace Jovanovich, 1971.

Kenkel, W. F. *The family in perspective.* New York: Appleton-Century-Crofts, 1966.

Kent, S. How do we age? *Geriatrics*, March 1976, 128–134.

Kessler, R., & McRae, J. The effects of wives' employment on the mental health of married men and women. *American Sociological Review*, 1982, *47*, 216–226.

Khachaturian, Z. Progress on research on Alzheimer's disease. *American Psychologist*, 1985, *40*, 1251–1255.

Kimmel, D. C. *Adulthood and aging* (2nd ed.). New York: Wiley, 1980.

Kinney, D. K., & Matthysse, S. Genetic transmission of schizophrenia. *Annual Review of Medicine*, 1978, *29*, 459–473.

Kinsey, A. C., Pomeroy, W. B., & Martin, C. C. *Sexual behavior in the human male.* Philadelphia: Saunders, 1948.

Kinsey, A. C., Pomeroy, W. B., & Martin, C. C. *Sexual behavior in the human female.* Philadelphia: Saunders, 1953.

Klahr, D., & Wallace, J. G. *Cognitive development: An information-processing view.* Hillsdale, NJ: Erlbaum, 1976.

Klaus, M., & Kennell, J. *Parent–infant bonding* (2nd ed.). St Louis: Mosby, 1982.

Kleck, R., Richardson, S., & Ronald, L. Physical appearance cues and interpersonal attraction in children. *Child Development*, 1974, *46*, 187–192.

Kleiman, D. When abortion becomes a birth: A dilemma of medical ethics shaken by new advances. *New York Times*, February 15, 1984, B1:B4.

Klein, R. Caregiving arrangements by employed women with children under 1 year of age. *Developmental Psychology*, 1985, *21*, 403–406.

Klocke, R. A. Influence of aging on the lung. In C. E. Finch & L. Hayflick (Eds.), *Handbook of the biology of aging.* New York: Van Nostrand Reinhold, 1977.

Klonoff, H., Low, M., Marcus, A. Neuropsychological effects of marijuana. *Canadian Medical Association Journal*, 1973, *108*, 150–156.

Kobasa, S. C. Stressful life events, personality, and health: An inquiry into hardiness. *Journal of Personality and Social Psychology*, 1979, *37*, 1–11.

Kobrin, F., & Waite, L. Effects of childhood family structure on the transition to marriage. *Journal of Marriage and the Family*, 1984, *46*, 807–816.

Kogan, N. Creativity and cognitive style: A lifespan perspective. In P. B. Baltes & K. W. Schaie (Eds.), *Life-span developmental psychology: Personality and socialization.* New York: Academic Press, 1973.

Kogan, N. Categorizing and conceptualizing styles in younger and older adults. *Human Development*, 1974, *17*, 218–230.

Kogan, N. Cognitive styles in older adults. In T. Fields, A. Huston, H. Quay, L. Troll, & G. Finley (Eds.), *Review of human development.* New York: Wiley, 1982.

Kogan, N. Stylistic variation in childhood and adolescence: Creativity, metaphor, and cognitive styles. In J. H. Flavell & E. M. Markman (Eds.), *Handbook of child psychology, Vol. III: Cognitive development.* New York: Wiley, 1983.

Kohlberg, L. The development of children's orientations towards a moral order: I. Sequence in the development of moral thought. *Vita Humana*, 1963, *6*, 11–33.

Kohlberg, L. Development of moral character and moral ideology. In M. L. Hoffman & L. W. Hoffman (Eds.), *Review of child development research.* New York: Russell Sage Foundation, 1964.

Kohlberg, L. A cognitive developmental analysis of children's sex-role concepts and attitudes. In E. Maccoby (Ed.), *The development of sex differences.* Stanford, CA: Stanford University Press, 1966.

Kohlberg, L. Continuities in child and adult moral development revisited. In P. Baltes & K. W. Schaie (Eds.), *Lifespan developmental psychology: Personality and socialization.* New York: Academic Press, 1973.

Kohlberg, L. Moral stages and moralization: The cognitive development approach. In T. Lickona (Ed.), *Moral development and behavior.* New York: Holt, Rinehart and Winston, 1976.

Kohlberg, L., & Gilligan, C. The adolescent as a philosopher: The discovery of the self in a postconventional world. *Daedalus,* 1971, *100,* 1051–1086.

Kohlberg, L., & Kramer, R. Continuities and discontinuities in childhood and adult moral development. *Human Development,* 1969, *12,* 93–120.

Kohn, R. R. Heart and cardiovascular system. In C. E. Finch & L. Hayflick (Eds.), *Handbook of the biology of aging.* New York: Van Nostrand Reinhold, 1977.

Kolata, G. Huntington's disease gene located. *Science,* 1983, *222,* 913–915.

Kolata, G. B. Obese children. *Science,* 1986, *232,* 20–21.

Korner, A., Zeanah, C., Linden, J., Berkowitz, R., Kraemer, H., & Agras, W. S. The relation between neonatal and later activity and temperament. *Child Development,* 1985, *56,* 36–42.

Kramer, D. A. Post-formal operation? A need for further conceptualization. *Human Development,* 1983, *26,* 91–105.

Krupnick, M. *Incest: Identification and reporting.* Carrier Foundation Letter, May 1984, *98,* 1–4.

Kübler-Ross, E. *On death and dying.* New York: Macmillan, 1969.

Kübler-Ross, E., & Warshaw, M. *To live until we say goodbye.* Englewood Cliffs, NJ: Prentice-Hall, 1978.

Kuchuk, A., Vibbert, M., & Bornstein, M. The perception of smiling and its experiential correlates in three-month-old infants. *Child Development,* 1986, *57,* 1054–1061.

Kuczaj, II, S. Language play and language acquisition. In H. Reese (Ed.), *Advances in child development and behavior* (Vol. 17). New York: Academic Press, 1982.

Kuhlen, R. G. Developmental changes in motivation during the adult years. In J. E. Birren (Ed.), *Relations of development and aging.* Springfield, IL: Charles C. Thomas, 1964.

Kuhn, D., Nash, S., & Brucken, L. Sex-role concepts of two- and three-year-olds. *Child Development,* 1978, *49,* 445–451.

Kuhn, T. S. *The structure of scientific revolutions* (2nd ed.). Chicago: University of Chicago Press, 1970.

Labouvie, E. W. The dialectical nature of measurement activities in the behavioral sciences. *Human Development,* 1975, *18,* 396–403.

Labouvie, E. W. Issues in life-span development. In B. Wolman (Ed.), *Handbook of developmental psychology.* Englewood Cliffs, NJ: Prentice-Hall, 1982.

Labouvie-Vief, G. Adaptive dimensions in adult cognition. In N. Datan & N. Lohmann (Eds.), *Transitions in aging.* New York: Academic Press, 1980. (a)

Labouvie-Vief, G. Beyond formal operations: Uses and limits of pure logic in life-span development. *Human Development,* 1980, *23,* 141–161. (b)

Labouvie-Vief, G. Dynamic development and mature autonomy: A theoretical prologue. *Human Development,* 1982, *25,* 161–191.

Labouvie-Vief, G. Intelligence and cognition. In J. E. Birren & K. W. Schaie (Eds.) *Handbook of the psychology of aging* (2nd ed.). New York: Van Nostrand Reinhold, 1985.

Labouvie-Vief, G., & Chandler, M. Cognitive development and lifespan developmental theory: Idealistic versus contextual perspectives. In P. Baltes (Ed.), *Lifespan development and behavior* (Vol. 1). New York: Academic Press, 1978.

Labouvie-Vief, G., & Schell, D. A. Learning and memory in later life. In B. Wolman (Ed.), *Handbook of developmental psychology.* Englewood Cliffs, NJ: Prentice-Hall, 1982.

Ladd, G. Social networks of popular, average, and rejected children in school settings. *Merrill-Palmer Quarterly,* 1983, *29,* 283–307.

Ladd, G., & Oden, S. The relationship between peer acceptance and children's ideas about helpfulness. *Child Development,* 1979, *50,* 402–408.

Lamaze, F. *Painless childbirth.* New York: Simon & Schuster, 1981.

Lamb, M. E. Interaction between eight-month-old children and their fathers and mothers. In M. Lamb (Ed.), *The role of the father in child development.* New York: Wiley, 1976.

Lamb, M. E. Parent behavior and child development in nontraditional families: An introduction. In M. E. Lamb (Ed.), *Nontraditional families: Parenting and child development.* Hillsdale, NJ: Erlbaum, 1982. (a)

Lamb, M. E. Sibling relationships across the lifespan. In M. E. Lamb & B. Sutton-Smith (Eds.), *Sibling relationships.* Hillsdale, NJ: Erlbaum, 1982. (b)

Lamb, M. E. What can research experts tell parents about effective socialization? In E. Zigler, M. Lamb, & I. Child (Eds.), *Socialization and personality development* (2nd ed.). New York: Oxford University Press, 1982. (c)

Lamb, M. E., Frodi, A., Hwang, C. P., Frodi, M., & Steinberg, J. Effects of gender and caretaking role on parent–infant interaction. In R. Emde & R. Harmon (Eds.), *The development of attachment and affiliative systems.* New York: Plenum, 1982.

Lane, B. Attitudes of youth toward the aged. *Journal of Marriage and the Family,* 1964, *26,* 229–231.

Langer, E. J., & Rodin, J. The effects of choice and enhanced personal responsibility for the aged: A field experiment in an institutional setting. *Journal of Personality and Social Psychology*, 1976, *34*, 191–198.

Largman, R. The social-emotional effects of age of entry into full time group care. Unpublished doctoral dissertation, University of California, Berkeley, 1976.

LaRue, A., & Jarvik, L. Old age and biobehavioral change. In B. Wolman (Ed.) *Handbook of developmental psychology*. Englewood Cliffs, NJ: Prentice-Hall, 1982.

Laska, S. B., & Micklin, M. The knowledge dimension of occupational socialization: Role models and their social influences. *Youth and Society*, 1979, *10*, 360–378.

Lasky, R., Tyson, J., Rosenfeld, C., & Gant, N. Maternal–infant interactions at one year adjusted age in infants at low and high-risk as newborns. *Early Human Development*, 1984, *9*, 145–152.

Lavee, Y., McCubbin, H., & Olson D. The effects of stressful life events and transitions on family functioning and well-being. *Journal of Marriage and the Family*, 1987, *49*, 857–873.

Laws, J. L. Female sexuality through the lifespan. In P. Baltes & O. Brim (Eds.), *Life-span development and behavior* (Vol. 3). New York: Academic Press, 1980.

Lawton, M. Community supports for the aged. *Journal of Social Issues*, 1981, *37*, 102–115.

Lazar, I., & Darlington, R., with H. Murray, J. Royce, & A. Snipper. Lasting effects of early education: A report from the consortium for longitudinal studies. *Monographs of the Society for Research in Child Development*, 1982, *47*, nos. 2–3, serial no. 195.

Lazarus, R. S. Little hassles can be hazardous to health. *Psychology Today*, July 1981, 58–62.

Lazarus, R. S., & DeLongis, A. Psychological stress and coping in aging. *American Psychologist*, 1983, *38*, 245–254.

Lazarus, R. S., & Folkman, S. *Stress, appraisal, and coping.* New York: Springer, 1984.

Lazarus, R. S., & Launier, R. Stress-related transactions between person and environment. In L. A. Pervin & M. Lewis (Eds.), *Perspectives in interactional psychology*. New York: Plenum, 1978.

LeBel, J., & Zuckerman, B. Feeding problems, obesity. In S. Gabel (Ed.), *Behavioral problems in childhood: A primary care approach*. New York: Grune & Stratton, 1981.

Lee, G., & Ellithorpe, E. Intergenerational exchange and subjective well-being among the elderly. *Journal of Marriage and the Family*, 1982, *44*, 217–224.

Lee, G., & Ihinger-Tallman, M. Sibling interaction and morale: The effects of family relations on older people. *Research on Aging*, 1980, *2*, 367–391.

Lee, J. A., & Pollack, R. H. The effects of age on perceptual problem-solving strategies. *Experimental Aging Research*, 1978, *4*, 37–54.

Lehman, H. C. *Age and achievement*. Princeton, NJ: Princeton University Press, 1953.

Lemon, B. W., Bengston, V. L., & Peterson, J. A. An exploration of the activity theory of aging: Activity types and life satisfaction among in-movers to a retirement community. *Journal of Gerontology*, 1972, *27*, 511–523.

Lempers, J. D., Flavell, E. R., & Flavell, J. H. The development in very young children of tacit knowledge concerning visual perception. *Genetic Psychology Monographs*, 1977, *95*, 3–53.

Lenneberg, E. *Biological foundations of language*. New York: Wiley, 1967.

Leon, G. R., Gillum, B., Gillum, R., & Gouze, M. Personality stability and change over a 30-year period—Middle age to old age. *Journal of Consulting and Clinical Psychology*, 1979, *47*, 517–524.

Lerner, J. *Children with learning disabilities* (2nd ed.). Boston: Houghton Mifflin, 1976.

Lerner, J., & Galambos, N. Maternal role satisfaction, mother–child interaction, and child temperament: A process model. *Developmental Psychology*, 1985, *21*, 1157–1164.

Lerner, J., & Lerner, R. Temperament and adaptation across life: Theoretical and empirical issues. In P. Baltes & O. Brim (Eds.), *Life-span development and behavior* (Vol. 5). New York: Academic Press, 1983.

Lerner, R. M., & Korn, S. J. Development of body build stereotypes in males. *Child Development*, 1972, *45*, 908–920.

LeShan, E. *The wonderful crisis of middle age*. New York: David McKay, 1973.

Leskow, S., & Smock, C. D. Developmental changes in problem-solving strategies: Permutations. *Developmental Psychology*, 1970, *2*, 412–422.

Lester, B., Garcia-Coll, C., Valcarcel, M., Hoffman, J., & Brazelton, T. B. Effects of atypical patterns of fetal growth on newborn (NBAS) behavior. *Child Development*, 1986, *57*, 11–19.

Levine, L. "Mine" self-definition in 2-year-old boys. *Developmental Psychology*, 1983, *19*, 544–549.

Levine, M. Scientific method and the adversary model: Some preliminary thoughts. *American Psychologist*, 1974, *29*, 661–677.

Levinson, D. *The seasons of a man's life*. New York: Knopf, 1978.

Levinson, D. A conception of adult development. *American Psychologist*, 1986, *41*, 3–13.

Levinson, D., Darrow, C., Klein, E., Levinson, M., & McKee, B. Periods in the adult development of men: Ages 18 to 45. In A. G. Sargent (Ed.), *Beyond the sex roles*. New York: West, 1977.

Lewis, M., & Brooks-Gunn, J. *Social cognition and the acquisition of the self*. New York: Plenum, 1979.

Lewis, R. A. A longitudinal test of a developmental framework for premarital dyadic formation. *Journal of Marriage and the Family*, 1973, *35*, 16–25.

Lewis, R.A, Frenau, P. J., & Roberts, C. L. Fathers and the postparental transition. *The Family Coordinator*, 1979, *28*, 514–520.

Liang, J., Dvorkin, L., Kahana, E., & Mazian, F. Social integration and morale: A re-examination. *Journal of Gerontology*, 1980, *35*, 746–757.

Lieberman, M. A. The relation of mortality rates to entrance to a home for the aged. *Geriatrics*, 1961, *16*, 515–519.

Lieberman, M. A. Psychological correlates of impending death: Some preliminary observations. *Journal of Gerontology,* 1965, *20,* 181–190.

Lieberman, M., & Coplan, A. Distance from death as a variable in the study of aging. *Developmental Psychology,* 1970, *2,* 71–84.

Liebert, R., Sprafkin, J., & Davidson, E. *The early window: Effects of television on children and youth* (2nd ed.). New York: Pergamon, 1982.

Lifton, B. J. *Lost and found.* New York: Dial Press, 1979.

Lindemann, E. The symptomatology and management of acute grief. *American Journal of Psychiatry,* 1944, *101,* 141–148.

Lindgren, S., DeRenzi, E., & Richman, L. Cross-national comparisons of developmental dyslexia in Italy and the United States. *Child Development,* 1985, *56,* 1404–1417.

Lipsitt, L. The synchronicity of respiration, heart rate and sucking behavior in the newborn. *Biological and clinical aspects of brain development: Mead Johnson Symposium on Perinatal and Developmental Medicine,* Evansville, IN: Mead Johnson & Company, 1975, no. 6, 67–72.

Lipsitt, L., & Kaye, H. Conditional sucking in the human newborn. *Psychonomic Science,* 1964, *1,* 29–30.

Lipsitz, J. S. Adolescent development: Myths and realities. *Children Today,* October 1979, 2–7.

Livson, N. Developmental dimensions of personality: A lifespan formulation. In P. Baltes & K. W. Schaie (Eds.), *Lifespan developmental psychology: Personality and socialization.* New York: Academic Press, 1973.

Livson, N., & Peskin, H. Perspectives on adolescence from longitudinal research. In J. Adelson (Ed.), *Handbook of Adolescent Psychology,* New York: Wiley, 1980.

Loehlin, J. C., & Nichols, R. C. *Heredity, environment and personality.* Austin: University of Texas Press, 1976.

Loftus, E., & Loftus, G. *Mind at play: The psychology of video games.* New York: Basic Books, 1983.

Lonetto, R. *Children's conceptions of death.* New York: Springer, 1980.

Lonkey, E., Kaus, C., & Roodin, P. Life experience and mode of coping: Relation to moral judgment in adulthood. *Developmental Psychology,* 1984, *20,* 1159–1167.

Lopata, H. Z. Widows as a minority group. *The Gerontologist,* 1971, *11,* 67–77.

Lopata, H. Z. *Widowhood in an American city.* Cambridge, MA: Schenkman, 1973.

Lopata, H. Z. The meaning of friendship in widowhood. In L. Troll, J. Israel, & K. Israel (Eds.), *Looking ahead: A woman's guide to the problems and joys of growing older.* Englewood Cliffs, NJ: Prentice-Hall, 1977.

Lopata, H. Z. *Women as widows: Support systems.* New York: Elsevier, 1979.

Lorenz, K. *On aggression.* New York: Harcourt, 1966.

Lowenthal, M. F., & Boler, D. Voluntary versus involuntary social withdrawal. *Journal of Gerontology,* 1975, *20,* 363–371.

Lowenthal, M. F., & Haven, C. Interaction and adaptation: Intimacy as a critical variable. *American Sociological Review,* 1968, *33,* 20–30.

Lowenthal, M. F., Thurnher, M., & Chiriboga, D. *Four stages of life: A comparative study of women and men facing transitions.* San Francisco: Jossey-Bass, 1975.

Lowry, E. H. (Ed.) *Growth and development of children.* Chicago: Year Book Medical Publishers, Inc., 1967.

Luke, B. Maternal alcoholism and the fetal alcohol syndrome. *American Journal of Nursing,* December 1977, 1924–1926.

Lynch, J. *The broken heart: Medical consequences of loneliness.* New York: Basic Books, 1977.

Maccoby, E. *Social development: Psychological growth and the parent–child relationship.* New York: Harcourt, Brace, Jovanovich, 1980.

Maccoby, E. Socialization and developmental change. *Child Development,* 1984, *55,* 317–328.

Maccoby, E., & Jacklin, C. *The psychology of sex differences.* Stanford,

CA: Stanford University Press, 1974.

Maccoby, E., & Jacklin, C. Sex differences in aggression. A rejoinder and reprise. *Child Development,* 1980, *51,* 964–980.

Maccoby, E., & Martin, J. Socialization in the context of the family: Parent–child interaction. In E. M. Hetherington (Ed.), P. H. Mussen (Series Ed.), *Handbook of child psychology,* Vol. 4: *Socialization, personality and social development.* New York: Wiley, 1983.

MacFarlane, A, What a baby knows. *Human Nature,* February 1978.

Macklin, E. D. Nonmarital heterosexual cohabitation. *Marriage and Family Review.* 1978, *1,* 1–12.

Madden, D. Adult age differences in memory driven selective attention. *Developmental Psychology,* 1985, *21,* 655–665.

Maddox, G. Persistence of life style among the elderly. In B. Neugarten (Ed.), *Middle-age and aging.* Chicago: University of Chicago Press, 1968.

Maddox, G. L. Retirement as a social event in the United States. In B. L. Neugarten (Ed.), *Middle age and aging.* Chicago: University of Chicago Press, 1968.

Madison, L. S., Madison, J. K., & Adubato, S. A. Infant behavior and development in relation to fetal movement and habituation. *Child Development,* 1986, *57,* 1475–1482.

Magenis, R. E., Overton, K. M., Chamberlin, J., Brady, T., & Lovrein, E. Parental origins of the extra chromosome in Down's syndrome. *Human Genetics,* 1977, *37,* 7–16.

Mahler, M., Pine, F., & Bergman, A. *The psychological birth of the human infant.* New York: Basic Books, 1975.

Main, M., & George, C. Responses of abused and disadvantaged toddlers to distress in agemates: A study in the daycare setting. *Developmental Psychology,* 1985, *21,* 407–413.

Makinodan, T. Immunity and aging. In C. E. Finch & L. Hayflick (Eds.), *Handbook of the biology of aging.* New York: Van Nostrand Reinhold, 1977.

Malatesta, C. Z., Grigoryev, P., Lamb, C., Albin, M., & Culver, C. Emotion socialization and expressive development in preterm and full-term infants. *Child Development*, 1986, *57*, 316–330.

Malatesta, C. Z., & Haviland, J. M. Learning display rules: The socialization of emotion expression in infancy. *Child Development*, 1982, *53*, 991–1003.

Malina, R. M. Adolescent changes in size, build, composition and performance. *Human Biology*, 1974, *46*, 117–131.

Malina, R. M. Adolescent growth and maturation: Selected aspects of current research. *Yearbook of Physical Anthropology*, 1978, *21*, 63–94.

Malina, R. M. Secular changes in size and maturity: Causes and effects. In A. F. Roche (Ed.), *Secular trends in human growth, maturation and development. Monographs of the Society for Research in Child Development*, 1979, *44*, 59–102.

Mall, J. A study of U.S. teenage pregnancy rates. *Los Angeles Times*, March 17, 1985, Part 7, 27.

March of Dimes Birth Defects Foundation. *Birth Defects*, 1983. White Plains, NY.

Marcia, J. E. Development and validation of ego-identity status. *Journal of Personality and Social Psychology*, 1966, *3*, 551–558.

Marcia, J. E. Identity six years later: A follow-up study. *Journal of Youth and Adolescence*, 1976, *5*, 145–160.

Marcia, J. E. Identity in adolescence. In J. Adelson (Ed.), *Handbook of adolescent psychology*. New York: Wiley, 1980.

Marcus, D. E., & Overton, W. F. The development of cognitive gender and constancy and sex role preferences. *Child Development*, 1978, *49*, 434–444.

Maret, E., & Finlay, B. The distribution of household labor among women in dual earner families. *Journal of Marriage and the Family*, 1984, *46*, 357–364.

Margolin, L., & White, L. The continuing role of physical attractiveness in marriage. *Journal of Marriage and the Family*, 1987, *49*, 21–27.

Markman, E., & Hutchinson, J. Children's sensitivity to constraints on word meaning: Taxonomic versus thematic relations. *Cognitive Psychology*, 1984, *16*, 1–27.

Marsh, G. R., & Thompson. L. W. Psychophysiology of aging. In J. E. Birren & K. W. Schaie (Eds.), *Handbook of the psychology of aging*. New York: Van Nostrand Reinhold, 1977.

Martin, B. Parent–child relations. In F. D. Horowitz (Ed.), *Review of child development research* (Vol. 4). Chicago: University of Chicago Press, 1975.

Martin, C., & Halverson, C. A schematic processing model of sex typing and stereotyping in children. *Child Development*, 1981, *52*, 1119–1134.

Masnick, G., & Bane, M. J. *The nation's families: 1960–1990*. Cambridge, MA: Joint Center for Urban Studies, 1980.

Masten, A. Humor and competence in school-aged children. *Child Development*, 1986, *57*, 461–473.

Masters, W. H., & Johnson, V. E. *Human sexual response*. Boston: Little, Brown, 1966.

Masters, W. H., & Johnson, V. E. *The pleasure bond: A new look at sexuality and commitment*. Boston: Little, Brown, 1975.

Masters, W. H., & Johnson, V. E. Sex and the aging process. *Journal of the American Geriatric Society*, 1981, *29*, 385–390.

Masterson, J. F. *The psychiatric dilemma of adolescence*. Boston: Little, Brown, 1967.

Matheny, A., Riese, M., & Wilson, R. Rudiments of infant temperament: Newborn to 9 months. *Developmental Psychology*, 1985, *21*, 486–494.

Mathes, E. The effects of physical attractiveness and anxiety on heterosexual adjustment over a series of five encounters. *Journal of Marriage and the Family*, 1975, *37*, 769–773.

Matthews, K. A. Psychological perspectives on the Type A behavior pattern. *Psychological Bulletin*, 1982, *91*, 293–323.

Matthews, K. A., & Brunson, B. I. Allocation of attention and the Type A coronary-prone behavior pattern. *Journal of Personality and Social Psychology*, 1979, *37*, 2081–2090.

Matthews, K., & Angulo, J. Measurement of the Type A behavior patterns in children: Assessment of children's competitiveness, impatience-anger, and aggression. *Child Development*, 1980, *51*, 466–475.

Maurer, A. The child's knowledge of non-existence. *Journal of Existential Psychiatry*, 1961, *2*, 193–212.

Maurer, A. What children fear. *Journal of Genetic Psychology*, 1965, *106*, 265–277.

Maurer, D., & Salapatek, P. Developmental changes in the scanning of faces by young infants. *Child Development*, 1976, *47*, 523–527.

Mayer, J. Obesity during childhood. In M. Winick (Ed.), *Childhood Obesity*. New York: Wiley, 1975.

Mayle, P. *Where did I come from?* Secaucus, NJ: Lyle Stuart, 1973.

McCall, R. B., Eichorn, D. H., & Hogarty, P. S. Transitions in early mental development. *Monographs of the Society for Research in Child Development*, 1977, *42*, serial no. 171.

McCandless, B., & Evans, E. *Children and youth: Psychosocial development*. Hillsdale, IL: Dryden, 1973.

McCartney, K. The effects of quality of day-care environment on children's language development. *Developmental Psychology*, 1984, *20*, 244–250.

McClelland, K. A. Adolescent subculture in the schools. In T. Field, A. Huston, H. C. Quay, L. Troll, & G. E. Finley (Eds.), *Review of human development*. New York: Wiley-Interscience, 1982.

McCormick, K. An exploration of the functions of friends and best friends. Unpublished doctoral dissertation. Rutgers University, New Jersey, 1982.

McDavid, J., & Harari, M. Stereotyping of names and popularity in grade school children. *Child Development*, 1966, *37*, 453–459.

McGee, J., & Wells, K. Gender typing and androgeny in later life. *Human Development*, 1982, *25*, 116–139.

McGhee, P. *Humor: Its origin and development.* San Francisco: Freeman, 1979.

McKain, W. C. A new look at older marriages. *Family Coordinator,* 1972, *21,* 61–69.

McKinney, J., Hotch, D., & Truhon, S. The organization of behavioral values during late adolescence: Change and stability across two eras. *Developmental Psychology,* 1977, *13,* 83–84.

McKinney, J., & Moore, D. Attitudes and values during adolescence. In B. B. Wolman (Ed.), *Handbook of Human Development.* Englewood Cliffs, NJ: Prentice-Hall, 1982.

Mclearn, G., & Foch, T. Behavioral genetics. In J. E. Birren & K. W. Schaie (Eds.), *Handbook of the psychology of aging* (2nd ed.). New York: Van Nostrand Reinhold, 1985.

McPherson, B. *Aging as a social process.* Toronto: Butterworths, 1983.

McPherson, B., & Guppy, N. Pre-retirement life-style and the degree of planning for retirement. *Journal of Gerontology,* 1979, *34,* 254–263.

Meier, J. Prevalence and characteristics of learning disabilities found in second grade children. *Journal of Learning Disabilities,* 1971, *4,* 1–16.

Melamed, B., & Siegel, L. Reduction of anxiety in children facing hospitalization and surgery by use of filmed modeling. In E. M. Hetherington & R. Parke (Eds.), *Contemporary readings in child psychology* (2nd ed.). New York: McGraw-Hill, 1981.

Meltzoff, A. Immediate and deferred imitation in fourteen- and twenty-four-month-old infants. *Child Development,* 1985, *56,* 62–72.

Meltzoff, A. Infant imitation and memory: Nine-month-olds in immediate and deferred tests. *Child Development,* 1988, *59,* 217–225.

Meltzoff, A., & Moore, K. M. Imitation of facial and manual gestures by human neonates. *Science,* 1977, *198,* 75–78.

Meltzoff, A., & Moore, M. The origins of imitation in infancy: Paradigm, phenomena and theories. In L. P. Lipsitt & C. K. Rovee-Collier (Eds.), *Advances in infancy research* (Vol. 2). Norwood, NJ: Ablex, 1983.

Mendelson, B., & White, D. Development of self-body esteem in overweight youngsters. *Developmental Psychology,* 1985, *21,* 90–96.

Mendelson, E., Robinson, S., Gardner, H., & Winner, E. Are preschoolers' renamings intentional category violations? *Developmental Psychology,* 1984, *20,* 187–192.

Mendelson, M. A. *Tender loving greed: How the incredibly lucrative nursing home "industry" is exploiting old people and defrauding us all.* New York: Knopf, 1974.

Meredith, H. V. Research between 1960 and 1970 on the standing height of young children in different parts of the world. In H. W. Reese and L. P. Lipsitt (Eds.), *Advances in child development and behavior* (Vol. 12). New York: Academic Press, 1978.

Meredith, H. V. Research between 1950 and 1980 on urban–rural differences in body size and growth rate of children and youths. In H. Reese (Ed.), *Advances in child development and behavior* (Vol. 17). New York: Academic Press, 1982.

Mergler, N. L., & Goldstein, M. D. Why are there old people? Senescence as biological and cultural preparedness for the transmission of information. *Human Development,* 1983, *26,* 72–90.

Messer, S. B. Reflection–impulsivity: A review. *Psychological Bulletin,* 1976, *83,* 1026–1052.

Messer, S., & Schacht, T. A cognitive-dynamic theory of reflection-impulsivity. In J. Masling (Ed.), *Empirical studies of psychoanalytic theories* (Vol. 2). Hillsdale, NJ: Erlbaum, 1986.

Meyerhoff, M., & White, B. Making the grade as parents. *Psychology Today,* September 1986, 30–45.

Miller, B., & Gerard, D. Family influences on the development of creativity in children: An integrative review. *The Family Coordinator,* 1979, *28,* 295–312.

Miller, B., & Sollie, D. Normal stresses during the transition to parenthood. *Family Relations,* 1980, *29,* 459–465.

Miller, M. *Childstress.* New York: Doubleday, 1982.

Miller, N., & Marayama, G. Ordinal position and peer popularity. *Journal of Personality and Social Psychology,* 1976, *33,* 123–131.

Miller, P. H. *Theories of developmental psychology.* San Francisco: Freeman, 1983.

Miller, P. H., & Bigi, L. Children's understanding of how stimulus dimensions affect performance. *Child Development,* 1977, *48,* 1712–1715.

Miller, P., Haynes, V., DeMarie-Dreblow, D., & Woody-Ramsey, J. Children's strategies for gathering information in three tasks. *Child Development,* 1986, *57,* 1429–1439.

Milne, A. A. *Winnie-the-Pooh.* New York: E. P. Dutton, 1926.

Minde, K. Disorders of attention. In P. Steinhauer & Q. Rae-Grant (Eds.), *Psychological problems of the child in the family* (2nd ed.). New York: Basic Books, 1983.

Minnett, A., Vandell, D. L., & Santrock, J. The effects of sibling status on sibling interaction: Influence of birth order, age spacing, sex of child and sex of sibling. *Child Development,* 1983, *54,* 1064–1072.

Mischel, W. Sex typing and socialization. In P. Mussen (Ed.), *Carmichael's manual of child psychology* (3rd ed., vol. II), New York: Wiley, 1970.

Mitchell, J., Pyle, R., & Eckert, E. Frequency and duration of binge eating episodes in patients with bulimia. *American Journal of Psychiatry,* 1981, *138,* 835–836.

Moen, P. The two-provider family: Problems and potentials. In M. Lamb (Ed.), *Nontraditional families: Parenting and child development.* Hillsdale, NJ: Erlbaum, 1982.

Molfese, D., Molfese, V., & Carrell, P. Early language development. In B. Wolman & G. Stricker (Eds.), *Handbook of developmental psychology.* Englewood Cliffs, NJ: Prentice-Hall, 1982.

Money, J., & Ehrhardt, A. *Man and woman, boy and girl: The differentia-*

tion and dimorphism of gender identity from conception to maturity. Baltimore: Johns Hopkins University, 1972.

Montagu, M. F. A. *Prenatal influences.* Springfield, IL: Charles C Thomas, 1962.

Monthly vital statistics report advance report of final natality statistics, 1982, National Center for Health Statistics, *33*, no. 6, supplement.

Moore, D., & Hotch, D. Late adolescents' conceptualizations of home-leaving. *Journal of Youth and Adolescence, 1981, 10*, 1–10.

Moore, K., & Waite, L. Early childbearing and educational attainment. *Family Planning Perspectives,* 1977, *9*, 220–225.

Moos, R., & Lemke, S. Specialized living environments for older people. In J. Birren & K. Schaie (Eds.), *Handbook of the psychology of aging* (2nd ed.). New York: Van Nostrand Reinhold, 1985.

Morgan, L. A. A reexamination of widowhood and morale. *Journal of Gerontology*, 1976, *31*, 687–695.

Morrison, F., Lord, C., & Keating, D. Applied developmental psychology. In F. Morrison, C. Lord & D. Keating (Eds.), *Applied developmental psychology.* New York: Academic Press, 1984.

Morrison, I. The elderly primigravida. *American Journal of Obstetrics and Gynecology,* 1975, *15,* 465–470.

Morrison, J., & Stewart, M. The psychiatric status of the legal families of adopted hyperactive children. *Archives of General Psychiatry,* 1973, *28*, 888–891.

Moshman, D., & Neimark, E. Four aspects of adolescent cognitive development. In T. Field, A. Huston, H. C. Quay, L. Troll, & G. E. Finley (Eds.), *Review of human development.* New York: Wiley-Interscience, 1982.

Moursand, J. *Learning and the learner.* Monterey, CA: Brooks/Cole, 1976.

Mueller, D., & Cooper, P. Children of single parent families: How they fare as young adults. *Family Relations,* 1986, *35*, 169–176.

Mueller, E., & Lucas, T. A developmental analysis of peer interactions in playgroup setting. In M.

Lewis & L. A. Rosenblum (Eds.), *Friendships and peer relations.* New York: Wiley, 1975.

Munnichs, J. *Old age and finitude.* Basel, Switzerland: Karger, 1966.

Murphy, J. M., & Gilligan, C. Moral development in late adolescence and adulthood: A critique and reconstruction of Kohlberg's theory. *Human Development, 1980, 23,* 77–104.

Murphy, L. B. Infants' play and cognitive development. In M. W. Piers (Ed.), *Play and development: A symposium.* New York: Norton, 1972.

Murstein, B. I. Stimulus–value–role: A theory of marital choice. *Journal of Marriage and the Family,* 1970, *32,* 465–481.

Murstein, B. I. *Who will marry whom? Theories and research in marital choice.* New York: Springer, 1976.

Murstein, B. I. Marital choice. In B. Wolman (Ed.), *Handbook of developmental psychology.* Englewood Cliffs, NJ: Prentice-Hall, 1982.

Mussen, P. H., & Eisenberg-Berg, N. *Roots of caring, sharing and helping.* San Francisco: Freeman, 1977.

Mussen, P. H., & Jones, M. C. Self-conceptions, motivations, and interpersonal attitudes of late- and early-maturing boys. *Child Development,* 1957, *28,* 243–256.

Myers, N., & Perlmutter, M. Memory in the years from two to five. In P. A. Ornstein (Ed.), *Memory development in children,* Hillsdale, NJ: Erlbaum, 1978.

Nagy, M. The child's theories concerning death. *Journal of Genetic Psychology,* 1948, *73*, 3–27.

Nash, S. C., & Feldman, S. S. Sex role and sex-related attributions: Constancy and change across the family life cycle. In M. Lamb & A. Brown (Eds.), *Advances in developmental psychology* (Vol 1). Hillsdale, NJ: Erlbaum, 1981.

Nathanson, C., & Lorenz, G. Women and health: The social dimensions of biomedical data. In J. Giele (Ed.), *Women in the middle years.* New York: Wiley, 1982.

National Audience Demographics Report 1985. Northbrook, IL: A.C. Nielsen Company, 1985.

National Center for Health Statistics, *Monthly Vital Statistics Report, Advance Report of Final Natality Statistics,* 1982, *33,* no. 6, supplement.

National Children and Youth Fitness Study. Washington, DC: Office for Disease Prevention and Health Promotion, U.S. Public Health Service, 1984.

National Commission on the Reform of Secondary Education. *The reform of secondary education.* New York: McGraw-Hill, 1973.

National Commission on Youth. *The transition of youth to adulthood: A bridge too long.* Boulder, CO: Westview Press, 1980.

National Institute of Health, *Osteoporosis.* Consensus development conference statement, 5, no. 3. Bethesda, MD: U.S. Government Printing Office, 1984, 421–132: 4652.

National Panel on High School and Adolescent Education. *The education of adolescents.* Washington, DC: U.S. Government Printing Office, 1976.

Natterson, J., & Knudson, A. Observations concerning fear of death in fatally ill children and their mothers. *Psychosomatic Medicine,* 1960, *22,* 456–466.

Naylor, H. Reading disabilities and lateral assymmetry: An information processing analysis. *Psychological Bulletin,* 1980, *87,* 531–545.

Neimark, E. D. Intellectual development during adolescence. In F. Horowitz (Ed.), *Review of child development research* (Vol 4). Chicago: University of Chicago Press, 1975.

Neimark, E. D. Confounding with cognitive style factors: An artifact explanation for the apparent nonuniversal incidence of formal operations. In I. Sigel, D. Brodzinsky, & R. Golinkoff (Eds.), *New directions in Piagetian theory and practice.* Hillsdale, NJ: Erlbaum, 1981.

Neimark, E. D. Adolescent thought: Transition to formal operations. In B. Wolman (Ed.), *Handbook of developmental psychology.* Englewood Cliffs, NJ: Prentice-Hall, 1982.

Neimark, E. D., Slotnik, N., & Ulrich, T. Development of memorization strategies. *Developmental Psychology,* 1971, *5,* 427–432.

Nelson, C., & Dolgin, K. The generalized discrimination of facial expressions by seven-month-old infants. *Child Development,* 1985, *56,* 56–61.

Nelson, M., & Nelson, G. K. Problems of equity in the reconstituted family: A social exchange analysis. *Family Relations,* 1982, *31,* 223–231.

Neugarten, B. L. *Personality in middle and late life.* New York: Atherton Press, 1964.

Neugarten, B. L. The awareness of middle age. In R. Owen (Ed.), *Middle age.* London: British Broadcasting Corporation, 1967.

Neugarten, B. L. Adult personality: Toward a psychology of the life cycle. In B. L. Neugarten (Ed.), *Middle age and aging.* Chicago: University of Chicago Press, 1968.

Neugarten, B. L. Personality change in late life: A developmental perspective. In C. Eisdorfer & M. P. Lawton (Eds.), *Psychology of adult development and aging.* Washington, DC: American Psychological Association, 1973.

Neugarten, B. L. Personality and aging. In J. E. Birren & K. W. Schaie (Eds.), *Handbook of the psychology of aging.* New York: Van Nostrand Reinhold, 1977.

Neugarten, B. L. Time, age, and the life cycle. *American Journal of Psychiatry,* 1979, *136,* 887–894.

Neugarten, B. L., Moore, J. W., & Lowe, J. C. Age norms, age constraints, and adult socialization. *American Journal of Sociology,* 1965, *70,* 710–717.

Neugarten, B. L., & Weinstein, K. K. The changing American grandparent. *Journal of Marriage and the Family,* 1964, *26,* 199–203.

Neugarten, B. L., Wood, V., Kraines, R., & Loomis, B. Women's attitude toward the menopause. *Vita Humana,* 1963, *6,* 140–151.

Nevid, J. Sex differences in factors of romantic attraction. *Sex Roles,* 1984, *11,* 401–411.

Newcomb, P. R. Cohabitation in America: An assessment of consequences. *Journal of Marriage and the Family,* 1979, *41,* 597–603.

Newman, P. R. The peer group. In B. Wolman (Ed.), *Handbook of developmental psychology.* Englewood Cliffs, NJ: Prentice-Hall, 1982.

Niemi, R. G., & Sobieszek, B. I. Political socialization. *Annual Review of Sociology,* 1977, *3,* 209–233.

Nisan, M., & Kohlberg, L. Universality and variation in moral judgment: A longitudinal and cross-sectional study in Turkey. *Child Development,* 1982, *53,* 865–876.

Nisbet, J. D. Intelligence and age: Retesting with twenty-four years interval. *British Journal of Educational Psychology,* 1957, *27,* 190–198.

Niswander, K. R., & Gordon, M. (Eds.) *The collaborative perinatal study of The National Institute of Neurological Diseases and Stroke: Women and their pregnancies.* Washington, DC: U.S. Government Printing Office, 1972.

Nock, S. L. The life-cycle approach to family analysis. In B. Wolman (Ed.), *Handbook of developmental psychology.* Englewood Cliffs, NJ: Prentice-Hall, 1982.

Norman, J., & Harris, M. *The private life of the American teenager.* New York: Rawson Wade, 1981.

Norris, J., & Rubin, K. Peer interaction and communication: A life-span perspective. In P. Baltes & O. Brim (Eds.), *Life-span development and behavior* (Vol. 16). Orlando, FL: Academic Press, 1984.

Northcott, H. C. Women, work, health, and happiness. *International Journal of Women's Studies,* 1981, *4,* 268–276.

Norton, A., & Moorman, J. Current trends in marriage and divorce among American women. *Journal of Marriage and the Family,* 1987, *49,* 3–14.

NYCA. *Facts on alcoholism.* New York: National Council on Alcoholism, 1978.

O'Brien, M., & Huston, A. Development of sex-typed play behavior in toddlers. *Developmental Psychology,* 1985, *21,* 866–871.

O'Connell, M., & Rogers, C. *Child care arrangements for working mothers: June 1982.* Current Population Reports, series P-23, no. 129. Washington, DC: U.S. Government Printing Office, 1983.

Oden, S., & Asher, S. R. Coaching children in social skills for friendship making. *Child Development,* 1977, *48,* 495–506.

Offer, D. *The psychological world of the teenager: A study of normal adolescence.* New York: Basic Books, 1969.

Offer, D., Ostrov, E., & Howard, K. *The adolescent: A psychological self-portrait.* New York: Basic Books, 1981.

O'Hara, D., & Kahn, J. Communication and contraceptive practices in adolescent couples. *Adolescence,* 1985, *20,* 33–43.

Okun, M. A., & DiVesta, F. J. Cautiousness in adulthood as a function of age and instructions. *Journal of Gerontology,* 1976, *31,* 371–376.

Okun, M. A., & Elias, C. S. Cautiousness in adulthood as a function of age and payoff structure. *Journal of Gerontology,* 1977, *32,* 311–316.

Oldershaw, L., Walters, G., & Hall, D. Control strategies and noncompliance in abusive mother–child dyads: An observational study. *Child Development,* 1986, *57,* 722–732.

Olmstead, A. H. From the journal of a newly retired man. *New York Times,* August 13, 1975, p. 33.

Olson, G. M., & Sherman, T. Attention, learning and memory in infants. In P. H. Mussen (Ed.), *Handbook of child psychology, Vol. II: Infancy and developmental psychobiology.* (4th ed.). New York: Wiley, 1983.

Oren, D. L. Cognitive advantages of bilingual children related to labeling ability. *Journal of Educational Research,* 1981, *74,* 164–169.

Orlofsky, J. L., Marcia, J. E., & Lesser, I. M. Ego identity status and the intimacy versus isolation crisis of young adulthood. *Journal of Personality and Social Psychology,* 1973, *27,* 211–219.

Oskamp, S., & Mindick, B. Personality and attitudinal barriers to contraception. In D. Byrne & W. A. Fisher (Eds.), *Adolescents, sex, and contraception.* New York: McGraw-Hill, 1981.

Osterweis, M., Solomon, F., & Green, M., *Bereavement: Reactions, consequences, and care.* Washington, DC: National Academy of Sciences, Institutes on Medicine, 1984.

Overton, W. F., & Newman, J. L. Cognitive development: A competence-activation/utilization approach. In T. Field, A. Huston, H. C. Quay, L. Troll, & G. E. Finley (Eds.), *Review of human development.* New York: Wiley-Interscience, 1982.

Overton, W. F., & Reese, H. W. Models of development: Methodological implications. In J. R. Nesselroade & H. W. Reese (Eds.), *Life-span developmental psychology: Methodological issues.* New York: Academic Press, 1973.

Pagelow, M. D. Research on woman battering. In J. B. Fleming (Ed.), *Stopping wife abuse.* Garden City, NY: Anchor Press, 1979.

Paige, K. E., & Paige, J. M. *Politics and reproductive rituals.* Berkeley, CA: University of California Press, 1981.

Palkovitz, R. Father's birth attendance, early contact and extended contact with their newborns: A critical review. *Child Development,* 1985, *56,* no. 2, 392–406.

Palmore, E., *Social patterns in normal aging: Findings from the Duke longitudinal study.* Durham, NC: Duke University Press, 1981.

Palmore, E., Burchett, B., Fillenbaum, G., George, L., & Wallman, L. *Retirement: Causes and consequences.* New York: Springer, 1985.

Palmore, E., & Cleveland, W. Aging, terminal decline and the terminal drop. *Journal of Gerontology,* 1976, *31,* 76–81.

Panek, P. E., Barrett, G. V., Sterns, H. L., & Alexander, R. A. Age differences in perceptual style, selective attention, and perceptual-motor reaction time. *Experimental Aging Research,* 1978, *4,* 377–387.

Papalia, D. E. The status of several conservation abilities across the life span. *Human Development,* 1972, *15,* 229–243.

Papalia, D. E., & Bielby, D. Cognitive functioning in middle- and old-age adults: A review of research based on Piaget's theory. *Human Development,* 1974, *17,* 424–443.

Papousek, H., & Bernstein, P. The functioning of conditioning stimulation in human neonates and infants. In A. Ambrose (Ed.), *Stimulation in early infancy.* New York: Academic Press, 1969.

Parents on the brink of child abuse get crisis aid. *New York Times,* April 17, 1983, pp. 1, 29.

Park, D., Pulisi, J., & Smith, A. Memory for pictures. *Psychology and aging,* 1986, *1,* 11–17.

Parke, R. Father–infant interaction and infant social responsiveness. In J. Osofsky (Ed.), *The handbook of infant development.* New York: Wiley, 1979.

Parke, R. D. Punishment in children: Effects, side effects, and alternative strategies. In Harry L. Horn, Jr., and Paul Robinson (Eds.), *Psychological processes in early education.* New York: Academic Press, 1977.

Parke, R., & Lewis, N. The family in context: A multilevel interactional analysis of child abuse. In R. W. Henderson (Ed.), *Parent–child interaction: Theory, research and prospect.* New York: Academic Press, 1980.

Parke, R., & Sawin, D. The family in early infancy: Social interactional and attitudinal analysis. In. F. A. Pedersen (Ed.), *The father–infant relationship: Observational studies in a family setting.* New York: Praeger, 1980.

Parke, R., & Slaby, R. Aggression: A multilevel analysis. In E. M. Hetherington (Eds.), *Handbook of child psychology: Socialization, personality and social development* (4th ed.). New York: Wiley, 1983.

Parkes, C. M. The first year of bereavement: A longitudinal study of the reaction of London widows to the death of their husbands. *Psychiatry,* 1970, *33,* 444–467.

Parkes, C. M. *Bereavement,* London: Tavistock, 1972.

Parmelee, A. H., & Stern, E. S. Development of states in infants. In C. Clemente, D. Purpura, & F. Mayer (Eds.), *Sleep in the maturing nervous system.* New York: Academic Press, 1972.

Parpal, M., & Maccoby, E. Maternal responsiveness and subsequent child compliance. *Child Development,* 1985, *56,* 1326–1334.

Patterson, G. Mothers: The unacknowledged victims. *Monographs of the Society for Research in Child Development,* 1980, *45,* no. 5, serial no. 186.

Patterson G., & Stouthamer-Loeber, M. The correlation of family management practices and delinquency. *Child Development,* 1984, *55,* 1299–1307.

Pattison, E. Death through the life cycle. In E. Pattison (Ed.), *The experience of dying.* Englewood Cliffs, NJ: Prentice-Hall, 1977.

Peal, E., & Lambert, W. The relation of bilingualism to intelligence. *Psychological Monographs,* 1962, *76,* no. 546, 1–23.

Pearce, K., & Denney, N. A lifespan study of classification preference. *Journal of Gerontology,* 1984, *39,* 458–464.

Peck, R. Psychological development in the second half of life. In B. L. Neugarten (Ed.), *Middle age and aging.* Chicago: University of Chicago Press, 1968.

Pelton, L. Child abuse and neglect: The myth of classlessness. *American Journal of Orthopsychiatry,* 1978, *48,* 608–617.

Perlmutter, M., & List, J. Learning in later adulthood. In T. Field, A. Huston, H. Quay, L. Troll, & G. Finley (Eds.), *Review of human development.* New York: Wiley, 1982.

Peskin, H. Influence of the developmental schedule of puberty on learning and ego functioning. *Journal of Youth and Adolescence,* 1973, *2,* 273–290.

Peterson, A. Those gangly years. *Psychology Today,* 1987, *21,* 28–34.

Peterson, A. C. Female pubertal development. In M. Sugar (Ed.), *Female adolescent development.* New York: Brunner/Mazel, 1979.

Pfeiffer, E. Psychopathology and social pathology. In J. E. Birren & K. W. Schaie (Eds.), *Handbook of the psychology of aging.* New York: Van Nostrand Reinhold, 1977.

Pfeiffer, E., Verwoerdt, A., & Davis, G. C. Sexual behavior in middle life. *American Journal of Psychiatry,* 1972, *128,* 82–87.

Philblad, C., & Adams, D. Widowhood, social participation, and life satisfaction. *International Journal of Aging and Human Development,* 1972, *3,* 323–330.

Phillips, J. *Piaget's theory: A primer.* San Francisco: Freeman, 1981.

Piaget, J. *The language of the child.* (M. Warden, trans.) New York: Harcourt, 1926.

Piaget, J. *The child's conception of time.* (A. J. Pomerans, trans.) New York: Ballantine Books, 1971. (Originally published 1927.)

Piaget, J. *The child's conception of the world.* New York: Harcourt & Brace, 1929.

Piaget, J. *The child's conception of number.* New York: Humanities, 1952. (a)

Piaget, J. *The origins of intelligence in children.* New York: International Universities Press, 1952. (b)

Piaget, J. *The language and thought of the child* (3rd ed.) London: Routledge, Kegan Paul, 1959.

Piaget, J. *The moral judgment of the Child.* New York: Free Press, 1965.

Piaget, J. *The child's conception of the world.* Totowa, NJ: Littlefield, Adams, 1967.

Piaget, J. *Psychology of intelligence.* Totowa, NJ: Littlefield, Adams, 1969.

Piaget, J. The definition of stages of development. In J. Tanner & B. Inhelder (Eds.), *Discussions on child development.* (Vol. 4). New York: International Universities Press, 1970. (a)

Piaget, J. Piaget's theory. In P. Mussen (Ed.), *Carmichael's manual of child psychology* (Vol. 1). New York: Wiley, 1970. (b)

Piaget, J. Intellectual evolution from adolescence to adulthood. *Human Development,* 1972, *15,* 1–12.

Piaget, J., & Inhelder, B. *Psychology of the child.* New York: Basic Books, 1969.

Piers, E., & Harris, D. *The Piers-Harris children's self-concept scale.* Nashville, TN: Counselor Recordings & Tests, 1969.

Pineo, P. C. Disenchantment in the later years of marriage. *Marriage and Family Living,* 1961, *23,* 3–11.

Pleck, J. H. The work-family role system. *Social Problems,* 1977, *24,* 417–427.

Pleck, J. H. Men's family work: Three perspectives and some new data. *The Family Coordinator,* 1979, *28,* 481–487.

Pleck, J., & Rustad, M. *Husbands' and wives' time in family work and paid work in the 1975–76 study of time use.* Wellesley, MA: Wellesley College Research Center on Women, 1980.

Plomin, R., & DeFries, J. C. Genetics and intelligence: Recent data. *Intelligence,* 1980, *4,* 15–24.

Pohlman, E. Childlessness, intentional and unintentional: Psychological and social aspects. *Journal of Nervous and Mental Disease,* 1970, *151,* 2–12.

Polivy, J., & Herman, C. Dieting and binging: A causal analysis. *American Psychologist,* 1985, *40,* 193–201.

Pope, H. G., Jr., Hudson, J., Yurgelun-Todd, D., & Hudson, M. Prevalence of anorexia nervosa and bulimia in three student populations. *International Journal of Eating Disorders,* 1984, *3,* 45–51.

Population Institute. *The youth values project: An inquiry conducted by teenagers themselves, into the attitudes, values, and experiences of teenagers in New York City regarding sex, contraception, and their life goals.* Washington, DC, 1978.

Powell, R. R. Psychological effects of exercise therapy upon institutionalized geriatric mental patients. *Journal of Gerontology,* 1974, *29,* 157–161.

Power, T., & Parke, R. Patterns of mother and father play with their 8-month-old infant: A multiple analysis approach. *Infant Behavior and Development,* 1983, *6,* 453–459.

Powers, E., Bultena, G. Sex differences in intimate friendships in college. *Journal of Marriage and the Family,* 1976, *38,* 739–747.

President's Science Advisory Committee. *Youth: Transition to adulthood.* Chicago: University of Chicago Press, 1974.

Presser, H. Social factors affecting the timing of the first child. In W. Miller & F. Newman (Eds.),

The first child and family formation. Chapel Hill: Carolina Population Center, 1978.

Pressey, S., Janey, T., & Kuhlen, R. *Life: A psychological survey.* New York: Harper, 1939.

Puig-Antich, J., Greenhill, L., Sassin, J., & Sachar, E. Growth hormone prolactin and cortisol responses and growth patterns in hyperkinetic children treated with dextroamphetamine: Preliminary findings. *Journal of American Academy of Child Psychiatry,* 1978, *17,* 457–475.

Putallaz, M. Predicting children's sociometric status from their behavior. *Child Development,* 1983, *54,* 1417–1426.

Quay, H. C. Adolescent aggression. In T. Field, A. Huston, H. C. Quay, L. Troll, & G. E. Finley (Eds.), *Review of human development.* New York: Wiley-Interscience, 1982.

Quindlen, A. Relationships: Independence vs. intimacy. *New York Times,* November 28, 1977, p. 36.

Quinn, R., Staines, G., & McCullough, M. *Job satisfaction: Is there a trend?* U. S. Department of Labor, Manpower, and Research Monograph no. 30. Washington, DC: GPO, 1974.

Rader, N., Bausano, M., & Richards, J. On the nature of the visual-cliff-avoidance response in human infants. *Child Development,* 1980, *51,* 61–68.

Radke-Yarrow, M., Cummings, E. M., Kuczynski, L., & Chapman, M. Patterns of attachment in two- and three-year-olds in normal families and families with parental depression. *Child Development,* 1985, *56,* 884–893.

Rahe, H., Mahan, J., & Arthur, R. J. Prediction of near future health change from subjects preceding life change. *Journal of Psychosomatic Research,* 1970, *14,* 401–406.

Ramey, C., & Mills, P. Social and intellectual consequences of day care for high-risk infants. In R. Webb (Ed.), *Social development in childhood: Day care programs and research.* Baltimore, MD: Johns Hopkins University Press, 1977.

Ramey, C., & Smith, B. Assessing the intellectual consequence of early intervention with high-risk infants. *American Journal of Mental Deficiency*, 1977, *81*, 318–324.

Ramsay, D. S., Campos, J. J., & Fenson, L. Onset of bimanual handedness in infants. *Infant Behavior and Development*, 1979, *2*, 69–76.

Rando, T. An investigation of grief and adaptation in parents whose children have died from cancer. *Journal of Pediatric Psychology*, 1983, *8*, 3–20.

Rapoport, R., & Rapoport, R. *Dual-career families re-examined: New integrations of work and family*. New York: Hoper-Colophon, 1976.

Rathus, S. A. *Human sexuality*. New York: Holt, Rinehart and Winston, 1983.

Reaves, J., & Roberts, A. The effects of the type of information on children's attraction to peers. *Child Development*, 1983, *54*, 1024–1031.

Rebok, G. *Life-span cognitive development*. New York: Holt, Rinehart and Winston, 1987.

Reedy, M. N., Birren, J. E., & Schaie, K. W. Age and sex differences in satisfying love relationships across the adult life span. *Human Development*, 1981, *24*, 52–66.

Reese, H. W., & Overton, W. F. Models of development and theories of development. In L. R. Goulet & P. B. Baltes (Eds.), *Lifespan developmental psychology: Theory and research*. New York: Academic Press, 1970.

Regan, M., & Roland, H. Rearranging family and career priorities: Professional women and men of the eighties. *Journal of Marriage and the Family*, 1985, *47*, 985–992.

Reichard, S., Livson, F., & Peterson, P. Adjustment to retirement. In B. Neugarten (Ed.), *Middle age and aging*. Chicago: University of Chicago Press, 1962.

Reilly, T., Hasazi, J., & Bond, L. Children's conceptions of death and personal mortality. *Journal of Pediatric Psychology*, 1983, *8*, 21–31.

Reinert, G. Prolegomena to a history of life-span developmental psychology. In P. B. Baltes & O. G. Brim (Eds.), *Life-span development and behavior* (Vol. 2). New York: Academic Press, 1979.

Reinisch, J. Prenatal exposure to synthetic progesterone increases potential for aggression in humans. *Science*, 1981, *211*, 1171–1173.

Reisberg, B. *Brain failure: An introduction to current concepts of senility*. New York: Macmillan, 1981.

Reisman, J. Adult friendships. In S. Duck & R. Gilmour (Eds.), *Personal relationships, Vol. 2. Developing personal relationships*. New York: Academic Press, 1981.

Reiss, I. L. *Family systems in America* (3rd ed.). New York: Holt, Rinehart and Winston, 1980.

Reschly, D. Psychological testing in educational classification and placement. *American Psychologist*, 1981, *36*, 1094–1102.

Rest, J. Morality. In P. H. Mussen (Ed.), *Handbook of child psychology: Cognitive development* (4th ed., Vol. 3). New York: Wiley, 1983.

Rest, J., & Thoma, S. Relation of moral judgment development to formal education. *Developmental Psychology*, 1985, *21*, 709–714.

Rexroat, C., & Shehan, C. The family life cycle and spouses' time in housework. *Journal of Marriage and the Family*, 1987, *49*, 737–750.

Rhodes, S. R. Age-related differences in work attitudes and behavior: A review and conceptual analysis. *Psychological Bulletin*, 1983, *93*, 329–367.

Rholes, W., & Ruble, D. Children's understanding of dispositional characteristics of others. *Child Development*, 1984, *55*, 550–560.

Rice, M. The role of television in language acquisition. *Developmental Review*, 1983, *3*, 221–224.

Richards, M. P. M., & Bernal, J. F. Social interactions in the first few days of life. In H. Schaffer (Ed.), *The origins of human social relations*. New York: Academic Press, 1971.

Richardson, D. W., & Short, R. V. Time of onset of sperm production in boys. *Journal of Biosocial Science*, 1978, *5*, 15–25.

Rickards, L., Zuckerman, D., & West, P. Alzheimer's disease: Current congressional response. *American Psychologist*, 1985, *40*, 1256–1261.

Ricks, M. The social transmission of parental behavior: Attachment across generations. In Bretherton, I., & Waters, E. (Eds.) *Growing points of attachment theory and research, Monographs of the Society for Research in Child Development*, 1985, serial no. 209, *50*, nos. 1–2.

Riegel, K. F. Developmental psychology and society: Some historical and ethical considerations. In J. R. Nesselroade & H. W. Reese (Eds.), *Life-span developmental psychology: Methodological issues*. New York: Academic Press, 1973 (a).

Riegel, K. F. Dialectic operations: The final period of cognitive development. *Human Development*, 1973, *16*, 346–370 (b).

Riegel, K. F. Adult life crises: A dialectical interpretation of development. In N. Datan & L. H. Ginsberg (Eds.), *Lifespan developmental psychology: Normative life crises*. New York: Academic Press, 1975.

Riegel, K. F., & Riegel, R. Development, drop and death. *Developmental Psychology*, 1972, *6*, 306–319.

Riley, M. W., Riley, J. W., Jr., & Johnson, M. F. *Aging and society, Vol. 1: An inventory of research findings*. New York: Russell Sage, 1968.

Ringness, T. A. Identification patterns, motivation, and school achievement of bright junior high school boys. *Journal of Educational Psychology*, 1967, *58*, 93–102.

Ritchie, R., & Moses, J. Assessment center correlates of women's advancement into middle management: A 7-year longitudinal analysis. *Journal of Applied Psychology*, 1983, *68*, 227–231.

Robbins, D. R., Alessi, N. E., Cook, S. C., Poznanski, E. O., & Yanchyshyn, G. W. The use of the research diagnostic criteria (RDC) for depression in adolescent psychiatric inpatients. *Journal of the American Academy of Child Psychiatry*, 1982, *21*, 251–255.

Robertson, J. F. Grandparenthood: A study of role conceptions. *Journal of Marriage and the Family*, 1977, *34*, 165–174.

Robins, L. N. Sturdy childhood predictors of adult antisocial behavior: Replications from longitudinal studies. *Psychological Medicine,* 1978, *8,* 611–622.

Roche, A. F. Secular trends in stature, weight, and maturation. In A. F. Roche (Ed.), Secular trends in growth, maturation, and development of children. *Monographs of the Society for Research in Child Development,* 1979, *44,* 3–27.

Roche, A. F., & Davila, G. H. Late adolescent growth in stature. *Pediatrics,* 1972, *50,* 874–880.

Roche, A. F. The adipocyte-number hypothesis. *Child Development,* 1981, *52,* 31–43.

Rockstein, M., & Sussman, M. *Biology of aging.* Belmont, CA: Wadsworth, 1979.

Rodgers, W., & Thornton, A. Changing patterns of first marriage in the United States. *Demography,* 1985, *22,* 265–279.

Rodin, J., & Langer, E. J. Long-term effects of a control-relevant intervention with the institutionalized aged. *Journal of Personality and Social Psychology,* 1977, *35,* 897–902.

Rodin, J., Striegel-Moore, R., & Silberstein. L. *A prospective study of bulimia among college students on three U.S. campuses.* First unpublished progress report, Yale University, New Haven, CT, 1986.

Rollins, B. C., & Feldman, H. Marital satisfaction over the family life cycle. *Journal of Marriage and the Family,* 1970, *32,* 20–37.

Rollins, J., & White, P. The relationship between mothers' and daughters' sex role attitudes and self concepts in three types of family environment. *Sex Roles,* 1982, *8,* 1141–1155.

Romaniuk, J., & Romaniuk, M. Creativity across the life span: A measurement perspective. *Human Development,* 1981, *24,* 366–381.

Romaniuk, J., & Romaniuk, M. Participation motives of older adults in higher education: The Elderhostel experience. *Gerontologist,* 1982, *22,* 364–368.

Romaniuk, M., McAuley, W. J., & Arling, G. An examination of the prevalence of mental disorders among the elderly in the community. *Journal of Abnormal Psychology,* 1983, *92,* 458–467.

Rose, R. M., & Abplanalp, J. M. The premenstrual syndrome. *Hospital Practice,* June 1983, 129–141.

Rosen, B. C., & Aneshensel, C. S. Sex differences in the educational-occupational expectation process. *Journal of Social Forces,* 1978, *57,* 164–186.

Rosenbaum, M. B. The changing body image of the adolescent girl. In M. Sugar (Ed.), *Female adolescent development.* New York: Brunner/Mazel, 1979.

Rosenberg, M. *Conceiving the self.* New York: Basic Books, 1979.

Rosenberg, M. *Society and the adolescent self-image.* Princeton, NJ: Princeton University Press, 1965.

Rosenman, R., & Friedman, M. Relationship of type A behavior pattern to coronary heart disease. In H. Selye (Ed.), *Selye's guide to stress research* (Vol. 2). New York: Scientific and Academic Editions, 1983.

Rossi, A. S. Transitions to parenthood. *Journal of Marriage and the Family,* 1968, *30,* 26–39.

Rossman, I. Bodily changes with aging. In E. W. Busse & D. G. Blazer (Eds.), *Handbook of geriatric psychiatry.* New York: Van Nostrand Reinhold, 1980.

Rovee-Collier, C. K. The ontogeny of learning and memory in human infancy. In R. Kail & N. E. Spear (Eds.), *Comparative perspectives on the development of memory.* Hillsdale, NJ: Erlbaum, 1984.

Rowland, K. Environmental events predicting death for the elderly. In L. Bugen (Ed.), *Death and dying: Theory, research, and practice.* Boston: W. C. Brown, 1979.

Rubin, J., Provenzano, F., & Luria, Z. The eyes of the beholder: Parents' views on sex of newborns. *American Journal of Orthopsychiatry,* 1974, *44,* 512–519.

Rubin, K. Recent perspectives on social competence and peer status: Some introductory remarks. *Child Development,* 1983, *54,* 1383–1385.

Rubinstein, E. Television and behavior: Research conclusions of the 1982 NIMH Report and their policy implications. *American Psychologist,* 1983, *38,* 820–825.

Ruble, D. N. The development of social comparison processes and their role in achievement-related self-socialization. In E. T. Higgins, D. N. Ruble,, & W. W. Hartup (Eds.), *Social cognition and social behavior: Developmental perspectives.* New York: Cambridge University Press, 1983.

Ruble, D. Premenstrual symptoms: A reinterpretation. *Science,* 1977, *197,* 291–292.

Ruble, D. N., & Brooks-Gunn, J. The experience of menarche. *Child Development,* 1982, *53,* 1557–1566.

Rugh, R., & Shettles, L. *From conception to birth: The drama of life's beginnings.* New York: Harper & Row, 1971.

Runciman, A. Problems older clients present in counseling about sexuality. In I. M. Burnside (Ed.), *Sexuality and aging.* Los Angeles: University of Southern California Press, 1975.

Ruopp, R., & Travers, J. Janus faces day care: Perspective on quality and cost. In E. Zigler and E. W. Gordon (Eds.), *Day care: Scientific and social policy issues.* Boston: Auburn House, 1982.

Rupley, W., Garcia, J., & Longnion, B. Sex role portrayal in reading materials: Implications for the 1980's. *The Reading Teacher,* 1981, *34,* 786–791.

Ruopp, R., Travers, J., Glantz, F., & Coelen, C. *Children at the center.* Cambridge, MA: Abt Associates, 1979.

Russell, C. S. Transitions to parenthood: Problems and gratifications. *Journal of Marriage and the Family,* 1974, *36,* 294–301.

Russell, G. Bulimia nervosa: An ominous variant of anorexia nervosa. *Psychological Medicine,* 1979, *9,* 429–448.

Russell, O. *Freedom to die: Moral and legal aspects of euthanasia* (rev. ed.). New York: Human Sciences, 1977.

Rutter, M. Proactive factors in children's responses to stress and disadvantage. In M. Kent & J. E. Rolf (Eds.), *Primary prevention of psychopathology, Vol. III: Social competence in children.* Hanover, NH: University Press of New England, 1979.

Rutter, M., & Garmesy, N. Developmental psychopathology. In E. M. Hetherington (Ed.), *Handbook of child psychology, Vol IV: Socialization, personality, and social development* (4th ed.). New York: Wiley, 1983.

Rutter, M., Tizard, J., & Whitmore, K. (Eds.). *Education, health, and behavior.* London: Longmans, 1970.

Rychlak, J. F. *A philosophy of science for personality theory.* Boston: Houghton Mifflin, 1968.

Sacher, G. A. Longevity, aging, and death: An evolutionary perspective. *Gerontologist,* 1978, *18,* 112–119.

Safier, G. A study in relationships between life and death concepts in children. *Journal of Genetic Psychology,* 1964, *105,* 283–294.

Sagar, H. A., Schofield, J., & Snyder, H. Race and gender barriers: Preadolescent peer behavior in academic classrooms. *Child Development,* 1983, *54,* 1032–1040.

Salkind, N., & Nelson, C. A note on the development of reflection–impulsivity. *Developmental Psychology,* 1980, *16,* 237–238.

Sallade, J. B. A comparison of psychological adjustment of obese vs. non-obese children. *Journal of Psychosomatic Research,* 1973, *17,* 89–96.

Salthouse, T. *Adult cognition: An experimental psychology of human aging.* New York: Springer-Verlag, 1982.

Sameroff, A. Developmental systems: Contexts and evaluation. In P. H. Mussen (Ed.), *Handbook of child psychology, Vol. I: History, theory and methods.* New York: Wiley, 1983.

Sameroff, A. J., & Cavanagh, P. J. Learning in infancy: A developmental perspective. In J. D. Osofsky (Ed.), *Handbook of infant development.* New York: Wiley, 1979.

Santrock, J. The relation of type and onset of father absence to cognitive development. *Child Development,* 1972, *43,* 455–469.

Santrock, J., & Tracy, R. Effects of children's family structure status on the developmental stereotypes by children. *Journal of Educational Psychology,* 1978, *70,* 754–757.

Santrock, J., & Warshak, R. Father custody and social development in boys and girls. *Journal of Social Issues,* 1979, *35,* 112–125.

Santrock, J., Warshak, R., Lindberg, V., & Meadows, L. Children's and parents' observed social behavior in stepfather families. *Child Development,* 1982, *53,* 471–480.

Sants, H. J. Genealogical bewilderment in children with substitute parents. *British Journal of Medical Psychology,* 1964, *37,* 133–141.

Savin-Williams, R. C. Social interactions of adolescent females in natural groups. In H. C. Foot, A. J. Chapman, & J. R. Smith (Eds.), *Friendship and social relations in children.* New York: Wiley, 1980.

Savin-Williams, R., & Demo, D. Developmental change and stability in adolescent self concept. *Developmental Psychology,* 1984, *20,* 1100–1110.

Scales, P. Sex education and the prevention of teenage pregnancy: An overview of policies and programs in the United States. In T. Ooms (Ed.), *Teenage pregnancy in family context: Implications for policy.* Philadelphia: Temple University Press, 1981, 213–254.

Scanlon, J. *Young adulthood.* New York: Academy for Educational Development, 1979.

Scanzoni, J. *Sex role, life styles, and childbearing.* New York: Free Press, 1975.

Scanzoni, J. Contemporary marriage types: A research note. *Journal of Family Issues,* 1980, *1,* 125–140.

Scarr, S. *Mother care/other care.* New York: Basic Books, 1984.

Schacter, D., & Moscovitch, M. Infants, amnesics, and dissociable memory systems. In M. Moscovitch (Ed.), *Infant Memory.* New York: Plenum, 1984.

Schacter, D., Moscovitch, M., Tulving, E., McLachlan, D., & Freedman, M. Mnemonic precedence in amnesic patients: An analogue of the AB error in infants? *Child Development,* 1986, *57,* 816–823.

Schaefer, R., & Bayley, N. Maternal behavior, child behavior and their intercorrelations from infancy through adolescence. *Monographs of the Society for Research in Child Development,* 1963, *28,* (3), whole no. 87.

Schafer, W. *Stress management for wellness.* New York: Holt, Rinehart and Winston, 1987.

Schaffer, R. *Mothering.* Cambridge, MA: Harvard University Press, 1977.

Schaie, K. W. Transitions in gerontology—from lab to life: Intellectual functioning. *American Psychologist,* 1974, *29,* 802–807.

Schaie, K. W. The primary mental abilities in adulthood: An exploration in the development of psychometric intelligence. In P. B. Baltes & O. G. Brim, Jr. (Eds.), *Life-span development and behavior* (Vol. 3). 67–115. New York: Academic Press, 1979.

Schaie, K. W. (Ed.). *Longitudinal studies of adult psychological development.* New York: Guilford Press, 1983.

Schaie, K. W., & Hertzog, C. Longitudinal methods. In B. Wolman (Ed.), *Handbook of developmental psychology.* Englewood Cliffs, NJ: Prentice-Hall, 1982.

Schaie, K. W., & Hertzog, C. Fourteen-year cohort-sequential analyses of adult intellectual development. *Developmental Psychology,* 1983, *19,* 531–543.

Schaie, K. W., & Parham, I. A. Stability of adult personality: Fact or fable? *Journal of Personality and Social Psychology,* 1976, *34,* 146–158.

Schmeck, H. Fetal defects discovered early by new method. *New York Times,* October 18, 1983, p. C1.

Schoen, R., & Nelson, V. E. Marriage, divorce, and mortality: A life table analysis. *Demography,* 1974, *11,* 267–290.

Schram, R. W. Marital satisfaction over the family life-cycle: A critique and proposal. *Journal of Marriage and the Family,* 1979, *41,* 7–40.

Schultz, N. R., Jr., Kaye, D. B., & Hoyer, W. J. Intelligence and spontaneous flexibility in adulthood and old age. *Intelligence,* 1980, *4,* 219–231.

Schulz, D. A. *The changing family: Its function and future.* Englewood Cliffs, NJ: Prentice-Hall, 1972.

Schulz, R. *The psychology of death, dying and bereavement.* New York: Addison-Wesley, 1978.

Schulz, R., & Brenner, A. Relocation in the aged: A review and theoretical analysis. *Journal of Gerontology,* 1977, *32,* 323–333.

Schwebel, M. Effects of the nuclear war threat on children and teenagers: Implications for professionals. *American Journal of Orthopsychiatry,* 1982, *52,* 608–617.

Scott, J. Siblings and other kin. In T. Brubaker (Ed.), *Family relationships in later life.* Beverly Hills, CA: Sage Publications, 1983.

Sears, R., Maccoby, E., & Levin, H. *Patterns of child rearing.* Evanston, IL: Row Peterson, 1957.

Sears R., Rau, L., & Alpert, R. *Identification and child rearing.* Stanford, CA: Stanford University Press, 1965.

Seavey, C., Katz, P., & Zalk, S. Baby X: The effects of gender labels on adult responses to infants. *Sex Roles,* 1975, *1,* 103–109.

Seefeldt, F. M. Formal operations and adolescent painting. *The Genetic Epistemologist,* 1979, *8,* 5–6.

Segal, J., & Yahraes, H. *A child's journey: Forces that shape the lives of our young.* New York: McGraw-Hill, 1979.

Seligman, M. *Helplessness: On depression, development, and death.* San Francisco: Freeman, 1975.

Seligman, M. E. P., & Peterson, C. A learned helplessness perspective on childhood depression: Theory and research. In M. Rutter, C. E. Izard, & P. Read (Eds.), *Depression in childhood: Developmental perspectives.* New York: Guilford Press, 1983.

Selman, R. *The growth of interpersonal understanding.* New York: Academic Press, 1980.

Selman, R. L. The child as a friendship philosopher: A case study in the growth of interpersonal understanding. In S. R. Asher & J. M. Gottman (Eds.), *The development of children's friendships.* Cambridge: Cambridge University Press, 1981.

Serbin, L., & O'Leary, K. How nursery schools teach girls to shut up. *Psychology Today,* December 1975, *9,* 56–58.

Serbin, K., & Sprafkin, C. The salience of gender and the process of sex typing in three-to-seven-year-old children. *Child Development,* 1986, *57,* 1188–1199.

Shanas, E. Social myth as hypothesis: The case of the family relations of old people. *The Gerontologist,* 1979, *19,* 3–9.

Shanas, E. Older people and their families: New pioneers. *Journal of Marriage and the Family,* 1980, *42,* 9–18.

Shanas, E., & Sussman, M. The family in later life: Social structure and social policy. In R. W. Fogel, E. Hatfield, S. B. Kiesler & E. Shanas (Eds.), *Aging: Stability and change in the family.* New York: Academic Press, 1981.

Shanas, E., Townsend, P., Weddenburn, D., Friis, H., Hilhoj, P., & Stehouwer, I. *Older people in three industrial societies.* New York: Atherton, 1968.

Shantz, C. V. Social cognition. In J. H. Flavell & E. Markman (Eds.), *Handbook of child psychology, Vol. 3: Cognitive development* (4th ed.). New York: Wiley, 1983.

Shapiro, D., & Crowley, J. Aspirations and expectations of youth in the United States. P. 2: Employment activity. *Youth and Society,* 1982, *14,* 33–58.

Sheehy, G. *Passages: Predictable crises of adult life.* New York: Dutton, 1976.

Sheffield, M. *Where do babies come from?* New York: Knopf, 1972.

Sheppard, H., & Belitsky, A. *The job hunt.* Baltimore: Johns Hopkins Press, 1966.

Shirley, M. The first two years: A study of twenty-five babies. *Child Welfare Monograph,* 1933, *11,* no. 7.

Shneidman, E. The college student and death. In H. Feifel (Ed.), *New meanings of death.* New York: McGraw-Hill, 1977.

Shock, N. W. Biological theories of aging. In J. E. Birren & K. W. Schaie (Eds.), *Handbook of the psychology of aging.* New York: Van Nostrand Reinhold, 1977.

Sidorowicz, L., & Lunney, G. S. Baby X revisited. *Sex Roles,* 1980, *6,* 67–73.

Siegel, M. Congenital malformations following chicken pox, measles, mumps and hepatitis. *Journal of American Medical Association,* 1973, *226,* 1521–1524.

Siegel, O. Personality development in adolescence. In B. Wolman (Ed.), *Handbook of developmental psychology.* Englewood Cliffs, NJ: Prentice-Hall, 1982.

Siegler, I., McCarty, S., & Logue, P. Wechsler memory scale scores, selective attrition, and distance from death. *Journal of Gerontology,* 1982, *37,* 176–181.

Siegler, R. Information processing approaches to development. In P. H. Mussen (Ed.), *Handbook of child psychology, Vol. I: History, theory and methods.* New York: Wiley, 1983.

Sigel, I. E., & Brodzinsky, D. Individual differences: A perspective for understanding intellectual development. In H. L. Hom & P. A. Robinson (Eds.), *Psychological processes in early education.* New York: Academic Press, 1977.

Sigel, R. S. Students' comprehension of democracy and its application to conflict situations. *International Journal of Political Education,* 1979, *2,* 47–65.

Sigel, R. S., & Hoskin, M. B. *The political involvement of adolescents.* New Brunswick, NJ: Rutgers University Press, 1981.

Silverman, P. Widowhood and preventive intervention. In M. Bloom (ed.), *Life span development: Bases for preventive and interventive helping.* (2nd ed.). New York: Macmillan, 1985.

Simeonsson, R., Buckley, L., & Monson, L. Conceptions of illness causality in hospitalized children. *Journal of Pediatric Psychology,* 1979, *4,* 77–84.

Simmons, R. G., & Rosenberg, F. Sex, sex roles, and self-image. *Journal of Youth and Adolescence,* 1975, *4,* 225–258.

Simpson, J., Campbell, B., & Berscheid, E. The association between romantic love and marriage: Kephart (1967) twice revisited. *Personality and Social Psychology Bulletin,* 1986, *12,* 363–372.

Singer, L., Brodzinsky, D., Ramsay, D., Stein, M., & Waters, E. Mother–infant attachment in adoptive families. *Child Development*, 1985, *56*, 1543–1551.

Singer, J. L., and Singer, D. G. *Television, imagination and aggression. A study of preschoolers.* Hillsdale, NJ: Erlbaum, 1981.

Singer, J., & Singer, D. Psychologists look at television: Cognitive, developmental, personality and social policy implications. *American Psychologist*, 1983, *38*, 826–834.

Skinner, B. F. *Verbal behavior.* New York: Appleton-Century-Crofts, 1957.

Skinner, B. F. *The behavior of organisms: An experimental analysis.* New York: Appleton, 1938.

Skinner, B. F., & Vaughan, M. E. *Enjoy old age.* New York: Norton, 1983.

Slobin, D. Children and language: They learn the same way all around the world. *Psychology Today*, July 1972, p. 18.

Slobin, D. On the nature of talk to children. In E. H. Lenneberg & E. Lenneberg (Eds.), *Foundations of language development* (Vol. 1). New York: Academic Press, 1975.

Slobin, D. (Ed.). *The cross-cultural study of language acquisition.* Hillsdale, NJ: Erlbaum, 1982.

Slocum, W. L., & Nye, F. I. Provider and housekeeper roles. In F. I. Nye et al. (Eds.), *Role structure and analysis of the family.* Beverly Hills, CA: Sage Foundation, 1976.

Smiley, S. S., & Brown, A. L. Conceptual preference for thematic or taxonomic relations: A nonmonotonic age trend from preschool to old age. *Journal of Experimental Child Psychology*, 1979, *28*, 249–257.

Smith, D. Historical change in the household structure of the elderly in economically developed societies. In R. Fogel, E. Hatfield, S. B. Kiesler, & E. Shanas (Eds.), *Aging: Stability and change in the family.* New York: Academic Press, 1981.

Smith, P. K., & Daglish, L. Sex differences in parent and infant behavior in the home. *Child Development*, 1977, *48*, 1250–1254.

Smith, S. N. Recent cross-ethnic research on the adolescent. *Journal of Negro Education*, 1979, *48*, 302–323.

Smuts, A. B., & Hagen, J. W. History and research in child development. *Monographs of the Society for Research in Child Development*, 1985, *50*, 4–5, serial no. 211.

Smyser, A. Hospices: Their humanistic and economic value. *American Psychologist*, 1982, *37*, 1260–1262.

Snarey, J., Reimer, J., & Kohlberg, L. Development of social-moral reasoning among kibbutz adolescents: A longitudinal cross-cultural study. *Developmental Psychology*, 1985, *21*, 3–17.

Snarey, J., Son, L. Kuehne, V., Hauser, S., & Vaillant, G. The role of parenting in men's psychosocial development: A longitudinal study of early adulthood infertility and midlife generativity. *Developmental Psychology*, 1987, Vol. 23, 596–603.

Snow, C. E. The uses of initiation. *Journal of Child Language*, 1981, *8*, 205–212.

Snyder, R. D. Congenital mercury poisoning. *New England Journal of Medicine*, 1971, *284*, 1014–1016.

Sokol, R. J., Miller, S. I., & Reed, G. Alcohol abuse during pregnancy: An epidemiologic study. *Alcoholism*, 1980, *4*, 135–145.

Sokoloff, B. Alternative methods of reproduction: Effects on the child. *Clinical Pediatrics*, 1987, *26*, 11–16.

Sontag, L. W. Implications of fetal behavior and environment for adult personalities. *Annals of the New York Academy of Sciences*, 1966, *134*, 782–786.

Sontag, L. W., & Wallace, R. F. The effect of cigarette smoking during pregnancy upon the fetal heart rate. *American Journal of Obstetrics and Gynecology*, 1935, *29*, 77–83.

Sorce, J., Emde, R., Campos, J., & Klinnert, M. Maternal emotional signaling: Its effect on the visual cliff behavior of 1-year-olds. *Developmental Psychology*, 1985, *21*, 195–200.

Sorensen, R. *Adolescent sexuality in contemporary America.* New York: William Collins, 1973.

Sorosky, A. D., Baran, A., & Pannor, R. *The adoption triangle: The effects of the sealed record on adoptees, birth parents, and adoptive parents.* Garden City, NY: Anchor Press, 1978.

Sosa, R., Kennel, J., Klaus, M., Robertson, S., & Urrutia, J. The effect of a supportive companion on perinatal problems, length of labor, and mother–infant interaction. *New England Journal of Medicine*, 1980, *303* (11), 597–600.

Spanier, G. B., & Lewis, R. A. Marital quality: A review of the seventies. *Journal of Marriage and the Family*, 1980, *42*, 825–839.

Spanier, G. B., Lewis, R. A., & Cole, L. C. Marital adjustment over the family life cycle: The issue of curvilinearity. *Journal of Marriage and the Family*, 1975, *37*, 262–275.

Spanier, G. B., Roos, P., & Shockey, J. Marital trajectories of American women: Variations in the life course. *Journal of Marriage and the Family*, 1985, *47*, 993–1003.

Speece, M., & Brent, S. Children's understanding of death: A review of three components of a death concept. *Child Development*, 1984, *55*, 1671–1686.

Spinetta, J. The dying child's awareness of death: A review. *Psychological Bulletin*, 1974, *81*, 256–260.

Spinetta, J., & Rigler, D. The child-abusing parent: A psychological review. *Psychological Bulletin*, 1972, *72*, 296–304.

Spinetta, J., Swarner, J., & Sheposh, J. Effective parental coping following the death of a child from cancer. *Journal of Pediatric Psychology*, 1981, *6*, 251–263.

Spitz, R. Hospitalism: An inquiry into the genesis of psychiatric conditions in early childhood. *Psychoanalytic Study of the Child*, 1945, *1*, 53–74.

Spreitzer, E., & Riley, L. E. Factors associated with singlehood. *Journal of Marriage and the Family*, 1974, *36*, 533–542.

Squire, S. *The slender balance: Causes and cures for bulimia, anorexia, and the weight-loss/weight-gain seesaw.* New York: Putnam, 1983.

Sroufe, L. A. Attachment and the roots of competence. *Human Nature*, October 1978, 50–57.

Sroufe, L. A. Socioemotional development. In J. Osofsky (Ed.),

Handbook of infant development. New York: Wiley, 1979.

Sroufe, L. A. Attachment classification from the perspective of infant caregiver relationships and infant temperament. *Child Development*, 1985, *56*, 1–14.

Stagner, R. Postscripts and prospects. In A. S. Glickman (Ed.), *The changing composition of the work force: Implications for research and its application.* New York: Plenum, 1982.

Stankov, K. Aging, attention and intelligence. *Psychology and Aging*, 1988, *3*, 59–74.

Statistical Abstract of the United States Washington, DC: Department of Commerce, 1981; National Center for Health Statistics, *Monthly Vital Statistics Report, 33,* no. 9, Hyattsville, MD: Public Health Service, December 1984.

Stein, A., & Friedrich, L. Impact of television on children and youth. In E. M. Hetherington, J. Hagen, R. Kron, & A. H. Stein (Eds.), *Review of child development research* (Vol. 5). Chicago: University of Chicago Press, 1975.

Stein, P. J. Singlehood: An alternative to marriage. In J. Henslin (Ed.), *Marriage and the family in a changing society.* New York: Free Press, 1980.

Stein, S. *Making babies.* New York: Walker, 1974.

Steinberg, L. Bound to bicker. *Psychology Today*, 1987, *21*, 36–39.

Steinberg, L. Stability of type A behavior from early childhood to young adulthood. In P. Baltes, D. Featherman, & R. Lerner (Eds.), *Life-span development and behavior* (Vol. 8). Hillsdale, NJ: Erlbaum, 1988.

Steinberg, L., Greenberger, E., Garduque, L., Ruggiero, M., & Vaux, A. Effects of working on adolescent development. *Developmental Psychology*, 1982, *18*, 385–395.

Steinberg, L., & Silverberg, S. The vicissitudes of autonomy in early adolescence. *Child Development*, 1986, *57*, 841–851.

Steinberg, L., & Silverberg, S. Influences on marital satisfaction during the middle stages of the family life cycle. *Journal of Marriage and the Family*, 1987, *49*, 751–760.

Stenberg, C., Campos, J., & Emde, R. The facial expression of anger in seven-month-old infants. *Child Development*, 1983, *54*, 178–184.

Stern, G., Caldwell, B., Hersher, L., Lipton, E., & Richmond, E. A factor-analytic study of the mother–infant dyad. *Child Development*, 1969, *40*, 163–182.

Stern, M., & Hildebrandt, K. Prematurity stereotyping: Effects on mother–infant interaction. *Child Development*, 1986, *57*, 308–315.

Sternglanz, S. H., & Serbin, L. Sex role stereotyping in children's television programs. *Developmental Psychology*, 1974, *10*, 710–715.

Stevens, J. Black grandmothers' and black adolescent mothers' knowledge about parenting. *Developmental Psychology*, 1984, *20*, 1017–1025.

Stevens-Long, J. *Adult life: Developmental processes.* Palo Alto, CA: Mayfield, 1979.

Stewart, R. Sibling attachment relationships: Child–infant interactions in the strange situation. *Developmental Psychology*, 1983, *19*, 192–199.

Stinnett, N., Carter, L. M., & Montgomery, J. E. Older persons' perceptions of their marriages. *Journal of Marriage and the Family*, 1972, *34*, 665–670.

Stinnett, N., & Walters, J. *Relationships in marriage and family.* New York: Macmillan, 1977.

Stipek, D. A developmental analysis of pride and shame. *Human Development*, 1983, *26*, 42–54.

Stoddard, S. *The hospice movement: A better way of caring for the dying.* Briarcliff Manor, NY: Stein and Day, 1978.

Stoddart, T., & Turiel, E. Children's concepts of cross gender activities. *Child Development*, 1985, *56*, 1241–1252.

Stoneman, Z., Brody, G., & MacKinnon, C. Naturalistic observations of children's activities and roles while playing with their siblings and friends. *Child Development*, 1984, *55*, 617.

Stott, D. H., & Latchford, S. A. Prenatal antecedents of child health, development, and behavior: An epidemiological report of inci-

dence and association. *Journal of the American Academy of Child Psychology*, 1976, *15*, 161–191.

Streib, G. F. Social stratification and aging. In R. H. Binstock & E. Shanas (Eds.), *Handbook of aging and the social sciences.* New York: Van Nostrand Reinhold, 1977.

Streib, G. F., & Schneider, C. *Retirement in American society.* Ithaca, NY: Cornell University Press, 1971.

Streissguth, A., Martin, D., Barr, H., Sandman, B., Kirchner, G., & Darby, B. Intrauterine alcohol and nicotine exposure: Attention and reaction time in 4-year-old children. *Developmental Psychology*, 1984, *20*, 533–541.

Striegel-Moore, R., Silberstein, L., & Rodin, J. Toward an understanding of risk factors for bulimia. *American Psychologist*, 1986, *41*, 246–263.

Stroebe, M. S., & Stroebe, W. Who suffers more? Sex differences in health risks of the widowed. *Psychological Bulletin*, 1983, *93*, 279–301.

Strong, L. D. Alternative marital and family forms: Their relative attractiveness to college students and correlates of willingness to participate in nontraditional forms. *Journal of Marriage and the Family*, 1978, *40*, 493–503.

Stueve, A., & Fischer, C. Social networks and old women. Paper presented at the Workshop on Older Women, Washington, DC, September 1978.

Stults, H. Obesity in adolescents: Prognosis, etiology, and management. *Journal of Pediatric Psychology*, 1977, *2*, 122–126.

Stunkard, A., Thorkild, M., Sorenson, I., Hanis, C., Teasdale, T., Chakraborty, R., Schull, W., & Schulsinger, F. An adoption study of human obesity. *The New England Journal of Medicine*, 1986, *314*, 193–198.

Suedfeld, P., & Piedrahita, L. Intimations of mortality: Integrative simplification as a precursor of death. *Journal of Personality and Social Psychology*, 1984, *47*, 848–852.

Super, C. M. Secular trends in child development and the institutionalization of professional disciplines. SCRD *Newsletter,* Spring 1982, 10–11.

Super, D. E. *The psychology of careers.* New York: Harper & Row, 1957.

Super, D. E. *Career development: Self-concept theory.* New York: College Entrance Examination Board, 1963.

Sussman, M. B. Intergenerational family relationships and social role changes in middle age. *Journal of Gerontology,* 1960, *15,* 71–75.

Sussman, M. B. Relationships of adult children with their parents in the United States. In E. Shanas & G. Streib (Eds.), *Social structure and the family: Generational relations.* Englewood Cliffs, NJ: Prentice-Hall, 1965.

Sutker, P. B. Adolescent drug and alcohol behaviors. In T. Field, A. Huston, H. C. Quay, L. Troll, & G. E. Finley (Eds.), *Review of human development.* New York: Wiley-Interscience, 1982.

Sutton-Smith, B. Birth order and sibling status effects. In M. E. Lamb & B. Sutton-Smith (Eds.), *Sibling relationships: Their nature and significance across the life span.* Hillsdale, NJ: Erlbaum, 1982.

Sutton-Smith, B., & Rosenberg, B. *The sibling.* New York: Holt, Rinehart and Winston, 1970.

Svejda, M. J., Campos, J. J., & Emde, R. N. Mother–infant "bonding": Failure to generalize. *Child Development,* 1980, *51,* 775–779.

Swanson, J., & Kinsbourne, M. Food dyes impair performance of hyperactive children on a laboratory learning test. *Science,* 1980, *207,* 1485–1487.

Sweetland, J. *Mid-career perspectives: The middle-aged and older population.* Scarsdale, NY: Work in America Institute, 1978.

Swensen, C., Eskew, R., & Kohlhepp, K. Stage of family life cycle, ego development, and the marriage relationship. *Journal of Marriage and the Family,* 1981, *43,* 841–853.

Talland, G. A. Three estimates of the word span and their estimates over the adult years. *Quarterly Journal of Experimental Psychology,* 1965, *17,* 301–307.

Tamir, L. *Men in their forties: The transition to middle age.* New York: Springer, 1982.

Tanfer, K. Patterns of premarital cohabitation among never married women. *Journal of Marriage and the Family,* 1987, *49,* 483–497.

Tangri, S. S. Determinants of occupational role innovations among college women. In M. T. S. Mednick, S. S. Tangri, & L. W. Hoffman (Eds.), *Women and achievement: Social and motivational analysis.* Washington, DC: Hemisphere, 1975.

Tanner, J. M. *The physique of the Olympic athlete.* London: Allen and Unwin, 1964.

Tanner, J. M. Physical growth. In P. H. Mussen (Ed.), *Carmichael's manual of child psychology.* New York: Wiley, 1970.

Tanner, J. M. *Fetus into man: Physical growth from conception to maturity.* Cambridge, MA: Harvard University Press, 1978.

Taussig, H. B. The thalidomide syndrome. *Scientific American,* 1962, *107,* 29–35.

Tavris, C., & Offir, C. *The longest war: Sex differences in perspective.* New York: Harcourt Brace Jovanovich, 1977.

Tavris, C., & Wade, C. *The longest war: Sex differences in perspective.* New York: Harcourt Brace Jovanovich, 1984.

Teller, M. N. Age changes and immune resistance to cancer. *Advances of Gerontological Research,* 1972, *4,* 25–43.

Terman, L. M. *Genetic studies of genius: Mental and physical traits of a thousand gifted children* (Vol. 1). Stanford, CA: Stanford University Press, 1925.

Terman, L. M., & Merrill, M. *Stanford-Binet Intelligence Scale: Manual for the third revision of form L-M.* Boston: Houghton Mifflin, 1973.

Tesch, S. A. Review of friendship development across the life span. *Human Development,* 1983, *26,* 266–276.

Theorell, T., & Rahe, R. H. Psychosocial factors and myocardial infarction. I: An inpatient study in Sweden. *Journal of Psychosomatic Research,* 1974, *15,* 25–31.

Thomas, A., & Chess, S. *Temperament and development.* New York: Brunner/Mazel, 1977.

Thompson, L., & Walker, A. Mothers and daughters: Aid patterns and attachment. *Journal of Marriage and the Family,* 1984, *46,* 313–322.

Thompson, R. A., Lamb, M. E., & Estes, D. Stability of infant–mother attachment and its relationship to changing life circumstances in an unselected middle class sample. *Child Development,* 1982, *53,* 144–148.

Thoresen, C., Eagleston, J., Kirmil-Gray, K., & Bracke, P. *Type A children.* Paper presented at the annual meeting of the American Psychological Association. Los Angeles, August 1985.

Thurnher, M., Spence, D., & Lowenthal, M. F. Value conflict and behavior conflict in intergenerational relations. *Journal of Marriage and the Family,* 1974, *36,* 308–319.

Tibbitts, C. Older Americans in the family context. *Aging,* 1977, *270–271,* 6–11.

Tierney K., & Corwin, D. Exploring intrafamilial child sexual abuse: A systems approach. In D. Finkelhor, R. J. Gelles, G. T. Hotaling, & M. A. Straus (Eds.), *The dark side of families: Current family violence research.* Beverly Hills, CA: Sage Publications, 1983.

Timiras, P. S. *Developmental physiology and aging.* New York: Macmillan, 1972.

Tinklenberg, J. R., & Darley, C. F. Psychological and cognitive effects of cannabis. In P. H. Cornell & N. Dorn (Eds.), *Cannabis and man.* New York: Churchill Livingstone, 1975.

Tinsley, B. R., & Parke, R. D. Grandparents as support and socialization agents. In M. Lewis (Ed.), *Beyond the dyad.* New York: Plenum, 1983.

Tisdale, S. *Harvest Moon: Portrait of a nursing home.* New York: Henry Holt, 1987.

Tobias, S. Sexist equations. *Psychology Today,* January 1982, *15,* 14–18.

Tobin, S. S., & Lieberman, M. A. *Last home for the aged.* San Francisco: Jossey-Bass, 1976.

Townes, B., & Wold, D. Childhood leukemia. In E. Pattison (Ed.), *The experience of dying.* Englewood Cliffs, NJ: Prentice-Hall, 1979.

Townsend, C. *Old age, the last segregation: The report on nursing homes.* Ralph Nader's Study Group Reports. New York: Grossman, 1971.

Treas, J., & Van Hilst, A. Marriage and remarriage rate among older Americans. *The Gerontologist,* 1976, *16,* 132–136.

Treffert, D. A. Marijuana use in schizophrenia: A clear hazard. *American Journal of Psychology,* 1978, *135,* 10.

Troll, L. E. The family of later life: A decade review. *Journal of Marriage and the Family,* 1971, *33,* 263–290.

Troll, L. E. *Early and middle adulthood.* Monterey, CA: Brooks/Cole, 1975.

Troll, L. E. Grandparenting. In L. Poon (Ed.), *Aging in the 1980s: Psychological issues.* Washington, DC: American Psychological Association, 1980.

Troll, L. E. *Continuations: Adult development and aging.* Monterey, CA: Brooks/Cole, 1982.

Troll, L. E. Grandparents: The family watchdog. In T. Brubaker (Ed.), *Family relationships in later life.* Beverly Hills, CA: Sage, 1983.

Troll, L. E., & Bengston, V. Intergenerational relations throughout the life span. In B. Wolman (Ed.), *Handbook of developmental psychology.* Englewood Cliffs, NJ: Prentice-Hall, 1982.

Troll, L. E., Miller, S. J., & Atchley, R. C. *Families in later life.* Belmont, CA: Wadsworth, 1979.

Troll, L. E., & Smith, J. Attachment through the life span: Some questions about dyadic bonds among adults. *Human Development,* 1976, *19,* 156–170.

Troll, L. E., & Turner, B. F. Sex differences in problems of aging. In E. Gomberg & V. Franks (Eds.), *Gender and disordered behavior.* New York: Brunner/Mazel, 1980.

Tuckman, J., & Lorge, I. Attitudes toward old people. *Journal of Social Psychology,* 1953, *37,* 249–260.

Tuma, N. B., & Hallinan, M. T. The effects of sex, race, and achievement on schoolchildren's friendships. *Social Forces,* 1979, *57,* 1265–1285.

Turiel, E. Social regulations and domains of social concept. *New Directions for Child Development,* 1978, *1,* 45–74.

Turkington, C. Parents found to ignore sex stereotypes. *APA Monitor,* April 1984, p. 12.

Unger, R. K. *Female and male: Psychological perspectives.* New York: Harper & Row, 1979.

U. S. Bureau of Labor Statistics. Rise in mothers' labor force activity includes those with infants. *Monthly Labor Review,* 1986, *109,* 43–45.

U. S. Bureau of the Census. *Statistical Abstracts of the United States, 1980* (101st Annual Ed.). Washington, DC: Government Printing Office, 1980.

U. S. Bureau of the Census. *Statistical Abstracts of the United States, 1981.* Washington, DC: Government Printing Office, 1981.

U. S. Bureau of the Census. *Statistical Abstracts of the United States, 1982–83* Washington, DC: Government Printing Office, 1982.

U. S. Bureau of the Census. *Statistical Abstracts of the United States, 1982,* Vol. 83, (103rd Annual Ed.). Washington, DC: Government Printing Office, 1983.

U. S. Bureau of the Census. *Statistical Abstracts of the United States.* Washington, DC: Government Printing Office, 1984.

U. S. Bureau of the Census. Households, families, marital status and living arrangements: March 1985, Advanced Report, *Current Population Reports,* series P-20, no. 402. Washington, DC: Government Printing Office, 1985.

U. S. Department of Commerce, Bureau of the Census. The sex differential in earnings by age, 1975. *Current Population Reports,* series P-60, no. 105. Washington, DC: Government Printing Office, 1977.

U. S. Department of Commerce, Bureau of the Census. *Marital status and living arrangements, March 1978.* Current Population Reports, series P-20, no. 338. Washington, DC: Government Printing Office, 1979.

U. S. Department of Health, Education and Welfare. *Monthly vital statistics report: final mortality statistics, 1976.* Washington, DC: Government Printing Office, 1978.

U. S. Department of Health, Education and Welfare. Public Health Service. *Facts about Down's syndrome for women over 35.* Public Health Service, NIH Publication No. 80–536, December 1979.

U. S. Department of Health and Human Services. *Consumer memo: Caffeine and pregnancy.* Public Health Service, Food and Drug Administration, Rockville, MD, Publication No. 80, 1979.

U. S. Department of Labor, Bureau of Statistics. *Students, graduates, and dropouts in the labor market, October, 1976.* Special Labor Force Report No. 200. Washington, DC: Government Printing Office, 1977.

U. S. Department of Labor, Bureau of Labor Statistics. *Monthly labor statistics, November, 1979.* Washington, DC: Government Printing Office, 1979.

U. S. Department of Labor. *Perspectives on working women: A databook.* Bulletin 2080. Washington, DC: U. S. Bureau of Labor Statistics, 1980.

U.S. Department of Labor, Bureau of Labor Statistics, *Monthly Labor Review,* September 1987.

U. S. News and World Report. Why a surge of suicide among the young? July 10, 1978.

Vaillant, G. E. *Adaptation to life.* Boston: Little, Brown, 1977.

Valdes-Dapena, M. *Sudden unexplained infant death 1970 through 1975.* U. S. Dept. of Health, Education and Welfare. DHEW Publication No. 80–5255, 1980.

Vander Linde, E., Morrongiello, B., & Rovee-Collier, C. Determinants of retention in 8-week-old infants. *Developmental Psychology,* 1985, *21,* 601–613.

Van Velsor, E., & O'Rand, A. Family life cycle, work career patterns and women's wages at midlife. *Journal of Marriage and the Family,* 1984, *46,* 365–373.

Vega-Lahr, N., & Field, T. Type A behavior in preschool children. *Child Development,* 1986, *57,* 1333–1348.

Veroff, J., Reuman, D., & Feld, S. Motives in American men and women across the adult life span. *Developmental Psychology,* 1984, *20,* 1142–1158.

Vincent, C. E. Socialization data in research on young marrieds. *Acta Sociologica,* 1964, August 8.

Vinovskis, M. The historian and the life course: Reflections on recent approaches to the study of American family life in the past. In P. Baltes, D. Featherman, & R. Lerner (Eds.), *Life-span development and behavior* (Vol. 8). Hillsdale, NJ: Erlbaum, 1988.

Vishner, E. B., & Vishner, J. S. Major areas of difficulty for stepparent couples. *International Journal of Family Counseling,* 1978, *6,* 71–72.

Vore, D. Prenatal nutrition and postnatal intellectual development. *Merrill-Palmer Quarterly,* 1973, *19,* 253–260.

Vurpillot, E. The development of scanning strategies and their relation to visual differentiation. *Journal of Experimental Child Psychology,* 1968, *6,* 632–650.

Vygotsky, L. *Thought and language.* Cambridge, MA: MIT Press, 1962.

Wachs, T., & Gruen, G. *Early experience and human development.* New York: Plenum, 1982.

Wagner, C. A. Adolescent sexuality. In J. F. Adams (Ed.), *Understanding adolescence: Current development in adolescent psychology* (4th ed.). Boston: Allyn Bacon, 1980.

Walberg, H. J. Families as partners in educational productivity. *Phi Delta Kappan,* 1984, *65,* 397–400.

Walker, K. Time spent by husbands in household work. *Family Economics Review,* 1970, *14,* 8–11.

Wallach, M. Ideology, evidence and creative research. *Contemporary Psychology,* 1973, *18,* 162–164.

Wallerstein, J. S., & Kelly, J. B. *Surviving the breakup: How children and parents cope with divorce.* New York: Basic Books, 1980.

Walster, E., Aronson, V., Abrahams, D., & Rottmann, L. Importance of physical attractiveness in dating behavior. *Journal of Personality and Social Psychology,* 1966, *4,* 508–516.

Walters, G., & Grusec, J. *Punishment.* San Francisco: Freeman, 1977.

Wapner, J., & Conner, K. The role of defensiveness in cognitive impulsivity. *Child Development,* 1986, *57,* 1370–1374.

Waterman, A. S. Identity development from adolescence to adulthood: An extension of theory and a review of research. *Developmental Psychology,* 1982, *18,* 341–358.

Waterman, A. S. Identity in the context of adolescent psychology. In Alan S. Waterman (Ed.), *Identity in adolescence: Processes and contents. New directions in child development* (Vol. 30). San Francisco: Jossey-Bass, 1985.

Waterman, A. S., Geary, P. S., & Waterman, C. K. A longitudinal study of changes in ego identity status from freshman to the senior year of college. *Developmental Psychology,* 1974, *10,* 387–392.

Watson, E. H., & Lowrey, G. H. *Growth and development of children* (5th ed.). Chicago: Year Book Medical Publishers, 1967.

Watson, J. B., & Raynor, R. Conditioned emotional reactions. *Journal of Experimental Psychology,* 1920, *3,* 14.

Watson, M., & Amgott-Kwan, T. Transitions in children's understanding of parental roles. *Developmental Psychology,* 1983, *19,* 659–666.

Waugh, W. C., & Norman, D. A. Primary memory. *Psychological Review,* 1965, *72,* 89–104.

Weber, R. A., Levitt, M. J., & Clark, M. C. Individual variation in attachment security and strange situation behavior: The role of maternal and infant temperament. *Child Development,* 1986, *57,* 56–65.

Weg, R. B. Changing physiology of aging: Normal and pathological. In D. S. Woodruff & J. E. Birren (Eds.), *Aging: Scientific perspectives and social issues.* New York: Van Nostrand, 1975.

Weg, R. B. More than wrinkles. In L. Troll, J. Israel, & K. Israel (Eds.), *Looking ahead: A woman's guide to the problems and joys of growing older.* Englewood Cliffs, NJ: Prentice-Hall, 1977.

Weg, R. B. The physiology of sexuality in aging. In R. L. Solnick (Ed.), *Sexuality and aging.* Los Angeles, CA: University of Southern California Press, 1978.

Weideger, P. *Menstruation and menopause: The physiology and psychology: The myth and the reality.* New York: Knopf, 1976.

Weidner, G., & Mathews, K. A. Reported physical symptoms elicited by unpredictable events and the Type A coronary-prone behavior pattern. *Journal of Personality and Social Psychology,* 1978, *36,* 1213–1220.

Weiner, A. S. Cognitive and social-emotional development in adolescence. *Journal of Pediatric Psychology,* 1977, *2,* 87–92.

Weiner, I. *Child and adolescent psychopathology.* New York: Wiley, 1982.

Weinraub, M., Clemens, L. P., Sockloff, A., Ethridge, T., Gracely, E., & Myers, B. The development of sex role stereotypes in the third year: Relationships to gender labeling, gender identity, sex typed toy preference, and family characteristics. *Child Development,* 1984, *55,* 1493–1503.

Weinraub, M., & Wolf, B. Effects of stress and social supports on mother–child interactions in single- and two-parent families. *Child Development,* 1983, *54,* 1297–1311.

Weisler, A., & McCall, R. Exploration and play. *American Psychologist,* 1976, *31,* 492–508.

Weiss, R. Growing up a little faster: The experience of growing up in a single-parent household. In T. E. Levitin (Ed.), Children of divorce. *Journal of Social Issues,* 1979, *35,* 97–111.

Weissberg, J., & Paris, S. Young children's remembering in different contexts: A reinterpretation of Istomina's study. *Child Development,* 1986, *57,* 1123–1129.

Weissman, M., Prusoff, B., Gammon, G. D., Merikangas, K., Leckman, J., & Kidd, K. Psychopathology in the children (ages 6–18) of depressed and normal parents. *Journal of the American Academy of Child Psychiatry*, 1984, *23*, 78–84.

Welford, A. T. Psychomotor performance. In J. E. Birren (Ed.), *Handbook of aging and the individual*. Chicago: University of Chicago Press, 1959.

Wellberg, H. Families as partners in educational productivity. *Phi Delta Kappan*, February 1984, *65*, 397–400.

Wellman, H., & Estes, D. Early understanding of mental entities: A reexamination of childhood realism. *Child Development*, 1986, *57*, 910–923.

'Wellness epidemic' spreads. *Trenton Times*, November 8, 1987, p. A10.

Werner, H. The concept of development from a comparative and organismic point of view. In D. Harris (Ed.), *The concept of development: An issue in the study of human behavior*. Minneapolis: University of Minnesota Press, 1957.

Wessel, J. A., & Van Huss, W. D. The influence of physical activity and age on exercise adaptation of men 20–69 years. *Journal of Sports Medicine*, 1969, *9*, 173–180.

West, D. J. *Delinquency: Its roots, careers and prospects*. London: Heinemann, 1982.

Whalen, C., & Henker, B. Type A behavior in normal and hyperactive children: Multi-source evidence of overlapping constructs. *Child Development*, 1986, *57*, 688–699.

White, B. *Human infants: Experience and psychological development*. Englewood Cliffs, NJ: Prentice-Hall, 1971.

White, B. *Educating the infant and toddler*. Lexington, MA: Lexington Books, 1988.

White, R. *Lives in progress* (3rd ed.). New York: Holt, Rinehart and Winston, 1975.

Whorf, B. *Language, thought and reality*. New York: Wiley, 1956.

Wilkes, R. Robert L. Coles: Doctor of crisis. *New York Times Magazine*, March 26, 1978.

Wilkinson, A. C. Children's partial knowledge of the cognitive skill of

counting. *Cognitive Psychology*, 1984, *6*, 28–64.

Willems, E. P., & Alexander, J. L. The naturalistic perspective in research. In B. Wolman (Ed.), *Handbook of developmental psychology*. Englewood Cliffs, NJ: Prentice-Hall, 1982.

Williams, D. *The search for leadership*. Unpublished manuscript prepared for The Conference Board, New York, 1977.

Williams, J., & Stith, M. *Middle childhood behavior and development* (2nd ed.). New York: Macmillan, 1980.

Wilson, R., & Matheny, A. Assessment of temperament in infant twins. *Developmental Psychology*, 1983, *19*, 172–183.

Winch, R. F. Complementary needs and related notions about voluntary mate selection. In R. F. Winch & G. B. Spanier (Eds.), *Selected studies in marriage and the family*. New York: Holt, Rinehart and Winston, 1974.

Windle, M., & Lerner, R. The role of temperament in dating relationships among young adults. *Merrill Palmer Quarterly*, 1984, *30*, 163–175.

Winick, M. (Ed.) *Childhood obesity*. New York: Wiley, 1975.

Winick, M. *Malnutrition and brain development*. New York: Oxford University Press, 1976.

Wiseman, R. Crisis theory and the process of divorce. *Social Casework*, 1975, *56*, 205–212.

Witken, H. A., & Goodenough, D. R. Field dependence and interpersonal behavior. *Psychological Bulletin*, 1977, *84*, 661–689.

Witken, H. A., & Goodenough, D. R. Cognitive styles: Essence and origins. *Psychological Issues: Monograph 51*. New York: International Universities Press, 1981.

Witken, H. A., Goodenough, D. R., & Karp, S. A. Stability of cognitive style from childhood to young adulthood. *Journal of Personality and Social Psychology*, 1967, *7*, 291–300.

Witken, H. A., Mednick, S., Schulsinger, F., Bakkestrom, E., Christiansen, K., Goodenough, D., Hirschhorn, K., Lundsteen, C., Owen, D., Philip, J., Rubin, D., &

Stocking, M. Criminality in XYY and XXY men. *Science*, 1976, *193*, 547–555.

Wolff, P. H. Observations on newborn infants. *Psychosomatic Medicine*, 1959, *21*, 110–118.

Wolk, S., & Kurtz, J. Positive adjustment and involvement during aging and expectancy for internal control. *Journal of Consulting and Clinical Psychology*, 1975, *43*, 173–178.

Women on Words and Images. *Dick and Jane as victims*. Princeton, NJ: 1975.

Wood, V., & Robertson, J. F. Friendship and kinship interaction: Differential effect on the morale of the elderly. *Journal of Marriage and the Family*, 1978, *40*, 367–375.

Woodruff, D. S., & Birren, J. E. Age changes and cohort differences in personality. *Developmental Psychology*, 1972, *6*, 252–259.

Wright, J., & Huston, A. A matter of form: Potentials of television for young viewers. *American Psychologist*, 1983, *38*, 835–843.

Wyden, B. Growth: 45 crucial months. *Life*, December 17, 1971, 93–95.

Wylie, R. C. *The self-concept* (Vol. 2. Rev. Ed.). Lincoln, NB: University of Nebraska Press, 1979.

Yankelovich, D. *The new morality: A profile of American youth in the 70s*. New York: McGraw-Hill, 1974.

Yankelovich, D. *New rules: Searching for self-fulfillment in a world turned upside down*. New York: Random House, 1981.

Yankelovich, Skelly, & White, Inc. *Raising children in a changing society*. Minneapolis: General Mills, 1977.

Yarrow, L. Everything you want to know about teen-agers (but are afraid to ask). *Parents Magazine*, 1979, *54*, 68.

Yarrow, L. J., Rubenstein, J., & Pedersen, F. *Infant and environment*. New York: Wiley, 1975.

Yarrow, M. R., Campbell, J., & Burton, R. *Child rearing: An inquiry into research and methods*. San Francisco: Jossey-Bass, 1968.

Yllo, K. Nonmarital cohabitation: Beyond the college campus. *Alternative Lifestyles*, 1978, *1*, 37–54.

Yonas, A., Granrud, C., & Pettersen, L. Infants' sensitivity to relative size information for distance. *Developmental Psychology*, 1985, *21*, 161–167.

Young, R. D., & Avdze, E. The effects of obedience–disobedience and obese–nonobese type on social acceptance by peers. *Journal of Genetic Psychology*, 1979, *134*, 43–49.

Youniss, J., & Smollar, J. *Adolescent relations with mothers, fathers, and friends.* Chicago: University of Chicago Press, 1985.

Youniss, J., & Volpe, J. A relationship analysis of children's friendship. In W. Damon (Ed.), *Social cognition (New directions for child development, No. 1).* San Francisco: Jossey-Bass, 1978.

Yudkin, M. When kids think the unthinkable. *Psychology Today*, April 1984, *18*, 18–25.

Zabin, L. S., Hirsch, M. B., Smith, E. A., & Hardy, J. B. Adolescent sexual attitudes and behavior: Are they consistent? *Family Planning Perspectives*, 1984, *16*, 181.

Zacharias, P., Rand, W., & Wurtman, R. A prospective study of sexual development and growth in American girls: The statistic of menarche. *Obstetrical and Gynecological Survey*, 1976, *31*, 323–337.

Zahn-Waxler, C., Cummings, E. M., McKnew, D., & Radke-Yarrow, M. Altruism, aggression and social interaction in young children with a manic–depressive parent. *Child Development*, 1984, *55*, 112–122.

Zahn-Waxler, C., Iannotti, R., & Chapman, M. Peers and prosocial development. In K. H. Rubin and H. S. Ross (Eds.), *Peer relationships and social skills in childhood.* New York: Springer-Verlag, 1982.

Zelnik, M., & Kantner, J. Sexual activity, contraceptive use and pregnancy among metropolitan-area teenagers, 1971–1979. *Family Planning Perspectives*, 1980, *12*, 230–237.

Zelnik, M., Kantner, J., & Ford, K. *Sex and pregnancy in adolescence*, Beverly Hills, CA: Sage Publications, 1981.

Zelnik, M., & Kim Y. Sex education and its association with teenage sexual activity, pregnancy, and contraceptive use. *Family Planning Perspectives.* May–June 1982, *14*, 117–126.

Zelniker, T., & Jeffrey, W. Reflective and impulsive children: Strategies of information processing underlying differences in problem solving. *Monographs of the Society for Research in Child Development.* 1976, *41*, no. 5, serial no. 168.

Zelniker, T., & Jeffrey, W. Attention and cognitive style in children. In G. Hale & M. Lewis (Eds.), *Attention and cognitive development.* New York: Plenum, 1979.

Zelson, C. Infant of the addicted mother. *New England Journal of Medicine*, 1973, *288*, 1393–1395.

Zelson, C., Lee, S. J., & Casalino, M. Neonatal narcotic addiction: Comparative effects of maternal intake of heroin and methadone. *New England Journal of Medicine*, 1973, *289*, 1216–1220.

Zeskend, P., & Marshall, T. The relation between variations in pitch and maternal perceptions of infant crying. *Child Development*, 1988, *59*, 193–196.

Zigler, E. Controlling child abuse: Do we have the knowledge and/or will? In G. Gerbner, C. Ross, & E. Zigler (Eds.), *Child abuse: An agenda for action.* New York: Oxford University Press, 1980.

Zigler, E. Controlling child abuse in America: An effort doomed to failure. In E. Zigler, M. Lamb, & I. Child (Eds.), *Socialization and personality development.* New York: Oxford University Press, 1982.

Zigler, E., & Gorden, E. (Eds.), *Day care: Scientific and social policy issues.* Boston: Auburn House, 1982.

Zill, N., & Peterson, J. *Trends in the behavior and emotional well-being of U.S. children: Findings from a national survey.* Paper presented at the meeting of the American Association for the Advancement of Science, Washington, DC, January, 1982.

Zimmerman, B. J. Social learning theory and cognitive constructivism. In I. Sigel, D. Brodzinsky, & R. Golinkoff (Eds.), *New directions in Piagetian theory and practice.* Hillsdale, NJ: Erlbaum, 1981.

Acknowledgments

LITERARY CREDITS

Figure 2.3 (page 48). From *Know Your Genes* by Aubrey Milunski, MD, p. 18. Copyright © 1977 by Aubrey Milunski, MD. Reprinted by permission of Houghton Mifflin Company.

Figures 2.6 and 2.7 (pages 57, 60). Figure 10.6 and Figure 10.2 from *Psychology: Science, Behavior, and Life* by Robert L. Crooks and Jean Stein, copyright © 1988 by Holt, Rinehart and Winston, Inc. Reprinted by permission of the publisher.

Figure 2.9 (page 68). After Ortho Diagnostic Systems, Inc.

Table 2.2 (page 65). NIH Publication 80-536 (December 1979), U.S. Department of Health, Education and Welfare.

Figure 3.1 (page 94). From J. L. Conel, *The Postnatal Development of the Human Cortex*. Cambridge, Mass.: Harvard University Press, 1939. Vol. i. Reprinted by permission.

Figure 3.2 (page 98). After N. Bayley, *Bayley Scales of Infant Development*. New York: The Psychological Corporation, 1969.

Table 4.2 (page 123). From J. Osofsky (ed.), *Handbook of Human Development*. New York: Wiley, 1979.

Table 5.1 (page 153). From Ernest H. Watson and George H. Lowrey, *Growth and Development of Children*, 5th ed.; data from tables 10-A through 10-D (pp. 89–92). Copyright 1967 by Year Book Medical Publishers, Inc.

Table 5.2 (page 157). Adapted from D. L. Gallahue, *Motor Development Experiences for Young Children* (New York: Wiley, 1976), pp. 65–66.

Table 5.3 (page 174). Reprinted by permission of the publisher from *Educating the Infant and Toddler* by Burton L. White (Lexington, Mass.: Lexington Books, D. C. Heath and Co.). Copyright 1988 D. C. Heath and Co. Page 24.

Table 5.4 (page 175). From D. Slobin, Children and language: They learn the same way all around the world. *Psychology Today*, July 1972, 18.

Figure 5.3 (page 168). Adapted from Vurpillot, The development of scanning strategies and their relation to visual differentiation. *Journal of Experimental Child Psychology* 6, pp. 632–650.

Figure 6.1 (page 213). U.S. Bureau of the Census, Current Population Reports Series P-20.

Table 6.2 (page 209). A. Clarke-Stewart, *Day Care*. Cambridge, Mass.: Harvard University Press, 1982.

Figure 7.2 (page 249). From J. Kagan, Impulsive and reflective children, in J. D. Krumboltz (ed.), *Learning and the Educational Process*. Skokie, Ill.: Rand McNally, 1965.

Table 7.3 (page 151). Reprinted with permission of The Riverside Publishing Company from page 127 of *Stanford-Binet Intelligence Scale Technical Manual*, 4th ed., by R. L. Thorndike, E. P. Hagen, and J. M. Sattler. The Riverside Publishing Company, 8420 W. Bryn Mawr Avenue, Chicago, Ill. 60631. Copyright 1986.

Figure 8.1 (page 273). Sociogram from S. Coopersmith, *The Antecedents of Self-esteem*. New York: Freeman, 1967.

Figure 9.1 (page 297). From G. B. Forbes. Growth of the lean body mass in man. *Growth* 36 (1972): 325-338.

Table 9.1 (page 316). Adapted from J. Adelson (ed.), *Handbook of Adolescent Psychology*. New York: Wiley, 1980. Page 565.

Figure 10.1 (page 323). Based on Czikszentmihaly and Larson, *Being Adolescent: Conflict and Growth in the Teenage Years* (New York: Basic Books, 1984).

Table 10.2 (page 331). Reprinted by permission of Plenum Press.

Figure 11.1 (page 360). Reproduced, with permission, from the *Annual Review of Psychology*, Volume 31. © 1980 by Annual Reviews, Inc.

Figure 11.2 (page 377). From Daniel J. Levinson. A conception of adult development. *American Psychologist* 41 (1986), 3–13.

Table 11.2 (page 363), Table 13.4 (page 454), and Table 15.1 (page 519). From *Developmental Tasks and Education*, 3rd ed., by Robert J. Havighurst. Copyright © 1972 by

Longman Inc. Reprinted by permission of publisher.

Table 11.3 (page 376). Copyright © 1978 by Roger Gould, MD. Reprinted by permission of Simon & Schuster, Inc.

Figure 12.1 (page 400). From Bernard I. Murstein, *Who Will Marry Whom?* (New York: Springer, 1976), p. 123. Reprinted by permission of the author.

Table 12.1 (page 394). Based on E. M. Duvall. *Marriage and Family Development,* 5th ed. (Philadelphia: Lippincott, 1977), p. 148.

Table 12.3 (page 411). Reprinted by permission of Plenum Press.

Table 13.2 (page 435). Reprinted with permission from *Psychology Today.* Copyright © 1981 American Psychological Association.

Table 14.1 (page 475). From L. E. Troll, *Early and Middle Adulthood* (Monterey, Calif: Brooks/Cole, 1975), p. 12.

Figure 14.1 (page 470). From B. C. Rollins and H. Feldman, Marital satisfaction over the family life cycle. *Journal of Marriage and the Family* 32 (1970), figure 4, p. 26. Copyrighted 1970 by the National Council on Family Relations, 1910 West County Road B, Suite 147, St. Paul, Minnesota 55113. Reprinted by permission.

Figure 16.1 (page 530). From M. N. Reedy, J. E. Birren, and K. W. Schale, Age and sex differences in satisfying love relationships across the adult life span. *Human Development* 24 (1981), 52–66. Reprinted by permission of S. Karger AG, Basel, Switzerland.

Figure 16.2 (page 547). Phases of retirement. From R. C. Atchley, *The Sociology of Retirement.* Rochester, Vt.: Schenkman Books, 1979.

Figure 17.1 (page 580). Reprinted with permission of Concern for Dying, 250 West 57th Street, New York, NY 10107; telephone (212) 246-6926.

PHOTO CREDITS

Cover: Ted Horowitz/The Stockmarket

Chapter 1: p. 11, Bettmann Newsphotos; p. 13, Charles Anderson/Monkmeyer Press Photo; p. 14, Jeffrey W. Myers/Stock, Boston; p. 19, Christopher S. Johnson/Stock, Boston; p. 20, © Hella Hammid/Photo Researchers, Inc.; p. 23, © Joe Munroe/Photo Researchers, Inc.; p. 24, © Jack Spratt/The Image Works; p. 27, Mimi Forsyth/Monkmeyer Press Photo; p. 29, Ken Robert Buck/The Picture Cube.

Part Opener I: David R. Austin/Stock, Boston

Chapter 2: p. 44, Hank Morgan Photo Researchers, Inc.; p. 47, Science Source/Photo Researchers, Inc.; p. 50, Photo Researchers, Inc.; p. 57 (left), Elizabeth Crews; p. 57 (right), Mike Mazzaschi/Stock, Boston; p. 58, Mimi Forsyth/Monkmeyer Press Photo; p. 61, Petit Format/Nestle/Science Source/Photo Researchers, Inc.; p. 63 (both) Petite Format/Nestle/Photo Researcher Inc.; p. 64 (both) Petit Format/Nestle/Photo Researchers, Inc. p. 73 (all) Pat Hansen p. 75, Courtesy of Dane-Brooke Productions.

Chapter 3: p. 82, Pat Hansen; p. 88, Spencer Grant/Photo Researchers, Inc.; p. 89 (left), Pat Hansen; p. 89 (right), © Ed Lettau/Photo Researchers, Inc.; p. 90, Monkmeyer Press Photo; p. 91, Peter Menzel/Stock, Boston; p. 97, Lew Merrim/Monkmeyer Press Photo; p. 101 (top), A.N. Meltzoff & M.K. Moore, *Science* 1977, Vol. 198, p. 75–78; p. 101 (left), Enrico Ferorelli/Dot Photos; p.

106 (both), George Zimbel/Monkmeyer Press Photo; p. 109, David Strickler/The Picture Cube.

Chapter 4: p. 118, Barbara Alper/Stock, Boston; p. 119, Ann McQueen/Stock, Boston; p. 122, Elizabeth Crews/The Image Works, Inc.; p. 127, Elizabeth Crews, p. 132, Elizabeth Crews; p. 133, Alice Kandell/Photo Researchers, Inc.; p. 134, Anne Gormly, p. 141, Pat Hansen; p. 143, Betsy Cole/The Picture Cube.

Part Opener 2: Pat Hansen

Chapter 5: p. 153, Gabor Demjen/Stock, Boston; p. 158 (top), Miro Vintoniv/Stock, Boston; p. 158, (bottom) Anne Gormly; p. 163 (both), Alan Carey/The Image Works, Inc.; p. 165, Elizabeth Crews; p. 180, Elizabeth Crews; p. 181, Arlene Collins/Monkmeyer Press Photo; p. 183, Elizabeth Crews.

Chapter 6: p. 192, Peter Vandermark/Stock, Boston; p. 193, © Erika Stone/Peter Arnold, Inc.; p. 194, © Alan Carey/The Image Works, Inc.; p. 195, Betsy Lee/Taurus Photos; p. 198, Alexander Lowry; p. 201, George W. Gardner/The Image Works, Inc.; p. 203, © Ann L. Reed/Taurus Photos; p. 217, James R. Holland/Stock, Boston; p. 220, © Elizabeth Crews.

Part Opener 3: © Charles Krebs/The Stock Market

Chapter 7: p. 231 (top), Rosemary Porter/The Image Works, Inc.; p. 231 (bottom), Pam Hasegawa; p. 232, Blair Seitz; p. 238, Stock, Boston; p. 239, Pat Hansen; p. 241, Bruce Roberts/Photo Researchers, Inc.; p. 245, Pat Hansen.

Chapter 8: p. 260 (left), © 1980 Victor Englebert/Photo Researchers, Inc.; p. 260 (right), © Robert A. Isaacs/Photo Researchers, Inc.; p. 262, Peter Vandermark/Stock, Boston; p. 267, © Joseph Schuyler/Stock, Boston; p. 268, © Barbara Rios/Photo Researchers, Inc.; p. 270, Elizabeth Crews; p. 271, © Barbara Rios/Photo Researchers, Inc.; p. 274, © Steve Takatsuno/The Picture Cube; p. 277, © David Wells/The Image Works, Inc.; p. 278, © George W. Gardner/Stock, Boston; p. 282, © Gale Zucker/Stock, Boston; p. 284, © Ulrike Welsch/Photo Researchers, Inc.

Part Opener 4: Thomas Braise/The Stock Market

Chapter 9: p. 295, Photo Researchers, Inc.; p. 302, courtesy, Anne Gormly; p. 304, James D. Wilson/The Image Works, Inc.; p. 306, © Katherine McGlynn/The Image Works, Inc.; p. 307, courtesy of Anne Gormly; p. 308, Monkmeyer Press Photo; p. 309, © Mike Maple 1982/Woodfin Camp & Associates; p. 310, courtesy of Anne Gormly; p. 314, © 1985 Michael Manheim/The Stock Market; p. 317, © 1987 Miriam White/The Stock Market.

Chapter 10: p. 324, Wide World Photos; p. 325, © Ellis Herwig/Stock, Boston; p. 330, Michael Weisbrot/Stock, Boston; p. 332, © Lynne Jaegar Weinstein 1986/Woodfin Camp & Associates; p. 334 (left), Paul Conklin/Monkmeyer Press Photo; p. 334 (right), Rick Mansfield/The Image Works, Inc.; p. 339 © Elizabeth Crews The Image Works, Inc.; p. 341, © Carolyn Hine/The Picture Cube; p. 343, Mary Ellen Mark/Archive Pictures; p. 349, © Frank Siteman/Stock, Boston.

Part Opener 5: © 1986 John Lawlor/The Stock Market

Chapter 11: p. 359, Bettmann Newsphotos; p. 362, Mimi Forsyth/Monkmeyer Press Photo; p. 364, George Bellerose/Stock, Boston; p. 365 (top), © Richard Wood/The Picture Cube; p. 365 (left), Wide World Photos;

Name Index

Subject Index